PRAXIS™:
Preparing for the Praxis I Pre-Professional Skills Tests (PPST®s) and the Praxis II® Principles of Learning and Teaching (PLT)

Related Titles

Becoming a Teacher

Best Careers for Teachers

Praxis II®: Para Pro Test Prep (0755-1755)

Praxis II®: Elementary Education Content Knowledge

PRAXIS™:
Preparing for the Praxis I Pre-Professional Skills Tests (PPST®s) and the Praxis II® Principles of Learning and Teaching (PLT)

Fifth Edition

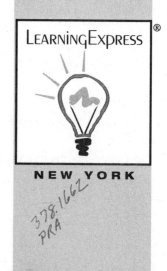

LEARNINGEXPRESS®

NEW YORK

ISBN-13 978-1-57685-930-8

Printed in the United States of America

9 8 7 6 5 4 3 2 1

For more information or to place an order, contact LearningExpress at:
  80 Broad Street
  Suite 410
  New York, NY 10004

Or visit us at:
  www.learningexpressllc.com

PRAXIS™, PPST®, PRAXIS II®, and the PRAXIS Series™ are registered trademarks of Educational Testing Service (ETS). This product is not endorsed or approved by ETS.

CONTENTS

CONTENTS

CONTRIBUTOR ▶

Cindy Lassonde, PhD, is a professor in the Elementary Education and Reading Department at the State University of New York College at Oneonta. She moved to the college level after teaching for more than 20 years at the elementary level. Currently, she teaches undergraduate and graduate courses in literacy, special education, and early childhood education. She is the 2010 recipient of the SUNY Chancellor's Award for Excellence in Teaching, and the author of 13 books and numerous journal articles.

HOW TO USE ▶
THIS BOOK

The Praxis Series™ of tests is used by many teacher education institutions and state education agencies that train and license new educators. Most states choose tests from the Praxis Series tests because of their proven capability for determining scholastic and pedagogical aptitudes of applicants. Scores from the Praxis Series tests help ensure those entering a teacher-training program—and ultimately the teaching workforce—are proficient and knowledgeable. The purpose of the Praxis Series of tests is to ensure you are qualified to teach, and LearningExpress's goal is to ensure you pass the tests!

This book is designed to give you the test-taking skills and background knowledge you need to tackle the Praxis I Pre-Professional Skills Tests (PPSTs) and the Praxis II Principles of Learning and Teaching (PLT), whether you decide to take the paper-based tests or the computer-based tests. It contains all the information you need to improve your score in the shortest amount of time possible. This chapter serves as a guide for using this book effectively, so you get the most out of your time and effort.

The Book

This book includes:

- a chapter explaining all about the Praxis Series of tests
- a full-length PPST Diagnostic Test, complete with answers and explanations
- three review chapters covering the three subjects of the PPSTs
- two full-length Praxis I practice exams, complete with answers and explanations
- a review chapter covering the categories of the Praxis II PLT
- four full-length Praxis II PLT practice exams, complete with answers and explanations

To begin, consult the teacher education institution or your state education agency to determine which test or tests you are required to pass. Go to your state's Education Department website, or visit www.ets.org/praxis/states to find state requirements. Then, start with Part I, "About the Praxis Series of Tests." Chapter 1, "The Praxis Series of Tests," tells you how to register for the exams and where to find testing sites. It also gives you an overview of the tests' content and formats. Even if you are already familiar with this information, it's still a good idea to review this chapter.

Next, read Part II, "Test Preparation." Chapter 2, "The LearningExpress Test Preparation System," teaches you how to effectively prepare for any test using LearningExpress's proven test-taking strategies. You will learn to:

- set up a personalized study plan, utilizing the lessons and tests in this book
- use your study time efficiently
- make educated guesses when you are unsure of an answer
- overcome test anxiety

After you have mastered these skills, move on to Part III, "Focusing on the Praxis I PPST." Try taking the full-length PPST Diagnostic Pretest in Chapter 3 before moving on to the reading, math, and writing reviews in Chapters 4, 5, and 6. This way, you can better assess your personal strengths and weaknesses, allowing you to focus your time where you need it most.

Once you have taken the PPST Diagnostic Pretest and read through the answer explanations, you are ready to get started with your study plan and move on to the review chapters. All three of the review chapters are effective tools for studying for each of the PPSTs. Each includes examples and explanations so you can practice as you learn. You should read all the review chapters, putting more emphasis on the subjects that were problematic for you on the PPST Diagnostic Pretest.

Chapter 4, the "Praxis I Reading Test Review," is designed to review the reading skills you will need to pass the PPST Reading test. Since you will be timed on test day, you will learn how to be an active reader. In other words, this chapter shows you how to read passages to quickly spot the differences between the main ideas and supporting ideas and to pinpoint key concepts in a reading passage. Also, you will learn to skim through the less important information, so that unnecessary and irrelevant information will not bog you down.

The reading review also demonstrates how to make logical inferences, draw likely conclusions, and gauge an author's attitude based on the information given in a reading passage. And, like each of the review chapters in this book, there are several practice questions that allow you to apply what you have just learned. There's nothing like having a lot of practice under your belt to make you feel confident when you go into the real exam.

Chapter 5 is the "Praxis I Mathematics Test Review." The review is designed to be as clear and concise as possible to bolster your confidence. All the basics are covered, including mathematical terms, arithmetic, algebraic foundations and equations, percentages, ratios, measurement, and geometry. Plus, you will learn strategies for solving word problems, analyzing data, interpreting graphs and tables, spotting trends and patterns, and recognizing various ways for solving problems. Since many problems you will face on the PPST Mathematics test will require a combination of math skills to get the correct answer, you should review the examples throughout the chapter.

The "Praxis I Writing Test Review" in Chapter 6 is an efficient crash course in writing. You will learn how to tackle the two separate sections of the writing exam: the multiple-choice questions and the essay-writing section. The writing multiple-choice review covers the basics in the areas of grammar, mechanics, word usage, and sentence structure. For the essay portion, you will find useful writing strategies so you can compose a clear, well-organized essay and effectively state your objective. Whether you choose to write your essay on paper or on the computer, you (or a trusted friend) should score it using the scoring criteria included in the lesson.

Next, go to Part IV, "Praxis I PPST Practice Exams." Chapter 7, "Praxis I Practice Exam 1," measures your improvement since you took the PPST Diagnostic Pretest. Check your answers and read the answer explanations for any questions you may have guessed on or answered incorrectly. At this point, you should read sections of the review chapters again (if needed), adding to your bank of knowledge in any areas that still require improvement.

In Chapter 8, you will find the final full-length PPST practice exam. By taking this test, you will practice your test-taking skills, continue to diagnose your weakest areas, and discover where you might still need improvement. Try taking this test under timed conditions—just like the real exam.

In Part V, "Focusing on the Praxis II PLT," the book turns to the review and sample test and answer chapters for the PLT part of the Praxis II. Chapter 9, "Praxis II Principles of Learning and Teaching Review," looks at principles of learning, instruction, assessment, communication, and teacher professionalism in education. This chapter addresses content that will appear on all levels of the Praxis II PLT: Early Education, Grades K–6, Grades 5–9, and Grades 7–12.

Part VI, "Praxis II PLT Practice Exams" contains four PLT practice exams. Chapter 10 is "Practice Exam 3: PLT: Early Childhood," Chapter 11 is "Practice Exam 4: PLT: Grades K–6," Chapter 12 is "Practice Exam 5: PLT: Grades 5–9," and Chapter 13 is "Practice Exam 6: PLT: Grades 7–12." Select the appropriate chapters to match your degree program or expected area or areas of certification.

Part VII provides the answers and explanations for the PPLT Diagnostic Pretest and each of the two PPLT practice exams and the four PLT practice exams. They are all grouped together so that you can find them easily.

Finally, the appendix is a chart of all the Praxis II tests. Codes and fees are provided for your information.

You

You already have a valuable tool for passing the test—this book; now the rest is up to you. Ultimately, you will have to rely on yourself to succeed. Remain disciplined, follow your study schedule, and do not give up. Most important—practice, practice, practice. Plenty of practice will improve your skills and build your confidence.

Good luck!

PART

ABOUT THE PRAXIS SERIES OF TESTS

1 ▶ THE PRAXIS SERIES OF TESTS

CHAPTER SUMMARY

This chapter familiarizes you with the Praxis Series of tests, which are administered by the Educational Testing Service (ETS). (Go to www.ets.org/praxis.) This chapter also discusses all the pertinent information about the Praxis Series, including contact information, the registration process, examination fees, and test formats and content. Additionally, you will learn about scoring, what the scores are used for, and how they are reported.

A ll the exams in the Praxis Series of tests are designed to measure the scholastic and pedagogical capability of teachers at different stages of their careers. The first exam in the Praxis Series, the Praxis I Pre-Professional Skills Test (PPST), may be taken early in a student's college career to qualify for entry into a teaching credential program. It is also taken by prospective teachers to be considered for a license in states not requiring education degrees. The Praxis I PPST is comprised of individual tests that measure basic skills in reading, mathematics, and writing. The second group of exams in the Praxis Series, the Praxis II, is taken by individuals entering the teaching profession as part of their state's teacher licensing and certification process. The Praxis II consists of three groups of tests that measure subject-specific content knowledge, general pedagogical knowledge, and teaching foundations. See the appendix for a list of these tests.

The Praxis Series of tests is administered in both a paper- and computer-based format. This chapter discusses both in detail. Although both forms of the test cover the same content, the procedures for registering and taking the tests are very different; therefore, these steps are discussed separately in this chapter.

PURPOSES OF THE PRAXIS SERIES OF TESTS

Praxis I is generally taken to gain entry into a teaching credential program and for state licensing. Some educational organizations require that you achieve passing PPST scores to gain membership. These organizations include the American Speech-Language-Hearing Association (ASHA), the Department of Defense Education Activity (DODEA), and the National Association of School Psychologists (NASP). **Praxis II** is taken by would-be teachers who are applying for state licensure as a teacher.

States Using the Praxis Series of Tests

Each state sets its own requirement for which tests to take and what score will be accepted as passing. Information regarding specific state or organization requirements may change from time to time. For accurate, up-to-date information, refer to the official Praxis website at www.ets.org/praxis/ and your state's Education Department.

Note: Although some information for the requirements of California is included on the Praxis website, those interested in meeting them should contact the California Commission on Teacher Credentialing (CTC) online at www.ctc.ca.gov.

IMPORTANT CONTACT INFORMATION

ETS—*The Praxis Series*
P.O. Box 6051
Princeton, NJ 08541-6051
Phone: 609-771-7395, M–F 8 A.M. to 7:45 P.M. (EST) (except for U.S. holidays)
Phone for the Hearing Impaired: 609-771-7714
Fax: 609-530-0581 or 609-771-7906
Website: www.ets.org/praxis/
E-mail directly through the website at www.ets.org/praxis/contact

What Is the Praxis I Like?

The Praxis I PPST is designed to see whether you have the academic skills to be an effective teacher. How are your basic skills in:

- Reading?
- Math?
- Writing?

All the questions on the Praxis I, with the exception of the essay portion of the PPST Writing test, are in multiple-choice format. Each multiple-choice question has five answer choices and is worth one point. Because test scoring is based only on the number of items answered correctly, you are not penalized for incorrect answers on the PPSTs—so be sure to fill in all the answer blanks rather than leaving difficult questions unanswered. Even a guess is better than leaving an answer blank!

Let's look at each test.

Reading

The PPST Reading test measures your ability to comprehend, analyze, and evaluate written information. You will be asked to read a number of passages (which may vary in length from 100 to 200 words) and then answer questions that test your ability to comprehend what you have read. The genre and reading levels of the passages will vary. You will be tested only on your ability to understand and analyze the selection; you will not be required to have specific knowledge about the topics discussed in the passages. Chapter 4, "Praxis I Reading Test Review," provides more detailed coverage of the question types you will face. The following are general types of questions that you may be asked:

Literal Comprehension
- main idea questions
- supporting idea questions
- organization questions
- vocabulary questions

Critical and Inferential Comprehension
- argument evaluation questions
- inferential reasoning questions
- generalization questions

Mathematics

The PPST Mathematics test measures your proficiency in math. Generally speaking, the test requires a competency at the high school or first-year college level. The lessons in Chapter 5, "Praxis I Mathematics Test Review," will give you more in-depth coverage of test content. Here are the four main math skills that will be tested:

Numbers and Operations
- order
- equivalence
- numeration and place value
- number properties
- operation properties
- computation
- estimation
- ratio, proportion, and percent
- numerical reasoning

Algebra
- equations and inequalities
- algorithmic thinking
- patterns
- algebraic representations
- algebraic reasoning

Geometry and Measurement
- geometric properties
- the xy-coordinate plane
- geometric reasoning
- systems of measurement

Data Analysis and Probability
- data interpretation
- data representation
- trends and inferences
- measures of center and spread
- probability

Writing

The PPST Writing test is divided into two sections: The first section consists of multiple-choice questions that require you to find and/or correct errors in standard English; the second part asks you to write a 30-minute essay on an assigned topic, which will represent 50% of your total writing test score. The "Praxis I Writing Test Review" (Chapter 6) provides detailed information on how to approach both sections of the writing test.

The multiple-choice section of the writing test is designed to measure your ability to use standard English correctly and effectively and is divided into two parts: usage and sentence correction.

Usage questions test your knowledge of:
- structural and grammatical relationships
- mechanics
- idiom or word choice

Usage questions also test your ability to identify error-free sentences.

Sentence Correction questions test your ability to:
- select the best way to state a given phrase or sentence
- correct sentences with errors in grammar, mechanics, idioms, or word choice

You are not expected to know formal grammatical terminology.

The essay portion of the PPST Writing test is designed to evaluate your ability to express ideas clearly and effectively in standard written English. You will be presented with a topic and asked to state an opinion in essay form. The given topics present situations that are generally familiar to all educated people and do not require any specialized knowledge in a particular field. Although you will be posing an argument and drawing conclusions based on examples from personal experience or observation, you will not be graded on your opinion—you will be scored only on how effectively you are able to get your ideas across.

The following qualities will be taken into consideration when your essay is scored:

- *Appropriateness:* whether your essay was written appropriately for the task and intended audience
- *Organization:* your ability to organize and develop the essay logically and make clear connections between ideas
- *Unity and focus:* your ability to devise and sustain a clear thesis throughout the essay
- *Development:* the ability to develop your essay through examples and details that clearly and logically support the ideas presented in your essay
- *Mechanical conventions:* demonstration of a proficient use of the English language and ability to use proper syntax
- *Sentence structure:* the ability to effectively construct sentences, free from error, in standard written English

NONSCORABLE QUESTIONS

From time to time, the ETS needs to try out new questions to see whether they are suitable for use in future editions of the test. These questions will not be identified because the ETS is trying to determinine how examinees will respond under real testing conditions. The questions are unscored, meaning that they do not count toward or against your score. Not all tests include unscored questions.

What about Scores?

Your official score report will be available online about four weeks after your test date. Your score report will also be sent to the recipients (for example, schools) you designated on your registration form.

The report shows a separate test score for each PPST subject that you take. Reading and math test scores are based on the number of items answered correctly. There is no penalty for answering a question incorrectly. The writing test score is based on the number of multiple-choice questions answered correctly combined with the essay score, which is scored on a scale of 1 to 6.

Your score report will show your score, whether or not you passed, the raw points earned in each content category, and the range of possible scores. If you took any test previously within the past 10 years, it will also show your highest scores on each test.

Can I Cancel My Scores?

For the paper-based test, you may cancel your scores for a particular test by submitting a *Request for Score Cancellation* form to the ETS within one week after the test date. If you take a computer-based test, you are given the option to cancel your scores at the end of your test session before viewing the scores (once you have viewed your computerized scores, you cannot cancel them). All score cancellations are permanent, and refunds are not given.

Passing Scores

Each state or institution determines its own passing score. The first thing you will want to do with your scores is to compare them to the passing scores set by your state. Along with your test scores, you will receive the *Understanding Your Praxis Scores* booklet that gives the passing scores for each state. The Praxis Series website (www.ets.org/praxis/) also has a complete state-by-state listing of required tests and passing scores.

Retaking the Tests

If you don't pass one or more PPST tests, you will be allowed to take them again. How many times or how often you may retake each PPST is determined by the policies of individual states or institutions. The ETS does not limit how many times you can take the paper-based tests. However, the ETS does mandate that you may take each of the computer-based tests only once per 30-day period and no more than six times in one year. Individual states may have further restrictions. Consult your scores from previous tests to see which areas require more study, so that you will pass the tests the next time you take them.

What to Bring to the Test

If you are taking the paper-based test, you will need to bring valid photo identification, your admittance ticket (which is mailed to you following registration or printed after online registration), several #2 pencils, a good eraser, and (if you are taking the writing test) blue or black ink pens. You may also choose to bring a watch, as long as it does not have calculator or keyboard functions.

For the computer-based test, you will need your photo identification and your admission ticket. You may not bring calculators, cell phones, smartphones or any other electronic devices, pencils or pens, books, bags, scratch paper, or other people into the test room with you. The test administrator will designate an area where you may keep your personal belongings during the test.

Time Allowed

Paper-Based Tests

For each paper-based test, you will have 60 minutes of actual testing time. The test administrator will begin timing after all test booklets and Scantron sheets have been handed out and the instructions have been given. You should allow about one and a half hours (90 minutes) for each individual test or four and a half hours if you are taking all three tests on the same day.

Computer-Based Tests

You will be allowed two hours for each individual computer-based test or four and a half hours for the combined computer-based tests. This allows time for tutorials and the collection of background information. Please see "The Computer-Based Test at a Glance (CPPST)" box on page 15 for the time allotted for each individual test.

On test day, allow plenty of time in the morning to get to your test location, especially if you are unfamiliar with the area where the test is given. You should arrive at least 30 minutes before your test to sign in, present your identification, and get yourself settled.

Payment Options

You may pay using a Visa, MasterCard, American Express, Discover Network, or JCB credit card. You can also use a debit card, bank check, or money order made payable to ETS—*Praxis*. Cash is never accepted. Fee waivers are available to applicants with financial need. Refund policies and a fee waiver application form may be found on the ETS website (www.ets.org/praxis).

How Do I Register?

Usually you will need to register at least four weeks prior to the test date.

To register by mail, you must download and complete the appropriate Praxis Registration Form.

FEES FOR THE PAPER-BASED AND COMPUTER-BASED TESTS

PPST Reading:	$ 85
PPST Math:	$ 85
PPST Writing:	$ 85
Register to take two tests on the same day:	$125
Register to take three tests on the same day (combined test):	$135

Special Service Fees

Extended registration:	$ 45
Test, test center, or test date change:	$ 30
Emergency registration:	$ 75
Telephone reregistration:	$ 35
File correction:	$ 40
Scores by phone:	$ 30 (per request)
Additional score reports:	$ 40 (per report)
Test surcharge (Nevada only):	$ 5
Score verification:	$ 40 (multiple choice); $55 (constructed response)

Approximately one week before your test date, you will receive a testing admission ticket by mail, which you will need to bring for entrance into the test. If you lose your ticket, do not receive it at least one week prior to your test day, or if there is an error on your ticket, contact ETS immediately.

You can also register online at www.ets .org/praxis/. To register online, you will need a valid e-mail address, mailing address, and phone number. Order confirmations and test admission tickets will be e-mailed to your e-mail address—you will not be sent a paper admission ticket by postal mail when you register online. Print out the ticket provided for you online. Online registration is available only to those not needing special accommodations such as considerations for disabilities or Monday testing.

If you have previously created a Praxis account online, you can register by phone with a credit card. There will be a nonrefundable $35 surcharge for the transaction, in addition to the standard registration and test fees. To register by phone, call 800-772-9476, 8 A.M. to 7:45 P.M. (EST), Monday through Friday.

Emergency Registration

Those trying to register for a desired test date after the regular and late registration deadlines may still be able to take the test on that date by using the emergency registration service for an additional $75 fee. This service guarantees a seat at a test center. Emergency registration is not available for individuals needing special accommodations.

To Cancel or Reschedule Your Test

If you are absent the day of the test or arrive too late to take the test, you are not eligible for a refund. You may cancel or reschedule a test for paper-delivered tests by logging into your Praxis account online, calling ETS at 1-800-772-9476, or completing and mailing a Change Request Form (see www.ets.org/praxis/ register/changes) to:

ETS—*The Praxis Series*
P.O. Box 6051
Princeton, NJ 08541-6051

You are eligible to receive a refund of 50 percent of your test fees if the change is received by ETS at least three days prior to the test date. Special service fees are nonrefundable. Registration deadlines are updated and posted on the website. Refunds are mailed approximately four to six weeks after receipt of your request. If you used a credit card to make a payment, the refund will be credited to your credit card account.

The Paper-Based Test

The paper-based test is offered six times during a testing year at testing centers around the country. Questions are presented in multiple-choice format in a test booklet, and answers are entered onto a Scantron form. The essay portion of the PPST Writing test must be handwritten in blue or black ink.

SPECIAL ARRANGEMENTS

Special arrangements may be available for individuals with documented disabilities or for test takers whose primary language is not English (PLNE). Monday test dates are available to those who cannot test on a Saturday test date due to religious convictions or military orders. These accommodations may vary from state to state. You should contact the ETS long before the test date to make inquiries.

THE PAPER-BASED TEST AT A GLANCE

PPST	TEST CODE	NUMBER OF QUESTIONS	TIME ALLOWED
Reading	0710	40 multiple-choice	60 minutes
Mathematics	0730	40 multiple-choice (no calculators)	60 minutes
Writing	0720	38 multiple-choice	30 minutes
		1 essay	30 minutes

Breakdown of Paper-Based Tests

The following table provides the approximate number and percentage of each question type on the paper-based PPSTs.

QUESTION TYPE	NUMBER OF QUESTIONS	PERCENTAGE OF TEST
PPST Reading		
Literal Comprehension	18	45%
Critical and Inferential Comprehension	22	55%
PPST Math		
Numbers and Operations	13	32.5%
Algebra	8	20%
Geometry and Measurement	9	22.5%
Data Analysis and Probability	10	25%
PPST Writing		
Grammatical Relationships	13	17%
Structural Relationships	14	18.5%
Word Choice and Mechanics	11	14.5%
Essay	1	50%

The Computer-Based Test

The Praxis I: Academic Skills Assessments are also available as computer-based tests in over 300 locations throughout the United States. In many ways, the computer-based test is more convenient than the paper-based version. It is given more frequently. The Praxis I tests are available continuously. You don't have to know much about computers to take the computer-based version—each test begins with a tutorial on the use of the computer. You are encouraged to spend as much time as needed on the tutorial.

About the Computer-Based PPST (CPPST)

With the exception of the essay portion of the writing test, all questions are in multiple-choice format. The questions are presented on the computer screen, and you choose your answers by selecting one choice or highlighting a section. The computer-based tests now have a special "mark" function, which allows you to "mark" a question that you would like to temporarily skip and come back to at a later time during the same section on the test. Test takers will have a review screen to see whether a question has been answered, not seen yet, or "marked." The computer-based test is designed to ensure fairness, because each test taker receives:

- the same distribution of content
- the same amount of testing time
- the same test directions
- the same tutorials on computer use

THE COMPUTER-BASED TEST AT A GLANCE (CPPST)

CPPST	TEST CODE	NUMBER OF QUESTIONS	TIME ALLOWED
Reading	5710	46 multiple-choice	75 minutes
Mathematics	5730	46 multiple-choice (no calculators)	75 minutes
Writing	5720	44 multiple-choice	38 minutes
		1 essay	30 minutes

Breakdown of Computer-Based Tests

The following table provides the approximate number and percentage of each question type on the computer-based PPSTs:

QUESTION TYPE	NUMBER OF QUESTIONS	PERCENTAGE OF TEST
CPPST Reading		
Literal Comprehension	21	45%
Critical and Inferential Comprehension	25	55%
CPPST Math		
Numbers and Operations	15	32.5%
Algebra	9	20%
Geometry and Measurement	10	22.5%
Data Analysis and Probability	12	25%
CPPST Writing		
Grammatical Relationships	15	17%
Structural Relationships	16	18.5%
Word Choice and Mechanics	13	14.5%
Essay	1	50%

REMINDER

Again, you may take the computer-based test only once a month, and no more than six times over the course of a year. This even applies to situations where you may have canceled your scores. If you violate this rule, your retest scores will not be reported, and your fees will not be refunded.

NONSTANDARD TESTING ACCOMMODATIONS

If you have a documented disability, you may be able to receive nonstandard testing accommodations for either the paper- or computer-delivered tests. Among a list of accommodations, you may qualify for

- extended test time
- a test reader
- a separate location
- a Braille test
- someone to record your answers

Online, you will find the *Bulletin Supplement for Test Takers with Disabilities or Health-Related Needs*, which contains contact information, registration procedures, and special registration forms.

If you are requesting accommodations, you must register by mail. At least six weeks before the registration date, send your completed requests for testing accommodations to:

ETS Disability Services
P.O. Box 6054
Princeton, NJ 08541-6054

What Is the Praxis II Like?

The Praxis II Subject Assessments include over 120 tests. These tests measure knowledge of specific K–12 content areas, from Agriculture to World and U.S. History. They also test teaching knowledge and skills. In this book we focus on the Principles of Learning and Teaching (PLT) tests, which assess pedagogical knowledge at the early childhood, grades K–6, grades 5–9, and grades 7–12 levels. These tests consist of constructed-response and multiple-choice questions that ask you to demonstrate what you know about educational theory and foundational knowledge, and to apply your understandings to practical situations. See Chapters 9 through 13 for a review of the principles and a practice exam at each level. Let's take a closer look here at the PLT tests.

Each level of the PLT tests presents 70 multiple-choice questions and 4 constructed-response questions related to two case histories. You will have two hours to complete the test. The PLTs are paper-delivered or computer-delivered tests.

The general information about test registration and payment, explained in "What Is the Praxis I Like?" also pertains to the Praxis II, so we won't repeat it all here. However, here is information that pertains specifically to the PLT.

Breakdown of Topics on the PLT

The following table provides the approximate percentage of each question type on the PLT tests.

TOPIC	QUESTION TYPE	PERCENTAGE OF TEST
Students as Learners	21 multiple-choice	22.5%
Instructional Process	21 multiple-choice	22.5%
Assessment	14 multiple-choice	15%
Professional Development, Leadership and Community	14 multiple-choice	15%
Analysis of Instructional Scenarios	4 constructed-response	25%
Students as Learners	(1–2)	
Instructional Process	(1–2)	
Assessment	(0–1)	
Professional Development, Leadership and Community	(0–1)	

TOPICS				
TEST CODE				
PAPER	COMPUTER	NAME OF TEST	HOURS ALLOTTED	FEE
0621	5621	PLT: Early Childhood	2	$139
0622	5622	PLT: Grades K–6	2	$139
0623	5623	PLT: Grades 5–9	2	$139
0624	5624	PLT: Grades 7–12	2	$139

Although the Praxis II tests are not available continuously as the Praxis I tests are, the Praxis II tests are available to take within frequent testing windows. Go to www.ets.org/praxis/register/centers_dates for a listing of current testing centers and dates.

How Is the PLT Scored?

Each multiple-choice question is worth one point. Each of the four constructed responses is worth two points based on the following scoring guide:

A response receiving 2 points
- shows that the writer thoroughly understands the relevant aspects of the case.
- reflects that the writer responded fully to all components of the question.
- demonstrates that if an explanation was required, the writer strongly explained and supported the explanation with relevant evidence.
- provides evidence that the writer has a strong knowledge of pedagogical concepts, facts, theories, methodologies, and procedures relevant to the question.

A response receiving 1 point
- shows that the writer has a basic understanding of the relevant aspects of the case.
- reflects that the writer responded fully to one component of the question only.
- demonstrates that if an explanation was required, the writer provided a weak explanation but supported the explanation with relevant evidence.

- provides evidence that the writer has some knowledge of pedagogical concepts, facts, theories, methodologies, and procedures relevant to the question.

A response receiving 0 points
- shows that the writer misunderstood the relevant aspects of the case.
- reflects that the writer failed to respond appropriately to the question.
- demonstrates that the writer cannot support the response with relevant evidence.
- provides little evidence that the writer has much knowledge of pedagogical concepts, facts, theories, methodologies, and procedures relevant to the question.

Where Do I Begin?

You have already taken the first step by reading this chapter and familiarizing yourself with the Praxis Series of tests. Perhaps you have even started researching to see which tests you need to take, when the tests are offered, and where you would like to take them. Now you should begin your study program: Start with "The LearningExpress Test Preparation System" (Chapter 2). This exclusive system gives you valuable test-taking techniques and will help you devise a study schedule that works best for you. If you stick with your study plan and concentrate on improving the areas in which you need help, you are sure to succeed. Good luck!

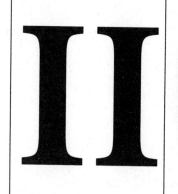

PART

II ▶ TEST PREPARATION

CHAPTER

2 ▶ THE LEARNINGEXPRESS TEST PREPARATION SYSTEM

CHAPTER SUMMARY

The Praxis Series of tests can be challenging. A great deal of preparation is necessary for achieving top scores and advancing your career. The LearningExpress Test Preparation System, developed by leading experts exclusively for LearningExpress, offers strategies for developing the discipline and attitude required for success.

Fact: Taking the Praxis Series of tests is not easy, and neither is getting ready for them. Your future career as a teacher depends on getting a passing score, but an assortment of pitfalls can keep you from doing your best. Here are some of the obstacles that can stand in the way of success:

- being unfamiliar with the exam format
- being paralyzed by test anxiety
- leaving your preparation to the last minute
- not preparing at all!
- not knowing vital test-taking skills: how to pace yourself through the exams, how to use the process of elimination, and when to guess
- not being in tip-top mental and physical shape
- messing up on test day by arriving late at the test site, having to work on an empty stomach, or feeling uncomfortable during the exams because the room is too hot or cold

What's the common denominator in all these test-taking pitfalls? One word: control. Who's in control, you or the exam?

Here's some good news: The LearningExpress Test Preparation System puts you in control. In nine easy-to-follow steps, you will learn everything you need to know to make sure that you are in charge of your preparation and your performance on the exams. Other test takers may let the tests get the better of them; other test takers may be unprepared or out of shape, but not you. You will have taken all the steps you need to take to get a high score on the Praxis tests.

Here's how the LearningExpress Test Preparation System works: Nine easy steps lead you through everything you need to know and do to get ready to master your exams. Each of the following steps includes both reading about the step and one or more activities. It's important that you do the activities along with the reading, or you won't be getting the full benefit of the system. Each step tells you approximately how much time that step will take you to complete.

Step 1: Get Information	50 minutes
Step 2: Conquer Test Anxiety	20 minutes
Step 3: Make a Plan	30 minutes
Step 4: Learn to Manage Your Time	10 minutes
Step 5: Learn to Use the Process of Elimination	20 minutes
Step 6: Know When to Guess	20 minutes
Step 7: Reach Your Peak Performance Zone	10 minutes
Step 8: Get Your Act Together	10 minutes
Step 9: Do It!	10 minutes
Total	**3 hours**

We estimate that working through the entire system will take you approximately three hours, though it's perfectly okay if you work faster or slower. If you take an afternoon or evening, you can work through the whole LearningExpress Test Preparation System in one sitting. Otherwise, you can break it up,

and do just one or two steps a day for the next several days. It's up to you—remember, you are in control.

Step 1: Get Information

Time to complete: 50 minutes
Activity: Read Chapter 1, "The Praxis Series of Tests."

Knowledge is power. The first step in the LearningExpress Test Preparation System is finding out everything you can about the Praxis tests. Once you have your information, the next steps in the LearningExpress Test Preparation System will show you what to do about it.

Part A: Straight Talk about the Praxis I

Why do you have to take rigorous exams, anyway? It's simply an attempt to be sure you have the knowledge and skills necessary to be a teacher.

It's important for you to remember that your scores on the Praxis tests do not determine how smart you are or even whether you will make a good teacher. There are all kinds of things exams like these can't test, such as whether you have the drive, determination, and dedication to be a teacher. Those kinds of things are hard to evaluate, while a test is easy to evaluate.

This is not to say that the exams are not important! The knowledge tested on the exams is knowledge you will need to do your job. And your ability to enter the profession you've trained for depends on passing. And that's why you are here—using the LearningExpress Test Preparation System to achieve control over the exams.

Part B: What's on the Tests

If you haven't already done so, stop here and read Chapter 1 of this book, which gives you an overview of the Praxis Series of tests. Then, go to the Internet and read the most up-to-date information about your exam directly from the test developers at www.ets.org/praxis.

Step 2: Conquer Test Anxiety

Time to complete: 20 minutes
Activity: Take the Test Anxiety Test.

Having complete information about the exams is the first step in getting control of them. Next, you have to overcome one of the biggest obstacles to test success: test anxiety. Test anxiety not only impairs your performance on the exams, but also keeps you from preparing. In Step 2, you will learn stress management techniques that will help you succeed. Learn these strategies now, and practice them as you work through the exams in this book so that they will be second nature to you by exam day.

Combating Test Anxiety

The first thing you need to know is that a little test anxiety is a good thing. Everyone gets nervous before a big exam—and if that nervousness motivates you to prepare thoroughly, so much the better. It's said that Sir Laurence Olivier, one of the foremost British actors of the twentieth century, felt ill before every performance. His stage fright didn't impair his performance; in fact, it probably gave him a little extra edge—just the kind of edge you need to do well, whether on a stage or in an examination room.

Below is the Test Anxiety Test. Stop and answer the questions to find out whether your level of test anxiety is something you should worry about.

TEST ANXIETY TEST

You don't need to worry about test anxiety unless it is extreme enough to impair your performance. The following questionnaire will provide a diagnosis of your level of test anxiety. In the blank before each statement, write the number that most accurately describes your experience.

0 = Never   1 = Once or twice   2 = Sometimes   3 = Often

_____ I have gotten so nervous before an exam that I simply put down the books and didn't study for it.

_____ I have experienced disabling physical symptoms such as vomiting and severe headaches because I was nervous about an exam.

_____ I have simply not shown up for an exam because I was afraid to take it.

_____ I have experienced dizziness and disorientation while taking an exam.

_____ I have had trouble filling in the little circles because my hands were shaking too hard.

_____ I have failed an exam because I was too nervous to complete it.

_____ **Total: Add up the numbers in the blanks.**

Your Test Anxiety Score

Here are the steps you should take, depending on your score. If you scored:

- **Below 3**, your level of test anxiety is nothing to worry about; it's probably just enough to give you that little extra edge.

- **Between 3 and 6**, your test anxiety may be enough to impair your performance, and you should practice the stress management techniques listed in this section to try to bring your test anxiety down to manageable levels.

- **Above 6**, your level of test anxiety is a serious concern. In addition to practicing the stress management techniques listed in this section, you may want to seek additional, personal help by contacting your academic counselor. Tell the counselor that you have a level of test anxiety that sometimes keeps you from being able to take an exam. The counselor may be willing to help you or may suggest someone else you should talk to.

Stress Management Before a Test

If you feel your level of anxiety getting the best of you in the weeks before a test, here is what you need to do to bring the level down again:

- **Get prepared.** There's nothing like knowing what to expect and being prepared for it to put you in control of test anxiety. That's why you are reading this book. Use it faithfully, and remind yourself that you are better-prepared than most of the people taking the test.
- **Practice self-confidence.** A positive attitude is a great way to combat test anxiety. This is no time to be humble or shy. Stand in front of the mirror and say to your reflection, "I am prepared. I am full of self-confidence. I am going to ace this test. I know I can do it." Record it and play it back once a day. If you hear it often enough, you will believe it.
- **Fight negative messages.** Every time someone starts telling you how hard the exam is or how it's almost impossible to get a high score, start telling them your self-confidence messages you learned about in the previous entry. Don't listen to the negative messages. Turn on your recorder and listen to your self-confidence messages.
- **Visualize.** Imagine yourself reporting for duty on your first day as a teacher or in your teacher training program. Visualizing success can help make it happen—and it reminds you of why you are doing all this work preparing for the exam.
- **Exercise.** Physical activity helps calm your body down and focus your mind. Besides, being in good physical shape can actually help you do well on the exam. Go for a run, lift weights, go swimming—and do it regularly.

Stress Management on Test Day

There are several ways you can bring down your level of anxiety on test day. They will work best if you practice them in the weeks before the test so that you know which ones work best for you.

- **Practice deep breathing.** Take a deep breath while you count to five. Hold it for a count of one, then let it out on a count of five. Repeat several times.
- **Move your body.** Try rolling your head in a circle. Rotate your shoulders. Shake your hands from the wrist. Many people find these movements very relaxing.
- **Visualize again.** Think of the place where you are most relaxed: lying on the beach in the sun, walking through the park, or wherever. Now close your eyes and imagine you are actually there. If you practice in advance, you will find that you only need a few seconds of this exercise to experience a significant increase in your sense of well-being.

When anxiety threatens to overwhelm you right there during the exam, there are still things you can do to manage your stress level:

- **Repeat your self-confidence messages.** You should have them memorized by now. Say them quietly to yourself, and believe them!
- **Visualize one more time.** This time, visualize yourself moving smoothly and quickly through the test, answering every question right and finishing just before time is up. Like most visualization techniques, this one works best if you have practiced it ahead of time.
- **Find an easy question.** Find an easy question, and answer it. Getting even one question finished gets you into the test-taking groove.

- **Take a mental break.** Everyone loses concentration once in a while during a long test. It's normal, so you shouldn't worry about it. Instead, accept what has happened. Say to yourself, "Hey, I lost it there for a minute. My brain is taking a break." Put down your pencil, close your eyes, and do some deep breathing for a few seconds. Then you are ready to go back to work.

Try these techniques ahead of time, and see if they work for you!

Step 3: Make a Plan

Time to complete: 30 minutes
Activity: Construct a study plan.

Maybe the most important thing you can do to get control of yourself and your exams is to make a study plan. Too many people fail to prepare simply because they fail to plan. Spending hours on the day before the exam poring over sample test questions not only raises your level of test anxiety, but it also is simply no substitute for careful preparation and practice over time.

Don't fall into the cram trap. Take control of your preparation time by mapping out a study schedule. On the following pages are two sample schedules, based on the amount of time you have before you take the Praxis I. If you are the kind of person who needs deadlines and assignments to motivate you for a project, here they are. If you are the kind of person who doesn't like to follow other people's plans, you can use the suggested schedules here to construct your own.

Even more important than making a plan is making a commitment. You have to set aside some time every day for study and practice. Try for at least 20 minutes a day. Twenty minutes daily will do you much more good than two hours on Saturday.

Don't put off your study until the day before the exam. Start now. A few minutes a day, with half an hour or more on weekends, can make a big difference in your score.

Schedule A: The 30-Day Plan for Praxis I

If you have at least a month before you take the Praxis I, you have plenty of time to prepare—as long as you don't waste it! If you have less than a month, turn to Schedule B.

TIME	PREPARATION
Days 1–4	Skim over any other study materials you may have. Make a note of areas you expect to be emphasized on the exam and areas you don't feel confident in. On Day 4, concentrate on those areas.
Day 5	Take the diagnostic pretest in Chapter 3.
Day 6	Score the pretest using the answers in Chapter 14. Identify two areas that you will concentrate on before you take the first practice exam.
Days 7–10	Study one of the areas you identified as a weak point. Don't forget, there is a Reading Test Review in Chapter 4, a Mathematics Test Review in Chapter 5, and a Writing Test Review in Chapter 6. Review one of these chapters in detail to improve your score on the practice test.
Days 11–14	Study the other area you identified as a weak point. Don't forget, there is a Reading Test Review in Chapter 4, a Mathematics Test Review in Chapter 5, and a Writing Test Review in Chapter 6. Review one of these chapters in detail to improve your score on the first practice test.
Day 15	Take the first practice exam in Chapter 7.
Day 16	Score the practice exam. Identify one area to concentrate on before you take the next practice exam.
Days 17–21	Study the one area you identified for review. Again, use the Reading, Mathematics, and Writing Test Reviews for help.
Day 22	Take the second practice exam in Chapter 8.
Day 23	Score the test. Note how much you have improved!
Days 24–28	Study any remaining topics you still need to review. Use the review chapters for help.
Day 29	Take an overview of all your study materials, consolidating your strengths and improving on your weaknesses.
Day before the exam	Relax. Do something unrelated to the exam and go to bed at a reasonable hour.

Schedule B: The Ten-Day Plan for Praxis I

If you have two weeks or less before you take the exam, use this ten-day schedule to help you make the most of your time.

TIME	PREPARATION
Day 1	Take the diagnostic pretest in Chapter 3 and score it using the answers in Chapter 14. Note which topics you need to review most.
Day 2	Review one area that gave you trouble on the pretest. Use the Reading Test Review in Chapter 4, the Mathematics Test Review in Chapter 5, and the Writing Test Review in Chapter 6. Review one of these chapters in detail to improve your score on the first practice test.
Day 3	Review another area that gave you trouble on the pretest. Again, use the Reading Test Review in Chapter 4, the Mathematics Test Review in Chapter 5, and the Writing Test Review in Chapter 6.
Day 4	Take the first practice exam in Chapter 7 and score it.
Day 5	If your score on the first practice exam doesn't show improvement on the two areas you studied, review them. If you did improve in those areas, choose a new weak area to study today.
Days 6–7	Continue to use the review chapters to improve some skills and reinforce others.
Day 8	Take the second practice exam in Chapter 8 and score it.
Day 9	Choose your weakest area from the second practice exam to review.
Day 10	Use your last study day to brush up on any areas that are still giving you trouble. Use the review chapters.
Day before the exam	Relax. Do something unrelated to the exam and go to bed at a reasonable hour.

For the Praxis II PLT, construct a study schedule that allows for plenty of time to self-assess your needs (use Figure 9.1 in Chapter 9) and review. Use Schedules A and B for the Praxis I as guides.

Step 4: Learn to Manage Your Time

Time to complete: 10 minutes to read, many hours of practice!

Activity: Practice these strategies as you take the sample tests in this book.

Steps 4, 5, and 6 of the LearningExpress Test Preparation System put you in charge of your exams by showing you test-taking strategies that work. Practice these strategies as you take the sample tests in this book, and then you will be ready to use them on test day.

First, take control of your time on the exams. It's a terrible feeling to know there are only five minutes left when you are only three-quarters of the way through a test. Here are some tips to keep that from happening to you:

- **Follow directions.** You may choose to take the computer-based Praxis exam. You should take your time taking the computer tutorial before the exam. Read the directions carefully and ask questions before the exam begins if there's anything you don't understand.

- **Pace yourself.** If there is a timer on the screen as you take the exam, keep an eye on it. This will help you pace yourself. For example, when one-quarter of the time has elapsed, you should be a quarter of the way through the test, and so on. If you are falling behind, pick up the pace a bit. If you do not take your exam on a computer, use your watch or the clock in the testing room to keep track of the time you have left.

- **Keep moving.** Don't waste time on one question. If you don't know the answer, skip the question and move on. You can always go back to it later.

- **Don't rush.** Although you should keep moving, rushing won't help. Try to keep calm and work methodically and quickly.

Step 5: Learn to Use the Process of Elimination

Time to complete: 20 minutes

Activity: Complete the worksheet on Using the Process of Elimination.

After time management, your next most important tool for taking control of your exam is using the process of elimination wisely. It's standard test-taking wisdom that you should always read all the answer choices before choosing your answer. This helps you find the right answer by eliminating wrong answer choices. And, sure enough, that standard wisdom applies to your exam, too.

You should always use the process of elimination on tough questions, even if the right answer

jumps out at you. Sometimes the answer that jumps out isn't right after all. You should always proceed through the answer choices in order. You can start with answer choice **a** and eliminate any choices that are clearly incorrect.

If you are taking the test on paper, like the practice exams in this book, it's good to have a system for marking good, bad, and maybe answers. We're recommending this one:

    X = bad
    ✔ = good
    ? = maybe

If you don't like these marks, devise your own system. Just make sure you do it long before test day—while you're working through the practice exams in this book—so you won't have to worry about it just before the exam.

Even when you think you are absolutely clueless about a question, you can often use the process of elimination to get rid of one answer choice. If so, you are better prepared to make an educated guess, as you will see in Step 6. More often, the process of elimination allows you to get down to only two possibly right answers. Then you are in a strong position to guess. And sometimes, even though you don't know the right answer, you find it simply by getting rid of the wrong ones.

Try using your powers of elimination on the questions in the worksheet Using the Process of Elimination beginning on the next page. The questions aren't about teaching; they're just designed to show you how the process of elimination works. The answer explanations for this worksheet show one possible way that you might use the process to arrive at the right answer.

The process of elimination is your tool for the next step, which is knowing when to guess.

Use the process of elimination to answer the following questions.

1. Ilsa is as old as Meghan will be in five years. The difference between Ed's age and Meghan's age is twice the difference between Ilsa's age and Meghan's age. Ed is 29. How old is Ilsa?
   a. 4
   b. 10
   c. 19
   d. 24

2. "All drivers of commercial vehicles must carry a valid commercial driver's license whenever operating a commercial vehicle." According to this sentence, which of the following people need NOT carry a commercial driver's license?
   a. a truck driver idling his engine while waiting to be directed to a loading dock
   b. a bus operator backing her bus out of the way of another bus in the bus lot
   c. a taxi driver driving his personal car to the grocery store
   d. a limousine driver taking the limousine to her home after dropping off her last passenger of the evening

3. Smoking tobacco has been linked to
   a. increased risk of stroke and heart attack.
   b. all forms of respiratory disease.
   c. increasing mortality rates over the past ten years.
   d. juvenile delinquency.

4. Which of the following words is spelled correctly?
   a. incorrigible
   b. outragous
   c. domestickated
   d. understandible

Answers

Here are the answers, as well as some suggestions as to how you might have used the process of elimination to find them.

1. d. You should have eliminated choice **a** immediately. Ilsa cannot be 4 years old if Meghan is going to be Ilsa's age in five years. The best way to eliminate other answer choices is to try plugging them into the information given in the problem. For instance, for choice **b**, if Ilsa is 10, then Meghan must be 5. The difference in their ages is 5 years. The difference between Ed's age, 29, and Meghan's age, 5, is 24. Is 24 two times 5? No. Then choice **b** is wrong. You could eliminate choice **c** in the same way and be left with choice **d**.

2. c. Note the word *not* in the question, and go through the answers one by one. Is the truck driver in choice **a** "operating a commercial vehicle"? Yes, idling counts as "operating," so he needs to have a commercial driver's license. Likewise, the bus operator in choice **b** is operating a commercial vehicle; the question does not say the operator has to be on the street. The limo driver in choice **d** is operating a commercial vehicle, even if it does not have a passenger in it. However, the cabbie in choice **c** is *not* operating a commercial vehicle, but his own private car.

3. a. You could eliminate choice **b** simply because of the presence of the word *all*. Such absolutes hardly ever appear in correct answer choices. Choice **c** looks attractive until you think a little about what you know—are there not fewer people smoking these days, rather than more? So how could smoking be responsible for a higher mortality rate? (If you did not know that *mortality rate* means the rate at which people die, you might keep this choice as a possibility, but you would still be able to eliminate two answers and have only two to choose from.) Choice **d** is plain silly, so you could eliminate that one, too. Now you are left with the correct choice, **a**.

4. a. How you used the process of elimination here depends on which words you recognized as being spelled incorrectly. If you knew that the correct spellings were *outrageous*, *domesticated*, and *understandable*, then you were home free. You probably knew that at least one of those words was spelled wrong.

Step 6: Know When to Guess

Time to complete: 20 minutes
Activity: Complete the worksheet on Your Guessing Ability.

Armed with the process of elimination, you are ready to take control of one of the big questions in test taking: Should I guess? The answer is: *Yes.* Some exams have what's called a "guessing penalty," in which a fraction of your wrong answers is subtracted from your right answers—the Praxis Series of tests does NOT work like that. The number of questions you answer correctly yields your raw score. So you have nothing to lose and everything to gain by guessing.

The following are ten really hard questions. You are not supposed to know the answers. Rather, this is an assessment of your ability to guess when you don't have a clue. Read each question carefully, just as if you did expect to answer it. If you have any knowledge at all about the subject of the question, use that knowledge to help you eliminate wrong answer choices.

ANSWER GRID

1.	ⓐ	ⓑ	ⓒ	ⓓ
2.	ⓐ	ⓑ	ⓒ	ⓓ
3.	ⓐ	ⓑ	ⓒ	ⓓ
4.	ⓐ	ⓑ	ⓒ	ⓓ

5.	ⓐ	ⓑ	ⓒ	ⓓ
6.	ⓐ	ⓑ	ⓒ	ⓓ
7.	ⓐ	ⓑ	ⓒ	ⓓ
8.	ⓐ	ⓑ	ⓒ	ⓓ

9.	ⓐ	ⓑ	ⓒ	ⓓ
10.	ⓐ	ⓑ	ⓒ	ⓓ

1. September 7 is Independence Day in
   a. India.
   b. Costa Rica.
   c. Brazil.
   d. Australia.

2. Which of the following is the formula for determining the momentum of an object?
   a. $p = mv$
   b. $F = ma$
   c. $P = IV$
   d. $E = mc^2$

3. Because of the expansion of the universe, the stars and other celestial bodies are all moving away from each other. This phenomenon is known as
   a. Newton's first law.
   b. the big bang.
   c. gravitational collapse.
   d. Hubble flow.

4. American author Gertrude Stein was born in
   a. 1713.
   b. 1830.
   c. 1874.
   d. 1901.

5. Which of the following is NOT one of the Five Classics attributed to Confucius?
   a. *I Ching*
   b. *Book of Holiness*
   c. *Spring and Autumn Annals*
   d. *Book of History*

6. The religious and philosophical doctrine that holds that the universe is constantly in a struggle between good and evil is known as
   a. Pelagianism.
   b. Manichaeanism.
   c. neo-Hegelianism.
   d. Epicureanism.

7. The third Chief Justice of the U.S. Supreme Court was
   a. John Blair.
   b. William Cushing.
   c. James Wilson.
   d. John Jay.

8. Which of the following is the poisonous portion of a daffodil?
  a. the bulb
  b. the leaves
  c. the stem
  d. the flowers

9. The winner of the Masters golf tournament in 1953 was
  a. Sam Snead.
  b. Cary Middlecoff.
  c. Arnold Palmer.
  d. Ben Hogan.

10. The state with the highest per capita personal income in 1980 was
  a. Alaska.
  b. Connecticut.
  c. New York.
  d. Texas.

Answers

Check your answers against the correct answers that follow.
 1. c.
 2. a.
 3. d.
 4. c.
 5. b.
 6. b.
 7. b.
 8. a.
 9. d.
10. a.

How Did You Do?

You may have simply gotten lucky and actually known the answer to one or two questions. In addition, your guessing was more successful if you were able to use the process of elimination on any of the questions. Maybe you didn't know who the third chief justice was (question 7), but you knew that John Jay was the first. In that case, you would have eliminated choice **d** and therefore improved your odds of guessing correctly from one in four to one in three.

According to probability, you should get $2\frac{1}{2}$ answers correct, so getting either two or three right would be average. If you got four or more right, you may be a really terrific guesser. If you got one or none right, you may need to work on your guessing skills.

Keep in mind, though, that this is only a small sample. You should continue to keep track of your guessing ability as you work through the sample questions in this book. Circle the numbers of questions you guess on as you make your guess; or, if you don't have time while you take the practice exams, go back afterward and try to remember which questions you guessed at. Remember, on an exam with four answer choices, your chance of getting a right answer is one in four. So keep a separate guessing score for each exam. How many questions did you guess on? How many did you get right? If the number you got right is at least one-fourth of the number of questions you guessed on, you are at least an average guesser, maybe better—and you should always go ahead and guess on a real exam. If the number you got right is significantly lower than one-fourth of the number you guessed on, you would, frankly, be safe in guessing anyway, but maybe you would feel more comfortable if you guessed only selectively, when you can eliminate a wrong answer or at least have a good feeling about one of the answer choices.

Step 7: Reach Your Peak Performance Zone

Time to complete: 10 minutes to read; weeks to complete!
Activity: Complete the Physical Preparation Checklist.

To get ready for a challenge like a big exam, you have to take control of your physical, as well as your mental, state. Exercise, proper diet, and rest will ensure that your body works with, rather than against, your mind on test day, as well as during your preparation.

Exercise

If you don't already have a regular exercise program going, the time during which you are preparing for an exam is actually an excellent time to start one. And if you are already keeping fit—or trying to get that way—don't let the pressure of preparing for an exam fool you into quitting now. Exercise helps reduce stress by pumping wonderful good-feeling hormones called *endorphins* into your system. It also increases the oxygen supply throughout your body, including your brain, so you will be at peak performance on test day.

A half hour of vigorous activity—enough to raise a sweat—every day should be your aim. If you are really pressed for time, every other day is okay. Choose an activity you like and get out there and do it. Jogging with a friend always makes the time go faster, or take a radio.

But don't overdo it. You don't want to exhaust yourself. Moderation is the key.

Diet

First of all, cut out the junk. Go easy on caffeine and nicotine, and eliminate alcohol and any other drugs from your system at least two weeks before the exam. Promise yourself a treat the night after the exam, if need be.

What your body needs for peak performance is simply a balanced diet. Eat plenty of fruits and vegetables, along with protein and carbohydrates. Foods that are high in lecithin (an amino acid), such as fish and beans, are especially good "brain foods."

The night before the exam, you might carboload the way athletes do before a contest. Eat a big plate of spaghetti, rice and beans, or whatever your favorite carbohydrate is.

Rest

You probably know how much sleep you need every night to be at your best, even if you don't always get it. Make sure you do get that much sleep, though, for at least a week before the exam. Moderation is important here, too. Extra sleep will just make you groggy.

If you are not a morning person and your exam will be given in the morning, you should reset your internal clock so that your body doesn't think you are taking an exam at 3 A.M. You have to start this process well before the exam. The way it works is to get up half an hour earlier each morning, and then go to bed half an hour earlier that night. Don't try it the other way around; you will just toss and turn if you go to bed early without having gotten up early. The next morning, get up another half an hour earlier, and so on. How long you will have to do this depends on how late you are used to getting up. Use the Physical Preparation Checklist on the next page to make sure you are in tip-top form.

PHYSICAL PREPARATION CHECKLIST

For the week before an exam, write down what physical exercise you engaged in and for how long, and what you ate for each meal. Remember, you are trying for at least half an hour of exercise every other day (preferably every day) and a balanced diet that is light on junk food.

Exam minus 7 days

Exercise: _____ for _____ minutes

Breakfast: _____

Lunch: _____

Dinner: _____

Snacks: _____

Exam minus 6 days

Exercise: _____ for _____ minutes

Breakfast: _____

Lunch: _____

Dinner: _____

Snacks: _____

Exam minus 5 days

Exercise: _____ for _____ minutes

Breakfast: _____

Lunch: _____

Dinner: _____

Snacks: _____

Exam minus 4 days

Exercise: _____ for _____ minutes

Breakfast: _____

Lunch: _____

Dinner: _____

Snacks: _____

Exam minus 3 days

Exercise: _____ for _____ minutes

Breakfast: _____

Lunch: _____

Dinner: _____

Snacks: _____

Exam minus 2 days

Exercise: _____ for _____ minutes

Breakfast: _____

Lunch: _____

Dinner: _____

Snacks: _____

Exam minus 1 day

Exercise: _____ for _____ minutes

Breakfast: _____

Lunch: _____

Dinner: _____

Snacks: _____

Step 8: Get Your Act Together

Time to complete: 10 minutes to read; time to complete will vary
Activity: Complete the Final Preparations worksheet.

You are in control of your mind and body; you are in charge of test anxiety, your preparation, and your test-taking strategies. Now it's time to take charge of external factors, like the testing site and the materials you need to take to the exam.

Find Out Where the Exam or Exams Are, and Make a Trial Run

Do you know how to get to the testing site? Do you know how long it will take to get there? If not, make a trial run, preferably on the same day of the week at the same time of day as when you will be taking your test. Note, on the Final Preparations worksheet on the next page, the amount of time it will take you to get to the exam site. Plan on arriving 30–45 minutes early so you can get the lay of the land, use the bathroom, and calm down. Then figure out how early you will have to get up that morning, and make sure you get up that early every day for a week before the exam.

Gather Your Materials

The night before the exams, lay out the clothes you will wear and the materials you have to bring with you to the exam. Plan on dressing in layers; you won't have any control over the temperature of the examination room. Have a sweater or jacket that you can take off if it's warm. Use the checklist on the Final Preparations worksheet to help you pull together what you will need.

Don't Skip Breakfast

Even if you don't usually eat breakfast, do so on exam morning. A cup of coffee doesn't count. Don't eat doughnuts or other sweet foods, either. A sugar high will leave you with a sugar low in the middle of the exam. A mix of protein and carbohydrates is best: Cereal with milk and just a little sugar, or eggs with toast, will do your body a world of good.

Step 9: Do It!

Time to complete: 10 minutes, plus test-taking time
Activity: Ace the Praxis tests!

Fast-forward to exam day. You are ready. You made a study plan and followed through. You practiced your test-taking strategies while working through this book. You are in control of your physical, mental, and emotional state. You know when and where to show up and what to bring with you. In other words, you are better-prepared than most of the other people taking the exam. You are psyched.

Just one more thing. When you are finished with the exams, you will have earned a reward. Plan a celebration. Call up your friends and plan a party, or have a nice dinner for two—whatever your heart desires. Give yourself something to look forward to.

And then do it. Go into the exams full of confidence and armed with test-taking strategies you have practiced until they're second nature. You are in control of yourself, your environment, and your performance on the exam. You are ready to succeed. So do it. Go in there and ace the exam. And look forward to your future career as a teacher!

FINAL PREPARATIONS

Getting to the Exam Site

Location of exam site: _____

Date: _____

Departure time: _____

Do I know how to get to the exam site?   Yes _____   No _____   (If no, make a trial run.)

Time it will take to get to exam site _____

Things to Lay Out the Night Before

Clothes I will wear   _____

Sweater/jacket   _____

Watch   _____

Photo ID   _____

Admission ticket   _____

Four #2 pencils   _____ (paper-delivered test only)

Eraser   _____ (paper-delivered test only)

Other Things to Bring/Remember

Do not bring electronic devices into the testing site.

_____   _____

_____   _____

_____   _____

_____   _____

III

FOCUSING ON THE PRAXIS I PPST

C H A P T E R

3 ▶ PRAXIS I DIAGNOSTIC PRETEST

CHAPTER SUMMARY

This is the first of the three full-length PPST exams in this book that are based on the three elements of the Praxis I PPSTs of Reading, Mathematics, and Writing. Use this Praxis I Diagnostic Pretest to see how you would do if you were to take the Praxis I today.

This Praxis I Diagnostic Pretest contains three tests of the same type as the real exam you will be taking—that is, Reading (multiple-choice questions), Mathematics (multiple-choice questions), and Writing (multiple-choice questions and an essay).

As you take this pretest, do not worry too much about timing. Just take the three tests in as relaxed a manner as you can to find out in which areas you are skilled and in which ones you will need extra work.

The answer sheet you should use for the multiple-choice questions is on the following page. (You will write your essay on a separate piece of paper.) After you finish taking your test, you should review the answer explanations found in Chapter 14. Following the answer explanations in Chapter 14, you will find information on how to score your exam.

SKILLS TEST IN READING

1. (a) (b) (c) (d) (e)
2. (a) (b) (c) (d) (e)
3. (a) (b) (c) (d) (e)
4. (a) (b) (c) (d) (e)
5. (a) (b) (c) (d) (e)
6. (a) (b) (c) (d) (e)
7. (a) (b) (c) (d) (e)
8. (a) (b) (c) (d) (e)
9. (a) (b) (c) (d) (e)
10. (a) (b) (c) (d) (e)
11. (a) (b) (c) (d) (e)
12. (a) (b) (c) (d) (e)
13. (a) (b) (c) (d) (e)
14. (a) (b) (c) (d) (e)
15. (a) (b) (c) (d) (e)
16. (a) (b) (c) (d) (e)
17. (a) (b) (c) (d) (e)
18. (a) (b) (c) (d) (e)
19. (a) (b) (c) (d) (e)
20. (a) (b) (c) (d) (e)
21. (a) (b) (c) (d) (e)
22. (a) (b) (c) (d) (e)
23. (a) (b) (c) (d) (e)
24. (a) (b) (c) (d) (e)
25. (a) (b) (c) (d) (e)
26. (a) (b) (c) (d) (e)
27. (a) (b) (c) (d) (e)
28. (a) (b) (c) (d) (e)
29. (a) (b) (c) (d) (e)
30. (a) (b) (c) (d) (e)
31. (a) (b) (c) (d) (e)
32. (a) (b) (c) (d) (e)
33. (a) (b) (c) (d) (e)
34. (a) (b) (c) (d) (e)
35. (a) (b) (c) (d) (e)
36. (a) (b) (c) (d) (e)
37. (a) (b) (c) (d) (e)
38. (a) (b) (c) (d) (e)
39. (a) (b) (c) (d) (e)
40. (a) (b) (c) (d) (e)

SKILLS TEST IN MATHEMATICS

1. (a) (b) (c) (d) (e)
2. (a) (b) (c) (d) (e)
3. (a) (b) (c) (d) (e)
4. (a) (b) (c) (d) (e)
5. (a) (b) (c) (d) (e)
6. (a) (b) (c) (d) (e)
7. (a) (b) (c) (d) (e)
8. (a) (b) (c) (d) (e)
9. (a) (b) (c) (d) (e)
10. (a) (b) (c) (d) (e)
11. (a) (b) (c) (d) (e)
12. (a) (b) (c) (d) (e)
13. (a) (b) (c) (d) (e)
14. (a) (b) (c) (d) (e)
15. (a) (b) (c) (d) (e)
16. (a) (b) (c) (d) (e)
17. (a) (b) (c) (d) (e)
18. (a) (b) (c) (d) (e)
19. (a) (b) (c) (d) (e)
20. (a) (b) (c) (d) (e)
21. (a) (b) (c) (d) (e)
22. (a) (b) (c) (d) (e)
23. (a) (b) (c) (d) (e)
24. (a) (b) (c) (d) (e)
25. (a) (b) (c) (d) (e)
26. (a) (b) (c) (d) (e)
27. (a) (b) (c) (d) (e)
28. (a) (b) (c) (d) (e)
29. (a) (b) (c) (d) (e)
30. (a) (b) (c) (d) (e)
31. (a) (b) (c) (d) (e)
32. (a) (b) (c) (d) (e)
33. (a) (b) (c) (d) (e)
34. (a) (b) (c) (d) (e)
35. (a) (b) (c) (d) (e)
36. (a) (b) (c) (d) (e)
37. (a) (b) (c) (d) (e)
38. (a) (b) (c) (d) (e)
39. (a) (b) (c) (d) (e)
40. (a) (b) (c) (d) (e)

SKILLS TEST IN WRITING, SECTION 1

1. (a) (b) (c) (d) (e)
2. (a) (b) (c) (d) (e)
3. (a) (b) (c) (d) (e)
4. (a) (b) (c) (d) (e)
5. (a) (b) (c) (d) (e)
6. (a) (b) (c) (d) (e)
7. (a) (b) (c) (d) (e)
8. (a) (b) (c) (d) (e)
9. (a) (b) (c) (d) (e)
10. (a) (b) (c) (d) (e)
11. (a) (b) (c) (d) (e)
12. (a) (b) (c) (d) (e)
13. (a) (b) (c) (d) (e)
14. (a) (b) (c) (d) (e)
15. (a) (b) (c) (d) (e)
16. (a) (b) (c) (d) (e)
17. (a) (b) (c) (d) (e)
18. (a) (b) (c) (d) (e)
19. (a) (b) (c) (d) (e)
20. (a) (b) (c) (d) (e)
21. (a) (b) (c) (d) (e)
22. (a) (b) (c) (d) (e)
23. (a) (b) (c) (d) (e)
24. (a) (b) (c) (d) (e)
25. (a) (b) (c) (d) (e)
26. (a) (b) (c) (d) (e)
27. (a) (b) (c) (d) (e)
28. (a) (b) (c) (d) (e)
29. (a) (b) (c) (d) (e)
30. (a) (b) (c) (d) (e)
31. (a) (b) (c) (d) (e)
32. (a) (b) (c) (d) (e)
33. (a) (b) (c) (d) (e)
34. (a) (b) (c) (d) (e)
35. (a) (b) (c) (d) (e)
36. (a) (b) (c) (d) (e)
37. (a) (b) (c) (d) (e)
38. (a) (b) (c) (d) (e)

Skills Test in Reading

Directions: Read the following passages and answer the questions that follow.

Use the following passage to answer questions 1 and 2.

The English-language premiere of Samuel Beckett's play *Waiting for Godot* took place in London in August 1955. *Godot* is an avant-garde play with only five characters (not including Mr. Godot, who never arrives) and a minimal setting: one rock and one bare tree. The play has two acts; the second act repeats what little action occurs in the first with few changes: the tree, for instance, acquires one leaf. In a statement that was to become famous, the critic Vivian Mercer described *Godot* as "a play in which nothing happens twice." Opening night, critics and playgoers greeted the play with bafflement and derision. The line, "Nothing happens, nobody comes, nobody goes. It's awful," was met by a loud rejoinder of "Hear! Hear!" from an audience member. _____. However, Harold Hobson's review in the *Sunday Times* managed to recognize the play for what history has proven it to be, a revolutionary moment in theater.

1. Which sentence, if inserted in the blank space, would make the best sense in the context of the passage?
   a. The director, Peter Hall, had to beg the theater management not to close the play immediately but to wait for the Sunday reviews.
   b. Despite the audience reaction, the cast and director believed in the play.
   c. It looked as if *Waiting for Godot* was beginning a long run as the most controversial play of London's 1955 season.
   d. *Waiting for Godot* was in danger of closing the first week of its run and of becoming nothing more than a footnote in the annals of the English stage.
   e. The audience and critics all completely misunderstood Beckett's play.

2. Which of the following best describes the attitude of the author of the passage toward the play *Waiting for Godot*?
   a. It was a curiosity in theater history.
   b. It is the most important play of the twentieth century.
   c. It had no effect on theater.
   d. It is too repetitious.
   e. It represents a turning point in stage history.

Use the following passage to answer question 3.

In space flight there are the obvious hazards of meteors, debris, and radiation; however, astronauts must also deal with two vexing physiological foes—muscle atrophy and bone loss. Space shuttle astronauts, because they spend only about a week in space, undergo minimal wasting of bone and muscle. But when longer stays in microgravity or zero gravity are contemplated, as with the International Space Station or a two-year round-trip voyage to

Mars, these problems are of particular concern because they could become acute.

3. The most appropriate audience for the passage would be students in a(n)
   a. physiology class.
   b. engineering class.
   c. physics class.
   d. astronomy class.
   e. history of science class.

Use the following passage to answer question 4.

Jessie Street is sometimes called the Australian Eleanor Roosevelt. Like Roosevelt, Street lived a life of privilege, while at the same time devoting her efforts to working for the rights of the disenfranchised, including workers, women, refugees, and Aborigines. In addition, she gained international fame when she was the only woman on the Australian delegation to the conference that founded the United Nations—just as Eleanor Roosevelt was for the United States.

4. Which of the following inferences may be drawn from the information presented in the passage?
   a. Eleanor Roosevelt and Jessie Street worked together to include women in the United Nations Charter.
   b. Usually, people who live lives of privilege do not spend much time participating in political activities.
   c. Discrimination in Australia is much worse than it ever was in the United States.
   d. At the time of the formation of the United Nations, few women were involved in international affairs.
   e. The United Nations has been ineffective in helping the disenfranchised all over the world.

Use the following passage to answer questions 5 through 7.

Mental and physical health professionals may consider referring clients and patients to a music therapist for a number of reasons. It seems a particularly good choice for the social worker who is coordinating a client's case. Music therapists use music to establish a relationship with the patient and to improve the patient's health, using highly structured musical interactions. Patients and therapists may sing, play instruments, compose music, dance, or simply listen to music.

The course of training for music therapists is comprehensive. In addition to their formal musical and therapy training, music therapists are taught to discern what kinds of interventions will be most beneficial for each individual patient. Because each patient is different and has different goals, the music therapist must be able to understand the patient's situation and choose the music and activities that will do the most toward helping the patient achieve his or her goals. The referring social worker can help this process by clearly articulating each client's history.

Although patients may develop their musical skills, that is not the main goal of music therapy. Any client who needs particular work on communication or on academic, emotional, and social skills, and who is not responding to traditional therapy, is an excellent candidate for music therapy.

5. Which of the following would be the most appropriate title for this passage?
   a. "The Use of Music in the Treatment of Autism"
   b. "How to Use Music to Combat Depression"
   c. "Music Therapy: A Role in Social Work?"
   d. "Training for a Career in Music Therapy"
   e. "The Social Worker as Music Therapist"

6. Which of the following inferences can be drawn from the passage?
  a. Music therapy can succeed where traditional therapies have failed.
  b. Music therapy is a relatively new field.
  c. Music therapy is particularly beneficial for young children.
  d. Music therapy probably will not work well for psychotic people.
  e. Music therapy is appropriate in only a limited number of circumstances.

7. Which of the following best organizes the main topics addressed in this passage?
  a. I. the role of music therapy in social work
      II. locating a music therapist
      III. how to complete a music therapist referral
  b. I. using music in therapy
      II. a typical music therapy intervention
      III. when to prescribe music therapy for sociopaths
  c. I. music therapy and social work
      II. training for music therapists
      III. skills addressed by music therapy
  d. I. how to choose a music therapist
      II. when to refer to a music therapist
      III. who benefits the most from music therapy
  e. I. music therapy as a cost-effective treatment
      II. curriculum of a music therapy program
      III. music therapy and physical illness

Use the following passage to answer question 8.

According to a recent poll, the number of students in the high school environmental club has increased by 40% over the past three years. This increase is the reason why more students have begun recycling their paper and cans during this period.

8. Which of the following, if true, most significantly weakens the preceding argument?
  a. The school installed recycling bins in all classrooms five years ago.
  b. Most students join the environmental club in order to add one more activity to their college applications.
  c. Not all students participated in the poll.
  d. Two years ago, the school began giving detention to any student caught throwing recyclable materials in the regular trash.
  e. The environmental club has begun hanging up more posters about recycling.

Use the following passage to answer question 9.

The seemingly simple question of "What defines a sport?" has been the fodder for argument and conversation for years, among professional and armchair athletes alike. There seems to be no doubt that vigorous and highly competitive activities such as baseball, football, and soccer are truly sports, but when the subject of other activities such as darts, chess, and shuffleboard is broached we find ourselves at the heart of a controversy. Some people claim that a true sport first and foremost requires some form of physical exertion. Therefore, if a player does not break a sweat, what he or she plays is not a sport. Beyond that, more important criteria would be the need for decent hand-eye coordination, and the ever-present possibility of sustaining injury.

9. According to the criteria given in the passage, all of the following would be considered a true sport EXCEPT
   a. cheerleading.
   b. skiing.
   c. race car driving.
   d. horseshoes.
   e. gymnastics.

Use the following passage to answer questions 10 through 12.

Businesses today routinely keep track of large amounts of both financial and nonfinancial information. Sales departments keep track of current and potential customers; marketing departments keep track of product details and regional demographics; accounting departments keep track of financial data and issue reports. To be useful, all this data must be organized into a meaningful and useful system. Such a system is called a *management information system*, abbreviated MIS. The financial hub of the MIS is accounting.

Accounting is the information system that records, analyzes, and reports economic transactions, enabling decision makers to make informed choices when allocating scarce economic resources. It is a tool that enables the user, whether a business entity or an individual, to make wiser, more informed economic choices. It is an aid to planning, controlling, and evaluating a broad range of activities. A financial accounting system is intended for use by both the management of an organization and those outside the organization. Because it is important that financial accounting reports be interpreted correctly, financial accounting is subject to a set of stringent guidelines called generally accepted accounting principles (GAAP).

10. This passage is most likely taken from
    a. a newspaper column.
    b. an essay about modern business.
    c. a legal brief.
    d. a business textbook.
    e. a business machine catalog.

11. According to the information in the passage, which of the following is least likely to be a function of accounting?
    a. helping businesspeople make sound judgments
    b. producing reports of many different kinds of transactions
    c. assisting with the marketing of products
    d. assisting companies in important planning activities
    e. providing information to potential investors

12. According to the information in the first paragraph of the passage, all of the following would be included in a company's MIS EXCEPT
    a. potential customers.
    b. financial data.
    c. regional demographics.
    d. employee birthdates.
    e. product details.

Use the following passage to answer question 13.

The salesperson of the month at Smith's Used Cars sold 26 cars in February. Diana sold 22 cars in February.

13. Based only on the information above, which of the following must be true?
   a. Diana is not salesperson of the month at Smith's Used Cars.
   b. The salesperson of the month is the person who sold the most cars that month.
   c. Diana does not work at Smith's Used Cars.
   d. The salesperson of the month made more money in February than Diana did.
   e. The salesperson of the month is better at selling cars than Diana is.

Use the following passage to answer question 14.

Many studies make it clear that sleep deprivation is dangerous. Sleep-deprived people who are tested by using a driving simulator or by performing a hand-eye coordination task perform as badly as or worse than those who are intoxicated. Sleep deprivation also magnifies alcohol's effects on the body, so a fatigued person who drinks will become much more impaired than someone who is well rested. Since drowsiness is the brain's last step before falling asleep, driving while drowsy can—and often does—lead to disaster. Caffeine and other stimulants cannot overcome the effects of severe sleep deprivation.

14. In the passage, the term *impaired* most nearly means
   a. sentient.
   b. apprehensive.
   c. disturbed.
   d. blemished.
   e. hampered.

Use the following passage to answer question 15.

Because they have the ability to evoke an emotional response in readers, political cartoons can serve as a vehicle for swaying public opinion and can contribute to reform. Thomas Nast (1840–1902), the preeminent political cartoonist of the second half of the nineteenth century, demonstrated the power of his medium when he used his art to end the corrupt Boss Tweed Ring in New York City. His images, first drawn for *Harper's Weekly*, are still in currency today: Nast created the tiger as the symbol of Tammany Hall, the elephant for the Republican Party, and the donkey for the Democratic Party. Created under tight deadlines for ephemeral, commercial formats like newspapers and magazines, cartoons still manage to have lasting influence. Although they tackle the principal issues and leaders of their day, they often provide a vivid historical picture for generations to come.

15. The author cites Thomas Nast's depiction of an elephant for the Republican Party as an example of
   a. an image that is no longer recognized by the public.
   b. the saying, "the pen is mightier than the sword."
   c. art contributing to political reform.
   d. a graphic image that became an enduring symbol.
   e. the ephemeral nature of political cartooning.

Use the following passage to answer questions 16 and 17.

Typically people think of genius, whether it manifests in Mozart's composing symphonies at age five or Einstein's discovery of relativity, as having a quality not just of the supernatural, but also of the eccentric. People see genius as a "good" abnormality; moreover, they think of genius as a completely unpredictable abnormality. Until recently, psychologists regarded the quirks of genius as too erratic to describe intelligibly; however, Anna Findley's groundbreaking study uncovers predictable patterns in the biographies of geniuses. These patterns do not dispel the common belief that there is a kind of supernatural intervention in the lives of unusually talented men and women, however, even though they occur with regularity. For example, Findley shows that all geniuses experience three intensely productive periods in their lives, one of which always occurs shortly before their deaths; this is true whether the genius lives to 19 or 90.

16. Which of the following would be the best title for this passage?
a. "Understanding Mozarts and Einsteins"
b. "Predicting the Life of a Genius"
c. "The Uncanny Patterns in the Lives of Geniuses"
d. "Pattern and Disorder in the Lives of Geniuses"
e. "Supernatural Intervention in the Life of the Genius"

17. Given the information in the passage, which of the following statements is true?
a. Anna Findley is a biographer.
b. All geniuses are eccentric and unpredictable.
c. A genius has three prolific periods in his or her life.
d. Mozart discovered relativity.
e. Geniuses experience three fallow periods in their lives.

Use the following passage to answer question 18.

A study conducted by the Centers for Disease Control (CDC) found that high school students who take part in team sports or are physically active outside of school are less likely to engage in risky behaviors, like using drugs or smoking. Physical activity does not need to be strenuous to be beneficial. The CDC recommends moderate, daily physical activity for people of all ages, such as brisk walking for 30 minutes or 15 to 20 minutes of more intense exercise. A survey conducted by the National Association for Sport and Physical Education questioned teens about their attitudes toward exercise and about what it would take to get them moving. Teens chose friends (56%) as their most likely motivators for becoming more active, followed by parents (18%) and professional athletes (11%).

18. Which of the following techniques is used in the last sentence of the passage?
a. explanation of terms
b. comparison of different arguments
c. contrast of opposing views
d. generalized statement
e. illustration by example

Use the following passage to answer question 19.

Burgers, fries, pizza, raw fish. Raw fish? Fast food in America is changing. Sushi, the thousand-year-old Japanese delicacy, was once thought of in this country as unpalatable and too exotic. But tastes have changed, for a number of reasons. Beginning in the 1970s, Americans became increasingly more aware of diet and health issues, and began rejecting their traditional red-meat diets in favor of healthier, lower-fat choices such as fish, poultry, whole grains, rice, and vegetables. The way food was prepared began to change, too; rather than frying food, people started opting for broiled, steamed, and raw versions. Sushi, a combination of cold boiled rice and raw fish, fit the bill. In addition, that same decade saw Japan become an important global economic force, and companies began flocking to the country to do business. All things Japanese, including décor, clothing, and cuisine, became popular.

19. In the passage, *unpalatable* most nearly means
   a. not visually appealing.
   b. not tasting good.
   c. bad smelling.
   d. too expensive.
   e. rough to the touch.

Use the following passage to answer question 20.

The information on a standard compact disc (CD) is contained in a single spiral track of pits, starting at the inside of the disk and circling its way to the outside. This information is read by shining light from a 780 nm wavelength semiconductor laser. Information is read as the laser moves over the bumps (where no light will be reflected) and the areas that have no bumps, also known as *land* (where the laser light will be reflected off the

aluminum). The changes in reflectivity are interpreted by a part of the compact disc player known as the *detector*. It is the job of the detector to convert the information collected by the laser into the music that was originally recorded onto the disk.

20. What would happen if the detector on a CD player malfunctioned?
   a. The spiral track would not be read properly.
   b. The pits and land would look like one unit.
   c. The changes in reflectivity would be absorbed back into the laser.
   d. The music would play backward.
   e. The information read by the laser would not be converted into music.

Use the following passage to answer questions 21 through 24.

The Caribbean island of Saint Martin is a favorite vacation spot, one that is popular with tourists from various countries. The French and Dutch settled on the island in the 1600s. Today, the island is divided between the two. The French capital is Marigot; the Dutch capital is Philipsburg.

Tourists on vacation soon discover that Saint Martin has an intriguing history. Twelve hundred years ago, the Arawak Indians inhabited all the islands of the West Indies, and were a peaceful people living under the guidance of their chiefs. In the 1300s, three hundred years after the Arawaks first arrived on Saint Martin, they were defeated and forced to abandon the island by a more hostile tribe of Indians that originated in South America. This new tribe was called the Carib. The Caribbean Sea was named after them. Unlike the Arawaks, they had no permanent chiefs or leaders, except in times of strife. They were also extremely warlike. Worse, they were cannibalistic, eating the enemy warriors they captured. In fact, the very word *cannibal* comes from the Spanish name for the Carib Indians. The Spanish arrived in the fifteenth century and, unfortunately, they carried diseases to which the Indians had no immunity. Many Indians succumbed to common European illnesses. Others died from the hard labor forced upon them.

21. According to the passage, all of the following are true about the Carib Indians EXCEPT
   a. the sea was named after them.
   b. they were peaceful fishermen, hunters, and farmers.
   c. they ate human flesh.
   d. they settled after defeating the Arawak Indians.
   e. during times of war, they had temporary leaders.

22. According to the passage, the Carib Indians were finally defeated by
   a. sickness and forced labor.
   b. the more aggressive Arawak tribe.
   c. the Dutch West India Company.
   d. the French explorers.
   e. a cannibalistic tribe.

23. One can infer from the passage that the word *strife* means
   a. cannibalistic.
   b. war.
   c. labor.
   d. chief.
   e. Carib.

24. According to the article, present-day Saint Martin
   a. belongs to the Spanish.
   b. is independent.
   c. belongs to the Carib.
   d. is part of the U.S. Virgin Islands.
   e. is shared by the French and the Dutch.

Use the following passage to answer question 25.

Although protected by the Australian government, the Great Barrier Reef faces environmental threats. Crown-of-thorns starfish feed on coral and can destroy large portions of reef. Pollution and rising water temperatures also threaten the delicate coral. But the most preventable of the hazards to the reef are tourists. Tourists have contributed to the destruction of the reef ecosystem by breaking off and removing pieces of coral to bring home as souvenirs. The government hopes that by informing tourists of the dangers of this seemingly harmless activity they will quash this creeping menace to the fragile reef.

25. The primary purpose of this passage is to
   a. inform the reader that coral reefs are a threatened, yet broadly functioning, ecosystem.
   b. alert the reader to a premier vacation destination in the tropics.
   c. explain in detail how the Great Barrier Reef is constructed.
   d. recommend that tourists stop stealing coral off the Great Barrier Reef.
   e. dispel the argument that coral is a plant, not an animal.

Use the following passage to answer questions 26 and 27.

Although it is called Central Park, New York City's great green space has no "center"—no formal walkway down the middle of the park, no central monument or body of water, no single orienting feature. The paths wind, the landscape constantly shifts and changes, the sections spill into one another in a seemingly random manner. But this "decentering" was precisely the intent of the park's innovative design. Made to look as natural as possible, Frederick Law Olmsted's 1858 plan for Central Park had as its main goal the creation of a democratic playground—a place with many centers to reflect the multiplicity of its uses and users. Olmsted designed the park to allow interaction among the various members of society, without giving preference to one group or class. Thus Olmsted's ideal of a "common-place civilization" could be realized.

26. In the passage, the author describes specific park features in order to
  a. present both sides of the argument.
  b. suggest the organization of the rest of the passage.
  c. provide evidence that the park has no center.
  d. demonstrate how large the park is.
  e. show how well the author knows the park.

27. The main idea of this passage is that
  a. New York City is a democratic city.
  b. Olmsted was a brilliant designer.
  c. more parks should be designed without centers.
  d. Central Park is used by many people for many different purposes.
  e. Central Park is democratic by design.

Use the following passage to answer questions 28 and 29.

Could good dental hygiene be man's earliest custom? The findings of paleontologist Leslea Hlusko suggest that 1.8 million years ago early hominids used grass stalks to clean their teeth. Many ancient hominid teeth unearthed in archaeological digs have curved grooves near the gumline. Hlusko posited that these grooves were evidence of teeth cleaning by early man. A stalk of grass is also about the same width as the marks found on the ancient teeth. To prove her theory Dr. Hlusko took a baboon tooth and patiently rubbed a grass stalk against it for eight hours. As she suspected, the result was grooves similar to those found on the ancient hominid teeth. She repeated the experiment with a human tooth and found the same result.

It seems that our early human ancestors may have used grass, which was easily found and ready to use, to floss between their teeth. As Hlusko suggests in the journal *Current Anthropology*, "Toothpicking with grass stalks probably represents the most persistent habit documented in human evolution."

28. In the passage, the word *posited* most nearly means
  a. insisted.
  b. demanded.
  c. questioned.
  d. suggested.
  e. argued.

29. The passage suggests that the theory that early man used grass stalks as toothpicks is
  a. a possibility.
  b. very probable.
  c. absolutely certain.
  d. fanciful.
  e. uncorroborated.

Use the following passage to answer questions 30 and 31.

A recent *New York Times* "House and Home" article featured the story of a man who lives in a glass house. Every wall in his home is transparent; he has no walls to hide behind, not even in the bathroom. Of course, he lives in an isolated area, so he doesn't have neighbors peering in and watching his every move. But he has chosen to live without any physical privacy in a home that allows every action to be seen. He has created a panopticon—a place in which everything is in full view of others.

The term *panopticon* was coined by Jeremy Bentham in the late eighteenth century when he was describing an idea for how prisons should be designed. The prisoners' cells would be placed in a circle with a guard tower in the middle. All walls facing the center of the circle would be glass. In that way, every prisoner's cell would be in full view of the guards. The prisoners could do nothing unobserved, but the prisoners would not be able to see the guard tower. They would know they were being watched—or rather, they would know it was possible they were being watched—but because they could not see the observer, they would never know when the guard was actually monitoring their actions.

30. According to the passage, a *panopticon* is
   a. a prison cell.
   b. a place in which everything can be seen by others.
   c. a tower that provides a panoramic view.
   d. a house that is transparent.
   e. a place in which surveillance cameras and other monitoring equipment are in use.

31. The description of how the panopticon would work in a prison implies that the panopticon
   a. can be an effective tool for social control.
   b. should be used regularly in public places.
   c. is not applicable outside of the prison dynamic.
   d. is an effective tool for sharing information.
   e. will redefine privacy for the twenty-first century.

Use the following passage to answer questions 32 through 34.

The postwar era marked a period of unprecedented energy against the second-class citizenship accorded to African Americans in many parts of the nation. Resistance to racial segregation and discrimination with strategies such as civil disobedience, nonviolent resistance, marches, protests, boycotts, freedom rides, and rallies received national attention as newspaper, radio, and television reporters and cameramen documented the struggle to end racial inequality.

When Rosa Parks refused to give up her seat to a white person in Montgomery, Alabama, and was arrested in December 1955, she set off a chain of events that generated a momentum the Civil Rights movement had never before experienced. Local civil rights leaders were hoping for such an opportunity to test the city's segregation laws. Deciding to boycott the buses, the African-American community soon formed a new organization to supervise the boycott, the Montgomery Improvement Association (MIA). The young pastor of the Dexter Avenue Baptist Church, Reverend Martin Luther King, Jr., was chosen as the first MIA leader. The boycott, more successful than anyone hoped, led to a 1956 Supreme Court decision banning segregated buses.

In 1960, four African-American freshmen from North Carolina Agricultural and Technical College in Greensboro strolled into the F. W. Woolworth store and quietly sat down at the lunch counter. They were not served, but they stayed until closing time. The next morning they came with 25 more students. Two weeks later similar demonstrations had spread to several other cities, and within a year similar peaceful demonstrations took place in over a hundred cities in the North and South. At Shaw University in Raleigh, North Carolina, the students formed their own organization, the Student Nonviolent Coordinating Committee (SNCC, pronounced "Snick"). The students' bravery in the face of verbal and physical abuse led to integration in many stores even before the passage of the Civil Rights Act of 1964.

Source: Excerpt from the Library of Congress, "The African American Odyssey: A Quest for Full Citizenship."

32. The passage is primarily concerned with
  a. enumerating the injustices that African Americans faced.
  b. describing the strategies used in the struggle for civil rights.
  c. showing how effective sit-down strikes can be in creating change.
  d. describing the nature of discrimination and second-class citizenship.
  e. recounting the legal successes of the Civil Rights movement.

33. In the second paragraph, the word *test* most nearly means
  a. analyze.
  b. determine.
  c. prove.
  d. quiz.
  e. challenge.

34. The passage suggests that the college students in Greensboro, North Carolina,
  a. were regulars at the Woolworth lunch counter.
  b. wanted to provoke a violent reaction.
  c. were part of an ongoing national movement of lunch-counter demonstrations.
  d. inspired other students to protest peacefully against segregation.
  e. did not plan to create a stir.

Use the following passage to answer question 35.

The Environmental Protection Agency (EPA) has published regulations for schools to follow in order to protect against asbestos contamination and provide assistance to meet the requirements of the Asbestos Hazard Emergency Response Act (AHERA). These include performing an original inspection and periodic reinspections every three years for asbestos-containing material; developing, maintaining, and updating an asbestos management plan at the school; providing yearly notification to parent, teacher, and employee organizations regarding the availability of the school's asbestos management plan and any asbestos abatement actions taken or planned in the school; designating a contact person to ensure that the responsibilities of the local education agency are properly implemented; performing periodic surveillance of known or suspected asbestos-containing building material; and providing custodial staff with asbestos awareness training.

35. The main purpose of this passage is to
   a. teach asbestos awareness in schools.
   b. explain the specifics of the AHERA.
   c. highlight the dangers of asbestos to your health.
   d. provide a list of materials that may include asbestos.
   e. frighten parents.

Use the following passage to answer question 36.

The ability to defer gratification is an essential skill for negotiating the adult world. In a study of four-year-olds, each child was offered a marshmallow. The child could choose to eat the marshmallow right away or wait 15 minutes to eat the marshmallow and receive another marshmallow as a reward for waiting. Researchers followed the children and found that by high school those children who ate their marshmallow right away were more likely to be lonely, more prone to stress, and more easily frustrated. Conversely, the children who demonstrated self-control were outgoing, confident, and dependable.

36. Based on the information in the passage, one can infer that children who are unable to defer gratification are most unlikely to succeed because
   a. they are unpopular.
   b. they lack empathy.
   c. their parents neglected them.
   d. they are unable to follow directions.
   e. they lack self-discipline.

Use the following passage to answer question 37.

The pioneering example set by Althea Gibson paved the way for future generations of African-American tennis players, and proved that beyond her tennis glory she was a true champion of the human spirit. In 1950, she was the first African American to play in the national indoor tournament, where she finished second. That year, she was refused an invitation to the U.S. Nationals, despite her talent. An editorial by tennis champion Alice Marble caused a national uproar that quickly led tournament officials to finally extend Althea an invitation to play in the Nationals. The following year she was the first African American to compete at Wimbledon. Althea once said that her extraordinary success was the product of being "game enough to take a lot of punishment along the way."

37. The author uses Althea's quote about *being game enough* to illustrate that
   a. Althea's career was plagued with injuries.
   b. the sport of tennis is more grueling than people realize.
   c. Althea believed the discrimination she faced served only to make her a stronger competitor.
   d. Althea was often fined for yelling at the referee.
   e. Althea believed talent was more important than mental toughness.

Use the following passage to answer questions 38 and 39.

The doctrine of judicial review gives the court the authority to declare executive actions and laws invalid if they conflict with the U.S. Constitution. The court's ruling on the constitutionality of a law is nearly final—it can be overcome only by a constitutional amendment or by a new ruling of the court. Through the power of judicial review, the court shapes the development of law, assures individual rights, and maintains the Constitution as a living document by applying its broad provisions to complex new situations.

Despite the court's role in interpreting the Constitution, the document itself does not grant this authority to the court. However, it is clear that several of the founding fathers expected the court to act in this way. Alexander Hamilton and James Madison argued for the importance of judicial review in the *Federalist Papers*, a series of 85 political essays that urged the adoption of the Constitution. Hamilton argued that judicial review protected the will of the people by making the Constitution supreme over the legislature, which might only reflect the temporary will of the people. Madison wrote that if a public political process determined the constitutionality of laws, the Constitution would become fodder for political interests and partisanship. However, the practice of judicial review was, and continues to be, a controversial power because it gives justices—who are appointed rather than elected by the people—the authority to void legislation made by Congress and state lawmakers.

38. The passage suggests that the practice of judicial review allows the court to
   a. wield enormous power.
   b. determine foreign policy.
   c. make laws that reflect the principles of the Constitution.
   d. rewrite laws that are unconstitutional.
   e. make amendments to the Constitution.

39. The last sentence in the passage provides
   a. a specific example supporting the argument made earlier.
   b. a summary of the points made earlier.
   c. an explanation of the positions made earlier.
   d. a prediction based on the argument made earlier.
   e. a counterargument to the views referred to earlier.

Use the following passage to answer question 40.

If you have ever made a list of pros and cons to help you make a decision, you have used the utilitarian method of moral reasoning. One of the main ethical theories, utilitarianism posits that the key to deciding what makes an act morally right or wrong is its consequences. Whether our intentions are good or bad is irrelevant; what matters is whether the *result* of our actions is good or bad. To utilitarians, happiness is the ultimate goal of human beings and the highest moral good. Thus, if there is great unhappiness because of an act, then that action can be said to be morally wrong. Conversely, if there is great happiness because of an action, then that act can be said to be morally right.

40. In the passage, the author refers to a list of pros and cons in order to
   a. show that there are both positive and negative aspects of utilitarianism.
   b. suggest that making a list of pros and cons is not an effective way to make a decision.
   c. emphasize that utilitarians consider both the good and the bad before making a decision.
   d. indicate that readers will learn how to make decisions using pro and con lists.
   e. show readers that they are probably already familiar with the principles of utilitarian reasoning.

Skills Test in Mathematics

Directions: Choose the best answer to each of the following questions.

Use the following figure to answer question 1.

1. Find the area of the parallelogram.
   a. 48 cm^2
   b. 60 cm^2
   c. 72 cm^2
   d. 90 cm^2
   e. 240 cm^2

2. Four congruent squares are joined together to form one large square. If the perimeter of one of the original squares was $8x$ units, what is the perimeter of the new, large square?
   a. $16x$ units
   b. $20x$ units
   c. $24x$ units
   d. $32x$ units
   e. $64x$ units

3. All students at Central High School take math. Some students at Central High School take art. Charles takes math.

   If these statements are true, which of the following statements must also be true?
   a. Charles attends Central High School.
   b. All students at Central High School take art.
   c. Some students at Central High School take both math and art.
   d. Charles does not take art.
   e. Some students at Central High School do not take math.

4. Which of the following is equivalent to 150% of 0.0032?
   a. 0.48
   b. 0.048
   c. 0.0048
   d. 0.00048
   e. 0.000048

5. Which number is greatest?
   a. $\frac{7}{12}$
   b. $\frac{5}{7}$
   c. 0.079
   d. 0.63
   e. 0.0108

Use the following graph to answer question 6.

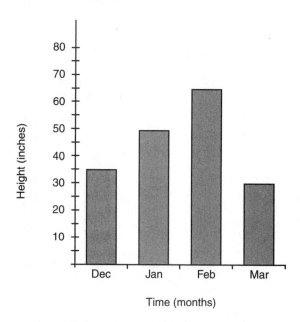

6. Which of the following represents the best choice for the title of the graph?
   a. "Average Rainfall per Month for Winter Months in Northern United States"
   b. "Average Number of Hours of Sunlight for Winter Months in Northern United States"
   c. "Daily Snowfall Rates for Winter Months in Northern United States"
   d. "Average Snowfall per Month for Winter Months in Northern United States"
   e. "Average Heating Oil Costs for Winter Months in Northern United States"

7. In Sunnyside, a special lottery is held for the elementary student who will attend the county's invention contest. There are 100 fifth graders, 150 fourth graders, and 200 third graders who qualify for the lottery. Each fifth grader's name is placed in the lottery three times; each fourth grader's name, twice; and each third grader's name, once. What is the probability that a fifth grader's name will be chosen?
   a. $\frac{1}{8}$
   b. $\frac{2}{9}$
   c. $\frac{2}{7}$
   d. $\frac{3}{8}$
   e. $\frac{1}{2}$

8. If three more than one-fourth of a number is three less than the number, what is the value of the number?
   a. $\frac{3}{4}$
   b. 4
   c. 6
   d. 8
   e. 12

9. A major city recently received a snowstorm that left a total of eight inches of snow. If it snowed at a constant rate of three inches every two hours, how much snow had fallen in the first five hours of the storm?
   a. 3 inches
   b. 3.3 inches
   c. 5 inches
   d. 7.5 inches
   e. 8 inches

Use the following graph to answer question 10.

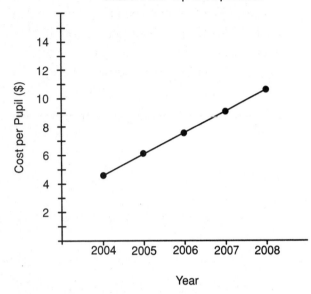

Cost of Field Trip Transportation

10. Based on the graph, if the current trend continues, what will be the approximate cost per pupil for field trip transportation in 2010?
a. $10.50
b. $11.50
c. $12.00
d. $13.00
e. $13.50

11. During the semester break, Marcus can wax the floors of five classrooms in an hour. Josie can wax four classrooms in an hour. If Marcus works for three hours and Josie works for two hours, what percentage of the 50 classrooms will be waxed?
a. 23%
b. 44%
c. 46%
d. 52%
e. 56%

Use the following graph to answer questions 12 through 14.

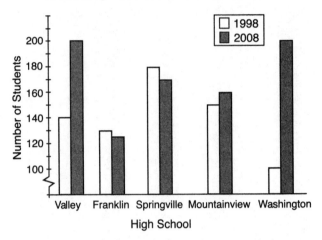

Graduating Class Size of Five High Schools

12. According to the graph, which of the schools doubled the size of its graduating class from 1998 to 2008?
a. Valley High
b. Franklin High
c. Springville High
d. Mountainview High
e. Washington High

13. Approximately how many more students graduated from Springville High than Valley High in 1998?
a. 15
b. 30
c. 45
d. 60
e. 140

14. According to the graph, which of the schools had an average increase of about six graduating students per year between 1998 and 2008?
a. Valley High
b. Franklin High
c. Springville High
d. Mountainview High
e. Washington High

Use the following graph to answer questions 15 through 17.

Stock Price of Two Companies over a Seven-Week Period

Company ABC
Company XYZ

Price per Share ($)

7.00
6.00
5.00
4.00
3.00
2.00
1.00

1   2   3   4   5   6   7

Week

15. According to the graph, if the trend of the past five weeks is expected to continue, at what point in the future should the price per share be the same for both companies?
a. week 12
b. week 11
c. week 10
d. week 9
e. week 8

16. What is the approximate average price per share of stock in Company ABC over the weeks shown in the graph?
a. $2.25
b. $2.57
c. $2.75
d. $2.86
e. $4.75

17. Based on the graph, in which week is the stock price for Company ABC exactly half the price per share for Company XYZ?
a. week 1
b. week 2
c. week 3
d. week 4
e. week 5

18. Which of the following has a 9 in the thousandths place?
a. 3.00950
b. 3.09050
c. 3.90050
d. 3.00590
e. 3.00509

19. Petra earns $10.40 per hour for the first eight hours that she works each day, and she earns time and a half for each hour after that. If she works an average of 9.5 hours per day, how much does she earn in a five-day workweek?
a. $83.20
b. $106.60
c. $416.00
d. $533.00
e. $790.40

Use the following figure to answer question 20.

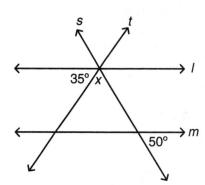

20. In the figure, line *l* is parallel to line *m*. What is the measure of the angle labeled *x*?
a. 15 degrees
b. 35 degrees
c. 50 degrees
d. 85 degrees
e. 95 degrees

21. Each teacher at Main Street School teaches at least three classes and at most five classes per day. Each of the classes is 40 minutes in length. Which of the following statements must be true?

   a. The average class time for the teachers at the school is 160 minutes per day.

   b. The teachers have an average of four classes per day.

   c. Each teacher has between 120 and 200 minutes of class time per day, inclusive.

   d. choices **a** and **c** only

   e. choices **a**, **b**, and **c**

22. A rectangular patio has one side that measures 15 feet and another side that is one-third as long. What is the area of the patio?

   a. 37.5 square feet

   b. 40 square feet

   c. 55 square feet

   d. 75 square feet

   e. 85 square feet

Use the following graph to answer question 23.

Time Spent on Various Activities During the School Day

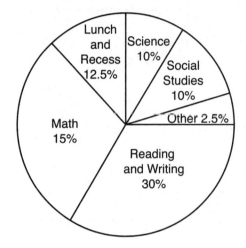

23. According to the information in the graph, if the school day consists of a total of 400 minutes, how many more minutes are spent during reading and writing than during social studies and science together?

   a. 20 minutes

   b. 40 minutes

   c. 60 minutes

   d. 80 minutes

   e. 120 minutes

24. According to recent statistics of a certain region of the United States, 5,000,000 students who took an aptitude test scored less than a perfect score, and 8,000 earned a perfect score. What is the ratio of students who earned a perfect score to the students who did not receive a perfect score?

   a. 1:624

   b. 1:625

   c. 1:626

   d. 625:1

   e. 626:1

25. The perimeter of a rectangular classroom is 148 feet. Its two longest sides add up to 86 feet. What is the length of each of the two shortest sides of the classroom?
  a. 31 feet
  b. 42 feet
  c. 62 feet
  d. 72 feet
  e. 74 feet

26. If a, b, and c represent distinct real numbers, which of the following equations must be true?
  a. $a \times b = b \times c$
  b. $a + (b \times c) = ab \times ac$
  c. $a(b + c) = ab + ac$
  d. $ab + bc = b(a \times c)$
  e. $a \times b + c = (a + b) \times (b + c)$

27. The East High School football team scored 20, 14, and 17 points in their last three games, respectively. What is the average number of points per game scored in their last three games?
  a. 20 points
  b. 19 points
  c. 17 points
  d. 14 points
  e. 12 points

28. Given the following statements, which statement must be true?

  All prime numbers are real numbers.
  Some number q is a real number.
  a. The number q is a prime number.
  b. All real numbers are prime numbers.
  c. No prime numbers are real numbers.
  d. Some real numbers are prime numbers.
  e. None of the above statements is necessarily true.

29. After three days, a group of hikers on a biology field trip discovers that they have used $\frac{2}{5}$ of their food supplies. They need enough food to make a round trip. At this rate, how many more days can they go forward before they have to turn around?
  a. 0.75 days
  b. 1.5 days
  c. 3.75 days
  d. 4.5 days
  e. 7.5 days

30. Which of the following numbers has the greatest value?
  a. $\frac{2}{7}$
  b. $\frac{4}{11}$
  c. $\frac{1}{3}$
  d. $\frac{3}{8}$
  e. $\frac{3}{10}$

31. An administrative assistant can file 26 forms per hour. If 5,600 forms must be filed in an eight-hour day, how many assistants must you hire for that day?
  a. 24 assistants
  b. 25 assistants
  c. 26 assistants
  d. 27 assistants
  e. 28 assistants

32. Heading toward each other, one train travels due east at 35 miles per hour, and a different train travels due west at 15 miles per hour. If the two trains start out 2,100 miles apart, how long will it take them to meet?
  a. 30 hours
  b. 42 hours
  c. 60 hours
  d. 105 hours
  e. 140 hours

33. During the spring bowling season, a bowler achieves the following scores: 116, 100, 104, 104, 114, 109, and 109. The bowler's three best scores are averaged for her final score on the season. What is her final score?

a. 105
b. 107
c. 109
d. 111
e. 113

Use the following graph to answer question 34.

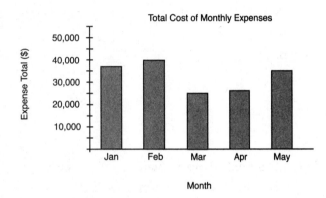

34. What were the total expenses for January, February, and April?

a. $78,000
b. $98,000
c. $105,000
d. $115,000
e. $132,000

Use the following information to answer question 35.

x	y
2	5
4	11
6	17
8	23
10	29

35. Based on the table, which of the following equations expresses the relationship between x and y?

a. $y = 2x + 3$
b. $y = 2x - 1$
c. $y = 3x + 2$
d. $y = x + 3$
e. $y = 3x - 1$

36. So far this week, Tory has worked a total of $26\frac{1}{4}$ hours at her job as a library clerk. If she is scheduled to work a total of $37\frac{1}{2}$ hours, how many more hours does she have to work this week?

a. $10\frac{1}{4}$ hours
b. $11\frac{1}{4}$ hours
c. $11\frac{3}{4}$ hours
d. $13\frac{1}{2}$ hours
e. $13\frac{3}{4}$ hours

Use the following information to answer question 37.

Survey Regarding Reading Habits

Books per Month	Percentage
0	13
1–3	27
4–6	32
>6	28

37. Which of the following graphs most accurately represents the information in the table?

a.

b.

c.

d.

e.

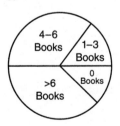

38. Some soccer players like to play in the rain.
All soccer players take science.
Sheila likes to play in the rain.

Based on this information, which of the following statements is true?
a. All soccer players like to play in the rain.
b. Only soccer players take science.
c. Sheila plays soccer.
d. Sheila takes science.
e. Some science students play soccer.

39. Tables in a cafeteria are arranged in four rows that are spaced 4 feet apart. Each table is 3 feet wide. If there is a distance of 4 feet from the wall to the rows of tables along the edges of the room, how wide is the cafeteria?
a. 20 feet
b. 28 feet
c. 32 feet
d. 36 feet
e. 40 feet

40. Kevin was half the age of his father 20 years ago. Kevin is 40. How old is Kevin's father?
a. 50
b. 60
c. 70
d. 80
e. 100

Skills Test in Writing— Section 1, Part A

Directions: Choose the letter for the underlined portion that contains a grammatical error. If there is no error in the sentence, choose **e**.

1. After the <u>director and assistant</u> director both
   a

   <u>resigned, we</u> could only guess <u>who would be</u>
   b   c

   hired to take <u>their</u> positions. <u>No error</u>
   d   e

2. The original shuttle bus <u>was</u> a horse-drawn
   a

   wooden <u>carriage with</u> spoke wheels, it carried
   b   c

   up to 15 ferryboat passengers <u>to and from</u> the
   d

   seaport. <u>No error</u>
   e

3. <u>Frightened,</u> the parakeet chirped <u>loud</u> as the
   a   b

   <u>neighbor's</u> curious cat <u>bounded up</u> to the
   c   d

   birdcage. <u>No error</u>
   e

4. *Kwanzaa,* a <u>S</u>wahili word meaning
   a

   <u>a harvest's first fruits,</u> is a nonreligious holiday
   b

   <u>that honors</u> African-American <u>heritage and</u>
   c   d
   culture. <u>No error</u>
   e

5. Last <u>Thursday,</u> as the <u>president of the university</u>
   a   b

   addressed the <u>student body, she</u> made an
   c

   <u>illusion to</u> the construction of a new stadium
   d

   for the football team. <u>No error</u>
   e

6. I thought <u>Johan's</u> dish of gumbo was
   a

   <u>more spicier</u> than <u>Harold's,</u> but the <u>judges</u>
   b   c   d

   disagreed. <u>No error</u>
   e

7. <u>Even as</u> the music industry pushes <u>further into</u>
   a   b

   the realm of the digital world, <u>there is</u> still a
   c

   large group of people who collect vinyl

   records and old-style <u>amplifiers and</u> speakers.
   d

   <u>No error</u>
   e

8. If you hate boring vacation places, travel off
   a   b

   the beaten path to such faraway locations

   such like Madagascar, New Guinea, or the
   c   d

   Himalayas. No error
             e

9. How will the president's new policies and
   a   b

   taxes effect the country's morale? No error
        c   d   e

10. Each of the players have had a half-hour
    a   b   c

    warm-up with his or her personal trainer.
            d

    No error
       e

11. To find the perimeter of a polygon, add the
    a   b

    lengths of it's sides. No error
       c   d   e

12. Of the three boys who have recently joined
                 a   b

    the school's hockey team, Martin is the taller.
                  c   d

    No error
       e

13. Cheryl can't hardly wait for election day;
           a   b

    she's very curious to see who will be the next
    c   d

    president. No error
             e

14. Although it usually has a metal frame and
           a   b

    exterior, some cars also have frames
                     c

    constructed completely out of plastics.
            d

    No error
       e

15. Despite the boa's daunting ten-foot length,
           a   b

    the snake will continue to grow; it still has not
           c   d

    reached maturity. No error
             e

16. The Department of State has foreign-policy
                      a

    responsibilities that include the promotion of
         b

    peace, must protect U.S. citizens abroad, and
           c   d

    the assistance of U.S. businesses in the foreign

    marketplace. No error
             e

17. My <u>history</u> class, which is taught by
           a

<u>Professor Mendes</u>, is held on
        b

<u>Tuesdays and Fridays</u> from 9:00 A.M. to
        c

11:30 A.M. in <u>Grange Hall</u>. <u>No error</u>
               d   e

18. <u>Today's</u> ski jackets are made with synthetic
     a

fabrics <u>that are</u> very light <u>but yet</u> provide
       b   c

exceptional <u>warmth and</u> comfort. <u>No error</u>
          d   e

19. Here <u>are</u> one of the three <u>scarves</u> you <u>left</u> at
      a   b   c

my house <u>yesterday</u> morning. <u>No error</u>
         d   e

20. The florist <u>refused to</u> sell his last <u>orchid</u>
         a   b

because the <u>flowers</u> petals were <u>deformed and</u>
        c   d

discolored. <u>No error</u>
      e

21. Because they <u>close</u> resemble each other, many
        a   b

people think that Sara and Heather <u>are</u>
                  c

identical <u>instead of</u> fraternal twins. <u>No error</u>
      d   e

Skills Test in Writing— Section 1, Part B

Directions: Choose the best replacement for the underlined portion of the sentence. If no revision is necessary, choose **a**, which always repeats the original phrasing.

22. Any <u>passenger who is getting off at the next stop</u> should move to the front.
  a. passenger who is getting off at the next stop
  b. passenger, who is getting off at the next stop
  c. passenger who is getting off at the next stop,
  d. passenger, who is getting off at the next stop,
  e. passenger, whom is getting off at the next stop,

23. The Tour de France is a grueling trek through <u>France; and covering</u> almost 3,400 kilometers over the course of three weeks.
  a. France; and covering
  b. France, and covering
  c. France; it covers
  d. France it covers
  e. France; it covered

24. Shortly after landing upon the Red Planet, the Mars rover took a picture of <u>some own tire tracks.</u>
  a. some own tire tracks.
  b. it's own tire tracks.
  c. their own tire tracks.
  d. its own tire tracks.
  e. the tire tracks.

25. When the mayor took office, his plan was to bolster the economy, clean up the subways, <u>, and reducing the crime rate.</u>
    a. , and reducing the crime rate.
    b. ; and reducing the crime rate.
    c. , and reduce the crime rate.
    d. , and reduction of the crime rate.
    e. ; and to reduce the rates of unlawful illegal criminal activities.

26. Our coach emphasizes teamwork <u>over individual accomplishment in his game plans.</u>
    a. over individual accomplishment in his game plans.
    b. onto individual accomplishment in his game plans.
    c. less better over individual accomplishment in his game plans.
    d. in his game plans over individual accomplishment instead.
    e. in his game plans with individual accomplishment instead.

27. <u>This was the third of the three assignments the professor gave during this the month of October.</u>
    a. This was the third of the three assignments the professor gave during this the month of October.
    b. Of the three assignments the professor gave during October, this was the third one.
    c. Thus far during the month of October, the professor gave three assignments and this was the third.
    d. This third assignment of the professor's given during the month of October was one of three assignments.
    e. This was the third assignment the professor gave during the month of October.

28. The horror film had <u>a frighteningly and unexpected ending.</u>
    a. a frighteningly and unexpected ending.
    b. a frighteningly and unexpectedly ending.
    c. an ending that was frightening and unexpectedly.
    d. a frightening and unexpected ending.
    e. an ending that was frightening and it was also an unexpected one.

29. An American writer of the twentieth century, <u>Jack Kerouac's collection of poems, *Mexico City Blues,*</u> celebrates freedom and individualism.
    a. Jack Kerouac's collection of poems, *Mexico City Blues,*
    b. *Mexico City Blues*, a collection of poems by Jack Kerouac,
    c. a collection of poems, *Mexico City Blues*, by Jack Kerouac,
    d. Jack Kerouac published poems, collected as *Mexico City Blues*, that
    e. Jack Kerouac published a collection of poems, *Mexico City Blues*, which

30. We loved our trip to the top of the <u>Empire State Building where you could see</u> the Statue of Liberty, all of New York's bridges, and the tiny people on the streets below.
    a. Empire State Building where you could see
    b. Empire State Building; you could see
    c. Empire State Building; where we saw
    d. Empire State Building; we saw
    e. Empire State Building in that you saw

31. <u>Conflicting to what stories you may have heard,</u> there was no curse written upon the entrance of King Tut's tomb.
- **a.** Conflicting to what stories you may have heard,
- **b.** Contrary in what you may have heard,
- **c.** Contrary to what you may have heard,
- **d.** To contrary what you have heard,
- **e.** Many stories of conflict you may have heard,

32. The senator did not <u>agree for the president's proposed tax hike.</u>
- **a.** agree for the president's proposed tax hike.
- **b.** agree the tax hike the president proposed with.
- **c.** agree with the president's proposed tax hike.
- **d.** agree with the tax hike that the president will propose.
- **e.** agree for the tax hike that the president will propose.

33. The student council has accused the members of the eighth-grade dance committee <u>with being careless with the spending of</u> the dance budget.
- **a.** with being careless with the spending of
- **b.** as to carelessness in the spending of
- **c.** of carelessness in the spending of
- **d.** of careless spending to
- **e.** with spending carelessly of

34. <u>Although England is surrounded by water,</u> it has always been important for the British to have a very powerful navy.
- **a.** Although England is surrounded by water,
- **b.** Although England was surrounded by water,
- **c.** England is surrounded by water,
- **d.** Because England is surrounded by water,
- **e.** Because England is surrounded by water;

35. The <u>principle objective of the documentary is to show you how global warming will effect</u> climates around the world.
- **a.** principle objective of the documentary is to show you how global warming will effect
- **b.** principle objective of the documentary is to show you how global warming will affect
- **c.** principal objective of the documentary is to show you how global warming will affect
- **d.** principal objective of the documentary is to show you how global warming will effect
- **e.** principle objective of the documentary is to show you how global warming will have effected

36. <u>Built in Boston, the *U.S.S. Constitution* was given the nickname "Old Ironsides" because her thick oak planks had deflected</u> many deadly cannonballs in battle.
- **a.** Built in Boston, the *U.S.S. Constitution* was given the nickname "Old Ironsides" because her thick oak planks had deflected
- **b.** Built in Boston, the *U.S.S. Constitution* was given the nickname "Old Ironsides" because her thick oak planks deflect
- **c.** The *U.S.S. Constitution*, being built in Boston, is nicknamed "Old Ironsides" because her thick oak planks had deflected
- **d.** Built in Boston, the *U.S.S. Constitution* will be given the nickname "Old Ironsides" because her thick oak planks had deflected
- **e.** The *U.S.S. Constitution*, to be built in Boston, was given the nickname "Old Ironsides" because her thick oak planks had deflected

37. Joe DiMaggio, the son of Italian immigrants, he was one of the most talented athletes of his generation and was later inducted into the baseball Hall of Fame.

- **a.** Joe DiMaggio, the son of Italian immigrants, he
- **b.** Joe DiMaggio, being the son of Italian immigrants,
- **c.** As he was the son of Italian immigrants, Joe DiMaggio
- **d.** The son of Italian immigrants, Joe DiMaggio
- **e.** Joe DiMaggio, the son of Italian immigrants, and he

38. The Gulf Stream is a warm current on the Atlantic's surface, it originates in the Gulf of Mexico and flows northeast.

- **a.** Atlantic's surface, it originates
- **b.** Atlantics' surface; it originates
- **c.** Atlantic's surface. Originating
- **d.** Atlantics' surface, and originating
- **e.** Atlantic's surface; it originates

Skills Test in Writing— Section 2, Essay Writing

Carefully read the essay topic that follows. Plan and write an essay that addresses all points in the topic. Make sure that your essay is well organized and that you support your central argument with concrete examples. Allow 30 minutes for your essay.

School boards often discuss books that should not be included in a reading curriculum. Some think that some books should not only be part of the curriculum, but also be required reading for students. Is there a book that you feel should be required reading for everyone? Choose a book you think should be required reading and write an essay persuading your audience why they should read this book. Be sure to support your position with logical arguments and specific examples.

PRAXIS I READING TEST REVIEW

CHAPTER SUMMARY

Reading comprehension is an important skill to have in life and on tests. This chapter covers the most essential reading and reading comprehension strategies for success. You will learn to become an active reader, to understand the difference between main ideas and supporting ideas, and to recognize information that is implied, but not stated, in a passage.

Developing strong reading comprehension skills is crucial for success as a prospective teacher. The PPST Reading test measures your ability to understand written passages and demonstrate insight and discrimination about what you read. The test contains passages of varying lengths: long passages of about 200 words, shorter passages of approximately 100 words, and short statements of a few sentences. One or more multiple-choice questions follow each passage or statement. You will be asked to answer 40 questions in 60 minutes (46 questions in 75 minutes on the computer version of the test).

The topics presented in the passages reflect a range of subjects, from art, science, politics, and history to real-life situations. Although you do not need any specialized knowledge or a background in the subject to answer the questions, you do need to show that you can extract information from the passage. Some questions will focus on the explicit information offered in a passage: its main purpose, supporting details, and organization. Other questions will ask you to interpret and evaluate the assumptions that are implicit in the passage: the text's underlying message, arguments, and logic.

Although the content of the computer-based Praxis I Reading test is similar to that of the paper-based test, the format of the two exams varies slightly. The way you view reading passages and related questions on the computer-based test is different from the paper test. You will view a split screen on your computer, with the reading passage displayed on the left-hand side and a question on the right-hand side;

you will view one question at a time. By using a special marking tool, you can check off a difficult question so that you can go back to it later and review or change it. A review screen will tell you whether a question is marked for review. Other differences between the two formats are outlined here:

	COMPUTER-BASED TEST	PAPER-BASED TEST
Total time	75 minutes	60 minutes
Number of questions	46 multiple-choice questions: 21 literal comprehension questions 25 critical and inferential comprehension questions	40 multiple-choice questions: 18 literal comprehension questions 22 critical and inferential comprehension questions

Types of Questions

Some of the questions on the PPST Reading test focus on *what* information is presented in a passage, while others deal with *how* information is presented. The questions fall into two basic categories: literal comprehension and critical and inferential comprehension. About 45% of the test questions deal with literal comprehension, whereas 55% focus on critical and inferential comprehension.

Literal Comprehension

Literal comprehension questions measure your ability to understand the literal content of a passage. You might be asked to identify the main purpose of a passage, locate a fact or detail, describe how the passage is organized, or define how a word is used in a passage. There are four types of literal comprehension questions:

1. **Main Idea.** For this question type, you need to be able to identify the main idea of the passage or a specific paragraph in the passage.

Examples
- The passage is primarily concerned with . . . ?
- What is the author's main purpose in this passage?
- Which of the following would be the best title for this passage?

2. **Supporting Idea.** This question type asks you to summarize a supporting idea in the passage. You will need to be able to locate specific information in the passage, such as a fact, figure, or name.

Examples
- According to the passage, how many people in the United States have Type II diabetes?
- The passage states that a lunar eclipse occurs when . . . ?
- Which of the following is NOT mentioned as one of the reasons for the Cuban Missile Crisis?

3. **Organization.** In this type of question, you will be asked to recognize how a reading passage is organized. Organization questions may ask you to identify how a passage uses transitions and key phrases or how ideas within a passage relate to each other.

Examples

- Which of the following best describes the organization of the passage?
- This passage is most likely taken from a . . . ? (newspaper column, textbook, etc.)
- The phrase *the contrast in meaning and tone* refers to the contrast between . . . ?
- Why is the word *indescribably* used in sentence 4?

4. **Vocabulary.** This question type asks you to determine the meaning of a word as it is used in the passage.

Examples

- Which of the following words, if substituted for the word *indelible* in the passage, would introduce the least change in the meaning of the sentence?
- The word *protest* in the passage could best be replaced by . . . ?
- Which of the following is the best meaning of the word *experience* as it is used in the passage?

Critical and Inferential Comprehension

Whereas literal comprehension questions are straightforward, critical and inferential comprehension questions ask you to read between the lines of a text. These questions are about what is *implied* in the passage or statement. They ask you to identify the author's assumptions and attitudes and evaluate the weaknesses and strengths of the author's argument or logic. Critical and inferential comprehension questions include three types:

1. **Evaluation.** This question type asks you to evaluate the strengths and weaknesses of the argument presented in a passage. Evaluation questions will ask you to judge whether something is fact or opinion, or whether the evidence presented supports the message of the passage.

Examples

- In order to evaluate the validity of the author's claim regarding Jackson Pollock, it would be most helpful to know which of the following?
- Which of the following is NOT mentioned in the passage as a weakness in the new law?
- Which of the following numbered sentences of the passage expresses a fact rather than an opinion?

2. **Inference.** This type of question asks you to make an inference (draw a logical conclusion) based on the content of the passage. Inference questions ask you to determine an author's underlying assumptions or attitude toward the subject of the passage.

Examples

- Which of the following is an unstated assumption made by the author of the passage?
- It can be inferred from the passage that the art of Picasso and Matisse differs in all of the following ways EXCEPT . . .
- This passage suggests that Greek tragedies are still so powerful because . . .
- The author would be least likely to agree with which of the following statements?

3. **Generalization.** This question type requires you to apply the ideas of a passage to new situations, recognize similar situations, and draw conclusions about the content of the passage.

Examples

- Which of the following conclusions can you make based on the passage?
- Given the information in the passage, what appeared to be an important post-World War II trend in the United States?

Now that you have a better idea of what to expect on the PPST Reading test, you can begin to review some reading comprehension skills and test-taking strategies. By honing these skills, you will be better equipped to understand reading passages and to do your best on the exam.

Reading Skill Builders

Reading may seem like a passive activity—after all, you are sitting, looking at words on a page. However, to improve your reading comprehension you need to read *actively*, meaning that you need to interact with the text. Incorporate these active-reading techniques into your study plan for the PPST Reading test. Each time you read a magazine, newspaper, or book, sharpen your reading comprehension skills using these strategies:

- **Skim ahead.** Scan the text *before* you read. Look at how the text is organized: How is it broken into sections? In what order are the topics presented? Note key words and ideas that are highlighted in boldface type or in bulleted lists.
- **Jump back.** Review the text after you read. By looking at summaries, headings, and highlighted information, you increase your ability to remember information and make connections between ideas.
- **Look up new words.** Keep a dictionary on hand as you read. Look up unfamiliar words and list them with their definitions in a notebook or make flash cards. To help you remember new words, connect them to something in your life or reading. Make a point to use new words in your writing and conversation. By increasing

your vocabulary, you build your reading comprehension.

- **Highlight key ideas.** As you read, highlight or underline key terms, main ideas, or concepts that are new to you. Be selective—if you highlight too much of the text, nothing will stand out for you on the page. (If you don't own the book, use a notebook to jot down information.)
- **Take notes.** Note-taking can help you remember material, even if you never look at your notes again. That's because it's a muscle activity, and using your muscles can actually aid your memory. Record your questions, observations, and opinions as you read. Write down the main idea of the passage, the author's point of view, and whether you agree with the author.
- **Make connections.** When you connect two ideas, you improve your chances of remembering the material. For example, if you are reading about a current presidential race, you may note how it is similar to or different from past elections. How have circumstances changed? You may also connect the topic to your own experience: How did you feel about the past election versus the current race?

Locate the Main Idea

When standardized reading tests ask you to find the main idea of a passage, they are asking you to determine an overall feeling or thought that a writer wants to convey about her subject. To find the main idea, think about a **general statement** that brings together all of the ideas in a paragraph or passage. Look out for statements that are too specific—a main idea

MAIN TOPIC VERSUS MAIN IDEA

Topic/subject: what the passage is about
Main idea: what the author wants to say about a subject

must be broad enough to contain all the concepts presented in a passage. Test takers often confuse the main idea of a passage with its main topic. The topic is the *subject*—what the passage is about. The main idea is what the author wants to express *about* the subject.

Textbook writing and the passages on the PPST Reading test often follow a basic pattern of **general idea → specific idea**. In other words, a writer states her main idea (makes a general claim about her subject) and then provides evidence for it through specific details and facts. Do you always find main ideas in the first sentence of the passage? The answer is no; although a first sentence may contain the main idea, an author may decide to build up to her main point. In that case, you may find the main idea in the last sentence of an introductory paragraph, or even in the last paragraph of the passage.

Read the following paragraph and answer the practice question that follows.

Experts say that if you feel drowsy during the day, even during boring activities, you haven't had enough sleep. If you routinely fall asleep within five minutes of lying down, you probably have severe sleep deprivation, possibly even a sleep disorder. *Microsleep*, or a very brief episode of sleep in an otherwise awake person, is another mark of sleep deprivation. In many cases, people are not aware that they are experiencing microsleeps. The widespread practice of "burning the candle at both ends" in western industrialized societies has created so much sleep deprivation that what is really abnormal sleepiness is now almost the norm.

Source: National Institute of Neurological Disorders and Stroke, National Institutes of Health, www.ninds.nih.gov.

What is the main point of this passage?
   a. If you fall asleep within five minutes every time you lie down, you are sleep deprived.
   b. If you experience enough microsleeps, you can attain the sleep you need to function.
   c. Sleep deprivation is a pervasive problem in the United States and other western nations.
   d. If trends in sleep deprivation continue, our society will experience grave consequences.
   e. Sleep deprivation is responsible for approximately 100,000 car accidents each year.

Choice **a** is a true statement, but too specific to be a main idea. Choice **b** is a false statement. Choice **d** is a speculative statement that is not implied in the passage, and choice **e** is a detail or fact that is not supported by the information in the paragraph. Only choice **c** represents a general or umbrella statement that covers all the information in the paragraph. Notice that in the sample passage, the author does not present the main idea in the first sentence, but rather builds up to the main point, which is expressed in the last sentence of the paragraph.

Find Essential Facts

Some of the literal comprehension questions on the PPST Reading test will ask you to identify a paraphrase or rewording of supporting details. How can you distinguish a main idea from a supporting idea? Unlike main ideas, supporting ideas present facts or **specific information**. They often answer the questions *what? when? why?* or *how?*

How can you locate a supporting detail in a passage that is 200 words long? One thing you don't have to do is memorize the passage. This test does not require that you have perfect recall. Instead, it measures your ability to read carefully and know where to look for specific information. Here are some tips for finding supporting details.

■ **Look for language clues.** Writers often use transitional words or phrases to signal that they are introducing a fact or supporting idea. As you read, keep your eye out for these common phrases:

for example	for instance	in particular
in addition	furthermore	some
other	specifically	such as

■ **Focus on key words from the question.** Questions often contain two or three important words that signal what information to look for in the passage. For example, a question following a passage about the American car industry reads, "The passage states that hybrid automobiles work best if. . . ." The key words are *hybrid automobiles* and *best*. They tell you to look for a sentence that contains the phrase *hybrid automobiles* and describes an optimal situation. Instead of rereading the passage, *skim* through the paragraphs looking for the key word. Keep in mind that the passage may use a slightly different wording than the key word. As you scan, look for words that address the same idea.

■ **Pay attention to the structure of the passage.** Take note of how the passage is organized as you read. Does the author begin with or build to his main point? Is information presented chronologically? Where does the author offer evidence to back up his main point? Understanding how a passage is structured can help you locate the information you need. Read on for more about common organizational models.

Read the following paragraph, focusing on its main idea and the details that support the main idea. Then, answer the practice questions that follow.

(1) The history of microbiology begins with a Dutch haberdasher named Antoni van Leeuwenhoek, a man of no formal scientific education. (2) In the late 1600s, Leeuwenhoek, inspired by the magnifying lenses used by drapers to examine cloth, assembled some of the first microscopes. (3) He developed a technique for grinding and polishing tiny, convex lenses, some of which could magnify an object up to 270 times. (4) After scraping some plaque from between his teeth and examining it under a lens, Leeuwenhoek found tiny squirming creatures, which he called "animalcules." (5) His observations, which he reported to the Royal Society of London, are among the first descriptions of living bacteria.

1. What inspired Leeuwenhoek's invention of the microscope?
   a. his training in science
   b. the great microbiologists of his era
   c. the lenses used by the practitioners of his profession
   d. the desire to observe bacteria
   e. the common practice of teeth scraping

2. In which sentence does the author give Leeuwenhoek's description of living bacteria?
   a. sentence 1
   b. sentence 2
   c. sentence 3
   d. sentence 4
   e. sentence 5

Answers

1. c. The first paragraph provides the supporting detail to answer this question. Leeuwenhoek, a haberdasher, was *inspired by the magnifying lenses used by drapers to examine cloth*. One of the key words from the question—*inspired*—leads you to the location of the detail in the passage. Choice **a** is refuted by a detail presented in the line *a man of no formal scientific education*. Choice **b** is untrue because the first sentence of the passage states that *the history of microbiology begins with* Leeuwenhoek. Choice **d** is also incorrect because Leeuwenhoek did not know *what* he would discover under his microscope. Choice **e** is a silly choice used as a distracter.

2. d. You can find Leeuwenhoek's description of bacteria in sentence 4: *tiny squirming creatures, which he called "animalcules."* You may have been tricked into selecting choice **e** because of its repetition of the phrase *descriptions of living bacteria*, from sentence 5. Be sure to always refer back to the passage when answering a question—do not rely on your memory. Choice **e** is incorrect because it does not refer to Leeuwenhoek's own description, but rather the significance of his observation. This question highlights the importance of taking note of where crucial details are located in a passage. Again, do not try to memorize or learn facts or details, but have an idea about where to find them.

All about Organization

Organization questions on the PPST Reading test ask you to identify how a passage is structured. You need to be able to recognize organizational patterns, common transitional phrases, and how ideas relate within a passage. Understanding the structure of a passage can also help you locate concepts and information, such as the main idea or supporting details.

To organize their ideas effectively, writers rely on one of several basic organizational patterns. The four most common strategies are:

1. chronological order
2. order of importance
3. comparison and contrast
4. cause and effect

Chronological order arranges events by the order in which they happened, from beginning to end. Textbooks, instructions and procedures, essays about personal experiences, and magazine feature articles may use this organizing principle. Passages organized by chronology offer language cues—in the form of transitional words or phrases—to signal the passage of time and link one idea or event to the next. Here are some of the most common chronological transitions:

first, second, third, etc.	before	after	next	now
then	when	as soon as	immediately	suddenly
soon	during	while	meanwhile	later
in the meantime	at last	eventually	finally	afterward

Order of importance organizes ideas by rank instead of by time. Instead of describing what happened next, this pattern presents what is most, or least, important. The structure can work two ways: Writers can organize their ideas either by increasing importance (least important idea → most important idea) or by decreasing importance (most important idea → least important idea).

Newspaper articles follow the principle of decreasing importance; they cover the most important information in the first sentence or paragraph (the *who, what, when, where,* and *why* about an event). As a result, readers can get the facts of an event without reading the entire article. Writing that is trying to persuade its readers or make an argument often uses the pattern of increasing importance. By using this structure, a writer creates a snowball effect, building and building upon her idea. "Saving the best for last" can create suspense for the reader and leave a lasting impression of the writer's main point.

Just as a chronological arrangement uses transitions, so does the order of importance principle. Watch for the following common transitional words and phrases:

first and foremost	most important	more important	moreover
above all	first, second, third	last but not least	finally

Comparison and contrast arranges two things or ideas side by side to show the ways in which they are similar or different. This organizational model allows a writer to analyze two things and ideas and determine how they measure up to one another. For example, this description of the artists Pablo Picasso and Henri Matisse uses comparison and contrast:

> The grand old lions of modernist innovation, Picasso and Matisse, originated many of the most significant developments of twentieth-century art [comparison]. However, although they worked in the same tradition, they each had a different relationship to painting [contrast]. For example, Picasso explored signs and symbols in his paintings, whereas Matisse insisted that the things represented in his paintings were merely things: The oranges on the table of a still life were simply oranges on the table [contrast].

Writers use two basic methods to compare and contrast ideas. In the **point-by-point** method, each aspect of idea A is followed by a comparable aspect of idea B, so that a paragraph resembles this pattern: ABABABAB. In the **block** method, a writer presents several aspects of idea A, followed by several aspects of idea B. The pattern of the block method looks like this: AAAABBBB.

Again, transitions can signal whether a writer is using the organizing principle of comparison and contrast. Watch for these common transitions:

TRANSITIONS SHOWING SIMILARITY		
similarly	in the same way	likewise
like	in a like manner	just as
and	also	both

TRANSITIONS SHOWING DIFFERENCE		
but	alternatively	yet
however	on the contrary	in contrast
conversely	whereas	unlike

Cause and effect arranges ideas to explain why an event took place (cause) and what happened as a result (effect). Sometimes one cause has several effects, or an effect may have several causes. For example, a historian writing about World War I might investigate several causes of the war (assassination of the heir to the Austro-Hungarian throne, European conflicts over territory and economic power), and describe the various effects of the war (10 million soldiers killed, weakened European powers, enormous financial debt).

Key words offer clues that a writer is describing cause and effect. Pay attention to these words as you read:

WORDS INDICATING CAUSE	
because	created by
since	caused by

WORDS INDICATING EFFECT	
therefore	so
hence	consequently
as a result	

A writer might also describe a **contributing** cause, which is a factor that *helps* to make something happen but can't make that thing happen by itself. On the opposite end of the spectrum is a **sufficient** cause, which is an event that, by itself, is strong enough to make the event happen. Often an author will offer her opinion about the cause or effect of an event. In that case, readers must judge the validity of the author's analysis. Are the author's ideas logical? Does she support the conclusions that she comes to?

Read the following excerpt and answer the practice question.

When Rosa Parks refused to give up her seat to a white person in Montgomery, Alabama, and was arrested in December 1955, she set off a train of events that generated a momentum the Civil Rights movement had never before experienced. Local civil rights leaders were hoping for such an opportunity to test the city's segregation laws. Deciding to boycott the buses, the African-American community soon formed a new organization to supervise the boycott, the Montgomery Improvement Association (MIA). The young pastor of the Dexter Avenue Baptist Church, Reverend Martin Luther King, Jr., was chosen as the first MIA leader. The boycott, more successful than anyone hoped, led to a 1956 Supreme Court decision banning segregated buses.

Source: Excerpt from the Library of Congress, "The African American Odyssey: A Quest for Full Citizenship."

The author implies that the action and arrest of Rosa Parks directly resulted in
  a. the 1956 Supreme Court decision banning segregated buses.
  b. Martin Luther King, Jr.'s ascendancy as a civil rights leader.
  c. the formation of the Civil Rights movement in Montgomery, Alabama.
  d. the bus boycott in Montgomery, Alabama.
  e. the birth of a nationwide struggle for civil rights.

The correct answer is choice **d**. According to the passage, Rosa Parks's action directly inspired local civil rights leaders to institute the Montgomery bus boycott. Although Rosa Parks's action may have been a *contributing* factor to King's emergence as a civil rights leader (choice **b**) and the Supreme Court's later decision to ban segregated buses (choice **a**), it was not the *direct* cause of these events, according to the passage. Choice **c** is incorrect because the passage makes clear that a local Civil Rights movement already existed and was not the result of Rosa Parks's refusal to give up her bus seat. Likewise, choice **e** is incorrect. Rosa Parks may have furthered the national Civil Rights movement, but she was not its direct cause.

Strategies for Vocabulary Questions

If you encounter an unfamiliar word when you are reading, you may likely grab a dictionary and look it up. During the PPST Reading test, you can't use a dictionary to check the meaning of new words. However, you can use a number of strategies to figure out what a word means.

Vocabulary questions measure your word power, but they also evaluate an essential reading comprehension skill, which is your ability to determine the meaning of a word from its **context**. The sentences that surround the word offer important clues about its meaning. For example, see if you can figure out the meaning of the word *incessant* from this context:

> The incessant demands of the job are too much for me. The responsibilities are endless!

The word *incessant* most nearly means
  a. inaccessible.
  b. difficult.
  c. unceasing.
  d. compatible.
  e. manageable.

The best answer is choice **c**. The second sentence, *The responsibilities are endless*, restates the phrase in the first sentence, *incessant demands*. This restatement, or elaboration, suggests the meaning of *incessant*: continuing or following without interruption.

If the context of an unfamiliar word does not restate its meaning, try these two steps to figure out what the word means:

1. **Is the word positive or negative?** Using the context of the passage, determine whether the unfamiliar word is a positive or negative term. If a word is used in a positive context, you can eliminate the answer choices that are negative. In the preceding example, you can guess that the word *incessant* is used negatively. The phrase, *too much for me*, suggests that the demands of the job are overwhelming and negative. Thus, you can eliminate choices **d** and **e** because they represent positive terms.
2. **Replace the vocabulary word** with the remaining answer choices, one at a time. Does the choice make sense when you read the sentence? If not, eliminate that choice. In the previous example, choice **a**, *inaccessible*, simply does not make sense in the sentence. Choice **b**, *difficult*, is too general to be a likely synonym. Only choice **c**, *unceasing*, makes sense in the context.

Fact versus Opinion

Just because something is in print does not mean that it is fact. Most writing contains some *bias*—the personal judgment of a writer. Sometimes a writer's beliefs unknowingly affect how he or she writes about a topic. In other cases, a writer deliberately attempts to shape the reader's reaction and position. For example, a writer may present only one perspective about a subject or include only facts that support his or her point of view. Critical and inferential questions on the PPST Reading test—specifically evaluation questions—will ask you to judge the strengths or weaknesses of an author's argument. You will be required to distinguish between fact and opinion, and decide whether the supporting details or evidence effectively back up the author's main point.

To separate fact from opinion, consider these differences:

- A **fact** is a statement that can be verified by a reliable source.
- An **opinion** is a statement about the beliefs or feelings of a person or group.

When determining whether a statement is factual, consider whether a source gives researched, accurate information. The following is an example of a factual statement—it can be supported by the recent national census:

> The U.S. population is growing older—in fact, adults over age 85 are the fastest-growing segment of today's population.

Opinions, on the other hand, reflect judgments that may or may not be true. Opinions include speculation or predictions of the future that cannot be proven at the present time. The following statement represents an opinion—it offers a belief about the future. Others may disagree with the prediction:

> Many believe that the population boom among elderly Americans will create a future healthcare crisis.

Language clues can alert you to a statement that reflects an opinion. Look for these common words that introduce opinions:

likely	should/could	say
possibly	think	charge
probably	believe	attest

EXHIBIT A—EVIDENCE

Most writing presents *reasonable opinions* based on fact: A writer asserts her opinion and supports it with facts or other evidence. A writer can use different types of evidence to build an argument—some forms of proof are more reliable than other types. When you read, look for the forms of evidence listed here and consider how accurate each might be.

observations

interviews

surveys and questionnaires

experiments

personal experience

expert opinions

Reading Between the Lines

Inference questions on the PPST Reading test will ask you to make an inference, or draw a logical conclusion, about what you read. Sometimes a writer does not explicitly state his main idea or offer a conclusion. The reader must infer the writer's meaning. To determine a writer's underlying assumptions or attitude, you need to look for clues in the context of the passage. One revealing clue to the writer's meaning is his word choice.

Word choice, also called **diction,** is the specific language the writer uses to describe people, places, and things. Word choice includes these forms:

- particular words or phrases a writer uses
- the way words are arranged in a sentence
- repetition of words or phrases
- inclusion of particular details

Consider how word choice affects the following sentences:

    a. Lesson preparation benefits a teacher's performance in the classroom.

    b. Lesson preparation improves a teacher's performance in the classroom.

The only difference between the two sentences is that sentence **a** uses *benefits*, and sentence **b** uses *improves*. Both sentences state that lesson preparation has a positive influence on a teacher's performance in the classroom. However, sentence **a** is stronger because of word choice: *to benefit* means to be useful or advantageous, whereas *to improve* means to enhance in value. The writer of sentence **b** believes that preparation is not only useful, it actually increases a teacher's effectiveness. The writer doesn't have to spell this out for you, because his word choice makes his position clear.

Denotation and Connotation

Even words with similar dictionary definitions (**denotations**) can have different suggested meanings (**connotations**). Consider the different implied meanings of the following word pairs:

- slim/thin
- perilous/dangerous
- rich/wealthy

Although they are nearly synonyms, these word pairs suggest varying degrees and have subtle differences in their effect. The word *slim* suggests fitness and grace. *Thin* is more neutral, or possibly negative, implying someone may be too skinny to be healthy.

Perilous suggests a greater threat of harm than the term *dangerous*: It has a more ominous connotation and implies a more life-threatening situation. The subtle difference between *rich* and *wealthy* is, again, one of degree: *rich* implies having more than enough to fulfill normal needs; *wealthy* suggests an established and elevated societal class.

Euphemism and Dysphemism

Writers also reveal their attitude toward a subject through the use of euphemism or dysphemism. Here is a quick definition of the terms:

- **euphemism**—a neutral or positive expression used in place of a negative one
- **dysphemism**—a negative expression substituted for a neutral or positive one

A euphemism is the substitution of an agreeable description of something that might be unpleasant. In contrast, a dysphemism is an offensive, disagreeable, or disparaging expression that describes something neutral or agreeable.

For example, a student who fails a test might use a euphemistic statement when reporting the grade to her parents:

"I didn't do very well on the test."

The student might feel more comfortable using a dysphemism when talking to her classmates:

"I bombed that test. I tanked!"

Another example might be the sentence "I've been fired." A euphemism for this statement is "I've been let go," whereas a dysphemism for the statement is "I've been axed."

Style

Just as word choice can alert you to a writer's underlying message, so can other aspects of a writer's style. **Style** is the distinctive way in which a writer uses language to inform or promote an idea. In addition to word choice, a writer's style consists of three basic components:

1. sentence structure
2. degree of detail or description
3. degree of formality

When you read a magazine, newspaper, or book, consider how the writer uses sentences. Does the writer use short, simple sentences or long, complex sentences, packed with clauses and phrases? Writers use different **sentence structures** to create different effects: They may make short declarative statements in order to persuade readers or long descriptions to create a flow that pleases the reader's ear.

Degree of detail refers to how specific an author is in describing something. For example, a writer may use a general term (dog, beach, government) or specific terms (German shepherd, Crane's Beach, British Parliament). In evaluating the strength of a writer's argument, consider whether terms are too general to provide adequate evidence.

Degree of formality refers to how formal or casual the writer's language is. Technical jargon or terminology is an example of formal language. Colloquial phrases and slang are examples of casual language. Writers create distance and a sense of objectivity when they use formal language, whereas slang expresses familiarity. The degree of formality a writer uses should be appropriate to his purpose and message. For example, a business missive that uses slang is likely to put off its audience, whereas a novel aimed at teenage readers may use slang to appeal to its audience.

Emotional Language

When writers want to persuade a reader of something, they may rely on emotional language. **Emotional language** targets a reader's emotions—fears, beliefs, values, prejudices—instead of appealing to a reader's reason or critical thinking. Just as advertising often uses emotional language to sell a product, writers use emotional appeals to sell an idea. Here are five techniques to look out for as you read:

1. **Bandwagon.** The basic message of a bandwagon appeal is that "everyone else is doing something, so you should, too." It appeals to the reader's desire to join the crowd or be on the winning team. Examples from advertising include: "Americans buy more of our brand than any other brand," or "the toothpaste picky parents choose."

2. **Common man.** In this approach, writers try to convince a reader that their message is just plain old common sense. Colloquial language or phrases and well-known jokes are examples of this technique.

3. **Generalities.** In this approach, writers use words or phrases that evoke deep emotions and carry strong associations for most people. By doing so, a writer can appeal to readers' emotions so that they will accept his message without evaluating it. Generalities are vague so that readers supply their own interpretations and do not ask further questions. Examples of generalities are *honor, peace, freedom,* or *home.*

4. **Labeling or name-calling.** This method links a negative label, name, or phrase to a person, group, or belief. Name-calling can be a direct attack that appeals to hates or fears, or it can be indirect, appealing to a sense of ridicule. Labels such as *communist* or *terrorist* can evoke deep emotions. Others can be negatively charged, depending on the situation: *yuppie, slacker, reactionary.*

You can detect a writer's tone—his mood or attitude as conveyed through language—from a writer's choices about point of view, language use, and style. PPST questions will sometimes ask you to evaluate and summarize a writer's tone. When you read material in preparation for the exam, always think about the tone of each passage. Here are some common words that describe tone:

cheerful	apologetic	sarcastic
complimentary	critical	playful
hopeful	humorous	authoritative
gloomy	ironic	indifferent

5. **Testimonial.** In advertising, athletes promote a range of products, from cereal to wristwatches. Likewise, a writer may use a public figure, expert, or other respected person to endorse an idea or support the writer's argument. Because readers may respect or admire the person, they may be less critical and more willing to accept an idea.

Point of View

One strategy that writers use to convey their meaning to readers is through **point of view**. Point of view is the person or perspective through which the writer channels her information and ideas. It determines *who* is speaking to the reader. Depending on the writer's intentions, she may present a **subjective** point of view (a perspective based on her own thoughts, feelings, and experiences) or an **objective** one (one that discounts the writer's personal feelings and attempts to offer an unbiased view). Understanding the point of view of a passage will help you answer questions that ask you to identify an author's assumptions or attitude. Here are three approaches to point of view.

First-person point of view expresses the writer's personal feelings and experiences directly to the reader using these pronouns: *I, me, mine, we, our, us.* The first person creates a sense of intimacy be-

tween the reader and writer because it expresses a *subjective* point of view.

This excerpt from Walt Whitman's *Leaves of Grass* provides an example of first-person perspective:

> As I ponder'd in silence,
> Returning upon my poems, considering,
>   lingering long,
> A Phantom arose before me with distrustful
>   aspect,
> Terrible in beauty, age, and power,
> The genius of poets of old lands,
> As to me directing like flame its eyes,
> With finger pointing to many immortal songs,
> And menacing voice, What singest thou? it said,
> Know'st thou not there is but one theme for
>   ever-enduring bards?

Second-person point of view is another personal perspective in which the writer speaks directly to the reader, addressing the reader as *you*. Writers use the second person to give directions or to make the reader feel directly involved with the argument or action of their message. The following excerpt from Mark Twain's *The Adventures of Huckleberry Finn* uses the second person.

> The widow rung a bell for supper, and you
> had to come to time. When you got to the

table you couldn't go right to eating, but you had to wait for the widow to tuck down her head and grumble a little over the victuals, though there warn't really anything the matter with them—that is, nothing only everything was cooked by itself.

Third-person point of view expresses an impersonal point of view by presenting the perspective of an outsider (a third person) who is not directly involved with the action. Writers use the third person to establish distance from the reader and present a seemingly *objective* point of view. The third person uses these pronouns: *he, him, his; she, her, hers; it, its;* and *they, them, theirs.* Most PPST passages are written in the third person. The following is an example of the third-person perspective.

The Sami are an indigenous people living in the northern parts of Norway, Sweden, Finland, and Russia's Kola peninsula. Originally, the Sami religion was animistic; that is, for them, nature and natural objects had a conscious life, a spirit.

Practice

Read the following passage and answer the practice questions. Consider the writer's choice of words, style, and point of view and how they affect the message presented in the text.

Jane Austen died in 1817, leaving behind six novels that have since become English classics. Most Austen biographers accept the image of Jane Austen as a sheltered spinster who knew little of life beyond the drawing rooms of her Hampshire village. They accept the claim of Austen's brother, Henry: "My dear sister's life was not a life of events."

Biographer Claire Tomalin takes this view to task. She shows that Jane's short life was indeed tumultuous. Not only did Austen experience romantic love (briefly, with an Irishman), but her many visits to London and her relationships with her brothers (who served in the Napoleonic wars) widened her knowledge beyond her rural county, and even beyond England. Tomalin also argues that Austen's unmarried status benefited her ability to focus on her writing. I believe that Jane herself may have viewed it that way. Although her family destroyed most of her letters, one relative recalled that "some of her [Jane's] letters, triumphing over married women of her acquaintance, and rejoicing in her freedom, were most amusing."

1. In order to evaluate the validity of the author's claim that Austen's marital status helped her writing, it would be helpful to know which of the following?
   a. why the author mentions the biographer Claire Tomalin
   b. how single women were regarded in Austen's time period
   c. whether marriage would actually prevent a woman from writing during Austen's era
   d. the reliability of the source of the quotation at the end of the passage
   e. more details about Austen's tumultuous life

2. What best describes the tone of the passage?
   a. somber
   b. critical
   c. apathetic
   d. appreciative
   e. playful

Answers

1. d. This evaluation question asks you to consider the evidence used to support the author's claim that Jane Austen viewed her unmarried status as a benefit to her writing. Because the author employs a quotation from one of Austen's relatives to back up her claim, it would be helpful to know more about the source. A greater degree of detail and description (which relative? can the relative be considered reliable?) would strengthen the author's argument.

2. b. To determine the tone of the passage, you need to look at the author's point of view, style, and word choice. Because the author's style and word choice are not formal, you can eliminate choice **a**, *somber.* Her style and word choice are not overly casual, either, so you can strike choice **e**, *playful.* The author uses the third-person point of view for most of the passage, signaling that the passage is attempting to be objective. Because the author uses the first-person point of view to make a claim, you can infer that the author is not *apathetic* (choice **c**) about her subject. Although the author may indeed be *appreciative* (choice **d**) about her subject, her word choice does not support this.

Test-Taking Tips

Now that you have reviewed the components that will help you understand and analyze what you read, you are ready to consider some specific test-taking strategies. The following techniques will help you read the PPST passages quickly and effectively and answer the multiple-choice questions strategically so that you can boost your score.

Reading passages for a standardized test is different than reading at home. For one thing, you have a time limit. You have one hour to complete 40 questions (the computer-based test gives 75 minutes for 46 questions). This means that you have about 90 seconds to answer each question! And the time you spend reading each passage detracts from the time you have to answer questions. Here are some basic guidelines for keeping you moving through the test in a time-efficient way:

- **Spend no more than two minutes on a question.** Circle difficult questions and return to them if you have time.
- **Skim and answer short passages quickly.** Short passages have only one or two questions, so you should move through them with speed. Give yourself a bit more time for long passages that are followed by four or more questions.
- **Guess, if necessary.** The PPST Reading test does not penalize for wrong answers. Make sure to answer each question, even if you think you might return to it later.
- **Circle, underline, and make notes.** You can write in your test booklet, so be sure to mark up the passage as you read. Scribble down quick notes that will help you answer the questions.
- **Target the first part of the passage.** The first third of many reading passages is packed with essential information. Often you can answer main-idea questions based on the information at the start of a passage. Likewise, for longer passages of 200 words, you will often find what each paragraph is about from its first two sentences.
- **Locate details, but don't learn them.** Detail-heavy portions of passages can be dense and difficult to read. Don't spend precious time rereading and absorbing details—just make sure you know where to find them in the passage. That way you can locate a detail if a question asks about it.

Eliminating Wrong Answers

Test makers use "distracters" in test questions that can confuse you into choosing an incorrect answer. Familiarizing yourself with some of the common distraction techniques that test makers use will increase your chances of eliminating wrong answers and selecting the right answer.

- **The choice that does too little.** This distracter type often follows main idea questions. The answer choice makes a true statement, but it is too narrow or too specific to be a main idea of the passage. It zeros in on select elements or supporting ideas of a passage instead of expressing a main idea.

- **The choice that does too much.** This distracter also relates to main idea questions. Unlike the type just discussed, this answer choice goes too far beyond the scope of the passage. It may be a true statement, but it cannot be supported by what the author expresses in the text.

- **The close, but not close enough, choice.** This type of answer is very close to the correct answer, but is wrong in some detail.

- **The off-topic choice.** Test takers often find this answer choice the easiest to spot and eliminate. It may have nothing at all to do with the passage itself.

- **The irrelevant choice.** This option uses language found in the text—elements, ideas, phrases, or words—but does not answer the question correctly. These distracters are tricky because test designers bait them with a good deal of information from the passage.

- **The contradictory choice.** This answer may in fact be opposite or nearly opposite to the correct answer. If two of the answer choices seem contrary to each other, there is a good chance that one of these choices will be correct.

- **The choice that is too broad.** This distracter relates to supporting detail questions. Although it may be a true statement, it is too general and does not address the specifics the question is looking for.

TYPES OF READERS

How you approach a reading passage may show what kind of reader you are. Each of the approaches listed here has some merit. When you practice reading passages as part of your PPST study plan, experiment with some of these different styles to see what works best for you.

- The **concentrator** reads the passage thoroughly before looking at the questions. By concentrating on the passage, you can locate answers quickly if you don't already know the answer.

- The **skimmer** skims the passage before looking at the questions. Once you understand how the passage is arranged, you can go back and find the answers.

- The **cautious reader** reads the questions and answer choices first. Because you know what questions to expect, you can be on the lookout as you read the passage.

- The **game player** reads the questions first and answers them by guessing. By guessing the answers, you become familiar with the questions and can recognize the answers when you read the passage.

- The **educated guesser** reads the questions first, but not the answers. When you find the answer in the passage, you can quickly look among the answer choices for the right one.

- The **efficiency expert** reads the questions first, looking for key words that indicate where an answer is located. By doing this, you can skim the passage for answers instead of reading the whole passage.

Look Out for Absolutes

Reading comprehension questions that use words that represent absolutes should alert you to the likely presence of clever distracters among the answer choices. Two or more answers may be close contenders—they may reflect language from the passage and be true in general principle, but not true in *all* circumstances. Beware of these commonly used absolutes in reading questions:

best	most closely	always	all
primarily	most nearly	never	none

Five-Step Approach to Answering Reading Questions

If you feel daunted by the task of quickly reading and understanding dense passages, here is a quick approach that you can use. Feel free to adapt it to your style or change the order of the steps, but try to incorporate each of the five steps somewhere in your process.

Step 1—Preview

To get an idea of the content and organization of a passage, begin by skimming it. With practice, you will quickly discern topic sentences and key adjectives. Often, the first two sentences in a paragraph are topic sentences—they will tell you what a paragraph is about. If the passage is several paragraphs long, read the first and last sentence of each paragraph. You can't depend 100% on this technique, though; use your judgment to determine whether a sentence is truly a topic sentence.

Step 2—Skim the Questions

Quickly take in the question or questions that follow a passage, marking important words and phrases. Don't bother reading the multiple-choice answers.

You simply want to gather clues about what to look for when you read.

Step 3—Read Actively

Although you do not want to memorize or analyze the passage, you do need to read it. Keep your pencil handy to mark the passage as you read, looking for information that applies to the questions you skimmed. Circle or underline topic sentences, main ideas, or phrases that reveal the author's point of view. Check important names, dates, or difficult words. Mark transitions and phrases, such as *however*, *most importantly*, *but*, or *except* that help you to follow the author's direction or the organization of the passage.

As you read, ask yourself some of the following questions:

- What is the main theme or idea in the passage?
- What is the author's purpose or goal?
- How do ideas in the passage relate to the main idea?
- What is the tone or mood of the passage? Informative? Critical? Playful?
- How is the passage structured?

Step 4—Review the Passage

After actively reading the passage, take a few seconds to look over the main idea, the topic sentences, or other elements you have marked. Ask yourself what you have just read. Your goal is not to understand the passage thoroughly, but rather to get the gist of it. Quickly summarize it in your own words.

Don't get hung up on difficult phrasing or technical elements in the passage that you might not even need to know. Instead of focusing on absorbing specific details, just know the location of details in the passage. Remember, you can refer back to the passage several times while answering the questions. Focus on identifying the general direction, main ideas, organization, purpose, and point of view of the passage, rather than learning details.

Step 5—Answer the Questions

Now it's time to answer the questions. Base your answers only on what is stated and implied in the passage. Some answer choices will try to trick you with information that is beyond the scope of the passage. Read *all* five multiple-choice answers before rushing to choose one. Eliminate and mark off as many choices as possible. If you eliminate three of the answer choices, reach your decision quickly between the remaining two. After you have timed yourself working with the practice tests in this book, you will have a good idea of your time limitations.

Using the Five-Step Approach

This practice applies the five-step approach to a sample passage. You may want to review the five-step approach before you begin.

Sample Passage

Read the following passage to answer questions 1 and 2.

In his famous study of myth, *The Hero with a Thousand Faces*, Joseph Campbell writes about the archetypal hero who has ventured outside the boundaries of the village and, after many trials and adventures, has returned with the boon that will save or enlighten his fellows. Like Carl Jung, Campbell believes that the story of the hero is part of the collective unconscious of all humankind. He likens the returning hero to the sacred or tabooed personage described by James Frazier in *The Golden Bough*. Such an individual must, in many instances of myth, be insulated from the rest of society, "not merely for his own sake but for the sake of others; for since the virtue of holiness is, so to say, a powerful explosive which the smallest touch can detonate, it is necessary in the interest of

the general safety to keep it within narrow bounds."

There is much similarity between the archetypal hero who has journeyed into the wilderness and the poet who has journeyed into the realm of imagination. Both places are dangerous and full of wonders, and both, at their deepest levels, are journeys that take place into the kingdom of the unconscious mind, a place that, in Campbell's words, "goes down into unsuspected Aladdin caves. There not only jewels but dangerous jinn abide. . . ."

1. Based on the passage, which of the following best describes the story that will likely be told by Campbell's returning hero and Frazier's sacred or tabooed personage?
   a. a radically mind-altering story
   b. a story that will terrify people to no good end
   c. a warning of catastrophe to come
   d. a story based on a dangerous lie
   e. a parable aimed at establishing a religious movement

2. Which of the following is the most accurate definition of the word *boon* as it is used in the passage?
   a. present
   b. blessing
   c. charm
   d. prize
   e. curse

You can answer these questions by following the five-step approach explained in the previous lesson.

Preview

Read the first sentence of each paragraph: "In his famous study of myth . . ." and "There is much similarity. . . ." Because of the length of the sentences in each passage, you may or may not wish to read the ending sentences in each paragraph. Underline the topic sentences.

Skim the Questions

Now, skim the questions and mark them.

- Based on the passage, which of the following best describes the story that will likely be told by Campbell's returning hero and Frazier's sacred or tabooed personage? An important word in this question is *story*. Also note the use of the absolute, *best*. This means that more than one answer choice may be true, but only one is the best answer. Circle or mark these terms. You may also notice that this is an inference question; it asks you to infer something based on the information of the passage.

- Which of the following is the most accurate definition of the word *boon* as it is used in the passage? This is a vocabulary question that measures your literal comprehension. The most important elements in this question are *definition* and *boon*. Mark these words. Again, note that the question asks for the *most accurate* definition—more than one answer choice may apply, but only one offers the best answer.

Read Actively

Now, read actively, marking the passage. The following marked passage is an example of which things you might choose to circle or underline in the passage:

In his famous study of myth, *The Hero with a Thousand Faces*, Joseph Campbell writes about the archetypal hero who has ventured outside the boundaries of the village and, after many **trials** and **adventures**, has returned with the **boon** that will **save** or **enlighten** his fellows. Like Carl Jung, Campbell believes that the story of the

hero is part of the collective unconscious of all humankind. He likens the returning **hero** to the **sacred or tabooed personage** described by James Frazier in *The Golden Bough*. [**comparison here**] Such an individual must, in many instances of myth, be insulated from the rest of society, "not merely for his own sake but for the sake of others; for since the virtue of holiness is, so to say, a powerful explosive which the smallest touch can detonate, it is necessary in the interest of the general safety to keep it within narrow bounds."

There is much similarity between the archetypal hero who has journeyed into the wilderness and the poet who has journeyed into the realm of imagination. [**comparison here**] Both places are **dangerous** and **full of wonders**, and both, at their deepest levels, are journeys that take place into the kingdom of the **unconscious mind**, a place that, in Campbell's words, "goes down into unsuspected Aladdin caves. There not only jewels but dangerous jinn abide. . . ."

Like many reading comprehension passages, the sample text features topic sentences that begin each paragraph. Then, the paragraphs become detail-heavy. Although you may have marked different terms in the sample passage, you should underscore the word *boon* in the first sentence because it applies to the second question. The information you need to infer the answer to the first question (the story that is likely told by Campbell's hero and Frazier's sacred or tabooed personage) is also contained in the first paragraph. The quotation at the end of the first paragraph is dense and somewhat difficult to read and understand. Don't bother rereading difficult parts of a passage—in this case, you can answer the questions without completely comprehending the quotation.

Your system of marking this passage may vary. You may underline topic sentences, circle words that cue important details, or put a star beside words that indicate the author's attitude or purpose. The important thing is to mark the passage in a way that will help you answer the questions.

Depending on the answers you are seeking, you may jot down notes or make observations as you read:

- Regarding the main idea, it seems that the author is proposing that the act of creating is similar to the journey undertaken by Campbell's mythic hero—both make a kind of passage and return with a vital message for others. (This would apply to a question that asks you to summarize the main idea.)
- The passage uses comparison to describe Campbell's study of myth: it compares Jung and Campbell, Campbell and Frazier, and the hero and the poet. (This would apply to a question about the organization of the passage.)
- The author cites quotes by Campbell to support the main idea. (This would apply to an evaluation question in which you are asked to look at the strengths and weaknesses of the author's argument.)
- The tone of the passage is measured and analytical. (This would apply to a question about the author's attitude or point of view.)

Review the Passage

Take a few seconds to summarize in your own words what the passage is about. Look again at how you have marked the passage.

The passage is about Joseph Campbell's mythic hero and how his journey and return home relate to the experience of a poet.

Answer the Questions

Look again at question 1:

1. Based on the passage, which of the following best describes the story that will likely be told by Campbell's returning hero and Frazier's sacred or tabooed personage?
   a. a radically mind-altering story
   b. a story that will terrify people to no good end
   c. a warning of catastrophe to come
   d. a story based on a dangerous lie
   e. a parable aimed at establishing a religious movement

The passage states that the hero's tale will *save* and *enlighten* his fellows, but that it will also be *dangerous*. Choice **a** is the best answer. You can infer from the information of the passage that such a story would surely be radically mind-altering. Choice **b** is directly contradicted in the passage. If the hero's tale would terrify people to no good end, it could not possibly be enlightening. There is nothing in the passage to imply that the tale is a warning of catastrophe, a dangerous lie, or a parable (choices **c**, **d**, and **e**).

Now, look again at question 2:

2. Which of the following is the most accurate definition of the word *boon* as it is used in the passage?
   a. present
   b. blessing
   c. charm
   d. prize
   e. curse

Even if you don't know the dictionary definition of the word *boon*, you can determine its meaning from the context of the passage. You can determine that *boon* is a positive term because the passage states that the hero's boon *will save or enlighten his fellows.* Therefore, you can eliminate choice **e**, *curse*, which is negative. You can also guess from the context of the passage that a boon is likely to be intangible, and not a concrete *present*, *charm*, or *prize* (choices **a**, **c**, and **d**). Choice **b** offers the most accurate definition of *boon*, which is a timely benefit, favor, or blessing.

Take the skills you have learned or honed in this review and apply them to Practice Exam I.

5 ▶ PRAXIS I MATHEMATICS TEST REVIEW

CHAPTER SUMMARY
This review covers the math skills you need to know for the PPST Mathematics test. First you will learn about the test, including question types, and then you will learn about arithmetic, measurement, algebra, geometry, and data analysis.

The PPST Mathematics test measures those mathematical skills and concepts that an educated adult might need. Many of the problems require the integration of multiple skills to achieve a solution. This test covers several types of questions, and several types of math. Before you start reviewing math concepts, you should familiarize yourself with the test.

Numbers and Operations
- **Order:** These questions require an understanding of order among integers, fractions, and decimals.
- **Equivalence:** These questions require an understanding that numbers can be represented in more than just one way.
- **Numeration and place value:** These questions require an understanding of how numbers are named, place value, and order of value.
- **Number properties:** These questions require an understanding of the properties of whole numbers.

- **Operation properties:** These questions require an understanding of the properties (commutative, associative, and distributive) of the basic operations (addition, subtraction, multiplication, and division).
- **Computation:** These questions require an ability to perform computations, change the result of a computation to fit the context of a problem, and recognize what is needed to solve a problem.
- **Estimation:** These questions require an ability to estimate and to determine the validity of an estimate.
- **Ratio, proportion, and percent:** These questions require an ability to solve problems dealing with ratio, proportion, and percent.
- **Numerical reasoning:** These questions require the ability to interpret statements that use logical connectives or quantifiers, to use reasoning to determine whether an argument is valid or invalid, and to identify a generalization or an assumption.

Algebra

- **Equations and inequalities:** These questions require an ability to solve simple equations and inequalities and to guess the result of changing aspects of a problem.
- **Algorithmic thinking:** These questions require an ability to understand an algorithmic view. In other words, you must follow procedure, understand different ways to solve a problem, identify or evaluate a procedure, and recognize patterns.
- **Patterns:** These questions require an ability to understand patterns in data, including variation.
- **Algebraic representations:** These questions require an ability to understand the relationship between verbal or symbolic expressions and graphical displays.

- **Algebraic reasoning:** These questions require the ability to interpret statements that use logical connectives or quantifiers, to use reasoning to determine whether an argument is valid or invalid, and to identify a generalization or an assumption.

Geometry and Measurement

- **Geometric properties:** These questions require an ability to use geometric properties and relationships in real-life applications.
- **The *xy*-coordinate plane:** These questions require you to use coordinate geometry to represent geometric concepts.
- **Geometric reasoning:** These questions require the ability to interpret statements that use logical connectives or quantifiers, to use reasoning to determine whether an argument is valid or invalid, and to identify a generalization or an assumption.
- **Systems of measurement:** These questions require an ability to demonstrate basic understanding of the U.S. customary and metric systems of measurement. You should be able to convert from one unit to another and recognize the correct units for making measurements.
- **Measurement:** These questions require an ability to recognize the measurements needed to solve a problem. You must also be able to solve for area, volume, and length, including using formulas, estimation, rates, and comparisons.

Data Analysis and Probability

- **Data interpretation:** These questions require an ability to read and interpret displays of information, including bar graphs, line graphs, pie charts, pictographs, tables, scatter plots, schedules, simple flowcharts, and diagrams. You must also have the ability to recognize relationships and understand statistics.
- **Data representation:** These questions require an understanding of the correspondence between data sets and their graphical displays.
- **Trends and inferences:** These questions require an ability to recognize, compare, contrast, and predict based on given information and an ability to make conclusions or inferences from given data.
- **Measures of center and spread:** These questions involve mean, median, mode, and range.
- **Probability:** These questions require an ability to evaluate numbers used to express simple probability and to figure the probability of a possible outcome.

Computer versus Paper

There are small differences between the Praxis I written and computer-based tests.

	PAPER-BASED PRE-PROFESSIONAL SKILLS TEST: MATH	COMPUTER-BASED PRE-PROFESSIONAL SKILLS TEST: MATH
Test code	0730	5730
Time allotment	60 minutes	75 minutes
Number of questions	40, with 5 answer choices each	46, with 5 answer choices each
Format	Multiple-choice questions (calculators prohibited)	Multiple-choice questions (calculators prohibited)

TOPIC	PAPER-BASED TEST	COMPUTER-BASED TEST
Numbers and Operations	13 questions (32.5%)	15 questions (32.5%)
Algebra	8 questions (20%)	9 questions (20%)
Geometry and Measurement	9 questions (22.5%)	10 questions (22.5%)
Data Analysis and Probability	10 questions (25%)	12 questions (25%)

Now that you know more about the test specifications, following are the math skills you will need to review to succeed.

Arithmetic

This section covers the basics of mathematical operations and their sequence. It also reviews variables, integers, fractions, decimals, and square roots.

Numbers and Symbols

Numbers and the Number Line

- **Counting numbers** (or natural numbers): 1, 2, 3, . . .
- **Whole numbers** include the counting numbers and zero: 0, 1, 2, 3, 4, 5, 6, . . .
- **Integers** include the whole numbers and their opposites. Remember, the opposite of zero is zero: . . . −3, −2, −1, 0, 1, 2, 3, . . .
- **Rational numbers** are all numbers that can be written as fractions, where the numerator and denominator are both integers, but the denominator is not zero. For example, $\frac{2}{3}$ is a rational number, as is $\frac{-6}{5}$. The decimal form of these numbers is either a terminating (ending) decimal, such as the decimal form of $\frac{3}{4}$ which is 0.75; or a repeating decimal, such as the decimal form of $\frac{1}{3}$, which is 0.3333333 . . .
- **Irrational numbers** are numbers that cannot be expressed as terminating or repeating decimals (i.e., nonrepeating, nonterminating decimals such as π, $\sqrt{2}$, $\sqrt{12}$).

The number line is a graphical representation of the order of numbers. As you move to the right, the value increases. As you move to the left, the value decreases.

If we need a number line to reflect certain rational or irrational numbers, we can estimate where they should be.

Comparison Symbols

The following table illustrates some comparison symbols.

=	is equal to	5 = 5
≠	is not equal to	4 ≠ 3
>	is greater than	5 > 3
≥	is greater than or equal to	$x \geq 5$ (x can be 5 or any number > 5)
<	is less than	4 < 6
≤	is less than or equal to	$x \leq 3$ (x can be 3 or any number < 3)

Symbols of Addition

In addition, the numbers being added are called **addends**. The result is called a **sum**. The symbol for addition is called a **plus** sign. In the following example, 4 and 5 are addends and 9 is the sum:

$$4 + 5 = 9$$

Symbols of Subtraction

In subtraction, the number being subtracted is called the **subtrahend**. The number being subtracted *from* is called the **minuend**. The answer to a subtraction problem is called a **difference**. The symbol for subtraction is called a **minus** sign. In the following example, 15 is the minuend, 4 is the subtrahend, and 11 is the difference:

$$15 - 4 = 11$$

Symbols of Multiplication

When two or more numbers are being multiplied, they are called **factors**. The answer that results is called the **product**. In the following example, 5 and 6 are factors and 30 is their product:

$$5 \times 6 = 30$$

There are several ways to represent multiplication in this mathematical statement.

- A dot between factors indicates multiplication:
  $$5 \cdot 6 = 30$$
- Parentheses around any one or more factors indicate multiplication:
  $$(5)6 = 30, 5(6) = 30, \text{ and } (5)(6) = 30.$$
- Multiplication is also indicated when a number is placed next to a variable:
  $$5a = 30.$$
  In this equation, 5 is being multiplied by *a*.

Symbols of Division

In division, the number being divided *by* is called the **divisor**. The number being divided *into* is called the **dividend**. The answer to a division problem is called the **quotient**.

There are a few different ways to represent division with symbols. In each of the following equivalent expressions, 3 is the divisor and 8 is the dividend:

$$8 \div 3, 8/3, \frac{8}{3}, \text{ and } 3\overline{)8}$$

Prime and Composite Numbers

A positive integer that is greater than the number 1 is either prime or composite, but not both.

- A **prime** number is a number that has exactly two factors: 1 and itself.

  Examples
  2, 3, 5, 7, 11, 13, 17, 19, 23

- A **composite** number is a number that has more than two factors.

  Examples
  4, 6, 8, 9, 10, 12, 14, 15, 16

- The number 1 is neither prime nor composite since it has only one factor.

Operations

Addition

Addition is used when it is necessary to combine amounts. It is easiest to add when the addends are stacked in a column with the place values aligned. Work from right to left, starting with the ones column.

Example
Add 40 + 129 + 24.

1. Align the addends in the ones column. Because it is necessary to work from right to left, begin to add starting with the ones column. The ones column totals 13, and 13 equals 1 ten and 3 ones, so write the 3 in the ones column of the answer, and regroup or "carry" the 1 ten to the next column as a 1 over the tens column to be added with the other tens:

$$\begin{array}{r} \overset{1}{} \\ 40 \\ 129 \\ +\ 24 \\ \hline 3 \end{array}$$

2. Add the tens column, including the regrouped 1.

$$\begin{array}{r} \overset{1}{} \\ 40 \\ 129 \\ +\ 24 \\ \hline 93 \end{array}$$

3. Then add the hundreds column. Because there is only one value, write the 1 in the answer.

$$\begin{array}{r} \overset{1}{} \\ 40 \\ 129 \\ +\ 24 \\ \hline 193 \end{array}$$

Subtraction

Subtraction is used to find the difference between amounts. It is easiest to subtract when the minuend and subtrahend are in a column with the place values aligned. Again, just as in addition, work from right to left. It may be necessary to regroup.

Example

If Becky has 52 clients and Claire has 36, how many more clients does Becky have?

1. Find the difference between their client numbers by subtracting. Start with the ones column.

Because 2 is less than the number being subtracted (6), regroup or "borrow" a ten from the tens column. Add the regrouped amount to the ones column. Now subtract 12 − 6 in the ones column.

$$\begin{array}{r} \overset{4}{\cancel{5}}\overset{10}{2} \\ -\ 36 \\ \hline 6 \end{array}$$

2. Regrouping 1 ten from the tens column left 4 tens. Subtract 4 − 3 and write the result in the tens column of the answer. Becky has 16 more clients than Claire. Check by addition: 16 + 36 = 52.

$$\begin{array}{r} \overset{4}{\cancel{5}}\overset{10}{2} \\ -\ 36 \\ \hline 16 \end{array}$$

Multiplication

In multiplication, the same amount is combined multiple times. For example, instead of adding 30 three times, 30 + 30 + 30, it is easier to simply multiply 30 by 3. If a problem asks for the product of two or more numbers, the numbers should be multiplied to arrive at the answer.

Example

A school auditorium contains 54 rows, each containing 34 seats. How many seats are there in total?

1. In order to solve this problem, you could add 34 to itself 54 times, but we can solve this problem more easily with multiplication. Line up the place values vertically, writing the problem in columns. Multiply the number in the ones place of the top factor (4) by the number in the ones place of the bottom factor (4): $4 \times 4 = 16$. Because 16 = 1 ten and 6 ones, write the 6 in the

ones place in the first partial product. Regroup or carry the ten by writing a 1 above the tens place of the top factor.

$$
\begin{array}{r}
\overset{1}{34} \\
\times\ \ 54 \\
\hline
6
\end{array}
$$

2. Multiply the number in the tens place in the top factor (3) by the number in the ones place of the bottom factor (4): $4 \times 3 = 12$. Then add the regrouped amount: $12 + 1 = 13$. Write the 3 in the tens column and the 1 in the hundreds column of the partial product.

$$
\begin{array}{r}
\overset{1}{34} \\
\times\ \ 54 \\
\hline
136
\end{array}
$$

3. The last calculations to be done require multiplying by the tens place of the bottom factor. Multiply 5 (tens from bottom factor) by 4 (ones from top factor); $5 \times 4 = 20$, but because the 5 really represents a number of tens, the actual value of the answer is 200 ($50 \times 4 = 200$). Therefore, write the two zeros under the ones and tens columns of the second partial product and regroup or carry the 2 hundreds by writing a 2 above the tens place of the top factor.

$$
\begin{array}{r}
\overset{2}{34} \\
\times\ \ 54 \\
\hline
136 \\
00
\end{array}
$$

4. Multiply 5 (tens from bottom factor) by 3 (tens from top factor); $5 \times 3 = 15$, but because the 5 and the 3 each represent a number of tens, the actual value of the answer is 1,500 ($50 \times 30 = 1,500$). Add the two additional hundreds carried over from the last multiplication: $15 + 2 =$

17 (hundreds). Write the 17 in front of the zeros in the second partial product.

$$
\begin{array}{r}
\overset{2}{34} \\
\times\ \ 54 \\
\hline
136 \\
1,700
\end{array}
$$

5. Add the partial products to find the total product:

$$
\begin{array}{r}
\overset{2}{34} \\
\times\ \ 54 \\
\hline
136 \\
+\ \ 1,700 \\
\hline
1,836
\end{array}
$$

Note: It is easier to perform multiplication if you write the factor with the greater number of digits in the top row. In this example, both factors have an equal number of digits, so it does not matter which is written on top.

Division

In division, the same amount is subtracted multiple times. For example, instead of subtracting 5 from 25 as many times as possible, $25 - 5 - 5 - 5 - 5 - 5$, it is easier to simply divide, asking how many 5s are in 25: $25 \div 5$.

Example

At a road show, three artists sold their beads for a total of $54. If they share the money equally, how much money should each artist receive?

1. Divide the total amount ($54) by the number of ways the money is to be split (3). Work from left to right. How many times does 3 divide evenly into 5? Write the answer, 1, directly above the 5 in the dividend because both the 5 and the 1 represent a number of tens. Now multiply: since

1(ten) × 3(ones) = 3(tens), write the 3 under the 5, and subtract: 5(tens) − 3(tens) = 2(tens).

$$\begin{array}{r} 1 \\ 3\overline{)54} \\ \underline{-3} \\ 2 \end{array}$$

2. Continue dividing. Bring down the 4 from the ones place in the dividend. How many times does 3 divide evenly into 24? Write the answer, 8, directly above the 4 in the dividend. Because 3 × 8 = 24, write 24 below the other 24 and subtract 24 − 24 = 0.

$$\begin{array}{r} 18 \\ 3\overline{)54} \\ \underline{-3\downarrow} \\ 24 \\ \underline{-24} \\ 0 \end{array}$$

Remainders

If you get a number other than zero after your last subtraction, this number is your remainder.

Example

9 divided by 4.

$$\begin{array}{r} 2 \\ 4\overline{)9} \\ \underline{-8} \\ 1 \end{array}$$

1 is the remainder.

The answer is 2 r1. This answer can also be written as $2\frac{1}{4}$ because there was one part left over out of the four parts needed to make a whole.

Working with Integers

Remember, an integer is a whole number or its opposite. Here are some rules for working with integers:

Adding

Adding numbers with the same sign results in a sum of the same sign:

(positive) + (positive) = positive   and
(negative) + (negative) = negative

When adding numbers of different signs, follow this two-step process:

1. Subtract the positive values of the numbers. Positive values are the values of the numbers without any signs.
2. Keep the sign of the number with the larger positive value.

Example

−2 + 3 =

1. Subtract the positive values of the numbers: 3 − 2 = 1.
2. The number 3 is the larger of the two positive values. Its sign in the original example was positive, so the sign of the answer is positive. The answer is positive 1.

Example

8 + −11 =

1. Subtract the positive values of the numbers: 11 − 8 = 3.
2. The number 11 is the larger of the two positive values. Its sign in the original example was negative, so the sign of the answer is negative. The answer is negative 3.

Subtracting

When subtracting integers, change the subtraction sign to addition and change the sign of the number being subtracted to its opposite. Then, follow the rules for addition.

Examples

$$(+10) - (+12) = (+10) + (-12) = -2$$
$$(-5) - (-7) = (-5) + (+7) = +2$$

Multiplying and Dividing

A simple method for remembering the rules of multiplying and dividing is that if the signs are the same when multiplying or dividing two quantities, the answer will be positive. If the signs are different, the answer will be negative.

$$(\text{positive}) \times (\text{positive}) = \text{positive} \qquad \frac{(\text{positive})}{(\text{positive})} = \text{positive}$$

$$(\text{positive}) \times (\text{negative}) = \text{negative} \qquad \frac{(\text{positive})}{(\text{negative})} = \text{negative}$$

$$(\text{negative}) \times (\text{negative}) = \text{positive} \qquad \frac{(\text{negative})}{(\text{negative})} = \text{positive}$$

Examples

$$(10)(-12) = -120$$
$$-5 \times -7 = 35$$
$$\frac{12}{-3} = -4$$
$$\frac{15}{3} = 5$$

Sequence of Mathematical Operations

There is an order in which a sequence of mathematical operations must be performed:

P: Parentheses/Grouping Symbols. Perform all operations within parentheses first. If there is more than one set of parentheses, begin to work with the innermost set and work toward the outside. If more than one operation is present within the parentheses, use the remaining rules of order to determine which operation to perform first.

E: Exponents. Evaluate exponents.

M/D: Multiply/Divide. Work from left to right in the expression.

A/S: Add/Subtract. Work from left to right in the expression.

This order is illustrated by the acronym PEMDAS, which can be remembered by using the first letter of each of the words in the phrase: **Please Excuse My Dear Aunt Sally**.

Example

$$\frac{(5+3)^2}{4} + 27$$
$$= \frac{(8)^2}{4} + 27$$
$$= \frac{64}{4} + 27$$
$$= 16 + 27$$
$$= 43$$

Properties of Arithmetic

There are several properties of mathematics:

- **Commutative Property:** This property states that the result of an arithmetic operation is not affected by reversing the order of the numbers. Multiplication and addition are operations that satisfy the commutative property.

Examples

$$5 \times 2 = 2 \times 5$$
$$5a = a5$$
$$b + 3 = 3 + b$$

However, neither subtraction nor division is commutative because reversing the order of the numbers does not yield the same result.

Examples

$$5 - 2 \neq 2 - 5$$
$$6 \div 3 \neq 3 \div 6$$

- **Associative Property:** If parentheses can be moved to group different numbers in an arithmetic problem without changing the result, then the operation is associative. Addition and multiplication are associative.

Examples

$2 + (3 + 4) = (2 + 3) + 4$

$2(ab) = (2a)b$

- **Distributive Property:** When a value is being multiplied by a sum or difference, multiply that value by each quantity within the parentheses. Then, take the sum or difference to yield an equivalent result.

Examples

$5(a + b) = 5a + 5b$

$5(100 - 6) = (5 \times 100) - (5 \times 6)$

This second example can be proved by performing the calculations:

$$5(94) = 5(100 - 6)$$
$$= 500 - 30$$
$$470 = 470$$

Additive and Multiplicative Identities and Inverses

- The **additive identity** is the value that, when added to a number, does not change the number. For all of the sets of numbers defined previously (counting numbers, integers, rational numbers, etc.), the additive identity is 0.

Examples

$5 + 0 = 5$

$-3 + 0 = -3$

Adding 0 does not change the values of 5 and −3, so 0 is the additive identity.

- The **additive inverse** of a number is the number that, when added to the number, gives you the additive identity.

Example

What is the additive inverse of −3?

This means, "What number can I add to −3 to give me the additive identity (0)?"

$-3 + \underline{\quad} = 0$

$-3 + 3 = 0$

The answer is 3.

- The **multiplicative identity** is the value that, when multiplied by a number, does not change the number. For all of the sets of numbers defined previously (counting numbers, integers, rational numbers, etc.) the multiplicative identity is 1.

Examples

$5 \times 1 = 5$

$-3 \times 1 = -3$

Multiplying by 1 does not change the values of 5 and −3, so 1 is the multiplicative identity.

- The **multiplicative inverse** of a number is the number that, when multiplied by the number, gives you the multiplicative identity.

Example

What is the multiplicative inverse of 5?

This means, "What number can I multiply 5 by to give me the multiplicative identity (1)?"

$5 \times \underline{\quad} = 1$

$5 \times \frac{1}{5} = 1$

The answer is $\frac{1}{5}$.

There is an easy way to find the multiplicative inverse of a number. It is the **reciprocal** of the number, which is obtained by reversing the numerator and denominator of a fraction. In the preceding example, the answer is the reciprocal of 5; 5 can be written as $\frac{5}{1}$, so the reciprocal is $\frac{1}{5}$.

Here are some numbers and their reciprocals:

4	$\frac{1}{4}$
$\frac{2}{3}$	$\frac{3}{2}$
$-\frac{6}{5}$	$-\frac{5}{6}$
$\frac{1}{6}$	6

Note: Reciprocals do not change sign.

Note: The additive inverse of a number is the opposite of the number; the multiplicative inverse is the reciprocal.

Factors and Multiples

Factors

Factors are numbers that can be divided into a larger number without a remainder.

Example

$12 \div 3 = 4$

The number 3 is, therefore, a factor of the number 12. Other factors of 12 are 1, 2, 4, 6, and 12. The common factors of two numbers are the factors that both numbers have in common.

Examples

The factors of 24 = 1, 2, 3, 4, 6, 8, 12, and 24.
The factors of 18 = 1, 2, 3, 6, 9, and 18.

From the examples, you can see that the common factors of 24 and 18 are 1, 2, 3, and 6. From this list it can also be determined that the *greatest* common factor of 24 and 18 is 6. Determining the **greatest common factor** (GCF) is useful for simplifying fractions.

Example

Simplify $\frac{16}{20}$.

The factors of 16 are 1, 2, 4, 8, and 16. The factors of 20 are 1, 2, 4, 5, and 20. The common factors of 16 and 20 are 1, 2, and 4. The greatest of these, or

the GCF, is 4. Therefore, to simplify the fraction, both the numerator and the denominator should be divided by 4.

$$\frac{16 \div 4}{20 \div 4} = \frac{4}{5}$$

Multiples

Multiples are numbers that can be obtained by multiplying a number x by a positive integer.

Example

$5 \times 7 = 35$

The number 35 is, therefore, a multiple of the number 5 and of the number 7. Other multiples of 5 are 5, 10, 15, 20, and so on. Other multiples of 7 are 7, 14, 21, 28, and so on.

The common multiples of two numbers are the multiples that both numbers share.

Example

Some multiples of 4 are: 4, 8, 12, 16, 20, 24, 28, 32, and 36.
Some multiples of 6 are: 6, 12, 18, 24, 30, 36, 42, and 48.

Some common multiples of 4 and 6 are 12, 24, and 36. From the preceding it can also be determined that the *least* common multiple of the numbers 4 and 6 is 12, since this number is the smallest number that appeared in both lists. The **least common multiple**, or LCM, is used when performing addition and subtraction of fractions to find the least common denominator.

Example (using denominators 4 and 6 and LCM of 12)

$$\frac{1}{4} + \frac{5}{6} = \frac{1(3)}{4(3)} + \frac{5(2)}{6(2)}$$
$$= \frac{3}{12} + \frac{10}{12}$$
$$= \frac{13}{12}$$
$$= 1\frac{1}{12}$$

Decimals

The most important thing to remember about decimals is that the first place value to the right of the decimal point is the tenths place. The place values are as follows:

1	2	6	8	.	3	4	5	7
THOUSANDS	HUNDREDS	TENS	ONES	DECIMAL POINT	TENTHS	HUNDREDTHS	THOUSANDTHS	TEN THOUSANDTHS

In expanded form, this number can also be expressed as:

$1{,}268.3457 = (1 \times 1{,}000) + (2 \times 100) +$
$(6 \times 10) + (8 \times 1) + (3 \times .1) + (4 \times .01) +$
$(5 \times .001) + (7 \times .0001)$

Adding and Subtracting Decimals

Adding and subtracting decimals is very similar to adding and subtracting whole numbers. The most important thing to remember is to line up the decimal points. Zeros may be filled in as placeholders when all numbers do not have the same number of decimal places.

Examples
What is the sum of 0.45, 0.8, and 1.36?

```
 1 1
 0.45
 0.80
+1.36
 2.61
```

What is the difference of 1.06 and 0.35?
Take away 0.35 from 1.06.

```
 0 1
 1.06
-0.35
 0.71
```

Multiplication of Decimals

Multiplication of decimals is exactly the same as multiplication of integers, except one must make note of the total number of decimal places in the factors.

Example
What is the product of 0.14 and 4.3?
First, multiply as usual (do not line up the decimal points):

```
   4.3
 ×.14
   172
+430
   602
```

Now, to figure out the answer, notice that 4.3 has one decimal place and .14 has two decimal places. Add in order to determine the total number of decimal places that the answer must have to the right of the decimal point. In this problem, there are a total of three (1 + 2) decimal places. When finished multiplying, start from the right side of the answer, and move to the left the number of decimal places previously calculated.

$$.\underset{\curvearrowleft}{6}\underset{\curvearrowleft}{0}\underset{\curvearrowleft}{2}$$

In this example, 602 turns into .602 because there have to be three decimal places in the answer. If there are not enough digits in the answer, add zeros in front of the answer until there are enough.

Example
Multiply 0.03×0.2.

$$
\begin{array}{r}
.03 \\
\times\ .2 \\
\hline
6
\end{array}
$$

There are three total decimal places in the problem; therefore, the answer must contain three decimal places. Starting to the right of 6, move left three places. The answer becomes 0.006.

Dividing Decimals

Dividing decimals is a little different from integers for the setup, and then the regular rules of division apply. It is easier to divide if the divisor does not have any decimals. In order to accomplish that, simply move the decimal place to the right as many places as necessary to make the divisor a whole number. If the decimal point is moved in the divisor, it must also be moved the same number of spaces in the dividend in order to keep the answer the same as the original problem; $4 \div 2$ has the same solution as its multiples $8 \div 4$ and $28 \div 14$. Moving a decimal point in a division problem is equivalent to multiplying a numerator and denominator of a fraction by the same quantity, which is the reason the answer will remain the same.

If there are not enough decimal places in the answer to accommodate the required move, simply add zeros until the desired placement is achieved. Add zeros after the decimal point to continue the division until the decimal terminates, or until a repeating pattern is recognized. The decimal point in the quotient belongs directly above the decimal point in the dividend.

Example
What is $.425\overline{)1.53}$?

First, to make .425 a whole number, move the decimal point three places to the right: 425.

Now move the decimal point three places to the right for 1.53: 1,530.

The problem is now a simple long division problem.

$$
\begin{array}{r}
3.6 \\
425.\overline{)1,530.0} \\
-1,275\ \downarrow \\
\hline
2,550 \\
-2,550 \\
\hline
0
\end{array}
$$

Comparing Decimals

Comparing decimals is actually quite simple. Just line up the decimal points and then fill in zeros at the ends of the numbers until each one has an equal number of digits.

Example
Compare .5 and .005.

Line up decimal points.	.5
	.005
Add zeros.	.500
	.005

Now, ignore the decimal point and consider, which is bigger: 500 or 5?

500 is definitely bigger than 5, so .5 is larger than .005.

Rounding Decimals

It is often inconvenient to work with very long decimals. Often it is much more convenient to have an approximation for a decimal that contains fewer digits than the entire decimal. In this case, we round decimals to a certain number of decimal places. There are numerous options for rounding:

To the nearest integer: zero digits to the right of the decimal point

To the nearest tenth: one digit to the right of the decimal point (tenths unit)

To the nearest hundredth: two digits to the right of the decimal point (hundredths unit)

In order to round, we look at two digits of the decimal: the digit we are rounding to, and the digit to the immediate right. If the digit to the immediate right is less than 5, we leave the digit we are rounding to alone and omit all the digits to the right of it. If the digit to the immediate right is 5 or greater, we increase the digit we are rounding by one and omit all the digits to the right of it.

Example

Round $\frac{3}{7}$ to the nearest tenth and then to the nearest hundredth.

Dividing 3 by 7 gives us the repeating decimal .428571428571. . . . If we are rounding to the nearest tenth, we need to look at the digit in the tenths position (4) and the digit to its immediate right (2). Because 2 is less than 5, we leave the digit in the tenths position alone and drop everything to the right of it. So, $\frac{3}{7}$ to the nearest tenth is .4.

To round to the nearest hundredth, we need to look at the digit in the hundredths position (2) and the digit to its immediate right (8). Because 8 is more than 5, we increase the digit in the hundredths position by 1, thus giving us 3, and drop everything to the right of it. So, $\frac{3}{7}$ to the nearest hundredth is .43.

Fractions

To work well with fractions, it is necessary to understand some basic concepts.

Simplifying Fractions

Rule:

$$\frac{ac}{bc} = \frac{a}{b}$$

- To simplify fractions, identify the greatest common factor (GCF) of the numerator and the denominator, and divide both the numerator and the denominator by this number.

Example

Simplify $\frac{63}{72}$.

The GCF of 63 and 72 is 9, so divide 63 and 72 each by 9 to simplify the fraction:

$$\frac{63 \div 9}{72 \div 9} = \frac{7}{8}$$

$$\frac{63}{72} = \frac{7}{8}$$

Adding and Subtracting Fractions

Rules:

To add or subtract fractions with the same denominator:

$$\frac{a}{b} \pm \frac{c}{b} = \frac{a \pm c}{b}$$

To add or subtract fractions with different denominators:

$$\frac{a}{b} \pm \frac{c}{d} = \frac{ad \pm cb}{bd}$$

- To add or subtract fractions with like denominators, just add or subtract the numerators and keep the denominator.

Examples

$\frac{1}{7} + \frac{5}{7} = \frac{6}{7}$ and $\frac{5}{8} - \frac{2}{8} = \frac{3}{8}$

- To add or subtract fractions with unlike denominators, first find the least common denominator or LCD. The LCD is the smallest number divisible by each of the denominators.

For example, for the denominators 8 and 12, 24 would be the LCD because 24 is the smallest number that is divisible by both 8 and 12: $8 \times 3 = 24$, and $12 \times 2 = 24$.

Using the LCD, convert each fraction to its new form by multiplying both the numerator and denominator by the appropriate factor to get the LCD, and then follow the directions for adding/subtracting fractions with like denominators.

Example

$$\frac{1}{3} + \frac{2}{5} = \frac{1(5)}{3(5)} + \frac{2(3)}{5(3)}$$
$$= \frac{5}{15} + \frac{6}{15}$$
$$= \frac{11}{15}$$

Multiplication of Fractions
Rule:

$$\frac{a}{b} \times \frac{c}{d} = \frac{a \times c}{b \times d}$$

- Multiplying fractions is one of the easiest operations to perform. To multiply fractions, simply multiply the numerators and the denominators.

Example

$\frac{4}{5} \times \frac{6}{7} = \frac{24}{35}$

If any numerator and denominator have common factors, these may be simplified before multiplying. Divide the common multiples by a common factor. In the following example, 3 and 6 are both divided by 3 before multiplying.

Example

$$\frac{\overset{1}{\cancel{3}}}{5} \times \frac{1}{\underset{2}{\cancel{6}}} = \frac{1}{10}$$

Dividing Fractions
Rule:

$$\frac{a}{b} \div \frac{c}{d} = \frac{a}{b} \times \frac{d}{c} = \frac{a \times d}{b \times c}$$

- Dividing fractions is equivalent to multiplying the dividend by the reciprocal of the divisor. When dividing fractions, simply multiply the dividend by the divisor's reciprocal to get the answer.

Example

$\frac{1}{4} \div \frac{1}{2}$

(dividend) ÷ (divisor)

Determine the reciprocal of the divisor:

$\frac{1}{2} \rightarrow \frac{2}{1}$

Multiply the dividend ($\frac{1}{4}$) by the reciprocal of the divisor ($\frac{2}{1}$) and simplify if necessary.

$$\frac{1}{4} \div \frac{1}{2} = \frac{1}{4} \times \frac{2}{1}$$
$$= \frac{2}{4}$$
$$= \frac{1}{2}$$

Comparing Fractions

Rules:

$$\text{If } \frac{a}{b} = \frac{c}{d}, \text{ then } ad = bc$$

$$\text{If } \frac{a}{b} < \frac{c}{d}, \text{ then } ad < bc$$

$$\text{If } \frac{a}{b} > \frac{c}{d}, \text{ then } ad > bc$$

Sometimes it is necessary to compare the sizes of fractions. This is very simple when the fractions are familiar or when they have a common denominator.

Examples

$\frac{1}{2} < \frac{3}{4}$ and $\frac{11}{18} > \frac{5}{18}$

- If the fractions are not familiar and/or do not have a common denominator, there is a simple trick to remember. Multiply the numerator of the first fraction by the denominator of the second fraction. Write this answer under the first fraction. Then multiply the numerator of the second fraction by the denominator of the first one. Write this answer under the second fraction. Compare the two numbers. The larger number represents the larger fraction.

Examples

Which is larger: $\frac{7}{11}$ or $\frac{4}{9}$?

Cross multiply.

$7 \times 9 = 63 \qquad 4 \times 11 = 44$

$63 > 44$; therefore,

$$\frac{7}{11} > \frac{4}{9}$$

Compare $\frac{6}{18}$ and $\frac{2}{6}$.

Cross multiply.

$6 \times 6 = 36 \qquad 2 \times 18 = 36$

$36 = 36$; therefore,

$$\frac{6}{18} = \frac{2}{6}$$

Converting Decimals to Fractions

- To convert a nonrepeating decimal to a fraction, the digits of the decimal become the numerator of the fraction, and the denominator of the fraction is a power of 10 that contains that number of digits as zeros.

Example

Convert .125 to a fraction.

The decimal .125 means 125 *thousandths*, so it is 125 parts of 1,000. An easy way to do this is to make 125 the numerator, and since there are three digits in the number 125, the denominator is 1 with three zeros, or 1,000.

$$.125 = \frac{125}{1,000}$$

Then we just need to reduce the fraction.

$$\frac{125}{1,000} = \frac{125 \div 125}{1,000 \div 125} = \frac{1}{8}$$

- When converting a repeating decimal to a fraction, the digits of the repeating pattern of the decimal become the numerator of the fraction, and the denominator of the fraction is the same number of 9s as digits.

Example

Convert $.\overline{3}$ to a fraction.

You may already recognize $.\overline{3}$ as $\frac{1}{3}$. The repeating pattern, in this case 3, becomes our numerator. There is one digit in the pattern, so 9 is our denominator.

$$.\overline{3} = \frac{3}{9} = \frac{3 \div 3}{9 \div 3} = \frac{1}{3}$$

Example

Convert $.\overline{36}$ to a fraction.

The repeating pattern, in this case 36, becomes our numerator. There are two digits in the pattern, so 99 is our denominator.

$$.\overline{36} = \frac{36}{99} = \frac{36 \div 9}{99 \div 9} = \frac{4}{11}$$

Converting Fractions to Decimals

- To convert a fraction to a decimal, simply treat the fraction as a division problem.

Example
Convert $\frac{3}{4}$ to a decimal.

$$\begin{array}{r} .75 \\ 4\overline{)3.00} \end{array}$$

So, $\frac{3}{4}$ is equal to .75.

Converting Mixed Numbers to and from Improper Fractions
Rule:

$$a\frac{b}{c} = \frac{ac + b}{c}$$

- A mixed number is a number greater than 1 that is expressed as a whole number joined to a proper fraction. Examples of mixed numbers are $5\frac{3}{8}$, $2\frac{1}{3}$, and $-4\frac{5}{6}$. To convert from a mixed number to an improper fraction (a fraction where the numerator is greater than the denominator), multiply the whole number and the denominator, and then add the numerator. This becomes the new numerator. The new denominator is the same as the original in the fraction.

Note: If the mixed number is negative, temporarily ignore the negative sign while performing the conversion, and just make sure you replace the negative sign when you're done.

Example
Convert $5\frac{3}{8}$ to an improper fraction.

Using the conversion formula,

$$5\frac{3}{8} = \frac{5 \times 8 + 3}{8} = \frac{43}{8}.$$

Example
Convert $-4\frac{5}{6}$ to an improper fraction.

Temporarily ignore the negative sign and perform the conversion:
$$4\frac{5}{6} = \frac{4 \times 6 + 5}{6} = \frac{29}{6}.$$
The final answer includes the negative sign:
$$-\frac{29}{6}.$$

- To convert from an improper fraction to a mixed number, simply treat the fraction like a division problem and express the answer as a fraction rather than a decimal.

Example
Convert $\frac{23}{7}$ to a mixed number.

Perform the division:
$$23 \div 7 = 3\frac{2}{7}.$$

Percents
Percents are always "out of 100"; for example, 45% means 45 out of 100. Therefore, to write percents as decimals, move the decimal point two places to the left (to the hundredths place).

$$45\% = \frac{45}{100} = 0.45$$

$$3\% = \frac{3}{100} = 0.03$$

$$124\% = \frac{124}{100} = 1.24$$

$$0.9\% = \frac{.9}{100} = \frac{9}{1,000} = 0.009$$

Here are some conversions you should be familiar with:

FRACTION	DECIMAL	PERCENTAGE
$\frac{1}{2}$	.5	50%
$\frac{1}{4}$	.25	25%
$\frac{1}{3}$	.333 . . .	33.$\overline{3}$%
$\frac{2}{3}$	.666 . . .	66.$\overline{6}$%
$\frac{1}{10}$	.1	10%
$\frac{1}{8}$	.125	12.5%
$\frac{1}{6}$	.1666 . . .	16.$\overline{6}$%
$\frac{1}{5}$	.2	20%

Absolute Value

The absolute value of a number is the distance of that number from zero. Distances are always represented by positive numbers, so the absolute value of any number is positive. Absolute value is represented by placing small vertical lines around the value: $|x|$.

Examples

The absolute value of seven: $|7|$.

The distance from seven to zero is seven, so $|7| = 7$.

The absolute value of negative three: $|-3|$.

The distance from negative three to zero is three, so $|-3| = 3$.

Exponents

Positive Exponents

A positive exponent indicates the number of times a base is used as a factor to attain a product.

Example

Evaluate 2^5.

In this example, 2 is the base and 5 is the exponent. Therefore, 2 should be used as a factor 5 times to attain a product:

$$2^5 = 2 \times 2 \times 2 \times 2 \times 2 = 32$$

Zero Exponent

Any nonzero number raised to the zero power equals 1.

Examples

$$5^0 = 1 \qquad 70^0 = 1 \qquad 29,874^0 = 1$$

Negative Exponents

A base raised to a negative exponent is equivalent to the reciprocal of the base raised to the positive exponent (absolute value of the exponent).

Examples

$$5^{-1} = \frac{1}{5}$$
$$7^{-2} = \left(\frac{1}{7}\right)^2 = \frac{1}{49}$$
$$\left(\frac{2}{3}\right)^{-2} = \left(\frac{3}{2}\right)^2 = \frac{9}{4}$$

Exponent Rules

- When multiplying identical bases, you add the exponents.

   Examples
   $2^2 \times 2^4 \times 2^6 = 2^{12}$
   $a^2 \times a^3 \times a^5 = a^{10}$

- When dividing identical bases, you subtract the exponents.

   Examples
   $\dfrac{2^7}{2^3} = 2^4$ $\qquad\qquad \dfrac{a^9}{a^4} = a^5$

- If a base raised to a power (in parentheses) is raised to another power, you multiply the exponents together.

   Examples
   $(3^2)^7 = 3^{14}$ $\qquad (g^4)^3 = g^{12}$

Perfect Squares

The number 5^2 is read "5 to the second power," or, more commonly, "5 squared." Perfect squares are numbers that are second powers of other numbers. Perfect squares are always zero or positive because when you multiply a positive or a negative by itself, the result is always positive. The perfect squares are $0^2, 1^2, 2^2, 3^2 \ldots$

   Perfect squares: 0, 1, 4, 9, 16, 25, 36, 49, 64, 81, 100 . . .

Perfect Cubes

The number 5^3 is read "5 to the third power," or, more commonly, "5 cubed." (Powers higher than three have no special name.) Perfect cubes are numbers that are third powers of other numbers. Perfect cubes, unlike perfect squares, can be either positive or negative. This is because when a negative is multiplied by itself three times, the result is negative. The perfect cubes are $0^3, 1^3, 2^3, 3^3 \ldots$

   Perfect cubes: 0, 1, 8, 27, 64, 125 . . .

- Note that 64 is both a perfect square and a perfect cube.

Square Roots

The square of a number is the product of the number and itself. For example, in the statement $3^2 = 3 \times 3 = 9$, the number 9 is the square of the number 3. If the process is reversed, the number 3 is the square root of the number 9. The symbol for square root is $\sqrt{}$ and is called a **radical**. The number inside of the radical is called the **radicand**.

   Example
   $5^2 = 25$; therefore, $\sqrt{25} = 5$

   Because 25 is the square of 5, it is also true that 5 is the square root of 25.

   The square root of a number might not be a whole number. For example, the square root of 7 is 2.645751311. . . . It is not possible to find a whole number that can be multiplied by itself to equal 7. Square roots of nonperfect squares are irrational.

Cube Roots

The cube of a number is the product of the number and itself for a total of three times. For example, in the statement $2^3 = 2 \times 2 \times 2 = 8$, the number 8 is the cube of the number 2. If the process is reversed, the number 2 is the cube root of the number 8. The symbol for cube root is the same as the square root symbol, except for a small 3: $\sqrt[3]{}$. It is read as "cube root." The number inside of the radical is still called the radicand, and the 3 is called the index. (In a square root, the index is not written, but it has an index of 2.)

Example

$5^3 = 125$; therefore, $\sqrt[3]{125} = 5$.

Like square roots, the cube root of a number might be not be a whole number. Cube roots of non-perfect cubes are irrational.

Probability

Probability is the numerical representation of the likelihood of an event occurring. Probability is always represented by a decimal or fraction between 0 and 1, with 0 meaning that the event will *never* occur, and 1 meaning that the event will *always* occur. The higher the probability, the more likely the event is to occur.

A **simple event** is one action. Examples of simple events are drawing one card from a deck, rolling one die, flipping one coin, or spinning a hand on a spinner once.

Simple Probability

The probability of an event occurring is defined as the number of desired outcomes divided by the total number of outcomes. The list of all outcomes is often called the **sample space**.

$$P(\text{event}) = \frac{\text{\# of desired outcomes}}{\text{total number of outcomes}}$$

Example

What is the probability of drawing a king from a standard deck of cards?

There are four kings in a standard deck of cards, so the number of desired outcomes is 4. There are 52 ways to pick a card from a standard deck of cards, so the total number of outcomes is 52. The probability of drawing a king from a standard deck of cards is $\frac{4}{52}$. So, $P(\text{king}) = \frac{4}{52}$.

Example

What is the probability of getting an odd number on the roll of one die?

There are three odd numbers on a standard die (1, 3, and 5), so, the number of desired outcomes is 3. There are six sides on a standard die, so there are 6 possible outcomes. The probability of rolling an odd number on a standard die is $\frac{3}{6}$. So, $P(\text{odd}) = \frac{3}{6}$.

Note: It is not necessary to reduce fractions when working with probability.

Probability of an Event Not Occurring

The sum of the probability of an event occurring and the probability of the event *not* occurring = 1. Therefore, if we know the probability of the event occurring, we can determine the probability of the event *not* occurring by subtracting from 1.

Example

If the probability of rain tomorrow is 45%, what is the probability that it will *not* rain tomorrow?

45% = .45, and $1 - .45 = .55$ or 55%. The probability that it will not rain is 55%.

Probability Involving the Word *Or*

Rule:

$P(\text{event A or event B}) = P(\text{event A}) + P(\text{event B}) - P(\text{overlap of event A and B})$

When the word *or* appears in a simple probability problem, it signifies that you will be adding outcomes. For example, if we are interested in the probability of obtaining a king or a queen on a draw of a card, the number of desired outcomes is 8, because there are four kings and four queens in the deck. The probability of event A (drawing a king) is $\frac{4}{52}$, and the probability of event B (drawing a queen) is $\frac{4}{52}$. The overlap of event A and B would be any cards that are both a king and a queen at the same time, but there are no cards that are both a king and a queen at the same time. So the probability of obtaining a king or a queen is $\frac{4}{52} + \frac{4}{52} - \frac{0}{52} = \frac{8}{52}$.

Example
What is the probability of getting an even number or a multiple of 3 on the roll of a die?

The probability of getting an even number on the roll of a die is $\frac{3}{6}$ because there are three even numbers (2, 4, 6) on a die and a total of 6 possible outcomes. The probability of getting a multiple of 3 is $\frac{2}{6}$ because there are 2 multiples of three (3, 6) on a die. But because the outcome of rolling a 6 on the die is an overlap of both events, we must subtract $\frac{1}{6}$ from the result so we don't count it twice.

P(even *or* multiple of 3) = P(even) + P(multiple of 3) – P(overlap)
$$= \frac{3}{6} + \frac{2}{6} - \frac{1}{6} = \frac{4}{6}$$

Compound Probability
A **compound event** describes the performance of two or more simple events in succession. Drawing two cards from a deck, rolling three dice, flipping five coins, and having four babies are all examples of compound events.

This can be done "with replacement" (probabilities do not change for each event) or "without replacement" (probabilities change for each event).

The probability of event A followed by event B occurring is $P(A) \times P(B)$. This is called the **counting principle** for probability.

Note: In mathematics, the word *and* usually signifies addition. In probability, however, *and* signifies multiplication and *or* signifies addition.

Example
You have a jar filled with three red marbles, five green marbles, and two blue marbles. What is the probability of getting a red marble followed by a blue marble, with replacement?

"With replacement" in this case means that you will draw a marble, note its color, and then replace it back into the jar. This means that the probability of drawing a red marble does not change from one simple event to the next.

Note that there are a total of ten marbles in the jar, so the total number of outcomes is 10.

$P(\text{red}) = \frac{3}{10}$ and $P(\text{blue}) = \frac{2}{10}$, so P(red followed by blue) is $\frac{3}{10} \times \frac{2}{10} = \frac{6}{100}$.

If the problem was changed to say "without replacement," that would mean you are drawing a marble, noting its color, but not returning it to the jar. This means that for the second event, you no longer have a total number of 10 outcomes; you have only 9 because you have taken one red marble out of the jar. In this case,

$P(\text{red}) = \frac{3}{10}$ and $P(\text{blue}) = \frac{2}{9}$, so P(red followed by blue) is $\frac{3}{10} \times \frac{2}{9} = \frac{6}{90}$.

Statistics
Statistics is the field of mathematics that deals with describing sets of data. Often, we want to understand trends in data by looking at where the center of the data lies. There are a number of ways to find the center of a set of data.

Mean
When we talk about average, we usually are referring to the **arithmetic mean** (usually just called the **mean**). To find the mean of a set of numbers, add all

of the numbers together and divide by the quantity of numbers in the set.

average = (sum of set) ÷ (quantity of set)

Example

Find the average of 9, 4, 7, 6, and 4.

$$\frac{9 + 4 + 7 + 6 + 4}{5} = \frac{30}{5} = 6$$

The mean, or average, of the set is 6.
(Divide by 5 because there are five numbers in the set.)

Median

Another center of data is the **median**. It is literally the center number if you arrange all the data in ascending or descending order. To find the median of a set of numbers, arrange the numbers in ascending or descending order and find the middle value.

- If the set contains an odd number of elements, then simply choose the middle value.

Example

Find the median of the number set: 1, 5, 4, 7, 2.

First arrange the set in order—1, 2, 4, 5, 7—and then find the middle value. Because there are five values, the middle value is the third one: 4. The median is 4.

- If the set contains an even number of elements, simply average the two middle values.

Example

Find the median of the number set: 1, 6, 3, 7, 2, 8.

First arrange the set in order—1, 2, 3, 6, 7, 8— and then find the middle values, 3 and 6. Find the average of the numbers 3 and 6: $\frac{3+6}{2} = \frac{9}{2} = 4.5$. The median is 4.5.

Mode

Sometimes when we want to know the average, we just want to know what occurs most often. The **mode** of a set of numbers is the number that appears the greatest number of times.

Example

For the number set 1, 2, 5, 9, 4, 2, 9, 6, 9, 7, the number 9 is the mode because it appears most frequently.

Measurement

This section reviews the basics of measurement systems used in the United States (sometimes called *customary measurement*) and other countries, methods of performing mathematical operations with units of measurement, and the process of converting between different units.

The use of measurement enables a connection to be made between mathematics and the real world. To measure any object, assign a number and a unit of measure. For instance, when a fish is caught, it is often weighed in ounces and its length measured in inches. The following lesson will help you become more familiar with the types, conversions, and units of measurement.

Types of Measurements

The types of measurements used most frequently in the United States are listed here:

Units of Length

12 inches (in.) = 1 foot (ft.)
3 feet = 36 inches = 1 yard (yd.)
5,280 feet = 1,760 yards = 1 mile (mi.)

Units of Volume

8 ounces* (oz.) = 1 cup (c.)

2 cups = 16 ounces = 1 pint (pt.)

2 pints = 4 cups = 32 ounces = 1 quart (qt.)

4 quarts = 8 pints = 16 cups = 128 ounces = 1 gallon (gal.)

Units of Weight

16 ounces* (oz.) = 1 pound (lb.)

2,000 pounds = 1 ton (T.)

Units of Time

60 seconds (sec.) = 1 minute (min.)

60 minutes = 1 hour (hr.)

24 hours = 1 day

7 days = 1 week

52 weeks = 1 year (yr.)

12 months = 1 year

365 days = 1 year

*Notice that ounces are used to measure the dimensions of both volume and weight.

Converting Units

When performing mathematical operations, it may be necessary to convert units of measure in order to simplify a problem. Units of measure are converted by using either multiplication or division.

- To convert from a larger unit into a smaller unit, *multiply* the given number of larger units by the number of smaller units in only one of the larger units:

(given number of the larger units) × (the number of smaller units per larger unit) = answer in smaller units

For example, to find the number of inches in five feet, multiply 5, the number of larger units, by 12, the number of inches in one foot:

5 feet = $\underline{\ ?\ }$ inches

5 feet × 12 (the number of inches in a single foot) = 60 inches: 5 ft. × $\frac{12 \text{ in.}}{1 \text{ ft.}}$ = 60 in. Therefore, there are 60 inches in five feet.

Example

Change 3.5 tons to pounds.

3.5 tons = $\underline{\ ?\ }$ pounds

3.5 tons × $\frac{2{,}000 \text{ pounds}}{1 \text{ ton}}$ = 7,000 pounds

Therefore, there are 7,000 pounds in 3.5 tons.

- To change a smaller unit to a larger unit, *divide* the given number of smaller units by the number of smaller units in only one of the larger units:

$$\frac{\text{given number of smaller units}}{\text{the number of smaller units per larger unit}} =$$

answer in larger units

For example, to find the number of pints in 64 ounces, divide 64, the number of smaller units, by 16, the number of ounces in one pint.

64 ounces = $\underline{\ ?\ }$ pints

$$\frac{64 \text{ ounces}}{16 \text{ ounces per pint}} = 4 \text{ pints}$$

Therefore, 64 ounces equals four pints.

Example

Change 32 ounces to pounds.

32 ounces = $\underline{\ ?\ }$ pounds

$$\frac{32 \text{ ounces}}{16 \text{ ounces per pound}} = 2 \text{ pounds}$$

Therefore, 32 ounces equals two pounds.

Basic Operations with Measurement

You may need to add, subtract, multiply, and divide with measurement. The mathematical rules needed for each of these operations with measurement follow.

Addition with Measurements

To add measurements, follow these two steps:

1. Add like units.
2. Simplify the answer by converting smaller units into larger units when possible.

Example
Add 4 pounds 5 ounces to 20 ounces.

      4 lb. 5 oz.   Be sure to add ounces to ounces.
    +   20 oz.
    4 lb. 25 oz.

Because 25 ounces is more than 16 ounces (1 pound), simplify by dividing by 16:

$$\begin{array}{r} 1 \text{ lb. r9 oz.} \\ 16 \text{ oz.} \overline{)25 \text{ oz.}} \\ -16 \text{ oz.} \\ \hline 9 \text{ oz.} \end{array}$$

Then add the 1 pound to the 4 pounds:

4 pounds 25 ounces = 4 pounds +
1 pound 9 ounces = 5 pounds 9 ounces

Subtraction with Measurements
1. Subtract like units if possible.
2. If not, regroup units to allow for subtraction.
3. Write the answer in simplest form.

Example
What is 6 pounds 2 ounces subtracted from 9 pounds 10 ounces?

      9 lb. 10 oz.   Subtract ounces from ounces.
    − 6 lb. 2 oz.   Then subtract pounds from
      3 lb. 8 oz.   pounds.

Sometimes, it is necessary to regroup units when subtracting.

Example
Subtract 3 yards 2 feet from 5 yards 1 foot.

Because 2 feet cannot be taken from 1 foot, regroup 1 yard from the 5 yards and convert the 1 yard to 3 feet. Add 3 feet to 1 foot. Then subtract feet from feet and yards from yards:

$$\begin{array}{r} \overset{4}{\cancel{5}} \text{ yd. } \overset{4}{\cancel{1}} \text{ ft.} \\ - \ 3 \text{ yd. } 2 \text{ ft.} \\ \hline 1 \text{ yd. } 2 \text{ ft.} \end{array}$$

Therefore, 5 yards 1 foot − 3 yards 2 feet = 1 yard 2 feet.

Multiplication with Measurements
1. Multiply like units if units are involved.
2. Simplify the answer.

Example
Multiply 5 feet 7 inches by 3.

                     Multiply 7 inches by 3, then
    5 ft. 7 in.   multiply 5 feet by 3. Keep the
    ×   3   units separate.
    15 ft. 21 in.   Because 12 inches = 1 foot,
                     simplify 21 inches.

15 ft. 21 in. = 15 ft. + 1 ft. 9 in. = 16 ft. 9 in.

Example
Multiply 9 feet by 4 yards.

First, decide on a common unit: either change the 9 feet to yards, or change the 4 yards to feet. Both options are explained next:

Option 1:
To change yards to feet, multiply the number of feet in a yard (3) by the number of yards in this problem (4).

3 feet in a yard • 4 yards = 12 feet

Then multiply:

9 feet × 12 feet = 108 square feet.

(Note: feet • feet = square feet = ft.^{2})

Option 2:
To change feet to yards, divide the number of feet given (9) by the number of feet in a yard (3).

9 feet ÷ 3 feet in a yard = 3 yards

Then multiply:

3 yards × 4 yards = 12 square yards.

(Note: yards • yards = square yards = yd.^{2})

Division with Measurements
1. Divide into the larger units first.
2. Convert the remainder to the smaller unit.
3. Add the converted remainder to the existing smaller unit, if any.

4. Divide into smaller units.

5. Write the answer in simplest form.

Example

Divide 5 quarts 4 ounces by 4.

1. Divide into the larger unit:

$$
\begin{array}{r}
1\ \text{qt. r1 qt.} \\
4\overline{)5\ \text{qt.}} \\
-4\ \text{qt.} \\
\hline
1\ \text{qt.}
\end{array}
$$

2. Convert the remainder:

1 qt. = 32 oz.

3. Add remainder to original smaller unit:

32 oz. + 4 oz. = 36 oz.

4. Divide into smaller units:

36 oz. ÷ 4 = 9 oz.

5. Write the answer in simplest form:

1 qt. 9 oz.

Metric Measurements

The metric system is an international system of measurement also called the **decimal system**. Converting units in the metric system is much easier than converting units in the customary system of measurement. However, making conversions between the two systems is much more difficult. The basic units of the metric system are the meter, gram, and liter. Here is a general idea of how the two systems compare:

METRIC SYSTEM	CUSTOMARY SYSTEM
1 meter	A meter is a little more than a yard; it is equal to about 39 inches.
1 gram	A gram is a very small unit of weight; there are about 30 grams in one ounce.
1 liter	A liter is a little more than a quart.

Prefixes are attached to the basic metric units to indicate the amount of each unit. For example, the prefix *deci* means one-tenth ($\frac{1}{10}$); therefore, one decigram is one-tenth of a gram, and one decimeter is one-tenth of a meter. The following six prefixes can be used with every metric unit:

KILO	HECTO	DEKA	DECI	CENTI	MILLI
(k)	(h)	(dk)	(d)	(c)	(m)
1,000	100	10	$\frac{1}{10}$	$\frac{1}{100}$	$\frac{1}{1,000}$

Examples

- 1 hectometer = 1 hm = 100 meters
- 1 millimeter = 1 mm = $\frac{1}{1,000}$ meter = .001 meter
- 1 dekagram = 1 dkg = 10 grams
- 1 centiliter = 1 cL* = $\frac{1}{100}$ liter = .01 liter

- 1 kilogram = 1 kg = 1,000 grams
- 1 deciliter = 1 dL* = $\frac{1}{10}$ liter = .1 liter

*Notice that liter is abbreviated with a capital letter—*L*.

The following chart illustrates some common relationships used in the metric system:

LENGTH	WEIGHT	VOLUME
1 km = 1,000 m	1 kg = 1,000 g	1 kL = 1,000 L
1 m = .001 km	1 g = .001 kg	1 L = .001 kL
1 m = 100 cm	1 g = 100 cg	1 L = 100 cL
1 cm = .01 m	1 cg = .01 g	1 cL = .01 L
1 m = 1,000 mm	1 g = 1,000 mg	1 L = 1,000 mL
1 mm = .001 m	1 mg = .001 g	1 mL = .001 L

Conversions within the Metric System

An easy way to do conversions with the metric system is to move the decimal point either to the right or to the left, because the conversion factor is always ten or a power of ten. Remember, when changing from a large unit to a smaller unit, multiply. When changing from a small unit to a larger unit, divide.

Making Easy Conversions within the Metric System

When multiplying by a power of ten, move the decimal point to the right because the number becomes larger. When dividing by a power of ten, move the decimal point to the left because the number becomes smaller.

To change from a larger unit to a smaller unit, move the decimal point to the right.

$$\rightarrow$$

kilo hecto deka UNIT deci centi milli

$$\leftarrow$$

An easy way to remember the metric prefixes is to remember the mnemonic: "King Henry Died Of Drinking Chocolate Milk." The first letter of each word represents a corresponding metric heading from kilo down to milli: "King"—Kilo, "Henry"—Hecto, "Died"—Deka, "Of"—Original Unit, "Drinking"—Deci, "Chocolate"—Centi, and "Milk"—Milli.

To change from a smaller unit to a larger unit, move the decimal point to the left.

Example

Change 520 grams to kilograms.

1. Be aware that changing grams to kilograms is going from small units to larger units and, thus, requires that the decimal point move to the left.
2. Beginning at the unit (for grams), note that the kilo heading is three places away. Therefore, the decimal point will move three places to the left.

k   h   dk   unit   d   c   m

3. Move the decimal point from the end of 520 to the left three places.
520

←

.520

Place the decimal point before the 5: .520
The answer is 520 grams = .520 kilograms.

Example

Ron's supply truck can hold a total of 20,000 kilograms. If he exceeds that limit, he must buy stabilizers for the truck that cost $12.80 each. Each stabilizer can hold 100 additional kilograms. If he wants to pack 22,300,000 grams of supplies, how much money will he have to spend on the stabilizers?

1. First, change 22,300,000 grams to kilograms.

kg   hg   dkg   g   dg   cg   mg

2. Move the decimal point three places to the left: 22,300,000 g = 22,300.000 kg = 22,300 kg.
3. Subtract to find the amount over the limit: 22,300 kg − 20,000 kg = 2,300 kg.
4. Because each stabilizer holds 100 kilograms and the supplies exceed the weight limit of the truck by 2,300 kilograms, Ron must purchase 23 stabilizers:

2,300 kg ÷ 100 kg per stabilizer = 23 stabilizers.

5. Each stabilizer costs $12.80, so multiply $12.80 by 23:

$12.80 × 23 = $294.40.

Algebra

This section helps in mastering algebraic equations by reviewing variables, cross multiplication, algebraic fractions, reciprocal rules, and exponents. Algebra is arithmetic using letters called **variables** in place of numbers. By using variables, the general relationships among numbers can be easier to see and understand.

Algebra Terminology

A **term** of a polynomial is an expression that is composed of variables (and their exponents) and coefficients. A **variable** is a letter that represents an unknown number. Variables are frequently used in equations, in formulas, and in mathematical rules to help illustrate numerical relationships. When a number is placed next to a variable, indicating multiplication, the number is said to be the **coefficient** of the variable.

Examples

$8c$	8 is the coefficient of the variable c.
$6ab$	6 is the coefficient of both variables a and b.

Three Kinds of Polynomials

- **Monomials** are single terms that are composed of variables and their exponents and a positive or negative coefficient. The following are examples of monomials: x, $5x$, $-6y^3$, $10x^2y$, 7, 0.
- **Binomials** are two nonlike monomial terms separated by + or – signs. The following are examples of binomials: $x + 2$, $3x^2 - 5x$, $-3xy^2 + 2xy$.
- **Trinomials** are three nonlike monomial terms separated by + or – signs. The following are examples of trinomials: $x^2 + 2x - 1$, $3x^2 - 5x + 4$, $-3xy^2 + 2xy - 6x$.
- Monomials, binomials, and trinomials are all examples of **polynomials**, but we usually reserve the word *polynomial* for expressions formed by more than three terms.
- The **degree** of a polynomial is the largest sum of the terms' exponents.

Examples

- The degree of the trinomial $x^2 + 2x - 1$ is 2 because the x^2 term has the highest exponent of 2.
- The degree of the binomial $x + 2$ is 1 because the x term has the highest exponent of 1.
- The degree of the binomial $-3x^4y^2 + 2xy$ is 6 because the x^4y^2 term has the highest exponent sum of 6.

Like Terms

If two or more terms have exactly the same variable(s), and if these variables are raised to exactly the same exponents, they are said to be **like terms**. Like terms can be simplified when they are added and subtracted.

Examples

$7x + 3x = 10x$
$6y^2 - 4y^2 = 2y^2$

However, $3cd^2 + 5c^2d$ cannot be simplified. Since the exponent of 2 is on d in $3cd^2$ and on c in $5c^2d$, they are not like terms.

The process of adding and subtracting like terms is called **combining like terms**. It is important to combine like terms carefully, making sure that *the variables are exactly the same.*

Algebraic Expressions

An algebraic expression is a combination of monomials and operations. The difference between algebraic expressions and algebraic equations is that algebraic expressions are evaluated at different given values for variables, while algebraic equations are solved to determine the value of the variable that makes the equation a true statement.

There is very little difference between expressions and equations because equations are nothing more than two expressions set equal to each other. Their usage is subtly different.

Example

A mobile phone company charges a flat fee of $39.99 a month for the first 600 minutes of calls, with a charge of $0.55 for each minute thereafter.

Write an algebraic expression for the cost of a month's mobile phone bill:
$39.99 + 0.55x$, where x represents the number of additional minutes used.

Write an equation for the cost (C) of a month's mobile phone bill:

$C = \$39.99 + \$0.55x$, where x represents the number of additional minutes used.

In the preceding example, you might use the expression $\$39.99 + \$0.55x$ to determine the cost if you are given the value of x by substituting the value for x into the equation. You could also use the equation $C = \$39.99 + \$0.55x$ in the same way, but you can also use the equation to determine the value of x if you were given the cost.

Simplifying and Evaluating Algebraic Expressions

We can use the preceding mobile phone company example to illustrate how to simplify algebraic expressions. Algebraic expressions are evaluated by a two-step process: substituting the given value(s) into the expression, and then simplifying the expression by following the order of operations (PEMDAS).

Example

Using the cost expression $\$39.99 + \$0.55x$, determine the total cost of a month's mobile phone bill if the owner made 700 minutes of calls.

Let x represent the number of minutes over 600 used, so in order to find out the difference, subtract $700 - 600$; $x = 100$ minutes over 600 used.

Substitution: Replace x with its value, using parentheses around the value.

$\$39.99 + \$0.55x$

$\$39.99 + \$0.55(100)$

Evaluation: PEMDAS tells us to evaluate parentheses and exponents first. There is no operation to perform in the parentheses, and there are no exponents, so the next step is to multiply, and then add.

$\$39.99 + \$0.55(100)$

$\$39.99 + \$55 = \$94.99$

The cost of the mobile phone bill for the month is $94.99.

You can evaluate algebraic expressions that contain any number of variables, as long as you are given all the values for all the variables.

Simple Rules for Working with Linear Equations

A linear equation is an equation whose variables' highest exponent is 1. It is also called a **first-degree equation**. An equation is solved by finding the value of an unknown variable.

1. The equal sign separates an equation into two sides.
2. Whenever an operation is performed on one side, the same operation must be performed on the other side.
3. The first goal is to get all the variable terms on one side and all the numbers (called **constants**) on the other side. This is accomplished by *undoing* the operations that are attaching numbers to the variable, thereby isolating the variable. The operations are always done in reverse PEMDAS order: start by adding/subtracting, then multiply/divide.
4. The final step often will be to divide each side by the coefficient (the number in front of the variable), leaving the variable alone and equal to a number.

Example

$$5m + 8 = 48$$
$$\underline{-8 \quad -8}$$
$$\frac{5m}{5} = \frac{40}{5}$$
$$m = 8$$

Undo the addition of 8 by subtracting 8 from both sides of the equation. Then, undo the multiplication by 5 by dividing by 5 on both sides of the equation. The variable, m, is now isolated on the left side of the equation, and its value is 8.

Checking Solutions to Equations

To check an equation, substitute the value of the variable into the original equation.

Example

To check the solution of the previous equation, substitute the number 8 for the variable m in $5m + 8 = 48$.

$$5(8) + 8 = 48$$
$$40 + 8 = 48$$
$$48 = 48$$

Because this statement is true, the answer $m = 8$ must be correct.

Isolating Variables Using Fractions

Working with equations that contain fractions is almost exactly the same as working with equations that do not contain variables, except for the final step. The final step when an equation has no fractions is to divide each side by the coefficient. When the coefficient of the variable is a fraction, you will instead multiply both sides by the reciprocal of the coefficient. Technically, you could still divide both sides by the coefficient, but that involves division of fractions, which can be trickier.

Example

$$\frac{2}{3}m + \frac{1}{2} = 12$$
$$\qquad -\frac{1}{2} \qquad -\frac{1}{2}$$
$$\frac{2}{3}m = 11\frac{1}{2}$$
$$\frac{3}{2} \cdot \frac{2}{3}m = 11\frac{1}{2} \cdot \frac{3}{2}$$
$$\frac{3}{2} \cdot \frac{2}{3}m = \frac{23}{2} \cdot \frac{3}{2}$$
$$m = \frac{69}{4}$$

Undo the addition of $\frac{1}{2}$ by subtracting $\frac{1}{2}$ from both sides of the equation. Multiply both sides by the reciprocal of the coefficient. Convert the $11\frac{1}{2}$ to an improper fraction to facilitate multiplication. The

variable m is now isolated on the left side of the equation, and its value is $\frac{69}{4}$.

Equations with More than One Variable

Equations can have more than one variable. Each variable represents a different value, although it is possible that the variables have the same value.

Remember that like terms have the same variable and exponent. All the rules for working with variables apply in equations that contain more than one variable, but you must remember not to combine terms that are not alike.

Equations with more than one variable cannot be solved because if there is more than one variable in an equation, there is usually an infinite number of values for the variables that would make the equation true. Instead, we are often required to "solve for a variable," which instead means to isolate that variable on one side of the equation.

Example

Solve for y in the equation $2x + 3y = 5$.

There are an infinite number of values for x and y that would satisfy the equation. Instead, we are asked to isolate y on one side of the equation.

$$2x + 3y = 5$$
$$-2x \qquad\qquad -2x$$
$$\frac{3y}{3} = \frac{-2x + 5}{3}$$
$$y = \frac{-2x + 5}{3}$$

Cross Multiplying

Because algebra uses percents and proportions, it is necessary to learn how to cross multiply. You can solve an equation that sets one fraction equal to another by using **cross multiplication**. Cross multiplication involves setting the cross products of opposite pairs of terms equal to each other.

Example

$$\frac{x}{10} = \frac{70}{100}$$

$$100x = 700$$

$$\frac{100x}{100} = \frac{700}{100}$$

$$x = 7$$

Algebraic Fractions

Working with algebraic fractions is very similar to working with fractions in arithmetic. The difference is that algebraic fractions contain algebraic expressions in the numerator and/or denominator.

Example

A hotel currently has only one-fifth of its rooms available. If x represents the total number of rooms in the hotel, find an expression for the number of rooms that will be available if another tenth of the total rooms are reserved.

Because x represents the total number of rooms, $\frac{x}{5}$ (or $\frac{1}{5}x$) represents the number of available rooms. One-tenth of the total rooms in the hotel would be represented by the fraction $\frac{x}{10}$. To find the new number of available rooms, find the difference:

$$\frac{x}{5} - \frac{x}{10}.$$

Write $\frac{x}{5} - \frac{x}{10}$ as a single fraction.

Just like in arithmetic, the first step is to find the LCD of 5 and 10, which is 10. Then, change each fraction into an equivalent fraction that has 10 as the denominator.

$$\frac{x}{5} - \frac{x}{10} = \frac{x(2)}{5(2)} - \frac{x}{10}$$
$$= \frac{2x}{10} - \frac{x}{10}$$
$$= \frac{x}{10}$$

Therefore, $\frac{x}{10}$ rooms will be available after another tenth of the rooms are reserved.

Reciprocal Rules

There are special rules for the sum and difference of reciprocals. The reciprocal of 3 is $\frac{1}{3}$, and the reciprocal of x is $\frac{1}{x}$.

- If x and y are not 0, then $\frac{1}{x} + \frac{1}{y} = \frac{y}{xy} + \frac{x}{xy} = \frac{y+x}{xy}$.

- If x and y are not 0, then $\frac{1}{x} - \frac{1}{y} = \frac{y}{xy} - \frac{x}{xy} = \frac{y-x}{xy}$.

Translating Words into Numbers

The most important skill needed for solving word problems is the ability to translate words into mathematical operations. The following will be helpful in achieving this goal by providing common examples of English phrases and their mathematical equivalents.

Phrases meaning addition: *increased by*; *sum of*; *more than*; *exceeds by*.

Examples

A number increased by five: $x + 5$.
The sum of two numbers: $x + y$.
Ten more than a number: $x + 10$.

Phrases meaning subtraction: *decreased by*; *difference of*; *less/fewer than*; *diminished by*.

Examples

Ten less than a number: $x - 10$.
The difference of two numbers: $x - y$.

Phrases meaning multiplication: *times*; *times the sum/difference*; *product*; *of*.

Examples

Three times a number: $3x$.
Twenty percent of 50: $20\% \times 50$.
Five times the sum of a number and three: $5(x + 3)$.

Phrases meaning equals: *is*; *result is*.

Examples
Fifteen is 14 plus 1: $15 = 14 + 1$.
Ten more than two times a number is 15:
$2x + 10 = 15$.

Assigning Variables in Word Problems

It may be necessary to create and assign variables in a word problem. To do this, first identify any knowns and unknowns. The known may not be a specific numerical value, but the problem should indicate something about its value. Then let x represent the unknown you know the least about.

Examples
Max has worked for three more years than Ricky.
Unknown: Ricky's work experience $= x$
Known: Max's experience is three more years $= x + 3$

Heidi made twice as many sales as Rebecca.
Unknown: number of sales Rebecca made $= x$
Known: number of sales Heidi made is twice Rebecca's amount $= 2x$

There are six less than four times the number of pens than pencils.
Unknown: the number of pencils $= x$
Known: the number of pens $= 4x - 6$

Todd has assembled five more than three times the number of cabinets that Andrew has.
Unknown: the number of cabinets Andrew has assembled $= x$
Known: the number of cabinets Todd has assembled is five more than three times the number Andrew has assembled $= 3x + 5$

Percentage Problems

To solve percentage problems, determine what information has been given in the problem and fill this information into the following template:

_____ is _____% of _____

Then translate this information into a one-step equation and solve. In translating, remember that *is* translates to $=$ and *of* translates to $\times$. Use a variable to represent the unknown quantity.

Examples
Finding a percentage of a given number:
In a new housing development there will be 50 houses. 40% of the houses must be completed in the first stage. How many houses are in the first stage?

1. Translate.
   _____ is 40% of 50.
   $x = .40 \times 50$.

2. Solve.
   $x = .40 \times 50$
   $x = 20$
   20 is 40% of 50. There are 20 houses in the first stage.

Finding a number when a percentage is given:
40% of the cars on the lot have been sold. If 24 cars were sold, how many total cars were there on the lot originally?

1. Translate.
   24 is 40% of _____.
   $24 = .40 \times x$.

2. Solve.
   $\dfrac{24}{.40} = \dfrac{.40x}{.40}$
   $60 = x$
   24 is 40% of 60. There were 60 total cars on the lot.

Finding what percentage one number is of another:

Matt has 75 employees. He is going to give 15 of them raises. What percent of the employees will receive raises?

1. Translate.

   15 is _____% of 75.

   $15 = x \times 75$.

2. Solve.

   $\frac{15}{75} = \frac{75x}{75}$

   $.20 = x$

   $20\% = x$

   15 is 20% of 75. Therefore, 20% of the employees will receive raises.

Problems Involving Ratio

A **ratio** is a comparison of two quantities measured in the same units. It is symbolized by the use of a colon—*x:y*. Ratios can also be expressed as fractions ($\frac{x}{y}$) or by using words (*x* to *y*).

Ratio problems are solved using the concept of multiples.

Example

A bag contains a total of 60 screws and nails. The ratio of the number of screws to nails is 7:8. How many of each kind are there in the bag?

From the problem, it is known that 7 and 8 share a multiple and that the sum of their product is 60. Whenever you see the word *ratio* in a problem, place an "*x*" next to each of the numbers in the ratio, and those are your unknowns.

Let $7x$ = the number of screws.

Let $8x$ = the number of nails.

Write and solve the following equation:

$7x + 8x = 60$

$\frac{15x}{15} = \frac{60}{15}$

$x = 4$

Therefore, there are $(7)(4) = 28$ screws and $(8)(4) = 32$ nails in the bag.

Check: $28 + 32 = 60$ screws, $\frac{28}{32} = \frac{7}{8}$.

Problems Involving Variation

Variation is a term referring to a constant ratio in the change of a quantity.

- Two quantities are said to vary **directly** if their ratios are constant. Both variables change in an equal direction. In other words, two quantities vary directly if an increase in one causes an increase in the other. This is also true if a decrease in one causes a decrease in the other.

Example

If it takes 300 new employees a total of 58.5 hours to train, how many hours will it take to train 800 employees?

Because each employee needs about the same amount of training, you know that these values vary directly. Therefore, you can set the problem up the following way:

$\frac{\text{employees}}{\text{hours}} \rightarrow \frac{300}{58.5} = \frac{800}{x}$

Cross multiply to solve:

$(800)(58.5) = 300x$

$\frac{46,800}{300} = \frac{300x}{300}$

$156 = x$

Therefore, it would take 156 hours to train 800 employees.

- Two quantities are said to vary **inversely** if their products are constant. The variables change in opposite directions. This means that as one quantity increases, the other decreases, or as one decreases, the other increases.

Example

If two people can plant a field in six days, how many days will it take six people to plant the same field? (Assume each person is working at the same rate.)

As the number of people planting increases, the number of days needed to plant decreases. Therefore, the relationship between the number of people and days varies inversely. Because the field remains constant, the two products can be set equal to each other.

$$2 \text{ people} \times 6 \text{ days} = 6 \text{ people} \times x \text{ days}$$
$$2 \times 6 = 6x$$
$$\frac{12}{6} = \frac{6x}{6}$$
$$2 = x$$

Thus, it would take six people two days to plant the same field.

Rate Problems

In general, there are three different types of rate problems likely to be encountered in the workplace: cost per unit, movement, and work output. **Rate** is defined as a comparison of two quantities with different units of measure.

$$\text{rate} = \frac{x \text{ units}}{y \text{ units}}$$

Examples

$$\frac{\text{dollars}}{\text{hour}}, \frac{\text{cost}}{\text{pound}}, \frac{\text{miles}}{\text{hour}}$$

Cost per Unit

Some problems will require the calculation of unit cost.

Example

If 100 square feet of tile costs $1,000, how much does 1 square foot cost?

$$\frac{\text{total cost}}{\text{\# of square feet}} = \frac{\$1,000}{100 \text{ ft.}^2}$$
$$= \$10 \text{ per square foot}$$

Movement

In working with movement problems, it is important to use the following formula:

$$(\text{rate})(\text{time}) = \text{distance}$$

Example

A courier traveling at 15 mph traveled from his base to a company in $\frac{1}{4}$ of an hour less than it took when the courier traveled at 12 mph. How far away was his drop-off?

First, write what is known and unknown.
Unknown: time for courier traveling 12 mph = x
Known: time for courier traveling 15 mph = $x - \frac{1}{4}$.
Then, use the formula $(\text{rate})(\text{time}) = \text{distance}$ to find expressions for the distance traveled at each rate:

12 mph for x hours = a distance of $12x$ miles
15 mph for $x - \frac{1}{4}$ hours = a distance of $15x - \frac{15}{4}$ miles

The distance traveled is the same; therefore, make the two expressions equal to each other:

$$12x = 15x - 3.75$$
$$-15x \qquad -15x$$
$$\frac{-3x}{-3} = \frac{-3.75}{-3}$$
$$x = 1.25$$

Be careful: 1.25 is not the distance; it is the time. Now you must plug the time into the formula $(\text{rate})(\text{time}) = \text{distance}$. Either rate can be used.

$$12x = \text{distance}$$
$$12(1.25) = \text{distance}$$
$$15 \text{ miles} = \text{distance}$$

Work Output

Work-output problems are word problems that deal with the rate of work. The following formula can be used on these problems:

(rate of work)(time worked) = job or part of job completed

Example

Danette can wash and wax two cars in six hours, and Judy can wash and wax the same two cars in four hours. If Danette and Judy work together, how long will it take them to wash and wax one car?

Because Danette can wash and wax two cars in six hours, her rate of work is $\frac{2 \text{ cars}}{6 \text{ hours}}$, or one car every three hours. Judy's rate of work is $\frac{2 \text{ cars}}{4 \text{ hours}}$, or one car every two hours. In this problem, making a chart will help:

	(Rate)	(Time)	= Part of job completed
Danette	$(\frac{1}{3})$	(x)	$= \frac{1}{3}x$
Judy	$(\frac{1}{2})$	(x)	$= \frac{1}{2}x$

Because they are both working on only one car, you can set the equation equal to one: Danette's part + Judy's part = 1 car:

$$\frac{1}{3}x + \frac{1}{2}x = 1$$

Solve by using 6 as the LCD for 3 and 2 and clearing the fractions by multiplying by the LCD:

$$6(\tfrac{1}{3}x) + 6(\tfrac{1}{2}x) = 6(1)$$
$$2x + 3x = 6$$
$$\frac{5x}{5} = \frac{6}{5}$$
$$x = 1\tfrac{1}{5}$$

Thus, it will take Judy and Danette $1\frac{1}{5}$ hours to wash and wax one car.

Patterns and Functions

The ability to detect patterns in numbers is a very important mathematical skill. Patterns exist everywhere in nature, business, and finance.

When you are asked to find a pattern in a series of numbers, look to see whether there is some common number you can add, subtract, multiply, or divide each number in the pattern by to give you the next number in the series.

For example, in the sequence 5, 8, 11, 14 . . . you can add 3 to each number in the sequence to get the next number in the sequence. The next number in the sequence is 17.

Example

What is the next number in the sequence $\frac{3}{4}$, 3, 12, 48?

Each number in the sequence can be multiplied by the number 4 to get the next number in the sequence: $\frac{3}{4} \times 4 = 3$, $3 \times 4 = 12$, and $12 \times 4 = 48$, so the next number in the sequence is $48 \times 4 = 192$.

Sometimes it is not that simple. You may need to look for a combination of multiplying and adding, dividing and subtracting, or some combination of other operations.

Example

What is the next number in the sequence 0, 1, 2, 5, 26?

Keep trying various operations until you find one that works. In this case, the correct procedure is to square the term and add 1: $0^2 + 1 = 1$, $1^2 + 1 = 2$, $2^2 + 1 = 5$, and $5^2 + 1 = 26$, so the next number in the sequence is $26^2 + 1 = 677$.

Properties of Functions

A **function** is a relationship between two variables x and y where for each value of x, there is one and only one value of y. Functions can be represented in four ways:

1. a word problem
2. a graph
3. an equation
4. a table or chart

For example, the following four representations are equivalent to the same function.

Word Problem
Javier has one more than two times the number of books Susanna has.

Graph

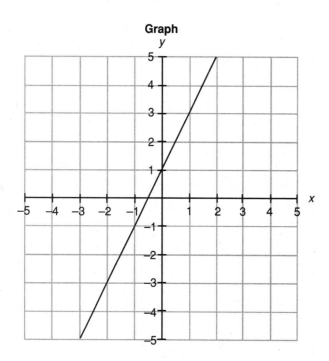

Equation

$y = 2x + 1$

Table

x	y
−3	−5
−2	−3
−1	−1
0	1
1	3
2	5

Helpful hints for determining whether a relationship is a function:

- If you can isolate y in terms of x using only one equation, it **is** a function.
- If the equation contains y^2, it will **not** be a function.
- If you can draw a vertical line anywhere on a graph such that it touches the graph in more than one place, it is **not** a function.
- If there is a value for x that has more than one y-value assigned to it, it is **not** a function.

x	y
5	2
3	-1
2	0
6	1
5	4

In this table, the
x-value of 5 has **two**
corresponding *y*-values,
2 and 4. Therefore,
it is **not** a function.

x	y
-2	5
-1	6
0	7
1	8
2	9

In this table, every
x-value
{−2, −1, 0, 1, 2, 3}
has **one** corresponding
y-value. This **is**
a function.

x	y
-2	3
-1	3
0	3
1	3
2	3

In this table, every
x-value
{−2, −1, 0, 1, 2, 3}
has **one** corresponding
y-value, even though
that value is 3
in every case.
This **is** a function.

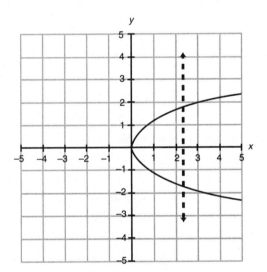

In this graph, there
is at least one vertical
line (the dotted line) that
can be drawn that intersects
the graph in more than one
place. Therefore, this is **not**
a function.

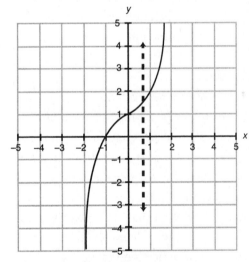

In this graph, there is no
vertical line that can be drawn
that intersects the graph
in more than one place.
This **is** a function.

Examples

$x = 5$ Contains no variable y, so you cannot isolate y. This is **not** a function.

$2x + 3y = 5$ Isolate y:

$$2x + 3y = 5$$
$$-2x \qquad\quad -2x$$
$$\frac{3y}{3} = \frac{-2x + 5}{3}$$
$$y = -\frac{2x}{3} + \frac{5}{3}$$

This is a **linear function**, of the form $y = mx + b$.

$x^2 + y^2 = 36$ Contains y^2, so it is **not** a function.

$|y| = 5$ There is no way to isolate y with a single equation; therefore, it is **not** a function.

Function Notation

Instead of using the variable y, often you will see the variable $f(x)$. This is shorthand for "function of x" to automatically indicate that an equation is a function. This can be confusing: $f(x)$ does not indicate that two variables f and x are multiplied together; it is a notation that means the single variable y.

Although it may seem that $f(x)$ is not an efficient shorthand (it has more characters than y), it is a very eloquent way of indicating that you are being given expressions to evaluate. For example, if you are given the equation $f(x) = 5x - 2$, and you are being asked to determine the value of the equation at $x = 2$, you need to write "evaluate the equation $f(x) = $ 5x − 2 when $x = 2$." This is very wordy. With function notation, you only need to write "determine $f(2)$." The x in $f(x)$ is replaced with a 2, indicating that the value of x is 2. This means that $f(2) = 5(2) - 2 = 10 - 2 = 8$.

All you need to do when given an equation $f(x)$ and told to evaluate $f(value)$ is to replace that $value$ for every occurrence of x in the equation.

Example

Given the equation $f(x) = 2x^2 + 3x + 1$, determine $f(0)$ and $f(-1)$.

$f(0)$ means replace the value 0 for every occurrence of x in the equation and evaluate.
$$f(0) = 2(0)^2 + 3(0) + 1$$
$$= 0 + 0 + 1$$
$$= 1$$

$f(-1)$ means replace the value −1 for every occurrence of x in the equation and evaluate.
$$f(0) = 2(-1)^2 + 3(-1) + 1$$
$$= 2(1) + -3 + 1$$
$$= 2 - 3 + 1$$
$$= 0$$

Families of Functions

There are a number of different types, or families, of functions. Each function family has a certain equation and its graph takes on a certain appearance. You can tell what type of function an equation is by just looking at the equation or its graph.

These are the shapes that some various functions have. They can appear thinner or wider, higher or lower, or upside down.

Linear Function
$f(x) = mx + b$
$y = mx + b$

Constant Function
$f(x) = c$
$y = c$
The equation contains no variable x.

Quadratic Function
$f(x) = ax^2 + bx + c$
$y = ax^2 + bx + c$
This is the function name for a parabola.

Square Root Function
The equation has to contain a square root symbol.

Cubic Function
$f(x) = ax^3 + bx^2 + cx + d$
$y = ax^3 + bx^2 + cx + d$

Absolute Value Function
The equation has to have an absolute value symbol in it.

Systems of Equations

A **system of equations** is a set of two or more equations with the same solution. Two methods for solving a system of equations are substitution and elimination.

Substitution

Substitution involves solving for one variable in terms of another and then substituting that expression into the second equation.

Example

$2p + q = 11$ and $p + 2q = 13$

■ First, choose an equation and rewrite it, isolating one variable in terms of the other. It does not matter which variable you choose.
$2p + q = 11$ becomes $q = 11 - 2p$.

■ Second, substitute $11 - 2p$ for q in the other equation and solve:
$p + 2(11 - 2p) = 13$
$p + 22 - 4p = 13$
$22 - 3p = 13$
$22 = 13 + 3p$
$9 = 3p$
$p = 3$

■ Now, substitute this answer into either original equation for p to find q.
$2p + q = 11$
$2(3) + q = 11$
$6 + q = 11$
$q = 5$

■ Thus, $p = 3$ and $q = 5$.

Elimination

The elimination method involves writing one equation over another and then adding or subtracting the like terms on the same sides of the equal sign so that one variable is eliminated.

Example
$x - 9 = 2y$ and $x - 3 = 5y$

- Rewrite each equation in the same form.
  $x - 9 = 2y$ becomes $x - 2y = 9$, and $x - 3 = 5y$ becomes $x - 5y = 3$.

- If you subtract the two equations, the "x" terms will be eliminated, leaving only one variable:
  Subtract:
  $$x - 2y = 9$$
  $$-(x - 5y = 3)$$
  $$\frac{3y}{3} = \frac{6}{3}$$
  $$y = 2$$

- Substitute 2 for y in one of the original equations and solve for x.
  $$x - 9 = 2y$$
  $$x - 9 = 2(2)$$
  $$x - 9 = 4$$
  $$x - 9 + 9 = 4 + 9$$
  $$x = 13$$

- The answer to the system of equations is $y = 2$ and $x = 13$.

If the variables do not have the same or opposite coefficients, as in the preceding example, adding or subtracting will not eliminate a variable. In this situation, it is first necessary to multiply one or both of the equations by some constant or constants so that the coefficients of one of the variables are the same or opposite. There are many different ways you can choose to do this.

Example
$3x + y = 13$
$x + 6y = -7$

We need to multiply one or both of the equations by some constant that will give equal or opposite coefficients of one of the variables. One way to do this is to multiply every term in the second equation by -3.

$$3x + y = 13$$
$$-3(x + 6y = -7) \rightarrow -3x - 18y = 21$$

Now if you add the two equations, the "x" terms will be eliminated, leaving only one variable. Continue as in the preceding example.

$$3x + y = 13$$
$$-3x - 18y = 21$$
$$\frac{-17y}{-17} = \frac{34}{-17}$$
$$y = -2$$

- Substitute -2 for y in one of the original equations and solve for x.
  $$3x + y = 13$$
  $$3x + (-2) = 13$$
  $$3x + (-2) + 2 = 13 + 2$$
  $$3x = 15$$
  $$x = 5$$

- The answer to the system of equations is $y = -2$ and $x = 5$.

Inequalities

Linear inequalities are solved in much the same way as simple equations. The most important difference is that when an inequality is multiplied or divided by a negative number, the inequality symbol changes direction.

Example

$10 > 5$, so $(10)(-3) < (5)(-3)$

$$-30 < -15$$

Solving Linear Inequalities

To solve a linear inequality, isolate the variable and solve the same way as you would in a linear equation. Remember to reverse the direction of the inequality sign if you divide or multiply both sides of the equation by a negative number.

Example

If $7 - 2x > 21$, find x.

- Isolate the variable.

$$7 - 2x > 21$$
$$\underline{-7 \qquad -7}$$
$$-2x > 14$$

- Because you are then dividing by a negative number, the inequality symbol changes direction.

$$\frac{-2x}{-2} > \frac{14}{-2}$$
$$x < -7$$

- The answer consists of all real numbers less than -7.

Solving Compound Inequalities

To solve an inequality that has the form $c < ax + b < d$, isolate the variable by performing the same operation on each part of the equation.

Example

If $-10 < -5y - 5 < 15$, find y.

- Add five to each part of the inequality.

$$-10 + 5 < -5y - 5 + 5 < 15 + 5$$
$$-5 < -5y < 20$$

- Divide each term by -5, changing the direction of both inequality symbols:

$$\frac{-5}{-5} < -\frac{5y}{-5} < \frac{20}{-5}$$
$$1 > y > -4$$

The solution consists of all real numbers less than 1 and greater than -4.

Geometry

This section familiarizes you with the properties of angles, lines, polygons, triangles, and circles, as well as with the formulas for area, volume, and perimeter.

Geometry is the study of shapes and the relationships among them. Basic concepts in geometry are detailed and applied in this section. The study of geometry always begins with a look at basic vocabulary and concepts; therefore, a list of definitions and important formulas is provided.

Geometry Terms

area	the space inside a two-dimensional figure
circumference	the distance around a circle
chord	a line segment that goes through a circle, with its endpoints on the circle
congruent	equal, in reference to lengths, measures of angles, or sizes of figures
diameter	a chord that goes directly through the center of a circle—the longest line segment that can be drawn in a circle
hypotenuse	the longest side of a right triangle, always opposite the right angle

leg	either of the two sides of a right triangle that make the right angle
perimeter	the distance around a figure
π (pi)	the ratio of any circle's circumference to its diameter (pi is an irrational number, but most of the time it is okay to approximate π with 3.14)
radius	a line segment from the center of a circle to a point on the circle (half of the diameter)
surface area	the sum of the areas of all of a three-dimensional figure's faces
volume	the space inside a three-dimensional figure

Coordinate Geometry

Coordinate geometry is a form of geometrical operations in relation to a coordinate plane. A **coordinate plane** is a grid of square boxes divided into four quadrants by both a horizontal *x*-axis and a vertical *y*-axis. These two axes intersect at one coordinate point, (0,0), called the **origin**. A **coordinate point**, also called an **ordered pair**, is a specific point on the coordinate plane, with the first number representing the horizontal placement and the second number representing the vertical placement. Coordinate points are given in the form of (*x,y*).

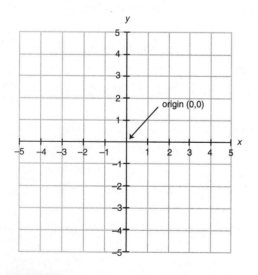

Graphing Ordered Pairs (Points)

- The *x*-coordinate is listed first in the ordered pair and tells you how many units to move to either the left or the right. If the *x*-coordinate is positive, move to the right. If the *x*-coordinate is negative, move to the left.
- The *y*-coordinate is listed second and tells you how many units to move up or down. If the *y*-coordinate is positive, move up. If the *y*-coordinate is negative, move down.

Example
Graph the following points: (2,3), (3,–2), (–2,3), and (–3,–2).

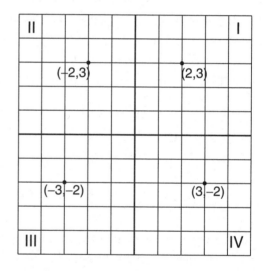

- Notice that the graph is broken up into four quadrants with one point plotted in each one. Here is a chart to indicate which quadrants contain which ordered pairs based on their signs:

Points	Sign of Coordinates	Quadrant
(2,3)	(+,+)	I
(–2,3)	(–,+)	II
(–3,–2)	(–,–)	III
(3,–2)	(+,–)	IV

Lines, Line Segments, and Rays

A **line** is a straight geometric object that goes on forever in both directions. It is infinite in length and is represented by a straight line with an arrow at both ends. Lines can be labeled with one letter (usually in italics) or with two capital letters near the arrows. **Line segments** are portions of lines. They have two endpoints and a definitive length. Line segments are named by their endpoints. **Rays** have an endpoint and continue straight in one direction. Rays are named by their endpoint and one point on the ray.

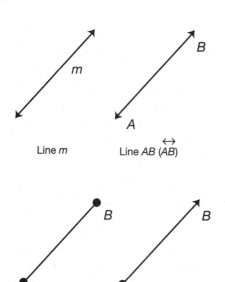

Line *m*   Line AB ($\overset{\leftrightarrow}{AB}$)

Line segment AB ($\overline{AB}$)   Ray AB ($\overrightarrow{AB}$)

Parallel and Perpendicular Lines

Parallel lines (or line segments) are a pair of lines that, if extended, would never intersect or meet. The symbol ‖ is used to denote that two lines are parallel. **Perpendicular lines** (or line segments) are lines that intersect to form right angles, and are denoted with the symbol ⊥.

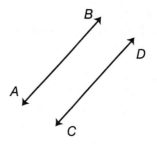

Parallel Lines *AB* and *CD*

$$\overset{\leftrightarrow}{AB} \parallel \overset{\leftrightarrow}{CD}$$

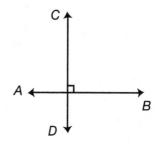

Perpendicular Lines *ABC* and *CD*

$$\overset{\leftrightarrow}{AB} \perp \overset{\leftrightarrow}{CD}$$

Lengths of Horizontal and Vertical Segments

Two points with the same *y*-coordinate lie on the same horizontal line, and two points with the same *x*-coordinate lie on the same vertical line. The distance between a horizontal or vertical segment can be found by taking the absolute value of the difference of the two points.

Example

Find the lengths of line segments $\overline{AB}$ and $\overline{BC}$.

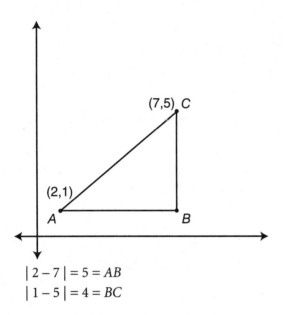

$$| 2-7 | = 5 = AB$$
$$| 1-5 | = 4 = BC$$

Distance of Coordinate Points

The distance between any two points is given by the formula $d = \sqrt{(x_2 - x_1)^2 + (y_2 - y_1)^2}$, where (x_1, y_1) represents the coordinates of one point and (x_2, y_2) is the other. The subscripts are used to differentiate between the two different coordinate pairs.

Example

Find the distance between points $A(-3,5)$ and $B(1,-4)$.

Let (x_1, y_1) represent point A, and let (x_2, y_2) represent point B. This means that $x_1 = -3$, $y_1 = 5$, $x_2 = 1$, and $y_2 = -4$. Substituting these values into the formula gives us:

$$d = \sqrt{(x_2 - x_1)^2 + (y_2 - y_1)^2}$$
$$d = \sqrt{(-3-1)^2 + (5-(-4))^2}$$
$$d = \sqrt{(-4)^2 + (9)^2}$$
$$d = \sqrt{16 + 81}$$
$$d = \sqrt{97}$$

Midpoint

The midpoint of a line segment is a point located at an equal distance from each endpoint. This point is in the exact center of the line segment, and is said to be **equidistant** from the segment's endpoints.

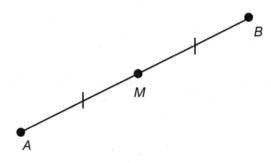

M is the midpoint of $\overline{AB}$

In coordinate geometry, the formula for finding the coordinates of the midpoint of a line segment whose endpoints are (x_1, y_1) and (x_2, y_2) is given by $M = (\frac{x_1 + x_2}{2}, \frac{y_1 + y_2}{2})$.

Example

Determine the midpoint of the line segment $\overline{AB}$ with $A(-3,5)$ and $B(1,-4)$.

Let (x_1, y_1) represent point A, and let (x_2, y_2) represent point B. This means that $x_1 = -3$, $y_1 = 5$, $x_2 = 1$, and $y_2 = -4$. Substituting these values into the formula gives us:

$$M = (\frac{-3+1}{2}, \frac{5+(-4)}{2})$$
$$M = (\frac{-2}{2}, \frac{1}{2})$$
$$M = (-1, \frac{1}{2})$$

Note: There is no such thing as the midpoint of a line, as lines are infinite in length.

Slope

The **slope** of a line (or line segment) is a numerical value given to show how steep the line is. A line or segment can have one of four types of slope:

1. A line with a **positive slope** increases from the bottom left to the upper right on a graph.
2. A line with a **negative slope** decreases from the upper left to the bottom right on a graph.
3. A horizontal line is said to have a **zero slope**.
4. A vertical line is said to have **no slope** (undefined).

Parallel lines have **equal slopes**.

Perpendicular lines have slopes that are negative reciprocals of each other.

Zero slope

Undefined (no) slope

Positive slope

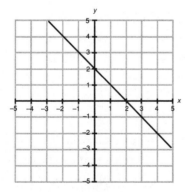

Negative slope

The slope of a line can be found if you know the coordinates of any two points that lie on the line. It does not matter which two points you use. Slope is found by writing the change in the y-coordinates of any two points on the line over the change in the corresponding x-coordinates. (This is also known as the *rise* over the *run*.)

The formula for the slope of a line (or line segment) containing points (x_1, y_1) and (x_2, y_2):
$m = \frac{y_2 - y_1}{x_2 - x_1}$.

Example

Determine the slope of the line containing points $A(-3,5)$ and $B(1,-4)$.

Let (x_1,y_1) represent point A, and let (x_2,y_2) represent point B. This means that $x_1 = -3$, $y_1 = 5$, $x_2 = 1$, and $y_2 = -4$. Substituting these values into the formula gives us:

$$m = \frac{y_2 - y_1}{x_2 - x_1}$$

$$m = \frac{-4 - 5}{1 - (-3)}$$

$$m = \frac{-9}{4}$$

Example

Determine the slope of the line graphed below.

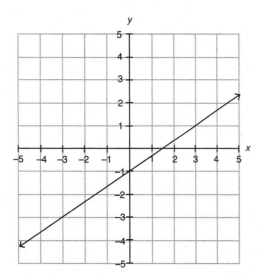

Two points that can be easily determined on the graph are $(3,1)$ and $(0,-1)$. Let $(3,1) = (x_1,y_1)$, and let $(0,-1) = (x_2,y_2)$. This means that $x_1 = 3$, $y_1 = 1$, $x_2 = 0$, and $y_2 = -1$. Substituting these values into the formula gives us:

$$m = \frac{-1 - 1}{0 - 3}$$

$$m = \frac{-2}{-3} = \frac{2}{3}$$

Note: If you know the slope and at least one point on a line, you can find the coordinates of other points on the line. Simply move the required number of units determined by the slope. For example, from $(8,9)$, given the

slope $\frac{7}{5}$, move up seven units and to the right five units. Another point on the line, thus, is $(13,16)$.

Determining the Equation of a Line

The equation of a line is given by $y = mx + b$, where:

- x and y are variables such that every coordinate pair (x,y) is on the line
- m is the slope of the line
- b is the **y-intercept**, or the y-value at which the line intersects (or intercepts) the y-axis

In order to determine the equation of a line from a graph, determine the slope and y-intercept and substitute them in the appropriate places in the general form of the equation.

Example

Determine the equation of the line in the following graph.

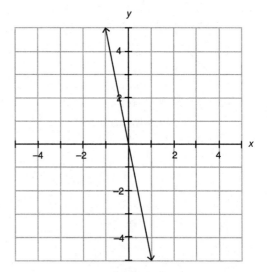

In order to determine the slope of the line, choose two points that can be easily determined on the graph. Two easy points are $(-1,5)$ and $(1,-5)$. Let $(-1,5) = (x_1,y_1)$, and let $(1,-5) = (x_2,y_2)$. This means that $x_1 = -1$, $y_1 = 5$, $x_2 = 1$, and $y_2 = -5$. Substituting these values into the formula gives us:

$$m = \frac{-5-5}{1-(-1)} = \frac{-10}{2} = -5.$$

Looking at the graph, we can see that the line crosses the y-axis at the point $(0,0)$. The y-coordinate of this point is 0, which is the y-intercept.

Substituting these values into the general formula gives us $y = -5x + 0$, or just $y = -5x$.

Example

Determine the equation of the line in the following graph.

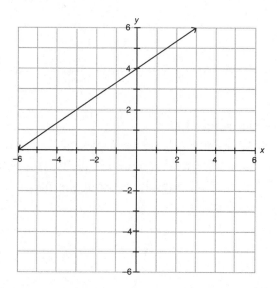

Two points that can be easily determined on the graph are $(-3,2)$ and $(3,6)$. Let $(-3,2) = (x_1,y_1)$, and let $(3,6) = (x_2,y_2)$. Substituting these values into the formula gives us:

$$m = \frac{6-2}{3-(-3)} = \frac{4}{6} = \frac{2}{3}.$$

We can see from the graph that the line crosses the y-axis at the point $(0,4)$. This means the y-intercept is 4.

Substituting these values into the general formula gives us $y = \frac{2}{3}x + 4$.

Angles

Naming Angles

An angle is a figure composed of two rays or line segments joined at their endpoints. The point at which the rays or line segments meet is called the **vertex** of the angle. Angles are usually named by three capital letters, where the first and last letter are points on the end of the rays, and the middle letter is the vertex.

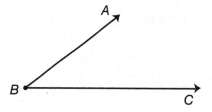

This angle can be named either $\angle ABC$ or $\angle CBA$, but because the vertex of the angle is point B, letter B must be in the middle.

We can sometimes name an angle by its vertex, as long as there is no ambiguity in the diagram. For example, in the preceding angle, we may call the angle $\angle B$ because there is only one angle in the diagram that has B as its vertex.

But in the following diagram, there are a number of angles that have point B as their vertex, so we must name each angle in the diagram with three letters.

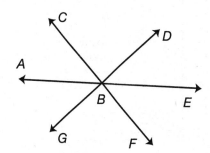

Angles may also be numbered (not measured) with numbers written between the sides of the angles, in the interior of the angle, near the vertex.

Classifying Angles

The unit of measure for angles is the degree.

Angles can be classified into the following categories: acute, right, obtuse, and straight.

- An **acute angle** is an angle that measures between 0 and 90 degrees.

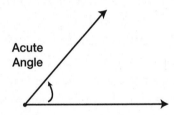

- A **right angle** is an angle that measures exactly 90°. A right angle is symbolized by a square at the vertex.

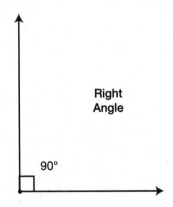

- An **obtuse angle** is an angle that measures more than 90°, but less than 180°.

- A **straight angle** is an angle that measures 180°. Thus, both of its sides form a line.

Special Angle Pairs

- **Adjacent angles** are two angles that share a common vertex and a common side. There is no numerical relationship between the measures of the angles.

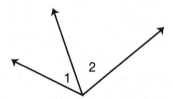

Adjacent angles ∠1 and ∠2

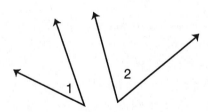

Nonadjacent angles ∠1 and ∠2

- A **linear pair** is a pair of adjacent angles whose measures add to 180°.
- **Supplementary angles** are any two angles whose sum is 180°. A linear pair is a special case of supplementary angles. A linear pair is always supplementary, but supplementary angles do not have to form a linear pair.

Linear pair (also supplementary)

Supplementary angles (but not a linear pair)

- **Complementary angles** are two angles whose sum measures 90 degrees. Complementary angles may or may not be adjacent.

Adjacent complementary angles

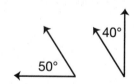

Nonadjacent complementary angles

Example

Two complementary angles have measures $2x°$ and $3x + 20°$. What are the measures of the angles?

Because the angles are complementary, their sum is 90°. We can set up an equation to let us solve for x:

$$2x + 3x + 20 = 90$$
$$5x + 20 = 90$$
$$5x = 70$$
$$x = 14$$

Substituting $x = 14$ into the measures of the two angles, we get $2(14) = 28°$ and $3(14) + 20 = 62°$. We can check our answers by observing that $28 + 62 = 90$, so the angles are indeed complementary.

Example

One angle is 40 more than 6 times the measure of its supplement. What are the measures of the angles?

Let x = one angle.
Let $6x + 40$ = its supplement.
Because the angles are supplementary, their sum is 180°. We can set up an equation to let us solve for x:

$$x + 6x + 40 = 180$$
$$7x + 40 = 180$$
$$7x = 140$$
$$x = 20$$

Substituting $x = 20$ into the measures of the two angles, we see that one of the angles is 20°, and its supplement is $6(20) + 40 = 160°$. We can check our answers by observing that $20 + 160 = 180$, proving that the angles are supplementary.

Note: A good way to remember the difference between supplementary and complementary angles is that the letter c comes before s in the alphabet; likewise, 90 comes before 180 numerically.

Angles of Intersecting Lines

Important mathematical relationships between angles are formed when lines intersect. When two lines intersect, four smaller angles are formed.

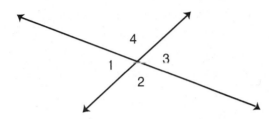

Any two adjacent angles formed when two lines intersect form a linear pair; therefore, they are supplementary. In this diagram, ∠1 and ∠2, ∠2 and ∠3, ∠3 and ∠4, and ∠4 and ∠1 are all examples of linear pairs.

Also, the angles that are opposite each other are called **vertical angles**. Vertical angles are angles that share a vertex and whose sides are two pairs of opposite rays. Vertical angles are congruent. In this diagram, ∠1 and ∠3 are vertical angles, so ∠1 ≅ ∠3; ∠2 and ∠4 are congruent vertical angles as well.

Note: Vertical angles is a name given to a special angle pair. Try not to confuse this with right angles or perpendicular angles, which often have vertical components.

Example

Determine the value of y in the following diagram:

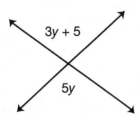

The angles marked $3y + 5$ and $5y$ are vertical angles, so they are congruent and their measures are equal. We can set up and solve the following equation for y:

$$3y + 5 = 5y$$
$$5 = 2y$$
$$2.5 = y$$

Replacing each instance of y with the value 2.5 gives us $3(2.5) + 5 = 12.5$ and $5(2.5) = 12.5$. This proves that the two vertical angles are congruent, with each measuring 12.5°.

Parallel Lines and Transversals

Important mathematical relationships are formed when two parallel lines are intersected by a third, nonparallel line called a **transversal**.

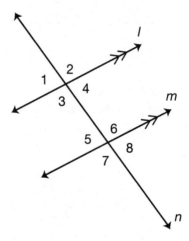

In the preceding diagram, parallel lines l and m are intersected by transversal n. Supplementary angle pairs and vertical angle pairs are formed in this diagram, too.

SUPPLEMENTARY ANGLE PAIRS		VERTICAL ANGLE PAIRS
$\angle 1$ and $\angle 2$	$\angle 2$ and $\angle 4$	$\angle 1$ and $\angle 4$
$\angle 4$ and $\angle 3$	$\angle 3$ and $\angle 1$	$\angle 2$ and $\angle 3$
$\angle 5$ and $\angle 6$	$\angle 6$ and $\angle 8$	$\angle 5$ and $\angle 8$
$\angle 8$ and $\angle 7$	$\angle 7$ and $\angle 5$	$\angle 6$ and $\angle 7$

Other congruent angle pairs are formed:

- Alternate interior angles are angles on the **interior** of the parallel lines and on **alternate** sides of the transversal: $\angle 3$ and $\angle 6$; $\angle 4$ and $\angle 5$.
- Corresponding angles are angles on **corresponding** sides of the parallel lines and on **corresponding** sides of the transversal: $\angle 1$ and $\angle 5$; $\angle 2$ and $\angle 6$; $\angle 3$ and $\angle 7$; $\angle 4$ and $\angle 8$.

Example
In the following diagram, line l is parallel to line m. Determine the value of x.

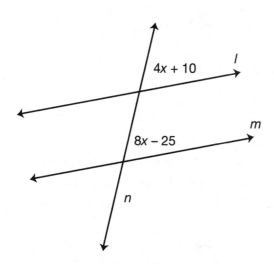

The two labeled angles are **corresponding** angle pairs because they are located on top of the parallel lines and on the same side of the transversal (same relative location). This means that they are congruent, and we can determine the value of x by solving the equation:

$$4x + 10 = 8x - 25$$
$$10 = 4x - 25$$
$$35 = 4x$$
$$8.75 = x$$

We can check our answer by replacing the value 8.75 for x in the expressions $4x + 10$ and $8x - 25$:

$$4(8.75) + 10 = 8(8.75) - 25$$
$$45 = 45$$

Note: If the diagram showed that the two angles were a vertical angle pair or an alternate interior angle pair, the problem would have been solved in the same way.

Area, Circumference, and Volume Formulas

Here are the basic formulas for finding area, circumference, and volume. They are discussed in detail in the sections that follow.

Circle

$C = 2r$
$A = r^2$

Rectangle

$A = lw$

Triangle

$A = \frac{1}{2}bh$

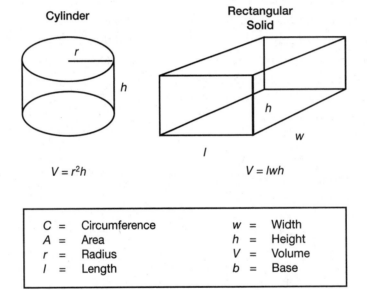

Cylinder

$V = r^2h$

Rectangular Solid

$V = lwh$

C	$=$	Circumference	w	$=$	Width
A	$=$	Area	h	$=$	Height
r	$=$	Radius	V	$=$	Volume
l	$=$	Length	b	$=$	Base

Triangles

The sum of the measures of the three interior angles of a triangle always equals 180°.

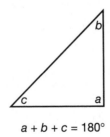

$a + b + c = 180°$

Exterior Angles

An **exterior angle** can be formed by extending a side from any of the three vertices of a triangle. Here are some rules for working with exterior angles:

- An exterior angle and an interior angle that share the same vertex are supplementary. In other words, exterior angles and interior angles form straight lines with each other.
- An exterior angle is equal to the sum of the nonadjacent interior angles.
- The sum of the exterior angles of a triangle equals 360°.

Example

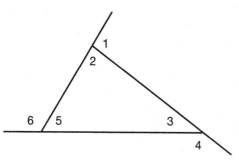

$$\angle 1 + \angle 2 = 180° \quad \angle 1 = \angle 3 + \angle 5$$
$$\angle 3 + \angle 4 = 180° \quad \angle 4 = \angle 2 + \angle 5$$
$$\angle 5 + \angle 6 = 180° \quad \angle 6 = \angle 3 + \angle 2$$
$$\angle 1 + \angle 4 + \angle 6 = 360°$$

Classifying Triangles

It is possible to classify triangles into three categories based on the number of congruent (indicated by the symbol ≅) sides. Sides are congruent when they have equal lengths.

SCALENE TRIANGLE	ISOSCELES TRIANGLE	EQUILATERAL TRIANGLE
no sides congruent	two congruent sides	all sides congruent

It is also possible to classify triangles into three categories based on the measure of the greatest angle:

ACUTE TRIANGLE	RIGHT TRIANGLE	OBTUSE TRIANGLE
greatest angle is acute	greatest angle is 90°	greatest angle is obtuse

Angle-Side Relationships

Knowing the angle-side relationships in isosceles, equilateral, and right triangles is helpful.

- In isosceles triangles, congruent angles are opposite congruent sides.

- In equilateral triangles, all sides are congruent and all angles are congruent. The measure of each angle in an equilateral triangle is always 60°.

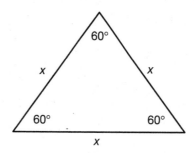

In a right triangle, the side opposite the right angle is called the **hypotenuse**, and the other sides are called **legs**. The box in the angle of the 90-degree angle symbolizes that the triangle is, in fact, a right triangle.

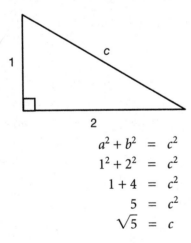

Pythagorean Theorem

The **Pythagorean theorem** is an important tool for working with right triangles. It states: $a^2 + b^2 = c^2$, where a and b represent the legs and c represents the hypotenuse.

This theorem makes it easy to find the length of any side of a right triangle as long as the measures of two sides are known. So, if leg $a = 1$ and leg $b = 2$ in the following triangle, it is possible to find the measure of the hypotenuse, c.

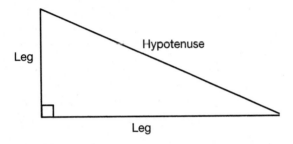

$$a^2 + b^2 = c^2$$
$$1^2 + 2^2 = c^2$$
$$1 + 4 = c^2$$
$$5 = c^2$$
$$\sqrt{5} = c$$

Pythagorean Triples

Sometimes, the measures of all three sides of a right triangle are integers. If three integers are the lengths of the sides of a right triangle, we call them **Pythagorean triples**. Some popular Pythagorean triples are:

3, 4, 5
5, 12, 13
8, 15, 17
9, 40, 41

The smaller two numbers in each triple represent the lengths of the legs, and the largest number represents the length of the hypotenuse.

Multiples of Pythagorean Triples

Whole-number multiples of each Pythagorean triple are also triples. For example, if we multiply each of the lengths of the triple 3, 4, 5 by 2, we get 6, 8, 10. This is also a triple.

Example

If given a right triangle with legs measuring 6 and x, and a hypotenuse measuring 10, what is the value of x?

3, 4, 5 is a Pythagorean triple, and a multiple of that is 6, 8, 10. Therefore, the length of the missing leg is 8.

Comparing Triangles

Triangles are said to be congruent (indicated by the symbol $\cong$) when they have exactly the same size and shape. Two triangles are congruent if their corresponding parts (their angles and sides) are congruent. Sometimes, it is easy to tell whether two triangles are congruent just by looking at them. However, in geometry, we must be able to prove that the triangles are congruent.

There are a number of ways to prove that two triangles are congruent:

Side-Side-Side (SSS): If the three sides of one triangle are congruent to the three corresponding sides of another triangle, the triangles are congruent.

Side-Angle-Side (SAS): If two sides and the included angle of one triangle are congruent to the corresponding two sides and included angle of another triangle, the triangles are congruent.

Angle-Side-Angle (ASA): If two angles and the included side of one triangle are congruent to the corresponding two angles and included side of another triangle, the triangles are congruent.

Used less often but also valid:

Angle-Angle-Side (AAS): If two angles and the non-included side of one triangle are congruent to the corresponding two angles and non-included side of another triangle, the triangles are congruent.

Hypotenuse-Leg (Hy-Leg): If the hypotenuse and a leg of one right triangle arc congruent to the hypotenuse and leg of another right triangle, the triangles are congruent.

Example
Determine whether these two triangles are congruent.

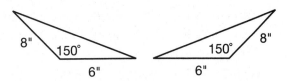

Although the triangles are not oriented the same, there are two congruent corresponding sides, and the angle between them (150°) is congruent. Therefore, the triangles are congruent by the SAS postulate.

Example
Determine whether these two triangles are congruent.

Although the triangles have two congruent corresponding sides and a corresponding congruent angle, the 150° angle is not included between them. This would be SSA, but SSA is not a way to prove that two triangles are congruent.

Area of a Triangle

Area is the amount of space inside a two-dimensional object. Area is measured in square units, often written as *unit²*. So, if the lengths of a triangle's sides are measured in feet, the area of the triangle is measured in *feet²*.

A triangle has three sides, each of which can be considered a **base** of the triangle. A perpendicular line segment drawn from a vertex to the opposite

base of the triangle is called the **altitude**, or the **height**. It measures how tall the triangle stands.

Acute Triangle   Right Triangle

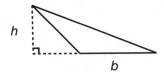

Obtuse Triangle

It is important to note that the height of a triangle is not necessarily one of the sides of the triangle. The correct height for the triangle below is 8, not 10. The height will always be associated with a line segment (called an **altitude**) that comes from one vertex (angle) to the opposite side and forms a right angle (signified by the box) with that side. In other words, the height must always be perpendicular to (form a right angle with) the base. Note that in an obtuse triangle, the height can be outside the triangle, and in a right triangle, the height is usually one of the sides.

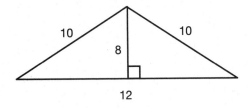

The formula for the area of a triangle is given by $A = \frac{1}{2}bh$, where b is the base of the triangle and h is the height.

Example

Determine the area of the following triangle.

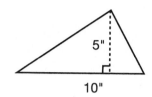

$A = \frac{1}{2}bh$

$A = \frac{1}{2}(5)(10)$

$A = 25 \text{ in.}^2$

Volume Formulas

A **prism** is a three-dimensional object that has matching polygons as its top and bottom. The matching top and bottom are called the **bases** of the prism. The prism is named for the shape of the prism's base, so a **triangular prism** has congruent triangles as its bases.

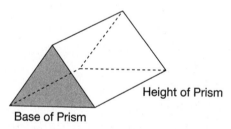

Note: This can be confusing. The **base** of the prism is the shape of the polygon that forms it; the **base** of a triangle is one of its sides.

Volume is the amount of space inside a three-dimensional object. Volume is measured in cubic units, often written as $unit^3$. So, if the edge of a triangular prism is measured in feet, the volume of the prism is measured in $feet^3$.

The volume of ANY prism is given by the formula $V = A_b h$, where A_b is the area of the prism's base and h is the height of the prism.

Example

Determine the volume of the following triangular prism:

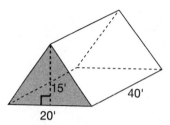

The area of the triangular base can be found by using the formula $A = \frac{1}{2}bh$, so the area of the base is $A = \frac{1}{2}(15)(20) = 150$. The volume of the prism can be found by using the formula $V = A_b h$, so the volume is $V = (150)(40) = 6{,}000$ cubic feet.

A **pyramid** is a three-dimensional object that has a polygon as one base, and instead of a matching polygon as the other base, there is a point. Each of the sides of a pyramid is a triangle. Pyramids are also named for the shape of their (non-point) base.

The volume of a pyramid is determined by the formula $V = \frac{1}{3}A_b h$.

Example

Determine the volume of a pyramid whose base has an area of 20 square feet and that stands 50 feet tall.

Because the area of the base is given to us, we only need to replace the appropriate values into the formula.

$V = \frac{1}{3}A_b h$

$V = \frac{1}{3}(20)(50)$

$V = 33\frac{1}{3}$

The pyramid has a volume of $33\frac{1}{3}$ cubic feet.

Polygons

A polygon is a closed figure with three or more sides—for example, triangles, rectangles, and pentagons.

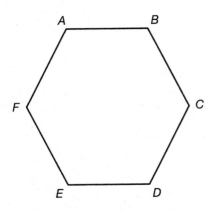

SHAPE	NUMBER OF SIDES
circle	0
triangle	3
quadrilateral (square/rectangle)	4
pentagon	5
hexagon	6
heptagon	7
octagon	8
nonagon	9
decagon	10

Terms Related to Polygons

- **Vertices** are the corner points, also called **endpoints**, of a polygon. The vertices in the polygon above are *A, B, C, D, E,* and *F,* and they are always labeled with capital letters.
- A **regular polygon** has congruent sides and congruent angles.
- An **equiangular polygon** has congruent angles.

Interior Angles

To find the sum of the interior angles of any polygon, use this formula:

$S = (x - 2)180°$, where x = the number of sides of the polygon.

Example

Find the sum of the interior angles in this polygon:

The polygon is a pentagon and has five sides, so substitute 5 for x in the formula:

$$S = (5 - 2) \times 180°$$
$$S = 3 \times 180°$$
$$S = 540°$$

Exterior Angles

Similar to the exterior angles of a triangle, the sum of the exterior angles of any polygon equals 360 degrees.

Similar Polygons

If two polygons are similar, their corresponding angles are congruent, and the ratios of the corresponding sides are in proportion.

Example

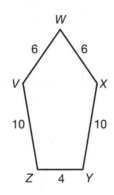

$$\angle A = \angle V = 140°$$
$$\angle B = \angle W = 60°$$
$$\angle C = \angle X = 140°$$
$$\angle D = \angle Y = 100°$$
$$\angle E = \angle Z = 100°$$

$$\frac{AB}{VW} = \frac{BC}{WX} = \frac{CD}{XY} = \frac{DE}{YZ} = \frac{EA}{ZV}$$

$$\frac{3}{6} = \frac{3}{6} = \frac{5}{10} = \frac{5}{10} = \frac{2}{4}$$

These two polygons are similar because their angles are congruent and the ratios of their corresponding sides are in proportion.

Quadrilaterals

A **quadrilateral** is a four-sided polygon. Because a quadrilateral can be divided by a diagonal into two triangles, the sum of its interior angles will equal 180 + 180 = 360°.

$$\angle 1 + \angle 2 + \angle 3 + \angle 4 + \angle 5 + \angle 6 = 360°$$

Parallelograms

A parallelogram is a quadrilateral with two pairs of parallel sides.

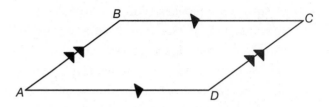

In the figure, $\overline{AB} \parallel \overline{CD}$ and $\overline{BC} \parallel \overline{AD}$. Parallel lines are symbolized with matching numbers of triangles or arrows.

A parallelogram has:

- opposite sides that are congruent ($\overline{AB} = \overline{CD}$ and $\overline{BC} = \overline{AD}$)
- opposite angles that are congruent ($\angle A = \angle C$ and $\angle B = \angle D$)
- consecutive angles that are supplementary ($\angle A + \angle B = 180°$, $\angle B + \angle C = 180°$, $\angle C + \angle D = 180°$, $\angle D + \angle A = 180°$)
- diagonals (line segments joining opposite vertices) that bisect each other (divide each other in half)

Special Types of Parallelograms

- A **rectangle** is a parallelogram that has four right angles.

- A **rhombus** is a parallelogram that has four equal sides.

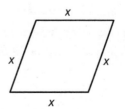

- A **square** is a parallelogram in which all angles are equal to 90 degrees and all sides are congruent. A square is a special case of a rectangle where all the sides are congruent. A square is also a special type of rhombus where all the angles are congruent.

Diagonals of Parallelograms

Rectangular *ABCD*
$\overline{AC} \cong \overline{BD}$

Rhombus *ABCD*   Square ABCD
$\overline{AC} \perp \overline{BD}$ $\overline{AB} \perp \overline{CD}, \overline{AC} \cong \overline{BD}$

In this diagram, parallelogram *ABCD* has diagonals $\overline{AC}$ and $\overline{BD}$ that intersect at point *E*. The diagonals of a parallelogram bisect each other, which means that $\overline{AE} \cong \overline{EC}$ and $\overline{BE} \cong \overline{ED}$.

In addition, the following properties hold true:

- The diagonals of a rhombus are perpendicular.
- The diagonals of a rectangle are congruent.
- The diagonals of a square are both perpendicular and congruent.

Example

In parallelogram *ABCD*, the diagonal $\overline{AC} = 5x + 10$, and the diagonal $\overline{BD} = 9x$. Determine the value of *x*.

Because the diagonals of a parallelogram are congruent, the lengths are equal. We can then set up and solve the equation $5x + 10 = 9x$ to determine the value of *x*.

$5x + 10 = 9x$ Subtract 5*x* from both sides of the equation.

$10 = 4x$ Divide 4 from both sides of the equation.

$2.5 = x$

Area and Volume Formulas

The area of any parallelogram can be found with the formula $A = bh$, where *b* is the base of the parallelogram and *h* is the height. The base and height of a parallelogram is defined the same way as in a triangle.

Note: Sometimes *b* is called the length (*l*) and *h* is called the width (*w*) instead. If this is the case, the area formula is $A = lw$.

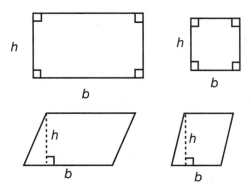

A **rectangular prism** (or **rectangular solid**) is a prism that has rectangles as bases. Recall that the formula for any prism is $V = A_b h$. Because the area of the rectangular base is $A = lw$, we can replace *lw* for A_b in the formula, giving us the more common and easier to remember formula, $V = lwh$. If a prism has a different quadrilateral-shaped base, use the general prisms formula for volume.

Note: A cube is a special rectangular prism with six congruent squares as sides. This means that you can use the $V = lwh$ formula for it, too.

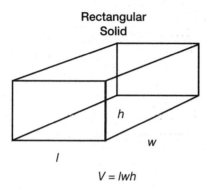

Rectangular
Solid

$V = lwh$

Circles

Terminology

A circle is formally defined as the set of points a fixed distance from a center point. The more sides a polygon has, the more it looks like a circle. If you consider a polygon with 5,000 small sides, it will look like a circle, but a circle is not a polygon. A circle contains 360 degrees around a center point.

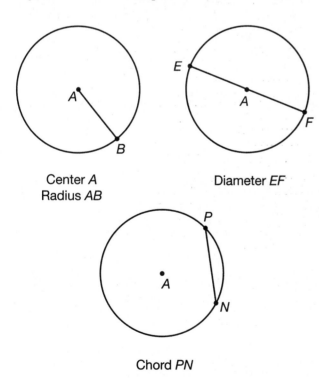

Center *A*
Radius *AB*

Diameter *EF*

Chord *PN*

- The midpoint of a circle is called the **center**.
- The distance around a circle (called **perimeter** in polygons) is called the **circumference**.
- A line segment that goes through a circle, with its endpoints on the circle, is called a **chord**.
- A chord that goes directly through the center of a circle (the longest line segment that can be drawn) in a circle is called the **diameter**.
- The line from the center of a circle to a point on the circle (half of the diameter) is called the **radius**.
- A **sector** of a circle is a fraction of the circle's area.
- An **arc** of a circle is a fraction of the circle's circumference.

Circumference, Area, and Volume Formulas

The area of a circle is $A = \pi r^2$, where r is the radius of the circle. The circumference (perimeter of a circle) is $C = 2\pi r$, or πd, where r is the radius of the circle and d is the diameter.

Example
Determine the area and circumference of this circle:

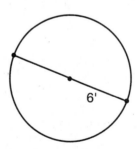

We are given the diameter of the circle, so we can use the formula $C = \pi d$ to find the circumference.

$$C = \pi d$$
$$C = \pi(6)$$
$$C = 6\pi = 18.85 \text{ feet}$$

The area formula uses the radius, so we need to divide the length of the diameter by 2 to get the length of the radius: $6 \div 2 = 3$. Then we can just use the formula.

$$A = \pi(3)^2$$
$$A = 9\pi = 28.27 \text{ square feet.}$$

Note: *Circumference* is a measure of length, so the answer is measured in *units*, whereas the *area* is measured in *square units*.

Area of Sectors and Lengths of Arcs

The area of a sector can be determined by figuring out what the percentage of the total area the sector is, and then multiplying that percentage by the area of the circle.

The length of an arc can be determined by figuring out what the percentage of the total circumference of the arc is, and then multiplying that percentage by the circumference of the circle.

Example

Determine the area of the shaded sector and the length of the arc AB.

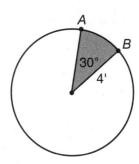

Because the angle in the sector is 30°, and we know that a circle contains a total of 360°, we can determine what fraction of the circle's area it is: $\frac{30°}{360°} = \frac{1}{12}$ of the circle.

The area of the entire circle is $A = \pi r^2$, so $A = \pi(4)^2 = 16\pi$.

So, the area of the sector is $\frac{1}{12} \times 16\pi = \frac{16\pi}{12} = \frac{4}{3}\pi \approx 4.19$ square inches.

We can also determine the length of the arc AB because it is $\frac{30°}{360°} = \frac{1}{12}$ of the circle's circumference.

The circumference of the entire circle is $C = 2\pi r$, so $C = 2\pi(4) = 8\pi$.

This means that the length of the arc is $\frac{1}{12} \times 8\pi = \frac{8\pi}{12} = \frac{2}{3\pi} \approx 2.09$ inches.

A prism that has circles as bases is called a **cylinder**. Recall that the formula for the volume of any prism is $V = A_b h$. Because the area of the circular base is $A = \pi r^2$, we can replace πr^2 for A_b in the formula, giving us $V = \pi r^2 h$, where r is the radius of the circular base and h is the height of the cylinder.

Cylinder

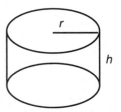

$$V = \pi r^2 h$$

A sphere is a three-dimensional object that has no sides. A basketball is a good example of a sphere. The volume of a sphere is given by the formula $V = \frac{4}{3}\pi r^3$.

Example

Determine the volume of a sphere whose radius is 1.5'.

Replace 1.5' for r in the formula $V = \frac{4}{3}\pi r^3$.

$$V = \frac{4}{3}\pi r^3$$
$$V = \frac{4}{3}\pi(1.5)^3$$
$$V = \frac{4}{3}(3.375)\pi$$
$$V = 4.5\pi \approx 14.14$$

The answer is approximately 14.14 cubic feet.

Example

An aluminum can is 6" tall and has a base with a radius of 2". Determine the volume the can holds.

Aluminum cans are cylindrical in shape, so replace 2" for r and 6" for h in the formula $V = \pi r^2 h$.

$$V = \pi r^2 h$$
$$V = \pi(2)^2(6)$$
$$V = 24\pi \approx 75.40 \text{ cubic feet}$$

Data Analysis

Data analysis simply means reading graphs, tables, and other graphical representations. You should be able to do the following:

- read and understand scatter plots, graphs, tables, diagrams, charts, figures, and so on
- interpret scatter plots, graphs, tables, diagrams, charts, figures, and so on
- compare and interpret information presented in scatter plots, graphs, tables, diagrams, charts, figures, and so on
- draw conclusions about the information provided
- make predictions about the data

It is important to read tables, charts, and graphs very carefully. Read all the information presented, paying special attention to headings and units of measure. This section covers tables and graphs. The most common types of graphs are scatter plots, bar graphs, and pie graphs. What follows is an explanation of each, with examples for practice.

Tables

All tables are composed of **rows** (horizontal) and **columns** (vertical). Entries in a single row of a table

usually have something in common, and so do entries in a single column. Look at the following table that shows how many cars, both new and used, were sold during particular months.

MONTH	NEW CARS	USED CARS
June	125	65
July	155	80
August	190	100
September	220	115
October	265	140

Tables are very concise ways to convey important information without wasting time and space. Just imagine how many lines of text would be needed to convey the same information. With the table, however, it is easy to refer to a given month and quickly know how many total cars were sold. It would also be easy to compare month to month. In fact, practice by comparing the total sales of July with that of October.

In order to do this, first find out how many cars were sold in each month. There were 235 cars sold in July (155 + 80 = 235) and 405 cars sold in October (265 + 140 = 405). With a little bit of quick arithmetic it can quickly be determined that 170 more cars were sold during October than during July (405 − 235 = 170).

Scatter Plots

Whenever a variable depends continuously on another variable, this dependence can be visually represented in a **scatter plot**. A scatter plot consists of the horizontal (x) axis, the vertical (y) axis, and collected data points for variable y, measured at variable x. The variable points are often connected with a line or a curve. A graph often contains a legend, especially if there is more than one data set or more than one variable. A legend is a key for interpreting the graph. Much like a legend on a map lists the symbols used to label an interstate highway, a railroad line, or a city, a legend for a graph lists the symbols used to label a particular data set. Look at the following sample graph. The essential elements of the graph—the *x*-axis and *y*-axis—are labeled. The legend to the right of the graph shows that diamonds are used to represent the variable points in data set 1, while squares are used to represent the variable points in data set 2. If only one data set exists, the use of a legend is not essential.

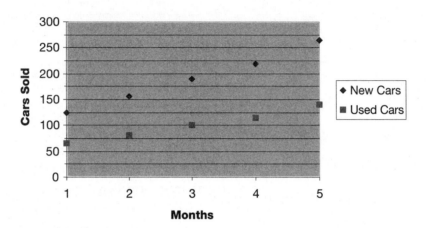

(Note: This data was used in the preceding example for tables.)

The *x*-axis represents the months after new management and promotions were introduced at an automobile dealership. The *y*-axis represents the number of cars sold in the particular month after the changes were made. The diamonds reflect the new cars sold, and the squares show the number of used cars sold. What conclusions can be drawn about the sales? Note that the new and used car sales are both increasing each month at a pretty steady rate. The graph also shows that new cars increase at a higher rate and that there are many more new cars sold per month.

Try to look for scatter plots with different trends:

- increase
- decrease

- rapid increase, followed by leveling off
- slow increase, followed by rapid increase
- rise to a maximum, followed by a decrease
- rapid decrease, followed by leveling off
- slow decrease, followed by rapid decrease
- decrease to a minimum, followed by a rise
- predictable fluctuation (periodic change)
- random fluctuation (irregular change)

Bar Graphs

Whereas scatter plots are used to show change, **bar graphs** are often used to indicate an amount or level of occurrence of a phenomenon for different categories. Consider the following bar graph. It illustrates the number of employees who were absent due to illness during a particular week in two different age groups.

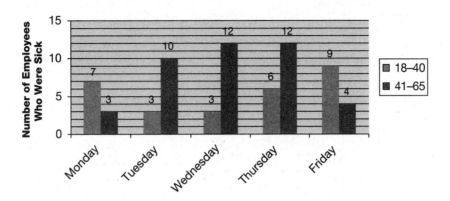

In this bar graph, the categories are the days of the week, and the frequency represents the number of employees who were sick. It can be immediately seen that younger employees were sick before and after the weekend. There is also an inconsistent trend for the younger employees, with data ranging all over the place. During midweek, the older crowd tends to stay home more often.

How many people on average were sick in the 41–65 age group? To find the average, you first must find out how many illnesses occurred each week in the particular age group. There were 41 illnesses in total for a five-day period (3 + 10 + 12 + 12 + 4 = 41). To calculate the average, just divide the total illnesses by the number of days for a total of 8.2 illnesses ($\frac{41}{5}$ = 8.2) or, more realistically, 8 absences per day.

Pictographs

Pictographs are very similar to bar graphs, but instead of bars indicating frequency, small icons are assigned a key value indicating frequency.

Number of Students at the Pep Rally

Freshmen	👤 👤 👤 👤 👤 👤 👤 👤 👤 👤 👤 👤
Sophomores	👤 👤 👤 👤 👤 👤
Juniors	👤 👤 👤 👤 👤
Seniors	👤 👤 👤

Key: 👤 indicates 10 people

In this pictograph, the key indicates that every icon represents 10 people, so it is easy to determine that there were 12 × 10 = 120 freshmen, 5.5 × 10 = 55 sophomores, 5 × 10 = 50 juniors, and 3 × 10 = 30 seniors.

Pie Charts and Circle Graphs

Pie charts and **circle graphs** are often used to show what percent of a total is taken up by different components of that whole. This type of graph is representative of a whole and is usually divided into percentages. Each section of the chart represents a portion of the whole, and all these sections added together will equal 100% of the whole. The following chart shows the three styles of model homes in a new development and what percentage of each there is.

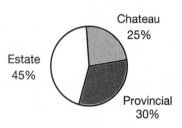

Models of Homes

The chart shows the different models of homes. The categories add up to 100% (25 + 30 + 45 = 100). To find the percentage of Estate homes, you can look at the pie chart and see that 45% of the homes are done in the Estate model.

Broken Line Graphs

Broken line graphs illustrate a measurable change over time. If a line is slanted up, it represents an increase, whereas a line sloping down represents a decrease. A flat line indicates no change.

In the following broken line graph, the number of delinquent payments is charted for the first quarter of the year. Each week the number of delinquent customers is summed and recorded.

There is an increase in delinquency for the first two weeks, and then the level is maintained for an additional two weeks. There is a steep decrease after week 5 (initially) until the ninth week, where it levels off again, but this time at 0. The 11th week shows a radical increase followed by a little jump up at week 12, and then a decrease to week 13. It is also interesting to see that the first and last weeks have identical values.

Diagrams

This diagram shows a sequence of events to construct two new objects out of one pipe and a few other parts. First, the instructions show that the pipe must be cut into two pieces with a saw. The next two levels show how the assembly will take place, first by adding the end pieces and then bolting in those pieces.

Diagrams can be used to show a sequence of events, a process, an idea, or the relationship between different events or people.

When you see a diagram, first ask what the purpose of it is. What is it trying to illustrate? Then look at the different labeled parts of the diagram. What is the function of each part? How are they interrelated? Take a look at the following diagram:

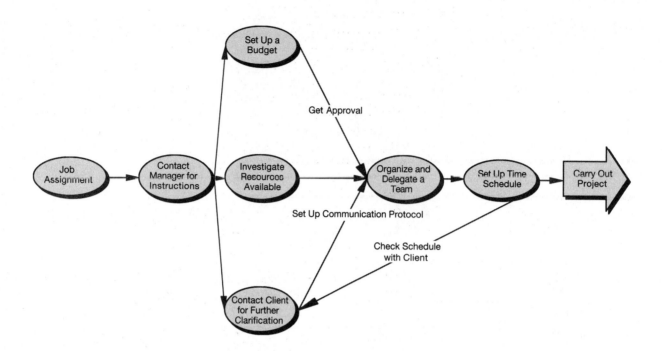

This diagram is a typical chart of how to start a new project. It starts (on the left) by learning about the assignment from the manager and then investigating several aspects of heading a project, including the client, resources, and budget. Once an overall picture is achieved, you will then know how many peo-ple will be required for the project in order to create an accurate schedule for the project. There are also reminders and further protocols within the diagram in the links.

Now, take the skills you have learned or honed in this review and apply them to Practice Exam I.

PRAXIS I WRITING TEST REVIEW

CHAPTER SUMMARY
Good writing skills are essential to success as a teacher. To be effective both in the classroom and with your colleagues, it's important to be able to communicate ideas clearly and accurately in written English. This chapter reviews the elements of good writing: basic grammar, sentence structure, verb and pronoun agreement, and idiomatic expressions.

The PPST Writing test is divided into two parts. Section 1 presents multiple-choice questions that measure your ability to identify errors in grammar or sentence structure, and to recognize the correct use of standard written English. Section 2 asks you to write a short essay about an assigned, general topic. The writing topics are designed so that you do not need any specialized knowledge to respond to the prompt. However, you will need to demonstrate that you can organize and support your thoughts effectively in writing. You will be given 30 minutes to create a clear, well-developed essay. The essay portion of the writing test is not designed to showcase creative writing; rather, it focuses on your ability to follow the rules of English grammar and avoid common errors.

The computerized writing test varies slightly from the paper-and-pencil test—these differences are outlined in the following chart.

	COMPUTER-BASED TEST	PAPER-BASED TEST
Total time	75 minutes	60 minutes
Section 1: Multiple-choice questions	38 minutes 44 multiple-choice questions	30 minutes 38 multiple-choice questions
Section 2: Essay	30 minutes 1 assigned topic	30 minutes 1 assigned topic

Types of Multiple-Choice Questions

In the first part of the writing test, you will not do any writing at all. Rather, you will answer multiple-choice questions that measure your knowledge of the basics of grammar, sentence construction, and appropriate word choice, and also your ability to locate errors. There are two basic types of multiple-choice questions in the writing test. To give yourself an advantage on test day, familiarize yourself with each type now.

Type 1—Usage Questions

In these questions, you need to be able to identify errors and oddities in sentences. You will be presented with a sentence that has four underlined words, phrases, or punctuation marks. You will choose the underlined portion that is *incorrect*. Some sentences are correct. In that case, you would select "No error," choice e. None of the sentences has more than one error. Here are some examples:

1. Acid rain <u>looks</u>, feels, even tastes <u>like</u> clean
        a   **b**

   rainwater, but it actually <u>contain</u> high levels
                           c

   <u>of pollutants.</u> <u>No error</u>
      d   **e**

2. <u>In science fiction</u>, writers <u>have</u> the opportunity
       a   **b**

   <u>to explore</u> and imagine what the world <u>will be</u>
      c   **d**

   like in the future. <u>No error</u>
                      e

Answers

1. **c.** The problem in this sentence is noun and verb agreement. The pronoun *it* (referring to the subject *acid rain*) is singular, so the verb should be singular as well—*contains*.

2. **e.** Because this sentence contains no grammatical, idiomatic, logical, or structural errors, the correct answer is choice **e**.

On the computer-based test, the underlined words or phrases do not correspond with the answer choices **a–e**. Instead, you simply highlight your answer choice by clicking on it. To alter your highlight, click on another underlined word or phrase in the sentence. If there are no problems in the sentence, click on "No error." Here is an example of what you will see on your computer screen:

Less teachers attended the conference this year, even though it offered more workshops and seminars. No error

Answer

Less teachers attended the conference this year, even though it offered more workshops and seminars. No error

The first underlined choice contains a grammatical error. The modifier *less* describes singular nouns that represent a quantity or degree. The modifier *fewer* would be correct in this context—it describes plural nouns, or things that can be counted.

Type 2—Sentence Correction

In these questions, you will demonstrate your ability to recognize and correct awkward sentence constructions and other grammatical elements. You will be shown a sentence with one part of it underlined. You will be asked to select one of five possible ways to rephrase the underlined part. Choice **a** always repeats the original phrasing, whereas choices **b–e** suggest changes to the underlined portion. Choose the phrasing that creates the most effective sentence with wording that is clear, exact, and without awkwardness or redundancy. If you think the original phrasing is better than the suggested alternatives, select the first answer choice. Here are some examples of this question type.

1. Lee Iacocca, the son of Italian immigrants, worked arduously to reach the top rungs of the Ford Motor Company corporate ladder.
   a. worked arduously
   b. worked arduous
   c. did worked arduously
   d. has work arduously
   e. had worked arduous

2. As an employee, one is eligible for the benefits we worked to attain, including health insurance, life insurance, and a retirement plan.
   a. As an employee, one is eligible
   b. We the employees are either eligible
   c. The employee is eligible
   d. Either the employee is eligible
   e. As employees, we are eligible

Answers

1. **a.** The sentence does not have any problems in its structure or meaning. Both the verb tense and the use of the adverb *arduously* are correct. Choices **b** and **e** incorrectly use the adjective *arduous*. Options **c** and **d** use the correct adverb, but have incorrect verb forms.

2. **e.** The problem with the original sentence is pronoun agreement. The underlined part of the sentence uses the singular pronoun *one*, which agrees with its singular antecedent *employee*. However, the plural pronoun *we* is used later in the sentence. To make a sentence with pronoun agreement, you must look for a choice that contains the pronoun *we* and the plural of *employee*.

Now that you are familiar with the format of the writing test and the two types of multiple-choice questions, you are ready to review some of the rules and patterns of English grammar, sentence structure, idioms, and word usage. This review will aid you in both parts of the writing test: the multiple-choice section and the essay section. The last part of this chapter covers the essay portion of the test in more detail: the kinds of writing prompts that you can expect, test-taking strategies, and essential information for organizing and creating a clear, well-supported essay.

Grammatical Relationships

For the multiple-choice section of the PPST Writing test, you must be able to identify problems in the relationships between the parts of a sentence. You need to be on the lookout for the incorrect use of adjectives and adverbs, subject-verb agreement, pronoun agreement, and verb tenses.

Adjectives and Adverbs

Adjectives and adverbs add spice to writing—they are words that describe, or modify, other words. However, adjectives and adverbs describe different parts of speech. Whereas adjectives modify nouns or pronouns, adverbs modify verbs, adjectives, or other adverbs.

> We enjoyed the *delicious* <u>meal</u>.
> The chef <u>prepared</u> it *perfectly*.

The first sentence uses the adjective *delicious* to modify the noun *meal*. In the second sentence, the adverb *perfectly* describes the verb *prepared*. Adverbs are easy to spot—most end in *-ly*. However, some of the trickiest adverbs do not end in the typical *-ly* form. The following are problem modifiers to look out for in the PPST Writing test:

Good/Well—Writers often confuse the adverb *well* with its adjective counterpart, *good*.
Ellie felt *good* about her test results.
(*Good* describes the proper noun, *Ellie*.)
Ruben performed *well* on the test.
(*Well* modifies the verb, *performed*.)

Bad/Badly—Similarly, writers confuse the function of these two modifiers. Remember to use the adverb *badly* to describe an action.
Henry felt *bad* after staying up all night before the exam. (*Bad* describes Henry.)
Juliet did *badly* in her first classroom presentation. (*Badly* describes the verb form, *did*.)
Fewer/Less—These two adjectives are a common pitfall for writers. To distinguish between them, look carefully at the noun modified in the sentence. *Fewer* describes *plural* nouns, or things that can be counted. *Less* describes *singular* nouns that represent a quantity or a degree.
The high school enrolls *fewer* students than it did a decade ago.
Emilia had *less* time for studying than Maggie.

Adjectives that follow verbs can also cause confusion. Although an adjective may come after a verb in a sentence, it may describe a noun or pronoun that comes before the verb. Here is an example:

> The circumstances surrounding Shakespeare's authorship seemed strange. (The adjective, *strange*, describes the subject, *circumstances*.)

Take special note of modifiers in sentences that use verbs that deal with the senses: *touch*, *taste*, *look*, *smell*, and *sound*. Here are some examples of sentences that use the same verb, but different modifiers:

Sarah felt sick after her performance review. (The adjective, *sick*, modifies *Sarah*.)
The archaeologist felt carefully through the loose dirt. (The adverb, *carefully*, modifies *felt*.)

The judge looked skeptical after the witness testified. (The adjective, *skeptical*, modifies *judge*.)
The judge looked skeptically at the flamboyant lawyer. (The adverb, *skeptically*, modifies *looked*.)

Subject-Verb Agreement

They goes together, or *they go together*? You probably don't even have to think about which subject goes with which verb in this clause—your ear easily discerns that the second version is correct. Subject-verb agreement is when the subject of a clause matches the verb *in number*. Singular nouns take singular verbs; plural nouns take plural verbs. However, some instances of subject-verb agreement are tricky. Look out for the following three problem areas on the writing test:

Phrases Following the Subject—Pay close attention to the subject of the sentence. Do not be misled by phrases that may follow the subject. These phrases may confuse you into selecting a verb that does not agree with the subject. Try this practice question:

1. Betty Friedan's 1963 book, <u>an exposé</u> of
                       a

   domesticity <u>that challenged</u> long-held
                  b

   American attitudes, <u>remain</u> an
                     c

   <u>important contribution</u> to feminism. <u>No error</u>
        d   **e**

The correct answer is choice **c**. The singular subject, *book*, needs a singular verb, *remains*. Don't be confused by the plural noun *attitudes*, which is part of a phrase that follows the subject.

Subjects Following the Verb—Be sure to locate the subject of the sentence. Test makers use subjects that come after the verb to confuse you. Sentence constructions that begin with *there is* or *there are* signal that the subject comes after the verb.

2. Although the Australian government protects the Great Barrier Reef, <u>there is environmental factors that continue to threaten</u> the world's largest coral reef ecosystem.
   a. there is environmental factors that continue to threaten
   b. there are fewer environmental factors that continue to threaten
   c. there are environmental factors that continue to threaten
   d. there are environmental factors that continued to threaten
   e. there is environmental factors that would continue to threaten

The correct answer is choice **c**. The plural subject *factors* requires a plural form of the verb, *are*. The verb *continue* is in the correct tense in the original sentence, so choices **d** and **e** are incorrect. The addition of the adjective *fewer* in choice **b** does not make sense in the sentence.

Special Singular Nouns—Some words that end in *s*, like *measles*, *news*, *checkers*, *economics*, *sports*, and *politics*, are often singular despite their plural form because we think of them as one thing. A watch for collective nouns—nouns that refer to a number of people or things that form a single unit. These words, such as *audience, stuff, crowd, government, group,* and *orchestra,* need a singular verb.

3. That <u>rowdy</u> group of drama students <u>were</u>
          a   b

labeled "the anarchists" <u>because</u> they took
                               c

over the university president's office

<u>in a protest</u> against the dress code. <u>No error</u>
      d   e

The correct answer choice is **b.** The collective noun *group* is the singular subject of the sentence. Notice how the position of the prepositional phrase *of drama students* following the subject is misleading.

Pronoun Agreement

Pronouns are words that take the place of a noun or another pronoun, called an **antecedent.** Just as subjects and verbs must agree in number, pronouns and their antecedents must match in number. If an antecedent is singular, the pronoun must be singular. If an antecedent is plural, the pronoun must be plural.

Pronouns also need to match their antecedent in case. **Case** refers to a word's grammatical relationship to other words in a sentence. A pronoun that takes the place of the subject of a sentence should be in the nominative case (*I, we, he, she, they*), whereas a pronoun that takes the place of the object in a sentence should be in the objective case (*me, us, him, her, them*). Here are some examples.

Matteo is funny, but *he* can also be very serious. (subject)
Bernadette hired Will, and she also fired *him.* (object)

In most cases, you will automatically recognize errors in pronoun agreement. The phrase *Me worked on the project with him* is clearly incorrect. However, some instances of pronoun agreement can be tricky. Review these common pronoun problems:

- **Indefinite pronouns** like *each, everyone, anybody, no one, one,* and *either* are singular.
  <u>Each</u> of the boys presented *his* science project.
- **Two or more nouns joined by *and*** use a plural pronoun.
  <u>Andy Warhol and Roy Lichtenstein</u> engaged popular culture in *their* art.
- **Two or more singular nouns joined by *or*** use a singular pronoun.
  <u>Francis or Andrew</u> will lend you *his* book.
- **He or she?** In speech, people often use the pronoun *they* to refer to a single person of unknown gender. However, this is incorrect—a singular antecedent requires a singular pronoun.
  <u>A person</u> has the right to do whatever *he or she* wants.

The following lists some pronouns that are commonly confused with verb contractions or other words. Watch out for these errors in the multiple-choice questions.

CONFUSING WORD	QUICK DEFINITION
its it's	belonging to it it is
your you're	belonging to you you are
their they're there	belonging to them they are describes where an action takes place
whose who's	belonging to whom who is *or* who has
who that which	refers to people refers to things introduces clauses that are not essential to the information in the sentence and do not refer to people

Try this practice sentence-correction question:

4. A child who is eager to please will often follow <u>everything that their parents say.</u>
  a. everything that their parents say.
  b. everything which their parents say.
  c. everything that his or her parents say.
  d. most everything that their parents say.
  e. everything that their parents said.

Choice **c** is the correct answer. The antecedent, *a child*, is singular. Even though you don't know the gender of the child, the possessive pronoun should be *his or her* in order to agree in number.

Pronoun Problem—Unclear Reference

When a pronoun can refer to more than one antecedent in a sentence, it is called an unclear, or ambiguous, reference. Ambiguous pronoun references also occur when there is no apparent antecedent. Look carefully for this common error in the PPST Writing test—a sentence may read smoothly, but it may still contain an unclear reference. Look at this practice usage question:

5. A regular feature in American newspapers

<u>since</u> the early nineteenth century, <u>they</u> use
  a   **b**

satirical humor to <u>visually</u> comment <u>on</u> a
              c   **d**

current event. <u>No error</u>
            e

The answer is choice **b**. Who or what uses satirical humor? You don't know how to answer, because the pronoun *they* does not have an antecedent. If you replace *they* with *political cartoons*, the sentence makes sense.

Verbs—Action Words

A verb is the action word of a sentence. The three basic verb tenses—present, past, and future—let you know when something happens, happened, or will happen. Test makers include some of these common verb trouble spots in the PPST Writing test:

Shifting Verb Tense—Verb tense should be consistent. If a sentence describes an event in the past, its verbs should all be in the past tense.

Incorrect: When Kate visited Japan, she sees many Shinto temples.

Correct: When Kate visited Japan, she saw many Shinto temples.

Past Tense for Present Conditions—It's incorrect to describe a present condition in the past tense.

Incorrect: My sister met her husband in a cafe. He was very tall.

Correct: My sister met her husband in a cafe. He is very tall.

Incomplete Verbs—Test makers may trick you by including the *-ing* form, or progressive form, of a verb without a helping verb (*is, has, has been, was, had, had been,* etc.). Make sure that verbs are complete and make sense in the sentence.

Incorrect: The major newspapers covering the story throughout the year because of the controversy.

Correct: The major newspapers have been covering the story throughout the year because of the controversy.

Subjunctive Mood—The subjunctive mood of verbs expresses something that is imagined, wished for, or contrary to fact. The subjunctive of *was* is *were.*

Incorrect: If I was a movie star, I would buy a fleet of Rolls-Royces.

Correct: If I were a movie star, I would buy a fleet of Rolls-Royces.

Now, practice answering this usage question.

6. <u>Unhappy</u> about the lack <u>of</u> parking at the old
      a   **b**

   stadium, season ticket holders <u>considering</u>
                                       c

   <u>boycotting</u> next week's game. <u>No error</u>
     d   **e**

The correct answer is **c**. *Considering* needs a helping verb to be complete and to make sense in this sentence. The clause should read *season ticket holders are considering boycotting next week's game.*

Structural Relationships

When you speak, you may leave your sentences unfinished or run your sentences together. Written expression makes a more permanent impression than speech. In writing, sentence fragments, run-on sentences, misplaced modifiers, and dangling modifiers are structural problems that obscure the meaning of a sentence. The parts of sentences need to have a clear relationship to each other in order to make sense. This section reviews common errors in sentence structure that will appear on the PPST Writing test, including comparison mistakes, incorrect use of independent and subordinate clauses, double negatives, and unparallel sentence construction.

Making Comparisons

One common writing problem involves comparisons. When a sentence compares two things or activities, the form, or part of speech, of the two entities must match. A writer can compare two nouns or, alternatively, two verb phrases, but he should not compare a noun with a verb phrase.

> *Incorrect:* For me, watching a psychological thriller is harder than a horror film.
>
> *Correct:* For me, watching a psychological thriller is harder than sitting through a horror film.

In the correct version of the sentence, the verb phrase *watching a psychological thriller* matches the form of the verb phrase *sitting through a horror film.* Try the following practice question.

7. Even though admired by some, <u>the innovations of Lewis Carroll's later novels were</u> not as well received as his *Alice's Adventures in Wonderland.*
   a. the innovations of Lewis Carroll's later novels were
   b. Lewis Carroll's later novels were
   c. the innovations about Lewis Carroll's later novels were
   d. the innovations of Lewis Carroll were
   e. Lewis Carroll was

Choice **b** is the correct answer. The original sentence compared *the innovations* of Carroll's later novels with the book, *Alice's Adventures in Wonderland.* The comparison becomes parallel when you simply compare Lewis Carroll's later novels with his early book. Another way to make the sentence parallel would be to compare the innovations of the later novels with the innovations of the early book.

Sentence Fragments

All inventory at reduced prices! Spectacular savings for you! Although pithy and popular with advertisers, sentence fragments are incomplete sentences that do not accurately communicate an idea. To be complete, a sentence needs more than punctuation at its end— it needs a subject and an active verb. A common fragment error that you will see on the PPST Writing test is the use of the *-ing* form of a verb without a helping verb.

> *Incorrect:* Emily sitting on the sofa, wondering what to do next.
>
> *Correct:* Emily was sitting on the sofa, wondering what to do next.

Another common type of sentence fragment is a **subordinate clause** that stands alone. To review, clauses are groups of words that have a subject and a verb. An **independent clause** is one that stands alone and expresses a complete thought. Even though a subordinate clause has a subject and a verb, it does not express a complete thought. It needs an independent clause to support it.

To identify a sentence fragment or a subordinate clause on the PPST Writing exam, look for the following joining words, called **subordinating conjunctions**. When a clause has a subordinating conjunction, it needs an independent clause to complete an idea.

after	because	once	though	when
although	before	since	unless	where
as, as if	if	that	until	while

Examples

The Canada goose that built a nest in the pond outside our building.

As if the storm never happened, as if no damage was done.

In the first example, removing the connector *that* would make a complete sentence. In the second example, the subordinate clauses need an independent clause to make logical sense: *As if the storm never happened, as if no damage was done, Esme remained blithely optimistic.* Try to locate the sentence fragment in the following practice question.

8. <u>One participant</u> of the civil rights movement
      a

<u>explained</u> that <u>in the heated atmosphere</u> of the
  b   **c**

1960s, <u>sit-in protests effective enough</u> to draw
              d

the attention of the nation. <u>No error</u>
                      e

The correct answer choice is **d**. In this question, the independent clause has a subject (*one participant*) and a verb (*explained*). However, the subordinate clause beginning with the connector *that* needs a verb to make sense. Adding the verb *were* completes the thought and fixes the fragment: *that in the heated atmosphere of the 1960s, sit-in protests were effective enough to draw the attention of the nation.*

Run-On Sentences

"Planning ahead and studying for a test builds confidence do you know what I mean?" In speech, you may run your sentences together, but if you do so in writing, you will confuse your reader. In a run-on sentence, two independent clauses run together as one sentence without being separated by proper punctuation.

There are four ways to correct a run-on sentence. Study how each fix listed below changes the following run-on sentence.

Example

We stopped for lunch we were starving.

1. **Add a period.** This separates the run-on sentence and makes two simple sentences. We stopped for lunch. We were starving.
2. **Add a semicolon.** We stopped for lunch; we were starving.
3. **Use a coordinating conjunction** (*and, but, or, for, nor, yet, so*) to connect the two clauses. We were starving, **so** we stopped for lunch.
4. **Use a subordinating conjunction** (see the preceding page for a list of subordinating conjunctions). By doing this, you turn one of the independent clauses into a subordinating clause. **Because** we were starving, we stopped for lunch.

On the PPST Writing test, be sure to watch for another common form of run-on sentence, the **comma splice**. A comma splice incorrectly uses a comma to separate two independent clauses.

Incorrect: Jacob bought the groceries, Lucy cooked dinner.

You can repair a comma splice in two ways: add a conjunction after the comma, or replace the comma with a semicolon.

Correct: Jacob bought the groceries, and Lucy cooked dinner.
             OR
             Jacob bought the groceries; Lucy cooked dinner.

Try this practice question.

9. *Citizen Kane*, Orson Welles's first full-length film, <u>is considered an American classic, however it did not manage</u> to garner the 1941 Academy Award for best picture.
   a. is considered an American classic, however it did not manage
   b. is considered an American classic. However, it did not manage
   c. is considered an American classic however it did not manage
   d. is considered an American classic however. It did not manage
   e. is considered an American classic because it did not manage

Choice **b** is correct. This original sentence is a run-on because the word *however* is used as if it were a conjunction. The words *however*, *therefore*, and *then* are not conjunctions, but rather a special kind of adverb that expresses a relationship between two clauses. Called **conjunctive adverbs**, these words cannot join two independent clauses the way a conjunction does. To repair this kind of run-on or comma splice, you can make two sentences (the way that choice **b** does). Another option for fixing the original sentence is to separate the two main clauses with a semicolon and set the adverb off from the rest of the clause with a comma. Note that you can move the adverb around in its clause without changing the meaning of the sentence.

- *Citizen Kane*, Orson Welles's first full-length film, is considered an American classic; however, it did not manage to garner the 1941 Academy Award for best picture.
- *Citizen Kane*, Orson Welles's first full-length film, is considered an American classic; it did

not manage, however, to garner the 1941 Academy Award for best picture.

More about Clauses

When a sentence contains two clauses that are linked in a logical way, they are **coordinated**. Subordinate clauses are joined to the independent clause by a conjunction (*as, after, although, because*) to complete a thought or idea. Problems occur when conjunctions are misused in a way that makes a sentence obscure and lacking in meaning. Notice below how in the first example, the conjunction *because* creates a confusing and illogical premise, whereas in the second example, the conjunction *although* sets up a contrast between the two clauses that makes sense.

Unclear: Because he was late again, the teacher let him off with just a warning.

Correct: Although he was late again, the teacher let him off with just a warning.

Another type of mistake is when a sentence has two or more subordinate clauses, but no independent clause. This is a problem with **subordination**. Here is an example:

Incorrect: Since the Industrial Revolution took place, because people have increased the concentration of carbon dioxide in the atmosphere by 30 percent by burning fossil fuels and cutting down forests.

The previous sentence contains two subordinate clauses: the first introduced by the conjunction *since*, and the second introduced by the conjunction because. By removing *because*, you create an independent clause, and the sentence makes sense. Try the following practice question.

10. When European settlers <u>arrived</u> in North
                              a

America <u>in the fifteenth century,</u> <u>where</u> they
              b   **c**

<u>encountered</u> diverse Native American cultures.
    d

<u>No error</u>
    e

The correct answer is choice **c**. If you remove the subordinating conjunction *where*, the second subordinating clause becomes an independent clause.

Misplaced Modifiers

Modifiers are phrases that describe nouns, pronouns, and verbs. In a sentence, they must be placed as closely as possible to the words they describe. If they are misplaced, you will end up with a sentence that means something other than what you intended. The results can be comical, but the joke may be on you!

Misplaced Modifier:	My uncle told me about feeding cows in the kitchen. (Why are there cows in the kitchen?)
Correct:	In the kitchen, my uncle told me about feeding cows.

Misplaced Modifier:	A huge python followed the man that was slithering slowly through the grass. (Why was the man slithering through the grass?)

Correct:	Slithering through the grass, a huge python followed the man. OR A huge python that was slithering slowly through the grass followed the man.

Most of the misplaced modifier problems on the PPST Writing are **dangling modifiers**. Dangling modifiers are phrases, located at the beginning of a sentence and set off by a comma, that mistakenly modify the wrong noun or pronoun. To be correct, modifying phrases at the beginning of a sentence should describe the noun or pronoun (the subject of the sentence) that directly follows the comma.

Dangling Modifier:	Broken and beyond repair, Grandma threw the serving dish away. (Why was Grandma broken?)
Correct:	Broken and beyond repair, the serving dish was thrown away by Grandma. OR Grandma threw away the serving dish that was broken and beyond repair.

Try the following sentence-correction question.

11. Subsidized by the federal government, <u>students can get help financing their post-secondary education through the Federal Work-Study Program.</u>

    a. students can get help financing their post-secondary education through the Federal Work-Study Program.

    b. since students finance their post-secondary education through the Federal Work-Study Program.

    c. to students who need help financing their post-secondary education.

    d. financing a post-secondary education is possible through the Federal Work-Study Program.

    e. the Federal Work-Study Program helps students finance their post-secondary education.

The correct answer is choice **e**. In the original sentence, the modifying phrase incorrectly describes the subject *students*. In choice **d**, the modifying phrasing incorrectly describes *financing*. Choices **b** and **c** are subordinate clauses, and, therefore, incorrect. Only choice **e** answers the question "What is subsidized by the federal government?" in a way that makes sense.

Double Negatives

When you use two negatives such as *not* or *no* in a sentence, you may think that you are emphasizing your point. In fact, you are obscuring your meaning. As in math, two negatives result in a positive. When you write, "I don't have no money," you are actually saying that you do have money. Always avoid using double negatives—they are considered grammatically incorrect. *No* and *not* are obvious negatives,

but on the PPST Writing test, watch for any sentence that doubles up on any of the following words:

no one	neither	nobody	scarcely
nothing	nowhere	hardly	barely

Try this usage question:

12. <u>Children</u> <u>don't hardly</u> need computers in the
     a   b

classroom <u>in order</u> <u>to learn</u> basic skills like
          c   d

math and reading. <u>No error</u>
              e

The correct answer is choice **b**. The negative verb *don't* and the adverb *hardly* cancel each other out. The double negative obscures the meaning of the sentence. To rewrite the sentence in a way that makes sense, you could remove either word.

Parallel Structure

When a sentence has a parallel structure, it means that its words and phrases follow the same grammatical structure. Parallel structure makes sentences easier to read and helps express ideas clearly. Parallel construction is important in sentences that make lists or describe a series of events. Each part of the list or series must be in the same form, or part of speech, as the others.

Not Parallel: Every day, I went to school, worked part-time, and was exercising. (Two verbs are in the past tense; one is a past participle.)

Parallel: Every day, I went to school, worked part-time, and exercised.

Not Parallel: We are looking for a teaching assistant who is smart, reliable, and will come on time. (Two characteristics are adjectives, whereas the third consists of a verb phrase.)

Parallel: We are looking for a teaching assistant who is smart, reliable, and punctual.

Parallel construction is also crucial when a sentence uses a *not only/but also* pattern. Review the following examples.

The author not only <u>raised several important questions</u>, but she also <u>made a convincing argument</u>. (Notice how the phrases following the *not only/but also* pattern are in the same form. Each has a verb in the past tense and a noun.)

The contract dispute was a result not only <u>of a breakdown in communication</u> but also <u>of the town's budgetary crisis.</u> (Here the words following the *not only/but also* pattern are in the form of prepositional phrases.)

Practice answering this sentence-correction question:

13. Expressing yourself clearly and effectively in writing means knowing the basic mechanics of language, eliminating ambiguity, choosing the right words, <u>and correct punctuation.</u>
   a. and correct punctuation.
   b. or correct punctuation
   c. and use correct punctuation.
   d. and having used correct punctuation.
   e. and using correct punctuation.

Choice **e** is correct because it follows the grammatical pattern of the sentence: a list of phrases beginning with **gerunds** (a gerund is a noun created from the *-ing* form of a verb).

Idioms and Word Choice

Idioms—words, phrases, or expressions used in everyday language—make up a large part of English. If your native language is not English, the use of idioms may challenge you. That is because idioms often have unusual grammatical structures or have a meaning that does not make sense if you simply add up the meanings of each word. Native English speakers recognize most idioms *by ear*—the words just sound right. The PPST Writing test will require you to identify both the proper use of idioms and correct word choice.

Prepositional Idioms

Prepositions are words that express the relationship in time or space between words in a sentence. They are generally short words, such as *in, on, around, above, between, beside, by, before,* or *with,* that introduce prepositional phrases in a sentence. The PPST Writing exam tests the idiomatic use of prepositions—word combinations that often go together. Review and familiarize yourself with this list of common prepositional idioms:

according to	depend on	next to
afraid of	equal to	of the opinion
anxious about	except for	on top of
apologize for (something)	fond of	opposite of
apologize to (someone)	from now on	prior to
approve of	from time to time	proud of
ashamed of	frown on	regard to
aware of	full of	related to
blame (someone) for	glance at/through	rely on
blame (something) on	grateful for (something)	respect for
bored with	grateful to (someone)	responsible for
capable of	in accordance with	satisfied with
compete with	incapable of	similar to
complain about	in conflict	sorry for
composed of	inferior to	suspicious of
concentrate on	insist on	take care of
concerned with	interested in	thank (someone) for
congratulate on	in the habit of	tired of
conscious of	in the near future	with regard to
consist of	knowledge of	

Keep your ear attuned to the use of prepositional idioms in this practice usage question.

14. The <u>period of</u> intellectual development known
     a

as the Renaissance <u>corresponded toward</u> a
         b

<u>time of</u> political stability <u>in western Europe</u>.
 c   **d**

<u>No error</u>
 e

The answer is choice **b**. The word combination *corresponded toward* is simply not idiomatic. When followed by a thing, such as a time period, either *corresponded with* or *corresponded to* are the correct prepositional idioms. When followed by a person, use *correspond with*.

Redundancy and Wordiness

You may be asked to identify redundant or wordy language. Your ability to write concisely and clearly will also be an important part of the essay portion of the test. To eliminate unnecessary repetitions or excessive wordiness, look for words that add no new information to a sentence.

Redundant: <u>Due to the fact that</u> the circumstances of the case were <u>sensitive in nature</u>, the proceedings were kept confidential.

Correct: <u>Because</u> the circumstances of the case were <u>sensitive</u>, the proceedings were kept confidential.

Redundant: Charles <u>returned back</u> to his room <u>at 10 A.M. in the morning</u>.

Correct: Charles <u>returned</u> to his room <u>at 10 A.M.</u>

Commonly Confused Words

A misused word can significantly alter the meaning of a sentence. The following list contains some commonly confused words. If you find some that you frequently confuse, study them and practice using them correctly in a sentence.

CONFUSING WORD	QUICK DEFINITION
accept	recognize, receive
except	excluding
affect (verb)	to influence
effect (noun)	result
effect (verb)	to bring about
all ready	totally prepared
already	by this time
allude	make indirect reference to
elude	evade
illusion	unreal appearance
all ways	every method
always	forever
among	in the middle of several
between	in an interval separating (two)
assure	to make certain (assure someone)
ensure	to make certain
insure	to make certain (financial value)
beside	next to
besides	in addition to

CONFUSING WORD (continued)	QUICK DEFINITION
complement	match
compliment	praise
continual	constant
continuous	uninterrupted
disinterested	no strong opinion either way
uninterested	don't care
elicit	to stir up
illicit	illegal
eminent	well known
imminent	pending
farther	beyond
further	additional
incredible	beyond belief, astonishing
incredulous	skeptical, disbelieving
loose	not tight
lose	unable to find
may be	something could possibly be
maybe	perhaps
overdo	do too much
overdue	late
persecute	to mistreat
prosecute	to take legal action
personal	individual
personnel	employees
precede	go before
proceed	continue
proceeds	profits
principal (adjective)	main
principal (noun)	person in charge
principle	standard
stationary	still, not moving
stationery	writing material
than	in contrast to
then	next
to	on the way to
too	also
weather	climate
whether	if

Mechanics

Knowing the mechanics of language means getting down to basics—the rules of punctuation and capitalization. Punctuation marks are standardized marks that clarify meaning for your reader and serve as traffic signs that direct the reader to pause, connect, stop, consider, and go. Although you have most likely studied and learned many of the basic rules of punctuation and capitalization, this section covers some common problem areas that may appear on the PPST Writing exam, including the misuse of commas, semicolons, colons, apostrophes, and capitalization.

Commas

Commas create pauses, clarify meaning, and separate different parts of a sentence. The comma splice is a common misuse of the comma—review this problem on page 173. For the PPST Writing exam, remember the six basic rules for using commas, outlined here.

Use a comma:

1. **To separate independent clauses** joined by a co-ordinating conjunction, such as *and, but, nor, so, for*, or *or*. Use a comma before the conjunction.
   My instinct was to solve the problem slowly and deliberately, *but* we only had a week before the deadline.
2. **To set off nonessential clauses.** A nonessential clause is one that can be removed from a sentence without changing its meaning.
   My friend Rebecca, *who is active in the local labor union,* is a fifth-grade teacher.
3. **To set off words or phrases that interrupt** the flow of thought in a sentence.
   The certification program, *however,* works well for me.
   Elena Alvarez, *my adviser and mentor,* was present at the meeting.

4. **To set off an introductory element,** such as a word or phrase that comes at the beginning of a sentence.
   Thrilled by the results, Phin presented the study to his colleagues.
5. **To set apart a series of words in a list.** Usually, the last item in a list is preceded by a conjunction. Although a comma is not necessary before the conjunction, it is preferred that you use one.
   Micah, Jose, and Sam attended the conference.
   Micah, Jose and Sam attended the conference.
6. **To separate elements of dates and addresses.** Commas are used to separate dates that include the day, month, and year. Dates that include just the month and year do not need commas. When the name of a city and state are included in an address, set off both with commas.
   Margaret moved to *Portsmouth, New Hampshire,* for the job.
   Maco came to Greensboro on *June 15, 2004,* right after she graduated from the program.
   Maco came to Greensboro in *June 2004* after she graduated from the program.

Semicolons

You may be asked to recognize errors involving the use of semicolons on the PPST Writing test. Review how to use this mark correctly in the following guidelines and examples:

1. **Use a semicolon to separate independent clauses** that are not joined by a conjunction.
2. **Use a semicolon to separate independent clauses that contain commas,** even if the clauses are joined by a conjunction.
3. **Use a semicolon to separate independent clauses connected with a conjunctive adverb,** such as *however, therefore, then, thus,* or *moreover.*

Colons

Colons are used to introduce elements and to show an equivalent relationship (almost like an equal sign in math). Follow these guidelines to recognize the correct use of colons:

1. **Use a colon to introduce a list** when the clause before the colon can stand as a complete sentence.

    These are the first-year teachers: Ellen, Ben, and Eliza.

    The first-year teachers are Ellen, Ben, and Eliza. (No colon here.)

2. **Use a colon to introduce a restatement or elaboration** of the previous clause.

    James enjoys teaching *Measure for Measure* each spring: it is his favorite play.

3. **Use a colon to introduce a word, phrase, or clause** that adds emphasis to the main body of the sentence.

    Carrie framed the check: it was the first paycheck she had ever earned.

4. **Use a colon to introduce a formal quotation.**

    Writer Gurney Williams offered this advice to parents: "Teaching creativity to your child isn't like teaching good manners. No one can paint a masterpiece by bowing to another person's precepts about elbows on the table."

Use the punctuation guidelines you have reviewed to answer this practice question.

15. Alternative medicine, which includes a range of
                       a

    practices outside of conventional medicine

    such as herbs, homeopathy, massage, yoga, and
                b

    acupuncture; holds increasing appeal for
           c   **d**

    Americans. No error
             e

Choice **c** is the correct answer. The semicolon does not work here because it does not separate two independent clauses. It should be replaced with a comma, setting off the nonessential clause that begins with the word *which*.

Apostrophes

Apostrophes are used to show possession, contractions, and so on. Consider these eight rules for using apostrophes:

1. **Add 's to form the singular possessive, even when the noun ends in *s*:**

    Mr. Summers's essay convinced me.

2. **Add 's to plural words not ending in *s* to show possession.**

    The *children's* ability to absorb foreign language is astounding.

    The workshops focus on working *women's* needs.

3. **Add ' to plural words ending in *s* to show possession.**

    The *students'* grades improved each semester.

4. **Add 's to indefinite pronouns that show ownership.**

    Everyone's ability level should be considered.

5. **Never use apostrophes with possessive pronouns.**

    This experiment must be *yours*.

6. **Use 's to form the plurals of letters, figures, and numbers, as well as expressions of time or money.**

    Mind your *p's* and *q's*.

7. **Add 's to the last word of a compound noun, compound subject, or name of a business or institution to show possession.**

    The *president-elect's* speech riveted the audience.

    Gabbie and Michael's wedding is in October.

    The *National Science Teachers Association's* meeting will take place next week.

8. **Use apostrophes to show that letters or words are omitted in contractions.**

> Abby *doesn't* (does not) work today.
> *Who's* (who is) on first?

Capitalization

Capitalization is necessary both for specific words and to start sentences and quotations. The following are six instances when capitalization is needed:

1. the first word of the sentence
2. proper nouns (names of *specific* people, places, and things)
3. the first word of a complete quotation, but not a partial quotation
4. the first, last, and any other important words of a title
5. languages
6. the pronoun *I*, and any contractions made with it

Sometimes knowing when to capitalize a word is tricky. Look for these trouble spots on the PPST Writing test:

- **Compass directions**, such as *east* or *west*, are not capitalized unless they refer to a specific geographical area.
    > The American Civil War was fought between the *North* and the *South*.
- **Family relationships** are not capitalized when they are preceded by a pronoun.
    > I met *my mother* for lunch.
    > *Uncle Russ* agreed to babysit, so that I could meet *Mother* for lunch.
- **Seasons and parts of the academic year** are not capitalized.
    > I'll register for the course this *fall*.
- **Words modified by proper adjectives** are not capitalized, unless they are part of a proper name.
    > Jacob recommended the *Italian restaurant* in his neighborhood.

Practice answering this usage question.

16. When Thomas Jefferson sent explorers Lewis

    and Clark into the <u>West,</u> he patterned their
                 a

    mission on the <u>Enlightenments'</u> scientific
                b

    methods<u>:</u> to observe, collect, document, and
         c   **d**

    classify. <u>No error</u>
            e

The answer is choice **b**. As a proper noun, *the Enlightenment* is correctly capitalized; however, the apostrophe is misplaced. To show possession, add *'s* to a singular noun. The *West* is correctly capitalized because it refers to a geographical region of the United States.

Introducing the Essay

Essay tests can intimidate anyone—even prospective teachers. You know you will be asked to write an essay, but you don't know your topic beforehand. And you are under pressure: You have only 30 minutes to complete the task. Even though this sounds nerve-racking, with preparation, you will be ready to produce your best writing. The good news is that because the time limit is brief, your essay doesn't need to be long (about four to five paragraphs). Furthermore, because you are provided with a topic, you don't need to spend valuable time deciding what to write about. Also, you can be confident that you will be able to answer the question: All the topics, or writing prompts, on the PPST Essay test are designed to be general so that you do not need any specialized knowledge or experience to write about them.

Creative, innovative writing is not the goal of the Praxis essay. Instead, it aims to measure your ability to generate ideas and support them through details and evidence in clear, concise writing. It tests how effectively and logically you organize your thoughts, and it evaluates your ability to use correct grammar and appropriate word choice. Do not spend a lot of time trying to produce a masterpiece—simply express your views through precise, direct language. To learn more about the criteria on which your essay will be judged, review the rubrics provided in the answer explanations found after each practice exam.

What to Expect

All the possible writing prompts in the PPST Essay test present a statement and ask you to respond to it. Be ready to explain and back up your position with specific reasons and examples from your personal experience, observations, or reading. You do not need any background knowledge to respond to the prompt. **Do not write about a topic other than the one provided.** To receive a score, you must write in English. These are some examples of the general topics you might find on the PPST Essay exam:

- "We live in a culturally diverse society. In-depth study of different cultures should be mandatory for all students."
- "Celebrities are just ordinary people with high-profile jobs. They don't have more responsibility than other adults to act as role models for children."
- "Because of the prevalence of information technology in society, computer training should be required for all teachers, regardless of the subject the instructor will teach."
- "Using a grade scale of A–F creates unnecessary competition and negative stress. Colleges and universities should replace the grade scale with a pass/fail report."

Essay Prompts Online

You can find more than 70 typical writing prompts at the Educational Testing Service (ETS) website. The essay prompt you get at exam time may not be included in this list, but reviewing the list will familiarize you with common types of prompts and topics. You can follow these instructions:

- Go to www.ets.org/praxis/prcparc/materials/ praxisi_writing.
- Under "*Praxis I®* (*PPST®*) Writing Test (0720 and 5720)," click on the "Test at a Glance" that applies to the test you are taking:
  – (5720) for the computerized test
  – (0720) for the paper-based test
- In the left-hand manu bar, select "Download PDF."

Your computer must be able to read pdf files.

Manage Your Time

You have 30 minutes to produce a clear, strong essay. Should you jump right into the writing or take time to plan your response? Even with a time limit, your ability to craft a well-organized, well-written essay improves if you take time to plan your essay. Allow time for each step of the writing process: planning, writing, and proofreading. You can break down the 30 minutes this way:

5–10 minutes	Plan (choose your thesis, brainstorm, and organize).
15–20 minutes	Write.
5 minutes	Proofread (read for errors or adjust word choice).

Steps to a Strong Essay

The prewriting—or planning—process is essential to developing a clear, organized essay. Because of the time limit, you may be tempted to skip the prewriting stage. However, the 5–10 minutes that you spend planning will be worth it. Prewriting consists of some quick, basic steps: carefully reading and understanding the writing prompt, formulating a thesis, brainstorming for examples that will support your thesis, and drafting an outline or basic structure for your essay.

Step 1—Create a Clear Thesis

To begin, carefully read the statement presented in the writing prompt. Make sure that you fully understand it. Then, decide what your position is: Do you agree or disagree with the statement? Consider to what extent you agree or disagree with the position: Are you in 100% agreement or do you only partly agree with the statement? Your answer to these questions will make up the main idea or **thesis** of your essay. It will form the foundation of your essay and will determine what kind of support, or examples, you will provide.

A strong thesis does not merely repeat or rephrase the question or prompt, and it does not state how *others* might respond to it. Rather, it presents *your* point of view.

A thesis statement should:

- answer the question given in the writing prompt
- tell the reader what your subject is
- inform the reader what you think and feel about the subject
- use clear, active language

Don't waste time making your thesis statement a masterpiece. You will be able to grab the reader's attention by clearly stating your purpose in simple words.

Consider the following prompt:

"Focusing on fashion and clothes can distract students from learning. School uniforms should be mandatory for all high-school students."

Discuss the extent to which you agree or disagree with this opinion. Support your views with specific reasons and examples from your own experience, observations, or reading.

The following sentences are *not* thesis statements:

- Many private schools already require school uniforms.
- Some students prefer school uniforms, while others detest them.
- Why do schools use uniforms?

The following *are* thesis statements; they relate directly to the prompt:

- School uniforms discourage high-school students from learning responsibility and developing individuality.
- School uniforms are effective in creating a positive learning environment.

Remember that you can also impose some conditions on your answer. For example, if you disagree with mandatory school uniforms, you can still qualify your answer: "I disagree that students should be required to wear school uniforms, but I believe a dress code helps create an effective learning atmosphere."

Step 2—Brainstorm for Ideas

Your answer to the question in the writing prompt will form the argument that you present in your essay. Once you have decided what your position will be, you will begin to brainstorm—think up ideas—that support your thesis. For your PPST essay, try to generate about three to five reasons that back up your main idea.

Brainstorming is a prewriting process in which you imagine or write down any ideas that come to mind. To brainstorm effectively, do not judge your ideas initially—simply put them down on paper. If you are stuck for ideas, try these brainstorming strategies:

- Try the **freewriting** technique in which you write nonstop for two minutes. Keep your pen to paper and your hand moving. Doubtlessly, your ideas will emerge.
- **List** as many ideas as you can. Don't edit for grammar or structure; just write down whatever comes to mind.
- Now get selective. Choose three to five of your strongest ideas for your essay.

For example, here's how you might brainstorm supporting ideas for the writing prompt mentioned earlier:

Thesis: Mandatory school uniforms are not effective tools for creating a positive, learning environment.

Examples
Why?
Uniforms don't give students the opportunity to make choices.
Uniforms send a message to students that they cannot be trusted.
Students find distractions in class even when they are wearing uniforms.
Teenage years are a time of self-exploration.
Learning isn't only something you read in a book—it's about finding out who you are.
Students need to learn about making good choices.

Personal experience—In my parochial high school, kids wore uniforms.
Lack of trust—We couldn't be trusted to do even a simple thing like dressing ourselves.
Found other ways to rebel—smoking, wearing makeup, dyeing our hair to attract attention
Distractions in class other than clothes—note writing, gossip, cell phones
Self-exploration—Clothes let teens try on different identities (sporty, punk, artistic).
Learning about good choices—Introduce a forum for students where they can talk about making choices? Encourage kids to talk about how they present themselves when they wear different clothes; talk about choices teens make that can be dangerous; talk about choices adults face.

Step 3—Outline Your Essay

To make sure that your essay is well-developed and organized, draft an outline. An outline will help you put your ideas into a logical order and identify any gaps in your supporting details. Essays follow a basic three-part structure:

1. **Introduction:** Present your position to your readers. State your thesis.
2. **Body:** Provide specific support for your thesis.
3. **Conclusion:** Bring closure to your essay and restate your thesis.

Your PPST essay should follow this basic structure, too. Because the essay is short, plan on writing about five paragraphs, listing one point on your outline for each paragraph. The body of your essay will be broken down into three supporting ideas:

1. Introduction
2. Body: support 1

3. Body: support 2
4. Body: support 3
5. Conclusion

Although you don't have to follow this model exactly, keep in mind that developing three supporting paragraphs is a good guide for the PPST essay. By providing three supporting paragraphs, you will give enough support to make a strong case for your argument.

Essay Structure

Where you put your introduction and conclusion is obvious. However, you need a pattern, or structure, to organize the ideas in the body of your essay. The four most common patterns are **chronological order**, **order of importance**, **comparison and contrast**, and **cause and effect**. The following chart lists each organizing principle's key characteristics and effective uses in writing:

ORGANIZATIONAL PATTERN	CHARACTERISTICS	EFFECTIVE USES
chronological order	uses time as organizing principle; describes events in the order in which they happened	historical texts, personal narratives, fiction
order of importance	arranges ideas by rank instead of time	persuasive essays, newspaper articles
comparison and contrast	places two or more items side by side to show similarities and differences	comparative essays
cause and effect	explains possible reasons why something took place	historical analysis, analysis of current events

What is the most effective way to organize your PPST essay when you don't have much time to consider the options? Because the prompts on the writing exam ask you to take a position on a subject, you are essentially developing a brief argument in your essay. A logical and effective strategy for making an argument is to organize your ideas by their importance, or rank. Using this pattern, you can arrange your ideas in two ways:

1. by increasing importance (Begin with your least important idea and build up to your most important idea.)
2. by decreasing importance (Start with your strongest, most persuasive, idea and end with your least important idea.)

Either arrangement works. However, if you develop your essay by the principle of increasing importance, you save your strongest idea for last, creating a greater impact in your conclusion.

Now it's time to make a detailed outline based on the writing prompt described earlier in the chapter. The outline organizes the supporting ideas by increasing importance. It includes reasons that support the thesis and examples that support each reason. Because this outline is so detailed, it offers a guide for almost every sentence in the body of the essay.

Introduction
Thesis: Mandatory school uniforms are not effective tools for creating a positive learning environment.
Reason 1: When students feel that they are not trusted, they "live down" to expectations.

Examples: Feel need to prove individuality through attention to makeup, hair; draw attention through risky behaviors like smoking; continue to find distractions like gossip, note passing, cell phones

Reason 2: School uniforms discourage self-discovery and individuality.

Examples: Can't try out looks that come with different identities (sporty, punk, artistic); fashion is harmless way to find out who you are

Reason 3: Students don't learn to make good choices.

Examples: Students aren't prepared for making decisions, simple (clothes, nutrition) or big (college, jobs, whether or not to engage in risky behaviors, friends, romantic relationships)

Conclusion:
Robbing students of choice discourages self-discovery and does not prepare students for making decisions. Allow students to make choices about their clothes, but also provide a class or forum for discussing how to make good choices, both big and small.

Target Your Audience

Effective writing pays close attention to its *audience*. Effective writers consider their readers: Who are they? What do they know about the subject? What preconceived notions do they have? What will hold their attention?

On the PPST, you will be writing to a general audience, meaning that your readers are people with a variety of interests and backgrounds. Knowing your audience helps you make key writing decisions about your level of formality and detail. Your level of formality determines whether you will use slang, an informal tone, technical jargon, or formal language in your writing. A good guide for the PPST Writing test is a balanced approach:

- Treat your readers with respect.
- Don't put off your readers with language that is too formal or pretentious. Don't try to use big, important-sounding words.
- Avoid slang (too informal) or jargon (technical or specialized language).
- Aim for a natural tone, without being too informal.

Your level of detail is also based on your audience. Because you are writing for a general audience and not for friends or family, your readers will not be familiar with your background or experiences. For example, if you are arguing against mandatory student uniforms, do not assume that your readers know whether your high school implemented such a rule. Give your readers adequate context by briefly describing your experience as it applies to your argument.

First Impression—The Introduction

Once you have completed your detailed outline, you are ready to write. Because you only have 15–20 minutes to write, you don't have time to perfect the wording of your introduction. Instead, use clear, direct language to introduce your reader to your thesis and focus. A good way to begin is to restate in your own words the quotation given in the prompt and then state your thesis. Here is an example using the prompt discussed earlier:

> *Although fashion and clothes can sometimes distract students, mandatory school uniforms are not the answer to creating a good learning environment.*

Another useful technique for creating a strong introduction is to begin with your thesis and then give a summary of the evidence (supporting details) you will be presenting in the body of your essay. Here is an expanded version of the preceding thesis statement:

> *Although fashion and clothes can sometimes distract students, mandatory school uniforms are not the answer to creating a good learning environment. School uniforms can be a negative influence in that they send a message that students can't be trusted to make good choices. High school students need to explore different identities through the harmless means of fashion.*

Notice how this introduction outlines the first two main points of the essay's body: how mandatory school uniforms (1) send a negative message about students' ability to make decisions and (2) discourage self-discovery.

Supporting Paragraphs— The Body of the Essay

Working from your detailed outline, begin composing the body of your essay (about three paragraphs long). Treat each of your paragraphs like a mini-essay, with its own thesis (a topic sentence that expresses the main idea of the paragraph) and supporting details (examples). Follow these guidelines for creating supporting paragraphs:

- **Avoid introducing several ideas within one paragraph.** By definition, a paragraph is a group of sentences about the *same* idea.

- **Use at least one detail** or example to back up each main supporting idea.
- **Aim for about three or four sentences in each paragraph.** Your PPST essay will be short. If you write more sentences for each paragraph you may run short on time and space. If you write fewer sentences, you may not develop your idea adequately.
- **Use transitions.** Key words and phrases can help guide readers through your essay. You can use these common transitions to indicate the order of importance of your material: *first and foremost*, *most important*, *first*, *second*, *third*, *moreover*, *finally*, and *above all*. Do not use "firstly," "secondly," or "thirdly"—these forms are incorrect and awkward.

Active versus Passive Voice

For precise, direct writing, use the active voice. In English grammar, *voice* expresses a relationship between the verb and the subject of the sentence or its direct object. When you write in the *active voice*, the subject of the sentence causes, or is the source of, the action (verb). When you use the *passive voice*, the subject does not perform the action, but rather is acted upon. Sentences in the passive voice are often wordier and more difficult to understand. Here are some examples of active versus passive voice:

Active: We suggest that you organize your ideas by importance.

Passive: It is suggested that you organize your ideas by importance. (Note that this sentence does not say *who* performed the action.)

Active: Her brother typed the letter.

Passive: The letter was typed by her brother. (Here the *doer* of the action is the direct object *brother*, not the subject of the sentence, *letter*.)

Sentence Variety

A strong PPST essay will show your ability to manipulate sentence structure for effect. Sentence structure is an important element of style. If all of your sentences have the same pattern, your writing will be monotonous and dull:

School uniforms are negative. They don't boost students' confidence. They don't make students feel trustworthy. They don't let students explore different styles and personalities.

Although these sentences are simple and direct, they are unlikely to captivate a reader. Because they all have the same length and structure, they create a monotonous pattern. Here is the same paragraph, revised to show variety in sentence structure:

School uniforms are negative because they do not boost students' confidence or make them feel trustworthy. Fashion choices allow students to explore different styles and personalities.

Four sentences are reduced to two; the pronoun *they* is no longer repeated; and verb choices are active and varied. You can also create emphasis in your writing through sentence structure. The best place to put sentence elements that you want to emphasize is at the end. What comes last lingers longest in the reader's mind.

He is tall, dark, and handsome. (The emphasis is on *handsome*. If *tall* is the most important characteristic, then it should come last.)

You can also use a dash to set off a part of a sentence for emphasis:

He is tall, dark, handsome—and married.

The dash emphasizes the last element, heightening the sense of disappointment the writer is trying to convey.

Your Conclusion

The last paragraph of your essay should sum up your argument. Avoid introducing new ideas or topics. Instead, your concluding paragraph should restate your thesis, but in *new words.* Your conclusion should demonstrate that you covered your topic fully and should convince readers that they have learned something meaningful from your argument. Here's an example:

> *School uniforms might be the easy answer: They create conformity and minimize distractions in the classroom. However, in order to teach students how to make good choices when they face tough decisions, school administrators need to invest students with the responsibility to practice everyday choices—like deciding what they wear to school.*

The Last Step—Proofread

On the timed essay test, you should take about five minutes to proofread—a time allowance that does not let you substantially revise or rewrite your piece. Much of what happens when you rewrite—like reorganizing your argument or making sure you present adequate support—must occur during the *prewriting* process, when you are outlining your essay. The goal of proofreading is to give your essay a final polish, by checking your spelling, correcting grammatical errors, and if needed, changing word order or word choice. To proofread, carefully read your essay, paying attention to anything that doesn't sound right. The following checklist outlines some basic grammatical problems to look out for as you proofread. (All of these grammar trouble spots are discussed earlier in the chapter.)

- **Make sure nouns and verbs agree.** The subject of the sentence must match the verb in number. If the subject is singular, the verb is singular. If the subject is plural, the verb is plural.
- **Make sure pronouns and antecedents agree.** Pronouns and the nouns they represent (antecedents) must agree in number. If the antecedent is singular, the pronoun is singular; if the antecedent is plural, the pronoun is plural.
- **Check your modifiers.** Look out for modifiers that are easy to confuse, like *good/well, bad/badly,* and *fewer/less.* Remember: Adjectives modify nouns and pronouns; adverbs describe verbs, adjectives, or other adverbs.
- **Avoid double negatives.** Do not use two negative words, like *no, not, neither, hardly,* or *barely,* in one sentence. See page 175 for a list of other negatives.
- **Keep your verb tense consistent.** Switching tense within a sentence can change its meaning. Generally, a sentence or paragraph that begins in the present tense should continue in the present tense.
- **Review prepositional idioms.** If you have studied the list of prepositional idioms on page 177, you may be able to "hear" whether a preposition (*to, of, about, for, with, about, on, upon*) sounds right with a particular phrase or verb.
- **Check your sentence structure.** Look for sentence fragments, run-on sentences, comma splices, and misplaced or dangling modifiers.

Now, take the skills you have learned or honed in this review and apply them to Practice Exam I.

P A R T

IV ▶ PRAXIS I PPST PRACTICE EXAMS

CHAPTER

7

PRAXIS I
PRACTICE EXAM 1

CHAPTER SUMMARY
Here is a full-length test based on the three elements of the Praxis I, the Pre-Professional Skills Tests (PPSTs) of Reading, Mathematics, and Writing. Now that you have completed the review chapters, take this exam to see how much your score has improved.

Like the real Praxis I, the exam that follows is made up of three tests: Reading (multiple-choice questions), Mathematics (multiple-choice questions), and Writing (multiple-choice questions and one essay).

With this practice exam, you should simulate the actual test-taking experience as closely as you can. Find a quiet place to work where you won't be disturbed. Use the answer sheet on the next page and write your essay on a separate piece of paper. Allow yourself an hour for the Reading test, an hour for the Mathematics test, 30 minutes for Section 1 of the Writing test, and 30 minutes for Section 2 of the Writing test (your essay).

Set a timer or stopwatch for each part of the exam, but do not worry too much if you go over the allotted times on this practice exam. You can work more on timing when you take the Praxis I Practice Exam 2 in Chapter 8.

After the exam, use the answer explanations to learn more about the questions you missed, and use the scoring guide to figure out how you did.

LEARNINGEXPRESS ANSWER SHEET

SKILLS TEST IN READING

1. (a) (b) (c) (d) (e)
2. (a) (b) (c) (d) (e)
3. (a) (b) (c) (d) (e)
4. (a) (b) (c) (d) (e)
5. (a) (b) (c) (d) (e)
6. (a) (b) (c) (d) (e)
7. (a) (b) (c) (d) (e)
8. (a) (b) (c) (d) (e)
9. (a) (b) (c) (d) (e)
10. (a) (b) (c) (d) (e)
11. (a) (b) (c) (d) (e)
12. (a) (b) (c) (d) (e)
13. (a) (b) (c) (d) (e)
14. (a) (b) (c) (d) (e)
15. (a) (b) (c) (d) (e)
16. (a) (b) (c) (d) (e)
17. (a) (b) (c) (d) (e)
18. (a) (b) (c) (d) (e)
19. (a) (b) (c) (d) (e)
20. (a) (b) (c) (d) (e)
21. (a) (b) (c) (d) (e)
22. (a) (b) (c) (d) (e)
23. (a) (b) (c) (d) (e)
24. (a) (b) (c) (d) (e)
25. (a) (b) (c) (d) (e)
26. (a) (b) (c) (d) (e)
27. (a) (b) (c) (d) (e)
28. (a) (b) (c) (d) (e)
29. (a) (b) (c) (d) (e)
30. (a) (b) (c) (d) (e)
31. (a) (b) (c) (d) (e)
32. (a) (b) (c) (d) (e)
33. (a) (b) (c) (d) (e)
34. (a) (b) (c) (d) (e)
35. (a) (b) (c) (d) (e)
36. (a) (b) (c) (d) (e)
37. (a) (b) (c) (d) (e)
38. (a) (b) (c) (d) (e)
39. (a) (b) (c) (d) (e)
40. (a) (b) (c) (d) (e)

SKILLS TEST IN MATHEMATICS

1. (a) (b) (c) (d) (e)
2. (a) (b) (c) (d) (e)
3. (a) (b) (c) (d) (e)
4. (a) (b) (c) (d) (e)
5. (a) (b) (c) (d) (e)
6. (a) (b) (c) (d) (e)
7. (a) (b) (c) (d) (e)
8. (a) (b) (c) (d) (e)
9. (a) (b) (c) (d) (e)
10. (a) (b) (c) (d) (e)
11. (a) (b) (c) (d) (e)
12. (a) (b) (c) (d) (e)
13. (a) (b) (c) (d) (e)
14. (a) (b) (c) (d) (e)
15. (a) (b) (c) (d) (e)
16. (a) (b) (c) (d) (e)
17. (a) (b) (c) (d) (e)
18. (a) (b) (c) (d) (e)
19. (a) (b) (c) (d) (e)
20. (a) (b) (c) (d) (e)
21. (a) (b) (c) (d) (e)
22. (a) (b) (c) (d) (e)
23. (a) (b) (c) (d) (e)
24. (a) (b) (c) (d) (e)
25. (a) (b) (c) (d) (e)
26. (a) (b) (c) (d) (e)
27. (a) (b) (c) (d) (e)
28. (a) (b) (c) (d) (e)
29. (a) (b) (c) (d) (e)
30. (a) (b) (c) (d) (e)
31. (a) (b) (c) (d) (e)
32. (a) (b) (c) (d) (e)
33. (a) (b) (c) (d) (e)
34. (a) (b) (c) (d) (e)
35. (a) (b) (c) (d) (e)
36. (a) (b) (c) (d) (e)
37. (a) (b) (c) (d) (e)
38. (a) (b) (c) (d) (e)
39. (a) (b) (c) (d) (e)
40. (a) (b) (c) (d) (e)

SKILLS TEST IN WRITING, SECTION 1

1. (a) (b) (c) (d) (e)
2. (a) (b) (c) (d) (e)
3. (a) (b) (c) (d) (e)
4. (a) (b) (c) (d) (e)
5. (a) (b) (c) (d) (e)
6. (a) (b) (c) (d) (e)
7. (a) (b) (c) (d) (e)
8. (a) (b) (c) (d) (e)
9. (a) (b) (c) (d) (e)
10. (a) (b) (c) (d) (e)
11. (a) (b) (c) (d) (e)
12. (a) (b) (c) (d) (e)
13. (a) (b) (c) (d) (e)
14. (a) (b) (c) (d) (e)
15. (a) (b) (c) (d) (e)
16. (a) (b) (c) (d) (e)
17. (a) (b) (c) (d) (e)
18. (a) (b) (c) (d) (e)
19. (a) (b) (c) (d) (e)
20. (a) (b) (c) (d) (e)
21. (a) (b) (c) (d) (e)
22. (a) (b) (c) (d) (e)
23. (a) (b) (c) (d) (e)
24. (a) (b) (c) (d) (e)
25. (a) (b) (c) (d) (e)
26. (a) (b) (c) (d) (e)
27. (a) (b) (c) (d) (e)
28. (a) (b) (c) (d) (e)
29. (a) (b) (c) (d) (e)
30. (a) (b) (c) (d) (e)
31. (a) (b) (c) (d) (e)
32. (a) (b) (c) (d) (e)
33. (a) (b) (c) (d) (e)
34. (a) (b) (c) (d) (e)
35. (a) (b) (c) (d) (e)
36. (a) (b) (c) (d) (e)
37. (a) (b) (c) (d) (e)
38. (a) (b) (c) (d) (e)

Skills Test in Reading

Directions: Read the following passages and answer the questions that follow.

Use the following passage to answer question 1.

James Carruthers' recent essays attempt to redefine arts criticism as a play of critical intelligence that can take place free from the bonds of political partisanship. In Carruthers' view, this play of the mind, working itself free from constraints, is the only ethical approach to the arts.

1. What is the best definition of the word *play* as it is used in the passage?
   a. acting or conducting oneself in a specified way
   b. moving or operating freely
   c. pretense; mimicry
   d. careless or indifferent behavior
   e. a stake or wager in a game

Use the following passage to answer question 2.

Rhesus monkeys use facial expressions to communicate with each other and to enforce social order. For example, the "fear grimace," although it looks ferocious, is actually given by a subordinate monkey that is intimidated by a dominant member of the group.

2. In the passage, the word *subordinate* most nearly means
   a. playful.
   b. powerful.
   c. angry.
   d. lower in status.
   e. sick.

Use the following passage to answer questions 3 through 5.

O'Connell Street is the main thoroughfare of Dublin City. Although it is not a particularly long street, Dubliners will tell the visitor proudly that it is the widest street in all of Europe. This claim usually meets with protests, especially from French tourists, claiming the Champs Elysees of Paris as Europe's widest street. But the witty Dubliner will not relinquish bragging rights easily and will trump the French visitor with a fine distinction: the Champs Elysees is a boulevard; O'Connell is a street.

Divided by several important monuments running the length of its center, the street is named for Daniel O'Connell, an Irish patriot. His monument stands at the lower end of the road, that is, the end closest to the river Liffey that bisects Dublin. O'Connell stands high above the unhurried crowds of shoppers, businesspeople, and students on a sturdy column, surrounded by four serene angels seated at each corner of the monument's base. Further up the street is the famous General Post Office that the locals affectionately call "the GPO." During the 1916 rebellion, the GPO was taken over and occupied by the Irish rebels to British rule, sparking weeks of armed combat in the city's center. To this day, the angels of O'Connell's monument bear the marks of the fighting: One sits reading calmly, apparently unaware of the bullet hole dimpling her upper arm; another, reaching out to stroke the ears of a huge bronze Irish wolfhound, has survived what should be a mortal wound to her heart.

3. Which of the following would be the best title for this passage?

    a. "Dublin's Famous Monuments"

    b. "The Irish Take Pride in Their Capital City"

    c. "The Widest Street in Europe"

    d. "Sights and History on Dublin's O'Connell Street"

    e. "Tourism in Dublin"

4. What is the best definition for the word *trump* as it is used in the first paragraph of the passage?

    a. to trumpet loudly, to blare or drown out

    b. to trample

    c. to get the better of by using a key or hidden resource

    d. to devise a fraud, to employ trickery

    e. to use a particular suit of cards

5. With which of the following statements about the people of Dublin would the author of the passage most likely agree?

    a. They are proud of their history but lack industry.

    b. They are playful and tricky.

    c. They are rebellious and do not like tourists.

    d. They are witty and relaxed.

    e. They are unaware of their history.

Use the following passage to answer questions 6 and 7.

The fictional world of Toni Morrison's novel *Sula*—the African-American section of Medallion, Ohio, a community called "the Bottom"—is a place where people, and even natural things, are apt to go awry, to break from their prescribed boundaries, a place where bizarre and unnatural happenings and strange reversals of the ordinary are commonplace. The very name of the setting of *Sula* is significant; the Bottom is located high up in the hills. The novel is furthermore filled with images of mutilation, both psychological and physical. A great part of the lives of the characters, therefore, is taken up with making sense of the world, setting boundaries and devising methods to control what is essentially uncontrollable. One of the major devices used by the people of the Bottom is the seemingly universal one of creating a _____—in this case, the title character Sula—upon which to project both the evil they perceive outside themselves and the evil in their own hearts.

6. Which of the following words would best fit into the blank in the final sentence of the passage?

    a. victim

    b. hero

    c. leader

    d. scapegoat

    e. outcast

7. Why does the writer of this passage mention that *the Bottom is located high up in the hills*?

    a. to show that ordinary expectations are reversed in this community

    b. to tell the reader where the novel is set

    c. to explain why natural things often go wrong there

    d. to describe the weather in the Bottom

    e. to emphasize that *Sula* is a work of fiction

Use the following passage to answer question 8.

When Maria plays in a softball game for her company's team, she plays catcher. If she is unable to attend a game, either Christine or Thomas plays catcher.

8. Based only on the information in the passage, which of the following is a valid conclusion?
- **a.** Christine and Thomas don't like playing catcher as much as Maria does.
- **b.** Christine and Thomas are equally good softball players.
- **c.** If Maria and Thomas both play in a game, Maria plays catcher.
- **d.** Maria is the best catcher on the team.
- **e.** Maria often misses softball games.

Use the following passage to answer question 9.

Wondering what to do with that old Atari Home Video Game in the attic? It's on the wish list of the Computer Museum of America, in San Diego, California, which hopes you will donate it to their holdings. The museum was founded in 1983 to amass and preserve historic computer equipment, such as calculators, card punches, and typewriters, and now owns one of the world's largest collections. In addition, it has archives of computer-related magazines, manuals, and books that are available to students, authors, researchers, and others for historical research.

9. All of the following are probably part of the collection of the Computer Museum of America EXCEPT
- **a.** adding machines.
- **b.** old computers.
- **c.** operation manuals for calculators.
- **d.** card punch machines.
- **e.** kitchen scales.

Use the following passage to answer question 10.

In 1904, the U.S. Patent Office granted a patent for a board game called "The Landlord's Game," which was invented by a Virginia Quaker named Lizzie Magie. Magie was a follower of Henry George, who started a tax movement that supported the theory that the renting of land and real estate produced an unearned increase in land values that profited a few individuals (landlords) rather than the majority of the people (tenants). George proposed a single federal tax based on land ownership; he believed this tax would weaken the ability to form monopolies, encourage equal opportunity, and narrow the gap between rich and poor.

Lizzie Magie wanted to spread the word about George's proposal, making it more understandable to a majority of people who were basically unfamiliar with economics. As a result, she invented a board game that would serve as a teaching device. The Landlord's Game was intended to explain the evils of monopolies, showing that they repressed the possibility for equal opportunity. Her instructions read in part: "The object of this game is not only to afford amusement to players, but to illustrate to them how, under the present or prevailing system of land tenure, the landlord has an advantage over other enterprisers, and also how the single tax would discourage speculation."

10. In paragraph 2, what does *repressed the possibility for equal opportunity* mean?
- **a.** Monopolies led to slavery.
- **b.** Monopolies were responsible for the single tax problems.
- **c.** Monopolies made it impossible for poorer people to follow Henry George.
- **d.** Monopolies were responsible for Lizzie Magie's $500 payment and Charles Darrow's millions.
- **e.** Monopolies made it impossible for poorer people to have the same chances as the wealthy.

Use the following passage to answer questions 11 through 14.

The roots of the modern-day sport of lacrosse are found in tribal stick and ball games developed and played by many native North American tribes dating back as early as the fifteenth century. The Native American names for these games reflected the bellicose nature of those early contests, many of which went far beyond friendly recreational competition. For example, the Algonquin called their game Baggattaway, which meant "they bump hips." The Cherokee Nation and the Six Tribes of the Iroquois called their sport Tewaarathon, which translated into "Little Brother of War." Rules and style of play differed from tribe to tribe and games could be played by as few as 15 to as many as 1,000 men and women at a time. These matches could last for three days, beginning at dawn each day and ending at sunset. The goals could be specific trees or rocks, and were a few hundred yards to a few miles apart. Despite these differences, the sole object of every game was the same: to score goals by any means necessary. Serious injuries caused by blows from the heavy wooden sticks used in the games were not uncommon, and often expected. Not surprisingly, the Native Americans considered these precursors to today's lacrosse excellent battle preparation for young warriors, and games were often used to settle disputes between tribes without resorting to full-blown warfare.

11. The author translates the Native American names for their games in order to
   a. demonstrate a strong knowledge of Native American languages.
   b. highlight the differences between the various tribes.
   c. revive the use of ancient tribal languages.
   d. prove that lacrosse has existed for centuries.
   e. emphasize the warlike aspects of these games.

12. In the second sentence, *bellicose* most closely means
   a. beautiful.
   b. warlike.
   c. peaceful.
   d. family-minded.
   e. clumsy.

13. Which of the following titles would be the most appropriate for this passage?
   a. "Little Brother of War"
   b. "Lacrosse: America's Most Violent Sport"
   c. "The Origins of the Modern Lacrosse Stick"
   d. "The Six Tribes"
   e. "Hockey: The Little Brother of Lacrosse"

14. Near the end of the passage, the author's use of the phrase *by any means necessary* emphasizes
   a. the unpredictable nature of the game.
   b. the mild nature of the game.
   c. the violent nature of the game.
   d. the fact that both women and men participated in the games.
   e. the importance of scoring goals.

Use the following passage to answer questions 15 and 16.

Among traditional societies of the Pacific Northwest—including the Haidas, Kwakiutls, Makahs, Nootkas, Tlingits, and Tsimshians—the gift-giving ceremony called potlatch was a central feature of social life. The word *potlatch*, meaning "to give," comes from a Chinook trading language that was used all along the Pacific Coast. Each nation, or tribe, had its own particular word for the ceremony, and the tribes all had different potlatch traditions. However, the function and basic features of the ceremony were universal among the tribes.

Each nation held potlatches to celebrate important life passages, such as birth, coming of age, marriage, and death. Potlatches were also held to honor ancestors and to mark the passing of leadership. A potlatch, which could last four or more days, was usually held in the winter when the tribes were not engaged in gathering and storing food. Each potlatch included the formal display of the host family's crest and masks. The hosts performed ritual dances and provided feasts for their guests. However, the most important ritual was the lavish distribution of gifts to the guests. Some hosts might give away most or all of their accumulated wealth in one potlatch. The more a host gave away, the more status was accorded him. In turn, the guests, who had to accept the proffered gifts, were then expected to host their own potlatches and give away gifts of equal value.

15. According to the passage, *potlatch* is best defined as a
  a. ceremony with rigid protocol to which all Pacific Northwest tribes adhered.
  b. generic term for a gift-giving ceremony celebrated in the Pacific Northwest.
  c. socialist ritual of the Pacific Northwest.
  d. lavish feast celebrated in the Pacific Northwest.
  e. wasteful ritual that was banned in the 1880s.

16. According to the passage, the gift-giving central to the potlatch can best be characterized as
  a. reciprocal.
  b. wasteful.
  c. selfless.
  d. spendthrift.
  e. commercialized.

Use the following passage to answer question 17.

Moscow has a history of chaotic periods of war that ended with the destruction of a once largely wooden city and the building of a new city on top of the rubble of the old. The result is a layered city, with each tier holding information about a part of Russia's past. In some areas of the city, archaeologists have reached the layer from 1147, the year of Moscow's founding. Among the findings from the various periods of Moscow's history are carved bones, metal tools, pottery, glass, jewelry, and crosses.

17. From the passage, the reader can infer that
   a. the people of Moscow are more interested in modernization than in preservation.
   b. the Soviet government destroyed many of the historic buildings in Russia.
   c. Moscow is the oldest large city in Russia, founded in 1147.
   d. Moscow has a history of invasions, with each new conqueror razing past structures.
   e. Moscow has endured many periods of uprising and revolution.

Use the following passage to answer question 18.

Beliefs are easily the most enduring and distinctive aspects of maritime culture. Common examples include beliefs about good and bad luck, signs for predicting the weather, interpretations of supernatural happenings, and remedies for sickness and injury. Commercial fishing is considered to be the most hazardous of all industrial occupations in the United States. Statistics show that fishermen are seven times more likely to die than workers in the next most dangerous occupation. Adhering to a system of beliefs most likely helps bring sense and order to a world in which natural disasters and misfortune are a part of daily life. Many fishermen also make a precarious living at best. Maritime beliefs contain the collective wisdom of generations and following these traditions may help fishermen catch more fish without taking unnecessary risks.

18. The purpose of the statistic in the passage is to
   a. qualify the statement that fishing is hazardous.
   b. prove that fishing is an undesirable occupation.
   c. illustrate the relative ease of other professions.
   d. quantify the hazardous nature of commercial fishing.
   e. demonstrate that fishermen need a system of beliefs.

Use the following poem by Alfred, Lord Tennyson to answer question 19.

The Eagle
He clasps the crag with crooked hands;
Close to the sun in lonely lands,
Ringed with the azure world he stands.

The wrinkled sea beneath him crawls;
He watches from his mountain walls,
And like a thunderbolt he falls.

19. Given the tone of the poem, and especially noting the last line, what is the eagle most likely doing in the poem?
   a. dying of old age
   b. hunting prey
   c. learning joyfully to fly
   d. keeping watch over a nest of young eagles
   e. battling another eagle

Use the following passage to answer questions 20 and 21.

Elizabeth Blackwell was the first woman to receive an M.D. degree since the Renaissance, graduating from Geneva Medical College, in New York State, in 1849. She supported women's medical education and helped many other women's careers. By establishing the New York Infirmary in 1857, she offered a practical solution to one of the problems facing women who were rejected from internships elsewhere but determined to expand their skills as physicians. She also published several important books on the issue of women in medicine, including *Address on the Medical Education of Women* in 1864 and *Medicine as a Profession for Women* in 1860.

In her book *Pioneer Work in Opening the Medical Profession to Women*, published in 1895, Dr. Blackwell wrote that she was initially repelled by the idea of studying medicine. She said she had "hated everything connected with the body, and could not bear the sight of a medical book. . . . My favorite studies were history and metaphysics, and the very thought of dwelling on the physical structure of the body and its various ailments filled me with disgust." Instead she went into teaching, then considered more suitable for a woman. She claimed that she turned to medicine after a close friend who was dying suggested she would have been spared her worst suffering if her physician had been a woman.

20. The passage is primarily concerned with
   a. the inevitable breaking down of social barriers for women.
   b. the effect of adversity in shaping a person's life.
   c. one woman's determination to open the field of medicine to females.
   d. one woman's desire to gain prestige.
   e. the quality of healthcare available in the 1800s.

21. The passage implies that Blackwell's attitude toward studying and practicing medicine changed from
   a. tenacious to wavering.
   b. uninterested to resolute.
   c. cynical to committed.
   d. idealized to realistic.
   e. theoretical to practical.

Use the following passage to answer question 22.

Jazz, from its early roots in slave spirituals and the marching bands of New Orleans, had developed into the predominant American musical style by the 1930s. In this era, jazz musicians played a lush, orchestrated style known as *swing*. Played in large ensembles, also called *big bands*, swing filled the dance halls and nightclubs. Jazz, once considered risqué, was made more accessible to the masses with the vibrant, swinging sounds of these big bands, whose musicians improvised from the melody to create original performances. Then came *bebop*. In the mid-1940s, jazz musicians strayed from the swing style and developed a more improvisational method of playing known as bebop. Jazz was transformed from popular music to an elite art form.

22. The swing style can be most accurately characterized as
   a. complex and inaccessible.
   b. appealing to an elite audience.
   c. lively and melodic.
   d. lacking in improvisation.
   e. played in small groups.

Use the following passage to answer question 23.

The youngest member of the Greenville High School track team can run a mile in 5.2 minutes. Sarah runs a mile in 4.9 minutes.

23. Based only on the information in the passage, which of the following must be true?
   a. A runner's speed is related to his or her age.
   b. Other members of the track team can run a mile faster than Sarah.
   c. Sarah is not the youngest member of the track team.
   d. Sarah is not a member of the Greenville High School track team.
   e. Sarah is the best runner on the team.

Use the following passage to answer questions 24 through 26.

Cuttlefish are intriguing little animals. Cuttlefish resemble rather large squid and are, like the octopus, members of the order of cephalopods. Although they are not considered the most highly evolved of the cephalopods, they are extremely intelligent. While observing them, it is hard to tell who is doing the observing, you or the cuttlefish, especially since the eye of the cuttlefish is very similar in structure to the human eye. Cuttlefish are also highly mobile and fast creatures. They come equipped with a small jet located just below the tentacles that can expel water to help them move. Ribbons of flexible fin on each side of the body allow cuttlefish to hover, move, stop, and start. By far their most intriguing characteristic is their ability to change their body color and pattern.

The cuttlefish is sometimes referred to as the "chameleon of the sea" because it can change its skin color and pattern instanta-neously. Masters of camouflage, cuttlefish can blend into any environment for protection, but they are also capable of the most imaginative displays of iridescent, brilliant color and intricate designs, which scientists believe they use to communicate with each other and for mating displays. However, judging from the riot of ornaments and hues cuttlefish produce, it is hard not to believe they paint themselves so beautifully just for the sheer joy of it. At the very least, cuttlefish conversation must be the most sparkling in all the sea.

24. Which of the following is correct according to the information given in the passage?
   a. Cuttlefish are a type of squid.
   b. Cuttlefish use jet propulsion as one form of locomotion.
   c. The cuttlefish does not have an exoskeleton.
   d. Cuttlefish are the most intelligent cephalopods.
   e. Cuttlefish always imitate the patterns and colors of their environment.

25. Which of the following best outlines the main topics addressed in the passage?
   a. I. explanation of why cuttlefish are intriguing
   II. communication skills of cuttlefish
   b. I. classification and difficulties of observing cuttlefish
   II. scientific explanation of modes of cuttlefish communication
   c. I. explanation of the cuttlefish's method of locomotion
   II. description of color displays in mating behavior
   d. I. comparison of cuttlefish with other cephalopods
   II. usefulness of the cuttlefish's ability to change color
   e. I. general classification and characteristics of cuttlefish
   II. uses and beauty of the cuttlefish's ability to change color

26. Which of the following best describes the purpose of the passage?
   a. to prove the intelligence of cuttlefish
   b. to explain the communication habits of cuttlefish
   c. to produce a fanciful description of the chameleon of the sea
   d. to persuade scuba divers of the interest in observing cuttlefish
   e. to describe the chameleon of the sea informatively and entertainingly

Use the following passage to answer question 27.

Public art fulfills several functions essential to the health of a city and its citizens. It educates about history and culture—of the artist, the neighborhood, the city, the nation. Public art is also a "place-making device" that instantly creates memorable, experiential landmarks, fashioning a unique identity for a public place, personalizing it and giving it a specific character. It stimulates the public, challenging viewers to interpret the art and arousing their emotions, and it promotes community by stimulating interaction among viewers. In serving these multiple and important functions, public art beautifies the area and regenerates both the place and the viewer.

27. Which sentence best sums up the main idea of the passage?
   a. Public art serves several important functions in the city.
   b. Public art is often in direct competition with private art.
   c. Public art should be created both by and for members of the community.
   d. In general, public art is more interesting than private art.
   e. Few people are aware of how much public art is around them.

Use the following passage from Jack London's The Cruise of the Snark *to answer questions 28 through 30.*

[N]ow to the particular physics of surf-riding. Get out on a flat board, six feet long, two feet wide, and roughly oval in shape. Lie down upon it like a small boy on a coaster and paddle with your hands out to deep water, where the waves begin to crest. Lie out there quietly on the board. Sea after sea breaks before, behind, and under and over you, and rushes in to shore, leaving you behind. When a wave crests, it gets steeper. Imagine yourself, on your board, on the face of that steep slope. If it stood still, you would slide down just as a boy slides down a hill on his coaster. "But," you object, "the wave doesn't stand still." Very true, but the water composing the wave stands still, and there you have the secret. If ever you start sliding down the face of that wave, you'll keep on sliding and you'll never reach the bottom. Please don't laugh. The face of that wave may be only six feet, yet you can slide down it a quarter of a mile, or half a mile, and not reach the bottom. For, see, since a wave is only a communicated agitation or impetus, and since the water that composes a wave is changing every instant, new water is rising into the wave as fast as the wave travels. You slide down this new water, and yet remain in your old position on the wave, sliding down the still newer water that is rising and forming the wave.

28. The author compares surfing to
   a. an ever-increasing hole forming in the water.
   b. a chemistry experiment gone wrong.
   c. a boy sledding down a hill on a coaster.
   d. a transformation of time and space.
   e. flying through the air like a bird.

29. As used in the passage, the word *impetus* most nearly means
  a. a moving force.
  b. a serious obstacle.
  c. a slight annoyance.
  d. a slight hindrance.
  e. an area of very warm water.

30. What is the secret referred to in the passage?
  a. why a good wave for surfing must be at least six feet tall
  b. A six-foot wave is between a quarter mile and a half mile in length.
  c. how a surfer can slide down a six-foot wave for a quarter of a mile
  d. The smarter surfers paddle out to the deep water to catch the best waves.
  e. The water that composes a wave remains with the wave until it reaches the shore.

Use the following passage to answer question 31.

Today's shopping mall has as its antecedents historical marketplaces, such as Greek agoras, European piazzas, and Asian bazaars. The purpose of these sites, as with the shopping mall, is both economic and social. People go not simply to buy and sell wares, but also to be seen, catch up on news, and be part of the human drama. Both marketplace and its descendant, the mall, might also contain restaurants, banks, theaters, and professional offices.

31. The statement that people went to marketplaces to *be part of the human drama* suggests that people
  a. prefer to shop anonymously.
  b. like to act on stage rather than shop.
  c. seem to be more emotional in groups.
  d. like to be in community, interacting with one another.
  e. prefer to be entertained rather than shop for necessities.

Use the following passage to answer question 32.

The Great Depression, which began during the presidency of Herbert Hoover, led to the election of President Franklin D. Roosevelt in 1932. Roosevelt introduced relief measures that would revive the economy and bring needed relief to Americans who were suffering the effects of the depression. In his first hundred days in office, Roosevelt and Congress passed major legislation that saved banks from closing and regained public confidence. These measures, called the New Deal, included the Agricultural Adjustment Act, which paid farmers to slow their production in order to stabilize food prices; the Federal Deposit Insurance Corporation, which insured bank deposits in case banks fail; and the Securities and Exchange Commission, which regulated the stock market. Although the New Deal offered relief, it did not end the depression. The economy sagged until the nation entered World War II. However, the New Deal changed the relationship between government and American citizens by expanding the role of the central government in regulating the economy and creating social assistance programs.

32. The content of the passage would most likely support which of the following statements?
  a. The New Deal policies were not radical enough in challenging capitalism.
  b. The economic policies of the New Deal brought about a complete business recovery.
  c. The Agricultural Adjustment Act paid farmers to produce surplus crops.
  d. The federal government became more involved in caring for needy members of society.
  e. The New Deal measures went too far in turning the country toward socialism.

Use the following passage to answer questions 33 through 35.

In the summer of 1919, the Cleveland Indians and the New York Yankees were two of the strongest teams in baseball's American League, but one team stood head and shoulders above the rest: the Chicago White Sox. The Chicago White Sox, called the White Stockings until 1902, were owned by an ex-ballplayer named Charles Comiskey. Between the years of 1900 and 1915, the White Sox had won the World Series only once, and Comiskey was determined to change that. In 1915, he purchased the contracts of three of the most promising stars in the league. Comiskey only had to wait two years for his plan to come to fruition; the 1917 White Sox, playing in a park named for their owner, won the World Series. Two years later they had the best record in all of baseball and were again on their way to the World Series.

Baseball players' salaries in that era were much different than the exorbitant paychecks of today's professional athletes. Often, ballplayers would have second careers in the off-season because of the mediocrity of their pay. To make matters worse, war-torn 1918 was such a horrible year for baseball attendance that many owners cut player salaries for the following season. However, it is said in all of baseball there was no owner as parsimonious as Charles Comiskey. In 1917 he reportedly promised every player on the White Sox a bonus if they won the American League Championship. After winning the championship, they returned to the clubhouse to receive their bonus—a bottle of inexpensive champagne. Unlike other owners, Comiskey also required the players to pay for the cleaning of their uniforms. The White Sox had the best record in baseball, but they were paid the least, were the most discontented, and wore the dirtiest uniforms.

33. In the fourth sentence of the second paragraph, the word *parsimonious* most nearly means
  a. generous.
  b. stingy.
  c. powerful.
  d. friendly.
  e. jovial.

34. According to facts from the passage, what was the name of the White Sox's ballpark?
  a. Chicago Park
  b. Comiskey Park
  c. Sullivan Stadium
  d. White Sox Park
  e. Sox Field

35. According to the passage, how many World Series did the White Sox win between 1900 and 1919?
  a. none
  b. one
  c. two
  d. three
  e. four

Use the following passage from Charlotte Brontë's Jane Eyre *to answer questions 36 through 38.*

I went to my window, opened it, and looked out. There were the two wings of the building; there was the garden; there were the skirts of Lowood; there was the hilly horizon. My eye passed all other objects to rest on those most remote, the blue peaks: it was those I longed to surmount; all within their boundary of rock and heath seemed prison-ground, exile limits. I traced the white road winding round the base of one mountain, and vanishing in a gorge between two: how I longed to follow it further! I recalled the time when I had traveled that very road in a coach; I remembered descending that hill at twilight: an age seemed to have elapsed since the day which brought me first to Lowood, and I had never quitted it since. My vacations had all been spent at school: Mrs. Reed had never sent for me to Gateshead; neither she nor any of her family had ever been to visit me. I had had no communication by letter or message with the outer world: school-rules, school-duties, school-habits and notions, and voices, and faces, and phrases, and costumes, and preferences, and antipathies: such was what I knew of existence. And now I felt that it was not enough: I tired of the routine of eight years in one afternoon. I desired liberty; for liberty I gasped; for liberty I uttered a prayer; it seemed scattered on the wind then faintly blowing. I abandoned it and framed a humbler supplication; for change, stimulus: that petition, too, seemed swept off into vague space: "Then," I cried, half desperate, "grant me at least a new servitude!"

36. It can be inferred from the passage that life at Lowood was
   a. very unconventional and modern.
   b. very structured and isolated.
   c. harsh and demeaning.
   d. liberal and carefree.
   e. urban and sophisticated.

37. The passage suggests that the narrator
   a. will soon return to Lowood.
   b. was sent to Lowood by mistake.
   c. is entirely dependent on the people at Lowood.
   d. has run away from Lowood before.
   e. is naturally curious and rebellious.

38. In the final lines of the passage, the narrator reduces her petition to simply *a new servitude* because she
   a. doesn't believe in prayer.
   b. is not in a free country.
   c. has been offered a position as a servant.
   d. knows so little of the real world.
   e. has been treated like a slave at Lowood.

Use the following passage to answer questions 39 and 40.

In the 1980s, I was just beginning as an internist, working in a private practice. Then in my late twenties, I felt pity for my patients who talked to me about a surgical fix for their wrinkles or other signs of aging. I felt that if they had a developed sense of self-esteem, they would not feel the need to surgically alter their appearance. I also felt a certain degree of envy for my cosmetic-surgeon colleagues, some of whom worked across the hall. To my "green" eye, they looked like slick salespeople reaping large financial rewards from others' insecurity and vanity. It was difficult for me to reconcile the fact that patients were willing to fork over thousands of dollars for cosmetic fixes, while primary care physicians struggled to keep their practices financially viable.

Since that time, my attitude has changed. Although cosmetic surgery sometimes produces negative outcomes—the media often highlights surgery disasters—for the most part, the health risk for cosmetic procedures is low and patient satisfaction is high. Often, people who have been hobbled by poor body image all of their lives walk away from cosmetic surgery with confidence and the motivation to lead healthier lives. In addition, reconstructive surgery for burn and accident victims or to those disfigured from disease restores self-esteem and well-being in a way that other therapies cannot. I believe it is time for members of the medical community to examine the benefits and results of cosmetic surgery without prejudice or jealousy.

39. The argument in the passage would be most effectively strengthened by which of the following?
   a. information about making plastic surgery more affordable
   b. anecdotes about incompetent plastic surgeons
   c. facts to support the author's claim that health risks are low for cosmetic procedures
   d. a description of the author's personal experience with patients
   e. a description of the psychological benefits of improved body image

40. Which audience is the author most likely addressing?
   a. burn or accident victims
   b. women with poor body image
   c. plastic surgeons
   d. healthcare providers
   e. baby boomers

Skills Test in Mathematics

Directions: Choose the best answer to each of the following questions.

Use the following figure to answer question 1.

Note: Figure not drawn to scale.

1. Pierre's usual route between Center City and Forest Grove is 85 miles long, as shown in the diagram above. Because of construction, he must now take a detour through Redmont first before driving the 75 miles between Redmont and Forest Grove. How much longer is the detoured route than his regular route between Center City and Forest Grove?
   a. 10 miles
   b. 30 miles
   c. 40 miles
   d. 75 miles
   e. 115 miles

Use the following information to answer question 2.

Cost of Car Rental by Mileage

2. The graph shows the cost of renting a car according to the number of miles the car is driven. Which equation represents the equation of the line that is determined by the data in the scatter plot?
- **a.** $y = 2x + 10$
- **b.** $y = \frac{1}{2}x + 10$
- **c.** $y = 10x + 15$
- **d.** $y = 5x + 10$
- **e.** $y = -5x + 15$

Use the following information to answer questions 3 and 4.

The cost of tickets to the school play is $7.50 for adults and $5 for children ages 12 and under. On Saturday and Sunday afternoon, there is a special matinee price: $5.50 for adults and $3 for children ages 12 and under. Special group discounts are available for groups of 30 or more people.

3. Which of the following can be determined from the information given in the passage?
- **a.** how much it will cost a family of four to buy tickets to the school play on Saturday afternoon
- **b.** the difference between the cost of two tickets to the school play on Tuesday night and the cost of one ticket on Sunday afternoon
- **c.** how much tickets to the school play will cost each person if he or she is part of a group of 40 people
- **d.** the difference between the cost of a ticket to the school play for an adult on Friday night and a ticket to the school play for a 13-year-old on Saturday afternoon
- **e.** the total amount of money saved by a group of 35

4. Using the passage, how can you find the difference in price between a ticket to the school play for an adult and a ticket for a child under the age of 12 if they are attending the show on Saturday afternoon?
- **a.** subtract $3.00 from $7.50
- **b.** subtract $3.00 from $5.50
- **c.** subtract $5.00 from $7.50
- **d.** subtract $7.50 from $5.50
- **e.** add $5.50 and $3.00 and divide by 2

5. There were 504 candies in a jar. Between 8 o'clock and 9 o'clock, $\frac{1}{8}$ of the candies were given out. Between 9 o'clock and 10 o'clock, $\frac{2}{9}$ of the remaining candies were handed out. If in the following hour, $\frac{1}{7}$ of the remaining candies are distributed, how many candies will be left?
- **a.** 441
- **b.** 343
- **c.** 294
- **d.** 188
- **e.** 96

6. Joe has exactly 720 hours until his vacation begins. How many days are there before his vacation begins?
   a. 30
   b. 60
   c. 72
   d. 144
   e. 17,280

7. Which of the following is equivalent to $3 \times 5 + 3 \times 8$?
   a. $3 + 5 \times 3 + 8$
   b. $3(5 \times 8)$
   c. $(3 \times 5) + 8$
   d. $3(5 + 8)$
   e. $(3 \times 5) \times (3 \times 8)$

Use the following table to answer question 8.

Class Time Schedule

Period	Start Time	End Time
1	7:55	8:35
2	8:39	9:19
3		10:03
4	10:07	10:47
5	10:51	11:31
6	11:35	12:15
7	12:19	12:59
8	1:03	
9	1:47	2:27

8. According to the table, what is the starting time of period 3 and the ending time of period 8, respectively?
   a. 9:24, 1:43
   b. 9:23, 1:44
   c. 9:29, 1:59
   d. 9:23, 1:43
   e. 9:24, 1:44

Use the following information to answer question 9.

A grocery store has a total of 55 different varieties of candy bars. Twelve are made of milk chocolate, 5 are made of white chocolate, and 15 are made of dark chocolate. The candy bars are made by three different companies: Hometown Confections, Cocoa Inc., and Taste of Chocolate.

9. Which of the following facts can be determined from the information given?
   a. the number of candy bars made by Hometown Confections
   b. the ratio of milk chocolate candy bars to white chocolate candy bars
   c. the number of toffee candy bars
   d. the cost of a milk chocolate candy bar made by Cocoa Inc.
   e. the ratio of milk chocolate peanut butter candy bars to dark chocolate candy bars with nuts

Use the following information to answer questions 10 and 11.

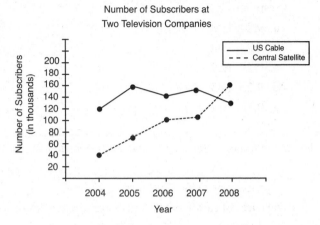

Number of Subscribers at
Two Television Companies

10. Approximately what percentage of the total subscribers to both services subscribed to US Cable in 2006?

a. 33%

b. 40%

c. 58%

d. 71%

e. 85%

11. Which of the following most accurately depicts the information in the graph?

a.

b.

c.

d.

e.

12. Out of 100 students polled at a local university, 80 said they would favor being offered a course in web page development. If there are 30,000 students enrolled at this university, how many would you expect to favor being offered such a course?
a. 2,400
b. 6,000
c. 16,000
d. 22,000
e. 24,000

13. Jacob pays a $19 flat fee for his cellular phone service each month, which includes the first 120 minutes of airtime he uses. He is then charged $0.32 per minute for each minute after that. If x represents the total airtime he uses each month, and he always uses more than 120 minutes of airtime each month, which of the following expressions can be used to calculate his monthly cellular phone bill?
a. $19 + 0.32x$
b. $19x + 0.32$
c. $19(x - 120) + 0.32x$
d. $19 + 0.32(x - 120)$
e. $19x + 0.32(x - 120)$

14. What is 56.73647 rounded to the nearest hundredth?
a. 57
b. 56.7
c. 56.73
d. 56.74
e. 56.736

Use the following graph to answer question 15.

15. Which equation is best represented by the graph?
a. $y = -x^2 + 2x + 4$
b. $y = -x^2 + 2x - 4$
c. $y = x^2 + 2x + 4$
d. $y = x^2 + 2x - 4$
e. $y = -x^2 - 2x - 4$

16. A factory operates 20 machines that make granola bars. Each machine can make between 80 and 100 granola bars per minute. Which of the following could be the number of granola bars produced per hour if all 20 machines are working at the same time?
a. 1,800
b. 5,000
c. 18,000
d. 100,000
e. 125,000

17. Ridgefield Stadium has a total of 36,042 seats. At the first home game of the year, every seat was sold out, and 16,534 of the people in attendance were male. Approximately how many more women attended this game than men?
   a. 1,500
   b. 2,000
   c. 3,000
   d. 4,000
   e. 4,500

18. If a, b, and c represent nonzero real numbers, which of the following statements are equivalent?
   I. $a + (b + c)$
   II. $(a + b) + (a + c)$
   III. $(a + b) + c$
   a. I and II
   b. I and III
   c. II and III
   d. I, II, and III
   e. None of the statements is equivalent.

19. An aquarium has a base length of 12 inches and a width of 5 inches. If the aquarium is 10 inches tall, what is the total volume?
   a. 480 cubic inches
   b. 540 cubic inches
   c. 600 cubic inches
   d. 720 cubic inches
   e. 1,200 cubic inches

Use the following chart to answer questions 20 and 21.

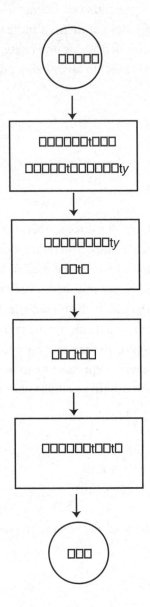

20. If $y = 4$, what is the result when steps 3 and 4 are reversed?
   a. 10
   b. 12
   c. 13
   d. 17
   e. 22

21. According to the flow chart on the preceding page, no matter what whole number is inputted, the resulting number will always be
   a. odd.
   b. even.
   c. prime.
   d. a multiple of 6.
   e. an integer.

Use the following chart to answer question 22.

Enrollment by Division

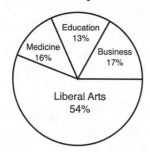

22. The pie chart shows the semester enrollment for four different divisions of a university. Which of the following combinations make up 70% of the total enrollment?
   a. Education and Business
   b. Education and Liberal Arts
   c. Business and Liberal Arts
   d. Business and Medicine
   e. Liberal Arts and Medicine

23. Mrs. Savoie noted the number of absences from her psychology class for the past six days. There were 11, 4, 0, 5, 4, and 6 students absent those six days, respectively. On those particular days, what was the average number of students absent?
   a. 4
   b. 5
   c. 6
   d. 7
   e. 8

24. Jacqueline was $\frac{1}{3}$ as young as her grandmother 15 years ago. If the sum of their ages is now 110, how old is Jacqueline's grandmother?
   a. 80
   b. 75
   c. 65
   d. 60
   e. 50

25. Which of the following fractions is between $\frac{1}{3}$ and $\frac{1}{4}$?
   a. $\frac{1}{2}$
   b. $\frac{1}{5}$
   c. $\frac{2}{3}$
   d. $\frac{2}{5}$
   e. $\frac{2}{7}$

Use the following graph to answer question 26.

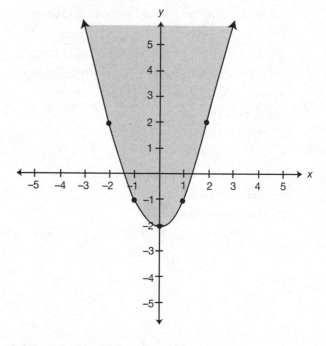

26. Which of the following inequalities is represented by the preceding graph?
   a. $y \geq x^2 + 2$
   b. $y \leq x^2 - 2$
   c. $y \geq x^2 + 2x$
   d. $y \geq x^2 - 2$
   e. $y \leq x^2 + 2$

27. If a function is defined as $f(x) = 3x^2 - \frac{1}{2}x + 7$, what is $f(\frac{1}{2})$?

a. $\frac{15}{2}$

b. $-\frac{15}{2}$

c. 8

d. $\frac{17}{2}$

e. $-\frac{17}{2}$

28. Given the equation $y = 5 + 4x$, what is the value of y when $x = 3$?

a. 6

b. 9

c. 12

d. 17

e. 20

29. At the grocery store, if Lucinda purchases a total of $30 or less, she will pay with cash. If Lucinda spends an amount between $30 and $70, she will pay with a check. If Lucinda spends $70 or more, she will use a credit card. If Lucinda recently paid for a grocery bill using a check, which of the following statements could be true?

a. The bill was $20.

b. The bill was $80.

c. If the bill was $20 more, she would have paid with cash.

d. The bill was at least $70.

e. The bill was more than $25.

Use the following figure to answer question 30.

30. If the figure is a tile in the shape of a regular decagon with a center at Q, what is the measure of the indicated angle?

a. 36°

b. 45°

c. 80°

d. 90°

e. 108°

31. Solve for x in the following equation:

$2x - 3(x - 1) = -12$

a. 11

b. 15

c. −11

d. 9

e. −15

Use the following figure to answer question 32.

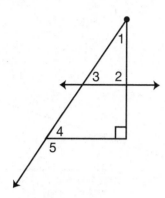

32. If angle 1 is 30°, and angle 2 is a right angle, what is the measure of angle 5?
a. 30°
b. 60°
c. 120°
d. 150°
e. 180°

33. A circle drawn on a gymnasium floor for a basketball court has an area of 78.5 square feet. What is the length of the diameter of this circle? Use $\pi = 3.14$.
a. 25 feet
b. 15 feet
c. 12.5 feet
d. 10 feet
e. 5 feet

34. A certain county has an annual spending budget of about $490,000. The largest area of allocation is regional transportation, in which the county spends about $98,000 per year. Which fraction most accurately portrays the portion of spending on regional transportation with respect to the total annual budget of the county?
a. $\frac{1}{5}$
b. $\frac{1}{4}$
c. $\frac{2}{9}$
d. $\frac{3}{4}$
e. $\frac{4}{5}$

35. Which of the following is NOT equivalent to the others?
a. $3(21 + 55) - 10$
b. $3(55 + 21) - 10$
c. $3 \times 55 + 3 \times 21 - 10$
d. $(55 + 21) \times 3 - 10$
e. $10 - 3(21 + 55)$

36. Thirty percent of the students at a middle school are involved in the vocal and instrumental music programs. If 15% of the musicians are in the choir, what percentage of the whole school is in the choir?
a. 4.5%
b. 9.0%
c. 15%
d. 30%
e. 45%

Use the following table to answer question 37.

Use the following graph to answer question 39.

x	y
10	8
8	8.5
6	9
4	9.5
2	10

37. According to the information in the table, which of the following statements is true?

a. As x increases by $\frac{1}{2}$, y decreases by 2.

b. As x decreases by 2, y decreases by $\frac{1}{2}$.

c. As x increases by 1, y decreases by 2.

d. As x decreases by 2, y increases by $\frac{1}{2}$.

e. As x increases by 2, y decreases by $\frac{1}{2}$.

38. While competing in a swim meet, Jose finished three one-hundredths of a second ahead of his opponent. Which of the following is equivalent to this value?

a. 3.0

b. 0.003

c. 0.0003

d. 0.03

e. 0.3

39. According to the graph, what is the approximate speed of the car in miles per hour?

a. 10 miles per hour

b. 20 miles per hour

c. 33 miles per hour

d. 40 miles per hour

e. 50 miles per hour

Use the following figure to answer question 40.

Note: Figures are NOT drawn to scale.

40. Which of the following is proportional to the figure above?

a.

b.

c.

d.

e.

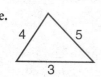

Skills Test in Writing— Section 1, Part A

Directions: Choose the letter for the underlined portion that contains a grammatical error. If there is no error in the sentence, choose **e**.

1. Elizabeth Blackwell, the first woman to be
                   a   **b**
   accepted into a medical school, she graduated
                              c
   from Geneva Medical College in 1849. No error
    d   **e**

2. The freshwater source of the Hudson River can
                                a
   be found in the Adirondack Mountains, at a
                         b
   small lake on Mount Marcy known as Lake
          c   **d**
   Tear of the Clouds. No error
                e

3. Considering the principal believed in school
    a   **b**
   uniforms, so he implemented a new rule in the
    c
   high school. No error
    d   **e**

4. Soon after Alison stopped to get some
                    a
   coffee; she realized that she had missed the
        b   **c**   **d**
   ferry. No error
         e

5. <u>Ronald</u> called <u>to say that</u> our new car <u>had</u>
   a   b   c

arrived and <u>asking</u> if we would pick it up by
           d

6:30. <u>No error</u>
          e

6. <u>Because</u> Nick <u>was</u> a confident <u>test taker, he</u>
    a   b   c

failed <u>horribly</u> on the math final. <u>No error</u>
      d   e

7. Albert Einstein <u>was</u> a genius in the world of
               a

science <u>and who</u> influenced the artists of his
  b   c

generation <u>as well</u>. <u>No error</u>
          d   e

8. We all <u>agreed</u> that the quick action of the
        a

security <u>officers'</u> thwarted the robbery attempt
        b

<u>yesterday</u> at the <u>bank</u>. <u>No error</u>
  c   d   e

9. In this travel guide, <u>you'll discover</u> great travel
                   a

deals, vacation hot spots, <u>and</u> unique exotic
                b

destinations <u>for even</u> the <u>more</u> experienced
         c   d

world travelers. <u>No error</u>
           e

10. The lifeguard staff at the <u>public</u> beach <u>deserve</u>
                  a   b

recognition for <u>winning</u> the annual
             c

"safest waters" award. <u>No error</u>
  d   e

11. <u>Any</u> player <u>who arrives</u> late to the soccer tryout
    a   b

will <u>give the coach</u> a bad first impression, <u>but</u>
      c   d

probably be cut from the team. <u>No error</u>
                      e

12. Pressed <u>sailors</u> in the time of <u>Lord Nelson</u> lived
       a   b

in cramped quarters, fought battles <u>on the high</u>
                        c

seas, <u>and learn to</u> understand the blessings of a
      d

mariner's life. <u>No error</u>
           e

13. All <u>students</u> with an excellent GPA <u>are eligible</u>
    a   b

for a full <u>scholarship</u>, including tuition, housing,
          c

meals, <u>and money</u> for books. <u>No error</u>
       d   e

14. The <u>person who</u> sold me the laptop, owns the
      a   b

electronics store on Melrose <u>A</u>venue and knows
                      c

all <u>there is</u> to know about computers. <u>No error</u>
    d   e

15. The <u>aorta</u> is the largest artery in the
       a

<u>human body;</u> it receives <u>oxygen-rich</u> blood
   b   c

from the <u>heart and</u> carries it to the rest of the
         d

body. <u>No error</u>
     e

16. Ernest Hemingway <u>and fellow</u> writer F. Scott
              a

Fitzgerald met as <u>expatriates</u> in Paris during
           b

the 1920s; <u>he</u> was the first of the two to move
        c

<u>there,</u> in 1921. <u>No error</u>
  d   e

17. <u>During</u> the summer season, boat owners should
  a

replace <u>their</u> oil filters at least once <u>a month;</u> a
     b   c

dirty filter <u>reduce</u> engine efficiency. <u>No error</u>
       d   e

18. In areas <u>or regions</u> of the world <u>that don't</u> get
      a   b

much <u>rain,</u> water-storing plants <u>dominate</u> the
    c   d

landscape. <u>No error</u>
     e

19. Our company <u>CEO</u> truly believes that money
        a

equals <u>happiness;</u> he's not <u>ashamed with himself</u>
     b   c

to admit <u>that</u> his first love is cash. <u>No error</u>
     d   e

20. <u>John Glenn</u>—the first American to orbit the
  a

<u>earth</u>—returned to space in <u>1998,</u> 36 years
  b   c

<u>after his first</u> historic space flight. <u>No error</u>
  d   e

21. The archaeologists excavating the ruins <u>were</u>
                      a

surprised to have <u>uncovered:</u> ancient <u>roads,</u>
         b   c

primitive <u>plumbing,</u> and personal items.
     d

<u>No error</u>
 e

Skills Test in Writing— Section 1, Part B

Directions: Choose the best replacement for the underlined portion of the sentence. If no revision is necessary, choose **a**, which always repeats the original phrasing.

22. <u>Along with your membership to our golf club goes</u> three free personal golf lessons.
    a. Along with your membership to our golf club goes
    b. Along with your membership to our golf club go
    c. With your membership to our golf club there is
    d. In addition to your membership to our golf club there's
    e. Added to your membership to our golf club,

23. When the doorbell <u>rung, Alvaro had been feeding</u> his fish.
    a. rung, Alvaro had been feeding
    b. rung, Alvaro was feeding
    c. rang, Alvaro was feeding
    d. had rung, Alvaro was feeding
    e. rang, Alvaro had feeded

24. There are a number of skeptics who don't believe in the <u>effects of global warming on the earths climate.</u>
    a. effects of global warming on the earths climate.
    b. effects' of global warming on the earth's climate.
    c. effect's of global warming on the earths climate.
    d. effect's of global warming on the earths' climate.
    e. effects of global warming on the earth's climate.

25. Vitellius "the Glutton" <u>was the greediest of all of the Roman emperors.</u>
    a. was the greediest of all of the Roman emperors.
    b. was the greedliest of all of the Roman emperors.
    c. was the greedier of all of the Roman emperors.
    d. was the most greedful of all of the Roman emperors.
    e. was the greedfullest of all of the Roman emperors.

26. <u>There wasn't never a comedian that was funnier.</u>
    a. There wasn't never a comedian that was funnier.
    b. There was never a comedian more funnier.
    c. Never was there a comedian more funnier.
    d. There never was a more funnier comedian.
    e. There never was a funnier comedian.

27. <u>The Doctor in Spokane can speak Italian, French, and Urdu.</u>
    a. The Doctor in Spokane can speak Italian, French, and Urdu.
    b. The doctor in spokane can speak italian, french, and urdu.
    c. The doctor in Spokane can speak Italian, French, and Urdu.
    d. The doctor in Spokane can speak italian, french, and urdu!
    e. The Doctor in spokane can speak Italian, French, and Urdu.

28. <u>I look forward to speaking with you and having</u> the opportunity to explain my views on the subject.
   a. I look forward to speaking with you and having
   b. I will look forward to our speaking and having
   c. As I look forward to our speaking and to have
   d. I look forward to speaking with you and have
   e. Looking forward to our speaking and hoping to have

29. Of the two cars, the <u>newest model is safest than the oldest one.</u>
   a. the newest model is safest than the oldest one.
   b. the newest model is safest than the older one.
   c. the newest model is more safe than the oldest one.
   d. the newer model is safer than the older one.
   e. the newer model is more safer than the older one.

30. The lacrosse team scored <u>less goals today than they did</u> last Monday.
   a. less goals today than they did
   b. today less goals than were scored
   c. fewer goals today then on
   d. fewer goals today than they did
   e. a lesser number of goals today then they did

31. <u>When twins have the same DNA, it is said to be identical.</u>
   a. When twins have the same DNA, it is said to be identical.
   b. When twins has the same DNA, it is said to be identical.
   c. Twins with the same DNA is said to be identical.
   d. They are identical when the said twins has the same DNA.
   e. When twins have the same DNA, they are said to be identical.

32. Athletic ability depends <u>not only on hand-eye coordination, but also</u> on mental acuity and physical fitness.
   a. not only on hand-eye coordination, but also
   b. not simply on hand-eye coordination, then too
   c. only just not on hand-eye coordination, also
   d. on hand-eye coordination alone, but also
   e. not only on hand-eye coordination, however, it also depends

33. <u>It snowed; so I tried to shovel the driveway.</u>
   a. It snowed; so I tried to shovel the driveway.
   b. It snowed, so I tried to shovel the driveway.
   c. It snowed, I tried to shovel the driveway.
   d. It's snowing, I tried to shovel the driveway.
   e. It will snow, so I tried to shovel the driveway.

34. <u>The Mississippi River, it originates in Minnesota,</u> empties into the Gulf of Mexico.

   a. The Mississippi River, it originates in Minnesota,

   b. The Mississippi River, that originates in Minnesota,

   c. The Mississippi River, who originates in Minnesota,

   d. The Mississippi River, which originates in Minnesota,

   e. The Mississippi River, whose originates in Minnesota,

35. The second layer of human skin is known as the <u>dermis, which is located</u> directly below the epidermis.

   a. dermis, which is located

   b. dermis, and which is located

   c. dermis but located

   d. dermis it is located

   e. that its location is

36. My favorite subjects <u>are gym and calculus, my second semester electives are Italian and physics.</u>

   a. are gym and calculus, my second semester electives are Italian and physics.

   b. are gym, and calculus; my second semester electives are Italian, and physics.

   c. are gym and calculus; my second semester electives are Italian and physics.

   d. are gym and calculus; my second semester electives are italian and physics.

   e. are gym, and calculus, my second semester electives are Italian, and physics.

37. <u>Because the economy is improving,</u> there are still many people who are unemployed.

   a. Because the economy is improving,

   b. Because the economy was improving,

   c. The economy is improving,

   d. Although the economy is improving,

   e. Although the economy is improving;

38. Nobody on the team <u>skates more graceful than me.</u>

   a. skates more graceful than me.

   b. skates more gracefully than I do.

   c. skates gracefuller than I do.

   d. skates more graceful than I do.

   e. skates more gracefully than me.

Skills Test in Writing— Section 2, Essay Writing

Carefully read the essay topic that follows. Plan and write an essay that addresses all points in the topic. Make sure that your essay is well organized and that you support your central argument with concrete examples. Allow 30 minutes for your essay.

There are more vegetarians in this country than ever before. Should school and workplace cafeterias accommodate these people by offering vegetarian selections? Use specific reasons and examples as support for your argument.

PRAXIS I
PRACTICE EXAM 2

CHAPTER SUMMARY

This is the last practice exam based on the three elements of the Praxis I, the Pre-Professional Skills Tests (PPSTs) of Reading, Mathematics, and Writing. This exam gives you another chance to master your test-taking skills and get ready for your exam.

Like the PPST Diagnostic Pretest and the previous practice exam in Chapter 7, this practice exam is made up of three tests: a Reading test (multiple-choice questions), a Mathematics test (multiple-choice questions), and a Writing test (multiple-choice questions and an essay).

Once again, you should pretend you are taking a real exam. Work in a quiet place, away from interruptions. Use a timer or stopwatch and allow yourself an hour for the Reading test, an hour for the Mathematics test, 30 minutes for Section 1 of the Writing test, and 30 minutes for Section 2 of the Writing test (your essay).

After the exam, study the answer explanations to learn about why you missed certain questions. Then, use the scoring section at the end of the exam to see how you did overall.

SKILLS TEST IN READING

1. ⓐ ⓑ ⓒ ⓓ ⓔ
2. ⓐ ⓑ ⓒ ⓓ ⓔ
3. ⓐ ⓑ ⓒ ⓓ ⓔ
4. ⓐ ⓑ ⓒ ⓓ ⓔ
5. ⓐ ⓑ ⓒ ⓓ ⓔ
6. ⓐ ⓑ ⓒ ⓓ ⓔ
7. ⓐ ⓑ ⓒ ⓓ ⓔ
8. ⓐ ⓑ ⓒ ⓓ ⓔ
9. ⓐ ⓑ ⓒ ⓓ ⓔ
10. ⓐ ⓑ ⓒ ⓓ ⓔ
11. ⓐ ⓑ ⓒ ⓓ ⓔ
12. ⓐ ⓑ ⓒ ⓓ ⓔ
13. ⓐ ⓑ ⓒ ⓓ ⓔ
14. ⓐ ⓑ ⓒ ⓓ ⓔ
15. ⓐ ⓑ ⓒ ⓓ ⓔ
16. ⓐ ⓑ ⓒ ⓓ ⓔ
17. ⓐ ⓑ ⓒ ⓓ ⓔ
18. ⓐ ⓑ ⓒ ⓓ ⓔ
19. ⓐ ⓑ ⓒ ⓓ ⓔ
20. ⓐ ⓑ ⓒ ⓓ ⓔ
21. ⓐ ⓑ ⓒ ⓓ ⓔ
22. ⓐ ⓑ ⓒ ⓓ ⓔ
23. ⓐ ⓑ ⓒ ⓓ ⓔ
24. ⓐ ⓑ ⓒ ⓓ ⓔ
25. ⓐ ⓑ ⓒ ⓓ ⓔ
26. ⓐ ⓑ ⓒ ⓓ ⓔ
27. ⓐ ⓑ ⓒ ⓓ ⓔ
28. ⓐ ⓑ ⓒ ⓓ ⓔ
29. ⓐ ⓑ ⓒ ⓓ ⓔ
30. ⓐ ⓑ ⓒ ⓓ ⓔ
31. ⓐ ⓑ ⓒ ⓓ ⓔ
32. ⓐ ⓑ ⓒ ⓓ ⓔ
33. ⓐ ⓑ ⓒ ⓓ ⓔ
34. ⓐ ⓑ ⓒ ⓓ ⓔ
35. ⓐ ⓑ ⓒ ⓓ ⓔ
36. ⓐ ⓑ ⓒ ⓓ ⓔ
37. ⓐ ⓑ ⓒ ⓓ ⓔ
38. ⓐ ⓑ ⓒ ⓓ ⓔ
39. ⓐ ⓑ ⓒ ⓓ ⓔ
40. ⓐ ⓑ ⓒ ⓓ ⓔ

SKILLS TEST IN MATHEMATICS

1. ⓐ ⓑ ⓒ ⓓ ⓔ
2. ⓐ ⓑ ⓒ ⓓ ⓔ
3. ⓐ ⓑ ⓒ ⓓ ⓔ
4. ⓐ ⓑ ⓒ ⓓ ⓔ
5. ⓐ ⓑ ⓒ ⓓ ⓔ
6. ⓐ ⓑ ⓒ ⓓ ⓔ
7. ⓐ ⓑ ⓒ ⓓ ⓔ
8. ⓐ ⓑ ⓒ ⓓ ⓔ
9. ⓐ ⓑ ⓒ ⓓ ⓔ
10. ⓐ ⓑ ⓒ ⓓ ⓔ
11. ⓐ ⓑ ⓒ ⓓ ⓔ
12. ⓐ ⓑ ⓒ ⓓ ⓔ
13. ⓐ ⓑ ⓒ ⓓ ⓔ
14. ⓐ ⓑ ⓒ ⓓ ⓔ
15. ⓐ ⓑ ⓒ ⓓ ⓔ
16. ⓐ ⓑ ⓒ ⓓ ⓔ
17. ⓐ ⓑ ⓒ ⓓ ⓔ
18. ⓐ ⓑ ⓒ ⓓ ⓔ
19. ⓐ ⓑ ⓒ ⓓ ⓔ
20. ⓐ ⓑ ⓒ ⓓ ⓔ
21. ⓐ ⓑ ⓒ ⓓ ⓔ
22. ⓐ ⓑ ⓒ ⓓ ⓔ
23. ⓐ ⓑ ⓒ ⓓ ⓔ
24. ⓐ ⓑ ⓒ ⓓ ⓔ
25. ⓐ ⓑ ⓒ ⓓ ⓔ
26. ⓐ ⓑ ⓒ ⓓ ⓔ
27. ⓐ ⓑ ⓒ ⓓ ⓔ
28. ⓐ ⓑ ⓒ ⓓ ⓔ
29. ⓐ ⓑ ⓒ ⓓ ⓔ
30. ⓐ ⓑ ⓒ ⓓ ⓔ
31. ⓐ ⓑ ⓒ ⓓ ⓔ
32. ⓐ ⓑ ⓒ ⓓ ⓔ
33. ⓐ ⓑ ⓒ ⓓ ⓔ
34. ⓐ ⓑ ⓒ ⓓ ⓔ
35. ⓐ ⓑ ⓒ ⓓ ⓔ
36. ⓐ ⓑ ⓒ ⓓ ⓔ
37. ⓐ ⓑ ⓒ ⓓ ⓔ
38. ⓐ ⓑ ⓒ ⓓ ⓔ
39. ⓐ ⓑ ⓒ ⓓ ⓔ
40. ⓐ ⓑ ⓒ ⓓ ⓔ

SKILLS TEST IN WRITING, SECTION 1

1. ⓐ ⓑ ⓒ ⓓ ⓔ
2. ⓐ ⓑ ⓒ ⓓ ⓔ
3. ⓐ ⓑ ⓒ ⓓ ⓔ
4. ⓐ ⓑ ⓒ ⓓ ⓔ
5. ⓐ ⓑ ⓒ ⓓ ⓔ
6. ⓐ ⓑ ⓒ ⓓ ⓔ
7. ⓐ ⓑ ⓒ ⓓ ⓔ
8. ⓐ ⓑ ⓒ ⓓ ⓔ
9. ⓐ ⓑ ⓒ ⓓ ⓒ
10. ⓐ ⓑ ⓒ ⓓ ⓔ
11. ⓐ ⓑ ⓒ ⓓ ⓔ
12. ⓐ ⓑ ⓒ ⓓ ⓔ
13. ⓐ ⓑ ⓒ ⓓ ⓔ
14. ⓐ ⓑ ⓒ ⓓ ⓔ
15. ⓐ ⓑ ⓒ ⓓ ⓔ
16. ⓐ ⓑ ⓒ ⓓ ⓔ
17. ⓐ ⓑ ⓒ ⓓ ⓔ
18. ⓐ ⓑ ⓒ ⓓ ⓔ
19. ⓐ ⓑ ⓒ ⓓ ⓔ
20. ⓐ ⓑ ⓒ ⓓ ⓔ
21. ⓐ ⓑ ⓒ ⓓ ⓔ
22. ⓐ ⓑ ⓒ ⓓ ⓔ
23. ⓐ ⓑ ⓒ ⓓ ⓔ
24. ⓐ ⓑ ⓒ ⓓ ⓔ
25. ⓐ ⓑ ⓒ ⓓ ⓔ
26. ⓐ ⓑ ⓒ ⓓ ⓔ
27. ⓐ ⓑ ⓒ ⓓ ⓔ
28. ⓐ ⓑ ⓒ ⓓ ⓔ
29. ⓐ ⓑ ⓒ ⓓ ⓔ
30. ⓐ ⓑ ⓒ ⓓ ⓔ
31. ⓐ ⓑ ⓒ ⓓ ⓔ
32. ⓐ ⓑ ⓒ ⓓ ⓔ
33. ⓐ ⓑ ⓒ ⓓ ⓔ
34. ⓐ ⓑ ⓒ ⓓ ⓔ
35. ⓐ ⓑ ⓒ ⓓ ⓔ
36. ⓐ ⓑ ⓒ ⓓ ⓔ
37. ⓐ ⓑ ⓒ ⓓ ⓔ
38. ⓐ ⓑ ⓒ ⓓ ⓔ

Skills Test in Reading

Directions: Read the following passages and answer the questions that follow.

Use the following passage to answer questions 1 and 2.

In 1899, Czar Nicholas II of Russia invited the nations of the world to a conference at The Hague. This conference—and a follow-up organized by Theodore Roosevelt in 1907—ushered in a period of vigorous growth in international law. This growth was in response to several factors, not the least of which was the increasing potential of modern warfare for destruction. The recently concluded Civil War in the United States made this potential clear.

During this growth, the subjects of international law were almost exclusively restricted to the relationships that countries had with one another. Issues of trade and warfare dominated both the disputes and the agreements of the period. _____, the developments of this period paved the way for further expansion of international law, which has occurred in the last several years. _____, organizations such as the United Nations and the International Court of Justice are greatly concerned not only with the way countries deal with one another, but the ways in which they treat their own citizens.

1. Which words or phrases, if inserted in order into the blanks in the passage, would help the reader understand the sequence of the author's ideas?
   a. Therefore; In addition
   b. However; Now
   c. Furthermore; Yet
   d. Even if; On the other hand
   e. As a result; Meanwhile

2. Which of the following is the best meaning of the phrase *ushered in* as it is used in the beginning of the passage?
   a. escorted
   b. progressed
   c. guarded
   d. heralded
   e. conducted

Use the following passage to answer question 3.

The 1964 report on smoking and health issued by the Surgeon General's office had a significant impact on public attitudes and policy. A Gallup survey conducted in 1958 found that only 44% of Americans believed smoking caused cancer, while 78% believed so by 1968. In the course of a decade, it had become common knowledge that smoking damaged health, and mounting evidence of health risks gave the 1964 report public resonance. Yet, while the report proclaimed that "cigarette smoking is a health hazard of sufficient importance in the United States to warrant appropriate remedial action," it remained silent on concrete remedies. That challenge fell to politicians. In 1965, Congress required all cigarette packages distributed in the United States to carry a health warning, and since 1970 this warning is made in the name of the Surgeon General. In 1969, cigarette advertising on television and radio was banned, effective September 1970.

3. The statement that the 1964 Surgeon General's report *remained silent on concrete remedies* implies that it
   a. served primarily as a manifesto that declared the views of the Surgeon General.
   b. would have recommended banning cigarette advertising if it were not for political pressure.
   c. was ignorant of possible remedial actions.
   d. maintained its objectivity by abstaining from making policy recommendations.
   e. did not deem it necessary to recommend specific actions that would confront the health problem of smoking.

Use the following passage to answer question 4.

Time is running out for the old-growth forests of Finland. The vast majority of Finland's valuable old-growth forests is owned by the state and logged by the state-owned company Metsähallitus. Metsähallitus' logging practices include clear-cutting, logging in habitats of threatened and vulnerable species, and logging in areas of special scenic or cultural value—including in areas that are critical for the reindeer herding of the indigenous people.

4. According to the passage, which is NOT a logging practice engaged in by Metsähallitus?
   a. employing the clear-cutting method
   b. logging in the habitat of reindeer
   c. logging near scenic Finnish vistas
   d. logging within the boundaries of the indigenous people
   e. logging in traditional Norwegian fjords

Use the following passage to answer questions 5 through 7.

By using tiny probes as neural prostheses, scientists may be able to restore nerve function in quadriplegics and make the blind see or the deaf hear. Thanks to advanced techniques, a single, small, implanted probe can stimulate individual neurons electrically or chemically and then record responses. Preliminary results suggest that the microprobe telemetry systems can be permanently implanted and replace damaged or missing nerves.

The tissue-compatible microprobes represent an advance over the typical aluminum wire electrodes used in studies of the cortex and other brain structures. Researchers accumulate much data using traditional electrodes, but there is a question of how much damage they cause to the nervous system. Microprobes, which are about as thin as a human hair, cause minimal damage and disruption of neurons when inserted into the brain.

In addition to recording nervous system impulses, the microprobes have minuscule channels that open the way for delivery of drugs, cellular growth factors, neurotransmitters, and other neuroactive compounds to a single neuron or to groups of neurons. Also, patients who lack certain biochemicals could receive doses via prostheses. The probes can have up to four channels, each with its own recording/stimulating electrode.

5. As it is used in the passage, *prostheses* most closely means
   a. medications.
   b. electrodes.
   c. artificial body parts.
   d. wires.
   e. brain cells.

6. Which of the following best expresses the main idea of the passage?
   a. Microprobes require further technological advances before they can be used in humans.
   b. Wire electrodes are antiquated as a means for delivering neuroactive compounds to the brain.
   c. Microprobes have great potential to help counteract neural damage.
   d. Technology now exists that may counteract the nervous system.
   e. Use of wire electrodes is being replaced by use of wire microprobes.

7. All of the following are mentioned in the passage as potential uses for prostheses EXCEPT
   a. transportation of medication.
   b. induction of physical movement.
   c. compensation for damaged nerves.
   d. transportation of growth factors.
   e. removal of biochemicals from the cortex.

Use the following passage to answer question 8.

In a recent Senate race, the Republican candidate dropped out because an illness made it difficult for him to campaign. The candidate who replaced him lost the election to the opposing Democrat.

8. According to the information given, which statement must be true?
   a. The first Republican candidate would have been elected if he had stayed in the race.
   b. It is unusual for Senate candidates to withdraw from a race.
   c. The first Republican candidate will never run for office again.
   d. Senate candidates may withdraw from a race due to illness.
   e. The Democratic candidate was the best choice for senator.

Use the following passage to answer question 9.

The U.S. population is going gray. A rising demographic tide of aging baby boomers—those born between 1946 and 1964—and increased longevity have made adults age 85 and older the fastest-growing segment of today's population. This unprecedented "elder boom" will have a profound effect on American society, particularly in the field of healthcare. Is the U.S. health system equipped to deal with the demands of an aging population? Although we have adequate physicians and nurses, many of them are not trained to handle the multiple needs of older patients. Only about 230 new geriatricians (physicians who are experts in aging-related issues) are certified each year. Some studies estimate a need for about 26,000 more geriatricians than are likely to be available by 2030.

9. The author uses the phrase *going gray* in order to
   a. maintain that everyone's hair loses its color eventually.
   b. suggest the social phenomenon of an aging population.
   c. depict older Americans in a positive light.
   d. demonstrate the normal changes of aging.
   e. highlight the tendency of American culture to emphasize youth.

Use the following passage to answer questions 10 through 12.

The history of microbiology begins with a Dutch haberdasher named Antoni van Leeuwenhoek, a man of no formal scientific education. In the late 1600s, Leeuwenhoek, inspired by the magnifying lenses used by drapers to examine cloth, assembled some of the first microscopes. He developed a technique for grinding and polishing tiny, convex lenses, some of which could magnify an object up to 270 times. After scraping some plaque from between his teeth and examining it under a lens, Leeuwenhoek found tiny squirming creatures, which he called "animalcules." His observations, which he reported to the Royal Society of London, are among the first descriptions of living bacteria. Leeuwenhoek discovered an entire universe invisible to the naked eye. He found more animalcules—protozoa and bacteria—in samples of pond water, rainwater, and human saliva. He gave the first description of red corpuscles, observed plant tissue, examined muscle, and investigated the life cycles of insects.

Nearly 200 years later, Leeuwenhoek's discovery of microbes aided French chemist and biologist Louis Pasteur to develop his "germ theory of disease." This concept suggested that disease derives from tiny organisms attacking and weakening the body. The germ theory later helped doctors to fight infectious diseases, including anthrax, diphtheria, polio, smallpox, tetanus, and typhoid.

10. According to the passage, Leeuwenhoek would best be described as a
   a. bored haberdasher who stumbled on scientific discovery.
   b. trained researcher with an interest in microbiology.
   c. proficient hobbyist who made microscopic lenses for entertainment.
   d. inquisitive amateur who made pioneer studies of microbes.
   e. talented scientist interested in finding a cure for disease.

11. In the second sentence of the passage, *inspired* most nearly means
   a. introduced.
   b. invested.
   c. influenced.
   d. indulged.
   e. inclined.

12. The author's attitude toward Leeuwenhoek's contribution to medicine is one of
   a. ecstatic reverence.
   b. genuine admiration.
   c. tepid approval.
   d. courteous opposition.
   e. antagonistic incredulity.

Use the following passage to answer question 13.

According to a poll of Smithtown residents, the number of adults who belong to a health club or gym is 25% higher than it was five years ago. This higher level of physical fitness among Smithtown adults must account for the reduced rate of heart disease during the same period.

13. Which of the following, if true, most weakens the author's argument?

   a. All the health clubs and gyms in Smithtown offer information on improving cardiac health.

   b. Smithtown has always had a relatively low rate of heart disease.

   c. Not all adults participated in the poll.

   d. A new cardiac clinic was established in Smithtown ten years ago.

   e. Most of the adults who have joined gyms in the past five years only work out a few times a month.

Use the following passage to answer question 14.

A book proposal has three major functions. First, it should sell a publisher on the commercial potential of the as-yet-to-be-written book. Second, the writing in the proposal itself should convince the publisher that the author has the ability to write the book. Finally, the proposal should show that the author has the background necessary to write the book.

14. Which of the following is the best meaning of the word *background* as it is used in the passage?

   a. something behind the main event

   b. something in a subordinated position

   c. one's ability to do something

   d. events leading up to something

   e. facts to help explain something

Use the following passage to answer question 15.

In the mid-1800s, the art world in England was rattled by the initials PRB. The PRB (or Pre-Raphaelite Brotherhood) was founded by William Holman Hunt, John Everett Millais, and Dante Gabriel Rossetti. These three burgeoning artists (the oldest of whom was 21) and their disdain for the artistic conventions of the time would have a dramatic influence on the art world for generations to come. During the era leading up to the PRB, the Royal Academy dominated British art. The Royal Academy advocated a style that was typically staid and relied heavily on the use of dark amber and brown tones to depict overly idealized landscapes, carefully arranged family portraits and still lifes, and overly dramatic nature scenes such as boats caught in stormy seas. By contrast, the PRB believed that art should present subjects that, by their very nature, had greater meaning and more accurately depicted reality.

15. The author's main purpose in this passage is to
   a. describe the lives of the founders of the PRB.
   b. describe the artistic principles of the PRB.
   c. compare and contrast revolutions in art.
   d. describe the controversy created by the PRB.
   e. describe how the PRB influenced future artists.

Use the following passage to answer questions 16 and 17.

(1) The Woodstock Music and Art Fair—better known to its participants and to history simply as "Woodstock"—should have been a colossal failure. (2) Just a month prior to its August 15, 1969, opening, the fair's organizers were informed by the council of Wallkill, New York, that permission to hold the festival was withdrawn. (3) Amazingly, not only was a new site found, but word also got out to the public of the fair's new location.

(4) At the new site, fences that were supposed to facilitate ticket collection never materialized, and all attempts at gathering tickets were abandoned. (5) Crowd estimates of 30,000 kept rising; by the end of the three days, some estimated the crowd at 500,000. (6) And then, on opening night, it began to rain. (7) Off and on, throughout all three days, huge summer storms rolled over the gathering. (8) In spite of these problems, most people think of Woodstock not only as a fond memory but also as the defining moment for an entire generation.

16. Which of the following would be the most appropriate title for this passage?
   a. "Woodstock as Metaphor"
   b. "Backstage at Woodstock"
   c. "Woodstock: From The Band to The Who"
   d. "Remembering Woodstock"
   e. "Woodstock: The Untold Story"

17. Which of the numbered sentences of the passage best represents an opinion rather than a fact?
   a. sentence 1
   b. sentence 2
   c. sentence 3
   d. sentence 4
   e. sentence 5

Use the following passage to answer question 18.

The Sami are an indigenous people living in the northern parts of Norway, Sweden, Finland, and Russia's Kola peninsula. Originally, the Sami religion was animistic; that is, for them, nature and natural objects had a conscious life, a spirit. One was expected to move quietly in the wilderness and avoid making a disturbance out of courtesy to these spirits. Ghengis Khan is said to have declared that the Sami were one people he would never try to fight again. Since the Sami were not warriors and did not believe in war, they simply disappeared in times of conflict. They were known as peaceful retreaters.

18. Based on the tone of the passage, which of the following words best describes the author's attitude toward the Sami people?
   a. admiring
   b. pitying
   c. contemptuous
   d. patronizing
   e. perplexed

Use the following passage to answer question 19.

From its beginnings in the 1920s, the modeling industry has provided beautiful people to help sell everything from magazines to computers to vacation destinations. John Robert Powers, who opened the first modeling agency in 1923, was a former actor who hired his actor friends to model for magazine advertisements. Cary Grant, Lucille Ball, and Princess Grace of Monaco were clients. However, for many models, "great-looking" was where their resumes began and ended. The height of popularity for them was in the 1980s and 1990s, the era of the supermodel. A handful of "perfect" women commanded salaries of up to $25,000 a day to walk catwalks at fashion shows, appear in print ads, and pose their way through commercials. They were celebrities, treated with all of the lavish attention usually paid to heads of state or rock stars.

19. The clause *"great-looking" was where their resumes began and ended* is
   a. a description of the models' work experience.
   b. meant to be taken literally.
   c. meant to be taken figuratively.
   d. a truthful statement.
   e. an example of pathos.

Use the following passage by Edith Wharton to answer question 20.

There are at least two reasons why a subject should find expression in novel form rather than as a tale; but neither is based on the number of what may be conveniently called incidents, or external happenings, which the narrative contains. There are novels of action which might be condensed into short stories without the loss of their distinguishing qualities. The marks of the subject requiring a longer development are, first, the gradual unfolding of the inner life of its characters, and secondly the need of producing in the reader's mind the sense of the lapse of time. Outward events of the most varied and exciting nature may without loss of probability be crowded into a few hours, but moral dramas usually have their roots deep in the soul, their rise far back in time; and the suddenest-seeming clash in which they culminate should be led up to step by step if it is to explain and justify itself.

20. The author's main purpose in this passage is to
  a. provide guidelines for choosing the narrator in a novel.
  b. provide tips for making short stories and novels more realistic.
  c. debunk several myths about writing novels.
  d. explain why some tales are better for novels than short stories.
  e. explain why novels are better than stories.

Use the following passage to answer questions 21 through 23.

Heat reactions usually occur when large amounts of water and/or salt are lost through excessive sweating following strenuous exercise. When the body becomes overheated and cannot eliminate this excess heat, heat exhaustion and heatstroke are possible.

Heat exhaustion is generally characterized by clammy skin, fatigue, nausea, dizziness, profuse perspiration, and sometimes fainting, resulting from an inadequate intake of water and the loss of fluids. First aid treatment for this condition includes having the victim lie down, raising the feet 8 to 12 inches, applying cool, wet cloths to the skin, and giving the victim sips of salt water (1 teaspoon per glass, half a glass every 15 minutes) over the period of an hour.

Heatstroke is much more serious; it is an immediately life-threatening situation. The characteristics of heatstroke are a high body temperature (which may reach 106°F or more); a rapid pulse; hot, dry skin; and a blocked sweating mechanism. Victims of this condition may be unconscious, and first aid measures should be directed at cooling the body quickly. The victim should be placed in a tub of cold water or repeatedly sponged with cool water until his or her temperature is lowered sufficiently. Fans or air conditioners will also help with the cooling process. Care should be taken, however, not to overchill the victim once the temperature is below 102°F.

21. The most immediate concern of a person tending a victim of heatstroke should be to
   a. get salt into the victim's body.
   b. raise the victim's feet.
   c. lower the victim's pulse rate.
   d. have the victim lie down.
   e. lower the victim's temperature.

22. Heatstroke is more serious than heat exhaustion because heatstroke victims
   a. have too little salt in their bodies.
   b. cannot take in water.
   c. do not sweat.
   d. have frequent fainting spells.
   e. may have convulsions.

23. On the basis of the information in the passage, symptoms such as nausea and dizziness in a heat exhaustion victim indicate that the person most likely needs to
   a. be immediately taken to a hospital.
   b. be immersed in a tub of water.
   c. be given more salt water.
   d. sweat more.
   e. go to an air-conditioned place.

Use the following passage to answer question 24.

After rock and roll exploded on the music scene in the 1950s, many rock artists began covering blues songs, thus bringing the blues to a mainstream audience and giving it true national and international exposure. In the early 1960s, the Rolling Stones, the Yardbirds, Cream, and others remade blues songs such as Robert Johnson's "Crossroads" and Big Joe Williams' "Baby Please Don't Go" to wide popularity. People all across America listened to songs with lyrics that were intensely honest and personal, songs that told about any number of things that give us the blues: loneliness, betrayal, unrequited love, a run of bad luck, being out of work or away from home or broke or brokenhearted.

24. In the sentence *"People all across America listened to songs with lyrics that were intensely honest and personal, songs that told about any number of things that give us the blues: loneliness, betrayal, unrequited love, a run of bad luck, being out of work or away from home or broke or brokenhearted,"* the author is
   a. defining blues music.
   b. identifying the origin of the blues.
   c. describing the lyrics of a famous blues song.
   d. explaining why blues cover songs were so popular.
   e. making a connection between the blues and the Civil Rights movement.

Use the following passage from Aristotle's Nicomachean Ethics *to answer questions 25 and 26.*

Good things are commonly divided into three classes: (1) external goods, (2) goods of the soul, and (3) goods of the body. Of these, we call the goods pertaining to the soul goods in the highest and fullest sense. But in speaking of "soul," we refer to our soul's actions and activities. Thus, our definition [of good] tallies with this opinion which has been current for a long time and to which philosophers subscribe. We are also right in defining the end as consisting of actions and activities; for in this way the end is included among the goods of the soul and not among external goods.

Also the view that a happy man lives well and fares well fits in with our definition: for we have all but defined happiness as a kind of good life and well-being.

Moreover, the characteristics which one looks for in happiness are all included in our definition. For some people think that happiness is a virtue, others that it is practical wisdom, others that it is some kind of theoretical wisdom; others again believe it to be all or some of these accompanied by, or not devoid of, pleasure; and some people also include external prosperity in its definition.

25. As it is used in the first paragraph of the passage, the word *tallies* means
   a. keeps count.
   b. records.
   c. labels.
   d. corresponds.
   e. scores.

26. The author's definition of happiness in the second paragraph of the passage is related to the definition of good in that
   a. living a good life will bring you happiness.
   b. happiness is the same as goodness.
   c. happiness is often sacrificed to attain the good.
   d. all things that create happiness are good things.
   e. happiness is a virtue.

Use the following passage to answer questions 27 and 28.

The inhabitants of the Trobriand Islands, an archipelago off the coast of Papua New Guinea in the South Pacific, are united by a ceremonial trading system called the *kula ring*. Kula traders sail to neighboring islands in large ocean-going canoes to offer either shell necklaces or shell armbands. The necklaces, made of red shells called *bagi*, travel around the trading ring clockwise, and the armbands, made of white shells called *mwali*, travel counterclockwise.

Each man in the kula ring has two kula trading partners—one partner to whom he gives a necklace for an armband of equal value, although the exchanges are made on separate occasions, and one partner with whom he makes the reverse exchange. Each partner has one other partner with whom he trades, thus linking all the men around the kula ring. For example, if A trades with B and C, B trades with A and D, and C trades with A and E, and so on. A man may have only met his own specific kula partners, but he will know by reputation all the men in his kula ring. It can take anywhere from two to ten years for a particular object to complete a journey around the ring. The more times an object has made the trip around the ring, the more value it accrues. Particularly beautiful necklaces and armbands are also prized. Some famous kula objects are known by special names and through elaborate stories. Objects also gain fame through ownership by powerful men, and, likewise, men can gain status by possessing particularly prized kula objects.

27. What is the best definition for *accrues* as it is used in the second paragraph of the passage?
   a. increases over time
   b. decreases over time
   c. becomes worthless
   d. steals
   e. exchanges

28. According to the passage, necklaces and armbands gain value through all the following means EXCEPT
   a. being in circulation for a long time.
   b. being especially attractive.
   c. being owned by a powerful man.
   d. being made of special shells.
   e. being known by a special name.

Use the following passage adapted from Ian Johnston's My Body the Billboard *to answer questions 29 through 32.*

Traditional body signage seems largely to have disappeared. Well, many of the old symbols and names are still around, of course, but they are part of the commercial range of options. Seeing someone in a Harvard or Oxford sweatshirt or a kilt or a military tie now communicates nothing at all significant about that person's life other than the personal choice of a particular consumer. Religious signs are still evocative, to be sure, but are far less common than they used to be. Why should this be? I suspect one reason may be that we have lost a sense of significant connection to the various things indicated by such signs. Proclaiming our high school or university or our athletic team or our community has a much lower priority nowadays, in part because we live such rapidly changing lives in a society marked by constant motion that the stability essential to confer significance on such signs has largely gone.

But we still must attach ourselves to something. Lacking the conviction that the traditional things matter, we turn to the last resort of the modern world: the market. Here there is a vast array of options, all equally meaningless in terms of traditional values, all equally important in identifying the one thing left to us for declaring our identity publicly, our fashion sense and disposable income. The market naturally manipulates the labels, making sure we keep purchasing what will most quickly declare us excellent consumers. If this year a Chicago Bulls jacket or Air Jordan shoes are so popular that we are prepared to spend our way into a trendy identity, then next year there will be something else.

29. The main purpose of the passage is to
   a. discuss basketball's importance in today's fashions.
   b. relate the tribal history of tattoos.
   c. tell a story about the good old days.
   d. help the reader discover his or her own true identity.
   e. discuss commercialism's powerful influence on personal identity.

30. The author would agree with all the following statements EXCEPT which one?
   a. A person wearing a New York Yankees baseball hat is not necessarily a fan or resident of New York.
   b. Pride in our school or community is not as strong today as it was years ago.
   c. In today's society, being trendy is more important than keeping tradition.
   d. You can tell a lot about somebody by what he or she is wearing.
   e. The last resort of the modern world is the marketplace.

31. Which statement best simplifies the author's point of view of today's society, as stated in the last sentence of paragraph 1?
   a. Times have changed.
   b. People's lives today are very similar to those of a generation ago.
   c. Fashion is very important in today's world.
   d. People today don't have proper nutrition.
   e. Life is short.

32. In the second paragraph, *disposable income* refers to
   a. recyclable goods.
   b. spending money.
   c. life savings.
   d. a donation to charity.
   e. garbage.

Use the following passage to answer question 33.

Emperor Charlemagne of the Franks was crowned in 800 A.D. The Frankish Empire at that time extended over what is now Germany, Italy, and France. Charlemagne died in the year 814, but his brief reign marked the dawn of a distinctly European culture. The artists and thinkers who helped create this European civilization drew on the ancient texts of the Germanic, Celtic, Greek, Roman, Hebrew, and Christian worlds. Many traditions of these cultures remained active in Frankish society for centuries. These mores in turn laid the groundwork for the laws, customs, and even attitudes of today's Europeans.

33. Which of the following is the best meaning of the word *culture* as it is used in the passage?
   a. the fashionable class
   b. a community of interrelated individuals
   c. a partnership
   d. a group of loosely associated outsiders
   e. an organized group with a common goal

Use the following passage to answer question 34.

Sir Isaac Newton, English mathematician, philosopher, and physicist, was born in 1642 in Woolsthorpe-by-Colsterworth, a hamlet in the county of Lincolnshire, England. Newton was educated at Grantham Grammar School. In 1661 he joined Trinity College, Cambridge, and continued there as Lucasian professor of mathematics from 1669 to 1701. In 1665 he originated the binomial theorem and began to develop a mathematical theory that would later become calculus. However, his most important discoveries were made during the two-year period from 1664 to 1666, when the university was closed due to the Great Plague. Newton retreated to his hometown and set to work on

developing calculus, as well as advanced studies on optics and gravitation. It was at this time that he formulated the Law of Universal Gravitation and discovered that white light is composed of all the colors of the spectrum. These findings enabled him to make fundamental contributions to mathematics, astronomy, and theoretical and experimental physics.

34. Which statement best summarizes the life of Sir Isaac Newton?
   a. distinguished inventor, mathematician, physicist, and great thinker of the seventeenth century.
   b. eminent mathematician, physicist, and scholar of the Renaissance
   c. noteworthy physicist, astronomer, mathematician, and British lord
   d. Lord Isaac Newton: from Woolsthorpe to Cambridge
   e. Isaac Newton: founder of calculus and father of gravity

Use the following passage to answer question 35.

Through the years, the U.S. Department of Transportation conducted polls concerning Daylight Saving Time and found that many Americans were in favor of it because of the extended hours of daylight and the freedom to do more in the evening hours. In further studies, the Department of Transportation also found that DST conserves energy by cutting the electricity usage in the morning and evening for lights and particular appliances. During the darkest winter months (November through February), the advantage of conserving energy in afternoon Daylight Saving Time is outweighed by needing more light in the morning because of late sunrise. In Britain, studies showed that there were fewer accidents on the road because of the increased visibility resulting from additional hours of daylight.

35. In which month does the need for more energy in the morning offset the afternoon conservation of energy by DST?
a. June
b. July
c. October
d. January
e. March

Use the following passage to answer questions 36 and 37.

An estimated 75 million Americans suffer from an allergic disease, which results from the immune system reacting to a normally innocuous substance, such as pollen or dust. An allergic response begins with a process called *sensitization*. When a foreign substance—an allergen such as pollen, for example—first enters the body of an allergic person, cells called *macrophages* engulf the invader, chop it into pieces and display the pieces on their surfaces. T-helper cells recognize certain allergen fragments and bind to the macrophages. This process causes the T-helper cells to secrete signaling molecules, including interleukin-4 (IL-4). IL-4, in turn, spurs nearby B cells to mature into plasma cells. Plasma cells produce Y-shaped antibody proteins.

36. An allergic disease occurs when the body's immune system reacts to a substance that is usually
a. common.
b. toxic.
c. irritating.
d. airborne.
e. harmless.

37. Cells that surround allergens within the body are known as
a. T-helper cells.
b. macrophage cells.
c. B cells.
d. plasma cells.
e. IL-4.

Use the following poem by Emily Dickinson to answer questions 38 and 39.

A Narrow Fellow in the Grass
A narrow fellow in the grass
Occasionally rides;
You may have met him did you not?
His notice sudden is.

The grass divides as with a comb,
A spotted shaft is seen,
And then it closes at your feet
And opens further on.

He likes a boggy acre,
A floor too cool for corn,
Yet when a boy, and barefoot,
I more than once at noon

Have passed, I thought, a whip-lash
Unbraiding in the sun,
When, stooping to secure it,
It wrinkled, and was gone.

Several of nature's people
I know and they know me;
I feel for them a transport
Of cordiality;

But never met this fellow,
Attended or alone,
Without a tighter breathing
And zero at the bone.

38. Who or what is the *fellow* in this poem?
a. a whip-lash
b. a weed
c. a snake
d. a gust of wind
e. a boy

39. The lines *Without a tighter breathing / And zero at the bone* most nearly indicate
a. fright.
b. cold.
c. grief.
d. awe.
e. relief.

Use the following passage to answer question 40.

Do you sing in the shower while dreaming of getting your own record deal? There are a couple of "reality" shows made just for you. Audition and make the cut so some British guy who has never sung a note can rip you to pieces on live television. At least you can take comfort in the knowledge that the winner probably wouldn't have been able to get a record deal in real life without the votes of a supportive audience. Or maybe you're lonely and fiscally challenged, and dream of walking down the aisle with a millionaire? Real marriage doesn't involve contestants who know each other for a couple of days. The people on these shows seem to be more interested in how they look on camera than in the character of the person they might spend the rest of their life with. Let's hope that reality TV isn't reality.

40. What does the author find most troublesome about reality TV?
a. It isn't original.
b. It can humiliate people.
c. It invades people's privacy.
d. It doesn't accurately show reality.
e. It shows how shallow people are.

Skills Test in Mathematics

Directions: Choose the best answer to each of the following questions.

Use the following figure to answer question 1.

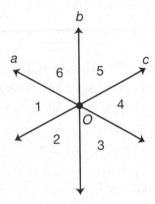

1. In the diagram, lines *a*, *b*, and *c* intersect at point *O*. Which of the following are NOT adjacent angles?
   a. ∠1 and ∠6
   b. ∠1 and ∠4
   c. ∠4 and ∠5
   d. ∠2 and ∠3
   e. All the angles are adjacent.

2. A middle school cafeteria has three different options for lunch.
   ■ For $2, a student can get either a sandwich or two cookies.
   ■ For $3, a student can get a sandwich and one cookie.
   ■ For $4, a student can get either two sandwiches, or a sandwich and two cookies.
   If Jimae has $6 to pay for lunch for her and her brother, which of the following is NOT a possible combination?
   a. three sandwiches and one cookie
   b. two sandwiches and two cookies
   c. one sandwich and four cookies
   d. three sandwiches and no cookies
   e. one sandwich and three cookies

3. The sequence of numbers 0, 2, 2, 4, 6, 10, 16 follows a pattern. Using this pattern, which of the following is the next number in the sequence?
   a. 16
   b. 20
   c. 22
   d. 26
   e. 32

4. A model of the ancient city of Rome uses a scale of 1 foot:100 yards. The Coliseum, a stadium built nearly 2,000 years ago, is about 617 feet long. Which is the length, in feet, of the Coliseum in the model, rounded to the nearest tenth?
   a. 1.5 feet
   b. 2.1 feet
   c. 6.2 feet
   d. 24.7 feet
   e. 60 feet

Use the following figure to answer question 5.

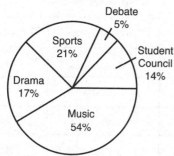

5. According to the graph, if 105 students at the school are involved in sports, how many are involved in the drama club?

a. 17

b. 35

c. 85

d. 105

e. 175

6. The average high temperature for the first five days in July was 90°. If the temperature the first four days was 95°, 85°, 88°, and 84°, respectively, what was the temperature on the fifth day?

a. 90°

b. 92°

c. 94°

d. 96°

e. 98°

7. A jar of coins contains 8 dimes, 10 quarters, 3 nickels, and 9 pennies. What is the probability of selecting either a nickel or a penny if drawing one coin from the jar?

a. $\frac{1}{10}$

b. $\frac{2}{5}$

c. $\frac{4}{15}$

d. $\frac{3}{10}$

e. $\frac{1}{3}$

8. What is the perimeter of a pentagon with three sides of 3 inches, and the remaining sides 5 inches long?

a. 24 inches

b. 19 inches

c. 14 inches

d. 12 inches

e. 9 inches

9. What is the product when 11 is multiplied by 0.032?

a. 0.032

b. 0.0352

c. 0.32

d. 0.352

e. 3.20

10. Amanda buys three T-shirts on sale at a, b, and c dollars each. If she gets a discount of 90%, which expression would determine the average price paid by Amanda for each T-shirt?

a. $\frac{a+b+c}{0.9}$

b. $(a+b+c) \times 0.9$

c. $\frac{a+b+c}{3}$

d. $3 \times \frac{a+b+c}{0.9}$

e. $\frac{0.9(a+b+c)}{3}$

11. Garth wants to know whether he has enough money to purchase several items at the grocery store. He needs three cans of soup, which cost $0.99 each, and two boxes of rice, which cost $3.49 each. He uses the expression $(3 \times \$0.99) + (2 \times \$3.49)$ to calculate how much the items will cost. Which of the following expressions could also be used?
   a. $3 \times (\$3.49 + \$0.99) - \$3.49$
   b. $3 \times (\$3.49 + \$0.99)$
   c. $(2 + 3) \times (\$3.49 + \$0.99)$
   d. $(2 \times 3) + (\$3.49 \times \$0.99)$
   e. $3 \times (\$3.49 + \$0.99) + \$3.49$

12. Tess finds the average of her three most recent history quiz scores by using the following expression, where a, b, and c are the three scores: $\frac{a+b+c}{3}$. Which of the following would also determine the average of her scores?
   a. $(\frac{a}{3} + \frac{b}{3} + \frac{c}{3})$
   b. $\frac{\frac{a+b+c}{3}}{100}$
   c. $(a + b + c) \times 3$
   d. $\frac{a \times b \times c}{3}$
   e. $\frac{a+b+c}{3+100}$

13. What is $\frac{2}{3}$ divided by $\frac{5}{12}$?
   a. $1\frac{3}{5}$
   b. $1\frac{5}{18}$
   c. $1\frac{7}{36}$
   d. $1\frac{5}{6}$
   e. $1\frac{2}{3}$

Use the following table to answer question 14.

Train Schedule

Train	Arrival Time	Departure Time
A	6:42 A.M.	6:53 A.M.
B	7:24 A.M.	7:34 A.M.
C	7:55 A.M.	8:06 A.M.
D	8:13 A.M.	8:24 A.M.
E	9:03 A.M.	9:11 A.M.
F	9:31 A.M.	9:42 A.M.

14. What is the difference between the arrival time for Train A and the departure time for Train D?
   a. 1 hour, 18 minutes
   b. 1 hour, 24 minutes
   c. 1 hour, 42 minutes
   d. 2 hours, 6 minutes
   e. 2 hours, 18 minutes

15. Which of the following represents the solution to the inequality $-4x - 1 \geq 11$?
   a. $x \leq 3$
   b. $x \geq 3$
   c. $x \geq -3$
   d. $x \leq -3$
   e. $x \geq 2\frac{1}{2}$

16. Given a polygon with four congruent sides, which of the following does NOT contradict the statement: "If a polygon has four congruent sides, then the polygon is a square"?
a. The polygon has five congruent sides.
b. The polygon does not have four congruent sides.
c. The polygon has exactly one pair of parallel sides.
d. The polygon is a triangle.
e. The polygon is also a rhombus.

17. Of the 6,251 teachers in a study of certification areas, 312 have dual certification in two subject areas. What is a reasonable estimate of the percentage of teachers in the study who have dual certification?
a. 0.5%
b. 2%
c. 5%
d. 20%
e. 50%

Use the following chart to answer questions 18 through 20.

MAJOR CAUSES OF HOME FIRES IN THE PREVIOUS FOUR-YEAR PERIOD		
CAUSE	FIRES (% OF TOTAL)	CIVILIAN DEATHS (% OF TOTAL)
heating equipment	161,500 (27.5%)	770 (16.8%)
cooking equipment	104,800 (17.8%)	350 (7.7%)
incendiary, suspicious	65,400 (11.1%)	620 (13.6%)
electrical equipment	45,700 (7.8%)	440 (9.6%)
other equipment	43,000 (7.3%)	240 (5.3%)
smoking materials	39,300 (6.7%)	1,320 (28.9%)
appliances, air-conditioning	36,200 (6.2%)	120 (2.7%)
exposure and other heat	28,600 (4.8%)	191 (4.2%)
open flame	27,200 (4.6%)	130 (2.9%)
child play	26,900 (4.6%)	370 (8.1%)
natural causes	9,200 (1.6%)	10 (0.2%)

18. What is the percentage of the total fires caused by both electrical equipment and other equipment combined?
- **a.** 7.8%
- **b.** 14.9%
- **c.** 15.1%
- **d.** 29.9%
- **e.** 30.0%

19. Of the causes listed in the table, which one has the highest ratio of the percentage of deaths to the percentage of total fires?
- **a.** heating equipment
- **b.** smoking materials
- **c.** exposure and other heat
- **d.** child play
- **e.** natural causes

20. Which of the following answer choices would most accurately show the percentages from the Fires column in the table?

a.

b.

c.

d.

e.

21. All the rooms on the main floor of an office building are rectangular, with 8-foot-high ceilings. Keira's office is 9 feet wide by 11 feet long. What is the combined surface area of the four walls of her office, including any windows and doors?

  a. 99 square feet
  b. 160 square feet
  c. 320 square feet
  d. 729 square feet
  e. 288 square feet

22. A springtime day had a temperature of 40°C. What was the temperature in degrees Fahrenheit? The formula for converting Celsius to Fahrenheit is $F = \frac{9}{5}C + 32$.

  a. 100°F
  b. 101°F
  c. 102°F
  d. 103°F
  e. 104°F

23. Which of the following fractions are in order from greatest to least?

  a. $\frac{1}{2}, \frac{6}{11}, \frac{3}{5}, \frac{5}{8}$
  b. $\frac{3}{5}, \frac{6}{11}, \frac{1}{2}, \frac{5}{8}$
  c. $\frac{5}{8}, \frac{6}{11}, \frac{3}{5}, \frac{1}{2}$
  d. $\frac{5}{8}, \frac{3}{5}, \frac{6}{11}, \frac{1}{2}$
  e. $\frac{3}{5}, \frac{1}{2}, \frac{5}{8}, \frac{6}{11}$

Use the following chart to answer question 24.

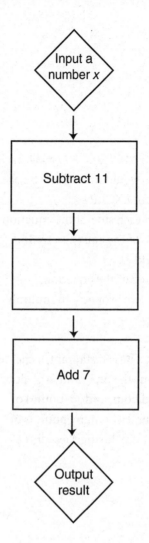

24. When the input is 63, the result is 11. What is the missing step?

  a. Divide by 4.
  b. Subtract 31.
  c. Subtract 41.
  d. Divide by 13.
  e. Divide by 2.

25. How much is one-eighth of one-sixth?

   a. $\frac{1}{48}$

   b. $\frac{1}{2}$

   c. $\frac{6}{8}$

   d. $\frac{1}{12}$

   e. $\frac{1}{6}$

26. Given the equation $14x + 2(x + 1) = 34$, each of the following steps would most likely be used to solve the problem EXCEPT

   a. subtract 2 from each side of the equation.

   b. divide each side of the equation by 16.

   c. combine $14x$ and $2x$.

   d. add 2 to each side of the equation.

   e. use the distributive property to multiply $2 \times (x + 1)$.

27. During her shift at a busy restaurant, a chef uses $2\frac{1}{4}$ pounds of flour the first hour, $4\frac{5}{8}$ pounds of flour the second hour, and $\frac{1}{2}$ pound of flour the third hour. How many pounds of flour does the chef use during these three hours?

   a. $6\frac{3}{8}$

   b. $6\frac{7}{8}$

   c. $7\frac{1}{4}$

   d. $7\frac{3}{8}$

   e. $7\frac{3}{4}$

28. A floor rug in the shape of a circle has a diameter of 152 cm. What is the approximate area of the rug?

   1 cm = 0.39 inches

   a. 878.53π in.^{2}

   b. 360π in.^{2}

   c. $3{,}514.12\pi$ in.^{2}

   d. $2{,}252.64\pi$ in.^{2}

   e. $5{,}776\pi$ in.^{2}

29. First-year members of an auto club have to purchase the membership at the full price of $84.50, but those who were also members last year get a 15% discount. Those who have been members for at least three years get an additional 10% off the discounted price. How much does a person who has been a member at least three years have to pay for their membership?

   a. $63.38

   b. $64.64

   c. $65.78

   d. $71.83

   e. $72.05

Use the following table to answer question 30.

h	k
3	4
6	5
9	6
12	7
15	8

30. Which of the following equations expresses the relationship between h and k in the table?

   a. $k = 3h + 3$

   b. $k = \frac{1}{3}h + 3$

   c. $h = \frac{1}{3}k + 3$

   d. $h = 3k + 3$

   e. $k = \frac{2}{3}h + 3$

Use the following table to answer question 31.

DISTANCE TRAVELED FROM CHICAGO WITH RESPECT TO TIME	
TIME (HOURS)	**DISTANCE FROM CHICAGO (MILES)**
1	60
2	120
3	180
4	240

31. A train moving at a constant speed of 60 miles per hour leaves Chicago for Los Angeles at time $t = 0$. If Los Angeles is 2,000 miles from Chicago, which of the following equations describes the distance from Los Angeles at any time t?
  a. $D(t) = 60t - 2,000$
  b. $D(t) = 60t$
  c. $D(t) = 2,000 - 60t$
  d. $D(t) = -2,000 - 60t$
  e. $D(t) = 2,000 + 60t$

32. At a baseball game, Deanna bought food for herself and her sister Jamie: one jumbo box of popcorn to share at $7 a box, two hot dogs for each of them (four total) at $3 a dog, and one soda for each at $4 apiece. Jamie paid for their tickets at $13 a ticket. Who spent more money and by how much?
  a. Deanna, by $1
  b. Deanna, by $3
  c. Jamie, by $1
  d. Jamie, by $2
  e. Jamie, by $4

Use the following figure to answer questions 33 and 34.

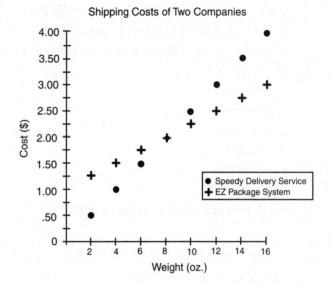

This double scatter plot compares the rates for different-weight packages for two companies.

33. Using the company with the better rate for each weight, which of the following combinations of packages would be the least expensive to ship?
  a. 8 oz. and 2 oz.
  b. 2 oz. and 6 oz.
  c. 2 oz. and 10 oz.
  d. one 12 oz. package
  e. 6 oz. and 8 oz.

34. At what weight is the cost for shipping at Speedy Delivery Service 20% more than the cost for the same-weight package at EZ Package System?
  a. 2 oz.
  b. 4 oz.
  c. 6 oz.
  d. 10 oz.
  e. 12 oz.

35. Felicia spent $5,618 on rent this year, and $5,085 the year before. She predicts she will be paying approximately $6,163 next year. To the nearest ten, what is the best estimate of the total amount she will spend on rent during this three-year span?
   a. $16,800
   b. $16,860
   c. $16,870
   d. $16,900
   e. $17,000

Use the following figure to answer question 36.

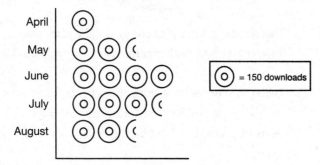

Music Downloads at Dina's Tunes Website

April
May
June
July
August

= 150 downloads

36. According to the figure, what is the average number of music downloads sold per month over the five-month period?
   a. 150
   b. 375
   c. 390
   d. 405
   e. 2,025

37. A triangle has two sides that measure 14 cm and 17 cm, respectively. Which of the following could be the length of the triangle's third side?
   a. 33 cm
   b. 31 cm
   c. 25 cm
   d. 44 cm
   e. 3 cm

38. One thousand students are participating in the regional math competition. An equal number of teams of five students are placed into four different gymnasiums. Each team has one adult coach. To find the total number of people (students and coaches) in each gymnasium you could
   a. divide 1,000 by 4, divide that result by 5, and then add that result and 1,000.
   b. divide 1,000 by 5, add that result to 1,000, and then divide that result by 4.
   c. divide 1,000 by 4, divide that result by 4, and then add that result and 1,000.
   d. divide 1,000 by 5, divide that result by 4, and then add that result and 50.
   e. divide 1,000 by 4, add 50 to that result, and then divide that result by 5.

39. Harold has two containers that he has filled with water. One is a rectangular plastic box with a base of 16 square inches, and the other is a cylindrical container with a base radius of 2 inches and a height of 11 inches. If the rectangular box is filled with water 9 inches from the bottom, and Harold pours the water into the cylinder without spilling, which of the following will be true?

a. The cylinder will overflow.

b. The cylinder will be exactly full.

c. The cylinder will be filled to an approximate level of 10 inches.

d. The cylinder will be filled to an approximate level of 8 inches.

e. The cylinder will be filled to an approximate level of 6 inches.

40. Robert, Linda, Miguel, and Sonja are friends. They all practice unique sports: One enjoys skiing, one enjoys fishing, one enjoys tennis, and one enjoys volleyball. The friend who fishes is Miguel's neighbor. Robert and Linda dislike sports that use balls. Sonja is older than both Robert and the friend who fishes. Who likes to fish?

a. Robert

b. Miguel

c. Sonja

d. Linda

e. The answer cannot be determined from the information given.

Skills Test in Writing— Section 1, Part A

Directions: Choose the letter for the underlined portion that contains a grammatical error. If there is no error in the sentence, choose **e**.

1. <u>As soon as</u> we stepped off of the water taxi,

　　a
   <u>which</u> pulled away from the <u>dock, leaving</u> both

b　　　　　　　　　　　**c**
   of us standing <u>in a puddle of</u> river water.

　　　　　　　d
   <u>No error</u>

e

2. <u>As the popularity</u> of professional lacrosse

　　a
   <u>continues</u> to grow, more and more companies

b
   are <u>investing</u> thousands of <u>dollars</u> to become

　　c　　　　　　　　**d**
   primary sponsors so they can get their brand
   names in front of television viewers. <u>No error</u>

　　　　　　　　　　　　　　　　　　e

3. <u>When</u> the casting agent called out her name,

a
   <u>she walked</u> rather <u>hesitant</u> to the front of the

b　　　　　　**c**
   stage and stood <u>there</u> shaking. <u>No error</u>

　　　　　　　d　　　　　　**e**

4. In John F. <u>Kennedy's</u> famous inaugural address

　　　　　　a
   in <u>1961, he</u> implored his <u>fellow Americans</u> to

　　b　　　　　　　**c**
   "<u>ask not</u> what your country can do for you,

　d
   ask what you can do for your country."

   <u>No error</u>

e

5. Corporate educators will often <u>use</u> analogies

　　　　　　　　　　　　　　　a
   and metaphors <u>from</u> sports <u>describing</u> business

　　　　　　b　　　　　**c**
   decision<u>s and</u> goals. <u>No error</u>

　　d　　　　　　**e**

6. I am looking for <u>an</u> assistant <u>who is</u> smart,

　　　　　　　a　　　　　**b**
   <u>reliable,</u> and <u>will come on time</u>. <u>No error</u>

c　　　　　**d**　　　　　　　**e**

7. The famous <u>composer</u> Igor Stravinsky <u>was born</u>

　　　　　a　　　　　　　　　　　**b**
   in <u>Russia,</u> his father was a <u>well-established</u>

　　c　　　　　　　　　**d**
   opera singer. <u>No error</u>

　　　　　　e

8. My <u>mother</u> <u>is</u> a teacher <u>and who</u> also has

　　a　　**b**　　　　　**c**
   <u>been a principal</u>. <u>No error</u>

d　　　　　　**e**

9. <u>During</u> the first act of the play, I <u>begun</u> to ask

a　　　　　　　　　　　　　**b**
   <u>myself</u> why I spent my hard-earned money on

c
   tickets <u>to</u> such a flop. <u>No error</u>

　　d　　　　　　**e**

10. A <u>captain</u> sailing a ship from <u>New York Harbor</u>

　a　　　　　　　　　**b**
    to <u>San Francisco Bay</u> can shave 7,872 miles off

　　c
    his <u>or</u> her trip by cutting through the Panama

　d
    Canal. <u>No error</u>

　　　　e

11. We <u>couldn't</u> barely hear the <u>Spanish</u> <u>lesson;</u> the
  a   b   c

teacher <u>spoke</u> in a very soft voice. <u>No error</u>
           d   e

12. The used car had been treated <u>bad</u> by <u>its</u>
                                       a   b

previous <u>owner, but</u> the people at the car
              c

dealership <u>worked hard</u> to fix it up like new.
                d

<u>No error</u>
    e

13. After <u>Pele's</u> final soccer <u>game, in</u> which he
          a   b

played for both <u>teams, players</u> from both
                    c

squads carried him off the field on <u>their</u>
                                        d

shoulders. <u>No error</u>
               e

14. The harsh <u>Winter</u> of <u>1777</u> tested the
                    a   b

<u>endurance and</u> spirit of the American
    c

<u>revolutionaries, but</u> it did not
    d

break them. <u>No error</u>
                e

15. The <u>principal's</u> decision at last <u>Monday's</u>
          a   b

teacher conference is sure to have an <u>affect</u> on
                                          c

all the <u>students</u> in the junior high school.
            d

<u>No error</u>
    e

16. The <u>biologist</u> <u>spoke at length</u> about his
          a   b

discovery of a new <u>species</u> of bacteria and <u>its</u>
                        c   d

possible uses in medicine. <u>No error</u>
                                e

17. <u>Although</u> the owner of the theater
    a

<u>acknowledged</u> that the ticket prices of $15.00
    b

for adults and $8.50 for children are too

expensive for some, <u>also noted</u> that many
                        c

moviegoers <u>can take advantage of</u> the matinee
                d

discounts. <u>No error</u>
               e

18. By mixing sounds from the <u>Jazz Age</u> with the
                                    a

beats of <u>contemporary modern</u> dance music,
              b

the DJ will show how twentieth-century

musicians <u>can be influenced</u> by the
                c

<u>sound and style</u> of early styles of music.
    d

<u>No error</u>
    e

19. Wolfgang <u>Amadeus</u> Mozart <u>began playing</u>
              a   b

music <u>on</u> a pianolike instrument called a
          c

<u>clavier.</u> <u>No error</u>
    d   e

20. As you read <u>them,</u> remember that this story
              a

    <u>is intended to be</u> a source of entertainment and
         b

    that <u>nothing</u> in it is <u>factual.</u> <u>No error</u>
         c   **d**   **e**

21. <u>Neither</u> the soldiers <u>nor</u> the sergeant <u>was</u> sure
     a   **b**   **c**

    of <u>their</u> location. <u>No error</u>
       d   **e**

Skills Test in Writing—Section 1, Part B

Directions: Choose the best replacement for the underlined portion of the sentence. If no revision is necessary, choose **a**, which always repeats the original phrasing.

22. <u>To determine the speed of pitches, radar is often used by baseball scouts.</u>
   a. To determine the speed of pitches, radar is often used by baseball scouts.
   b. To determine the speed of pitches, it is often necessary for baseball scouts to use radar.
   c. In determining the speed of pitches, the use of radar by baseball scouts is often employed.
   d. To determine the speed of pitches, baseball scouts often use radar.
   e. Radar by baseball scouts in determining the speed of pitches is often used.

23. The entire class signed the homework petition before <u>we submit it</u> to the teacher.
   a. we submit it
   b. one submits them
   c. you submit them
   d. we will submit it
   e. we submitted it

24. At 9 years old, Quvenzhané Wallis was the <u>younger</u> nominee ever for the Academy Award for Best Actress.
   a. younger
   b. more young
   c. most youngest
   d. youngest
   e. most youngly

25. Gloria has a multifaceted fitness regimen: <u>she swims laps, plays basketball, the weight machines, and surfing.</u>
   a. she swim laps, plays basketball, the weight machines, and surfing.
   b. she swims laps, plays basketball, lifts weights, and surfs.
   c. she swim laps, plays basketball, she lift weights, and surfs.
   d. swimming laps, basketball, lifting weights, and surfing.
   e. swims laps, plays basketball, lifting weights, and surfing.

26. Miles Davis, <u>a twentieth-century American trumpeter, is well known and renowned for creating</u> important improvisational jazz techniques.
   a. a twentieth-century American trumpeter, is well known and renowned for creating
   b. an American trumpeter who lived and played in the twentieth century, is well known for the creation of
   c. renowned and prominent, was known as a twentieth-century American trumpeter for creating
   d. he is an American trumpeter well known and renowned for creating
   e. a twentieth-century American trumpeter, is well known for creating

27. NASA scientists confirmed that the Mars rover's signal was lost for more than 24 hours.
    a. that the Mars rover's signal was lost for more than 24 hours.
    b. that the Mars rover's signal were lost for more than 24 hours.
    c. that the Mars rovers' signal were lost for more than 24 hours.
    d. that the Mars rovers' signal was lost for more than 24 hours.
    e. for more than 24 hours that the Mars rover lost its signal.

28. Reverend Martin Luther King, Jr. helped organize the famous 1963 March on Washington, which drew hundreds of thousands of civil rights supporters from all over the United States.
    a. which drew
    b. it drew
    c. but it drew
    d. that it drew
    e. and drawing

29. Please remember that I am older than him and have more experience in these matters.
    a. older than him and have
    b. oldest than him and have
    c. older than he and have
    d. more older than he and have
    e. less older than him and have

30. In 1978 the year I was born the average price of a new car was about $14,000.
    a. In 1978 the year I was born
    b. In 1978, the year I was born
    c. In 1978, the year I was born:
    d. In 1978, the year I was born,
    e. In 1978, the year I was born;

31. The likenesses of Washington, Jefferson, Lincoln, and Roosevelt is carved into the side of Mount Rushmore.
    a. is carved
    b. carved
    c. is been carved
    d. been carved
    e. are carved

32. A relationship between two dissimilar organisms that mutually benefits both organisms is called symbiosis.
    a. between two dissimilar organisms that mutually benefits
    b. among two dissimilar organisms that mutually benefits
    c. among two dissimilar organisms that mutually benefit
    d. between two dissimilar organisms that mutually benefit
    e. with two dissimilar organisms that mutually benefit

33. The CEO wished to insure the stockholders that their investment would be spent wisely.
    a. to insure the stockholders that their investment would be spent wisely.
    b. that the stockholders would be insured of investment wisely spent.
    c. in assuring the stockholders, that their investment would be wisely spent.
    d. to assure the stockholders that he would spend their investment wisely.
    e. to assure and promise the stockholders of his intentions to spend their investment wisely.

34. <u>Beside their use in jewelry,</u> silver has many uses in photography and electronics.
   a. Beside their use in jewelry,
   b. Beside jewelry,
   c. In addition also to its jewelry applications,
   d. Besides its use in jewelry,
   e. Besides your using it in jewelry,

35. It poured; <u>so I tried to run for cover.</u>
   a. It poured; so I tried to run for cover.
   b. It poured, so I tried to run for cover.
   c. It poured, I tried to run for cover.
   d. It's poured, I tried to run for cover
   e. It will pour, so I tried to run for cover.

36. The Beatles were <u>a big hit in America like England</u>.
   a. a big hit in America like England.
   b. as well a big hit in England as they were in America.
   c. as big a hit in America as they were in England.
   d. just as big a hit in America than in England.
   e. a big hit as well as in both England and America.

37. <u>The novel *The Grapes of Wrath* written by John Steinbeck in 1939 won the Pulitzer Prize in 1940.</u>
   a. The novel *The Grapes of Wrath* written by John Steinbeck in 1939 won the Pulitzer Prize, in 1940.
   b. The novel *The Grapes of Wrath*, written by John Steinbeck, in 1939 won the Pulitzer Prize, in 1940.
   c. The novel *The Grapes of Wrath* written by John Steinbeck, in 1939 won the Pulitzer Prize, in 1940.
   d. The novel, *The Grapes of Wrath*, written by John Steinbeck in 1939, won the Pulitzer Prize in 1940.
   e. The novel *The Grapes of Wrath*, written by John Steinbeck in 1939, won the Pulitzer Prize in 1940.

38. <u>Running toward the gate as the plane took off, leaving Aramis and I standing helplessly in the terminal.</u>
   a. Running toward the gate as the plane took off, leaving Aramis and I standing helplessly in the terminal.
   b. While running toward the gate and watching the plane take off, which left Aramis and me standing helplessly in the terminal.
   c. Left helplessly standing in the terminal after Aramis and me ran toward the gate and watched the plane take off.
   d. As we ran toward the gate, the plane took off, leaving Aramis and me standing helplessly in the terminal.
   e. After having run toward it, the plane taking off and leaving Aramis and me in the terminal, watching helplessly.

Skills Test in Writing— Section 2, Essay Writing

Carefully read the essay-writing topic that follows. Plan and write an essay that addresses all points in the topic. Make sure that your essay is well organized and that you support your central argument with concrete examples. Allow 30 minutes for your essay.

Many people would say that the Internet has become an indispensable aspect of our lives, affecting our work, our school, and our modes of communication. Write an essay in which you show how important or not the Internet is to modern life.

_____

_____

_____

_____

_____

_____

_____

_____

_____

_____

_____

_____

_____

_____

_____

FOCUSING ON THE PRAXIS II PLT

9 ▶ PRAXIS II PRINCIPLES OF LEARNING AND TEACHING REVIEW

CHAPTER SUMMARY

This chapter looks at principles of learning, instruction, assessment, communication, and teacher professionalism in education. It offers a broad base of information as it addresses information and ideas that are common to all levels of the Praxis II PLT. The principles reviewed here appear in each of the PLT tests: Early Childhood, Grades K–6, Grades 5–9, and Grades 7–12.

Teachers must have strong knowledge of educational psychology, child development, instructional design, lesson planning, assessment techniques, and classroom management. The Praxis II PLT measures your knowledge and understanding of basic theories and concepts in education and how to apply them to classroom situations. The test consists of two case histories. Each case presents a different teaching situation. You will be asked to write short constructed responses to two questions related to each case history. Each of these 4 constructed responses (2 case histories × 2 questions per case) will be scored on a scale of 0 to 2. The test also contains 70 multiple-choice questions. You will have two hours to complete the entire test. Plan to spend about 25 minutes on each of the two case histories and about 70 minutes on the 70 multiple-choice questions.

About the Case Histories

It will help you to know a bit more about the cases before you begin to review the content of the categories in this chapter. Cases are used on the Praxis II to determine how well you can apply the professional knowledge you have gained and respond to the situations presented in the cases in a meaningful way. These cases simulate actual teaching contexts and challenges you will face on a daily basis in the classroom. There may be several acceptable ways to respond to the questions that follow each case. As long as you can strongly support your explanation with logical evidence, your response will be valid. For scoring information and a scoring rubric for the PLT constructed responses, see Chapter 1, "The Praxis Series of Tests."

There are several characteristics of cases: They may be teacher-based, student-based, narrative, and/or document-based, or any combination of these. Descriptions of each follow:

- **teacher-based cases**—focus on practices used by one or more teachers
- **student-based cases**—focus on information about one or more students (i.e., their backgrounds, learning needs, and strengths)
- **narrative cases**—tell about something that happens in a classroom or school context
- **document-based cases**—provide several documents (i.e., a lesson plan, assignments, student work samples) relating to a student or a teacher

When constructing your response, be sure to make it clear to the scorer who will be reading your response that you clearly understand the case and the teaching practices related to the questions. Justify your responses by explaining why you answered as you did. Justification might include explaining an educational principle or theory, or referring specifically to a particular document in the case that supports your point.

With that said, it is time to proceed and review the categories that will be evaluated on the test. Keep in mind that some of these concepts will be assessed through multiple-choice questions and some by essays, which we refer to here as constructed responses. Be prepared to not only recall this information, but also to explain and apply it to educational contexts.

How to Use This Chapter

This chapter is divided into the four categories listed below. The percentage following each category is the approximate percentage of the total score attributed to that category. Knowing these percentages may be another contributing factor to help you decide how much time to spend studying and reviewing each category.

I.	Students as Learners	22.5%
II.	Instructional Process	22.5%
III.	Assessment	15%
IV.	Professional Development, Leadership, and Community	15%
V.	Analysis of Instructional Scenarios	25%

Remember, Category V, the case history constructed responses, which are worth 25% of the total score, includes questions related to two to four of Categories I through IV.

You are encouraged to begin your review of the principles of learning and teaching by self-assessing your areas of need and studying this chapter. However, to extend your studies, read widely. Consult other resources—books, professional journals, textbooks from past education courses, and the Internet—to become familiar with even more key concepts, names, theories, debates, and issues related to the topics you have identified as areas about which you want to increase your level of knowledge and confidence.

Finally, we recommend you join or form a study group of peers who are all preparing for the Praxis II PLT. Set a regular time to meet each week for several months before you are scheduled to take the test. Study meetings like this work best when each participant comes to the group prepared to share some information or to raise questions. Also, food can be a great motivator. Schedule your meetings around Thursday night pizza or Sunday morning lattés in the café!

When you meet, dedicate each meeting to one category. Decide beforehand the topics you will go over so that members can prepare by reading that section of this chapter. Note questions members of the group had as they were reading. Extend the readings by talking about related concepts and discussing how the topics can be applied to the classroom and pedagogy. Bring this book, a computer with Internet access, and other resources to the group meetings to guide and inform your discussion.

Use the Study Group Prompts inserted throughout this chapter to guide your discussion, and scribble your own prompts in the margins as you read to bring to the group. (The prompts provided offer open-ended discussion questions that aim to spark dialogue and thinking within the group; therefore, there are no "right" answers provided within this book.) When you come to an area your group wants to research further, search the Internet, find the information, and share information with the group immediately. If you cannot find the information right away, assign a member of the group to research it and report his or her findings to the group at the next meeting.

You may want to extend your study group by blogging or setting up some other form of online communication throughout the week. You could arrange something creative so that the group reviews one topic each day. For example, you might "assign" one day of the week to each member of the group. On that day, the member writes and posts a short Education Snippet of the Day to share with the group. Imagine the number of snippets you could accumulate over just a few weeks of posting. The idea is to study in small increments, collaborate with peers, discuss your understanding, and keep each other motivated by working together.

Good luck—and try to enjoy learning and preparing for your future career as an educator—as you prepare for the Praxis PLT II. Now, let's get started with the first category.

Category I: Students as Learners

Important Theorists

> **Study Group Prompt:** *What classroom practices reflect each of these theorists' beliefs?*

John Dewey—no, nothing to do with the Dewey Decimal System—was the foremost American educator of his day. In the late 1800s and early 1900s, Dewey proposed that schools should reflect the needs of society. When you think of Dewey, think of progressive education. Although Dewey didn't coin the phrase, we associate it with Dewey based on his rejection of authoritarian teaching methods and his belief that schools educate the whole child to help him or her become a well-rounded human being, not just a good student. Dewey's approach supported the introduction of the arts in education. Also, when you think of Dewey, think of democracy. He regarded democracy as a primary ethical value, and this idea shaped his educational theories. He believed there was a strong connection between social action and education in a democratic society. To be good citizens who can actively participate in a community, students should be encouraged to explore and inquire, solve problems and become critical thinkers, and work cooperatively with others. Students, Dewey believed, should participate in decisions that affect their learning. His book, *Pedagogic Creed*, became a guide for educators when it was published in 1897. His thinking challenged the more traditional methods of rote learning and authoritative teaching that were commonplace in that era. You can imagine how Dewey must have been seen as a radical in his day!

Around about the same time Dewey was changing education in America—the early 1900s—Maria Montessori was doing the same in Italy, India, and, by invitation, the United States. She founded the

Montessori approach of education, which emphasizes developmental, hands-on learning. Today, we associate hands-on learning with early childhood education; Montessori schools worked with students from birth through 18 years. Her schools, still around today, are known as child-centered settings worldwide. Montessori schools focus on teaching students how to develop skills at a pace they set themselves. Her approach uses a variety of equipment of increasing complexity to complement students' interests and hasten development. When a student shows a readiness to learn and an interest in learning a new or more difficult task, the teacher's job is to guide the student's first attempts to avoid any wasted effort and the development of wrong habits. Otherwise, the student develops on his or her own based on interest and open-ended research.

Jerome Bruner, whose work followed Dewey and Montessori in the middle through late 1900s, also made profound contributions to education and curriculum theory. Think of Bruner as the father of Discovery Learning. He believed learners create and think as they inquire and experience events. Discovery learning focuses on the active process of constructing knowledge and understanding through authentic experiences, rather than the ability to output information. To learn, students participate in problem-solving situations where they draw on existing knowledge and past experiences. Through discovering, exploring, experimenting, inquiring, wrestling with issues, and manipulating objects, they learn new relationships and truths and are more likely to remember concepts and knowledge. Furthermore, Bruner proposed that any child at any stage of development can learn any subject. This idea inspired the spiral curriculum that is still used today in most American schools: The spiral curriculum builds on basic ideas year after year. Of course, each year concepts and constructs become increasingly complex as the student develops and knowledge and insight build. Think of how the concepts of growth and change in biology would be introduced in preschool, elementary, and high-school classrooms. Visualize how the spiral swirls up and around, building on past understanding from grade level to grade level.

Terms Related to Learning Theory

There are three main learning theories: behaviorism, cognitivism, and constructivism. As a result of advances in media and technology, a theory of networked learning known as connectivism, which we briefly describe, has also emerged. Each theory makes certain assumptions about how people learn. Let's look at each one.

> **Study Group Prompt:** *How is each of these theories manifested in a classroom? For example, what classroom events imply a particular learning theory is true? And, how would a teacher instruct if he or she holds a particular theory to be true?*

Behaviorism assumes learners are passive. They start off as a clean slate and learn by responding to stimuli in the environment. Learning and behavior are shaped through a student's response to positive and negative reinforcements, punishment, and rewards. Learning is recognized as a change in the student's behavior. You probably remember B. F. Skinner and Pavlov's work with animals. Pavlov's dogs, for example, were conditioned to drool at the sound of a bell because they learned they would be fed when the bell rang. Much of the early work of behaviorists was done initially with animals and then generalized to humans. So, now you know why you start to drool when you hear the ice-cream truck's jingle!

Behaviorism was dominant until the 1960s, when **cognitivism** took over as the more popular learning paradigm. Cognitivism sees learners as problem-solvers who are able to think for themselves, and sees brains as computers that process, organize, and use information and produce certain outcomes. To teach students, then, we need to investigate phenomena such as memory, thinking, and what it means to know something. Cognitivists credit learning as a change in a student's schemata or mental constructions and say—unlike the behaviorists—that rational beings must participate actively in learning. This participation is a consequence of thinking. The changes noted in behavior are important to observe, but only because they indicate the cognitive learning that is taking place in the learner's mind.

Constructivism, which became very popular in the 1980s and 1990s, assumes learners build—or construct—knowledge and personal understanding based on their experiences coupled with the negotiation of meanings. Social constructivism presumes this happens within social contexts. That is, through approaches that encourage students to test hypotheses and talk with others about how they interpret events and concepts, they "grow" knowledge rather than acquire it or are conditioned. Learning occurs within an active context wherein students construct their own interpretations of events, concepts, and ideas. Constructivism is commonly misapplied in classrooms. Constructivists do not presume teachers should never directly teach students anything. Constructivism assumes learners use their previous knowledge to construct new understanding, regardless of how they are taught. Therefore, even when listening to a lecture, a student can be actively constructing new knowledge by interpreting the lecturer's words and the ideas presented based on what he or she already knows. However, typically, teachers in a constructivist classroom are seen as facilitators or coaches. Jean Piaget and Lev Vygotsky are often credited with planting the seeds of constructivism. Bruner's later work drew attention to constructivism.

Finally, **connectivism** is a learning theory that has come about as a result of the surge of media and technology advancements. It is consistent with recent brain research. Connectivists assume learners actively connect special sets of information. They see the connections that help us learn and the learner's ability to merge them as increasingly more important than one's current state of knowing. Connectivism is based on the idea that new information is continually acquired and changed. It is stored in multiple locations throughout the brain within a network. The more connections there are to a single piece of information, the more likely a student is to remember it. Learners must distinguish which information is valuable and which is not. Connectivists might say, "The world is changing so fast that it's more important to know how to learn by connecting and evaluating information from multiple sources than it is to bank knowledge for future use. Knowledge quickly becomes outdated and must be revised. Students must know how to negotiate diverse opinions."

> **Study Group Prompt:** *What type of visual graphic organizer could your group create to help you compare and contrast the theorists and the learning theories presented so far? Give it a try!*

Important Theorists with Major Progressions

> **Study Group Prompt:** *As you work through the following theorists and progressions of human development, discuss how each relates to classroom pedagogy. For example, how might preschool teachers shape their curriculum and pedagogy keeping Erikson's stages of personality development in mind?*

People develop cognitively, socially, emotionally, physically, and so on. When we look at human development theorists, we must consider the various domains of development. Let's look at several theorists whose work has greatly influenced education.

"I'm having an identity crisis!" This phrase should be associated with Erik Erikson and his psychosocial theory of human personality development. Erikson proposed that people continue to develop through adolescence and adulthood. Previous to his theory, we saw development ending much earlier in the life span. Erikson proposed that people move through eight stages of development. The first five stages are associated with school-age children:

1. **Trust versus Mistrust (birth to 1 year old):** Infants depend on parents for their every need.
2. **Autonomy versus Shame and Doubt (2 to 3 years old):** Toddlers gain control and begin to explore.
3. **Initiative versus Guilt (4 to 6 years old):** Children initiate actions and attempt to master their world.
4. **Industry versus Inferiority (7 to 11 years old):** Children diligently produce works and develop self-confidence with successes.
5. **Identity versus Role Confusion (12 to 19 years old):** Adolescents are concerned with who they are and how they appear to others.

Bowlby and Ainsworth studied attachment, which is the emotional bond that exists between people. They described several types of attachment and suggest secure attachments lead one to feel safe to explore the world. Their focus on relationships has many implications for childcare and education.

B. F. Skinner, whom we know as a behaviorist, focused on the ways the environment and interactions influence behavior and development. He considered development to be a reaction to stimuli and reinforcements, such as rewards and punishments.

Jean Piaget created a revolution in human development with his theory of cognitive development that dominated the study of child development in the 1970s and 1980s. He proposed there are four periods of growth. They are:

1. **Sensorimotor Stage (birth to 2 years old):** Infants move from instinctual, reflexive actions to the beginnings of developing symbolic thoughts.
2. **Preoperational Stage (2 to 7 years old):** Children demonstrate egocentrism.
3. **Concrete Operational Stage (7 to 11 years old):** Children can use logic to process seriation, classification, and conservation.
4. **Formal Operational Stage (11 years old into adulthood):** Adolescents and adults move beyond the concrete into abstract thinking and reasoning.

Whereas Piaget believed that developmental growth (moving through the stages) causes learning to happen, Lev Vygotsky believed that learning comes first and causes children to develop. See the twist there? Vygotsky's social development theory views learning—cognitive development—as a social process. Supportive adults and peers help scaffold learning. More about Piaget and Vygotsky appears in the following section on the impact of development on learning.

Finally, let's look at moral development. Lawrence Kohlberg thought that moral reasoning is the route of ethical behavior and listed six levels of moral development. At the lower level, children judge whether an action is moral by its immediate consequences. At the medial level, adolescents judge the morality of actions based on how society views them. At the higher levels, one's own perspective on what is right and what is wrong may take precedence over that of society.

The Impact of Development on Learning

When theories of learning and human development are applied to schooling, one can see how curriculum can become dependent on whether a child is deemed ready to learn something. For example, Piaget's stages of cognitive development would imply that educators would plan developmentally appropriate curriculum and practices that enhance students' cognitive growth. Very young students would not be expected to be able to think abstractly. Concrete operations would be more effective. Followers of Vygotsky would be sure to assess to establish where the student is working in his or her zone of proximal development—the point of learning between what the student can do independently and what he or she can do with the help of a more knowledgeable peer or adult. Sociocultural theorists who have applied and expanded Vygotsky's work would expect educators to scaffold students' learning by gradually decreasing support as students work toward independence. To this end, the student becomes an apprentice. Educators aware of Erikson's theory of personality development would create responsive, caring learning environments in which social skills, relationship-based teaching, and reflective practices are integrated into all aspects of the curriculum and reflective practices.

> **Study Group Prompt:** *What other theories on learning and human development influence pedagogy? Explain how.*

Development across Domains

There is more than one type of learning. The term *learning domain* refers to cognitive, affective, psychomotor, and interpersonal functions. Educators must analyze the type of domain they plan to access as they plan lessons so that they can determine the appropriate tasks, activities, and assessments. Presenting and assessing through multiple modes will increase the probability that students will reach high levels of learning. Let's look at each type of domain.

The **cognitive domain** centers on intellectual skills. You'll remember Bloom's Taxonomy of Learning Domains: knowledge, comprehension, application, analysis, synthesis, and evaluation. Bloom's

Taxonomy describes the progressively complex levels of cognitive skills. Students advance through the levels from beginner to more advanced. Methods such as providing graphic organizers, class notes, additional examples, and self-check quizzes will facilitate students' work in the cognitive domain. As students become more skilled in this domain, collaborative assignments will help them engage in problem-solving as they synthesize and evaluate.

> **Study Group Prompt:** *Discuss ways you might integrate Bloom's Taxonomy into lesson planning.*

The **affective domain** focuses on attitudes, engagement, and motivation. Stages of affective skills are:

- receiving (listening)
- responding (participating)
- valuing (being involved)
- organizing (advocating)
- characterizing (changing behavior or lifestyle)

Methods such as providing opportunities for students to experience success often; encouraging them to set personal goals; and offering support and meaningful, sincere feedback and encouragement have been proven to enhance students' work in the affective domain.

The **psychomotor domain** centers on demonstrating accuracy and skill through motor activities, such as laboratory, vocational, and physical education courses and the performing arts. The psychomotor domain is represented by levels or stages of action (basic movement), coordination (synchronized movement), formation (body movement), and production (combining verbal and nonverbal movements). Educators address this domain through hands-on demonstrations, simulations, and performances. When content is new to students, they generally find it helpful to be introduced to it through the psychomotor domain, so they are experiencing it physically in some way. As they become more expert, they will be increasingly able to learn from videos and pictures.

Finally, the **interpersonal domain** focuses on interactions among people or learners. Students move among skill levels as they seek and give information, propose ideas, help others build and support their ideas, exclude or involve others, offer differing opinions, negotiate, make compromises, lead others, and summarize ideas. Students learn skills best in this domain by seeing models, being coached, and practicing.

> **Study Group Prompt:** *How might educators present lessons that include all four domains? How might development in one domain affect performance in another domain?*

Understanding Diversity

> **Study Group Prompt:** *There are many ways to define diversity. How would you define it?*

Educators must recognize and understand that diversity includes differences in the ways students participate and learn based on various factors such as students' culture, race, gender, immigrant status, socioeconomic level, ethnicity, language, cognitive abilities, challenges, family support, and so on. Teachers, administrators, and all staff must be prepared to meet the diverse needs of students and their families on a daily basis. We should also reflect on our own biases and background so we can work best with our students.

As educators, it is our responsibility to become familiar with the cultures and languages of our students so we can best help students apply prior experiences to their current learning. Schools offer a number of approaches to accommodating and teaching second-language learners (SLLs) and bilingual students. While some schools immerse SLLs in the English language with some support, other schools provide instruction in English as a second language or offer two-way or transitional bilingual education. There are advantages and disadvantages to each approach.

> **Study Group Prompt:** *What might be some of the advantages and disadvantages of each of the types of language instruction? Which approach do you think is most child-centered and most effective? What types of instruction and assessment accommodations should be made for second-language learners?*

Learning Styles

Educators know that students learn in different ways; therefore, we have to be prepared to design lessons to maximize all students' learning styles. One approach comes from **Kolb's experiential learning theory**. This model proposes that we learn from concrete experiences by actively participating in new experiences, from reflective observations by watching others participate, from abstract conceptualizations by generating theories to explain experiences, and from active experimentation by applying theories to solve problems. According to Kolb, students benefit most when they engage in all four modes, and they tend to develop strengths in one or two modes as they practice them. As a result, they develop as:

- **convergers**—good at applying new ideas and deductive reasoning
- **divergers**—characterized as imaginative
- **assimilators**—good at inductive reasoning and producing theoretical models
- **accommodators**—actively engage in doing things rather than reading about them

Fleming's VARK model is one of the most widely known ways to categorize learning styles. VARK stands for visual, auditory, reading/writing-preference, and kinesthetic learning. Visual learners prefer learning through pictures, visual aids, handouts, and so on. They like to sit in the front of the classroom, and often take numerous, detailed notes. Auditory learners prefer listening through lectures and discussions. They often learn best by reading aloud and study by talking aloud. Reading/writing-preference learners prefer reading, taking notes, and being able to see and record what they hear. Kinesthetic learners prefer to move and actively explore. They are more likely to remember what was done versus what was said. They use many gestures when speaking. Educators should prepare lessons that incorporate each area. Also, students can identify their preferred learning style and then focus on the style from which they learn best.

Other learning styles have been identified as well. For example, some people learn best through interacting with others through discussions and debates. Others learn best through hands-on experiences, and still others learn best through their sense of smell or taste. If you've ever walked into a room and smelled an odor that reminds you of a past learning experience, you may be an olfactory learner.

> **Study Group Prompt:** *What kinds of physical changes could teachers make in their classroom environment to benefit every learning style?*

Multiple Intelligences

Howard Gardner's theory of multiple intelligences, which was developed in 1983, suggests there is more to intelligence than an IQ score. Gardner proposed these eight types of intelligence:

- linguistic intelligence—someone who is "word smart"
- logical-mathematical intelligence—someone who is "number or reasoning smart"
- spatial intelligence—someone who is "picture smart"
- bodily-kinesthetic intelligence—someone who is "body smart"

- musical intelligence—someone who is "music smart"
- interpersonal intelligence—someone who is "people smart"
- intrapersonal intelligence—someone who is "self smart"
- naturalist intelligence—someone who is "nature smart"

Although schools tend to value and recognize linguistic and logical-mathematical intelligences the most, Gardner proposes we should equally value the gifts other intelligences offer. In our schools, many students who are intelligent in the other areas struggle because they have unique ways of thinking and learning. The theory of multiple intelligences suggests teachers present their lessons in a variety of ways, such as through the arts, field trips, multimedia, and so on, especially if a teacher is having a hard time reaching students in the traditional ways.

> **Study Group Prompt:** *Take a sample lesson and discuss how you might teach it eight different ways to meet the needs of students who learn best through each of the eight intelligences.*

Gender Differences

Gender-specific personality traits can affect how children learn. We used to think in the 1960s and into the 1980s that gender differences were constructed socially by the way we treated boys and girls. However, the National Institutes of Health has found gender differences in personality are consistent across all cultures. There are significant differences in the ways girls and boys learn. These differences are even more significant than differences in age.

Girls and boys practice different learning strategies. For example, girls and boys differ in their performances in math and reading. Girls tend to do better in reading; boys tend to do better in math.

Girls are stronger at memorization, planning, organizing, and reflecting on their own learning. Teachers must question and challenge their expectations for both genders and motivate both genders to participate and reflect on their learning.

> **Study Group Prompt:** *What experiences have you had with gender biases in a school setting that may have influenced your learning? How might teachers have influenced your learning based on your gender?*

Culture

A culture is a group or community that shares common experiences, understandings, and traditions. There are many types of cultural differences, such as differences in the ways people communicate both verbally and nonverbally, in their learning style preferences, in the rules they follow for adult-child relationships and discourse, and in the ways they greet each other. These seemingly simple differences can greatly influence students' learning; therefore, it is very important for teachers to not only be aware of students' cultures, but also to be knowledgeable about how to set expectations regarding student-teacher relationships, classroom participation, and social interactions involving peer groups. If the teacher is not familiar with the traditions, expectations, and daily lifestyle of a culture, he or she should make it a priority to research the culture either firsthand by spending time immersed in it or by reading about it. A teacher's own cultural values and traditions may be very different from those of his or her students; therefore, the teacher must be sure to reflect and act on any biases that may exist.

Teachers should offer opportunities for students to share their cultural experiences with their classmates in a safe environment. Make multiculturalism and diversity a part of every lesson by bringing in diverse ways of doing things. Integrating multiculturalism within themes is much more effective than doing a once-a-year theme on multiculturalism and then omitting it from daily lessons. Involve parents and families in planning and instructional support to enhance learning and participation of all cultures.

Types of Exceptionalities

Students may be diverse in their exceptionalities. That is, students may have special needs in one or more areas. There are a number of areas in which students may have cognitive, physical, social, or emotional exceptionalities, including learning disabilities, vision and perception, physical or sensory disabilities, mental retardation, behavioral disorders, developmental delays, and attention-deficit or attention-deficit/hyperactivity disorder.

Teachers must know how to adapt and accommodate to meet students' needs. Students with special needs will be mainstreamed into the regular classroom, and it is the teacher's responsibility to teach all students. Therefore, you have to have an arsenal of methods and approaches that allow you to differentiate instruction to meet various needs.

Legislation and Responsibilities Regarding Exceptionalities

- **Americans with Disabilities Act (ADA)**—prohibits discrimination based on disability. It sets forth a national mandate that ensures the federal government prohibits this kind of discrimination. Go to www.ada.gov for complete information on ADA.
- **Individuals with Disabilities Education Act (IDEA)**—governs the provision of free and appropriate public education, early intervention, and related services for all students, preschool through age 21, with special needs. Go to http://idea.ed.gov for complete information on IDEA.
- Check what laws and specific regulations regarding exceptionalities exist in your state. Be familiar with provisions made to ensure students' rights are protected. You can find this in-

formation by searching your state's department of education website.

Study Group Prompt: *Discuss the implications of ADA, IDEA, and state laws regarding exceptionalities in a school setting.*

Terms Related to Legislation

- **inclusion**—when students with special needs are placed in the same classroom as children without disabilities
- **mainstreaming**—when students with special needs spend all or some of their days in a regular classroom setting
- **"least restrictive environment"**—an educational setting that allows students with special needs to learn to the best of their ability with the least number of restrictions present

Study Group Prompt: *What do you think some of the advantages and disadvantages might be to inclusion, mainstreaming, and placing a student in the least restrictive environment?*

- **Individualized Education Plan (IEP)**—an education plan that is designed and updated annually for school-age children who have been identified as having special needs. It is written and approved by educators and the child's family. IEPs must include a description of the child's present functioning, measurable goals and learning objectives and how they will be evaluated, description and duration of the services provided, and placement.
- **Section 504 of the Rehabilitation Services Act**—prohibits discrimination against students with special needs who do not meet the definition of a child with disabilities stipulated by

IDEA. Section 504 prohibits discrimination in after-school programs, care, and sports that are not covered by IDEA. Schools must identify and evaluate the students and, if eligible, the school must write a 504 plan, which is similar to (but not as lengthy as) an IEP. Families, teachers, and school staff are involved in the process.

- **due process**—a reporting procedure that protects the rights of students with special needs by granting families and schools the right to an impartial hearing to review placement and planning for the student. Due process rights are assured and outlined in IDEA.

How Can Educators Accommodate Diversity?

Three effective approaches for accommodating diverse needs are differentiated instruction, alternative assessments, and testing modifications. To differentiate instruction, teachers must be knowledgeable about exceptionalities and diverse needs, how to assess students' needs, and how to teach students with these exceptionalities and needs effectively. By differentiating instruction, teachers maximize students' learning by meeting each individual student where he or she is academically, emotionally, and physically and helping the student move to a higher level of understanding or skill. Differentiated instruction is student-centered. Teachers can differentiate by varying teaching methods, materials, strategies, the physical setting or design, assessment style, and lessons to accommodate learning styles and needs.

Study Group Prompt: *What kinds of strategies and teaching approaches lead to differentiated instruction?*

Alternative assessments—also called authentic assessments—consist of activities or tasks designed to equitably demonstrate a student's learning in nontraditional ways. They emphasize students' strengths rather than their weaknesses, and are not only different from traditional tests in their design and structure, but may also be graded differently. Examples of alternative assessments include demonstrations and performances that assess understanding through displays of interpretation rather than responding on a multiple-choice test. You can see how alternative assessments open the door for diverse students to express what they know in forms they can interact with more comfortably.

> **Study Group Prompt:** *What kinds of alternative assessments might English language learners favor over a written test essay response to reveal what they know about a topic?*

Testing modifications minimize the effects of the student's disability in testing situations by allowing support or assistance. They are not meant to compensate for the students' lack of understanding or skill; they are not meant to be a substitute for ability or knowledge. They can vary from one student, grade level, test, and state to another. Examples of testing modifications include extending the time allowed on a test, having the test read to the student, and moving the student from one setting to another.

What Are the Best Ways to Teach Second-Language Learners?

The change in demographics that has occurred in the United States over the past 20 years has greatly affected schools. As a nation, we are still trying to figure out how best to teach second-language learners who face many challenges in our schools. Learning English as a second language involves not just linguistic challenges; it introduces social and cultural challenges as well when students must put up with discrimination, prejudice, and ignorance based on their differences.

Educators must first observe and assess second-language learners to determine what strategies they are already using. For example, do they have frequent contact with all students? Do they ask for clarification when they do not understand? Which situations motivate students to use their first language, and which cause them to use English? These types of observations will inform instruction and indicate where the students' comfort and confidence levels are. Then educators can provide a wide variety of learning strategies to support students' learning styles, motivating factors, and strategy preferences.

> **Study Group Prompt:** *What relevant experiences have you had related to teaching or interacting with second-language learners?*

Student Motivation and the Learning Environment

What motivates you to study for the Praxis? Is it that you want to prepare to be the best teacher you can be? Is it that you want to get a good score? (It's probably a little of both. Right?) **Motivation** can be described as an **internal** (preparing for teaching) or **externally caused** (getting a good score) need or desire that can energize a person to act in a certain way (to study for the Praxis). Motivation causes students to want to learn and stimulates them to direct their behaviors in productive ways. Internal motivation is caused by the students' determination to achieve a self-set goal. You want to do well on the Praxis because it will make you feel confident about teaching. Externally caused motivation can be the result of receiving some favorable compensation from others, such as stickers, good grades, or extra recess time. Optimally, we want students to experience internal motivation to learn. This has been proven to be more effective over time than external rewards.

There are several theories of motivation that are based on the various theories of learning and development. You can see how your beliefs about how someone learns and develops would influence how you think he or she is motivated. For example, if you are a **behaviorist**, you would explain motivation based on your observation of students' behaviors. First, you would decide on and identify the student behaviors you want to change. Then, you would control students' behaviors by giving them rewards to reinforce the occurrence of what you want them to do and punish them (or not give a reward) to decrease the occurrence of the behavior. Here, you're using extrinsic rewards to motivate students. Through classical conditioning, you are causing biological responses to the stimuli that act to energize and direct the students' behaviors. What happens when the teacher leaves the room, though? Students haven't been internally motivated, so they are more than likely going to slip back into exhibiting the undesirable behaviors, unless they have internalized the desired goals and behaviors. If you've ever been a substitute teacher, you understand where we're going here! Typically, rewards and punishments work well for short-term but not long-term motivation and behavior changes.

If you follow, instead, the **cognitive** approach, you would say we process information and are motivated by how we perceive our ability, luck, effort, and the difficulty of the task. This theory is called **attribute theory**. These attributes are either perceived as controlled internally by the person or externally by others. Teachers must help students develop self-esteem ("I'm pretty smart and I value that about myself") and self-efficacy ("I can do this") so that they believe they have control over their behaviors, learning, and outcomes. For instance, we can teach students that they have control over the amount of effort they put into something. But, then, when learning that problems occur, students' learning behaviors may decrease because they feel they have no ability or control. Using appropriate teaching methods to meet students' needs can reengage them and teach them to take charge of their learning.

> **Study Group Prompt:** *What kinds of teaching methods would reengage disenchanted students?*

Another cognitive approach motivation theory is called **expectancy theory**. This theory proposes that if I expect I can be successful at a task, I see a connection between the task and success, and I value that success—motivating me. All factors have to be present for a high level of motivation.

Abraham Maslow offers a **humanistic approach** through his **Hierarchy of Needs**. He proposed that if we are hungry, thirsty, physically uncomfortable (physiological needs); if we feel unsafe (safety/security needs); if we feel unaccepted or unloved by others (belongingness needs); or if we feel incompetent and unrecognized (esteem needs), then we will be motivated to meet these needs before moving to his higher level of needs in the hierarchy. He thought our motivation to acquire these basic needs would energize, direct, and sustain—our definition of motivation—our behaviors. Once these four levels were achieved, then we could move on to the next four levels. They are the cognitive level, the aesthetic level, self-actualization or self-fulfillment, and self-transcendence. These final levels reflect enlightenment and empowerment, which are intrinsically motivating.

What Factors and Situations Foster Students' Motivation?

There are many "tricks of the trade" that highly skilled and effective teachers know and integrate into their daily planning and teaching to motivate students. Here are some of the most valuable that help motivate students intrinsically:

- Teachers must first believe the work is important and meaningful themselves to honestly portray their beliefs to their students.
- Teachers must believe—and frequently express to students—that all students are capable of achieving challenging, yet reasonable, expectations.
- Teachers and students make decisions about goals mutually so students are empowered and feel a sense of control over activities.
- Teachers should clearly explain the reasons why the content or skill is valuable.
- Lessons should be authentically related to real-life skills and expectations.
- Activities should vary and aim to meet all students' needs and learning styles.
- Students should be given choices.
- Materials and resources should be available to meet all students' reading and skill needs.
- Constructive feedback should be provided along the way.
- Teachers should provoke students' curiosity.
- Teachers should present activities in interesting contexts.

> **Study Group Prompt:** *What points can you add to this list that motivate you?*

Principles of Effective Classroom Management

Although educators aim for child-centered classrooms that encourage students to explore and inquire as they collaborate with peers, we still need to maintain an equitable and safe learning environment. How do we do this? Here are more "tricks of the trade" our best educators use:

- Establish daily routines so students can predict what comes next. Have a class schedule posted in the room. At the beginning of each school day, go over the schedule and announce any changes to the usual routine.
- Establish classroom rules—preferably composed mutually with the students—that are consistent so students know what to expect. Constructing the rules mutually makes them "our" rules versus the teacher's rules. Discuss the rationale behind each rule. Post the rules in a prominent place in the classroom for all to see. Refer to them often. Determine ahead of time what happens—what are the consequences?—when a rule is not followed?
- Provide positive guidance regularly. "Catch" them being good so that you are praising students who model good behaviors and work habits. Provide positive feedback frequently, as well.
- Model the behaviors you want from your students. Show them how you resolve conflicts, solve problems, and control your anger. Be kind to all students all the time. Never be sarcastic or rude. Promote academics by modeling your love of learning. For example, let the students "catch" you reading a book when they come into the classroom and tell them how much you enjoy reading.
- Keep accurate records that are always up to date. Be accountable.
- Communicate with students, their families, your administrator, and your colleagues on a regular basis.
- Respond to students' behaviors immediately. Don't ignore pushing or name-calling. Let your students know from the first day of school that you will not tolerate such behaviors. Always explain why.
- Provide a safe environment for all students. Allow adequate spaces in the classroom where students can go to be away from others sometimes.
- Spend time planning your lessons carefully to accommodate for classroom management is-

sues, such as movement of students and furniture, noise level needed so all students can function and concentrate, and how you will keep students on task.

■ After each day, take time to reflect on classroom management to see whether you can improve anything.

Category II: Instructional Process

Major Cognitive Processes Associated with Students' Learning

Educators are challenged to not only arouse students' curiosity and get them to think about things, but also to teach them to think in certain high-level ways. So, what does that mean? Isn't thinking just thinking? Well, no. There are lots of kinds of thinking. Benjamin Bloom showed us that with his Taxonomy of Learning Domains. According to Bloom, there are three domains: cognitive, affective, and psychomotor. Educators use the cognitive domain widely to plan lessons. The six levels of the cognitive domain are listed here, from the lowest level of cognition to the highest level.

■ **knowledge**—recalling information (defining, describing, identifying, labeling)
■ **comprehension**—making meanings; understanding things (defending, giving examples, summarizing)
■ **application**—using a concept in a new situation (demonstrating, modifying, relating)
■ **analysis**—separating concepts into their parts to understand how they're organized (making inferences, analyzing, comparing and contrasting)
■ **synthesis**—putting parts together to make new meanings (reconstructing, categorizing, compiling)

■ **evaluation**—making judgments (appraising, making conclusions, interpreting)

As teachers we also want to encourage students to think critically and creatively, be inductive and deductive thinkers, solve problems, invent, memorize, and recall things. The next section helps us think about—Bloom would say we'd be applying—ways to do that.

Instructional Strategies

Study Group Prompt: *Discuss some of the advantages and disadvantages to each of the following instructional strategies.*

Cooperative learning involves small groups of students who are at various levels of ability (heterogeneously grouped) interacting to help each other learn as they accomplish a task or multiple tasks around a subject. The groups not only learn about the subject but also experience how to work with others.

Direct instruction is often associated with the Direct Instruction System for Teaching Arithmetic and Reading (DISTAR) program, which was implemented by the U.S. government to help disadvantaged public schools. Direct instruction usually involves teachers following scripted lessons, which tell them how to run the lesson down to the detail of what to say. Direct instruction can also refer to teacher-directed instruction that is often referred to as the "meat and potatoes" of a lesson, where the teacher models and explains a skill or concept.

Student-centered models highlight students' needs, interests, skills, and learning styles as the focus of learning. The teacher's role is that of facilitator, as students' voices dominate the classroom.

Discovery learning and **inquiry** encourage students to follow their interests and questions within a topic. Students are allowed space to solve problems and learn from their past experiences.

Interdisciplinary instruction involves integrating the content areas. Commonly, in theme or unit approaches, interdisciplinary instruction is used to provide a full, contextualized picture of an issue or topic.

Concept mapping is an instructional strategy in which students construct a visual representation of a concept or topic that breaks down and organizes the concepts that compose a topic. Concept maps illustrate how ideas are connected within a topic.

Play has many benefits as an instructional strategy, especially for young children who become immersed in pretend play worlds to make clarifications, explore, and socialize. **Learning centers** can be organized in a classroom so students can participate in several small-group learning experiences in a row.

Small-group lessons allow teachers to interact intimately with a few students. Teachers can observe and assess students' needs closely and provide individual help immediately. Students learn from each other by listening and watching interactions.

Service learning projects integrate authentic community service with instruction and learning. Students learn about civic responsibility as they work with local or international communities in various capacities and reflect on their role in the community and the world.

Other methods that enhance students' learning are computers and Internet resources, audiovisual technologies, bringing in local experts, viewing and manipulating primary documents and artifacts, going on field trips, and visiting libraries.

Planning Instruction

Teachers have the benefit of consulting many resources to help them plan instruction. Not only are there state and national learning standards to guide our work with students, but there are also curriculum frameworks, guides, and webbing; and scope and sequence charts across disciplines. Publishing compa-

nies and professional organizations also offer curriculum packages, units, and lessons.

We cannot discount, though, how important it is to plan thoughtful lessons on a daily basis. Composing lesson plans or learning objectives (what you want students to learn from the lesson) that are connected to learning standards (what the state and national government have determined it is important for students to learn at a particular grade level), instruction (the teaching component), and assessments (how you'll determine whether students reached the objectives) helps teachers follow through with well-designed instruction and helps students see how materials and instruction are related to goals.

Learning objectives clearly tell what the intended learning outcome or end product of the lesson will be. Learning objectives should include cognitive, affective, speech and language, and psychomotor goals. Bloom's Taxonomy is often used as a way to categorize the types of objectives as we ask students to gain knowledge or skills in comprehension, application, analysis, synthesis, or evaluation. When writing behavioral objectives that reflect the particular behavior you'll be looking to assess to determine whether the student reached the objective, use verbs that are observable and measureable, such as *describes*, *reports*, *demonstrates*, or *analyzes*.

Other factors to consider when writing lesson plans and objectives follow.

- How will you integrate learning across the content areas?
- Will the lesson be teacher-led or student-led?
- What types of technology will enhance the lesson?
- How will you teach to meet the needs of all students' learning styles, strengths, and needs? How will you accommodate all students?
- How will you vary your teaching methods and instructional strategies?
- How will you encourage students to activate their prior knowledge of a topic and apply it to the new ideas of this lesson?

- What types of questions will you incorporate to encourage participation and to extend thinking and language?
- What is the best way to group students for this lesson?
- What materials, resources, and equipment will you need?
- How much time will you need to fully complete the lesson?
- How might you involve families and other community members?
- What is the best way to assess whether or not students have met the objectives?
- What will you do to help students who struggle and do not reach the objectives?

Before finishing up with techniques for planning instruction, we should mention two types of curricula: emergent and antibias. What are they? **Emergent curriculum** is based on the student's and the teacher's interests. How does it work? Instead of starting with a lesson plan and ideas to motivate students to learn and produce, emergent curriculum starts with observation, brainstorming, and flexibility. A teacher may introduce experiences or materials to get students interested in a general topic. Or the teacher may hear students talking about a topic with interest and use that topic as the base for instruction. Brainstorming and webbing are then used as a road map to decide what students and the teacher want to learn about the topic. One school system that follows this type of curriculum is the Reggio Emilia schools.

Antibias curriculum aims to eliminate bias by helping students form a solid understanding of the issues and problems of society. It helps students develop an understanding of social justice.

Creating Bridges Between Students' Experiences and Curriculum Goals

The following techniques capitalize on students' experiences to help them reach curriculum goals.

- **modeling**—Students watch and listen as a teacher or another more knowledgeable person demonstrates how to do something. When accompanied by the teacher thinking aloud about the processes that go with the actions, teaching can be quite effective.
- **guided practice**—As students work toward being able to perform a task independently, the teacher asks guiding questions and provides scaffolded instruction to assist students through the task.
- **activating prior knowledge**—When beginning a new topic, teachers help students think about other experiences they've had—books they've read, places they've visited, and so on—that are related to the topic. These discussions bring in the vocabulary and concepts that are relevant to the topic so students can make connections to what they know.

Other techniques include anticipating preconceptions about a topic, using transitioning techniques, assigning homework, encouraging problem-solving and exploring, and making predictions about what's coming up.

> **Study Group Prompt:** *What other teaching techniques have you experienced or heard about?*

Communication Techniques

In education, various assessments are used to determine what students know and do not understand. They can be either summative or formative. **Summative assessments** are usually given at the end of a unit of work to determine what the student learned. To remember this, you can connect summative with the word *summarize* because students' learning is summarized, such as it is with a unit test at the end of a unit of study. In contrast, **formative assessments** are diagnostic, in that they are given to see what the student currently knows and what he or she has yet to learn. You can remember that *form*ative assessments in*form* the teacher so he or she knows what to teach or reteach.

Assessments can also be categorized as formal or informal. **Formal assessments** are usually traditional in that paper-and-pencil tests and other methods are given a grade based on how well the student does on them. **Informal assessments** don't usually count toward the student's grade, but supplement the more formal types of assessment. Checklists, journals, self-evaluations, and observations are some examples of informal assessments.

Yet another way to categorize assessments is as norm- or criterion-referenced. Think of an IQ test when you think of **norm-referenced assessments** because they compare students to how other students have performed on the same test. They show what the *norm* did. **Criterion-referenced assessments** don't compare student to student. Instead, they compare the student's performance against an established criterion, such as whether the student can do something. Think of taking the driving test to get your license. You are assessed against a list of criteria to see whether you stand up to the assessor's expectations.

And, then, of course, there are these types of assessments and assessment tools: observations, checklists, paper-and-pencil, demonstrations, rubrics, portfolios, and so on.

Study Group Prompt: *Discuss the types of assessments you've experienced as a student and as a teacher. What do you see as the advantages, disadvantages, and uses of each?*

Characteristics of Assessments

Assessments should be varied to meet students' needs so that they best portray what the student knows about a topic. For example, a teacher wouldn't always want to assess what a student who struggles with writing understands about a topic by assigning an es-

say or written report where the student is expected to produce a lengthy piece of writing. The student may not be able to express his or her knowledge through writing but could dazzle the teacher with what he or she knows by constructing a model or verbal presentation about the topic. So, assessment should be fair and equitable.

Also, assessments should accurately reflect the objectives of a lesson. Ask yourself whether the chosen assessment truly shows whether the student can perform the task or skill or has reached the sought after level of understanding.

And, finally, students should always be told ahead of time how they will be assessed and what they will be expected to know to do well. Showing students the scoring rubric when introducing a topic and providing a study guide are two techniques that help direct students.

How Are Assessments Scored?

Two ways to score assessments are holistically or analytically. **Holistic scoring** means the student is given one score for his or her performance on the overall assignment or project rather than receiving separate grades for parts of it. A holistic rubric might score a student's writing based on an overall impression of the piece. **Analytic scoring** *analyzes* (remember that similarity) how students do on the parts of an assignment, then the final grade results from those separate grades. An analytic rubric might score a student's essay based on its content, grammar, and citations, then provide a final score based on these parts.

Category III: Assessment

Strategies for Assessment

Educators must keep the lines of communication open among students, families, peers, the community, and administrators. Classroom websites and newsletters, face-to-face meetings, e-mails, letters and notes, and phone calls are all examples of ways educators communicate with others. Frequent communication is recommended to keep all parties up-to-date and informed.

Communication can be either verbal or nonverbal. Nonverbal communication can be through facial expressions, body language, posture, gestures, or eye movement. As an educator, you want to model attentive body language and focused attention so that others see you as sincere and interested. How you say something in a classroom or at a family conference can be as important as what you say. Furthermore, being aware of nonverbal communication can help teachers better understand students' messages and feelings.

Communication through humor can be an effective teaching tool when done sincerely. Laughter can release stress and stimulate interest and attentiveness. Of course, there is no room for sarcasm and the belittling of students in any context. Also, the teacher who is aware of current trends and the popular culture of his or her students and finds time to talk with students informally does a lot to build rapport and trust with students.

How Culture and Gender Influence Classroom Communications

Teachers must be culture- and gender-competent communicators. To notice blocks in communication, teachers should be aware of their students' and their own belief systems about ethnocentrism (thinking, "My way is the best way"); discrimination (thinking, "I can't teach people like you"); stereotyping (thinking, "She's quiet because she's a girl"); cultural blindness (thinking, "As long as I'm sensitive to all students, I don't have to worry about their cultural differences"); and cultural imposition (thinking, "They should speak English like everyone else does").

Teachers must recognize any biases they may have and treat students equally. You don't want to interact with students in ways that manifest double standards. Do you think all girls are bad at math and science, so you don't encourage them to do their best? You should communicate with all students as individuals rather than labeling: boys, girls, blacks, whites, and so on. Correct communication patterns that treat groups unequally or in a biased way. Be sensitive to terminology used to identify ethnic groups because it changes over time.

Teachers should also be aware of current research and literature related to gender and cultural differences in education. See the previous sections on diversity for more information.

How Can Educators Stimulate Classroom Discussion?

Educators can stimulate classroom discussion in many ways. Here are several:

- During open forums, probe for students' understandings. Don't presume they know something. They may have misunderstandings or gaps of understanding that you aren't aware of until you start questioning, making clarifying statements, or listening even more carefully than you normally do.
- Help students articulate their ideas by adding to their vocabulary, sharing their thoughts with others, and listening to others closely.
- Encourage all students to take risks and solve problems. Along with this, however, it is vital that teachers model and teach students to accept other's ideas through the development of a caring community. Never ridicule a student for creative thoughts. Students should feel safe to express their opinions. The teacher will have to monitor, however, the degree of openness with which he or she (or school policy) feels comfortable on controversial topics.
- Stimulate and promote curiosity, the ability to rouse critical questions, and the use of both convergent and divergent thinking.

Category IV: Professional Development, Leadership, and Community

A **reflective practitioner** is one who looks at his or her practice critically and continuously asks:

How could I do this better?

How can I improve students' learning?

Resources Available for Professional Development

Reflection can be achieved through professional development conferences, meetings, workshops, and other experiences; reading professional literature; talking with colleagues; and belonging to and participating in professional associations. Reflective practitioners seek out and apply current research to their teaching practices. They may participate in action research to study their practices and students' learning in an effort to improve it. They may keep a teaching log or journal they use to record and reflect on trends and events. They may even initiate or join a study group that focuses on an issue in education. Personal reflection can take many forms. Technology today opens the doors to blogging and other forms of online professional development and reflection opportunities.

Study Group Prompt: *Of what types of professional development are you aware? What are the advantages and disadvantages of the different kinds of reflection mentioned?*

What Is a Teacher's Responsibility to the Larger Community?

Teachers and schools can be resources to the local community. With their training in child development and teaching techniques, educators have much to offer a community. They can reach out to communities in formal and informal ways. For example, they might donate time to the local library to help select appropriate books for children. Or they might initiate service learning projects to benefit community groups. The possibilities are only limited by their creativity and interest.

It is also a teacher's responsibility to be aware of the family circumstances his or her students face, influential community environments, and the health and economic conditions in the areas where students live. Active partnerships, such as shared decision-making and respectful, reciprocal communication can be developed among the community, the home, the school, and the teacher.

Educators must also be aware of and must advocate for students' rights. Students have a right to an equal education, confidentiality and privacy, appropriate treatment, and due process.

PART

VI ▶ PRAXIS II PLT PRACTICE EXAMS

10 ▶ PRACTICE EXAM 3: PLT: EARLY CHILDHOOD

CHAPTER SUMMARY

Here is a full-length test based on the Praxis II PLT for Early Childhood. Now that you have studied the review chapter, take this exam to get familiar with the test format and the types of questions on the test and see how you do.

L ike the real Praxis II PLT, the exam that follows is made up of 70 multiple-choice questions and four constructed-response questions based on two case histories. Use the answer sheet on the next page to record your answers to the multiple-choice questions. Write your answers to the constructed responses on a separate piece of paper. Allow yourself 70 minutes for the multiple-choice questions and 50 minutes for the constructed-response questions.

With this practice exam, you should simulate the actual test-taking experience as closely as you can. Find a quiet place to work where you won't be disturbed. Set a timer or stopwatch for each part of the exam to guide your pace.

When you have completed the exam, use the answer explanations in Chapter 17 to learn more about the questions you missed, and use the scoring guide to figure out how you did.

PLT Multiple-Choice Questions

1.	ⓐ	ⓑ	ⓒ	ⓓ	36.	ⓐ	ⓑ	ⓒ	ⓓ
2.	ⓐ	ⓑ	ⓒ	ⓓ	37.	ⓐ	ⓑ	ⓒ	ⓓ
3.	ⓐ	ⓑ	ⓒ	ⓓ	38.	ⓐ	ⓑ	ⓒ	ⓓ
4.	ⓐ	ⓑ	ⓒ	ⓓ	39.	ⓐ	ⓑ	ⓒ	ⓓ
5.	ⓐ	ⓑ	ⓒ	ⓓ	40.	ⓐ	ⓑ	ⓒ	ⓓ
6.	ⓐ	ⓑ	ⓒ	ⓓ	41.	ⓐ	ⓑ	ⓒ	ⓓ
7.	ⓐ	ⓑ	ⓒ	ⓓ	42.	ⓐ	ⓑ	ⓒ	ⓓ
8.	ⓐ	ⓑ	ⓒ	ⓓ	43.	ⓐ	ⓑ	ⓒ	ⓓ
9.	ⓐ	ⓑ	ⓒ	ⓓ	44.	ⓐ	ⓑ	ⓒ	ⓓ
10.	ⓐ	ⓑ	ⓒ	ⓓ	45.	ⓐ	ⓑ	ⓒ	ⓓ
11.	ⓐ	ⓑ	ⓒ	ⓓ	46.	ⓐ	ⓑ	ⓒ	ⓓ
12.	ⓐ	ⓑ	ⓒ	ⓓ	47.	ⓐ	ⓑ	ⓒ	ⓓ
13.	ⓐ	ⓑ	ⓒ	ⓓ	48.	ⓐ	ⓑ	ⓒ	ⓓ
14.	ⓐ	ⓑ	ⓒ	ⓓ	49.	ⓐ	ⓑ	ⓒ	ⓓ
15.	ⓐ	ⓑ	ⓒ	ⓓ	50.	ⓐ	ⓑ	ⓒ	ⓓ
16.	ⓐ	ⓑ	ⓒ	ⓓ	51.	ⓐ	ⓑ	ⓒ	ⓓ
17.	ⓐ	ⓑ	ⓒ	ⓓ	52.	ⓐ	ⓑ	ⓒ	ⓓ
18.	ⓐ	ⓑ	ⓒ	ⓓ	53.	ⓐ	ⓑ	ⓒ	ⓓ
19.	ⓐ	ⓑ	ⓒ	ⓓ	54.	ⓐ	ⓑ	ⓒ	ⓓ
20.	ⓐ	ⓑ	ⓒ	ⓓ	55.	ⓐ	ⓑ	ⓒ	ⓓ
21.	ⓐ	ⓑ	ⓒ	ⓓ	56.	ⓐ	ⓑ	ⓒ	ⓓ
22.	ⓐ	ⓑ	ⓒ	ⓓ	57.	ⓐ	ⓑ	ⓒ	ⓓ
23.	ⓐ	ⓑ	ⓒ	ⓓ	58.	ⓐ	ⓑ	ⓒ	ⓓ
24.	ⓐ	ⓑ	ⓒ	ⓓ	59.	ⓐ	ⓑ	ⓒ	ⓓ
25.	ⓐ	ⓑ	ⓒ	ⓓ	60.	ⓐ	ⓑ	ⓒ	ⓓ
26.	ⓐ	ⓑ	ⓒ	ⓓ	61.	ⓐ	ⓑ	ⓒ	ⓓ
27.	ⓐ	ⓑ	ⓒ	ⓓ	62.	ⓐ	ⓑ	ⓒ	ⓓ
28.	ⓐ	ⓑ	ⓒ	ⓓ	63.	ⓐ	ⓑ	ⓒ	ⓓ
29.	ⓐ	ⓑ	ⓒ	ⓓ	64.	ⓐ	ⓑ	ⓒ	ⓓ
30.	ⓐ	ⓑ	ⓒ	ⓓ	65.	ⓐ	ⓑ	ⓒ	ⓓ
31.	ⓐ	ⓑ	ⓒ	ⓓ	66.	ⓐ	ⓑ	ⓒ	ⓓ
32.	ⓐ	ⓑ	ⓒ	ⓓ	67.	ⓐ	ⓑ	ⓒ	ⓓ
33.	ⓐ	ⓑ	ⓒ	ⓓ	68.	ⓐ	ⓑ	ⓒ	ⓓ
34.	ⓐ	ⓑ	ⓒ	ⓓ	69.	ⓐ	ⓑ	ⓒ	ⓓ
35.	ⓐ	ⓑ	ⓒ	ⓓ	70.	ⓐ	ⓑ	ⓒ	ⓓ

Case History Questions

Directions: Two case histories and four constructed-response questions follow. You are not expected to include citations of specific texts, authors, or theories in your responses. Your answers will be evaluated, however, based on your use of professionally accepted practices and the principles in learning and teaching. Some questions have multiple parts, so be sure your that response addresses all components of each question.

PLT Case History 3.1: Mark Roberts

Scenario

It is September, and it is Mark Roberts's first year in a preschool classroom. At their initial meeting, Mark's mother reports to Ms. Salisbury, Mark's teacher, that four-year-old Mark is the youngest of five children in his family. He is the only boy. The girls are very active at home. They sometimes exclude Mark from their activities and call him "the baby." Mrs. Roberts concludes that, as a result, Mark has become withdrawn and seems to prefer playing by himself rather than with his sisters. Mrs. Roberts has asked Ms. Salisbury how Mark gets along with his peers at the preschool. So that she can take part in an informed discussion with Mark's family about this situation, Ms. Salisbury has asked a co-teacher, who works in her classroom two hours each day, to observe Mark and suggest ways to promote and develop Mark's language and social interactions with his peers. She has invited Mrs. Roberts to return for a follow-up conference in one week. The co-teacher's notes follow.

Document 1
Preobservation Interview Notes, September 15

Mark's mother says, "At home Mark mostly plays with his toys in his bedroom or in the living room. Most of the time when he plays, he pretends he is a construction foreman like his dad. His sisters have always been more interactive with each other than they are with Mark. They're off running around and playing games while Mark is inside doing his own, quiet thing."

Ms. Salisbury says, "I have seen Mark in the block corner every day. He builds roads and houses with another little boy, John, most days. He seems comfortable and relaxed when talking with John. They share ideas."

Document 2
Observation Notes of Ms. Salisbury's Class with Focus on Mark Roberts, September 17

As children enter the classroom at arrival time, they take off their coats and boots, chat with the teacher and each other, and move into the various play centers in the room. Mark enters the room alone. Unless spoken to, he does not interact with peers or adults. When he does respond to a question or remark, Mark's answers are one- or two-word utterances, such as "hi," "good," "yes," "no," "uh-huh," and "over there." He keeps a pleasant smile on his face, though.

Mark moves toward the block corner, briefly surveys who is there and what is going on, then drops to his knees and begins to build with the blocks. He plays alone for three minutes before he looks up. When he sees John has entered the area, he walks over to him and hands him a block. John says, "Thanks, Mark," then sits down and starts to build with the blocks. He begins to give Mark directions on what to build. John takes on the leadership and decision-making role. He tells Mark to "make that road go over there 'cause the workers have to get to that house," and Mark extends the row of blocks. This pattern continues for 15 minutes, with John giving directives and Mark following suit. Occasionally, Mark makes comments such as "dis way, John?" and "the wed (red) block here, John?" Based on the body language and tone of voice Mark uses, the observer feels the questions are more for acknowledgment and confirmation rather than for clarification and cooperation. Mark watches what John is doing and mimics his building of houses along the stretch of road.

Then, a noise draws the boys' attention to the reading center, where three children are pretending to read a big book on the easel. They are roaring like the lion in the book. John walks over to the book to see the lion. Mark follows John. They both start to roar and laugh with the other three children. Soon they become interested in the array of books on the table and sit down to look independently at books. At this point, the observer talks with Mark about the characters in a book. It is noted he is unable to identify some animals and common items in the book, such as a giraffe and a bicycle. The observer also notes there are some words in Mark's speech that are indistinguishable, and she detects an articulation problem that should be further investigated.

Throughout the two hours, Mark follows John around from activity to activity. Although he does not initiate conversations with his peers, others are friendly toward him once he joins a group. He is an accepted member of the class.

PLT Case History 3.1 Questions

Write your answers to questions 1 and 2 on a separate sheet of paper. Be sure to answer each component of the questions.

1. Ms. Salisbury and the co-teacher meet to discuss the interview and observation notes. One of their goals is to analyze Mark's rate of language acquisition.
   - Explain TWO factors that might be contributing to Mark's rate of language acquisition.
   - For EACH factor, describe what action you would recommend to Mrs. Roberts.
2. At the follow-up conference, you want to be prepared with ideas and suggestions to help Mark and his family.
   - Explain TWO goals that you would propose the school and home work toward to promote Mark's language and social development.

- For EACH goal, explain strategies that Mark's teachers and parents can use to promote further progress in Mark's language and social development. Base your response on principles of teaching language and appropriate, rewarding social interaction.

PLT Case History 3.2: Alexandria

Scenario
Alexandria was usually a bubbly, spirited four-year-old girl who always had a smile on her face. Today was a different story, though.

Document 1
Conversation between Ms. Lorenzo, Alexandria's Classroom Teacher, and Kitty, the School Bus Driver

Kitty: Good morning, Ms. Lorenzo. I didn't want to just drop Alexandria off this morning without telling you something.

Ms. Lorenzo: What is it, Kitty?

Kitty: When I picked Alexandria up at her house this morning, I saw her mother talking to her at the bus stop. Well, really, she was being pretty mean and almost yelling at her right out there on the curb of the street. When Alexandria got on the bus she was really quiet. Usually she gives me a big smile and talks to me on the way in, but not today.

Ms. Lorenzo: What was she like on the ride in?

Kitty: Well, that's really what I wanted to tell you. As soon as she sat down, she started to cry. She kept standing up, and I kept telling her she had to sit down. You know, for safety reasons, the kids all have to sit in their seats. Usually Alexandria follows that rule.

Ms. Lorenzo: Was she upset the whole ride in?

Kitty: Yes, she kept crying and looking out the window. And she didn't talk to any of the other kids, either.

Ms. Lorenzo: Thanks, Kitty. I'll keep an eye on her.

Document 2
Anecdotal Note Made by Ms. Lorenzo the Same Day during Centers Time

Alexandria is in the kitchen center with her best friend. She is not participating in the pretend play as she usually does this time of day. Instead, she is watching the other children "make breakfast." When Quinna comes over and asks Alexandria what is wrong and rubs her on the back, Alexandria starts to cry.

Document 3
Observation Made by the School Nurse

10:15 A.M. in Ms. Lorenzo's classroom, centers time (free play):

Ms. Lorenzo asked me to come down to her classroom this morning because she is concerned about Alexandria's unusual behavior. The child will not talk to the teacher or her peers.

During centers time she is watching her friends in the kitchen center but not participating in the pretend play. She is not crying, but her face shows she has been crying recently.

Ten minutes have passed. A good friend of Alexandria's begins to rub the girl's back to comfort her. Soon the two friends are drinking juice and munching on crackers. The crisis—whatever it had been—is apparently over, at least for the time being. The girls go on to play, but Alexandria is still quiet. Ms. Lorenzo comments to me that while Alexandria's bubbly personality has not returned, Alexandria does seem to be recovering.

10:45 A.M., transitioning to circle time:

When the train whistle was tooted to signal it was time for everyone to gather for circle time, Alexandria came to the circle and kneeled down. When asked to sit "on her bottom" as was the expectation at circle time so all the children could see what was going on around them, Alexandria complied. However, she kept wiggling and wincing.

Document 4
Ms. Lorenzo's Reflective Teaching Journal

I'm so upset about the situation that happened with Alexandria this morning. After talking to Kitty, I tried to talk to Alexandria. But she wouldn't tell me what was wrong. I kept my eye on her and observed her during free play time this morning. She just wasn't herself. I was really worried about her, so I asked Nurse Carolyn if she could come down to observe Alexandria. I thought maybe Alexandria was ill, but I couldn't understand why she wouldn't talk to me or to her friends.

Nurse Carolyn noticed the same behaviors, so she asked Alexandria to come down to her office with her for a minute. Nurse Carolyn told me she asked Alexandria if she could lift the back of Alexandria's dress. When she did, she saw red marks in the shape of an adult's hand across the child's backside. She saw raised welts forming on the child's body. Nurse Carolyn said Alexandria shuddered in pain when she lightly dropped the dress back down over the area. It was obvious to Nurse Carolyn that an adult had recently spanked the child repeatedly and with a great deal of force. She suspects Alexandria has been abused. However, there had been no history of abuse in the past of which the center was aware.

PLT Case History 3.2 Questions

Write your answers to questions 3 and 4 on a separate sheet of paper. Be sure to answer each component of the questions.

3. Alexandria was not verbally revealing what was upsetting her, so Ms. Lorenzo and Nurse Carolyn had to do their own forms of assessments to determine the problem and help Alexandria.
   - Describe TWO forms of assessment that Ms. Lorenzo and Nurse Carolyn used and relied on in this unfortunate situation.
   - Describe the use, strengths, and limitations of EACH form of assessment used.

4. Once Nurse Carolyn saw the red hand marks on Alexandria, she knew she had to take immediate action.
   - State TWO actions Nurse Carolyn should take immediately.
   - Explain how Nurse Carolyn and Ms. Lorenzo should follow up with EACH action taken.

PLT Multiple-Choice Questions

1. An anecdotal record is
   a. a purposeful observation written about students that can help the teacher gain an in-depth understanding of the learning process.
   b. a collection of graphic languages that documents the ideas, memories, and feelings of an event.
   c. a skill-sequenced, criterion-referenced checklist that helps the teacher keep track of children's progress.
   d. a collection of artifacts produced by the child that shows progress over time.

2. Which of the following is the best example of a developmentally-appropriate practice for assessing and evaluating preschoolers?
   a. assessing the children in relationship to groups, not as individuals
   b. assessing the children as individuals, not in relationship to groups
   c. observing children during authentic, not contrived, activities
   d. basing decisions that have an impact on children on a single developmental assessment or screening device

3. The Reggio Emilia approach
   a. is based on the philosophy that in the preschool years, children form who they are as individuals.
   b. is an educational philosophy focused on K–12 education.
   c. is based in the child's home, not a separate school location.
   d. originated in Spain.

4. According to Vygotsky,
   a. it is important not to work outside of a child's zone of proximal development.
   b. development leads learning.
   c. children should spend time on what they have already mastered.
   d. thought and action regulate a child's language use.

5. Scaffolding
   a. stretches the child's understanding to include new information.
   b. depends on the child's ability to solve problems independently.
   c. depends on the help of an adult teacher.
   d. depends on the child's developmental level.

6. According to brain-growth periodization studies, cognitively, young boys can be anywhere from _____ behind their female counterparts on average.
   a. 6 to 18 months
   b. 18 to 24 months
   c. 24 to 36 months
   d. 36 to 48 months

7. Jean Piaget
   a. was a developmental constructivist who thought that learning led development.
   b. thought that cognition was influenced by both children's experiences and maturation.
   c. was a behaviorist who thought that development led learning.
   d. regarded language as a critical bridge between the child and his or her mental functioning.

8. Most frequently, in an early childhood program that applies constructivist-based transactions in the classroom,
   a. children are treated as a cohort group rather than individuals.
   b. the entire class would be found listening to instructions on how to complete a task.
   c. paper-and-pencil tasks are used as the main source of assessment of skills.
   d. teacher and child are collaborating in meaningful discussions and explorations.

9. Which of the following statements about Abraham Maslow's hierarchy of needs pertains most accurately to educating young children?
   a. Maslow's work cannot be logically linked to education in any way.
   b. Maslow's pyramid implies teachers can more or less train children using behaviorist stimuli and reinforcements. For example, if we want a child to learn, we have to give him or her rewards.
   c. Maslow's pyramid implies children's more basic needs must be met before the more advanced needs can be achieved. For example, children's needs for enough food, sleep, and security must be met before they can be expected to become confident learners.
   d. Maslow's pyramid implies that parents are responsible for meeting children's basic needs before they are sent to school so that teachers can do their job of teaching the children. For example, if a child is not given breakfast at home, there is nothing the teacher can do to help the child learn.

10. Which of the following answers best completes this sentence? The National Association for the Education of Young Children (NAEYC) views early childhood professional development as
   a. an annual convention event.
   b. unnecessary once teachers have completed their teacher training.
   c. a forum for education administrators to come together and form partnerships with university professionals.
   d. a continuum of support and learning opportunities designed to get educators ready to work with and advocate for young children and their families.

11. An early childhood educator can help instill respect, responsibility, and compassion in today's young children by
   a. building classroom communities founded on caring and fairness.
   b. punishing children who are disrespectful to others in the classroom.
   c. modeling compliance to strict, inflexible class rules and routines.
   d. having a firm policy that those who are disrespectful to others will be timed-out from play time for five minutes.

12. Which teacher is most likely to use technology effectively in her classroom?
   a. Ann, who has a personal computer of her own at home and uses it for word processing
   b. Jill, who text messages her friends on her cell phone all the time
   c. Kelly, who has been teaching for twenty years and feels comfortable using technology with her students
   d. Cindy, who has been trained to integrate technology into her early childhood curriculum

13. Direct instruction is characterized as
   a. following the constructivist approach.
   b. incorporating random and infrequent assessment checks.
   c. slow-paced.
   d. systematic and scripted.

14. According to Bronfenbrenner's ecological model of child development,
   a. a child affects and is affected by his or her environment, and the most important setting for a child is the family (and school).
   b. a child's behavior is independent of his or her physical surroundings and is not influenced by community learning.
   c. proximal processes and learning are dominated by the child's formal academic schooling.
   d. the components of the complete ecological model are not connected.

15. An early childhood program seeking to be compliant with the Americans with Disabilities Act (ADA) must follow ADA requirements. The program should be sure it
   a. places a child with disabilities using placement procedures that are more stringent than those used for all children.
   b. offers curriculum, routines, and schedules for children with disabilities that are the same as those offered to all children.
   c. has policies and procedures that describe how accommodations will be made for children with disabilities.
   d. provides separate activities for children with disabilities if they will not be able to keep up with all children.

16. Which of the following is the best example of an event that would intrinsically motivate most young children to participate?

    a. A rewards program wherein students receive a gold star for each book they listen to a family member read to them, or that they read themselves. When they collect ten stars, they hand them in to their teacher for a prize from the treasure chest.

    b. The teacher sets the classroom up in learning centers. Students move from one center to the next in a rotating pattern every 20 minutes, experiencing all four different activities.

    c. The teacher smiles at the children before dismissing them to board the buses. She tells them they were all very well-behaved that day so, in return, they will all get a big hug from her as they go out the door.

    d. The teacher knows from observing the children that they seem to like animals. She displays a wide array of photographs and books on various animals in the classroom library, and pulls up the "National Geographic Kids" website on the class computer, inviting children to learn about animals in which they are interested.

17. In Bloom's Taxonomy, skills in the affective domain

    a. describe how children develop awareness in their feelings and react emotionally.

    b. revolve around children's ability to physically manipulate tools and develop changes in their behavior.

    c. involve developing and gaining knowledge, comprehension, application, analysis, synthesis, and evaluation skills.

    d. relate to the ability to create and defend opinions.

18. Which of the following depicts an example of a deficit model of teaching young children?

    a. The teacher opens a discussion using Socratic questioning.

    b. The teacher assesses which letters of the alphabet the child does not know, and then seeks to teach them.

    c. The teacher provides a variety of writing tools and papers in the writing center.

    d. The teacher helps the child articulate what she knows about animals through drawing.

19. Ms. D'Orazio's class is visiting the local assisted-living home for senior citizens. Each student is bringing his or her favorite book to share with the seniors. They will pair up with the seniors and tell them the story in the book. They will then share snacks they made and talk with the seniors about the book. Also, they will leave bookmarks they made for their new friends. This is an example of

    a. service learning.

    b. inductive reasoning.

    c. curriculum webbing.

    d. unit planning.

20. Which of the following is the most important reason for teachers to know and understand how children develop physically, emotionally, socially, and cognitively?
    a. so they can knowledgeably report the child's current levels of development to the child's family and the teacher the child will have the following school year
    b. so they can provide learning experiences that support and promote various levels of children's development
    c. so they can identify children with special needs who do not belong in the regular classroom
    d. It is only important to know and understand children's cognitive development in an academic school setting because teachers aim to improve cognitive development.

21. Which of the following statements about self-concept and self-esteem is most accurate?
    a. Self-concept is how we value others.
    b. Self-esteem generally refers to how we feel about others.
    c. Children are born with a certain self-concept that is not influenced by others.
    d. When a teacher models self-esteem, he or she can influence students to become confident and develop high self-esteem.

22. When feeding an infant,
    a. positions vary based on the size and posture of the child.
    b. the infant should not be positioned upright.
    c. apply hand pressure on the back of the child's head to cause the infant's body to extend.
    d. use bottle nipples with large-sized holes.

23. When teaching communicative behaviors to preschoolers with communication delays, it is most effective to
    a. ignore the child until he or she speaks appropriately.
    b. reward the child for correct responses.
    c. punish the child for inappropriate responses.
    d. create authentic opportunities and needs to cause the child to communicate.

24. One of the most important components of effective co-teaching is
    a. to teach with a teacher who has a different philosophy of teaching than you do.
    b. to build time into the schedule to consistently and regularly plan and evaluate the co-teaching experience.
    c. to practice before co-teaching with the children.
    d. to write out detailed lesson plans so both teachers know which activities and strategies will be taught.

25. When we say children learn best by doing, which theorist's model are we talking about?
    a. Dewey
    b. Bandura
    c. Bruner
    d. Kohlberg

26. When a school empowers students with positive images of self, family, and culture, language learning
    a. is not affected.
    b. is facilitated.
    c. is ensured.
    d. is hindered.

27. According to attribution theory, if we want children to persist, we should
   a. help them believe they are competent.
   b. help them believe things happen based on luck.
   c. tell them to give up when they fail at something.
   d. tell them natural talent, not effort, determines success.

28. A teacher sets up a table with various types of boats, airplanes, and cars. Children complete charts categorizing things that go in the air, on water, and on land. Then, during circle time, they read books about different means of travel. For math, they estimate how far each means of transportation could travel in one minute. These activities exemplify
   a. a thematic unit.
   b. a lesson plan.
   c. mapping.
   d. collaboration.

29. Which of the following questions is the best example of a question that effectively probes for content-area understanding?
   a. "We just read about firefighters. Let's talk about the firefighters and the fire station in our town. How is our fire station like the one in the book?"
   b. "We just read about a little girl who wants to be a firefighter when she grows up. What did you like about this story?"
   c. "We just read about firefighters. What do you want to be when you grow up?"
   d. "We just read about a fire dog named Sparky. If you had a dog, what would you name it?"

30. The three components of an early childhood assessment system are
   a. identification, evaluation, and instruction.
   b. selection, administration, and utilization.
   c. choosing, testing, and analyzing.
   d. determining, administering, and analyzing.

31. Which level of performance from the *High/Scope Preschool Child Observational Record* would the following observation indicate?
   12/18 During centers time, Anurrahda said, "Blocks."
   a. Level I: Child indicates a choice by pointing or another gesture.
   b. Level II: Child expresses choice in one or two words.
   c. Level III: Child expresses choice in a short sentence consisting of a few words.
   d. Level IV: Child plans his or her choice.

32. Which of the following is an acronym for a prominent early childhood professional organization?
   a. NAEYC
   b. AERA
   c. NRA
   d. NAACP

33. The danger of excluding a student's culture from the classroom is that
   a. the student will be labeled and stereotyped by peers.
   b. the school will not support the student's primary language.
   c. if a student's cultural identity is not included, the student may become oppositional.
   d. students whose cultures are excluded will occupy the same social status as their parents.

34. A mother wants to teach a child to say "thank you" when appropriate in interactions with others. When the child changes his behavior and says "thank you" appropriately, he is rewarded with a piece of candy. This reward system is an example of
   a. the hierarchy of need.
   b. self-esteem.
   c. punishment.
   d. operant conditioning.

35. A teacher is planning a lesson that involves small groups of students working in simultaneous learning centers. She is concerned about how best to meet the cognitive needs of a student who she expects will not understand the sequencing of the learning centers. Who would be the best person to ask for help when planning for the needs of the student?
   a. the library media specialist
   b. the school director
   c. the gifted-and-talented teacher
   d. the special education teacher

36. A teacher knows one of the keys to effective questioning is
   a. to give students 3 to 5 seconds to process a question before expecting them to answer with quality responses.
   b. to recognize that if students do not raise their hands to answer a question, they don't know the answer.
   c. to ask only inquiry-type questions that extend students' thinking.
   d. to ask only questions that require students to use high-level thinking.

37. A teacher leads students through a step-by-step process in which he begins with recall, observation, description, and identification questions and then guides them into synthesis, interpretation, and application questions and discussions. This type of questioning is known as
   a. inquiry questioning.
   b. discovery questioning.
   c. guided questioning.
   d. spiral questioning.

38. Which of the following is NOT an example of active listening?
   a. restating key points of what the child said
   b. interpreting information the child gives you
   c. asking follow-up questions
   d. starting a new topic

39. What is the value of early childhood assessment systems that screen for children at risk for developmental delays?
   a. Young children can be identified for intervention services at an early age.
   b. Children with delays can be removed from the regular classroom for special services.
   c. Teachers can label these students with an identified disability.
   d. Instruction can focus on the children who are not at risk.

40. Besides teacher observational rating scales, many of the developmentally appropriate assessment tools that the National Association for the Education of Young Children informs its members about for use with children ages 3 to 5 include
   a. standardized tests administered in a group situation.
   b. portfolios and teacher-parent summary reports.
   c. running records.
   d. informal reading inventories.

41. Someone who fosters someone else's educational career is referred to as a
a. mentor.
b. critical friend.
c. comrade.
d. companion teacher.

42. Miss Cindy finds her students learn best when they talk and work together. For example, in the library center she observes two girls sharing a book about horses. They tell each other what they know about horses as they look through the pictures and pretend-read the story. What kind of learning is this?
a. competitive learning
b. cooperative learning
c. avoidant learning
d. independent learning

43. After giving the class a two-minute warning, Rocky's teacher tells everyone it is time to clean up the toys they've been playing with. Rocky resists with, "I'm not done yet! I'm building a garage." The teacher replies, "It's time to clean up, Rocky. Would you like to put the blocks in the wheelbarrow, or would you like to carry them over to the shelves to stack them?" Rocky says, "I want to use the wheelbarrow!" He runs to get it. What most likely changed Rocky's resistant attitude?
a. The teacher had promised Rocky a reward.
b. He suddenly tired of building blocks and wanted to clean up.
c. He was given the power to make a choice.
d. The teacher sounded like Rocky was going to be punished if he didn't change his attitude.

44. What is the theoretical basis of having prekindergarten standards of learning?
a. to strengthen instruction in prekindergarten classrooms in all settings and help educators align pre-K standards and instruction with K-12 standards
b. to make it easier for prekindergartners who move from state to state to keep up with the curriculum
c. to identify which children are above, at, and below grade level
d. to teach prekindergartners how to take achievement tests

45. A teacher instructs her class to put their thumbs up if they think the lion will eat the mouse or put their thumbs down if they think the mouse will get away. This type of response is known as
a. a guessing game system.
b. an all-class response system.
c. an opinion system.
d. a Socratic seminar.

46. Which of the following is an example of proxemics?
a. When a teacher reprimands a child, she stands closer to him than usual and looks right into his eyes.
b. A teacher walks her class out to the playground.
c. When a child is interested in a subject, he blinks more frequently than usual.
d. The teacher lightly touches the child's arm to show affection.

47. Which of the following would be the most effective way to assess a preschooler's understanding of concepts of print?
   a. asking the child's parents what the child knows about concepts of print
   b. giving the student a short paper-and-pencil quiz about concepts of print
   c. observing the student in the classroom library and checking off evidence of concepts he knows on a checklist
   d. taking an anecdotal note about the child during a read-aloud

48. What would be the most important information to acquire at a parent-teacher conference?
   a. what kinds of books the child enjoys
   b. what concerns the parents have about the child's health, development, and behavior
   c. the child's hobbies and interests
   d. how well the child gets along with other children his own age

49. Once per month, a group of teachers get together after school and talk about selected articles they have read. They share research to support their teaching practices. This type of group may be referred to as
   a. a workshop.
   b. an independent research group.
   c. a study group.
   d. an internship.

50. Tina Marie is in a wheelchair. She is ensured certain accommodations based on her physical disabilities. Which of the following is NOT an allowable accommodation for a student with a physical disability?
   a. Tina Marie should be assigned to a classroom she can easily access in her wheelchair.
   b. Tina Marie's classroom space should allow her to move around comfortably while in her wheelchair.
   c. Tina Marie should have access to a wheelchair-accessible table.
   d. Tina Marie should be assigned to a male teacher who can more easily help Tina Marie with her wheelchair.

51. A young child is helping his grandmother write a shopping list. She tells him, "Oh, we need cereal, David. Be sure to put down cereal." David scribbles small shapes and says, "Okay. What else?" The grandmother looks at what David wrote. What would be the best feedback she could provide at this stage of David's writing development to encourage him to keep trying?
   a. "David, good writers use letters when they write, not shapes."
   b. "Good job, David."
   c. "Read that back to me, David. What's on our list so far?"
   d. "Okay. Thanks. Now I'll write the rest of the list."

52. Miss Johnson is preparing her four-year-olds to participate in a sink-or-float learning center. She has a bucket of water and a variety of objects on the table. The children are supposed to carefully place one object at a time into the bucket and determine whether it sinks or floats. Then, they mark an X in the proper column on the chart provided to indicate if the object sank or floated. Probably the best way to introduce her students to this activity to ensure they learn the difference between the concepts of sink and float is to

a. model and explain the procedure with one or two of the objects while the children watch.

b. give the children a list of written instructions on how to proceed.

c. post a chart of the directions near the learning center.

d. allow the children to proceed with the activity without any instructions and let them explore on their own.

53. All of the following are valid educational reasons for asking children questions EXCEPT

a. to gain information about what they know and do not know.

b. to help them clarify their understanding of a concept.

c. to interrogate them about their family life.

d. to encourage their oral language development.

54. Can nonverbal communication vary between cultures?

a. Yes, the greatest variances are apparent between the cultures of the northern and southern hemispheres.

b. No, body language is universal.

c. Yes, even facial expressions for fear, happiness, and sadness are dissimilar.

d. Yes, it varies; however, facial expressions for fear, happiness, and sadness are similar across cultures.

55. Ms. Finch asks students what they have learned each day. This practice is an example of

a. self-assessment.

b. divergent thinking.

c. problem solving.

d. risk taking.

56. Which of the following statements about assessment tools is correct?

a. Diagnostic tools can be used to exclude a child from preschool or kindergarten.

b. Assessment tools are interchangeable: One tool may address multiple purposes.

c. Screening tools and diagnostic tools are used for the same purpose.

d. Assessment tools may potentially be misused when a tool intended to measure for one purpose is used inappropriately for another purpose.

57. At the end of the day, Ms. Juene sits at her desk and thinks about her teaching. She writes about what went well and what she would do differently next time. Which choice best describes this practice?

a. a critical friend

b. a reflective journal

c. a peer observation

d. an incident analysis

58. The most important component to ensure successful collaboration is

a. for everyone to pull their own weight.

b. to agree on a purpose for the collaboration.

c. effective communication.

d. having a strong leader.

59. Ms. Tintle is about to read a book about the ocean to her students, but she knows many of them have never been to the seashore. How can she best help her students comprehend the story?

a. She should read the story fluently and with expression so the students will understand it.

b. Before reading the story, she should spend time showing them pictures of the ocean and beach and talking about any experiences they've had at the local lake.

c. She should give them a quiz about the ocean to see what they know.

d. She should let them play in the sandbox.

60. Young children have the right not to be bullied or harassed through which legislation?

a. equal access

b. privacy and confidentiality

c. intellectual freedom

d. due process

61. Which question would encourage students to transfer their knowledge from one context to another?

a. Which animal is taller, the giraffe or the zebra?

b. How tall are you?

c. If you grew taller and taller every day, how tall do you think you would become?

d. Which animal in our real world looks as tall as the storybook character Clifford the Big Red Dog?

62. It is policy that when parents question a teacher's practice, the director meets with the parent and the teacher to review what happened. Video is reviewed and the teacher reports past experiences that may be relevant to the event. The event is discussed until an understanding is reached. This type of experience is called

a. an incident analysis.

b. a peer observation.

c. a peer- and self-assessment.

d. a study group.

Questions 63 through 66 are based on the following passages. These passages reflect the debate about testing young children.

Why testing children before they enter kindergarten is not effective

Testing young children before they enter kindergarten is outrageous. As a preschool teacher, I spend my time observing and gaining an understanding of how the children learn and how they think about things. Now first-grade curriculum is being pushed down to kindergarten, and kindergarten curriculum is being pushed down to preschool. It seems the belief is that teaching preschoolers how to read and do math will make them perform better in kindergarten. In reality, the opposite is true. Children at this age are not developmentally ready to read. They are still developing emergent literacy skills like phonemic awareness. In European countries, formal education doesn't begin until the child is seven years old when, neurologically, the child is able to understand the concepts being taught. Here, that would be in first grade. If tests are going to act as tools to exclude children from entering kindergarten based on the determination that the child does not have the readiness skills required of a kindergartner, then this type of assessment is outrageous.

Why testing children before they enter kindergarten is effective

About 50 percent of the states have instituted readiness-assessment tools for children entering kindergarten even before the practice was highlighted in the Race to the Top, Early Learning Challenge funding competition. The development of these tests varies across states based on what areas of development and knowledge will be evaluated and how they will be used for practical and policy purposes. Such assessment tools have the potential to contribute greatly to identifying and meeting the needs of children in early childhood settings. Testing young children before they enter kindergarten is effective in promoting high-quality early childhood programs.

63. The teacher's opinion in the first passage asserts that certain proposed practices are developmentally inappropriate. This teacher would be most likely to recommend which of the following types of assessment tools as developmentally appropriate for the early childhood setting?
    a. administering ability tests in a group situation
    b. administering aptitude tests one-on-one with a child
    c. administering standardized tests in a group setting
    d. compiling ongoing observation data several times over the year to document the child's development over time

64. It can be inferred that the author of the second passage
    a. supports the use of standardized tests with young children.
    b. is an employee of a state's department of education.
    c. has never taught in an early childhood classroom before.
    d. is concerned about meeting the needs of young children.

65. The author of the first passage talks about first-grade curriculum being moved down into kindergarten. How does this comment connect to her belief that assessing preschoolers is "outrageous"?
    a. There really is no connection; the author goes off-topic and begins to ramble.
    b. The first author proposes that generally we are expecting too much in our assessment and instruction of preschoolers.
    c. The first author does not think assessment informs instruction.
    d. The first author thinks assessment informs instruction.

66. The authors of both passages take positions on a current topic in preschool education and assessment. Which of the following leadership roles are they demonstrating by speaking out about the topic?
    a. perceptions of teachers
    b. partnering with families
    c. shaping and advocating for their profession
    d. partnering with the community

67. Regularly, the Rocking Horse Nursery School takes in student teachers from a local community college to work with students. When this occurs, the administrators are adamant that no pictures be taken of the children and that the names of the children are not used outside of the classrooms. These policies ensure the protection of
a. each child's confidentiality and privacy.
b. the school's confidentiality and privacy.
c. the parents' right to due process.
d. the teacher's right to due process.

68. As a new teacher at the nursery school, Martha is asked to cite a professional development plan for the first two years of her career. What would be the most effective and appropriate plan to support this novice teacher's learning and growth at this level?
a. to attend workshops related to teaching elementary mathematics
b. to participate in a professional learning community networked with other preschool teachers
c. to take a photography course at the local community college
d. to blog with teachers across the country

69. Jon never takes the initiative to pick up a book during class. What would be the best recommendation the teacher could give to Jon's parents to support his interest in books?
a. There really isn't anything the parents can do. If Jon doesn't like books, he just doesn't like them.
b. Take all of Jon's toys away from him and give him books to read instead.
c. Buy Jon books for his birthday and for the holidays the family celebrates.
d. Bring Jon to a library and let him select several books he is interested in taking home. Then read the books with him, modeling your interest in them.

70. When dropping Jill off at school, her mother tells the teacher that Jill has been biting her little sister. If you were Jill's teacher, what might you suggest her mother do?
a. Tell her not to worry about it.
b. Tell her to scold Jill and give her a time-out when it happens.
c. Schedule a meeting with you so you can talk about the situation.
d. Tell her to note what else is happening around the time Jill bites to determine what is causing her actions.

PRINCIPLES OF LEARNING AND TEACHING STUDY CHART PRACTICE EXAM 3

STUDENTS AS LEARNERS	QUESTIONS
Student Development and Learning Process	4, 7, 9, 14, 20, 22, 25
Students as Diverse Learners	6, 15, 26, 33, 42, 50, 59
Student Motivation and Learning Environment	11, 16, 21, 27, 34, 43, 51
INSTRUCTIONAL PROCESS	
Planning Instruction	17, 28, 35, 44, 52
Instructional Strategies	3, 5, 8, 13, 19
Questioning Techniques	36, 37, 45, 53, 61
Communication Techniques	12, 23, 29, 38, 46, 54
ASSESSMENT	
Assessment and Evaluation Strategies	2, 18, 30, 39, 47, 55, 63
Assessment Tools	1, 31, 40, 48, 56, 64, 65
Professional Development, Leadership, and Community	10, 24, 32, 41, 49, 57, 58, 60, 62, 66, 67, 68, 69, 70
ANALYSIS OF INSTRUCTIONAL SCENARIOS	
Students as Learners	CR1
Instructional Process	CR2
Assessment	CR3
Professional Development, Leadership, and Community	CR4

PRACTICE EXAM 4: PLT: GRADES K–6

CHAPTER SUMMARY

Here is a full-length test based on the Praxis II PLT for Grades K–6. Now that you have studied the review chapter, take this exam to get familiar with the test format and the types of questions on the test and see how you do.

L ike the real Praxis II PLT, the exam that follows is made up of 70 multiple-choice questions and four constructed-response questions based on two case histories. Use the answer sheet on the next page to record your answers to the multiple-choice questions. Write your answers to the constructed responses on a separate piece of paper. Allow yourself 70 minutes for the multiple-choice questions and 50 minutes for the constructed-response questions.

With this practice exam, you should simulate the actual test-taking experience as closely as you can. Find a quiet place to work where you won't be disturbed. Set a timer or stopwatch for each part of the exam to guide your pace.

When you have completed the exam, use the answer explanations in Chapter 18 to learn more about the questions you missed, and use the scoring guide to figure out how you did.

PLT Multiple-Choice Questions

1.	ⓐ	ⓑ	ⓒ	ⓓ		36.	ⓐ	ⓑ	ⓒ	ⓓ
2.	ⓐ	ⓑ	ⓒ	ⓓ		37.	ⓐ	ⓑ	ⓒ	ⓓ
3.	ⓐ	ⓑ	ⓒ	ⓓ		38.	ⓐ	ⓑ	ⓒ	ⓓ
4.	ⓐ	ⓑ	ⓒ	ⓓ		39.	ⓐ	ⓑ	ⓒ	ⓓ
5.	ⓐ	ⓑ	ⓒ	ⓓ		40.	ⓐ	ⓑ	ⓒ	ⓓ
6.	ⓐ	ⓑ	ⓒ	ⓓ		41.	ⓐ	ⓑ	ⓒ	ⓓ
7.	ⓐ	ⓑ	ⓒ	ⓓ		42.	ⓐ	ⓑ	ⓒ	ⓓ
8.	ⓐ	ⓑ	ⓒ	ⓓ		43.	ⓐ	ⓑ	ⓒ	ⓓ
9.	ⓐ	ⓑ	ⓒ	ⓓ		44.	ⓐ	ⓑ	ⓒ	ⓓ
10.	ⓐ	ⓑ	ⓒ	ⓓ		45.	ⓐ	ⓑ	ⓒ	ⓓ
11.	ⓐ	ⓑ	ⓒ	ⓓ		46.	ⓐ	ⓑ	ⓒ	ⓓ
12.	ⓐ	ⓑ	ⓒ	ⓓ		47.	ⓐ	ⓑ	ⓒ	ⓓ
13.	ⓐ	ⓑ	ⓒ	ⓓ		48.	ⓐ	ⓑ	ⓒ	ⓓ
14.	ⓐ	ⓑ	ⓒ	ⓓ		49.	ⓐ	ⓑ	ⓒ	ⓓ
15.	ⓐ	ⓑ	ⓒ	ⓓ		50.	ⓐ	ⓑ	ⓒ	ⓓ
16.	ⓐ	ⓑ	ⓒ	ⓓ		51.	ⓐ	ⓑ	ⓒ	ⓓ
17.	ⓐ	ⓑ	ⓒ	ⓓ		52.	ⓐ	ⓑ	ⓒ	ⓓ
18.	ⓐ	ⓑ	ⓒ	ⓓ		53.	ⓐ	ⓑ	ⓒ	ⓓ
19.	ⓐ	ⓑ	ⓒ	ⓓ		54.	ⓐ	ⓑ	ⓒ	ⓓ
20.	ⓐ	ⓑ	ⓒ	ⓓ		55.	ⓐ	ⓑ	ⓒ	ⓓ
21.	ⓐ	ⓑ	ⓒ	ⓓ		56.	ⓐ	ⓑ	ⓒ	ⓓ
22.	ⓐ	ⓑ	ⓒ	ⓓ		57.	ⓐ	ⓑ	ⓒ	ⓓ
23.	ⓐ	ⓑ	ⓒ	ⓓ		58.	ⓐ	ⓑ	ⓒ	ⓓ
24.	ⓐ	ⓑ	ⓒ	ⓓ		59.	ⓐ	ⓑ	ⓒ	ⓓ
25.	ⓐ	ⓑ	ⓒ	ⓓ		60.	ⓐ	ⓑ	ⓒ	ⓓ
26.	ⓐ	ⓑ	ⓒ	ⓓ		61.	ⓐ	ⓑ	ⓒ	ⓓ
27.	ⓐ	ⓑ	ⓒ	ⓓ		62.	ⓐ	ⓑ	ⓒ	ⓓ
28.	ⓐ	ⓑ	ⓒ	ⓓ		63.	ⓐ	ⓑ	ⓒ	ⓓ
29.	ⓐ	ⓑ	ⓒ	ⓓ		64.	ⓐ	ⓑ	ⓒ	ⓓ
30.	ⓐ	ⓑ	ⓒ	ⓓ		65.	ⓐ	ⓑ	ⓒ	ⓓ
31.	ⓐ	ⓑ	ⓒ	ⓓ		66.	ⓐ	ⓑ	ⓒ	ⓓ
32.	ⓐ	ⓑ	ⓒ	ⓓ		67.	ⓐ	ⓑ	ⓒ	ⓓ
33.	ⓐ	ⓑ	ⓒ	ⓓ		68.	ⓐ	ⓑ	ⓒ	ⓓ
34.	ⓐ	ⓑ	ⓒ	ⓓ		69.	ⓐ	ⓑ	ⓒ	ⓓ
35.	ⓐ	ⓑ	ⓒ	ⓓ		70.	ⓐ	ⓑ	ⓒ	ⓓ

Case History Questions

Directions: Two case histories and four constructed-response questions follow. You are not expected to include citations of specific texts, authors, or theories in your responses. Your answers will be evaluated, however, based on your use of professionally accepted practices and principles in learning and teaching. Some questions have multiple parts, so be sure your response addresses all components of each question.

PLT Case History 4.1: Misao Tanaka

Scenario

Eight-year-old Misao Tanaka and his family recently moved to the United States from Japan. His parents have enrolled him in a school district in a rural area in central New York State. Misao was assigned to Mr. Sato's second-grade classroom. Mr. Sato is Japanese-American, speaks some Japanese, and practices Japanese traditions with his family. Misao and his parents speak and write some English. However, their English is not as strong as their native language.

Document 1
Excerpt from Interview with Parents
Mrs. Tanaka (An Interpreter's Words)

In Misao's school in Japan, things were very different than how they are in the United States. In Japan, students rose when the teacher entered the room, and school uniforms were required. There were almost twice as many children in the class in Japan. Teams of Japanese students were assigned to do daily school chores, such as serving lunch to classmates, cleaning the classroom, and cleaning the restrooms. Misao is trying to learn about and adjust to his new culture, classmates, and teacher.

Mr. Sato: Overall, Misao is doing well. He has made new friends even though verbal communication is sometimes difficult. The other children are in-terested in getting to know Misao and in helping him. I encourage the children to help Misao feel welcome by modeling a generous, compassionate attitude with Misao myself.

Document 2
Mr. Sato's Reflective Journal, 12/10

I am concerned about how to assess Misao's knowledge and skills. Misao's English hinders his ability to comprehend the resources and books he uses with the other children. Also, Misao is used to learning in a different style. In Japan students were not expected to participate in discussions very much. Due to Misao's quiet nature, sometimes it is difficult to assess what he knows and what he does not understand. Similarly, because English is Misao's second language, his written and oral language skills sometimes hinder his ability to express himself and what he understands. I am worried I will misinterpret what Misao understands and what he is trying to express.

PLT Case History 4.1 Questions

1. Mr. Sato is aware of the need to facilitate nonbiased assessment and instruction.
   - Describe TWO methods Mr. Sato should use to facilitate nonbiased assessment and instruction.
   - For EACH method, explain theories that relate to and support these practices.
2. Mr. Sato is concerned about Misao's ability to express himself in writing.
   - Describe TWO specific writing strategies that would be helpful to use with Misao to promote his ability to write English.
   - For EACH strategy, explain why they would be effective. Base your response on the principles of teaching writing to diverse learners.

PLT Case History 4.2: Ms. Isabella

Scenario

Ms. Isabella is a fourth-grade teacher at St. Joseph's Parish Elementary School. Lately she has been feeling very frustrated with the volume of materials she is responsible for including in her curriculum. Some days she feels like she is just throwing information at the students in an attempt to cover everything she is supposed to get through by the end of the school year.

Document 1
Conversation with a Colleague

Ms. Isabella: I'm exhausted. I can only imagine the whirlwind my students feel they're caught up in. There's so much to get through each day. I struggle to get through all of the subjects in one day. Today we had so much to do in math but we barely had 15 minutes after we finished the science lab. How do you get through everything?

Mr. Fletcher: I use organized units that integrate the content areas into meaningful themes. For example, we do a unit on water. Students role play and write skits about digging the Erie Canal. Teams write math word problems about topics like condensation and evaporation to challenge each other's calculation skills. I bring in a variety of resources, such as books at multiple reading levels, websites, pictures, DVDs, and primary resources for the students to explore and study. They construct questions they want to research and compose lessons to present to their classmates. The days go so quickly—not because we're shoving so much into them, but because we're excited about what we're doing.

Document 2
Ms. Isabella's Reflective Journal, 1/15

I want to learn more about thematic units and other ways to integrate literacy into the content areas. I've looked into professional development opportunities that might help and came across the International Reading Association's annual convention, which is coming up in May. I'm particularly interested in all of the workshops about content literacy that are advertised on the organization's website. I got permission and funding from the building administrator and plan to attend three days of the convention!

Document 2
Isabella's Reflective Journal, 6/1

While I was at the conference, I collected a number of strategies for integrating literacy skills across the curriculum. I spoke with colleagues who were experiencing the same feelings of frustration. By the end of the convention, I was eager to return to the classroom and try out what I had learned.

Document 3
Ms. Isabella's Reflective Journal, 6/15

It's been only two weeks and already I'm seeing marked student improvement in writing skills and reading comprehension as a result of using the strategies I learned about increasing and analyzing vocabulary.

I'm so excited by my students' improvement, I'm going to spend part of the summer break working on integrating literacy instruction into my social studies curriculum. I plan to start with social studies content as outlined in the state learning standards, and then move into the other content areas. I will reshape lessons to include the instruction of literacy skills within the social studies content and the use of literature and other literacy resources to teach content.

PLT Case History 4.2 Questions

3. Ms. Isabella is eager to improve her students' reading and writing skills while learning content knowledge.
   - Describe TWO methods Ms. Isabella should use to facilitate her students' reading and writing skills in the content areas.
   - For EACH method, provide specific examples of how she could teach specific literacy skills.

4. Ms. Isabella could consider integrating technology into her thematic units.
   - Describe TWO advantages of integrating technology in content-area instruction.
   - For EACH advantage, explain one method that would capitalize on it to promote learning. Base your response on the principles of using technology in the classroom.

Multiple-Choice Questions

1. According to Gardner's theory of multiple intelligences, students with strong kinesthetic intelligence
   a. are adept at reasoning.
   b. have sensitivity to pitch, rhythm, and melody.
   c. are athletically gifted.
   d. understand relationships and people.

2. Which of the following would be the most effective way for children to learn how the digestive system works?
   a. to read about it in a book
   b. to read about it in several different resources, such as books, websites, and illustrations
   c. to participate in teacher-led instruction that includes diagrams and note-taking
   d. small-group collaborative creation of a model of the system constructed by consulting various resources

3. Regular classroom teachers are responsible for knowing how to work effectively with children with special needs. Typically, it is the classroom teacher's responsibility to
   a. write the child's individualized education plan (IEP) and present it to the child's committee.
   b. determine which teaching strategies will help these children succeed.
   c. find the one solution to meeting the needs of children with special needs.
   d. group children with special needs together during small-group work.

4. The Individuals with Disabilities Education Act (IDEA) mandates that each student with a disability
   a. has an individualized education plan (IEP) stating modifications to be provided by teachers.
   b. is provided appropriate education within a private school setting.
   c. be separated from children without disabilities to receive diagnostic assessment and instruction from specialized educators trained to work with the child's disability.
   d. be removed from the regular classroom only if parents of the children who are not disabled complain.

5. Which of the following statements about classroom design reflects best teaching practices?

   a. The classroom design should reflect the teacher's pedagogical goals and students' needs.

   b. The seating arrangement of the classroom should not be changed so that students gain a sense of predictability and security among their peers.

   c. Students' desks should be arranged far enough away from each other so that students are not tempted to talk with each other.

   d. Students' desks should be arranged in a boy-girl-boy-girl pattern to discourage differences between sexes.

6. Lesson plan objectives

   a. should correspond to national and state learning standards.

   b. should be broad enough to meet the needs of all students in the class, even children with disabilities.

   c. describe what the students are able to do prior to the lesson.

   d. should not correspond with assessment criteria.

7. Which of the following is the best example of an approach to activating a student's prior knowledge about the sea?

   a. setting up a learning center with all kinds of shells from your trip to the sea last summer

   b. interactively reading and discussing a book about the seashore with the child

   c. assigning the child to read a book of his or her choice about the seashore

   d. singing "Down by the Sea" with the child

8. *Funds of knowledge* refers to

   a. the life and educational experiences of a family.

   b. the exchange of knowledge that occurs in a school setting.

   c. the financial exchange that takes place between tutors and their tutees.

   d. the exchange of labor for capital.

9. Which of the following is the best example of holistic scoring?

   a. A student receives two points for each correct multiple-choice answer on a quiz.

   b. A teacher adds the four separate scores the student earned on each part of the assignment to come up with the final score the student earns.

   c. A student self-assesses which words he or she still has to study for the weekly spelling test.

   d. A teacher gives a score based on his or her overall impression of an essay, not the separate elements within it.

10. *Brown v. Board of Education*

   a. declared schools had the right to house black students in schools that were separate from white students.

   b. was the first challenge to school segregation.

   c. caused far-reaching ideological and social implications about natural rights beyond children and education.

   d. supported the "separate but equal" doctrine.

11. If an educator followed John Dewey's philosophy of education, he or she would most likely
   a. take the class on a field trip to a "living museum" to experience how people lived in the Colonial Period.
   b. have the class research and write reports about geographic climates throughout the United States.
   c. learn mathematics by teaching each other.
   d. set up cross-grade level tutoring and mentoring programs within the school.

12. The *McGuffey Readers*
   a. were introduced in schools in the 18th century.
   b. were seminal in separating church and state in schools.
   c. were highly moralistic in nature, modeling honesty, kindness, and truthfulness.
   d. denounced autocratic educational practices.

13. Blended literacy instruction is best described as
   a. a combination of the emergent literacy and scientifically based reading research approaches to early literacy instruction.
   b. a combination of social constructivist and traditional approaches to instruction.
   c. the approach to literacy instruction that advocates for the integration of technology.
   d. the approach to literacy instruction that integrates media forms of literacy.

14. Which of the following statements about using technology in the classroom is accurate?
   a. When schools use Internet filtering systems, teachers do not have to worry about students' unsafe or inappropriate use of computers.
   b. Most teachers feel well-prepared to use technology effectively in their classrooms.
   c. Only high-achieving students benefit from the use of technology in the classroom.
   d. The poor use of technology in a classroom can distract students from reaching instructional objectives.

15. Which of the following is the best example of differentiated instruction?
   a. cross-grade-level reading buddies
   b. heterogeneously grouped instruction
   c. varying the expected outcomes or products of student learning to match students' attributes
   d. setting up learning centers in the classroom

16. How does measurement theory relate to K–6 instruction and assessment?
   a. It relates only to instruction and assessment for grades 7–12.
   b. It encourages educators to analyze the meaning of test scores and what tests are really assessing.
   c. It assumes all tests are invalid, so students should be assessed in alternative ways.
   d. It assumes all tests are valid, so it doesn't matter which ones teachers choose to use.

17. An example of a primary source is
  a. a letter written by Eleanor Roosevelt in which she resigns from the Daughters of the American Revolution.
  b. a report written by a fifth-grade student about the Daughters of the Revolution.
  c. the annual reenactment of Washington's crossing of the Delaware River.
  d. "Washington Crossing the Delaware," a sonnet by David Shulman written in 1936.

18. Instruction that incorporates visual literacy education
  a. can prepare K–6 students to decode media advertisements.
  b. is not developmentally appropriate for K–6 learners.
  c. requires the use of technology.
  d. assumes students are given rather than construct knowledge.

19. Of the following, the best example of formative assessment would be
  a. a final examination given to determine a student's final grade on a unit of study.
  b. pre-testing students to determine what they know about a topic before they begin a unit on it.
  c. a student self-assessing what he or she has learned after a field trip.
  d. an assessment given to determine whether or not an instructional module teaches what it is supposed to teach.

20. Which of the following best represents uses of graphic organizers?
  a. prewriting tools used to organize students' thoughts before writing.
  b. tools used by a student during reading to outline the key points in a passage.
  c. tools used by students to review materials already discussed.
  d. tools used at all stages of learning.

21. The best example of scope and sequence in a K–6 program would be
  a. teaching students to add and subtract because as adults they will need to be able to balance their checkbooks.
  b. using the Think-Pair-Share strategy.
  c. the social studies curriculum starting with a focus on the self and expanding outward into community, town, city, state, national, and international affairs over time.
  d. students work together in small groups to generate ideas, and then share their thoughts with the rest of the class.

22. Phonological awareness is an umbrella term that includes the ability to discriminate
  a. letters and their corresponding sounds.
  b. sentences and sentence fragments.
  c. numbers, letters, and symbols.
  d. onset and rime, syllables, and phonemes.

Questions 23 and 24 are based on the following passages about foreign-language courses.

Casie, a second-grade teacher, visits an education-related blog to see what people are talking about. She finds these two postings addressing the question from one blogger, "Should we teach Spanish in public elementary schools in America?"

One post had the following argument: "Yes. We should teach Spanish in American schools, beginning in kindergarten. The number of Spanish-speaking immigrants has increased drastically over the past decade. The children of these immigrants are in our schools and need our help *now*. Having Spanish classes will help these children learn English and will help English-speaking children communicate with the Spanish-speaking children. And it isn't good just for children whose first language is Spanish. English-speaking children will benefit, too, by learning a second language. It might help them when they go on to find a job and succeed in a global society. Studies show that foreign languages are best learned when we're young. So, I say, the sooner the better."

Another post presented a counter-argument: "No. We definitely should not waste our already depleted resources by teaching Spanish in American schools. Funds are limited. We need regular classroom teachers and supplies to support learning. We need to stick to the basics. Then students can learn a foreign language if they choose to later in life. If we teach American children how to speak Spanish, then the Spanish-speaking children will be less motivated to learn English. Let's act like Americans!"

23. How should Casie react to these postings?
   a. advocate for foreign language classes to be taught in her school
   b. work against foreign language classes being taught in her school
   c. not visit the blog again because there is too much debating going on among her colleagues
   d. do further reading in professional journals about the debate to inform her thinking

24. The author of the second passage would most likely feel that
   a. this is America, and we speak English. Let *them* learn *our* language.
   b. learning a foreign language might help children accept other cultures more readily.
   c. children will be motivated to learn a second language.
   d. additional teachers should be hired to teach foreign language classes.

25. A student comes across a new vocabulary word: *combustible*. Although she has never read the word before, she applies the phonics rules she knows and has used to decode other new words successfully. She uses what she knows about context clues to determine that it probably has something to do with exploding. How did the student construct an accurate understanding of the new word?
   a. by applying the knowledge she already had of words and context clues
   b. by making a random guess
   c. by consulting a reference, resource, or knowledgeable other
   d. Actually, the student did not construct an accurate understanding of the new word. She is totally wrong.

26. Macy is allowed certain accommodations in testing situations based on her individualized education plan. Which of the following is NOT an allowable accommodation for a student with a learning disability, such as Macy?
   a. Macy may be tested in a private room or alternative test site.
   b. Macy may be allowed to have a scribe record the answers she states orally.
   c. Macy may be allowed more time to finish the test.
   d. Macy may be excluded from taking the test altogether.

27. Which of the following is NOT one of the premises of Thorndike's theory of learning?
   a. Learning is incremental.
   b. If a situation is followed by a good effect, it will be strengthened.
   c. Reward is a stronger motivator than punishment.
   d. If a situation is followed by a bad effect, it will be weakened.

28. The theoretical basis of standards-based education is that
   a. standards motivate students to learn.
   b. it provides fodder for testing students.
   c. if we set academic standards for what students should be able to do and know, then we can use the standards to guide what we teach students.
   d. standards teach the basic concepts of predominant educational theories.

29. Responses to which of the following questions would reflect the highest order of thinking according to Bloom's Taxonomy?
   a. Do you think gun control is a good thing or a bad thing?
   b. What happened at a Connecticut school in the fall of 2012 that caused people to debate issues related to gun control?
   c. What differences exist between the Connecticut shooting (2012) and the Colorado shootings in Columbine (1999) and Aurora (2012)?
   d. Do you know of another instance when issues of gun control were debated?

30. All of the following are good reasons why a teacher should solicit students' participation in a classroom discussion EXCEPT
   a. so that students feel their questions and comments are valued.
   b. to prove to the students that their ideas are not accepted by the majority of their peers.
   c. to encourage the free exchange of ideas with one's peers.
   d. to build students' confidence in expressing themselves in public.

31. Norm-referenced and criterion-referenced tests are both examples of
   a. formal assessments.
   b. informal assessments.
   c. play-based assessments.
   d. observational assessments.

32. Standardized test data may be used effectively to design individualized intervention. However, prior to making any intervention decisions, the teacher should not only examine the percentile ranks and raw scores, but also the
   a. rank order.
   b. content area targets.
   c. average.
   d. total number of items in a particular subtest.

33. A teacher who offers a colleague counsel, provides information, serves as a role model, and acts as an advisor is known as
   a. a mentor.
   b. an intern.
   c. an independent researcher.
   d. a critical friend.

34. A viable research question for a second-grade action research project would be
   a. Do children like to read about people from their own culture?
   b. How does the implementation of Reader's Theater influence reading fluency with students who have learning disabilities?
   c. How long until I can retire?
   d. Does round-robin reading improve students' reading development?

35. Which of the following questions refers to validity?
   a. Will all items on the test be internally consistent?
   b. If students take the same test over and over, will they perform similarly each time?
   c. If several teachers score an assessment, will they all get similar results?
   d. Does the rubric used really measure the students' ability to summarize a passage?

36. Multiple examples of students' performance in the basic skills of reading, spelling, writing, and math are collected as "probes." Student performances are measured by some type of frequency count, such as the number of words read accurately. Results are used for the purposes of screening, instructional planning, program placement, and monitoring student progress. This type of assessment is referred to as
   a. curriculum-based measurement.
   b. portfolio assessment.
   c. a rating scale.
   d. probational assessment.

37. A student would most likely feel that a teacher is invading his personal space if she
   a. hands him a pencil.
   b. stands too close to him when she is speaking to him.
   c. tilts her head when speaking to him.
   d. maintains direct eye contact when speaking with him.

38. Which of the following is NOT an acceptable reason to question a student?
   a. to actively involve him in the lesson
   b. to evaluate his preparation
   c. to put him on the spot in front of his peers
   d. to nurture insights

39. The behaviorist theorist John B. Watson
   a. believed that the instinct for love is something we are born with.
   b. emphasized the nature side of the nature versus nurture debate.
   c. was one of the first psychologists to propose that children should be treated like children, not young adults.
   d. warned against the dangers of parents giving too much affection and love to their children.

40. Cindy learns best when she works with her peers. Discussing her ideas and others' perspectives on issues broadens her understanding in meaningful ways. Cindy is what kind of learner?
   a. a competitive learner
   b. a cooperative learner
   c. an avoidant learner
   d. an independent learner

41. Which of the following is an example of self-determination?
   a. giving a pop quiz to see if students read and understood the assigned readings
   b. assigning students readings to prepare them for the upcoming state tests
   c. giving students a topic to research and report about in small groups
   d. promoting the value of a task when assigning it

42. Research shows that when a teacher increases the amount of time he pauses after he has asked a question,
   a. interruptions increase.
   b. student-to-student interactions increase.
   c. responses are shortened.
   d. a greater number of lower cognitive responses occur.

43. Which of the following statements about communication and eye contact is correct?
   a. In some cultures, direct eye contact is a sign of disrespect or is given only to close friends and family.
   b. If a person looks down a lot when you are talking with her, it means she is shy, upset, or trying to hide something.
   c. When someone's eyes are looking far away, the person is probably in deep thought.
   d. A person who looks to the side may be nervous, distracted, or lying.

44. On a spelling test, Molly gets 15 out of 20 questions correct. She has earned a score of 75%. Last week she got 60% on the spelling test. What type of assessment is this?
   a. informal testing
   b. norm-referenced testing
   c. criterion-referenced testing
   d. rational testing

45. Standardized tests typically convert a student's raw score on the test to a common scale so that test scores can be compared over time. What do educators call this type of score?
   a. a standard deviation
   b. a stanine score
   c. a percentile
   d. a scaled score

46. To be highly effective, peer observations should consist of
   a. preobservation preparation, observation, and postobservation feedback.
   b. an observation instrument.
   c. a lesson plan and observation notes.
   d. a written reflective response from both the observer and the observed about how the lesson went.

47. Before beginning a research project with her sixth-grade language arts class, Ms. Tenache wants to ensure that the school has enough resources on topic choices so that all of the students will be able to gather information in a timely manner. Also, she must be sure there are resources to meet the reading and comprehension needs of all of her diverse students. Which member of the school's support staff would be the best person to talk with about these needs?
   a. the guidance counselor
   b. the school's library media specialist
   c. the para educator who works with her class
   d. the teacher of the gifted and talented students

48. A fourth-grade teacher, using peer assessment for the first time with her students, is skeptical because she knows that one of the disadvantages of peer assessment is that
   a. it generally encourages students to produce higher-quality work.
   b. it provides valuable insight about the product, assessment tool, and process that the peer assessor can apply to his own work.
   c. students can receive more feedback than they would if they just received a score from the teacher.
   d. students might not provide rigorous feedback about their peers based on nonacademic reasons.

49. One of the disadvantages of using scoring rubrics to evaluate a student's writing is that they typically
   a. give so much information that they might overwhelm the student.
   b. relay specifically why the student earned the grade he did.
   c. give students specific information on their writing.
   d. can save teachers time writing out responses to children's writing.

50. According to Gardner's Theory of Multiple Intelligences, some students learn best through listening. Which of the following communication techniques would most highlight auditory learning?
a. maps and pictures
b. performances
c. music and mnemonics
d. reading and writing

51. Ms. Henri asks the class, "What is the capital of New York State?" Carolina calls out, "New York City!" What would be the best way for her teacher to reply to encourage Carolina to continue to be engaged?
a. "No, Carolina. Does anyone else know the right answer?"
b. "Oh, very good try! You're thinking New York City because it's the largest city in New York, but the capital is actually a smaller city in upstate New York. What could it be, Carolina?"
c. "Good try, but not correct. Try again."
d. "I bet many of us would think it's New York City, but that isn't right."

52. A fifth-grade teacher wants to encourage his students to be intrinsically motivated to write poetry. Which of the following is NOT a good way to encourage intrinsic motivation?
a. Have a writing contest and give a prize to the author of the best poem.
b. Students share their poems with students in a younger grade.
c. Students write a poem as part of a class book of poems that is published and given out to each student's family.
d. Families come to a poetry night "slam" to hear students perform their original poems.

53. Research shows that poverty
a. affects achievement of Caucasian students only.
b. has no effect on student achievement.
c. slightly affects student achievement.
d. greatly affects student achievement.

54. A child who sneaks a cookie from the cookie jar judges the morality of his act by its direct consequences. He considers that it isn't wrong to do as long as he doesn't get caught. This kind of morality exemplifies which of Kohlberg's six stages of moral development?
a. self-interest orientation
b. obedience and punishment orientation
c. interpersonal accord and conformity
d. authority and social-order maintaining orientation

55. Educators know that students' learning benefits from a positive parent-teacher relationship. What type of relationship is least productive?
a. a confrontational relationship
b. a respectful relationship
c. a problem-solving relationship
d. a trusting relationship

56. Which acronym represents an international association that fosters the professional development of elementary language arts and reading teachers?
a. RAI
b. ACEI
c. SPA
d. IRA

57. What is the best way to explain standardized test stanine scores to a parent?
   a. "Stanine scores are like percentages and are based on the highest score of 100."
   b. "Stanine scores are determined by giving a test that is developed for one grade to students in another grade."
   c. "Stanine scores range from 1 to 9. Scores of 4 through 6 are average. Scores below 4 indicate areas where the child needs improvement. Scores above 6 indicate the child performed better in those areas than other children who took the same test."
   d. "Stanine scores are not helpful to determine a child's progress. They are used strictly by testing publishers to evaluate the reliability and validity of a test."

58. To best encourage students to reflect upon their learning, a teacher might prompt them to complete which of the following statements?
   a. The most significant part was . . .
   b. Now I understand that . . .
   c. A thought I especially liked was . . .
   d. This makes me think of . . .

59. To improve students' listening skills during a read-aloud, Mr. Whitcomb should teach the prelistening strategy of
   a. predicting what the book will be about and what vocabulary might be in the book.
   b. identifying the main idea.
   c. taking notes.
   d. listening for a particular detail.

60. Ms. Lassonde asks her students, "What do you know about your genealogy?" Most likely, what is her purpose for asking this question?
   a. to determine students' prior knowledge about a new topic
   b. to develop critical and creative thinking skills
   c. to guide their thinking
   d. to review previous lessons

61. All of the following exemplify ways to arrange classroom space effectively to facilitate inclusion EXCEPT
   a. placing student desks in groups of two to four desks per group to encourage cooperative learning, discussion, and collaboration.
   b. decorating in a way that does not create sensory overload and distraction.
   c. clearing items out of pathways to ensure all students can move around the room safely.
   d. setting student desks in rows facing the teacher's desk at the front of the classroom.

62. The legislation that was the first statute to declare civil rights for children and all people with disabilities and that paved the way for the Americans with Disabilities Act is
   a. the Qualified Individuals with Disabilities Act.
   b. Section 107 of the Rehabilitation Act.
   c. Section 504 of the Rehabilitation Act.
   d. the Individuals with Disabilities Education Act.

63. Kelly is an elementary student who is beginning to gain an understanding of cause and effect. She is eager to learn and is forming moral values. In school, she likes being recognized by teachers, her family, and her peers when she accomplishes hard tasks. Which of Erikson's stages of psychosocial development is Kelly in, most likely?
   a. basic trust versus mistrust
   b. industry versus inferiority
   c. autonomy versus shame and doubt
   d. initiative versus guilt

64. Educators advocate for their profession by becoming involved in the legislative process. Educators may write letters or visit their representatives. The best time to advocate in the legislative process is
   a. when a bill is introduced.
   b. when a bill is sent to full committee.
   c. when the bill is voted on by the House and Senate.
   d. throughout the process, right up to the time when the president signs or vetoes the bill.

65. While collaborating with colleagues on the development of a thematic unit to be used next year with their third graders, Candice was unexpectedly invited to speak at a state conference about a new method she is using with her students. She is honored that the state group recognizes her efforts, though she doesn't feel she has time to do both. What would be the best way to handle this situation?
   a. Since the unit isn't going to be used until next year, she should explain to her colleagues that an unexpected honor has come up. She should then ask if their collaboration can be put on hold until the presentation is done.
   b. Candice should not shirk her commitment to work on the collaborative theme. She should say no to the state conference invitation.
   c. Candice should continue to do both projects without telling her colleagues about the state conference. She may have to miss a few meetings, and they will have to understand.
   d. Candice should tell her colleagues they'll have to finish the theme without her because she wants to do the presentation instead.

66. Mr. Como is planning a lesson in which students will demonstrate their understanding of the main idea of a passage. Which of the following assessment formats would be the best way to assess that students have met the learning objective?
   a. performance
   b. portfolio
   c. essay
   d. observation

67. Ms. Gardenia has observed that when her students are listening to peers' presentations, some do not listen respectfully. They fidget while waiting for their turn to talk and don't listen to others. How might Ms. Gardenia best teach her students to listen respectfully to their peers and others?

   a. Provide negative reinforcement to those not listening respectfully.

   b. Provide positive reinforcement for those listening respectfully.

   c. Direct instruction on listening respectfully followed by practice using a self-assessment checklist.

   d. Videotape them when they are listening and critique inappropriate behaviors in a playback of the video.

68. To help students develop self-motivation, a teacher should do all of the following EXCEPT

   a. hold all grades and feedback until report cards come out so that students work for the intrinsic value rather than the external grades.

   b. assign tasks students view as valuable.

   c. include students in instructional decisions.

   d. provide frequent, positive feedback.

69. Every individual has the right to access and receive information and expressions of ideas from all points of view, without restriction. This right is known as

   a. due process.

   b. mandated reporting of child abuse.

   c. copyright.

   d. intellectual freedom.

70. Due process is intended to ensure that

   a. teachers have the right to an attorney when accused of a crime.

   b. all children are protected from abusive situations.

   c. children with disabilities receive a free, appropriate education.

   d. if teachers have a criminal record, they cannot teach young children.

12 ▶ PRACTICE EXAM 5: PLT: GRADES 5–9

CHAPTER SUMMARY

Here is a full-length test based on the Praxis II PLT for Grades 5–9. Now that you have studied the review chapter, take this exam to get familiar with the test format and the types of questions on the test and see how you do.

Like the real Praxis II PLT, the exam that follows is made up of 70 multiple-choice questions and four constructed-response questions based on two case histories. Use the answer sheet on the next page to record your answers to the multiple-choice questions. Write your answers to the constructed responses on a separate piece of paper. Allow yourself 70 minutes for the multiple-choice questions and 50 minutes for the constructed-response questions.

With this practice exam, you should simulate the actual test-taking experience as closely as you can. Find a quiet place to work where you won't be disturbed. Set a timer or stopwatch for each part of the exam to guide your pace.

When you have completed the exam, use the answer explanations in Chapter 19 to learn more about the questions you missed, and use the scoring guide to figure out how you did.

PLT Multiple-Choice Questions

1.	ⓐ	ⓑ	ⓒ	ⓓ	36.	ⓐ	ⓑ	ⓒ	ⓓ
2.	ⓐ	ⓑ	ⓒ	ⓓ	37.	ⓐ	ⓑ	ⓒ	ⓓ
3.	ⓐ	ⓑ	ⓒ	ⓓ	38.	ⓐ	ⓑ	ⓒ	ⓓ
4.	ⓐ	ⓑ	ⓒ	ⓓ	39.	ⓐ	ⓑ	ⓒ	ⓓ
5.	ⓐ	ⓑ	ⓒ	ⓓ	40.	ⓐ	ⓑ	ⓒ	ⓓ
6.	ⓐ	ⓑ	ⓒ	ⓓ	41.	ⓐ	ⓑ	ⓒ	ⓓ
7.	ⓐ	ⓑ	ⓒ	ⓓ	42.	ⓐ	ⓑ	ⓒ	ⓓ
8.	ⓐ	ⓑ	ⓒ	ⓓ	43.	ⓐ	ⓑ	ⓒ	ⓓ
9.	ⓐ	ⓑ	ⓒ	ⓓ	44.	ⓐ	ⓑ	ⓒ	ⓓ
10.	ⓐ	ⓑ	ⓒ	ⓓ	45.	ⓐ	ⓑ	ⓒ	ⓓ
11.	ⓐ	ⓑ	ⓒ	ⓓ	46.	ⓐ	ⓑ	ⓒ	ⓓ
12.	ⓐ	ⓑ	ⓒ	ⓓ	47.	ⓐ	ⓑ	ⓒ	ⓓ
13.	ⓐ	ⓑ	ⓒ	ⓓ	48.	ⓐ	ⓑ	ⓒ	ⓓ
14.	ⓐ	ⓑ	ⓒ	ⓓ	49.	ⓐ	ⓑ	ⓒ	ⓓ
15.	ⓐ	ⓑ	ⓒ	ⓓ	50.	ⓐ	ⓑ	ⓒ	ⓓ
16.	ⓐ	ⓑ	ⓒ	ⓓ	51.	ⓐ	ⓑ	ⓒ	ⓓ
17.	ⓐ	ⓑ	ⓒ	ⓓ	52.	ⓐ	ⓑ	ⓒ	ⓓ
18.	ⓐ	ⓑ	ⓒ	ⓓ	53.	ⓐ	ⓑ	ⓒ	ⓓ
19.	ⓐ	ⓑ	ⓒ	ⓓ	54.	ⓐ	ⓑ	ⓒ	ⓓ
20.	ⓐ	ⓑ	ⓒ	ⓓ	55.	ⓐ	ⓑ	ⓒ	ⓓ
21.	ⓐ	ⓑ	ⓒ	ⓓ	56.	ⓐ	ⓑ	ⓒ	ⓓ
22.	ⓐ	ⓑ	ⓒ	ⓓ	57.	ⓐ	ⓑ	ⓒ	ⓓ
23.	ⓐ	ⓑ	ⓒ	ⓓ	58.	ⓐ	ⓑ	ⓒ	ⓓ
24.	ⓐ	ⓑ	ⓒ	ⓓ	59.	ⓐ	ⓑ	ⓒ	ⓓ
25.	ⓐ	ⓑ	ⓒ	ⓓ	60.	ⓐ	ⓑ	ⓒ	ⓓ
26.	ⓐ	ⓑ	ⓒ	ⓓ	61.	ⓐ	ⓑ	ⓒ	ⓓ
27.	ⓐ	ⓑ	ⓒ	ⓓ	62.	ⓐ	ⓑ	ⓒ	ⓓ
28.	ⓐ	ⓑ	ⓒ	ⓓ	63.	ⓐ	ⓑ	ⓒ	ⓓ
29.	ⓐ	ⓑ	ⓒ	ⓓ	64.	ⓐ	ⓑ	ⓒ	ⓓ
30.	ⓐ	ⓑ	ⓒ	ⓓ	65.	ⓐ	ⓑ	ⓒ	ⓓ
31.	ⓐ	ⓑ	ⓒ	ⓓ	66.	ⓐ	ⓑ	ⓒ	ⓓ
32.	ⓐ	ⓑ	ⓒ	ⓓ	67.	ⓐ	ⓑ	ⓒ	ⓓ
33.	ⓐ	ⓑ	ⓒ	ⓓ	68.	ⓐ	ⓑ	ⓒ	ⓓ
34.	ⓐ	ⓑ	ⓒ	ⓓ	69.	ⓐ	ⓑ	ⓒ	ⓓ
35.	ⓐ	ⓑ	ⓒ	ⓓ	70.	ⓐ	ⓑ	ⓒ	ⓓ

Directions: Two case histories and four constructed-response questions follow. You are not expected to include citations of specific texts, authors, or theories in your responses. Your answers will be evaluated, however, based on your use of professionally accepted practices and principles in learning and teaching. Some questions have multiple parts, so be sure your response addresses all components of each question.

Case History Questions

PLT Case History 5.1: Mr. Tenace

Scenario

Throughout his past five years of teaching seventh-grade science, Matthew Tenace has observed variance in the ways males and females participate in his classes and labs. He has read that statistics indicate females are less represented than males in most science fields. Mr. Tenace has set a goal for himself this year to learn more about gender issues in science by studying his students' behaviors and reading up on the issue. He has invited a colleague who teaches eighth-grade science, Mrs. Parker, to work with him on this teacher research project. He plans to apply what he learns to his teaching practices.

Mr. Tenace and Mrs. Parker want to answer these questions:

1. How do males and females participate in science classes and labs?
2. Do males and females feel equally confident and competent in the field of science?

Document 1
Mr. Tenace's Project Plan

State Science Learning Standard
Students will compare and contrast structures and functions in living systems: animals.

Course Objective
Students will investigate the respiratory and circulatory systems of animals.

Activities
Students will

a. complete self-selected readings on animal systems and participate in class discussions to share what they have learned.
b. work in small groups to illustrate the process of respiration.
c. individually illustrate the process of the circulatory system for a homework assignment.
d. prepare a small-group oral presentation to be shared with the class to describe the interaction between the respiratory and circulatory systems.
e. dissect and label the respiratory and circulatory systems of a frog with a lab partner after the process has been modeled for the whole class by the instructor.
f. write individual essays comparing and contrasting the structures and functions of the respiratory and circulatory systems of a frog.
g. reflect upon and self-assess what they have learned about the structures and functions of the animal respiratory and circulatory systems.

Document 2
Observation by Mrs. Parker
Mr. Tenace asked Mrs. Parker to observe his class and document student participation, noting in particular any differences between male and female participation. Her notes follow:

Bell rings. Students enter lab talking rather loudly about the upcoming basketball game. One boy shoves past another and a seemingly friendly push-shove interaction results between the two young men. Several girls nearby duck out of the way of the skirmish.

Mr. Tenace: Respect for each other, please, gentlemen. We have young ladies present whom we don't want to hurt. Watch yourselves.

Tony: Oh, yeah. We don't want to hurt the young ladies.

Len: Ladies? Where are the ladies? I don't see any ladies.

Josephine (whines): Lenny!

Len: Oh, sorry Jo-Jo. Just kidding, m'lady. (He flourishes a royal bow to her.)

Students sit at their assigned seats with their lab partners. There are 12 mixed male-female groups and one group of two females.

Mr. Tenace: Okay, let's get started. We have a lot to do. Today is dissection day!

Dianne: Ugh! I'm going to be sick, Mr. Tenace.

Tonya: Do we have to do this? It's so gross.

Akim: We're gonna cut it open and squeeze its guts out. Ahhhh!

Giggles and conversations spring up around the room.

Mr. Tenace: All right now. Let's go over the procedure. I'll demonstrate the process. Watch and learn.

Dianne: Can we just watch our lab partner do it? We don't have to actually touch it, do we?

Mr. Tenace: That's up to you and your partner. Everyone has to participate in some way, though. We can't have any slackers here.

Dianne: (turning to her male partner) Okay, you're in charge. Just wake me when it's over. I'll take notes. Gross.

Document 3
Interview with a Female Student

Mr. Tenace: Do you like science?

Dianne: Mostly I like the classes when we're reading and talking about interesting stuff that relates to me or people in general. But I don't like labs. Mostly because I work with Jason and he just takes over. He's really interested in the experiments we do. And when we did the frog, I just let him go for it. I don't want him to think I'm vulgar and willing to cut up a frog. Girls aren't supposed to like that sort of stuff.

Mr. Tenace: What if you had a female lab partner?

Dianne: That would be interesting. I don't know. Maybe we'd work together better because it wouldn't be like the boy always trying to take over. One of us would have to do it. I kind of think if it were two girls as partners, they'd work together to split the work up.

Document 4
Interview with a Male Student

Mr. Tenace: Do you like science?

Len: Yeah, it's kind of cool. I like that we don't have to sit and listen all the time. We get to do things like the labs.

Mr. Tenace: How do you and your partner, Dianne, work together?

Len: She's a good speller and I'm not. So she does the writing and I do the hands-on stuff. She doesn't like to dissect frogs and stuff like that. You know, the typical girl. But we work well together.

Mr. Tenace: What if you had a male partner?

Len: Then who would do the writing? No, we definitely need to mix it up.

PLT Case History 5.1 Questions

1. Mr. Tenace's goal for himself this year is to learn more about gender issues in science. He has described his project plan.

   ■ Describe TWO strengths of Mr. Tenace's project plan.

- For EACH strength, describe how it depicts effective aspects of planning. Base your response on what you know about planning instruction.
2. The documents provide information about Mr. Tenace's class.
   - Describe TWO methods Mr. Tenace could use to equalize the roles of males and females in his science classes.
   - For EACH method described, identify specific evidence that indicates that the roles are not currently equalized. Base your response on what you know about gender role development and gender biases.

PLT Case History 5.2: Kim

Scenario

It is the beginning of the school year, and Ms. Lee is assessing all students' strengths and needs through various universal screening measures using a typical Response to Intervention model. She is also making observations and jotting down notes about students' behaviors and participation in a teaching log.

Kim is a fifth grader in Ms. Lee's class. In her review of the anecdotal notes she has made of various students over the past two weeks, Ms. Lee has noted the following about Kim:

Document 1
Anecdotal Notes

9/9, 8:30 A.M. Upon entering room, Kim does not respond to classmates who call to her from across the room. She appears to hear them but does not respond. Eventually, they come over to Kim and talk with her at her desk. Then Kim responds to them.

9/12, noon. During the class read-aloud time, the whole class was laughing and attentive except Kim. They all seem to be engaged in the book (Because of Winn-Dixie by Kate DiCamillo), but Kim just doesn't seem to be

attentive. She seems to be mimicking others when they laugh or react rather than demonstrating authentic, personal emotions.

9/18, 10 A.M. During literature circles time, I observed Kim's group. Kim's job was to be the Word Wizard. She was to record new, unusual vocabulary that stood out in the night's reading assignment. In her notes, she listed these words: except, especially, and independent. When asked why she chose those words, she said, "They were the biggest words I could find." I need to reteach the purpose of the role of the Word Wizard. Does she know these words or was she just confused about the directions? Further evaluation is needed.

Document 2
Ms. Lee's Analysis of the Anecdotal Notes

I am somewhat concerned about Kim's disorientation. She often appears on the fringes of the class, watching others rather than participating herself. She looks confused by expectations and directions, especially when they are given orally.

PLT Case History 5.2 Questions

3. Based on Ms. Lee's observations so far, she wants to inquire further into Kim's needs.
   - Identify TWO other types of assessment that Ms. Lee should use to further assess Kim's needs.
   - For EACH type of assessment you suggest, explain specifically what Ms. Lee might hope to learn or achieve.
4. After further assessment, Ms. Lee has determined that Kim would benefit from learning listening strategies to help her become a more active listener.
   - Describe TWO listening strategies that might help Kim develop her active listening skills.
   - Describe how Kim might use technology to practice or support the application of EACH strategy.

Multiple-Choice Questions

1. Mr. Fortuin is explaining an individual child's performance on a school-administered test to the child's parents. He explains that this particular test compares the child's performance to that of her classmates and other larger groups. It tells how well she did compared to her classmates on a given set of knowledge, but it does not indicate what information she does and does not know. The score will be given in a percentile, which was derived from raw scores obtained from testing a large population. The test Mr. Fortuin is describing is most likely
   a. an aptitude test.
   b. a criterion-referenced test.
   c. a norm-referenced test.
   d. a standard-score test.

2. During Piaget's concrete operational stage, children
   a. are egocentric thinkers who believe everyone thinks as they do.
   b. are able to handle abstract reasoning and understand hypothetical concepts.
   c. are not yet capable of concrete problem solving.
   d. begin to organize their thoughts and reason logically.

3. Robert Gagne, an experimental psychologist, published *The Conditions of Learning*, which
   a. outlined the relation of appropriate instructional designs to learning objectives.
   b. described the relation of child development to learning styles.
   c. defined the psychological strategies children must learn to be self-sufficient.
   d. is used widely by states to assess students' learning.

4. No Child Left Behind legislation
   a. authorized and funded the Goals 2000 program.
   b. set national educational goals for U.S. students that were to be achieved by the year 2000.
   c. identified eight national goals, including that all children in the United States would start school ready to learn.
   d. supports standards-based education reform, which proposes that setting high standards and establishing assessable goals will improve students' learning.

5. A writing approach designed for use at all grade levels, in which students have opportunities to choose writing topics and styles, and where teachers and peers act as mentor authors and confer with students as they advance their ways through the writing process, is known as
   a. writing with technology.
   b. guided writing.
   c. a writing workshop.
   d. individualized writing.

6. Which of the following learning theories views learning as a process whereby learners build new ideas and concepts?
   a. constructivism
   b. behaviorism
   c. cognitivism
   d. naturalism

7. Accommodations
   a. may lower the level of difficulty of a task so that students with special needs may experience success.
   b. may offer alternative ways for students to share what they are learning with others.
   c. reduce the standards of achievement for the learner.
   d. must be made for all children with special needs.

8. A school is seeking to use Title I funds to support a new literacy program at the grade five through grade nine levels. The school must investigate upon what research the new program is based. This is an example of
   a. due process.
   b. Section 504 of the Rehabilitation Services Act.
   c. using scientifically-based research to make critical decisions about programming.
   d. legislation related to the Americans with Disabilities Act.

9. A classroom teacher is concerned about the varying skill levels and learning styles in his ninth-grade classroom. To meet his students' needs, he plans to acquire materials across readability levels, present ideas orally and visually, and set up the classroom in interest centers that allow students to practice inquiry learning. These approaches are examples of
   a. learning theories.
   b. discriminatory practices.
   c. gender inequalities.
   d. differentiated instruction.

10. Mr. Bing's classroom is set up in problem-solving stations. Students move through the stations and use their prior knowledge to interact with the environment. They experiment, explore, and manipulate as they work their way through the stations with their classmates. This environment may best be described as
   a. discovery learning.
   b. skill and drill.
   c. service learning.
   d. antibias curriculum.

11. To best encourage students' divergent thinking, a teacher could ask
   a. What might be another solution to this problem?
   b. How did the author solve the problem?
   c. What is a fraction?
   d. When the settlers travelled across the nation, what did they pack in their wagons?

Use the following concept map to answer question 12.

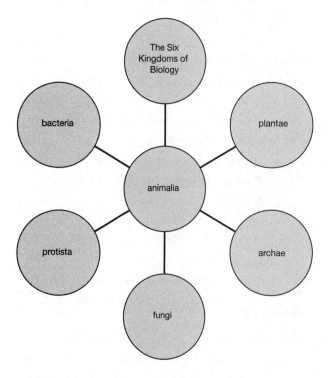

12. When given a blank concept map and asked to complete it showing the six kingdoms of biology in a graphic way, a seventh grader completed the map as shown. From looking at the map, a teacher could safely assess that the student
   a. does not understand the six kingdoms.
   b. does not understand the purpose of the concept map configuration.
   c. strayed off the topic.
   d. copied the information from another classmate or a book.

13. Culturally responsive educators
   a. encourage children to set aside their own nationalities and take on those of the majority race.
   b. teach multiculturalism during a two-week themed unit of the school year.
   c. incorporate a variety of instructional approaches and strategies that recognize all learning styles.
   d. call on students of color to represent the feelings and experiences of the people of their heritage.

14. Which method is most likely to be used in a direct instruction approach to teaching?
   a. coaching a student how to do long division step-by-step in small increments through clear instruction
   b. setting up learning centers and allowing students to flow from center to center throughout the morning
   c. teaching one student a skill and directing that student in how to teach the skill to his or her peers
   d. students determining what they will learn by constructing questions of inquiry

15. A child tells the teacher that his mother was upset because he came home with a low grade on a math quiz the night before, and he blames the teacher for his low grade. What is the best way for the teacher to respond?
   a. "It isn't my fault if you didn't study!"
   b. "I don't blame your mother for being upset; it was a terrible grade."
   c. "So, what are you going to do to get a better grade on your next test?"
   d. "How did you feel when your test grade upset your mother?"

16. One thing that influences how much time a teacher should plan to spend teaching a lesson is
   a. the complexity of the concept.
   b. the teacher's personal interest in the topic.
   c. students' interest in the topic.
   d. how much time is left in the class period.

17. An eighth-grade boy refers to a classmate as a "chick." What would be the best way to respond to this student?
   a. Ignore the comment, as he was just joking.
   b. Demand he apologize to the classmate.
   c. Have him write out all of the definitions of "chick" and substantiate his use of the word.
   d. Ask him why he thinks some females might find the term offensive.

18. Which of the following would most likely be the best way to motivate students to learn about history?
   a. Let them use an inquiry approach to determine what they want to learn, how they want to learn it, and how they want to report what they've learned.
   b. Have them write a report about American history using Microsoft Word.
   c. Let them read books of their choice about the founders of America.
   d. Let them research topics of their choice using Internet search engines.

19. Maslow's hierarchy of needs portrays self-actualization as
   a. the realization that we need water, food, air, and sleep to survive.
   b. the need for love and affection through friendships, romance, and family companionship.
   c. a person's desire for self-fulfillment, reflected through spontaneity, autonomy, and realism.
   d. knowing who we are and being satisfied with our self-worth.

20. Readers who read the title and main headings, glance through the pictures and graphics, and begin to form questions of what the text will be about before reading the text are activating valuable information. They are

a. determining where the answers to the questions at the end of the chapter are.

b. forming predictions of what the text will be about to increase their alertness to the text.

c. deciding what information will be on the next test the teacher gives them.

d. gathering information about the text so they can just skim the materials later.

21. Through which type of thinking do we begin by detecting patterns in specific observations, then formulating tentative hypotheses and then conclusions?

a. deductive

b. inductive

c. reasoning

d. inclusive

22. In the teachers' faculty room, Ms. Curtain tells Mr. Bassett that one of her student's parents who happens to live down the street from her was just arrested for assaulting another neighbor. A conversation ensues in which she reveals other family interactions she has observed also. Is Ms. Curtain within her bounds to share this information with her colleagues? What should she do? Select the best choice.

a. Ethically, because Ms. Curtain is the child's teacher, she should refrain from "gossiping" about the child's family. Nothing good can come from it.

b. The incidents all occurred in public, so Ms. Curtain is not obligated by confidentiality rules in this case.

c. Ms. Curtain is obligated to share everything she knows about her students to other teachers who may come in contact with the student.

d. If in doubt, Ms. Curtain should talk with the building principal or other administrator to determine what information is confidential and what information may be helpful for school personnel to be aware of.

Questions 23 and 24 are based on the following passages regarding the debate about national versus state control of educational institutions and policies.

Education should be controlled at the national level.

There are 50 states in the United States. When the national government controls educational policies, all states are uniform. Families can move from state to state and hold the same expectations for the schools their children will attend. Central management at the national level creates predictability and conformity to the same standards and a universal curriculum across states. If states were to be the locus of control for school policy, inequalities would exist, making it unfair for some populations.

Education should be controlled at the state level. People in a local community best know what the children in the area need as far as education is concerned. States should control school policies within their state because they understand what the school and students need better than the national government would. Funding stays local rather than going to another part of the country. It is too big an undertaking to try to control a whole nation of schools with any success.

23. The author of the first passage would most likely agree that
    a. states should set their own learning standards that are controlled by the national government.
    b. state taxes from New York should be used to support poor school districts in California.
    c. the national government should hold all schools to one set of learning standards.
    d. families should not be allowed to switch schools when they move from one state to another.

24. The second passage suggests that
    a. one state should have a say about how another state educates its children.
    b. it is too big a job for the state to control the educational policies within its state.
    c. children who move from state to state will not achieve the same caliber of education.
    d. state control takes into consideration the economic needs of a state.

25. McCalli is intensely interested in new things but his interest is usually short-lived. He prefers interactions with his peers instead of adults, and he prefers active versus passive learning. These characteristics reflect that McCalli is an adolescent
    a. whose brain development reinforces such typical adolescent behaviors.
    b. who is capable of retaining massive amounts of information at one time.
    c. who is moving from abstract to concrete thinking.
    d. who is incapable of thinking critically or controlling impulses.

26. Tammel's math teacher has observed that Tammel has difficulty using a separate answer sheet to respond to multiple-choice questions on a test. When reading aloud, Tammel keeps skipping lines of text or repeats the same line again and again. Tammel also has trouble understanding math equations. Which type of visual processing disorder does Tammel most likely have?
    a. visual memory
    b. visual sequencing
    c. visual discrimination
    d. visual figure-ground discrimination

27. Ms. Martini is a ninth-grade English teacher who is teaching a unit on identity through literary and informational texts. Throughout the unit, students are journaling to prompts such as "Who am I?" and "How do I fit in?" and "Where am I going in life?" She believes that by allowing her ninth-graders to explore, they will come to understand their own identities. Ms. Martini's goals closely resemble which of the following theories?
    a. Piaget's Theory of Cognitive Development
    b. Vygotsky's Social Learning Theory
    c. Erikson's Personality Development Theory
    d. Bruner's Information Processing Theory

28. Based on the cognitive development of adolescents, teachers should plan instruction that does all of the following EXCEPT
   a. limit the amount of new information presented at one time to accommodate adolescents' short-term memory capabilities.
   b. provide problem-solving activities to enhance and strengthen brain growth through practice.
   c. provide lessons that are varied and include lots of hands-on activities.
   d. cram in large amounts of information to encourage students' brains to grow and develop.

29. To best communicate objectives and procedures to his adolescent students, Mr. Griffin should do all of the following EXCEPT
   a. distribute assignment worksheets that clearly identify the objectives and timelines.
   b. establish, teach, and practice consistent routines.
   c. expect students to be told expectations once and then remember and follow the rules.
   d. provide graphic organizers and process charts to help students visualize and proceed toward objectives.

30. All of the following are informal assessments EXCEPT
   a. surveys and interviews.
   b. standardized tests.
   c. portfolios.
   d. observations.

31. Which of the following tests is a standardized test used to measure what a student has learned in a specific content area, such as mathematics or reading?
   a. an achievement test
   b. an intelligence test
   c. a proficiency test
   d. an aptitude test

32. Most professional educational associations offer all of the following forms of professional development EXCEPT
   a. websites with various resources.
   b. professional journals.
   c. conferences and conventions.
   d. accredited master's-level graduate programs.

33. Cici is a Latina young adult who closely identifies herself with her homeland culture. Her native language is important to maintaining her cultural identity. Cici's teachers can best enhance her academic success in an American middle school by
   a. providing opportunities for Cici to integrate her Latina language and culture into her learning experiences.
   b. providing opportunities for Cici to learn more about her homeland but encouraging her to leave her language behind and use only English.
   c. encouraging Cici to blend in with the other students by changing her cultural identity to reflect the dominant culture.
   d. treating all the students the same.

34. A student who is being bullied by her classmates decides there isn't anything that she can do to stop the situation. If she tells adults, the bullies will only be crueler to her. She feels powerless to change the situation. As a result of the student's resistance, the bullying gets even worse. The student begins to recede into clinical depression. This is an example of
   a. learning as experience.
   b. learned helplessness.
   c. reciprocal determinism.
   d. intrinsic punishment.

35. Colinda intently watches the teacher demonstrate a science experiment. She knows that if she forgets the procedure, she can refer to the handout the teacher distributed. She practices once, carefully using the handout to ensure she remembers the sequence correctly; however, the experiment fails. What went wrong? She doesn't intend to give up because she knows she can do this. With which of the following steps in the modeling process is Colinda experiencing difficulty?
   a. attention
   b. retention
   c. reproduction
   d. motivation

36. Ms. Camille wants her students to form new insights while reading *To Kill a Mockingbird*. Which of the following questions would lead toward that goal?
   a. How does Atticus try to instill conscience in Jem and Scout?
   b. What was Chapter 1 about?
   c. How did Chapter 1 make you feel?
   d. What is Atticus's relationship to Jem and Scout?

37. When using oral questioning techniques, Ms. Camille notes that her shy students are sometimes reluctant to participate. How could Ms. Camille encourage these shy students to be more willing to get involved?
   a. Call on them even if they do not raise their hands to participate.
   b. Provide a secure, noncritical classroom environment.
   c. Eliminate the use of oral questioning in the classroom and have students write responses.
   d. Have shy students whisper their responses to more outgoing students to share.

38. When speaking about culture and communication, educators know that context is key. What does this mean?
   a. You should not speak with someone from a culture different than your own until you have learned about the context of that person's familial culture.
   b. People have their own communication style preferences.
   c. How you communicate with one person, in one situation, or in one place, might be very different than how you communicate with another person, in another situation, or another place.
   d. How someone interprets what you are saying to them may be different from what you meant them to understand from your message.

39. Mr. Williams is administering the state examinations for the first time as a new teacher. As he starts the test, he says to his students, "Let's see, it says here that you have to listen to me, these directions, and everything. But you've done this stuff before, so just go ahead and start the test. If you need anything, just raise your hand." The special education teacher who is in the room covers for him and quickly steps in with, "Mr. Williams, you are such a kidder. You know we have to read everything they tell us to read. So, what were those directions?"

Does Mr. Williams have to read the directions to the students?

a. No. The students are supposed to read all parts of the test themselves.

b. No. It is up to the discretion of the teacher to determine how to administer the test.

c. Yes. He should read them to students if they raise their hand and don't know what to do.

d. Yes. Teachers should not deviate from test administration instructions on standardized tests, or the results may be invalid.

40. Which type of test is used by classroom teachers to monitor their students' performance on a day-to-day basis? The tests are based on the curriculum. Results from these tests help teachers determine how much the students have learned.

a. criterion-referenced tests

b. norm-referenced tests

c. achievement tests

d. aptitude tests

41. When teachers conduct research in their classrooms to determine the effectiveness of methods they are using, they collect data to analyze. All of the following are examples of types of data they might collect EXCEPT

a. student work samples.

b. Wikipedia resources.

c. interviews with the children and parents.

d. audiotapes of students' small-group, collaborative conversations.

42. Social learning theory consists of three core concepts. Which of the following choices is NOT one of these concepts?

a. People learn by observing others.

b. Internal reinforcements are important to learning.

c. Learning does not always lead to change in behavior.

d. Learning leads to permanent change in behavior.

43. Mrs. Flander's seventh-grade English class students tried to convince her that if she took away the homework that week, they would spend 30 minutes each night reading a good book of their choice. Taking away the homework to increase the desired behavior of reading a good book is an example of

a. negative reinforcement.

b. positive reinforcement.

c. reward.

d. punishment.

44. The student will use verb tense to convey various times.

Which learning domain does this objective address?

a. cognitive domain

b. affective domain

c. psychomotor domain

d. physical domain

45. Read the following dialogue, then identify what type of strategy Ms. Peek is using to support the student's attempts to articulate her ideas.

Amy: I'm so angry! I could burst!

Ms. Peek: You sound upset.

Amy: Yes, I can't get this math! I just don't understand it at all!

Ms. Peek: You're frustrated because you don't understand the math.

    a. wait-time strategy
    b. verbal prompting
    c. nonverbal prompting
    d. reflective-listening statements

46. What might be a disadvantage of having computers in the classroom?
    a. time lost due to connectivity issues
    b. use of different kinds of texts, graphics, videos, and pictures
    c. promotion of independent learning
    d. students learning IT skills along with the content

47. If the lesson plan objective is that, in small groups, students will research and report a panel presentation to the class on what they learned about electrical currents, the best assessment method to use would be
    a. a portfolio.
    b. an analytic rubric.
    c. a multiple-choice quiz.
    d. an essay.

48. At the end of seventh grade, students in the Altamont school district take a final exam in math. If the scores on this test correlate highly with the statewide math tests, these tests would be said to have high concurrent
    a. criterion.
    b. construction.
    c. reliability.
    d. validity.

49. Mr. Treesome is finding it difficult to develop a critical perspective when he reflects on his practice. What would be the best method for him to use to add this perspective to his reflection practice?
    a. Engage a critical friend to collaborate in the process.
    b. Start a teaching journal.
    c. Reread his reflections two weeks after writing them.
    d. Examine the underlying assumptions in the reflection.

50. Stacey plans how to approach a task, monitors her comprehension as she proceeds through the activity, and evaluates her progress as she completes the task. These are all examples of how Stacey is using her
    a. memory skills.
    b. regulatory processing skills.
    c. metacognitive skills.
    d. overview cognitive skills.

51. Standards of conduct must be taught at the beginning of the school year and reinforced throughout the year. These standards may include class rules regarding all of the following EXCEPT
    a. how, when, and where to hand in assignments.
    b. rules for the use of technology outside of school.
    c. what to bring to class in order to be prepared.
    d. expectations for students' collaborative work activities.

52. Ms. Carrie is designing a social studies unit in which students will help make some of the instructional decisions. Which of the following would NOT be an appropriate decision to leave up to students to make on their own?
a. final grades for themselves and their peers
b. what type of outcome products will represent the knowledge they gained during the unit
c. which resources may be used to research the topic
d. whether they will collaborate on the project or work independently

53. To encourage high levels of thinking, a teacher should guide students to do all of the following EXCEPT
a. reflect.
b. challenge assumptions.
c. find relationships.
d. use their body language.

54. When teaching students about active listening techniques, educators should model how to interpret information. An example of this is: Every ten minutes a man gets mugged in Los Angeles.
A speaker may mean that every ten minutes someone gets mugged, or that every ten minutes this one certain man gets mugged over and over again. The purpose of teaching this interpretation skill would be to teach students that sometimes the speaker's meaning and the sentence's meaning can confuse the listener. When this occurs, teach the students that they should
a. attend to the speaker.
b. ask a clarifying question.
c. be respectful of the speaker.
d. provide supportive feedback.

55. At the end of a two-week unit on change, Mr. Watson will administer which type of assessment to evaluate students' overall learning and modify and validate his instruction?
a. formative assessment
b. summative assessment
c. diagnostic assessment
d. standardized assessment

56. In norm-referenced assessments, a scale to determine the differences among scores and whether the scores are below average, average, or above average is known as
a. code patterns.
b. quantitative data.
c. frequency distribution.
d. standard deviation.

57. Most likely, all of the following people might be members of a child's individualized educational plan (IEP) EXCEPT
a. the child.
b. the parents.
c. the para educator.
d. the classroom teacher.

58. All of the following are key elements of diagnostic assessments except that they should
a. be connected to specific, predetermined learning objectives.
b. identify labels for students.
c. be built into the curriculum in a systematic way.
d. lead to what the student should learn next.

59. Jordan is going through sudden physical changes as an adolescent. As a result he may exhibit all of the following EXCEPT
a. hypersensitivity reaction.
b. self-consciousness.
c. sensitivity.
d. anxiety.

60. Ms. Carter, a tenured teacher and lifetime member of the community, was recently asked to speak at the Town Board meeting. The Board was interested in hearing about what teaching and learning looked like in the community. Ms. Carter was happy to talk with the Board to tell them about the efforts of her colleagues and to gain the Board's support. Ms. Carter's support for teaching and learning is known as

   a. teacher advocacy.
   b. stakeholding.
   c. teacher perception.
   d. collaboration.

61. Ms. Realia is beginning a new unit by having her students fill out a KWL chart like the one that follows. What is her strategy for using this KWL?

K	W	L
What do you **know** about the topic?	What do you **want** to know about the topic?	What have you **learned** about the topic?

   a. This is a writing exercise that will help students practice expressing their ideas about the topic.
   b. Ms. Realia wants to teach students how to take notes to aid their comprehension of the new topic.
   c. As students talk in small groups about their charts, they will learn what they wanted to learn about the topic.
   d. Ms. Realia wants to motivate her students to connect their prior knowledge and interests to new ideas and concepts.

62. A student came to Mr. Livingston and told him that a group of boys had been bullying him and then threatened him. Mr. Livingston told him to ignore the boys and they would stop. But they didn't. The boy was assaulted by the bullies, and he is in the hospital now. Legally, because Mr. Livingston knew about the threat and did not report it to his supervisor, he may be

   a. slanderous.
   b. malicious.
   c. liable.
   d. defamatory.

63. Students in Mr. Jay's class are working on writing specific, measurable, achievable, relevant, time-bound (SMART) goals for themselves. They will begin by setting personal learning targets, then work toward achieving those targets. Finally, they will evaluate the progress they've made toward the goal. This process is an example of

   a. reflective learning.
   b. student self-assessment.
   c. metacognition.
   d. selected response.

64. Mr. Biddle wants to use an assessment that will evaluate students' work as a whole, even while weighing its major elements. He doesn't want to become overly concerned with any one aspect of the project. What type of scoring should he use?

   a. incidental scoring
   b. guided scoring
   c. analytic scoring
   d. holistic scoring

65. Jack, an eighth grader, receives a score report from a standardized English language arts test taken recently by all eighth graders in the school district. The results indicate that Jack's national percentile rank is 47 and that his grade-equivalent score is 6.4. Jack's grade-equivalent score indicates that he

    a. did as well on this test as an average sixth grader in the fourth month of school would do on the same test.

    b. will encounter problems in English language arts when he gets into ninth grade.

    c. did as well on this test as the average sixth-grade student in the fourth month of school would do on an eighth-grade test.

    d. can do the same math a sixth grader in the fourth month of sixth grade can do.

66. If a teacher suspects a child has been abused, she

    a. should ask the parents if they are the abusers.

    b. can decide to report the incident to the authorities or not.

    c. is legally obligated to report it to the authorities.

    d. should ask the student who abused him or her.

67. Adelphia is a seventh-grade student who is capable of high levels of abstract thinking, can retrieve information quickly, and shows originality of thought. She is likely a candidate for which school program?

    a. future teachers program

    b. school counseling program

    c. the gifted-and-talented program

    d. library media specialty program

68. At the middle-school level, students develop the capacity to assume responsibility for reflecting on and documenting their academic progress. One effective way to encourage this development is to provide vital communication between the teacher and student concerning affective and academic matters. This type of assessment is known as

    a. a conference.

    b. an interview.

    c. a debriefing.

    d. a diary.

69. To foster a home environment that supports children as learners, teachers should stress

    a. critical concerns they have about students.

    b. critical concerns the teacher has about the parents' lack of support for the students.

    c. the importance of high parental aspirations for the children.

    d. student achievement rather than problems-centered discussions.

70. Gwen graduated from a teachers' college in Alabama. Her husband just got a job opportunity in New York State. How can Gwen find out if she will be certified to teach in New York?

    a. Gwen should call schools in New York to ask about teacher licensing.

    b. Gwen doesn't have to worry because once you graduate from a teachers' college, you can get a teaching job in any state.

    c. Gwen will have to check on New York licensing regulations through the State Education Department.

    d. Gwen will have to check Alabama's licensing regulations through Alabama's State Education Department.

13 ▶ PRACTICE EXAM 6: PLT: GRADES 7–12

CHAPTER SUMMARY

Here is a full-length test based on the Praxis II PLT for Grades 7–12. Now that you have studied the review chapter, take this exam to get familiar with the test format and the types of questions on the test and see how you do.

L ike the real Praxis II PLT, the exam that follows is made up of 70 multiple-choice questions and four constructed-response questions based on two case histories. Use the answer sheet on the next page to record your answers to the multiple-choice questions. Write your answers to the constructed responses on a separate piece of paper. Allow yourself 70 minutes for the multiple-choice questions and 50 minutes for the constructed-response questions.

With this practice exam, you should simulate the actual test-taking experience as closely as you can. Find a quiet place to work where you won't be disturbed. Set a timer or stopwatch for each part of the exam to guide your pace.

When you have completed the exam, use the answer explanations in Chapter 20 to learn more about the questions you missed, and use the scoring guide to figure out how you did.

PLT Multiple-Choice Questions

	a	b	c	d			a	b	c	d
1.	ⓐ	ⓑ	ⓒ	ⓓ	36.	ⓐ	ⓑ	ⓒ	ⓓ
2.	ⓐ	ⓑ	ⓒ	ⓓ	37.	ⓐ	ⓑ	ⓒ	ⓓ
3.	ⓐ	ⓑ	ⓒ	ⓓ	38.	ⓐ	ⓑ	ⓒ	ⓓ
4.	ⓐ	ⓑ	ⓒ	ⓓ	39.	ⓐ	ⓑ	ⓒ	ⓓ
5.	ⓐ	ⓑ	ⓒ	ⓓ	40.	ⓐ	ⓑ	ⓒ	ⓓ
6.	ⓐ	ⓑ	ⓒ	ⓓ	41.	ⓐ	ⓑ	ⓒ	ⓓ
7.	ⓐ	ⓑ	ⓒ	ⓓ	42.	ⓐ	ⓑ	ⓒ	ⓓ
8.	ⓐ	ⓑ	ⓒ	ⓓ	43.	ⓐ	ⓑ	ⓒ	ⓓ
9.	ⓐ	ⓑ	ⓒ	ⓓ	44.	ⓐ	ⓑ	ⓒ	ⓓ
10.	ⓐ	ⓑ	ⓒ	ⓓ	45.	ⓐ	ⓑ	ⓒ	ⓓ
11.	ⓐ	ⓑ	ⓒ	ⓓ	46.	ⓐ	ⓑ	ⓒ	ⓓ
12.	ⓐ	ⓑ	ⓒ	ⓓ	47.	ⓐ	ⓑ	ⓒ	ⓓ
13.	ⓐ	ⓑ	ⓒ	ⓓ	48.	ⓐ	ⓑ	ⓒ	ⓓ
14.	ⓐ	ⓑ	ⓒ	ⓓ	49.	ⓐ	ⓑ	ⓒ	ⓓ
15.	ⓐ	ⓑ	ⓒ	ⓓ	50.	ⓐ	ⓑ	ⓒ	ⓓ
16.	ⓐ	ⓑ	ⓒ	ⓓ	51.	ⓐ	ⓑ	ⓒ	ⓓ
17.	ⓐ	ⓑ	ⓒ	ⓓ	52.	ⓐ	ⓑ	ⓒ	ⓓ
18.	ⓐ	ⓑ	ⓒ	ⓓ	53.	ⓐ	ⓑ	ⓒ	ⓓ
19.	ⓐ	ⓑ	ⓒ	ⓓ	54.	ⓐ	ⓑ	ⓒ	ⓓ
20.	ⓐ	ⓑ	ⓒ	ⓓ	55.	ⓐ	ⓑ	ⓒ	ⓓ
21.	ⓐ	ⓑ	ⓒ	ⓓ	56.	ⓐ	ⓑ	ⓒ	ⓓ
22.	ⓐ	ⓑ	ⓒ	ⓓ	57.	ⓐ	ⓑ	ⓒ	ⓓ
23.	ⓐ	ⓑ	ⓒ	ⓓ	58.	ⓐ	ⓑ	ⓒ	ⓓ
24.	ⓐ	ⓑ	ⓒ	ⓓ	59.	ⓐ	ⓑ	ⓒ	ⓓ
25.	ⓐ	ⓑ	ⓒ	ⓓ	60.	ⓐ	ⓑ	ⓒ	ⓓ
26.	ⓐ	ⓑ	ⓒ	ⓓ	61.	ⓐ	ⓑ	ⓒ	ⓓ
27.	ⓐ	ⓑ	ⓒ	ⓓ	62.	ⓐ	ⓑ	ⓒ	ⓓ
28.	ⓐ	ⓑ	ⓒ	ⓓ	63.	ⓐ	ⓑ	ⓒ	ⓓ
29.	ⓐ	ⓑ	ⓒ	ⓓ	64.	ⓐ	ⓑ	ⓒ	ⓓ
30.	ⓐ	ⓑ	ⓒ	ⓓ	65.	ⓐ	ⓑ	ⓒ	ⓓ
31.	ⓐ	ⓑ	ⓒ	ⓓ	66.	ⓐ	ⓑ	ⓒ	ⓓ
32.	ⓐ	ⓑ	ⓒ	ⓓ	67.	ⓐ	ⓑ	ⓒ	ⓓ
33.	ⓐ	ⓑ	ⓒ	ⓓ	68.	ⓐ	ⓑ	ⓒ	ⓓ
34.	ⓐ	ⓑ	ⓒ	ⓓ	69.	ⓐ	ⓑ	ⓒ	ⓓ
35.	ⓐ	ⓑ	ⓒ	ⓓ	70.	ⓐ	ⓑ	ⓒ	ⓓ

Case History Questions

Directions: Two case histories and four constructed-response questions follow. You are not expected to include citations of specific texts, authors, or theories in your responses. Your answers will be evaluated, however, based on your use of professionally accepted practices and principles in learning and teaching. Some questions have multiple parts, so be sure your response addresses all components of each question.

PLT Case History 6.1: Mr. Granato

Scenario

It's conference day at Guilderland High School. Classes have been canceled; appointments have been made; family members and students are sitting in classrooms talking quietly—for the most part—with educators about students' progress, attitudes, and programs. It's a day to not only share reports and problem-solve, but it's also a day for families and educators to meet and get to know each other. Educators hope to gain some insight about the home environment of their students, so they can best help the students. Parents desire feedback about their high schooler so they can support their adolescent at home. Students listen and contribute, sometimes proudly and sometimes defensively.

Document 1
Narrative Description of
Mrs. Maynard's Conference

Mr. Granato has just finished his 8:15 A.M. appointment with his twelfth-grade English student Jeff, Jeff's mother, and his father. Mr. Granato found the family supportive but respective of Jeff's ability to manage his academic and sport schedules in a way that prioritized school work. Jeff was eager to do well his last year so he would be prepared for college. Jeff's father ended the conference with, "Well, you keep doing your job and we'll keep doing ours to get our boy ready. But the truth is that Jeff has it all under control. He knows what he wants out of life, and he's got a plan to get it. He's a good kid. We're proud of him."

Mr. Granato had a smile on his face thinking about the meeting when the Maynards—Cody and his mother—walked briskly into the room. He had a feeling by the look on Mrs. Maynard's face that this conference would be a bit different from his last one. Stress followed Mrs. Maynard into the room.

"Mr. Granato," Mrs. Maynard said as she held out her hand. She wore a business suit with black high-heels. "I'm a little early, I know; but, I have to be at work in a half hour. So, I hope you don't mind if we start early."

"That's fine, Mrs. Maynard. Hi, Cody. How ya doing?" Mr. Granato signaled the desks that were pulled together in a circle.

Before everyone was even seated, Mrs. Maynard took out a list and began to question Mr. Granato about its first item. "I sent you a couple of e-mails last week, Mr. Granato, with an agenda of what I'd like to cover in today's meeting. Did you get my e-mails? Did I send them to the right address? I called the school secretary and she said that yes, I had the right address? So, did you get my e-mails?"

"Oh, yes, I think I did. I was very busy last week grading the students' essays. I'm sorry I never got back to you. I always give my students' work priority over my other responsibilities. I saw your name in my inbox but just didn't get a chance to read what you wrote. I figured we were meeting today anyway, so we can talk now. So, let's get started." Mr. Granato admitted his neglect and was ready to move on to talk about Cody's work . . . or, actually, lack of work.

Cody was really quiet in class and often came unprepared. He had "senioritis," as he called it. He had already told Mr. Granato that he was just biding his time until he graduated, doing just enough to get through the course. His records showed he was an average student with average grades all through high school. Homework and tests just weren't motivating to him, according to notes from previous teachers. In short, Cody was an intelligent student who was unmotivated to perform. He saw no reason to make an effort to get an A or B when a C would suffice.

However, Mrs. Maynard saw things differently. She'd spent the past 13 years—Cody's academic years—doing the best she could to support him. She drove him to school and picked him up every day until he got his driver's license and she bought him his first pickup truck. She met with teachers, kept in touch with them through phone calls and e-mails between meetings, e-mailed when she had a question about Cody's assignments, checked over Cody's homework, asked him repeatedly about his progress, and tried to perk his interest as best she could. She'd tried punishing him, grounding him, praising him, and even paying him for good grades. Mrs. Maynard had a reputation with the teachers and administrators in the building as a "helicopter mom" who was always hovering around Cody and the school. (In fact, a colleague had told Mr. Granato at the very beginning of the school year to check Cody's work regularly to see if he was doing his homework—on nights when it was done at all—or if maybe someone else was micromanaging it just a bit too much.) Nothing seemed to have any effect on his class average. To Cody, school was a great place to go to see his friends; the academic part was something he just put up with.

PLT Case History 6.1 Questions

1. Parents who micromanage their children to a high degree have been referred to as "helicopter parents."

   - Discuss ONE advantage and ONE disadvantage of parents being highly involved in their children's academic lives.
   - For EACH advantage and disadvantage, provide an example from the scenario to support your points.

2. The narrative provided describes highlights of the first part of a parent-teacher conference.

   - Describe TWO goals Mr. Granato should have for this meeting.
   - For EACH goal, explain how Mr. Granato might accomplish them.

PLT Case History 6.2: Ms. Strub

Scenario

Dusti Strub is a first-year seventh-grade English teacher at Onteora Middle School. She has made it through the middle of her first month of teaching. Things have gone pretty smoothly, and she feels she is getting to know the students very well.

She spent time getting to know her students first. She had them write "I Am" poems—a formulaic poem about how authors see themselves—to introduce themselves. This activity also gave her an idea of their writing skills and their interests so she could use what she'd learned to plan her next writing assignment.

Ms. Strub connects well with this age group, she is finding. However, there is one student who Ms. Strub is particularly concerned about. Annie Morris is her name. She's a very quiet young girl with short blonde hair and big brown eyes. She rarely looks Ms. Strub in the eyes, even when Ms. Strub has stopped her in the hall just to converse. Ms. Strub has noticed that Annie seems to tag along with two girls who have very different personalities from her own. Ms. Strub would describe Annie's place in the threesome as more like an awkward third wheel than part of a close circle of friends. Ms. Strub has begun an observation journal about the students, and she is focusing on Annie at the moment. She is mostly concerned based on the I Am poem Annie wrote, but the young woman's behaviors and self-imposed isolation also have her concerned.

Document 1

Annie's I Am Poem

I am ugly and shy.
I wonder if there is life after death.
I hear people talking about me.
I see snickers and sneers.
I want to have lots of friends.
I am ugly and shy.
I pretend I am popular.

I feel like an alien on a strange planet.
I touch the stars and the far planets.
I worry about what other people say about me.
I cry when I am alone.
I am ugly and shy.
I understand that being popular isn't
    important, it's what's inside that has value.
I say, "I can get through this."
I dream about living in Australia.
I try to smile at people.
I hope they notice me.
I am ugly and shy.

PLT Case History 6.2 Questions

3. Ms. Strub expresses her concern for Annie.
   - Describe TWO concerns Ms. Strub should investigate further.
   - For EACH concern, explain what action Ms. Strub should take.

4. If unchecked or ignored, adolescents' social and emotional issues can lead to mental health issues.
   - Discuss TWO psychological issues that adolescents are susceptible to developing during this stage of development.
   - For EACH issue, describe how Ms. Strub could help Annie avoid these psychological issues.

Multiple-Choice Questions

1. Students learn to question, clarify, summarize, and predict to improve their ability to monitor their understanding of text as they apply strategies on their own through
   a. reciprocal teaching.
   b. guided teaching.
   c. extended text teaching.
   d. scaffolded teaching.

2. According to the Generating Interaction between Schemata and Text (GIST) approach, students
   a. add a main idea with supporting ideas to a writing prompt.
   b. construct a 15-word-limit summary of a text with topic statements that fit it.
   c. practice extending their writing by adding personal experiences to it.
   d. activate prior knowledge to interpret text.

3. An anticipation/reaction guide for the topic of dinosaurs might include which of the following?
   a. Most dinosaurs' names come from the Latin language.
   b. Explain how you feel about dinosaurs.
   c. What do you want to learn about dinosaurs?
   d. What do you already know about dinosaurs?

Use the following table to answer question 4.

	QUESTION 1	QUESTION 2	QUESTION 3	QUESTION 4	QUESTION 5
I think . . .					
Resource 1 says . . .					
Resource 2 says . . .					
Resource 3 says . . .					
Resource 4 says . . .					

4. The table is an example of
   a. a rubric.
   b. a portfolio.
   c. an interest chart.
   d. an inquiry chart.

5. The following graphic organizer—a network tree—would best be used to illustrate

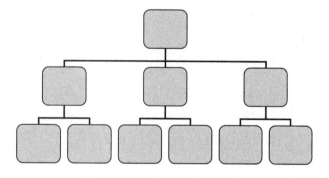

   a. the life cycle of a butterfly.
   b. the sequence of steps to conducting a lab experiment.
   c. the causal interaction of an election.
   d. attempted solutions to solving the national debt and their potential results.

6. The findings of the National Institute for Literacy indicate that
   a. content-area teachers are not responsible for improving adolescent literacy skills.
   b. the primary responsibility of content-area teachers should be to improve adolescents' literacy skills.
   c. content-area teachers must be aware of literacy instructional approaches that can be integrated within their existing curricula.
   d. the needs of diverse learners cannot be assessed accurately by content-area teachers.

7. Which of the following is an example of self-regulation?
   a. A student working in a collaborative group of peers is in charge of assessing that all members of the group are doing their assigned jobs.
   b. A reader is motivated, has prior knowledge about a topic, and uses effective strategies as she reads a passage.
   c. A writer directs his performance toward goals he wants to achieve.
   d. A writer perceives that she has control over her writing.

8. The most common form of formative assessment at the middle- and high-school levels is
   a. state tests across the content areas.
   b. teacher questioning.
   c. performance criteria.
   d. the use of student think alouds.

9. Morphology refers to
   a. the part of speech a word represents.
   b. the ability to use context clues to decipher the meaning of a word.
   c. the definition of a word.
   d. the roots and affixes in a word.

10. G. Stanley Hall was one of the first psychologists to study adolescents. He is noted for identifying the period between ages 12 and 25 as a period of
   a. childhood and adulthood.
   b. storm and stress.
   c. laughter and frivolity.
   d. fragility and strength.

11. According to the National Center for Education Statistics, the dropout rates of high school students between 2000 and 2008
   a. differed by race and ethnicity.
   b. increased drastically due to unemployment.
   c. increased drastically due to changes in housing.
   d. remained the same.

12. If a parent or a school district has concerns about the eligibility or placement of a child in a supportive special education program, either party has the legal right to
   a. request a due process hearing to resolve the dispute.
   b. enforce a solution they deem appropriate for the child.
   c. void the child's individualized education plan.
   d. place the child in the program based on assignment as the child's power of attorney.

13. Word identification or decoding refers to
   a. the ability to figure out the word a group of accurately sequenced letters makes.
   b. knowing the definition of a word in isolation.
   c. determining the meaning of a word by using context clues.
   d. the ability to pick the word a person dictates out of a list of words.

14. According to the Individuals with Disabilities Education Act (IDEA), children with disabilities require Individualized Education Programs (IEPs). The following information about the child must be included; however, this is not the only information that is required by law to be documented in the IEP. The IEP must include
   a. past performance, short- and long-term goals for the child, and health history of the child.
   b. past performance, current skills, goals, and special education services.
   c. current performance, annual goals, and special education and related services.
   d. needed transitional services, family history, and how progress will be measured.

15. Erikson's eight stages of development propose that adolescents (ages 12 to 18 years)

a. are developing a sense of industry accompanied by unresolved feelings of inferiority among their peers.

b. attempt to find their own identity and experience role confusion as they separate from family to be members of a wider society.

c. experience a desire to take initiative while they rely significantly on the basic family structure.

d. experience intimacy or isolation, depending on their success with this stage.

16. The main objective for PL 94-142 is to

a. mainstream and integrate students with handicaps into general education classes.

b. provide equal education for children of all cultures and races.

c. extend health insurance for all students living with their parents up to the age of 25.

d. restrict the working age for children to 16.

17. If a parent wanted to know what the goals of the science program of a high school were and what fundamental concepts would be explored, he or she would ask the administrator for a copy of

a. the school's individualized education program.

b. the school's mission statement.

c. the school's report card.

d. the school's curriculum guide.

18. At the beginning of each class, it is a good idea for educators to review with the students what happened in the previous class

a. to give students time to settle down and get ready for the day's lesson.

b. to reinforce students' understanding of where they are now and to determine if any reteaching is needed.

c. so that students can summarize what they are to do in this class.

d. because research indicates this is the best way to begin a class using the constructivist approach.

19. Which of the following is the best example of a question/prompt that would facilitate a student's factual recall?

a. How does the character John Proctor in *The Crucible* compare with other characters you know?

b. How did you get your answer to problem four?

c. Describe the contexts in which nominalization would be used.

d. Is the solution a reasonable one considering the situation?

20. Families are sometimes marginalized by cultural or linguistic differences and need the teacher's help to know effective ways to support school goals. When working with families that are marginalized, the teacher and school

    a. must not judge these families for the lack of interest they portray by not attending school events.

    b. should hold families accountable to attend school events.

    c. must find ways to accommodate families who are not able to attend school events.

    d. should not plan school events for these families because they will not be able to participate and will feel out of place.

21. Constructivist approaches are most effective

    a. when instructors are experts at teaching students how to construct answers, not at giving them answers.

    b. with unmotivated students.

    c. when teachers eliminate direct instruction from the curriculum.

    d. when students are not expected to memorize.

22. Nonfluent speakers typically will have difficulty articulating the English language when reading a text out loud. Therefore, the teacher should

    a. not call on these students to read text out loud in class so as not to embarrass them.

    b. recognize that the students cannot understand a passage if they cannot accurately pronounce the words out loud.

    c. understand that nonfluent speakers of the English language can comprehend what they are reading before they can correctly pronounce all of the sounds in the language.

    d. assume that the reading skills of the nonfluent speaker are well established and that it is just an articulation problem.

Questions 23 and 24 can be answered by reading the following passages. They are taken from a debate about the advantages and disadvantages of discussing controversial issues in the secondary classroom with students.

Controversial Issues Should Be Discussed with High-School Students

Teachers must accept the incredible responsibility of helping secondary students understand and make sense of today's social and political events. Today's youth are intelligent and world-savvy. They have access to media and news from around the world at the touch of a screen. Therefore, we cannot assume that they are disinterested in world, political, and social events. Neither should we assume that they can intelligently interpret all they hear without the guidance of those adults in their lives who have more education and experiences than the students have. High-school students are generally eager to discuss controversial issues. Frequently, it is the students who bring these topics up when they are inserted into classroom discussions. We owe it to our students to offer our classrooms as safe grounds for questioning and clarifying controversial issues so that students can make informed decisions and construct meaningful positions on them. Many times controversy is inherent in content areas; dismissing it would be irresponsible. Educators are supposed to help students develop skills needed to interpret today's world. It is the duty of educators to carefully plan contexts so that students can explore issues in a constructive manner.

High-School Classrooms Are Not the Place to Discuss Controversial Issues

Controversial issues are too risky and too unpredictable to bring into classroom conversations. Teachers are not equipped to know how to respond to current controversial issues. Even experts need time to understand causes and likely political and social effects of current issues to develop the knowledge and evidence needed to wisely counteract hearsay and speculation. Classroom discussions can cause students to compound their anxieties and fears. When they hear the speculations and fears of their classmates, they become doubtful and afraid. It is not the teacher's responsibility to bring controversial issues into the high-school classroom. It is the role of the family to address these concerns.

23. The author of the first article
   a. would support teachers telling their students about the World Trade Center attacks on September 11, 2001, but not discussing it beyond that.
   b. would not support teachers saying anything about the World Trade Center attacks.
   c. would support teachers opening the classroom to discuss the possible reasons for the World Trade Center attacks the day they happened.
   d. would advise teachers to carefully plan how they would lead a class discussion about the World Trade Center attacks.

24. The most important component missing from both articles is
   a. a timeline for discussing controversial issues so that teachers can implement it into their curriculum.
   b. a definition of the term *controversial issue* because readers don't even know to what types of issues the authors are referring.
   c. the authors' names so that we know what their political backgrounds are.
   d. the date the articles were written so that we know if they are current or dated.

25. Learning is a process. Educators know that the learning process begins when learners
   a. cue and retrieve their prior knowledge about a topic.
   b. integrate new information into their current beliefs.
   c. reposition their current beliefs to adjust to the new information.
   d. develop self-regulated learning.

26. Clarissa is a visual learner. She would learn the information in a required science chapter best by
   a. discussing the contents of the chapter with a small group of peers.
   b. using graphic organizers to diagram key concepts and clarify relationships among concepts.
   c. reading the chapter aloud.
   d. listening to the teacher lecture about the chapter's contents.

27. Ms. Pratt has set up book clubs in her class to motivate her students. Which of the following is the best reason for doing so?
   a. Students, especially English language learners, get to practice their speaking skills as they participate.
   b. Book clubs show that the students have done their required reading.
   c. Book clubs encourage students to talk about their reading experiences with their peers.
   d. Book clubs help students interpret the texts they read.

28. A math teacher is planning which strategy to use to help students understand a complex formulaic process in which students will have to follow a series of steps and problem-solve along the way to reach the right answer. Which of the following would be the least effective strategy or method to use?
   a. direct instruction
   b. thinking aloud
   c. modeling
   d. jigsawing

29. Which of the following is least likely to influence personal space and touching?
   a. a person's culture
   b. the gender of the parties involved
   c. the time of day
   d. the familiarity between the parties involved

30. Which of the following would be the most effective strategy for using a concept map as an assessment?
   a. to evaluate students' memorization of mathematical formulas
   b. to evaluate students' understanding of a content chapter
   c. to evaluate cooperation among group members in a collaborative project
   d. to evaluate students' writing skills

31. Mr. Montez's eleventh graders have just finished reading Chaucer's *The Canterbury Tales*. He tested the students on the learning objectives for the reading and has compared individual students' performance to their peers' performance. This type of evaluation is best described as
   I. norm-referenced.
   II. criterion-referenced.
   III. formative.
   IV. summative.
   a. I and III
   b. I and IV
   c. II and III
   d. II and IV

32. Mr. Kite is a member of a professional organization and receives its journals. He just read a research study published in one of these journals that described the use of a strategy he has tried unsuccessfully in his classroom. According to the research, the strategy was effective in improving students' learning. What is the most likely reason for the discrepancy in results if we assume that Mr. Kite and the researcher administered the strategy the same way?
   a. Mr. Kite's students were less motivated.
   b. The researcher's students were less motivated.
   c. The researcher skewed the results.
   d. Contextual factors and variables influenced the results in both classrooms.

33. Melissa is a student with Down syndrome. She has been placed in a classroom that has been determined to be the least restrictive educational environment that fits her specific needs as a learner. What is the purpose of this type of least-restrictive-environment placement?
    a. It provides opportunities for students with disabilities to be schooled with their peers rather than in isolation.
    b. Parents of students without disabilities share the cost of educating students with disabilities.
    c. It makes better use of public facilities, such as school transportation and buildings, and state employees.
    d. Least restrictive environment provides for equal access to education for all minorities.

34. Marco has learned that if he finishes the assigned math worksheet promptly, his teacher will only come and give him more math problems to do. So, he daydreams between problems and works inefficiently. What should Marco's teacher do to eliminate this practice and encourage efficient work habits?
    a. Double up the number of math problems on the worksheet so that no one will be able to finish within the time allotted.
    b. Reward students who work efficiently rather than giving them more work to do, which is apparently seen as a punishment to Marco.
    c. Allow students who finish early to socialize with their friends.
    d. Set up a routine for students who need help with the worksheet to have a chance to work with the teacher.

35. In French class, students stop raising their hands to answer questions because the teacher never praises or rewards their peers for doing so. This is an example of
    a. discovery learning.
    b. learning as experience.
    c. problem-based learning.
    d. vicarious extinction.

36. After Ms. Abermann asks a question, her students know not to raise their hands to respond right away. Ms. Abermann won't call on anyone until everyone has thought about the question for at least 10 seconds. Ms. Abermann follows this practice because she knows that when she gives this extra wait time,
    a. interruptions decrease.
    b. student-to-student interactions decrease.
    c. responses are shortened.
    d. a greater number of lower cognitive responses occur.

37. Students have just read an article about the causes of global warming. Ms. Abermann asks the following question:
    "What factors are said to contribute toward global warming?"
    This type of question will
    a. provide practice for students' development of divergent thinking.
    b. allow Ms. Abermann to check the students' understanding of the article.
    c. require students to think critically about the article.
    d. help students develop insight to interpret the author's meaning.

38. Teachers often expect students to maintain eye contact during conversations. However, some factors influence students to avoid making eye contact. Which of the following is the least acceptable reason for a student to avoid making eye contact with a teacher based on American school culture expectations?

  a. The student is not engaged in the conversation.

  b. The student's culture traditionally shows respect for elders by lowering the eyes.

  c. The student is showing disrespect for the teacher.

  d. The teacher is confronting the student.

39. Which of the following is the best reason to use essay questions to assess high-schoolers' work?

  a. Essays can be graded with a rubric.

  b. Essays can be written in an English language learner's native language, then converted to English for scoring.

  c. Essays prevent students from guessing at the right response.

  d. Essays can highlight students' thought processes and their ability to synthesize, apply, and analyze knowledge.

Questions 40 through 42 are based on the following passage about adolescents.

In high schools today, sports and athletics are often emphasized over academic accomplishments and achievement. Sports and athletics erroneously encourage adolescents to seek extrinsic rewards and accolades based on competition among peers. Changes in the school culture should be made to encourage adolescents to become active participants in their learning, assume leadership roles in advocating for their developmental needs, and engage in practices that focus on intrinsically-motivated learning.

40. The author of this passage would least likely support which of the following terms related to foundational motivation theory?

  a. extrinsic motivation

  b. self-determination

  c. attribution

  d. intrinsic motivation

41. If an educator wanted to access research or theories that presented alternative perspectives on this topic, what would be the best topic to search for on the Internet or in a database of professional articles?

  a. sports and athletics

  b. adolescent school culture

  c. motivating adolescents

  d. adolescents and academics

42. In high schools today, sports and athletics are often emphasized over academic accomplishments and achievement. Changes in the school culture should be made to encourage adolescents to become active participants in their learning, assume leadership roles in advocating for their developmental needs, and engage in practices that focus on intrinsically-motivated learning.

The author of this passage would support the intentional development of an academically focused peer

  a. clique.

  b. crowd.

  c. government.

  d. culture.

43. Mr. Burton is a twelfth-grade English teacher. He wants his students to graduate with a love of writing so that they will continue to write for pleasure for the rest of their lives. Which of the following is least likely to facilitate this type of love for writing?

   a. assigning each student a topic to write a research paper about

   b. assigning students to select their own topic from a list of topics to write a research paper about

   c. providing 15 minutes each day for students to write about a topic of their choice in a personal journal

   d. allowing students to write about their hopes and dreams for their future

44. In instructional planning, scope refers to

   a. the connection between objectives and standards.

   b. the order in which a teacher is going to teach lessons.

   c. how much a teacher is going to teach of a subject over the course of an academic year.

   d. the instructional method recommended for a particular lesson.

45. One of the advantages of the thematic unit method of teaching content is that students

   a. who miss a day of the unit may miss important connections needed to understand concepts.

   b. from another culture may not be able to access some concepts.

   c. who are not interested in the topic may be unwilling to participate for the duration of the unit.

   d. learn to transfer knowledge and skills they acquire in one content area to use or apply in another area.

46. Students are assigned readings on drone warfare. In the discussion that follows, one student brings up the morality issue. Opinions bubble up among multiple students as the class becomes engaged in an authentic exploration of the topic. Facilitating a discussion about this topic is an example of taking advantage of a

   a. teachable moment.

   b. collaborative environment.

   c. risk-taking environment.

   d. moral digression.

47. All of the following are good suggestions for writing essay questions EXCEPT

   a. to make sure each question is focused so that students know what is expected of them.

   b. to make the questions unpredictable so that students will not be able to prepare for them by studying the content.

   c. to provide specific guidelines about how the response will be scored.

   d. to link essay questions to unit objectives.

48. In science lab, a teacher has her students repeat a lab they have already done to see if they have the same results. She is teaching her students that repeating the same procedure in exactly the same way should yield the same results. This concept is known as

   a. brilliance.

   b. accuracy.

   c. validity.

   d. reliability.

49. Which of the following would be the least valuable topic for a study group of high school math teachers to pursue for the objective of improving students' learning?
  a. how to Skype with other math teachers
  b. how to integrate technology into the math curriculum
  c. strategies for helping students comprehend math text
  d. metacognitive writing in math class

50. Families and educators can help students with learning disabilities develop self-determination by doing all of the following EXCEPT
  a. encouraging them to make choices and explore opportunities.
  b. promoting self-advocacy, goal setting, and planning.
  c. encouraging dependence and cautious behaviors.
  d. encouraging them to take risks and develop problem-solving skills.

51. Based on what we know about the personality development of adolescents and theories related to this development, which of the following choices best completes the following sentence?
  Providing academic opportunities for adolescents to be creative motivates this age group, particularly because it allows them to
  a. avoid schoolwork.
  b. pursue their own unique identities.
  c. reflect on their learning.
  d. learn from adults.

52. Kelly is an animal lover and activist. She has always been against animal testing, but in science class she is learning how animal testing helps the medical field develop procedures that save people's lives. This new information does not fit with her current values and beliefs about animals' rights, but she also believes in helping people. This struggle to integrate this new knowledge into her current values and beliefs is known as
  a. cognitive dissonance.
  b. extrinsic motivation.
  c. attribution.
  d. self-determination.

53. A teacher has determined through diagnostic pretests that a small group of students is ready to learn strategies for critical writing. She designs cooperative learning exercises wherein students will receive appropriate assistance and enough support with this new task to learn and practice the strategies. Students will work at their
  a. operant conditioning.
  b. classical conditioning.
  c. transfer point.
  d. zone of proximal development.

54. Research on early adolescent reasoning provides evidence of all of the following except that
  a. academic achievement and the development of reasoning skills are linked.
  b. reasoning develops through isolation and independent thought.
  c. early adolescence is a time of transition in the development of reasoning.
  d. reasoning develops interactively.

55. How might guided thinking be used as an assessment of students' understanding of irony?
  a. By using the "After Instruction" column, the teacher can assess what students have learned about irony and the guided question.
  b. By using the "Guided Question" column, the student can frame a meaningful question about irony.
  c. In the "Prior to Instruction" column, the student can reflect on what he knows and wants to know about irony.
  d. In the "During Instruction" column, the student can account for what she is learning.

56. A teacher wants to know what the middle value is of all of her students' test scores. This value is known as the
  a. mean score.
  b. mode.
  c. median score.
  d. range.

57. Which of the following is the least effective way to increase communication with parents of high schoolers through technology?
  a. password-protected online gradebooks
  b. progress-report emails
  c. Facebook
  d. a class web page that posts homework daily

58. Which of the following choices best explains why plagiarism is illegal?
  a. It is copying someone's work.
  b. It is an act of fraud.
  c. It is borrowing someone's work.
  d. It is a scandalous act.

Questions 59 and 60 are based on the following excerpt from a student's education plan.

Terry has a recognized disability, type 2 diabetes. It requires the modifications and accommodations set forth in a prepared plan to ensure that Terry has the same conditions and opportunities for academic testing and instruction that his classmates do. Also, the plan includes information from Terry's medical file to prevent hyperglycemia.

59. Terry may not be discriminated against based on his disability according to one of the following laws. The civil rights act that prohibits discrimination against students like Terry for reasons related to their disabilities is known as
  a. Section 504 of the Rehabilitation Act of 1973.
  b. the Education for the Handicapped Act (EHA).
  c. the No Child Left Behind (NCLB) Act of 2001.
  d. the Individuals with Disabilities Education Act (IDEA).

60. Which of the following best explains the difference between an IEP and a 504 plan?
  a. An IEP provides remediation. A 504 plan levels the playing field.
  b. A 504 plan provides remediation. An IEP levels the playing field.
  c. An IEP falls under a civil rights law.
  d. A 504 plan falls under IDEA.

61. "I like the way you explain the Republican views on the fiscal cliff in your essay. It's a complicated issue, but you explained it in a way that made sense to me. I'd be interested in hearing more in your essay about how the Democrats view the same issue. How do you think adding alternative perspectives would add to your essay?"

What is most likely the teacher's motive for providing this type of feedback during a writing conference with a student writer?
a. to provide positive feedback
b. to establish standards of conduct
c. to include the student in instructional decisions
d. to motivate the student to think and write more critically

62. Which of the following best describes what a holistic rubric to assess a student's essay on Republican and Democratic perspectives might look like?
a. multiple levels of performance criteria grouped together under several numeric scores, such as 3, 2, and 1
b. several rows of criteria divided into columns of levels of performance for each criterion
c. ranges of percentile scores
d. a list of individual performance criteria with columns to check off levels of performance

63. Authentic assessment can include all of the following EXCEPT
a. open-ended questions based on the objectives of the lesson.
b. tests that don't match the content of the instruction.
c. oral presentations that demonstrate students' understandings of content.
d. portfolios that include artifacts as evidence of learning content.

64. Standardized test scores often provide the measure of how spread out students' scores are to help educators interpret test results. Knowing this measure provides a way of understanding what scores are below average, average, and above average. This measure is called the
a. percentile.
b. stanine score.
c. raw score.
d. standard deviation.

65. What does it mean if a student receives an 87th percentile on a standardized test?
a. The student achieved a score that is higher than 87% of all of the other students who took the same test.
b. The student scored lower than 87 out of 100 students taking the test.
c. The student scored higher than 87 out of 1,000 students taking the test.
d. The student got 87 out of 100 answers correct.

66. There are several kinds of portfolios. One type of portfolio involves students collecting items that reflect the content of the curriculum. Students write reflective comments to demonstrate their mastery of the objectives of the curriculum. This type of portfolio that documents what a student has learned is referred to as
a. a showcase portfolio.
b. a working portfolio.
c. an assessment portfolio.
d. a display portfolio.

67. Active listening can be used to clarify communication and avoid misunderstandings in cross-cultural dialogues in all of the following ways EXCEPT by
　a. attending to the speaker.
　b. restating key points.
　c. making assumptions.
　d. asking questions.

68. Which of the following is the best example of how a teacher can provide supportive feedback to help a student improve his essay writing?
　a. "I can see the amount of effort you've put into this already! I like that you've included _____. Have you considered adding _____ to support your claims?"
　b. "You've done a nice job so far. Don't forget to talk about ___, too."
　c. "I think you can do better. Go back and add ___, then bring it back to me to check again."
　d. "This is excellent! I'm so proud of you! I didn't realize you could write this way! Wow!"

69. Students in grades 7 through 12 are developing cognitive skills. They are able to reason in more idealistic, abstract, and logical ways. These cognitive skills exemplify which of the following stages of cognitive development, according to Piaget?
　a. sensorimotor stage
　b. preoperational stage
　c. concrete operational stage
　d. formal operational stage

70. Adolescents typically move from identifying with their parents to identifying with their peers. How does Bandura's theory of social learning connect with this idea?
　a. Bandura's theory explains that adolescents learn through hands-on experiences, so their tendency to identify with peers would indicate they would learn by interacting with others.
　b. Bandura's theory explains that adolescents establish a sense of personal identity. It would make sense that during the adolescent years, students would align their identity with their peers' identities.
　c. Bandura's theory states that people develop new skills and learn by observing the actions of others. It would make sense that during the adolescent years, students are learning by observing the actions of their peers.
　d. Bandura's theory states that early relation-ships with caregivers, like their parents, influence social relationships throughout life. It would make sense that even though they are identifying with peers, their relationship with their early caregivers will prevail.

VII ▶ ANSWERS AND EXPLANATIONS TO THE PPST EXAMS

14 ▶ ANSWERS AND EXPLANATIONS FOR PRAXIS I DIAGNOSTIC PRETEST

Answers and Explanations

Skills Test in Reading

1. d. It is logical that a play would close after such a bad first-night reception, and the sentence in choice **d** also uses a metaphor about stage history that is extended in the next sentence. Choices **a**, **b**, and **c** do not fit the sense or syntax of the paragraph, because the *however* in the next sentence contradicts them. Choice **e** claims that all critics misunderstood the play, whereas the last sentence states that the critic Harold Hobson did see the importance of the play.

2. e. Although the writer seems amused by the negative criticisms of the play, he or she does give the opinion that it was *revolutionary* (a word that literally means a turning point). Choice **a** underplays and choice **b** overestimates the importance of the work to the author of the passage. Choice **c** is contradicted by the last sentence of the passage, and choice **d** mistakes Vivian Mercer's opinion for the author's.

3. a. Although students in the other classes might find the passage's subject matter somewhat appropriate, the passage talks mainly about physiological changes to astronauts in space.

4. d. Because the author mentions two women who attended an international conference as an accomplishment for which at least one of them gained international fame, the reader can surmise that it was a rare occurrence and that choice **d** is the best answer. Choices **b**, **c**, and **e** are far beyond the scope of the passage; choice **a** might be true but would require information not contained in the passage.

5. c. This passage provides information to social workers about music therapy, as the title in choice **c** indicates. Choice **e** is incorrect because the first sentence speaks of mental and physical health professionals referring their clients and patients to music therapists; the second sentence indicates that *it* (meaning a referral) seems a particularly good choice for the social worker. Choice **d** is possible, but does not summarize the passage as well as choice **c**. Choices **a** and **b** refer to topics not covered in the passage.

6. a. Based particularly on the last sentence of the passage, choice **a** is the best inference. The other choices are beyond the scope of the passage.

7. c. Choice **c** provides the best outline of the passage. The other choices all contain points that are not covered by the passage.

8. d. If students have a strong motivation to recycle other than membership in the environmental club (i.e., fear of punishment), then this weakens the author's assertion that recycling has gone up because of increased membership in the club. Choice **a** is incorrect because it refers to a change made prior to the increase in the number of students recycling. Choice **b** is wrong because the students' motivation for joining the club is unrelated to whether they recycle. Choice **c** is incorrect because not all students need to participate in order for the poll to be valid. Finally, choice **e** is incorrect because it would strengthen the author's argument, not weaken it.

9. d. Cheerleading (choice **a**), skiing (choice **b**), race car driving (choice **c**), and gymnastics (choice **e**) are all strenuous activities that require good hand-eye coordination and run the risk of injury. Playing horseshoes (choice **d**) only requires good hand-eye coordination.

10. d. The passage contains objective language and straightforward information about accounting, such as one might find in a textbook.

11. c. The second sentence of the passage speaks of a marketing department separate from the accounting department.

12. d. All of the other choices are listed in the passage.

13. a. While all of the other choices may be true, the fact that Diana sold 22 cars in February and the salesperson of the month sold 26 means that they are not the same person. None of the other choices can be proven based on the information given.

14. e. The passage claims that lack of sleep *magnifies alcohol's effects on the body*, implying that it hampers a person's ability to function.

15. d. The author cites Thomas Nast's symbols for Tammany Hall and the Democratic and Republican Parties as examples of images that have entered the public consciousness and are *still in currency today*.

16. c. This title expresses the main point of the passage that, while there are predictable patterns in the life of a genius, the pattern increases the sense of something supernatural touching his or her life. Choices **a** and **b** are too general. Choice **d** is inaccurate because the passage does not talk about disorder in the life of a genius. Choice **e** covers only one of the two main ideas in the passage.

17. c. All the other statements are inaccurate.

18. e. The last sentence illustrates factors that motivate teenagers to exercise by using the results of a national survey to provide specific examples.

19. b. *Unpalatable* may be defined as not agreeable to taste (from the Latin *palatum*, which refers to the roof of the mouth). You know the word *palate* as the roof of the mouth, so unpalatable most likely has to do with the sense of taste. Another clue comes in the line that states that *tastes have changed*, indicating that sushi, which is now popular, was once considered unpleasant to eat.

20. e. The last sentence states that the detector's function is *to convert the information collected by the laser into . . . music.*

21. b. The Carib were not in any way described as peaceful, but rather as hostile people. Therefore, this answer is the exception. All other choices are descriptive of the Caribs and are explicitly mentioned in the passage.

22. a. The last two lines of the passage directly state what defeated the Caribs. Choice **b** is incorrect because the Arawaks were defeated by the Carib. Neither the Dutch nor the French nor another cannibalistic tribe was mentioned in the role of conquerors.

23. b. *Strife* means war. Choice **a** is mentioned as a characteristic of the Carib toward their enemies in times of strife; it is not the meaning of strife. Choices **c** and **e** are not mentioned in conjunction with being warlike or with strife. Choice **d** makes no sense because the times of strife were when the tribe allowed a chief to be chosen.

24. e. Present-day Saint Martin belongs to the French and the Dutch. Choices **b** and **d** have no support in the passage. Choices **a** and **c** are incorrect. The Spanish are mentioned in the passage only in conjunction with the Carib Indians.

25. a. This statement encapsulates the entire passage, not just a part of it. Choices **c** and **e** are too specific to be correct. Choices **b** and **d** are not supported by the passage.

26. c. The description of the winding paths, shifting landscape, and sections that *spill into one another* support the assertion that the park lacks a center.

27. e. The passage states that Olmsted wanted to create a *democratic playground*, so he designed the park to have many centers that would *allow interaction among the various members of society.*

28. d. To *posit* means to *suggest.* In this context, Hlusko suggests that grass stalks may have caused the grooves seen on early hominid teeth.

29. b. In the passage, the author states, *It seems that our early human ancestors may have used grass, which was easily found and ready to use, to floss between their teeth.* The use of *may* indicates that the author is not absolutely certain, but as the author does not suggest anything to contradict Dr. Hlusko's findings, we can conclude that the author finds her theory very probable.

30. b. The passage defines panopticon: *a place in which everything is in full view of others.* The second paragraph repeats this definition: *Every prisoner's cell would be in full view of the guards.*

31. a. In the second paragraph, the author states that people behave differently when they know they are being watched—and that when we are being watched, or even think we are being watched, we will act the way we think we should act when we are being observed by others. Thus, the panopticon would be a useful tool for social control. If prisoners know they may be being watched by guards, it is logical to conclude that they are less likely to engage in wrongdoing; thus, the panopticon helps maintain order.

32. b. The passage illustrates several protest strategies used in the Civil Rights movement. Choices **c** and **e** are true statements but are too specific to be the primary focus of the passage. Choices **a** and **d** are not described in detail in the passage.

33. e. One meaning of *to test* is to apply a test as a means of analysis or diagnosis. In this context, *test* refers to putting something to a test or challenging something.

34. d. The protest at the Greensboro Woolworth lunch counter inspired others. The passage states *two weeks later similar demonstrations had spread to several other cities, and within a year similar peaceful demonstrations took place in over a hundred cities in the North and South.*

35. a. While the passage does include the other choices except choice **e**, the overall purpose of the passage is to teach asbestos awareness in schools.

36. e. This passage links the ability to defer gratification with self-control. Hence, children who are unable to defer gratification are unlikely to succeed because they lack self-discipline, or self-control.

37. c. Althea Gibson was an extraordinarily gifted athlete, yet because of the color of her skin and the time in which she lived, her path to success from the very beginning was obstructed by segregation and discrimination. Althea's ability to put these distractions aside and excel was a triumph of mental toughness, and the author uses the quote to illustrate that fact.

38. a. The fact that judicial review can override decisions made by the legislative and executive branches implies that it gives the court great authority.

39. e. The last sentence offers a view in opposition to the points made earlier in the passage supporting the Supreme Court's power to interpret the Constitution.

40. e. The opening sentence tells readers that making a list of pros and cons is a technique of utilitarian reasoning. Thus, readers who have used this technique will realize they are already familiar with the basic principles of utilitarianism.

Skills Test in Mathematics

1. a. In order to find the area of the parallelogram, first find the height. The vertical, dashed line drawn is the height and also forms a right triangle on the left side. Because two sides of this triangle are given, use the Pythagorean theorem to find the missing side: $a^2 + b^2 = c^2$. In this case, $a = 3$, $c = 5$, and $b =$ the height. Substitute: $3^2 + b^2 = 5^2$. Evaluate the exponents: $9 + b^2 = 25$. Subtract 9 on both sides of the equation: $9 - 9 + b^2 = 25 - 9$; $b^2 = 16$. Therefore, $b = 4$. (The triangle is a 3–4–5 right triangle.) To find the area of the parallelogram, multiply the base of the figure by the height: $12 \times 4 = 48$ cm^2.

2. a. The perimeter of each small square is $8x$ units; therefore, the length of one side of each small square is $\frac{8x}{4} = 2x$ units. Because the new, large square is comprised of two sides from each of the four squares (the remaining four sides are now within the large square), the perimeter of the new, large square is equal to $4(2x + 2x) = 4(4x) = 16x$ units.

3. c. Because *all* students at Central High School take math and *some* students take art, then some of the students will take both math and art. Choice **a** is incorrect because there is no information that shows that Charles attends Central High School. Choice **b** is incorrect because the second given statement says that *some* students take art, and it cannot be assumed that this includes all students. Choice **d** is incorrect because there is no information given to prove that Charles does not also take art. Choice **e** is incorrect because the first given statement says that all students at Central High School do take math.

4. c. To find 150% of a number, multiply it by 1.5; 0.0032 multiplied by 1.5 is equal to 0.0048.

5. b. The fractions are changed to decimals by dividing: $\frac{7}{12} = 7 \div 12 = 0.58$ and $\frac{5}{7} = 5 \div 7 = 0.71$. Change all the numbers to decimals with the same number of digits after the decimal point: 0.5800, 0.7100, 0.6300, 0.0790, 0.0108. The decimal 0.71 is the greatest, which was $\frac{5}{7}$.

6. d. In the bar graph, the horizontal axis is labeled with four different months, and the vertical axis is labeled with height in inches. The title of this graph is then related to a quantity measured in inches that would occur during the winter months. The title in choice **d** represents a quantity (snowfall) that would be measured in inches during the winter. The amounts in the graph are not reasonable for rainfall amounts (choice **a**).

7. d. To determine the probability that a fifth grader's name will be chosen, you must determine the total number of fifth graders' names that are in the lottery and divide this number by the total number of names in the lottery. Because each fifth grader's name is placed in the lottery three times, there are $3 \times 100 = 300$ fifth-grade names. Likewise, there are $2 \times 150 = 300$ fourth-grade names and $1 \times 200 = 200$ third-grade names in the lottery. The probability that a fifth grader's name will be chosen is $\frac{300}{300 + 300 + 200} = \frac{300}{800} = \frac{3}{8}$.

8. d. This question translates into the equation $\frac{1}{4}x + 3 = x - 3$. First, subtract $\frac{1}{4}x$ from both sides of the equation: $3 = x - \frac{1}{4}x - 3$. Multiply both sides by 4: $12 = 4x - x - 12$. Combine like terms: $12 = 3x - 12$. Add 12 to both sides: $24 = 3x$. Divide both sides by 3: $8 = x$.

9. d. First, find the rate of snowfall per hour. Because it snowed at a constant rate of three inches every two hours, divide $\frac{3 \text{ inches}}{2 \text{ hours}}$ to get a rate of 1.5 inches per hour. The question asks for the amount of snow that fell in the first five hours, so multiply 1.5 inches per hour $\times$ 5 hours $= 7.5$ inches.

10. e. The cost of a field trip increases by approximately $1.50 each year. Because the cost per pupil in 2008 is $10.50 per pupil, the cost in 2009 will be approximately $10.50 + 1.50 = $12.00 and the cost in 2010 will be $12.00 + 1.50 = $13.50.

11. c. First, find the total number of floors they can wax in the specified time. This is found by multiplying the rate for each person by the amount of time spent working by each. Marcus waxes five floors an hour for three hours, or 15 floors; Josie waxes four floors an hour for two hours, or eight floors. Together they wax 23 floors. Because there are 50 classrooms total, the percentage waxed is $\frac{23}{50} = 0.46$, which is equal to 46%.

12. e. Be aware of the break in the scale on the vertical axis. This scale starts at zero, jumps to 100, and then increases by 10 at each mark. Washington High School has a graduating class size of approximately 100 students in 1998 and 200 students in 2008, thus doubling the size of its graduating class during that time.

13. b. Approximately 180 students from Springville High School and about 150 students from Valley High School graduated in 1998. Find the difference between them by subtracting $180 - 150 = 30$.

14. a. An average increase of six students per year over a period of ten years is an increase of about 60 students. Valley High School had about 140 students in the graduating class in 1998 and about 200 in 2008: $200 - 140 = 60$ students over the course of 10 years.

15. e. Over the five-week period between week 3 and week 7, Company ABC followed a pattern where the stock increased by $1 for week 4, decreased by $0.50 for week 5, increased by $1 for week 6, and decreased by $0.50 for week 7. If this trend continues, the price expected for week 8 would be $1 more than week 7, or $4.00 per share. Company XYZ decreased in price by $0.50 each week. Because the price for week 7 was $4.50, the expected price for week 8 would also be $4.00. The price per share for both companies would be the same for week 8.

16. b. To find the average price per share over the seven-week period, add the price per share for each week and divide the total by 7. By reading the graph, the price per share for each week is as follows: week 1 = $2.50, week 2 = $1.50, week 3 = $2.00, week 4 = $3.00, week 5 = $2.50, week 6 = $3.50, and week 7 = $3.00. Adding the price for each week results in a total of $18; $18 divided by 7 weeks equals approximately $2.57.

17. d. During week 4, the price per share for Company XYZ was $6.00 and the price per share of Company ABC was $3.00. Since 3 is half of 6, this is the week in which the stock price for Company ABC is exactly half that of Company XYZ.

18. a. The thousandths place is three places to the right of the decimal point. Choice **a** has a 9 in the thousandths place. In choice **b**, the 9 is in the hundredths place; in choice **c** it is in the tenths place; in choice **d** it is in the ten-thousandths place; and in choice **e** it is in the hundred-thousandths place.

19. d. First calculate her earnings for one day: $10.40 times 8 hours per day is equal to $83.20. For any amount of time she worked over 8 hours she earns time and a half, or 1.5 times her regular pay. This is equal to $10.40 × 1.5 = $15.60 per hour overtime. Because she worked $1\frac{1}{2}$ hours overtime on average, this is equal to $15.60 × 1.5 = $23.40 extra pay per day. Therefore, her total pay per day is equal to $83.20 + $23.40 = $106.60. Multiply this amount by 5 days per week to get her weekly pay: $106.60 × 5 = $533.00.

20. e. Because lines *l* and *m* are parallel, there are a number of angle relationships that allow you to solve for *x*. As shown in the following figure, the angle labeled 35° and its corresponding angle are congruent. In addition, the angle vertical to, or across from, the angle labeled 50° is also 50°.

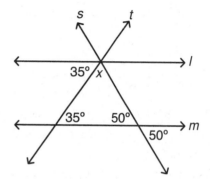

The two newly labeled angles and the angle labeled *x* are three interior angles of a triangle, so subtract the sum of the two known angles from 180 to solve for *x*: 180 − (50 + 35) = 180 − 85 = 95°.

21. c. The words *at least* and *at most* in the first sentence indicate that a teacher at this school teaches between three and five classes, inclusively, but no more and no less. Because the actual number of teachers at the school is not known, the average number of classes and the average time spent teaching cannot be determined. Therefore, it can only be concluded that each teacher has from three to five classes at 40 minutes each, for a total between 120 and 200 minutes per day, inclusive.

22. d. The area of the patio is found by multiplying the length times width. Because the length is 15 feet and the width is $\frac{1}{3}$ as long as the length, the width is $\frac{1}{3} × 15 = 5$ feet. Multiplying the length by the width yields the area: 15 feet × 5 feet = 75 square feet.

23. b. Use the percent of each section of the graph to find the total number of minutes spent in the specific areas. Because 30% of the day is spent on reading, multiply $0.30 \times 400 = 120$ minutes. Because 10% of the day is spent on social studies and another 10% on science, multiply $0.10 \times 400 = 40$ minutes for each. Therefore, the total time for reading (120 minutes) minus the total time for social studies and science together (80) is equal to 40 minutes.

24. b. The ratio is *number of perfect scores:number of nonperfect scores*. This unreduced ratio is 8,000:5,000,000 or 8:5,000. Because 5,000 divided by 8 equals 625, this ratio then becomes 1:625.

25. a. The first step in solving the problem is to subtract the length of the two known sides from the perimeter: $148 - 86 = 62$. This number is the sum of the two shorter sides. Divide 62 by 2 to get 31 feet, which is the measure of each of the shorter sides.

26. c. Choice **c** represents the distributive property of multiplication over addition. This property can be checked by substituting numbers for a, b, and c. For example, if $a = 3$, $b = 4$, and $c = 5$ the equation would become $3(4 + 5) = 3 \times 4 + 3 \times 5$. The equation simplifies to $3(9) = 12 + 15$, which becomes $27 = 27$. Because both sides are equal, the equation is true. Each of the other choices would not be true if different numbers were substituted in for a, b, and c.

27. c. To find the average number of points scored per game, you add the total points for each game and divide by the number of games: $\frac{20 + 17 + 14}{3} = \frac{51}{3} = 17$ average points per game.

28. d. Because it is given that all prime numbers are real numbers, then it can be inferred that at least *some* real numbers are also prime numbers. However, it cannot be assumed that *all* real numbers are also prime numbers (choice **b**). We know only that q is a real number, so it is not certain that it is also a prime number (choice **a**). Choice **c** contradicts the first statement that was given.

29. a. First, find out how long the entire hike can be, based on the rate at which the hikers are using their supplies: $\frac{\frac{2}{5}}{3} = \frac{1}{x}$, where 1 is the total amount of supplies and x is the number of days for the whole hike. Cross multiplying, you get $\frac{2}{5}x = 3$. Multiply each side of the equation by $\frac{5}{2}$ to get $x = \frac{5}{2} \times 3 = \frac{15}{2} = 7\frac{1}{2}$ days for the length of the entire hike, which includes the trip back. Because half of $7\frac{1}{2}$ is $3\frac{3}{4}$ or 3.75, the hikers could go forward for 3.75 days altogether before they would have to turn around. They have already hiked for three days, so $3.75 - 3 = 0.75$ (days) is the amount of time they can now go forward before they have to turn around.

30. d. Another way to complete the problem, or simply check your answer, is to change each of the fractions to decimal form to the nearest hundredth to compare: $\frac{2}{7} \approx 0.29$, $\frac{4}{11} \approx 0.36$, $\frac{1}{3} \approx 0.33$, $\frac{3}{8} \approx 0.38$, $\frac{3}{10} \approx 0.30$. Choice **d** is greater than the others.

31. d. Multiply: 26 forms times 8 hours is 208 forms per day per assistant. Divide the total forms that need to be filed by the amount of forms one assistant can file per day: 5,600 divided by 208 is approximately 26.9. You can't hire 0.9 of an assistant, so you have to hire 27 assistants for the day.

32. b. Because they are traveling toward each other, the trains' combined rate of travel is 35 miles per hour plus 15 miles per hour. This is equal to 50 miles per hour. Because distance = rate × time, time = $\frac{distance}{rate}$. Divide the rate of travel into the total distance that the trains need to go: 2,100 miles divided by 50 miles per hour equals 42 hours.

33. e. The bowler's three best scores are the highest three scores. These are 116, 114, and 109. To find the average, divide the sum of these three scores by 3: $\frac{116+114+109}{3} = \frac{339}{3} = 113$.

34. c. January's expenses are approximately $38,000, February's are approximately $41,000, and April's are approximately $26,000. These added together give a total of $105,000.

35. e. One of the best ways to solve a question such as this one is to substitute the values for x into the equations and see which one results in the matching y-values from the table. If 2 is substituted for x, only choices **d** and **e** result in a y-value of 5: $y = 2 + 3$; $y = 5$. $y = 3(2) - 1$; $y = 6 - 1$; $y = 5$. Now try each of these equations with other values from the table. If 4 is substituted for x, choice **d** gives a result of 7 and choice **e** gives a result of 11. Because 11 is the y-value in the table, the solution is choice **e**.

36. b. Subtract the number of hours she has worked so far this week from the total number of hours she needs to work. The expression becomes: $37\frac{1}{2} - 26\frac{1}{4} = 37\frac{2}{4} - 26\frac{1}{4} = 11\frac{1}{4}$ hours.

37. c. Three out of the four sections are each close to 30%, so look for the answer choice with three of the four sections about the same size and that together make up about 90% of the circle. Only choice **c** has three sections about the same size that take up most of the circle and the fourth section about half the size of one of the others.

38. e. Because all soccer players take science, then at least some of the science students are also soccer players. Only some soccer players like to play in the rain, so it cannot be concluded that *all* soccer players like to play in the rain. In addition, we cannot conclude from this information that *only* soccer players take science. The fact that Sheila likes to play in the rain does not give you any information as to whether she is a soccer player or whether she takes science. Thus, there is not enough information to draw a conclusion about answer choices **b**, **c**, or **d**.

39. c. The width of the room can be determined by two factors: (1) the width of each table and the number of tables across the width of the room, and (2) the width of the spaces between the tables and the walls, and the number of these spaces. Because there are four tables that are each 3 feet in width, there is $4 \times 3 = 12$ feet to include for the width of the tables. In addition, there are five spaces either between tables or between a table and the wall that measure 4 feet in width: $5 \times 4 = 20$ feet. Combine these two together: $12 + 20 = 32$ feet.

40. b. Kevin is 40, so 20 years ago he was $40 - 20 = 20$ years old. At that time in the past, Kevin's father was twice his age, so his father was 40, 20 years ago. Therefore, Kevin's father is $40 + 20 = 60$ years old now.

Skills Test in Writing— Section 1, Part A

1. **e.** Because there are no grammatical, idiomatic, logical, or structural errors in this sentence, choice **e** is the best answer.

2. **c.** The comma is incorrect punctuation. Because this sentence contains two independent clauses, a semicolon (;) should be used instead.

3. **b.** The word *loud* is an adjective and should modify a noun. In this sentence, the adverb *loudly* should be used because it would correctly modify the verb *chirped*.

4. **e.** Because there are no grammatical, idiomatic, logical, or structural errors in this sentence, choice **e** is the best answer.

5. **d.** This is an error in word choice. The use of the word *illusion* makes this sentence illogical. An illusion is something that is not what it seems. The correct word choice would be *allusion*, which means a reference or hint.

6. **b.** Using *more* or *most* before an adjective or adverb is an example of a double comparison. In this sentence, just using the word *spicier* is enough to establish the proper comparison between the two dishes of gumbo.

7. **e.** Because there are no grammatical, idiomatic, logical, or structural errors in this sentence, choice **e** is the best answer.

8. **c.** In this comparison the word *as* should be used instead of *like*. The use of *as* completes the idiom *such as*.

9. **c.** This is a word-choice error. In this sentence the verb *affect*, meaning to influence, should be used. *Effect* is most often used as a noun, but when it is used as a verb, it means to bring about. In this sentence, the use of *effect* as a verb makes this sentence illogical.

10. **b.** The error is grammatical; there is no subject-verb agreement in this sentence. The subject *each* is singular and requires a singular verb form. In this sentence, the correct form is *has had*.

11. **d.** This is a grammatical error. The contraction *it's* (meaning *it is*) should be replaced by the possessive pronoun *its*.

12. **d.** This sentence makes a comparison among Martin and two other boys (three people); therefore, the superlative *tallest* should be used. *Taller* is incorrect because it is the comparative form and should be used only when there is a comparison between two people.

13. **a.** The phrase *can't hardly* is an example of a double negative. In this sentence, the proper form would be to use *can hardly wait* or simply, *cannot wait*.

14. **a.** This is an error of agreement. The singular pronoun *it* does not agree with the plural noun *cars*. In this sentence *it . . . has* should be replaced by the plural *they . . . have*.

15. **e.** Because there are no grammatical, idiomatic, logical, or structural errors in this sentence, choice **e** is the best answer.

16. **c.** This is an error in sentence construction. For proper parallel construction in the sentence, *must protect* should be changed to *the protection of*.

17. **e.** Because there are no grammatical, idiomatic, logical, or structural errors in this sentence, choice **e** is the best answer.

18. **c.** Because the words *but* and *yet* mean the same thing, this sentence contains a redundancy. Either one of these words should be deleted.

19. a. This is an error in agreement. The singular noun *one* requires the singular verb *is*. When the subject (in this case *one*) follows the verb, as in a sentence beginning with *here* or *there*, be careful to determine the subject. In this sentence, the subject is not the plural noun *scarves*.

20. c. This is an error in the possessive case. The possessive indicates ownership (a flower's petals). With singular nouns, the possessive case is formed by adding an *'s*.

21. a. This is a grammatical error. Because the word modifies the verb *resemble*, the adverb *closely* should be used instead of the adjective *close*.

Skills Test in Writing— Section 1, Part B

22. a. The clause *who is getting off at the next stop* is a restrictive (essential) clause and should not be set off by commas. Choices **b**, **c**, **d**, and **e** are all punctuated incorrectly. In addition, choice **e** uses the pronoun *whom*, which is the wrong case.

23. c. This is the only choice in which the sentence construction is clear and error-free. Choices **a** and **b** create faulty subordination. In addition, choice **b** also uses incorrect punctuation between the two clauses. Choice **d** fails to include any punctuation between the two clauses. In choice **e**, *covered* represents an incorrect shift in verb tense.

24. d. This is the only choice that contains the pronoun (*its*) that grammatically agrees with the noun *Mars rover*. Choices **a** and **c** contain incorrect pronouns. Choice **b** mistakenly uses the contraction *it's* (*it is*), and choice **e** incorrectly implies that the rover did not create the tire tracks.

25. c. The item in the underlined portion of the sentence should be parallel with the rest of the sentence and possess the appropriate punctuation. Only choice **c** has the appropriate parallel construction and punctuation. Choices **a**, **b**, and **d** break the parallel flow of the sentence with the use of the words *reducing* or *reduction*. Choice **e** incorrectly uses a semicolon and is also unnecessarily wordy and redundant.

26. a. This sentence requires that the comparison between *teamwork* and *individual accomplishment* be logical and clear. Choice **b** is incorrect because the use of the preposition *onto* is confusing and does not observe standard usage conventions. The phrase *less better* in choice **c** makes no sense. Choices **d** and **e** result in an unclear comparison.

27. e. This is the only choice that does not contain excessive wordiness or a redundancy. In choice **a**, the phrase *the third of three* is a redundancy. Choice **b** also repeats by using both *three* and *third*. Choices **c** and **d**, although constructed differently, make the same error.

28. d. Adjectives modify nouns and adverbs modify verbs. In choice **d**, the adjectives *frightening* and *unexpected* correctly modify the noun *ending*. In choices **a** and **b**, *frighteningly* is an adverb incorrectly modifying a noun. In choice **c**, the adverb *unexpectedly* incorrectly modifies a noun. Choice **e** is incorrect because it is excessively wordy.

29. e. The opening phrase, *An American writer of the twentieth century*, should modify a noun that identifies the *writer*. Only choices **d** and **e** do this. In choices **a**, **b**, and **c**, either *collection* or *Mexico City Blues* is illogically credited with being the writer. Choice **d** is incorrect because the subject of the resulting dependent clause, *poems*, would not agree with its verb, *celebrates*.

30. d. Choice **d** is correctly punctuated with a semicolon between two independent clauses, and there is no shift in person (i.e., everything is in the first person). Choices **a**, **b**, and **e** are incorrect because the sentence shifts from the first person (*we*) to the second person (*you*). Choice **c** uses a semicolon when no punctuation is necessary.

31. c. This is the only choice that is clear, logical, and idiomatic. In this sentence *contrary to*, which means a viewpoint that is opposite to or in conflict with another viewpoint, is used correctly in this context. Choices **a** and **b** are incorrect because the prepositions *to* and *in* are inappropriately used with *conflicting* (choice **a**) and *contrary* (choice **b**). Similarly, choice **d** does not use standard-usage phrasing. Choice **e** simply does not make sense in context.

32. c. This is the only choice that is clear and idiomatic. In choice **a**, the preposition *for* is incorrectly paired with *agree*. In choice **b**, the sentence is awkward and does not make sense. Choice **d** is idiomatically correct, but like choice **e**, it uses awkward phrasing.

33. c. This choice is the only one that uses the idioms of standard English correctly. Choice **a** is wordy and awkward. Choices **b** and **e** also use awkward phrasing. Choice **d** is unclear and ambiguous; the use of the preposition *to* distorts the meaning of the sentence.

34. d. This is the only choice that employs the correct conjunction *because* and uses the proper punctuation between the two clauses. The use of the conjunction *although* in choices **a** and **b** sets up faulty coordination between the two clauses. In addition, the use of *was* in choice **b** is a verb tense error that creates a nonparallel sentence. Choice **c** lacks a proper conjunction, and is therefore incorrect. Choice **e** is properly coordinated, but the incorrect use of a semicolon instead of a comma creates a punctuation error.

35. c. The word *principle*, meaning rule, can only be used as a noun. *Principal*, meaning chief, can be used as a noun or as an adjective. In this sentence, it is clearly an adjective, which rules out choices **a**, **b**, and **e**. Choice **d** incorrectly uses the word *effect*. The verb *affect* means to produce an *effect* (noun) on something.

36. a. When constructing sentences, unnecessary shifts in verb tenses should be avoided. Choice **a** is best because all three verbs in the sentence indicate that the action occurred in the past (*built*, *was given*, and *had deflected*). In choice **b**, there is a shift to the present (*deflect*). Choice **c** begins in the present (*being built*, *is nicknamed*), and then shifts to the past (*had deflected*). Choice **d** starts in the past tense (*built*), shifts to the future (*will be given*), and then reverts back to the past (*had deflected*). Finally, choice **e** shifts from the future (*to be built*) to past tense (*was given*, *had deflected*).

37. d. This is the only choice that is both grammatically and logically correct. Choice **a** has a shift in construction; there are two subjects that mean the same thing (*Joe DiMaggio* and *he*). Choice **b** has a modifier problem; the sentence implies that Joe DiMaggio was a talented athlete because he was the son of immigrants. Choice **c**, though constructed differently, results in the same faulty logic. Choice **e** creates faulty subordination.

38. e. There are two potential problems in this sentence. One is the possessive form of the word *Atlantic*, and the other is the punctuation between the two clauses. Choice **e** uses the correct possessive form (there is only one Atlantic), and the correct punctuation (a semicolon should be used between two independent clauses). Choice **a** is incorrect because it creates a comma splice. Choice **b** uses the incorrect possessive form. Choice **c** creates a sentence fragment. Choice **d** creates faulty subordination.

Skills Test in Writing—Section 2, Essay Writing

Following are sample criteria for scoring a PPST essay.

A score "6" writer will

- create an exceptional composition that appropriately addresses the audience and given task.
- organize ideas effectively, include very strong supporting details, and use smooth transitions.
- present a definitive, focused thesis and clearly support it throughout the composition.
- include vivid details, clear examples, and strong supporting text to enhance the themes of the composition.
- exhibit an exceptional level of skill in the usage of the English language and the capacity to employ an assortment of sentence structures.
- build essentially error-free sentences that accurately convey intended meaning.

A score "5" writer will

- create a commendable composition that appropriately addresses the audience and given task.
- organize ideas, include supporting details, and use smooth transitions.
- present a thesis and support it throughout the composition.
- include details, examples, and supporting text to enhance the themes of the composition.
- generally exhibit a high level of skill in the usage of the English language and the capacity to employ an assortment of sentence structures.
- build mostly error-free sentences that accurately convey intended meaning.

A score "4" writer will

- create a composition that satisfactorily addresses the audience and given task.
- display satisfactory organization of ideas, include adequate supporting details, and generally use smooth transitions.
- present a thesis and mostly support it throughout the composition.
- include some details, examples, and supporting text that typically enhance most themes of the composition.
- exhibit a competent level of skill in the usage of the English language and the general capacity to employ an assortment of sentence structures.
- build sentences with several minor errors that generally do not confuse the intended meaning.

A score "3" writer will

- create an adequate composition that basically addresses the audience and given task.
- display some organization of ideas, include some supporting details, and use mostly logical transitions.

- present a somewhat underdeveloped thesis but attempt to support it throughout the composition.
- display limited organization of ideas, have some inconsistent supporting details, and use few transitions.
- exhibit an adequate level of skill in the usage of the English language and a basic capacity to employ an assortment of sentence structures.
- build sentences with some minor and major errors that may obscure the intended meaning.

A score "2" writer will

- create a composition that restrictedly addresses the audience and given task.
- display little organization of ideas, have inconsistent supporting details, and use very few transitions.
- present an unclear or confusing thesis with little support throughout the composition.
- include very few details, examples, and supporting text.
- exhibit a less than adequate level of skill in the usage of the English language and a limited capacity to employ a basic assortment of sentence structures.
- build sentences with a few major errors that may confuse the intended meaning.

A score "1" writer will

- create a composition that has a limited sense of the audience and given task.
- display illogical organization of ideas, include confusing or no supporting details, and lack the ability to effectively use transitions.
- present a minimal or unclear thesis.
- include confusing or irrelevant details and examples, and little or no supporting text.
- exhibit a limited level of skill in the usage of the English language and little or no capacity to employ basic sentence structure.

- build sentences with many major errors that obscure or confuse the intended meaning.

Sample 6 Essay

Most people know who Frankenstein is—or at least they think they do. Because of the way Mary Shelley's brilliant 1818 novel was adapted to film, most Americans think that Frankenstein is a towering, scar-faced monster who brings terror wherever he goes. In Shelley's novel, however, the real monster is Victor Frankenstein, the scientist who is the monster's creator. In her story of how Victor Frankenstein creates the monster and what he does after the monster comes to life, Shelley conveys several timeless messages about the dangers of science, the dangers of isolation, and the importance of being a good parent. It is a novel that everyone should read.

In the story, Frankenstein, eager for glory, wants to discover the "elixir of life" so that he can have the power to bring the dead back to life. He wants to create a new race of superhuman beings and wants them to worship him like a god. He wants to unlock the secrets of nature and use that power for his own selfish goals. Shelley's novel warns us that we must be careful what we do with science—how we apply the knowledge we discover. For when Frankenstein does discover the elixir of life, and when he does create a superhuman being, he creates a creature that is beyond his control. The creature is more powerful and more intelligent than Victor Frankenstein, and the creature engineers Frankenstein's demise.

Shelley's novel also warns us about the dangers of isolation. Frankenstein's creation is so revolting and dangerous in part because Frankenstein works completely alone. He becomes so absorbed with his project that he completely blocks out family and friends. He stops communicating with others and works secretly; he does not consult with anyone about his project, both because he knows that what he is doing is wrong, and because he wants all the glory. But because he does not work with others, and because he loses touch with his community of family and friends, he also loses touch with his responsibility to other human beings. When the creature comes to life, Frankenstein runs away, abandoning his creation even though he knows the creature might harm others.

This abandonment brings us to the novel's third timeless message: the importance of being a good parent. Frankenstein creates a living being and then abandons him because he is an "ugly wretch." He totally ignores his responsibility to the creature, who is born as innocent as a child, even though he is the size of a giant. The creature is abhorred by everyone he meets, and because no one has ever shown him love, he learns to hate. And the person he comes to hate most is the father who abandoned him. Shelley's message is clear: You are responsible for what you create, and if you are a parent, you must love your child, whatever his or her appearance.

In our age of cloning and genetic engineering, of scattered communities and neighbors who don't know each other's names, of abandoned children and neglectful parents, Shelley's book may have more importance than ever. But it is not just the message that makes this book great. It is also a great read, powerful and suspense-filled. Will Frankenstein capture the creature? Will he create a "bride" for the monster? Will Walton, the ship captain who records Frankenstein's story, learn from Frankenstein's tale? Shelley's *Frankenstein* should be required reading for everyone.

Sample 4 Essay

Frankenstein isn't who most people think he is—a monster. The real Frankenstein is the scientist who brings the monster to life. The confusion comes from the fact that many rely on the movie version of the story, rather than the original book by Mary Shelley. *Frankenstein* should be required reading for a number of reasons. It teaches some important lessons, which are maybe even more important to day than they were in Shelly's time (the 1800s.)

One lesson is about how to use science. Dr. Frankenstein in the story discovers how to bring a dead person back to life. But everything goes wrong after the creature wakes up. What was supposed to be a great thing that would bring Frankenstein glory and make him a master creator instead brought him and many other people all kinds of terrible horror. I think Mary is telling us to be very careful how we use science.

She also is telling us in this story to stay close to others. Frankenstein makes the creature by himself. While working on the monster; he doesn't talk to anyone, and no one in the university knows what he's up to. He's so obsessed that he doesn't consider what will happen once this giant creature comes to life. He doesn't think about being responsible to and for the creature.

Another lesson is that we need to be good parents. Frankenstein is like the creature's father and mother. He created him, and he needs to take care of him. But he doesn't, he just runs away. That's when the horror begins. The creature is hated by everyone and his life is really sad.

There are many other important lessons to be learned from Frankenstein, including the need to learn from other's mistakes. Walton, a ship captain, learns the story from Frankenstien, and then writes about it in letters to his sister.

The reader is left wondering if Walton will understand the messages of Frankenstein's story and live his life differently as a result.

Another message is the need to tell the truth, and the consequences of not doing so. Victor Frankenstein knows that the monster strangled his brother, but he does not want to tell anyone. Even when an innocent girl is accused of the crime, he keeps his silence. The girl is found guilty and executed as a result of his unwillingness to tell the truth. Shelley's *Frankenstein* is filled with important lessons, and I think it should be required reading for everyone.

Sample 1 Essay

Every school has a required reading list. They are filled with "the classics." Classics are books thought to be important by teachers. Some books leave the list, and others are added. But for the last century, many books have stayed the same. Some of them probably shouldn't be considered classics, but they remain on the list. Others are great books that are enjoyed by millions of people. One of these books is Mary Shelly's *Frankenstien.*

It is the story of a monster. Many people think the monster's name is Frankenstien, but this is really the name of the doctor who creates him. This is due to the 1931 movie version of the novel, which starred Boris Karloff. The movie was directed by James Whale. It was based on a play of the Shelly book. When people hear the name Frankenstien, they think of Boris Karloff.

In the book, Victor Frankenstien makes the monster out of dead body parts. Then he makes the monster come to life. But then he abandons the childlike monster and trouble starts. Everyone hates the monster, and he starts to hate, too. There is also a story about a sailor named Walton. He writes letters to someone in his family. They are about the story of Frankenstien. Frankenstine deserves to be on the list of classics.

Praxis I Scoring

Your scores on the multiple-choice parts of the exam are based on the number of questions you answered correctly; there is no "guessing penalty" for incorrect answers and no penalty for unanswered questions. The Educational Testing Service does not set passing scores for these tests, leaving this up to the institutions, state agencies, and associations that use the tests. Therefore, the interpretation of your score depends on the reason you are taking the test. For example, there will be a difference in the interpretation of your score if you are applying for a teacher-training program rather than a candidate for educational credentials or for teacher selection. Whatever the case, though, it is necessary for you to do well on all three segments of the Praxis I—Reading, Mathematics, and Writing—so you must figure your score on each test separately.

The Reading test, the Mathematics test, and the multiple-choice sections of the Writing test are scored the same way: First find the number of questions you got right on each test. As noted earlier, questions you skipped or got wrong don't count; just add up how many questions you got right. Then, divide the number of questions you got right by the number of questions in the section to arrive at a percentage. You can check your score against the passing scores in the state or organization that requires you to take the exam.

In addition to passing the multiple-choice questions, you must receive a passing score on the essay portion of the PPST Writing test. On this portion, the essay is read and scored by at least two writing experts, using a scale of 1 to 6, where 6 is the highest. The scores of the two experts are then combined. The scoring criteria are outlined in detail in the answer explanations. The best way to see how you did on the essay portion of the exam is to give your essay and the scoring criteria to a teacher or other reader whom you trust to see what scores he or she would assign.

What's much more important than your scores, for now, is how you did on each of the basic skills tested by the exam. You need to diagnose your strengths and weaknesses so that you can concentrate your efforts as you prepare for the exam.

Use your percentage scores in conjunction with the LearningExpress Test Preparation guide in Chapter 2 of this book to help you devise a study plan. Then, turn to the review chapters that cover each of the basic skills tested on the Praxis I. You should plan to spend more time on the lessons that correspond to the questions you found hardest and less time on the lessons that correspond to areas in which you did well.

15 ▶ ANSWERS AND EXPLANATIONS FOR PRACTICE EXAM 1

Answers and Explanations

Skills Test in Reading

1. b. The connotations of words like *bonds* and *constraints* in the passage suggest a confined space of criticism where the mind must be allowed to find some movement or *play*. None of the other choices makes sense in the context of the passage.

2. d. The passage says that the subordinate monkey grimaces when he is *intimidated by a dominant member of the group*. Because *intimidated* means *afraid*, and *dominant* means *powerful* or *in a leadership position*, one can infer that *subordinate* means *lower in status*.

3. d. The title "Sights and History on Dublin's O'Connell Street" touches on all the specific subjects of the passage—the sights to see on this particular street and the history connected to them.

4. c. The hidden or key resource mentioned in the passage is the fine distinction between the definitions of street and boulevard, which is used to win the argument with, or get the better of, tourists.

5. d. The author offers an example of Dublin wit and mentions the unhurried pace of Dublin crowds.

6. d. A *scapegoat* is one who is forced to bear the blame for others or upon whom the sins of a community are heaped.

7. a. In the beginning of the passage, the author describes the Bottom as a *place where bizarre and unnatural happenings and strange reversals of the ordinary are commonplace*. It is a reversal of the ordinary to name a hilltop community *the Bottom*, and the author mentions this in order to emphasize his or her point about the strangeness of this community.

8. c. This is the only conclusion that is supported by information in the passage.

9. e. The passage mentions calculators (adding machines), computers, card punches, and manuals. The only item not mentioned is kitchen scales.

10. e. Look back to the last sentence of the first paragraph, where George's single-tax proposal (the idea The Landlord's Game was meant to teach) is described as aiming to *weaken the ability to form monopolies, encourage equal opportunity, and narrow the gap between rich and poor*.

11. e. In the beginning of the passage, the author writes that these games *went far beyond friendly recreational competition*, and the end of the passage says that Native Americans viewed these games as *excellent battle preparation* for the young.

12. b. *Bellicose* most closely means *warlike*. There are two major clues in this passage to help you answer this question. The first clue lies in the translation of the name *Tewaarathon*, meaning "Little Brother of War." Another clue lies in the line where the author states that these games were *excellent battle preparation for young warriors*.

13. a. "Little Brother of War" is the best choice for the title of this passage because the games are described as fierce and warlike. At the end of the passage, the author writes that games were often used to settle disputes between tribes without resorting to full-blown warfare. Therefore, these games could be considered an alternative to war, or war's "little brother." The other choices do not fit because they are unsupported by the passage, or describe only a small portion of the passage.

14. c. The answer can be found in the two sentences that follow the phrase. The sentences state that the games were often high-stakes substitutes for war, and it was not uncommon for players to suffer serious injuries at the hands (and sticks) of others. These statements describe the fierce nature of the games and suggest that players would not hesitate to resort to violent tactics to score, *by any means necessary.* Choices **d** and **e** are true and mentioned in the passage, but they do not fit in context with the phrase.

15. b. The passage clearly states that a potlatch is a gift-giving ceremony. The author explains that *potlatch* is a generic word for the ceremony that comes from a shared trading language, while each nation has its own specific word for potlatch.

16. a. The passage states that guests were expected to give a potlatch with gifts of equal value to what they received. This arrangement can best be described as reciprocal. The other choices are not supported by the passage.

17. d. Choice **d** is the most accurate conclusion because the first sentence speaks of periods of war. The other choices, whether true or false, are not addressed in the selection.

18. d. The statistic provides numerical evidence of (quantifies) the degree to which commercial fishing is hazardous compared to the next most dangerous occupation.

19. b. Saying that the eagle watches and then falls *like a thunderbolt* implies alertness and striking, so the most logical conclusion is that the eagle is hunting.

20. c. The focus of the passage is Blackwell's efforts to open the profession of medicine to women. The first paragraph states that Blackwell *supported women's medical education and helped many other women's careers.*

21. b. Initially Blackwell was interested in teaching. However, she was inspired by her dying friend and went on to become not only the first woman doctor since the Renaissance, but also a supporter of medical education for women.

22. c. The passage describes swing as *vibrant,* a synonym for *lively.* It is also stated that the bands *improvised from the melody,* indicating that the music was *melodic.*

23. c. None of the other choices can be proven based on the information given.

24. b. The passage describes the cuttlefish's use of a water jet to move. Choice **a** is incorrect because the passage only describes cuttlefish as *resembling* squid.

25. e. This choice covers the most important ideas in the two paragraphs. All the other choices list more minor details from the paragraphs as the main subjects.

26. e. This choice includes both the informational content and light tone of the passage.

27. a. The passage discusses the many important functions of public art and its impact on the city.

28. c. In the passage, the author states a surfer should lie upon a surfboard *like a small boy on a coaster,* and then goes on to say that the surfer slides down a wave *just as a boy slides down a hill on his coaster.*

29. a. As it is used in the passage, *impetus* most nearly means *a moving force.* In this case, a wave is a moving force through the water. If you did not know the correct definition, the best way to answer this question would be to replace *impetus* in the sentence with each of the given answer choices to see which one makes the most sense in context.

30. c. The author compares surfing to sliding down a hill. But unlike a six-foot hill, a surfer can slide down a six-foot wave for more than a quarter of a mile without ever reaching the bottom. The author explains that this is possible because new water is rising into the wave as fast as the wave travels, preventing the surfer from reaching the bottom. So while a surfer is sliding along moving water, he or she is holding the same position on a wave as it moves through the water. That's the secret.

31. d. The passage explains that there was a social component to a trip to the marketplace. To be social means to be around others, suggesting that people sought out interaction with one another.

32. d. The end of the passage states that the New Deal expanded *the role of the central government in regulating the economy and creating social assistance programs.* Choices **b** and **c** are incorrect, and choices **a** and **e** require an opinion; the author does not offer his or her viewpoint about the New Deal measures.

33. b. *Parsimonious* is a word used to describe someone who is frugal to the point of stinginess. Comiskey's pay cuts, bonus of cheap champagne, and refusal to launder uniforms are all clues that should help you deduce the answer from the given choices.

34. b. Answering this question involves a bit of deductive reasoning. Though the actual name of the ballpark is never given in the passage, the passage states that the 1917 White Sox won the World Series playing in a park named for their owner.

35. c. The passage states between the years of 1900 and 1915 the White Sox had won the World Series only once, and then it tells us they won it again in 1917. Be careful not to mistakenly select choice **d**, three; the question asks for the number of World Series the Sox *won*, not the number of World Series they *played*.

36. b. The narrator describes the view from her window as a *prison-ground, exile limits*, and says *I had no communication . . . with the outer world.* Thus, it can be inferred that Lowood is both a structured and an isolated place.

37. e. The narrator's desire for freedom and to explore the world are evident in this passage; she longs to follow the road that leads away from Lowood, and she is *half desperate* in her cry for something new, something beyond Lowood and the rules and systems she *tired of . . . in one afternoon.*

38. d. Because Lowood had been the narrator's home for eight years and all she *knew of existence* was school rules, duties, habits, faces, and the like—because she had had *no communication . . . with the outer world*, it is likely that she feels her initial prayers were unrealistic. At least a *new servitude* would provide some familiar territory, and it therefore seems more realistic and attainable than *liberty* or *change.*

39. c. In the second paragraph, the author states that *the health risk for cosmetic procedures is low*, but does not give factual information to back this claim. The statement is important to the author's argument because he or she cites it as one of the reasons his or her attitude toward plastic surgery has changed.

40. d. The author directly invokes the audience he or she hopes to reach in the last sentence: *members of the medical community.*

Skills Test in Mathematics

1. b. The length of the regular route is the hypotenuse of a right triangle. The length of the detour is the sum of the legs of a right triangle. Use the Pythagorean theorem ($a^2 + b^2 = c^2$, or $\text{leg}^2 + \text{leg}^2 = \text{hypotenuse}^2$) to find the length of the missing side of the triangle: $x^2 + 75^2 = 85^2$. Evaluate the exponents: $x^2 + 5{,}625 = 7{,}225$. Subtract 5,625 from each side of the equation: $x^2 + 5{,}625 - 5{,}625 = 7{,}225 - 5{,}625$; $x^2 = 1{,}600$. Take the square root of each side of the equation: $x = 40$. Because the distance between Center City and Redmont is 40 miles and the distance between Redmont and Forest Grove is 75 miles, the length of the detour is $40 + 75 = 115$ miles. To find how much longer the detour is, subtract $115 - 85 = 30$ miles.

2. b. The scatter plot compares the number of miles driven with the total cost of renting a car. Because the points in the scatter plot form a straight line, the equation will be in the form $y = mx + b$, where m is the slope of the line and b is the y-intercept. To find the y-intercept, look on the graph for the point at 0 miles. This value is $10, so the y-intercept is 10. Moving from one point to another from left to right, as the cost increases by $5, the number of miles increases by 10. Because the slope of the line equals the change in y-values over the change in x-values, the slope of the line is $\frac{5}{10}$, which reduces to $\frac{1}{2}$. Thus, the equation is $y = \frac{1}{2}x + 10$.

3. d. Choices **a**, **b**, and **e** can be ruled out because there is no way to determine how many tickets are for adults and how many are for children. Choice **c** can be ruled out because the price of group tickets is not given.

4. b. The adult price on Saturday afternoon is $5.50; the child's price is $3.00. By subtracting $3.00 from $5.50, you can find the difference in price.

5. c. Remember that when taking a fraction *of* some number, you are actually *multiplying* that number by the fraction. Let's look at what happens hour by hour:

Time	Number of Candies
Start	504
8–9 o'clock	minus $\frac{1}{8} \cdot 504$, or $-63 = 441$
9–10 o'clock	minus $\frac{2}{9} \cdot 441$, or $-98 = 343$
10–11 o'clock	minus $\frac{1}{7} \cdot 343$, or $-49 = 294$

6. a. This problem is a straight conversion problem. Use the fact that there are 24 hours in one day to solve the problem. Remember, converting from a smaller unit to a larger unit requires division: $720 \div 24 = 30$. It is always a good idea to make sure the answer makes sense. Multiplying by 24 (instead of dividing) would result in choice **e**, which is not correct and does not make sense. If Joe had to wait 17,280 days before his vacation, that would mean he planned his vacation a little more than 47 years in advance!

7. d. This is an example of the distributive property of multiplication over addition. The number outside of the parentheses gets multiplied by each of the terms inside the parentheses. A way to solve this type of question, or to check your answer, is to simplify the expression in the question. Multiply first, then add: $3 \times 5 + 3 \times 8 = 15 + 24 = 39$. If each of the answer explanations is evaluated, the only one that also has a value of 39 is choice **d**.

8. d. First, examine the table to determine that there are 40 minutes in each class period and 4 minutes of passing time between each class. To determine the starting time of period 3, add 4 minutes to the ending time of period 2. Thus, the starting time of period 3 is 9:23. To calculate the ending time of period 8, add 40 minutes to the starting time. The ending time is 1:43. The answer choice with both of these times is choice **d**.

9. b. Because the only categories quantified are the types of chocolate in the candy bars, only the ratio of milk chocolate candy bars to white chocolate candy bars can be found. You would need additional information to determine any of the other choices.

10. c. The number of subscribers to US Cable in 2006 was 140,000. The number of subscribers to Central Satellite in 2006 was 100,000. The percent of US Cable subscribers can be found using the ratio $\frac{\text{part}}{\text{total}} = \frac{\%}{100}$. Because the total number of subscribers in 2006 was 140,000 + 100,000 = 240,000, the ratio becomes $\frac{140}{240} = \frac{x}{100}$. Cross multiply to get $240x = 14,000$. Divide each side of the equal sign by 240 to get $x \approx 58\%$.

11. d. Only choice **d** shows the heights of the bars at the same values for each year in the double-line graph. Choice **a** has each company's values by year increased by 10,000. Choice **b** has the values for US Cable and Central Satellite switched. Choice **c** has each of the values for US Cable decreased by 10,000. The graph in choice **e** has reversed the values for each company by starting with the amounts for 2008, instead of 2004, and sequentially going backward for the heights of the bars.

12. e. Because 80 students out of the 100 polled would prefer this class, 80 out of 100 is 80%. To find 80% of 30,000, multiply $0.80 \times 30,000$ to get 24,000.

13. d. His total bill will include the $19 flat fee plus $0.32 × the number of minutes of airtime over 120. If x = total airtime minutes, then $x - 120$ = total airtime minutes over 120. Therefore, the expression becomes $19 + 0.32(x - 120)$.

14. d. The hundredths place is two places to the right of the decimal point. In this case, the number in the hundredths place is 3. In order to round this number, look to the place directly to the right of the number to be rounded. If this number is 4 or less, keep the number and drop off the remaining numbers to the right. If this number is 5 or greater, add one to the number and drop off the remaining numbers to the right. Because the number to the right of 3 is 6, the 3 is rounded up to 4, and the entire rounded number becomes 56.74.

15. a. The standard form of a quadratic equation is $y = ax^2 + bx + c$, where a, b, and c are real numbers. Because the curve opens downward, the value of a, the number in front of the x^2 term, must be negative. Remember that $-x^2$ means $-1x^2$. This narrows down the choices to **a**, **b**, or **e**. Because the curve intercepts the y-axis at the point (0,4), the equation must have a c value of +4. Therefore, the answer must be choice **a**.

16. d. First, calculate the minimum number and the maximum number of granola bars that the 20 machines can make per minute. Because the minimum number per machine is 80, multiply 80×20 to get 1,600 as the minimum number of bars per minute for all 20 machines. The maximum number of bars per machine is 100, so multiply 100×20 to get 2,000 as the maximum number of bars per minute for all 20 machines. Be careful—although 1,800 is between 1,600 and 2,000, choice **a** is not correct. The minimum and maximum numbers found so far are per minute; the question asks for the number *per hour*. To find the minimum and maximum numbers per hour, multiply by 60 because there are 60 minutes in an hour.

minimum per hour = $1,600 \times 60 = 96,000$
maximum per hour = $2,000 \times 60 = 120,000$
Choice **d**, 100,000, is the only number between 96,000 and 120,000.

17. c. To estimate quickly, the numbers can be rounded to 36,000 and 16,500: 36,000 people minus 16,500 male attendees is equal to 19,500 female attendees. The difference between the number of females in attendance and the number of males in attendance can be found by subtracting $19,500 - 16,500 = 3,000$. There were approximately 3,000 more women than men.

18. b. Statements I and III illustrate the associative property of addition. In this property the association, or grouping, of the numbers changes, but the result is the same. Another way to approach this type of question is to substitute numbers for a, b, and c and look for the statements that give the same result. Try $a = 3$, $b = 4$, and $c = 5$. Statement I would then become $3 + (4 + 5) = 3 + 9 = 12$. Statement II would then become $(3 + 4) + (3 + 5) = 7 + 8 = 15$. Statement III would become $(3 + 4) + 5 = 7 + 5 = 12$. Because statements I and III both yield the same result, they are equivalent.

19. c. The volume of the aquarium can be found by using the formula $V = l \times w \times h$. Because the length is 12 inches, the width is 5 inches, and the height is 10 inches, multiply $V = 12 \times 5 \times 10$ to get a volume of 600 cubic inches.

20. e. To find the value, start with $y = 4$. Multiply 4 by 6 to get 24. Because step 3 and step 4 are switched, divide 24 by 2 to get 12. Add 10 to 12 to get a result of 22.

21. e. In this case, the only solution you are guaranteed when starting with a whole number is a value that is an integer. Remember that the set of integers is the whole numbers and their opposites. For example, if $y = 5$, the result is 20, which is even. However, if $y = 8$, the result is 29, which is odd and also prime. Each result is an integer.

22. e. In this problem, look for two sectors that when combined will add to 70%. The sector for Liberal Arts is 54%, and the sector for Medicine is 16%. Because $54\% + 16\% = 70\%$, the two sectors are Liberal Arts and Medicine.

23. b. The average is found by dividing the sum of the absences by the total number of days. The sum of the absences is $11 + 4 + 0 + 5 + 4 + 6 = 30$. Because there were six days, $\frac{30}{6} = 5$. There was an average of 5 students absent each day of the six-day period.

24. b. This uses two algebraic equations to solve for the age. Jacqueline (J) and her grandmother (G) have a sum of ages of 110 years. Therefore, $J + G = 110$. Jacqueline was $\frac{1}{3}$ as young as her grandmother 15 years ago. Therefore, $J - 15 = \frac{1}{3}(G - 15)$. Solve the first equation for J and substitute that value into the second equation: $J = 110 - G$; $(110 - G) - 15 = \frac{1}{3}(G - 15)$. This simplifies to $95 - G = \frac{1}{3}G - 5$. Add G and 5 to each side: $100 = \frac{4}{3}G$. Multiply each side of the equation by $\frac{3}{4}$ to get $G = 75$.

25. e. You can use the decimal equivalents to compare the numbers. Since $\frac{1}{3} \approx 0.33$ and $\frac{1}{4} = 0.25$, look for an answer choice that will be between those when written as a decimal: $\frac{1}{2} = 0.50$ (too large); $\frac{1}{5} = 0.20$ (too small); $\frac{2}{3} \approx 0.66$ (too large); $\frac{2}{5} = 0.40$ (too large). Because choice **e** is $\frac{2}{7} \approx 0.29$, it is the only choice between the two fractions.

26. d. This graph is a parabola with the y-axis as the axis, or line, of symmetry. Therefore, the line is in the general form $y = x^2$. The shading of the inequality is done above the graph, making the symbol used in the inequality *greater than or equal to*, or $\geq$. This narrows down the possible choices to **a, c,** or **d**. Because the graph has a y-intercept of -2, the inequality is $y \geq x^2 - 2$, which is choice **d**.

27. a. Substitute the value of $\frac{1}{2}$ in for each x in the function. The function then becomes $3(\frac{1}{2})^2 - \frac{1}{2}(\frac{1}{2}) + 7 = 3(\frac{1}{4}) - \frac{1}{4} + 7 = \frac{3}{4} - \frac{1}{4} + 7 = \frac{1}{2} + 7 = 7\frac{1}{2}$. This is equal to choice **a**, which is $\frac{15}{2}$.

28. d. Substitute $x = 3$ into the equation $y = 5 + 4x$. Thus, $y = 5 + 4(3)$. Multiply first and then add: $y = 5 + 12$, so $y = 17$.

29. e. The only choice that follows is choice **e**. Because Lucinda pays with a check only if an item costs more than $30, the item must have cost more than $25. Choice **a** is not correct because if the bill was $20, she would have paid with cash. Choice **b** is not correct because if the bill was $80, she would have used her credit card to pay. Choice **c** is not correct because she pays cash only for bills less than $30; if she has paid with a check, you can assume that the bill is already greater than this. Choice **d** is not correct because if the bill was at least $70, she would have used her credit card.

30. e. Because the figure is a regular decagon, it can be divided into ten equal triangular sections by straight lines passing through the center. The two lines that form the indicated angle also form an area equivalent to three of these ten sections. Therefore, to find the measure of the angle shown, find $\frac{3}{10}$ of 360: $\frac{3}{10} \times 360 = 0.3 \times 360 = 108°$.

31. b. First, eliminate the parentheses on the left side of the equation using the distributive property. The equation becomes $2x - 3x + 3 = -12$. Combine like terms on the left side of the equal sign: $-1x + 3 = -12$. Subtract 3 from both sides of the equal sign: $-1x + 3 - 3 = -12 - 3$. Simplify: $-x = -15$. Divide each side of the equal sign by -1 to get an answer of $x = 15$.

32. c. Because the measure of angle 2 is a right angle, its measure is 90° and is corresponding with the indicated right angle. Therefore, the two horizontal lines in the figure must be parallel. Because angle 1 is 30° and angle 2 is 90°, angle 3 must be 60° because the interior angles in a triangle have a sum of 180°. Angle 3 and angle 4 are also corresponding angles formed by two parallel lines, making the measure of angle 4 also equal to 60°. Because angle 4 and angle 5 form a linear pair, subtract to find the measure of angle 5: 180° − 60° = 120°.

33. d. The area of a circle can be found using the formula $A = \pi r^2$, where r is the radius of the circle. Because the area of 78.5 square feet is given, substitute $A = 78.5$ and $\pi = 3.14$ into the formula: $78.5 = 3.14r^2$. Divide each side of the equation by 3.14 to get $25 = r^2$. Take the square root of each side to get $r = 5$ feet. The diameter is twice the radius, and in this case, it is 10 feet.

34. a. Rounding to compatible numbers can help in this problem: 490,000 rounds to 500,000, and 98,000 rounds to 100,000. The question now becomes 100,000 compared to 500,000, which is equal to $\frac{100,000}{500,000}$. This reduces to $\frac{1}{5}$, which is choice **a**.

35. e. In each of the answer choices, the numbers remain the same but the order changes. The commutative property changes the order, but the result is the same. This property is true when used with addition or multiplication, but it does not hold for subtraction. Because the terms surrounding the subtraction sign in choice **e** are switched, this expression will most likely not have the same value as the others. To check, evaluate each expression to see which one results in a different value as the others. Be sure to use the correct order of operations (PEMDAS) when evaluating expressions. When evaluated, each answer choice gives a result of 218 except for choice **e**. Choice **e** evaluated becomes $10 − 3(76) = 10 − 228 = −218$.

36. a. In this question, you need to find 15% of the 30% of students who are in the music program. To find 15% of 30%, change the percents to decimal form and multiply. Because 30% = 0.30 and 15% = 0.15, multiply $(0.30)(0.15) = 0.045$. As a decimal, this is equivalent to 4.5%, which is choice **a**.

37. d. Examine the x column of the table. As the table is read downward, each value of x decreases by 2. At the same time, the y-values increase by 0.5, or $\frac{1}{2}$. Therefore, the answer is choice **d**.

38. d. The hundredths place in a decimal is two places to the right of the decimal point. Three one-hundredths of a second is written as a decimal with the number 3 in the hundredths place, or 0.03.

39. d. Because the graph has the unit of time in minutes, to convert to hours find a value that will be easy to work with. By reading the graph, in 30 minutes the car has traveled a total of 20 miles. The graph is a straight line, so it can be assumed that the speed, or slope, is constant. Therefore, because the distance in $\frac{1}{2}$ hour is 20 miles, the distance in 1 hour will be double that, or 40 miles. Thus, the car is traveling at a speed of 40 miles per hour.

40. e. The answer choice that is proportional to the given triangle will have sides that can be multiplied or divided by the same number in order to change to the values of the original triangle. In choice **e**, each of the sides from the original triangle of 12, 16, and 20 can be divided by 4 to get the sides 3, 4, and 5.

Skills Test in Writing— Section 1, Part A

1. c. There are two subjects, *Elizabeth Blackwell* and *she*, that mean the same thing. To correct this problem, the word *she* should be deleted from the sentence.

2. e. Because there are no grammatical, idiomatic, logical, or structural errors in this sentence, choice **e** is the best answer.

3. a. Starting the sentence with the conjunction *considering* is a subordination error because it creates two dependent clauses in this sentence. It should be deleted to make the sentence grammatically correct.

4. b. The semicolon should be replaced by a comma. This is a complex sentence; the first clause is dependent, and the second clause is independent. A semicolon should be used only when both clauses are independent.

5. d. In this sentence there is faulty parallelism. The word *asking* should be replaced by the verb *asked*. This sentence is in the past tense, so the two verbs *asked* and *called* should both be in the past tense.

6. a. The word *because* creates a coordination error between the two clauses in this sentence. Replacing *because* with another conjunction such as *although* or *even though* would make this sentence grammatically correct.

7. c. The use of *and who* in this sentence creates faulty parallelism between the two clauses. Deleting *and* would make the sentence parallel.

8. b. The apostrophe at the end of the word *officers* is incorrect and should be deleted. In this sentence, *officers* is not possessive.

9. d. This sentence makes a comparison. The comparative *more* is incorrect because the situation requires the superlative *most*. *More* is used only to compare two things.

10. b. The singular collective noun *staff* requires a singular verb form. Therefore, the plural form *deserve* should be replaced with the singular *deserves*.

11. d. The use of the word *but* makes this sentence illogical. The word *but* should be replaced by the word *and*.

12. d. There are three items in a series in this sentence: *lived in cramped quarters, fought battles,* and *learn to understand the blessings.* To make these three items parallel, the word *learn* in the underlined portion represented by choice **d** should be changed to *learned.*

13. e. Because there are no grammatical, idiomatic, logical, or structural errors in this sentence, choice **e** is the best answer.

14. b. The comma between the words *laptop* and *owns* is unnecessary and should be deleted. The clause *who sold me the laptop* is restrictive (essential) and should not be set off by commas.

15. e. Because there are no grammatical, idiomatic, logical, or structural errors in this sentence, choice **e** is the best answer.

16. c. The pronoun *he* does not have a definitive antecedent; it could be referring to either writer. Replacing *he* with *Hemingway* would make this sentence grammatically (and factually) correct.

17. d. The subject of the second independent clause is *dirty filter*, a singular noun. Therefore, the singular form of the verb should be used. The verb *reduce* should be replaced by the verb *reduces*.

18. a. Because the words *areas* and *regions* mean the same thing, this sentence contains a redundancy. To eliminate this redundancy, *or regions* should be deleted.

19. c. The phrase *ashamed with himself* is not idiomatic. The words *with himself* should be deleted.

20. e. Because there are no grammatical, idiomatic, logical, or structural errors in this sentence, choice **e** is the best answer.

21. b. This sentence contains a punctuation error. When using a colon, it is important to note that the preceding clause should have a subject and a predicate; in other words, it should be able to function as an independent clause. In this sentence, no colon is necessary.

Skills Test in Writing— Section 1, Part B

22. b. This is the correct choice because it is the only one where the subject and verb are in agreement. The subject *three months of free golf lessons* is plural and therefore agrees with the plural verb *go*.

23. c. The verbs *ring* and *feed* are irregular verbs, and this is the only choice to use the correct verb formations and the appropriate verb tense.

24. e. This is the only choice that contains the correct plural form of *effect* and the correct possessive form of *the earth*. To form the possessive case of a singular noun, add *'s*.

25. a. This is the correct choice because the sentence makes a comparison among many things (Roman emperors), and therefore requires the superlative, *greediest*. Do not be fooled by choices **b** and **e**; *greedliest* and *greedfullest* are in superlative form, but *greedly* and *greedful* (also in choice **d**) are not real words.

26. e. This is the correct choice because the sentence does not contain a double negative or a double comparison.

27. c. This is the only sentence with correct capitalization. A title (such as *doctor*) is capitalized only when it precedes a person's name or is used as a direct address. The names of cities and the names of languages should always be capitalized.

28. a. This sentence requires parallelism between the verbs *speak* and *have*, and choice **a** is the only choice that does this (*speaking* and *having*).

29. d. This is the only choice that uses the correct comparative form for the words *new, safe,* and *old.* When comparing two things (in this case, cars), use the comparative form (*-er*) for short modifiers of one or two syllables. Choice **e** uses the correct comparative form for the three modifiers, but the use of *more* before *safer* creates a double comparison and is therefore incorrect.

30. d. When a comparison is made, the word *fewer* is used with nouns that can be counted; the word *less* is used with quantities that cannot be counted.

31. e. This is the only sentence to have agreement between the subject and the verb and between the pronoun and its antecedent.

32. a. This sentence requires the comparison to be completed by *not only . . . but also.* The other choices create sentences that are ambiguous, unclear, and idiomatically incorrect.

33. b. The most common way to join two independent clauses is with a comma and a coordinating conjunction. The only sentence that correctly does both is choice **b.** Two closely related independent clauses can also be linked by a semicolon, but for choice **a** to be correct, the coordinating conjunction *so* needs to be deleted. Choice **d** lacks a proper coordinating conjunction and has faulty parallelism. Choice **e** contains a verb tense error.

34. d. This is the only choice that uses the correct pronoun, *which.* Use *which* when introducing clauses that are not essential to the information in the sentence, unless they refer to people (then use *who*). The second clause in choice **c** refers to a river, not a person, so the use of *who* is incorrect.

35. a. This is the only choice that does not have faulty subordination. The first part of the sentence is an independent clause; the second part is a dependent clause. Choice **a** is correct because the dependent clause is correctly introduced by the relative pronoun *which.*

36. c. This is the only choice that uses correct punctuation and contains no capitalization errors. Choice **d** uses correct punctuation, but *Italian* should be capitalized. Two independent clauses should be joined by a semicolon or a coordinating conjunction, not a comma, so choice **a** is incorrect. Choices **b** and **e** are incorrect because no commas are necessary when two items are linked by a conjunction (*gym and calculus; Italian and physics*).

37. d. This is the only choice that employs the correct conjunction *although* and uses the proper punctuation between the two clauses. The use of the conjunction *because* in choices **a** and **b** sets up faulty coordination between the two clauses. In addition, the use of *was* in choice **b** is a verb-tense error that creates a nonparallel sentence. Choice **c** lacks a proper conjunction and is incorrect. Choice **e** is properly coordinated, but the incorrect use of a semicolon instead of a comma creates a punctuation error.

38. b. This is the only choice that uses the adverb correctly and establishes the appropriate comparison. Choices **a, c,** and **d** are incorrect because an adverb (*gracefully*) is required to modify the verb *skates.* Choice **e** correctly uses the adverb, but it contains a comparison error: When the conjunction *than* is used to indicate a comparison, it should be followed by the nominative case, *I.*

Skills Test in Writing— Section 2, Essay Writing

Following are sample criteria for scoring a PPST essay.

A score "6" writer will

- create an exceptional composition that appropriately addresses the audience and given task.
- organize ideas effectively, include very strong supporting details, and use smooth transitions.
- present a definitive, focused thesis and clearly support it throughout the composition.
- include vivid details, clear examples, and strong supporting text to enhance the themes of the composition.
- exhibit an exceptional level of skill in the usage of the English language and the capacity to employ an assortment of sentence structures.
- build essentially error-free sentences that accurately convey intended meaning.

A score "5" writer will

- create a commendable composition that appropriately addresses the audience and given task.
- organize ideas, include supporting details, and use smooth transitions.
- present a thesis and support it throughout the composition.
- include details, examples, and supporting text to enhance the themes of the composition.
- generally exhibit a high level of skill in the usage of the English language and the capacity to employ an assortment of sentence structures.
- build mostly error-free sentences that accurately convey intended meaning.

A score "4" writer will

- create a composition that satisfactorily addresses the audience and given task.
- display satisfactory organization of ideas, include adequate supporting details, and generally use smooth transitions.

- present a thesis and mostly support it throughout the composition.
- include some details, examples, and supporting text that typically enhance most themes of the composition.
- exhibit a competent level of skill in the usage of the English language and the general capacity to employ an assortment of sentence structures.
- build sentences with several minor errors that generally do not confuse the intended meaning.

A score "3" writer will

- create an adequate composition that basically addresses the audience and given task.
- display some organization of ideas, include some supporting details, and use mostly logical transitions.
- present a somewhat underdeveloped thesis but attempt to support it throughout the composition.
- display limited organization of ideas, have some inconsistent supporting details, and use few transitions.
- exhibit an adequate level of skill in the usage of the English language and a basic capacity to employ an assortment of sentence structures.
- build sentences with some minor and major errors that may obscure the intended meaning.

A score "2" writer will

- create a composition that restrictedly addresses the audience and given task.
- display little organization of ideas, have inconsistent supporting details, and use very few transitions.
- present an unclear or confusing thesis with little support throughout the composition.
- include very few details, examples, and supporting text.
- exhibit a less than adequate level of skill in the usage of the English language and a limited

capacity to employ a basic assortment of sentence structures.

- build sentences with a few major errors that may confuse the intended meaning.

A score "1" writer will

- create a composition that has a limited sense of the audience and given task.
- display illogical organization of ideas, include confusing or no supporting details, and lack the ability to effectively use transitions.
- present a minimal or unclear thesis.
- include confusing or irrelevant details and examples, and little or no supporting text.
- exhibit a limited level of skill in the usage of the English language and little or no capacity to employ basic sentence structure.
- build sentences with many major errors that obscure or confuse the intended meaning.

Sample 6 Essay

It's a fact: More and more people across the United States are vegetarian, and school and workplace cafeterias should be required to provide vegetarian lunch options for them. There are many reasons why vegetarians choose this diet. Health concerns, moral issues, and religion are among them. Schools and workplaces should honor these reasons by making it easier for vegetarians to purchase healthful, meat-free lunches.

Some vegetarians are responding to the generally unhealthy American diet, which consists of plenty of fast food. They prefer more healthful choices, such as simply prepared salads, vegetables, and protein sources such as beans, soy-based products, and dairy products. However, this is not what may be found in most cafeterias. Cafeterias, both in schools and in businesses, tend to resemble fast food restaurants, offering such items as hamburgers, fried chicken, pizza, French fries, and sodas. If

they also stocked more healthful, meat-free choices, not only would the vegetarians be served, but also perhaps some of the overweight students and employees would eat them. This could improve the health of many people.

It would not be difficult to transform the typical school or workplace cafeteria into a vegetarian-friendly one. Many of the lunch selections currently offered could be made vegetarian, and therefore more healthy, with a few simple and inexpensive substitutions. Veggie burgers, for example, offered alongside beef burgers, would give vegetarians a satisfactory option. Tacos, burritos, and other Mexican entrees could be made with beans rather than ground beef. A salad bar would serve the dual purpose of providing both vegetarians and others concerned about their health and weight the opportunity for a satisfying meal. These changes, while relatively simple for cafeterias to incorporate, would provide vegetarians with acceptable lunch selections, and in the process, provide all the students or employees they serve with more healthful alternatives.

Sample 4 Essay

In the United States there are many people who are vegetarian. Many of these people are students or workers who eat lunch at their cafeterias on a daily basis. Surprisingly though, school and workplace cafeterias are not required to provide vegetarian options. That means that most often they don't. That means that vegetarians may be limited to lunches comprised of french fries, or pizza loaded with cheese. While these are vegetarian (non-meat), they are not healthy, especially if they are eaten every day.

Schools and businesses should have a wider variety of vegetarian options. Such as a salad bar, or perhaps even something with tofu.

Entrees that use beans or soy-based products instead of meat would also be good. It wouldn't cost cafeterias more money to provide vegetarian lunches. In fact, the ingredients used to make them (like beans) are typically much cheaper than their carnivorous counterparts (like ground beef). Salads require little preparation in comparison with French fries, which could save money on payroll. Also, cafeterias could buy premade vegetarian selections in bulk, just as they do nonvegetarian dishes. These premade foods are becoming more and more popular, and are not more expensive.

While cafeterias can't meet all the demands of those they serve, it is important to offer those committed to a vegetarian lifestyle the choice to eat healthfully and meat-free. Schools should create a menu that offers these options for all students.

Sample 1 Essay

Many people are vegetarian and don't eat meat. This may be because they are afraid of diseases found in meat, such as mad cow disease, salmanella, or avian influenza. Or, they may not eat meat because of their religion. Some care about animal rites, and others are vegetarian because they are concerned about their health. They believe a vegetarian diet will help them lose wieght and in general improve their health. But this is not necessarily the case. You could just eat French fries, cold cereal, and pizza every day and be a vegetarian. Vegetarians need to learn about how to eat this diet and make it healthy too. School and workplace cafeterias could help by offering them good selections at lunch.

Praxis I Scoring

Once again, in order to evaluate how you did on this practice exam, start by scoring the three parts of the PPST—Reading, Mathematics, and Writing—separately. You will recall that your scores on the PPST multiple-choice segments of the exam are based on the number of questions you answered correctly; there is no guessing penalty or penalty for unanswered questions. You will also recall that the Educational Testing Service has not set passing scores for these tests; this is left up to the institutions, state agencies, and associations that utilize the tests. Therefore, the interpretation of your score depends on the purpose for which you are taking the test.

If you are unsure of the passing score you will need, you can set yourself a goal of at least 70% of the answers right on each test of the Praxis I. To find the percent of questions you answered correctly, add up the number of correct answers and then divide by the total number of questions to find your percentage.

Even if you have scored well on the Reading test, the Mathematics test, and the multiple-choice subsections of the Writing test, don't forget that you must receive a passing score on the essay portion of the PPST Writing test. On this portion, your essay will be scored by at least two writing experts, and their combined score will be used to evaluate how you did. The scoring criteria are outlined in detail in the answer explanations. The best way to see how you did on the essay portion of the exam is to give your essay and the scoring criteria to a teacher or other reader whom you trust to see what scores he or she would assign.

You have probably seen improvement between your first practice exam score and this one; but if you didn't improve as much as you would like, ask yourself the following: Did I run out of time before I could answer all the questions? Did I go back and change my answers from right to wrong? Did I get flustered and sit staring at a difficult question for what seemed like hours? If you had any of these problems, be sure to go over the LearningExpress Test Preparation guide in Chapter 2 again to learn how to avoid them.

Once you have honed your test-taking skills, go back to the review chapters and study again the areas that gave you the most trouble. After working on your reading, writing, and math skills, take the third practice exam in Chapter 10 to see how much you have improved.

16 ▶ ANSWERS AND EXPLANATIONS FOR PRACTICE EXAM 2

Answers and Explanations

Skills Test in Reading

1. b. The context of the passage indicates that the sentences in question are pointing out an unforeseen consequence (*however*) and the current situation (*now*).

2. d. To *herald* means to give an indication of things to come; this word best fits the meaning of the sentence.

3. b. The author's statement implies that the report could have suggested specific actions to confront the health problem of smoking, but that it did not.

4. e. Choices **a** through **d** are all unauthorized logging practices performed by Metsähallitus in Finland. Choice **e** is an incorrect statement because it refers to another country.

5. c. The passage states that neural prostheses could *replace damaged or missing nerves.* Therefore, it can be inferred that prostheses are artificial body parts—in this case, artificial nerves.

6. c. The tone throughout the passage suggests the potential for microprobes. They can be permanently implanted, they have advantages over electrodes, they are promising candidates for neural prostheses, they will have great accuracy, and they are flexible.

7. e. According to the third paragraph, people who lack biochemicals could receive doses via prostheses. However, there is no suggestion that removing biochemicals would be possible.

8. d. None of the other choices is supported by the information given in the passage.

9. b. The author uses the phrase *going gray* as a euphemism for growing older. It describes the phenomenon of a large segment of a population growing older.

10. d. Although he was a man of no formal scientific education, Leeuwenhoek demonstrated a craving after knowledge. The phrase *stumbled on* in choice **a** is too accidental to describe Leeuwenhoek's perseverance. The words *hobbyist* and *entertainment* in choice **c** do not accurately describe Leeuwenhoek's skill and drive, which are depicted in the passage. Choices **b** and **e** are incorrect; Leeuwenhoek was not trained as a researcher, nor did he know that his discoveries would later help to cure disease.

11. c. *Inspired* means to exert an animating or enlivening influence on. In the context of the passage, Leeuwenhoek's creation of microscope lenses was influenced by the lenses used by drapers.

12. b. The tone of the passage is positive. However, ecstatic reverence (choice **a**) is too positive, and tepid approval (choice **c**) is not positive enough.

13. e. This is the choice that most significantly weakens the author's first assumption: that Smithtown adults are more physically fit overall than they were five years ago. If most of the new members do not work out regularly, it then cannot be assumed that they are in better shape than they were before, and therefore, increased gym membership is not necessarily a reason for the decline in heart disease. Choice **a** would strengthen, not weaken, the author's argument. Choice **b** is irrelevant to the argument, which focuses on the *decline* in heart disease in Smithtown. Choice **c** does not weaken the author's contention; it is not necessary to poll every adult in order for the survey to be accurate. While the establishment of a cardiac clinic may have contributed to the drop in heart disease, this occurred prior to the five-year period the author mentions.

14. c. Any of the choices may be a definition of *background*; however, the context of the passage indicates that the word refers to the education and training of the proposed author—that is, the author's ability to write the book.

15. b. In the passage, the author describes the principles of the PRB—why the group was formed and how the group defined itself in opposition to the dominant Royal Academy. There is little or no information offered about the other choices.

16. d. This is the most accurate title because the passage deals mainly with remembering the fair.

17. a. Sentence 1 contains the phrase *should have been a colossal failure*, which is an opinion of the author. The other sentences provide factual information about Woodstock.

18. a. To depict the Sami, the author uses words that point to their gentleness, which is an admirable quality: They moved quietly, displayed courtesy to the spirits of the wilderness, and were known as peaceful retreaters.

19. c. A resume is literally the summary of one's job experience, education, and skills. The author is saying that there is nothing one can say about these models except that they look great; their figurative resume has only one item on it. Being great-looking isn't work experience (choice **a**), one would not literally list "great-looking" alone on a resume (choices **b** and **d**), and pathos is a feeling of pity or sorrow (choice **e**).

20. d. After making it clear that subjects are not equally suitable for short stories and novels, Wharton explains what makes a particular subject suitable for the novel form and how the elements of time and character development are different in the short story.

21. e. This is stated in the last paragraph: *first aid measures should be directed at cooling the body quickly.*

22. c. Heatstroke victims have a blocked sweating mechanism, as stated in the third paragraph.

23. c. The second paragraph states that for the symptoms of heat exhaustion, which include nausea and dizziness, first aid treatment includes giving the victim sips of salt water. The other choices relate to heatstroke.

24. d. This sentence stating that the blues remakes were enjoyed by people all across America suggests why the songs were so popular by describing how the lyrics touch a common emotional chord in listeners, all of whom have had the blues from one or more of the sources listed in the sentence.

25. d. At the beginning of the passage, Aristotle notes that the definition of good *corresponds* with the current opinion about the nature of the soul.

26. a. In the second paragraph, Aristotle states that *we have all but defined happiness as a kind of good life and well-being.* Thus, the definitions of happiness and goodness are intertwined; living a good life will bring happiness.

27. a. If an object *accrues* value, it *increases* in value. This can be inferred from the next sentence, which says that beautiful objects are also *prized*, suggesting that an object that has made many trips around the ring is considered very valuable.

28. d. At the end of the passage, the author states the ways in which a kula object gains value; being made of special shells is not mentioned.

29. e. The author's primary purpose in writing this passage is to discuss his belief that commercialism's strong presence in today's society strongly influences a person's view of his or her personal identity. A good illustration of this can be found in the second paragraph, where the author states: *we are prepared to spend our way into a trendy identity.*

30. d. The statement that one *can tell a lot about somebody by what he or she is wearing* is directly contradicted by the claim the author makes in the first paragraph: *Seeing someone in a Harvard or Oxford sweatshirt or a kilt or a military tie now communicates nothing at all significant about that person's life other than the personal choice of a particular consumer.*

31. a. The author's point of view of today's society is that today's world is much smaller and more hectic than it used be, which makes it harder for people to put down solid roots and identify with a singular way of life. In short, *times have changed.*

32. b. The term *disposable income* refers to the specific amount of a person's income that is allotted as spending money. This is the only choice that makes sense in the context of the passage.

33. b. Although all the choices are possible definitions of culture, the passage is speaking of a community of interrelated individuals—Europeans.

34. a. Choice **a** is correct because it lists the proper accolades and the proper timeframe in which he lived. Choice **b** is incorrect because he did not live during the Renaissance; choices **c** and **d** are incorrect because he was not a lord, but a knight (indicated by the title *Sir*); and choice **e** is incorrect because it is not the best summary of his vast accomplishments.

35. d. Of all the choices, January is the only month that falls within the darkest period (November through February) mentioned in the passage.

36. e. The first sentence notes that an allergic disease results from the immune system *reacting to a normally innocuous substance.* Choices **b** and **c** are contradicted in the passage by this statement. Choices **a** and **d** are not reflected in the passage.

37. b. See the third sentence, which says that cells called macrophages engulf the invader (that is, the allergen).

38. c. The fellow frightens the speaker. Choices **a**, **b**, **d**, and **e** would not be frightening.

39. a. *Tighter breathing* indicates fear, as does *zero at the bone* (one is sometimes said to be cold with fear). Also, the subject is a snake, which is an animal that is commonly feared.

40. d. While there is evidence for the other choices, they are not most troublesome. Throughout the passage, beginning with the first mention of "reality," in quotation marks, the author emphasizes the fact that reality TV is not an accurate portrait of real life.

Skills Test in Mathematics

1. b. Adjacent angles share a vertex and a common side, but do not overlap. Angles 1 and 4 are the only ones given that are not adjacent, or next to, each other.

2. a. It will cost $3 for a sandwich and a cookie. To get two additional sandwiches, it would cost another $4. Therefore, it would cost $7 to get three sandwiches and a cookie. Because she has only $6 to spend, this combination is not possible.

3. d. After the first two terms, each term is obtained by adding the preceding two terms in the sequence: $10 + 16 = 26$.

4. b. One foot in the model represents 100 yards, or 300 feet. So you can use a proportion involving feet to solve this problem. Let l represent the actual length of the Coliseum in feet:

$$\frac{1 \text{ foot}}{300 \text{ feet}} = \frac{l}{617} \text{ feet}$$
$$300 \times l = 1 \times 617$$
$$l \approx 2.06$$

So, when rounded to the nearest tenth, the length of the Coliseum in the model is about 2.1 feet.

5. c. Because there are a total of 105 students involved in sports and this makes up 21% of the students involved in extracurricular activities, find the total number of students by using the proportion $\frac{105}{x} = \frac{21}{100}$. Cross multiply to get $21x = 10,500$. Divide each side of the equal sign by 21 to get $x = 500$. There are 500 students in extracurricular activities, so find 17% of 500 to find the number of students involved in drama: 17% of $500 = 0.17 \times 500 = 85$.

6. e. To find the average of the numbers, divide the sum of the numbers by the number of terms being averaged. In this case, let x represent the temperature on the fifth day and set the expression equal to the average temperature for the five days, which was 90: $\frac{95 + 85 + 88 + 84 + x}{5} = 90$. Simplify the expression to $\frac{352 + x}{5} = 90$ because the total sum of the first four days is 352. Cross multiply to get $352 + x = 450$. By subtracting 352 from each side, x is equal to 98. If unsure about this type of question, this problem could also be solved by trying each of the answer choices to see which one results in an average of 90°. When 98 is added to the temperatures for the first four days, the sum is 450; 450 divided by 5 is 90.

7. b. The probability of selecting a nickel or a penny is equal to the number of nickels and pennies in the jar divided by the total number of coins in the jar. In other words, $\frac{\text{nickels} + \text{pennies}}{\text{total coins}}$. Because there are 3 nickels and 9 pennies, the number in the numerator (or top) of the fraction is 12. There are a total of 30 coins in the jar, so the probability becomes $\frac{12}{30}$, which reduces to $\frac{2}{5}$.

8. b. The perimeter of an object is the distance around the object. This can be found by finding the sum of the sides of the object. Because this figure is a pentagon, it has five sides. Three of the sides measure 3 inches, and the remaining two sides measure 5 inches. Therefore, the sum of the sides is equal to $3 + 3 + 3 + 5 + 5 = 19$ inches.

9. d. When multiplied together, 11×0.032 is equal to 0.352. A quick way to solve a question that contains a number of decimal places is to first multiply the numbers as whole numbers: $11 \times 32 = 352$. Then, count the number of decimal places in the numbers being multiplied and apply the same number of places to the answer. Because there are three decimal places in the number 0.032, the result of 352 becomes 0.352.

10. e. The 90% discount is applied to all three of the items. Therefore, the total cost of the three T-shirts is equal to the sum of the items multiplied by 0.9. This is equal to $0.9 \times (a + b + c)$. To find the average cost of one T-shirt, divide the total cost of all three by 3. Therefore, the expression would become $\frac{0.9(a + b + c)}{3}$.

11. a. The expression in choice **a** uses the distributive property of multiplication over addition to find the total of purchasing three of each item, and then subtracts the cost of one box of rice because he is actually purchasing only two. Another way to solve this question is to find the total cost of the five items that are purchased ($9.95) and see that only choice **a** also results in this total when evaluated.

12. a. In the expression in the question, the terms a, b, and c are written over a common denominator of 3. Another way this can be expressed is to write each term individually over this common denominator of 3, as in choice **a**. Since the sum of the terms is still being divided by 3, this is equivalent to the original expression.

13. a. In order to divide two fractions, multiply the fraction being divided into by the reciprocal of the fraction being divided by. The expression $\frac{2}{3} \div \frac{5}{12}$ then becomes $\frac{2}{3} \times \frac{12}{5} = \frac{24}{15}$. This reduces to $\frac{8}{5}$, which is equal to $1\frac{3}{5}$ as a mixed number.

14. c. The arrival time of Train A is 6:42 A.M., and the departure time of Train D is 8:24 A.M. There are 18 minutes between 6:42 A.M. and 7:00 A.M., and there is one hour between 7:00 A.M. and 8:00 A.M. There are an additional 24 minutes between 8:00 A.M. and the departure time of 8:24 A.M. To find the difference of the times, add these values: 18 minutes + 1 hour + 24 minutes = 1 hour, 42 minutes.

15. d. To solve the inequality for x, first add 1 to each side of the inequality: $-4x - 1 + 1 \geq 11 + 1$ becomes $-4x \geq 12$. Next, divide each side of the inequality by -4. Note that when you divide or multiply each side of an inequality by a negative number, the inequality symbol reverses: $\frac{-4x}{-4} \geq \frac{12}{-4}$ simplifies to $x \leq -3$.

16. e. The only statement that does not contradict the original statement is choice **e** because a square is a special rhombus.

17. c. In order to look for a reasonable answer, use rounding to make the numbers in the question compatible: 6,251 can be rounded to 6,000 and 312 can be rounded to 300. To find the percentage of teachers that have dual certification, divide 300 by 6,000. This can also be thought of as $\frac{3}{60}$. Since 3 out of 50 would be equal to 6 out of 100, or 6%, the most reasonable answer choice is 5%. This answer can be checked by dividing 3 by 60 to get 0.05, which is equal to 5%.

18. c. To find the total percentage, add the percent for electrical equipment and the percent for other equipment together. Adding 7.8% (electrical equipment) and 7.3% (other equipment) results in a total of 15.1% for both causes.

19. b. To answer this question, you are looking for the greatest difference in percentage between the percentage of deaths and total fires. Because smoking materials account for only 6.7% of the fires but for 28.9% of the deaths, this area has the greatest discrepancy in the percentages. It therefore has the highest ratio of percentage of deaths to total fires.

20. d. There are 11 different causes listed in the table, so look for the answer choices that have 11 sections within the circle graphs. Answer choices **a** and **e** do not contain 11 sections, so they can be eliminated immediately. In answer choice **b**, the largest sector appears to be too large in relation to the next largest sector, and in answer choice **c**, the sectors are all too similar in size. The answer choice that has sectors that most reasonably represent the information in the table is choice **d**.

21. c. Each 9-foot wall has an area of 9×8 or 72 square feet. There are two such walls, so those two walls combined have an area of 72×2 or 144 square feet. Each 11-foot wall has an area of 11×8 or 88 square feet, and again there are two such walls: $88 \times 2 = 176$. To find the total surface area, add 144 and 176 to get 320 square feet.

22. e. Substitute the value of 40 for C into the given formula: $\frac{9}{5}(40) + 32 = 72 + 32 = 104$. Therefore, 40° Celsius is equal to 104° Fahrenheit.

23. d. A way to order the fractions is to change each to its decimal form and compare the values. Change a fraction to a decimal by dividing the numerator (top number) by the denominator (bottom number): $\frac{1}{2} = 0.50$, $\frac{6}{11} = 0.54$, $\frac{3}{5} = 0.60$, and $\frac{5}{8} = 0.625$. These four fractions are in order from least to greatest. Because the question asked for the fractions in order from greatest to least, the correct order is choice **d**.

24. d. If the input is 63, the first step of the flow chart is $63 - 11 = 52$. Because the next step is missing, take a look at the third step and the final result that is obtained. The third step will add 7 to the answer of the missing step and get a result of 11. Therefore, the result of the missing step must be $11 - 7 = 4$. To get an answer of 4 from 52, you must divide 52 by 13. Thus, the missing step is to divide by 13.

25. a. Write out the equation. Remember, *is* means equals and *of* means times. To find the answer, you first write one-eighth and one-sixth as fractions, and then you multiply straight across: $\frac{1}{8} \times \frac{1}{6} = \frac{1}{48}$.

26. d. In order to solve the equation $14x + 2(x + 1) = 34$, first use the distributive property to eliminate the parentheses. The equation then becomes $14x + 2x + 2 = 34$. Then, combine the like terms of $14x$ and $2x$ to get $16x + 2 = 34$. Subtract 2 from each side of the equation: $16x + 2 - 2 = 34 - 2$; $16x = 32$. Divide each side of the equation by 16 to get a result of $x = 2$. The only step not useful in solving this equation was choice **d**, add 2 to each side of the equation.

27. d. First, convert the two mixed numbers to improper fractions: $2\frac{1}{4}$ becomes $\frac{9}{4}$ and $4\frac{5}{8}$ becomes $\frac{37}{8}$. Use a common denominator of 8 in order to add the three fractions together: $\frac{1}{2} = \frac{4}{8}$ and $\frac{9}{4} = \frac{18}{8}$; $\frac{18}{8} + \frac{37}{8} + \frac{4}{8} = \frac{59}{8}$. This is equal to $7\frac{3}{8}$ as a mixed number, which is choice **d**.

28. a. In order to solve this problem, first calculate the area of the rug. Then convert the answer to square inches because each answer choice uses square inches as a label. The formula for the area of a circle is $A = \pi r^2$, where $r =$ the radius of the circle. Because each answer choice is left in terms of π, do not bother to substitute 3.14 for this symbol. The diameter of the rug is 152 cm, so the radius, which is half of this measure, must be 76 cm. Substitute into the area formula: $A = \pi(76)^2 = 5,776\pi$ cm^2. Because each answer choice is in square inches and 1 cm = 0.39 in., then 1 cm^2 = 0.1521 in.^{2}. Multiply the area by 0.1521 to convert cm^2 to in.^{2}: $5,776\pi \times 0.1521 = 878.53\pi$ in.^{2}.

29. b. Take caution in percent problems, especially when the percent is taken off of two different amounts. Figure the problem in two steps: first find 15% of $84.50, and then find 10% of the membership price *after* the 15% discount: 15% of $84.50 = 0.15×84.50 = 12.68; $84.50 − 12.68 = $71.82. Now, calculate 90% of $71.82 (remember, if you save 10%, you need to pay 90%): $0.90 \times 71.82 = $64.64.

30. b. Notice that each value in the first column (h) is a multiple of three. If a multiple of three is multiplied by $\frac{1}{3}$, the result will be an integer. Because each number in the second column is an integer, try choice **b** first. If $h = 3$, then $k = \frac{1}{3} \times 3 + 3 = 1 + 3 = 4$. If $h = 6$, then $k = \frac{1}{3} \times 6 + 3 = 2 + 3 = 5$. If $h = 9$, then $k = \frac{1}{3} \times 9 + 3 = 3 + 3 = 6$. If $h = 12$, then $k = \frac{1}{3} \times 12 + 3 = 4 + 3 = 7$. If $h = 15$, then $k = \frac{1}{3} \times 15 + 3 = 5 + 3 = 8$. Each pair of values in the table satisfies the equation in choice **b**.

31. c. The speed of the train is 60 miles per hour, so as each hour increases by 1 the number of miles increases by 60. Therefore, the distance from Chicago would be equal to $60t$ because distance = rate × time. However, as the train moves on, the distance decreases from Los Angeles, so there must be a function of $−60t$ in the equation. At time $t = 0$, the distance is 2,000 miles, so the function is $2,000 − 60t$.

32. a. This problem has multiple steps. First, figure out what Deanna spent: $7 for popcorn, 2 hot dogs × 2 girls × $3 each = $12, 2 sodas × $4 = $8. Then add them up: $7 + $12 + $8 = $27. Next, figure out what Jamie spent: $13 × 2 = $26. Last, subtract the two numbers: $27 − $26 = $1. Deanna spent $1 more.

33. b. Because you are looking for the best rate for each weight, use the lesser amount in each weight category. The cost for a 2 oz. and a 6 oz. is $0.50 + $1.50, respectively, which is equal to a total of $2.00. The total cost for choice **a** is $2.50, choice **c** is $2.75, choice **d** is $2.50, and choice **e** is $3.50. Because choice **b** has the lowest cost, it is the least expensive.

34. e. The cost for 12 ounces at Speedy Delivery Service is $3.00, and the cost for 12 ounces at EZ Package System is $2.50. The difference between these amounts is $0.50. To find the percent of the difference, substitute these amounts into the proportion: $\frac{\text{change}}{\text{original amount}} = \frac{\%}{100}$. The proportion becomes $\frac{.50}{2.50} = \frac{x}{100}$. Cross multiply to get $2.5x = 50$. Divide 50 by 2.5 to get $x = 20\%$.

35. c. One way to solve this problem is to round each of the amounts to the nearest ten and then add the rounded amounts together; 5,618 rounds to 5,620, 5,085 rounds to 5,090, and 6,163 rounds to 6,160. The sum of $5,620 + 5,090 + 6,160$ is equal to 16,870. Another approach would be to add the unrounded numbers first, and then round the answer to the nearest ten. When added, the sum of the numbers before rounding is 16,866. This number is also equal to 16,870 when rounded to the nearest ten.

36. d. Recall that to find an average (arithmetic mean), divide the sum of the terms by the total number of terms in the situation. To find the average number sold per month for the five-month period, first find the total number of music downloads sold and divide this number by 5. To find the total downloads represented, count the total number of symbols in the figure. There are 12 whole symbols and three half-symbols, making a total of 13.5 symbols in the figure. Because each symbol represents 150 downloads sold, multiply $13.5 \times 150 = 2,025$. Divide this amount by 5 to get an average of 405 downloads sold per month.

37. c. The third side of the triangle must be less than the sum of the other two sides $(17 + 14)$ and greater than their difference $(17 - 14)$. This means that the third side must be less than 31 and greater than 3. Only choice **c** fits these criteria.

38. b. Because there are 1,000 students and there are five students on a team, $1,000 \div 5 = 200$ teams. Therefore, there are a total of $1,000 + 200 = 1,200$ people involved; $1,200 \div 4$ gymnasiums is equal to 300 in each gym.

39. a. First determine the amount of water held in each container by finding the volume of each. The volume of water held by the rectangular box is found by multiplying the area of the base by the height of the water: $V = 16$ in.$^2 \times 9$ in. $= 144$ in.^{3}. The total volume of the cylindrical container can be found by using the formula $V = \pi r^2 h$, where $r =$ the radius of the base, $h =$ the height of the container, and $\pi = 3.14$: $V = (3.14)(2)^2(11) = (3.14)(4)(11) = 138.16$ in.^{3}. Because there is more water in the rectangular box to begin with, the cylinder will overflow.

40. d. Keep in mind that in this question you are only looking for the person who likes to fish. Because it is stated that the friend who fishes is Miguel's neighbor, the person who fishes is not Miguel. Robert and Linda dislike sports that use balls, so the person who fishes must be one of them (it must not be Sonja and Miguel who like tennis and volleyball). The statement *Sonja is older than both Robert and the friend who fishes* allows you to conclude that Robert is not the person who fishes. Therefore, the person who likes to fish must be Linda.

Skills Test in Writing— Section 1, Part A

1. b. This is not a complete sentence because it has no subject. To correct this problem, the word *which* should be replaced by the word *it*, which then becomes the subject of the sentence.

2. e. Because there are no grammatical, idiomatic, logical, or structural errors in this sentence, choice **e** is the best answer.

3. c. The verb *walked* should be modified by an adverb, not an adjective. The adverb *hesitantly* should replace the incorrect adjective *hesitant*.

4. e. Because there are no grammatical, idiomatic, logical, or structural errors in this sentence, choice **e** is the best answer.

5. c. The gerund *describing* is incorrect in this sentence. The infinitive *to describe* should be used.

6. d. This sentence has faulty parallelism. Two of the assistant's characteristics are adjectives (*smart*, *reliable*), while the third characteristic consists of a verb phrase and prepositional phrase (*will come on time*). To create proper parallelism, make all three characteristics adjectives by changing *will come on time* to *punctual* or *timely*.

7. c. The error is in punctuation. The two clauses in this compound sentence are independent and should be separated by a semicolon, not a comma.

8. c. This sentence contains faulty coordination. Using the conjunction *and* in this sentence creates an illogical link between the dependent and independent clauses. To make the sentence grammatically correct, you must delete *and*.

9. b. The error is in verb formation. The sentence requires the past tense of the verb *begin*. To correct this error, the past participle *begun* should be replaced with the past tense *began*.

10. e. Because there are no grammatical, idiomatic, logical, or structural errors in this sentence, choice **e** is the best answer.

11. a. When a negative word such as *no* or *not* is added to a sentence that already contains a negative, a double negative results. Because *barely* is a negative word, the use of *not* in this sentence creates a double negative. To correct this, change *couldn't* to *could*.

12. a. The verb *treated* should be modified by an adverb. *Bad* is an adjective and is used incorrectly; it should be replaced by the adverb *badly*.

13. e. Because there are no grammatical, idiomatic, logical, or structural errors in this sentence, choice **e** is the best answer.

14. a. This sentence contains a capitalization error. The names of seasons are not capitalized, so *Winter* should be lowercase (*winter*).

15. c. Here, the word *affect* is used incorrectly as a noun. *Affect* is a verb meaning to influence. As a noun, *effect* means result, which is how it is used in this sentence.

16. e. Because there are no grammatical, idiomatic, logical, or structural errors in this sentence, choice **e** is the best answer.

17. c. This is a sentence fragment; the independent clause does not have a subject. The first clause in the sentence is dependent and therefore does not stand alone. The subject must occur in the second clause. To correct this structural problem, a subject (*she*, *he*, or a person's name) should be added before the underlined *also noted*.

18. b. *Contemporary* and *modern* mean the same thing, so one of those words should be deleted to avoid a redundancy.

19. e. Because there are no grammatical, idiomatic, logical, or structural errors in this sentence, choice **e** is the best answer.

20. a. This sentence has an agreement problem. The plural pronoun *them* does not agree with the singular noun *story*. Therefore, *them* should be replaced by the singular pronoun *it*.

21. d. This sentence contains a pronoun error. When antecedents are connected with a *neither . . . nor* phrase, the pronoun should agree with the closer antecedent. In this sentence, the two antecedents are *soldiers* and *sergeant*. Because *sergeant* is the antecedent closer to the pronoun, the pronoun should be singular—either *his* or *her*—not the plural *their*. However, because *their location* makes more sense, a better solution would be to reverse the two antecedents.

Skills Test in Writing— Section 1, Part B

22. d. This choice is best because it is written in the active voice, and the sentence is constructed so that all modifiers are appropriately placed.

23. e. This is the correct choice because there is no shift in verb tense, and there is agreement between the noun *petition* and the pronoun *it*.

24. d. This is the correct choice because the sentence makes a comparison among many things (every Best Actress nominee ever), and therefore requires the superlative, *youngest*. Do not be fooled by choice **c**, *most youngest*. Using *most* before *youngest* creates a double comparison, and therefore makes the sentence grammatically incorrect. In choice **e,** *youngly* is not a real word.

25. b. The second clause of this sentence requires a parallel construction. Choice **b** is the only one in which all four elements are parallel.

26. e. This is the only choice that maintains the structure and meaning of the sentence and does not contain a redundancy.

27. a. This is the only choice that uses correct possession and the correct verb tense. Because *signal* is a singular noun, it needs a singular verb (*was*). Choice **e** implies that the scientists were in the act of confirming for 24 hours.

28. a. The other choices create either faulty subordination or a comma splice.

29. c. This is the only choice that contains both the correct pronoun and comparative form. The verb *is* is understood, so the sentence requires the subject pronoun *he*, not the object pronoun *him*. Because the comparison in this sentence is between only two people, the comparative form (*-er*) is required, not the superlative form (*-est*.) The use of *more* in choice **d** creates a double comparison, and is therefore incorrect. Besides containing the incorrect pronoun, choice **e** is incorrect because *less older* makes no sense.

30. d. Commas should be used to avoid ambiguity and to separate parenthetical elements. The phrase *the year I was born* is parenthetical.

31. e. The verb *are carved* is in agreement with the plural noun *likenesses*.

32. a. There are two possible errors in this sentence: One is subject-verb agreement, and the other is the use of the words *between* and *among*. *Between* is used to compare two things; *among* is used to compare more than two. In this sentence *between* is correct, so choices **b** and **c** can be ruled out. Choices **d** and **e** are wrong because the verb *benefit* does not agree with the subject relationship.

33. d. The word *insure* is incorrect in this sentence. The word that should be used here to make the sentence clear and logical is *assure*.

34. **d.** The word *beside* means *at the side of*; the word *besides* means *other than* or *together with*. Choice **d** also corrects the subject-verb agreement error.

35. **b.** The most common way to join two independent clauses is with a comma and a coordinating conjunction. The only sentence that correctly does both is choice **b.** For choice **a** to be correct, the coordinating conjunction *so* needs to be deleted. Choice **d** lacks a proper coordinating conjunction and has faulty parallelism. Choice **e** contains a verb tense error.

36. **c.** The comparison in this sentence between America and England requires *as . . . as.* Choice **c** establishes the proper comparison and creates the only sentence that is clear and logical.

37. **e.** This is the only choice that properly places the commas between the three clauses in the sentence.

38. **d.** In this complex sentence, choice **d** is the only complete sentence.

Skills Test in Writing— Section 2, Essay Writing

Following are sample criteria for scoring a PPST essay.

A score "6" writer will

- create an exceptional composition that appropriately addresses the audience and given task.
- organize ideas effectively, include very strong supporting details, and use smooth transitions.
- present a definitive, focused thesis and clearly support it throughout the composition.
- include vivid details, clear examples, and strong supporting text to enhance the themes of the composition.
- exhibit an exceptional level of skill in the usage of the English language and the capacity to employ an assortment of sentence structures.

- build essentially error-free sentences that accurately convey intended meaning.

A score "5" writer will

- create a commendable composition that appropriately addresses the audience and given task.
- organize ideas, include supporting details, and use smooth transitions.
- present a thesis and support it throughout the composition.
- include details, examples, and supporting text to enhance the themes of the composition.
- generally exhibit a high level of skill in the usage of the English language and the capacity to employ an assortment of sentence structures.
- build mostly error-free sentences that accurately convey intended meaning.

A score "4" writer will

- create a composition that satisfactorily addresses the audience and given task.
- display satisfactory organization of ideas, include adequate supporting details, and generally use smooth transitions.
- present a thesis and mostly support it throughout the composition.
- include some details, examples, and supporting text that typically enhance most themes of the composition.
- exhibit a competent level of skill in the usage of the English language and the general capacity to employ an assortment of sentence structures.
- build sentences with several minor errors that generally do not confuse the intended meaning.

A score "3" writer will

- create an adequate composition that basically addresses the audience and given task.
- display some organization of ideas, include some supporting details, and use mostly logical transitions.

- present a somewhat underdeveloped thesis but attempt to support it throughout the composition.
- display limited organization of ideas, have some inconsistent supporting details, and use few transitions.
- exhibit an adequate level of skill in the usage of the English language and a basic capacity to employ an assortment of sentence structures.
- build sentences with some minor and major errors that may obscure the intended meaning.

A score "2" writer will

- create a composition that restrictedly addresses the audience and given task.
- display little organization of ideas, have inconsistent supporting details, and use very few transitions.
- present an unclear or confusing thesis with little support throughout the composition.
- include very few details, examples, and supporting text.
- exhibit a less than adequate level of skill in the usage of the English language and a limited capacity to employ a basic assortment of sentence structures.
- build sentences with a few major errors that may confuse the intended meaning.

A score "1" writer will

- create a composition that has a limited sense of the audience and given task.
- display illogical organization of ideas, include confusing or no supporting details, and lack the ability to effectively use transitions.
- present a minimal or unclear thesis.
- include confusing or irrelevant details and examples, and little or no supporting text.
- exhibit a limited level of skill in the usage of the English language and little or no capacity to employ basic sentence structure.

- build sentences with many major errors that obscure or confuse the intended meaning.

Sample 6 Essay

In the twenty-first century, the first place people turn to when there is a question to be answered, information to be located, or people to be contacted, is often the Internet. The Internet has supplanted the traditional encyclopedia, as well as a number of other reference sources, such as telephone books and travel agents. On it, one can make reservations, plan vacations, play interactive games, learn a language, listen to music or radio programs, read the newspaper, and find out about a medical condition, without coming face-to-face with another person. Clearly, the Internet is an invaluable tool in modern life.

There is no limit to the subject matter that can be researched on the Internet. Search engines such as Yahoo! or Google, with a few keywords or Web addresses, can summon links to more sources than one could imagine. The Internet allows those at home in front of their computers to shop no matter what they wish to purchase. If that happens to be a bargain or an unusual item, popular auction sites are available with millions of unique items for sale.

If, however, one wishes to speak directly to another person, there are chat rooms and e-mail on the Internet that enable such dialogue. On almost any given topic, groups of people converse with one other. They may be giving opinions about a perfect travel itinerary, a book, or even a political party. Chat rooms can be a place to meet people, exchange ideas, or learn a new skill. The most prevalent use of the Internet, however, is the sending and receiving of e-mail messages. It is possible through e-mail to communicate instantly with anyone, anywhere, as long as there is an Internet connection. In a world where people frequently travel, and where family members do not necessarily live in the same state, e-mail is a means of making simple, inexpensive, immediate contact. In addition to verbal messages, digital cameras allow pictures to be taken and instantly transmitted on the Internet.

Unfortunately, there are individuals who subvert the opportunities offered by this technology. They are less than honest, disguise their identity, bilk people in financial scams, and entice unsuspecting people, including children, into giving them personal information. Caveats about these problems are currently being publicized so Internet users will not be victimized.

Of course, Internet providers, such as Verizon, Comcast, and Time Warner, are in business to make a profit, so there is usually a monthly fee for access. To increase profits, these providers sell advertising space. Some is easy to ignore, such as banners at the top and bottom of the screen. However, some advertising comes in the form of pop-ups that appear on the subscriber's screen and require the user to stop and respond, either positively or negatively, to the ads.

When one considers that, among other things, you can hear a concert, read a book, visit a museum and view its contents, visit the websites of numerous individuals and organizations, play a game with one or more people, and pay your bills, it becomes obvious that the uses of the Internet are too vast for a short list. Most would agree that much has been added to people's lives by connecting them to the Internet, and that we probably cannot anticipate what new purposes will be explored in the future.

Sample 4 Essay

The Internet has many important purposes. It has connected people all over the world in a way that has never been done before. You can send and receive e-mail from friends and colleagues whenever you want. You can also meet people through the Internet, and make friends. These facts prove the importance of the Internet in people's daily lives.

The internet is also good for research. If you want to get information about just about any topic, you can look it up. You don't have to go to the library. You can also use the Internet for recreation purposes. There are also good games and music that you can download, often for free.

Shopping may also be done on the Internet. You can buy things at home, without having to go the store.

For providers, the internet is a way for them to make money. They sell subscriptions, and also sell advertising space. Some provide good service, while others seem to want to make the most profit, and don't hire many technical people to help when there is a problem.

While the internet has its downside, such as identity theft problems and stalkers, these problems are found off the internet, too. You just have to be careful when using the internet, and you can enjoy the countless ways in which it has improved our lives.

Sample 1 Essay

The Internet has lots of purposes. It has been around for about ten years and it has really taken off. Most people have at least one computer in their house. Most of them have an internet connection. If you ask them why they have it, they will probably tell you about the useful purposes.

One of the best things you can do on the Internet is play games, such as chess and backgammon, with people you don't even know. Sometimes you have to pay for the games, and sometimes they are free. Sometimes you play against a really tough opponent, and sometimes you can win every game. I prefer the latter. It's also fun to listen to music on the internet. You can find just about any kind you like. These are some purposes of the Internet.

Praxis I Scoring

Again, evaluate how you did on this practice exam by scoring the three tests of the Praxis I—Reading, Mathematics, and Writing—separately. First, find the number of questions you got right in each section. Questions you skipped or got wrong don't count; just add up the number of correct answers, and then divide by the number of questions in the section to come up with a percentage. Remember, if you don't know the score you need, try to aim for at least 70%.

You must also receive a passing score on the essay portion of the PPST Writing test. On this portion, the combined score of at least two writing experts will be used to evaluate how you did. The scoring criteria are outlined in detail in the answer explanations. Once again, take your essay and the scoring criteria to a teacher or a trusted friend and ask that person to assign a score to your essay.

You have probably seen improvement between your second practice exam score and this one; if you didn't improve as much as you had hoped for, here are some options you may wish to consider.

- If you scored below 60%, you should seriously consider whether you are ready for the Praxis I at this time. A good idea would be to take some brushup courses, either at a university or community college nearby or through correspondence, in the areas you feel less sure of. If you don't have time for a course, you might try private tutoring.

- If your score is in the 60–70% range, you need to work as hard as you can to improve your skills. Also, reread and pay close attention to all the advice in Chapters 2, 4, 5, and 6 of this book in order to improve your score. It might also be helpful to ask friends and family to make up mock test questions and quiz you on them.

- If your score is between 70% and 90%, you could still benefit from additional work by going back to Chapters 4, 5, and 6 and brushing up your reading, writing, and general math skills before the exam.

- If you scored above 90%, that's great! This kind of score should make you a success in the academic program of your choice or in a teaching position. Don't lose your edge, though; keep studying right up to the day before the exam.

The key to success in almost any pursuit is to prepare for all you are worth. By taking the practice exams in this book, you have made yourself better prepared than other people who may be taking the exam with you. You have diagnosed where your strengths and weaknesses lie and learned how to deal with the various kinds of questions that will appear on the test. So go into the exam with confidence, knowing that you're ready and equipped to do your best.

17 ▶ ANSWERS AND EXPLANATIONS FOR PRACTICE EXAM 3

Scoring the Constructed-Response Case History Questions

Constructed responses are scored on a range from 0 to 2. First, this section presents the criteria for scoring constructed responses to the PLT case histories. Then it provides sample level 2 responses for each question based on the scoring criteria that follow.

Criteria for Scoring

For a score of 2, the response must

- show that the writer has a thorough understanding of the parts of the case history that relate to the question.
- appropriately address all components of the question.
- provide a strong explanation (if requested) and support it with relevant evidence.

- provide evidence that the writer possesses strong knowledge of pedagogical concepts, facts, theories, methodologies, or procedures relevant to the question.

For a score of 1, the response must

- show that the writer has a basic understanding of the parts of the case history that relate to the question.
- appropriately address one component of the question.
- provide a weak explanation (if requested) but still be supported with relevant evidence.
- provide evidence that the writer possesses some knowledge of pedagogical concepts, facts, theories, methodologies, or procedures relevant to the question.

For a score of 0, the response must

- show that the writer misunderstood the parts of the case history that relate to the question.
- fail to address the question.
- not be supported by relevant evidence.
- provide little evidence that the writer possesses some knowledge of pedagogical concepts, facts, theories, methodologies, or procedures relevant to the question.

A sample question and responses follow. They are based on the Chapter 10, Case History 3.1, Mark Roberts scenario and documents. Read the case history to understand how we have used the criteria to score three responses to the following question.

Sample Constructed-Response Question

The documents provide information about Mark's language and social interaction skills.

- Explain TWO factors that you note regarding Mark's development.

- For EACH factor, describe a theory of language or social development that supports your comments.

Sample of a Short Answer That Would Receive a 2

Developmentally, Mark's language skills appear to be slightly below the level of his four-year-old peers. From the observation, we know that he does know the names of familiar animals and some colors, and he engages in pretend play and make-believe. However, he does not verbalize very much when he is engaged in activities and has not mastered the vocabulary to identify many common objects in picture books that most four-year-olds would be able to name. Some of his speech is not intelligible, and he exhibits some articulation problems. Socially, he appears to be developing confidence in sharing interactions with his peers through social play. Although play does not necessarily develop sequentially from parallel to social to cooperative play, typically preschoolers participate in all three types of play. From the observation notes, we have evidence that he is playing alongside peers (parallel play) and playing socially (cooperative). Further observation would be needed to determine to what extent he is also playing cooperatively with others (taking on complementary roles and shared purposes). We see him taking directions from John, but not cooperating in the sense that he contributes to and helps form the purposes of the play and roles. He does not appear to be an equal partner in social play and interactions, but rather a quiet follower.

Rationale: This is a sample of a level 2 response because it meets all of the following criteria.

- By discussing specific details from the class observation and incorporating them into the response, this writer shows a thorough understanding of the parts of the case history that relate to the question.

- There are several components to the question: The writer is asked to address how Mark's development compares to that of his peers, whether his skills are developmentally appropriate, and pertinent theories of language and social development. All components of the question have been fully addressed.
- The writer explains the answer and discusses the relevant evidence the passage offers to support the explanation.
- The use of concepts and facts about development and play shows strong knowledge of theories and methods.

Sample of a Short Answer That Would Receive a 1

I would say Mark is developmentally delayed because he lacks confidence, based on his interactions with his sisters at home. They probably talk for him a lot, which has caused him not to talk for himself. He basically waits for others to tell him what to do. His skills are not developmentally appropriate because usually four-year-olds talk more and play and interact more openly with peers. He is following his friend around a lot. Although he talks some, his articulation should be assessed. Mark is in the egocentric stage of development. Maybe that's why he is quiet: He's focused on himself more than others.

Rationale: This is a sample of a level 1 response because it meets the following criteria.

- The response includes discussion of notes from the observation, but the level of understanding of Mark's development is basic at best. The response lacks clear insight.
- The writer does respond to the first part of the question by answering that Mark is delayed developmentally.
- The writer's explanation is weak, but it is somewhat supported by the theory of egocentrism.

- Mentioning concepts such as articulation and egocentrism shows that the writer possesses some knowledge of pedagogical concepts, facts, theories, methodologies, or procedures relevant to the question.

Sample Short Answer That Would Receive a 0

Mark's mother shouldn't let his sisters pick on him. When I was young, I was the youngest boy in the family. I had two older brothers. They always picked on me, and I think that's probably why I decided to become a teacher. I want to be able to help students like Mark develop into confident, smart people who have a lot to offer the world. I think it's wrong to have another teacher follow Mark around and watch everything he's doing. Doesn't he have any privacy rights? The poor kid is getting picked on at home, and then when he comes to school he gets followed around and told what to do. Mark should be taken out of that school and put into a better one.

Rationale: This is a sample of a level zero response for the following reasons.

- The writer seems to have misunderstood the whole purpose of the observation. Instead of seeing the observation as a way to assess the student's needs, the writer took it as a sort of punishment.
- The writer fails to answer any part of the question with any real insight about child development or pedagogy.
- No evidence from the case history is brought into the response to support the writer's perspective.
- The writer brings in no theories or pedagogical concepts to show knowledge of how they might apply to this case history.

Answers and Explanations

PLT Case History 3.1: Mark Roberts

1. One factor that might contribute to Mark's rate of language acquisition is his gender. Mrs. Roberts has four older girls. She should be wary of comparing their language development with Mark's because he is a different gender. Whether it is due to nature or nurture, most girls typically talk earlier than most boys. Also, most late-talkers are young boys. Mrs. Salisbury should recommend that Mark's language development be observed and documented to determine if there is a developmental delay. If there is a noted delay, the parent, the school's speech and language specialist, and the child's physician should be informed so that follow-up assessments may be arranged. Another factor that might contribute to the rate of language acquisition is medical concerns. Temporary medical problems, such as otitis media, when left unattended, can cause language delays. Also, more serious congenital conditions, such as neurological problems, could cause delays. Mrs. Salisbury should look for and remind Mrs. Roberts to look for symptoms of ear infections, such as earaches, fever, loss of hearing ability, and unclear speech. If symptoms appear, the parents should notify the child's physician for follow-up diagnosis, care, and assessment of hearing loss and potential language delay.

2. Two goals that Mark should work on in school and at home are

   1. to improve his speaking vocabulary so he can participate developmentally and appropriately in social situations with his peers.

   2. to increase his frequency of language interactions with peers in social situations.

   Two suggested strategies Mark's teachers and parents can use to promote Mark's language and social development follow: First, early childhood teachers and parents of young children should demonstrate and model language and socialization skills by using vocabulary-rich language to talk about the world with children. Children will attempt to do what they see and hear others do. For example, reading aloud with children will cause them to independently pick up books and mimic the kind of language found in books, thereby expanding their language growth. Modeling functional uses of language and print for various purposes will cause children to learn the practical uses of language. In Mark's case, explicit modeling of appropriate social interactions, such as how Mark could ask other children if he could join their play, might be beneficial. Initial adult involvement in play interactions among peers would provide opportunities for Mark to witness appropriate ways to interact with his peers. Second, language acquisition is a process that occurs through social interactions among children and supportive adults. Therefore, adults must provide opportunities for children to play and work together in literacy-rich environments. In Mark's case, because he is the youngest child and the only boy sibling, the teacher might recommend inviting John and other peers over for play dates with Mark. Children learn by not only watching and listening, but by practicing, copying, and experiencing the social acts and language that occur around them. Therefore, teachers and parents should surround children with a language- and print-rich environment that involves children in interaction with functional print and language through play. Children will act as coaches for each other's learning.

PLT Case History 3.2: Alexandria

3. Two forms of assessment Ms. Lorenzo and Nurse Carolyn used were an anecdotal note and an observation. These are both informal types of assessment that supplement more formal

types of assessment. Ms. Lorenzo documented particular behaviors in a brief anecdotal note. The note reflects an objective description of what Ms. Lorenzo noticed about Alexandria. Nurse Carolyn was asked to come in and observe Alexandria in the context of play events because Ms. Lorenzo was concerned with Alexandria's physical and emotional health. She felt the school nurse would be able to lend her expertise as a health professional to interpret the behaviors Alexandria was demonstrating.

Anecdotal notes are quick notes teachers make while or immediately after observing or working with children. They help teachers see patterns over time and aid the teacher's memory for instructional purposes. They can be limiting, however, if the teacher does not make it her practice to regularly review, reflect on, and analyze the notes. Also, the teacher must be sure to observe objectively rather than subjectively.

Anecdotal notes are based on observations, but a more formal, invited observation was performed by Nurse Carolyn. Observations are also objective ways of recording students' behavior. Observation reports may be narrative, as we see in this scenario, or they may also be reported with checklists. Narrative observations should include the setting, context, verbalizations, and length of the observation. They are helpful for reflecting on the behaviors and surrounding context of a situation. In this case, the school nurse was an outside health expert who contributed her perspective. This different perspective was a strength of the assessment measure. However, observations can be limiting when the observer is not trained to know what types of behaviors to look for or note.

4. Most state governments mandate that when teachers and other school personnel suspect or witness child abuse, they are required to report it to the state authorities. Alexandria's teacher and nurse must report this to the state and the school administrator or day-care owner immediately. Ms. Lorenzo most likely must return to her class. So Nurse Carolyn could make the call. Typically, states have a toll-free number for reporting abuse and methods for maintaining anonymity of the reporter. After the report has been made, the state officials will follow up and investigate the situation. The teacher and nurse do not have to follow up the legal action.

Nurse Carolyn and Ms. Lorenzo should also notify the school administrator or day-care owner of the situation and ask for his or her advice. This is not the kind of problem that anyone should solve alone, due to the public nature of schools. The situation should be discussed and carefully considered. The teacher may be advised to encourage the parent to continue to volunteer in the classroom and participate in parent meetings. Or some other solution may be devised. With the help of people trained and skilled in helping the abuser—whomever he or she turns out to be—there is hope.

Ms. Lorenzo should provide a responsive, predictable environment for Alexandria so she feels safe and cared for. Ms. Lorenzo can act as Alexandria's primary provider—a person who provides repeated and consistently warm responsiveness—so the child understands that she can obtain comfort from adults through appropriate social relationships. Ms. Lorenzo should help Alexandria express herself and understand her range of emotions.

Multiple-Choice Questions

1. a. It is particularly helpful to take the time to record informal observations of children as they play and participate in activities throughout the day. The implications for doing this on a regular basis are profound because these mini-reports can potentially be used in creating instructional tasks that are developmentally appropriate for the child.

2. c. The National Association for the Education of Young Children's (NAEYC) guidelines for developmentally-appropriate assessment include the principles that children should be assessed for what they can do independently as well as what they can do with help from other children or adults. The guidelines also state that assessment relies on observations of development and performance during authentic activities, and that multiple sources of relevant information should be relied upon.

3. a. The natural development and inquisitive nature of children lead the Reggio Emilia philosophy. The school, which focuses on preschool and primary education, originated in Italy; however, it has spread throughout the world. The approach is based on the principles that children should help control their learning as they learn through experiences; children must be encouraged to explore their environment and relationships with others; and children should be given endless ways to express themselves.

4. a. Vygotsky believed that learning occurs on a continuum. On one end of the continuum was the child's ability to solve problems on his or her own. On the other end was the child's ability to solve the problem with a maximum amount of adult help or peer collaborative assistance. He called this continuum the *zone of proximal development*, or ZPD. He believed children should work within this ZPD for optimum learning.

5. a. Invented by Wood and Middleton (not by Vygotsky, as is commonly assumed), the term *scaffolding* consists of involving children in joint problem solving with an adult or another, more knowledgeable, peer. As the two collaborate toward the common goal, the child gains new understandings and is guided by the adult, who points out the bridge between the child's prior knowledge and the new information.

6. a. Gender differences have been found to influence cognitive development. Boys are at greater risk for language disorders, reading and spelling difficulties, attention-concentration deficiencies, oral language problems, memory sequencing problems, directional confusion, and linguistic deficiencies. Boys can be anywhere from 6 to 18 months behind their female same-age peers.

7. b. Piaget, a developmental constructivist who thought that development led learning, saw cognitive development as the result of maturation and experience. He proposed that children move through a series of developmental stages.

8. d. Constructivist-based classrooms provide a multitude of opportunities for meaningful discussions and explorations involving both teacher-child and child-child collaborative and cooperative learning. Activities related to the curriculum are designed to be useful and engaging to the children.

9. c. Maslow was a humanist who believed that humans strive for the highest level of consciousness and wisdom they can reach. To achieve their highest levels, however, first their basic needs must be met. Maslow believed educators must respond to the potential all students have to reach self-actualization, the highest level of Maslow's hierarchy of needs.

10. d. NAEYC promotes a variety of resources for early childhood professional development. Their website (www.naeyc.org) offers links to resources and information on their annual convention, publications, and training sessions. Membership benefits include reduced rates on conference registrations, access to the association's network of affiliate groups, and subscription to their peer-reviewed professional journals.

11. a. Teachers can encourage the building of classroom communities that instill respect, responsibility, and compassion by modeling and expecting caring and fairness among all members of the classroom community. Rich classroom communities build a foundation for cognitive, emotional, and social growth and development.

12. d. Computers and other forms of technology should be placed in classrooms where teachers have been trained in integrating them successfully into the curriculum. Simply dumping computers into a classroom and expecting children to use them on their own can be highly inappropriate and a waste of funds. The effects of technology on learning should be closely monitored.

13. d. Direct instruction, commonly referred to as DI, is an instructional method that is characterized by explicit, systematic curriculum design; a prescribed script for the teacher to read and follow; ability grouping; accelerated student progress through a fast pace and efficiency; frequent assessment; and careful monitoring of embedded professional development.

14. a. The child is the center of Bronfenbrenner's ecological model of child development. The model proposes that a child interacts and is connected with his or her family, early education and care, health, and other community learning. Child development is influenced by what the child experiences in various settings. These experiences are called *proximal processes* and are considered by Bronfenbrenner to be essential in human development.

15. c. The ADA (Public Law 101-336) prohibits discrimination against people with disabilities. It was signed into law in 1990 by President George Bush.

16. d. Intrinsic motivation suggests students are motivated through their own accord, as opposed to being extrinsically motivated by some outside fuel or motivating factor. Examples of intrinsic motivation would be studying something just because you are interested in it, not because you want any recognition or reward for learning; doing something just because you feel it is the right thing to do; and creatively composing a poem to express your inner feelings.

17. a. Bloom's Taxonomy categorizes educational objectives into three domains. The affective domain relates to emotions and feelings; the psychomotor domain includes development in behavior and skills; and the cognitive domain involves the skills traditional education tends to focus on (e.g., knowledge, comprehension, application, analysis, synthesis, and evaluation).

18. b. The deficit model of teaching assumes children do not learn or do not understand something because they are lacking in some way. The deficit model contrasts the idea that a teacher's role is to facilitate understanding and learning by drawing out learners' tacit knowledge.

19. a. Service learning is a teaching method that integrates instruction and reflection with meaningful community service. The objective of this type of hands-on learning is to transform all involved—the community members, educators, and students. It offers participants opportunities to address the needs, concerns, and ambitions of their community.

20. b. Teachers must know and understand child development across various disciplines, not just in the cognitive realm. Being a teacher involves responding to a child emotionally, physically, cognitively, and socially. To most effectively support a child's overall development, teachers must be aware of the differences in children's development and how they influence their learning. Children develop at different rates. Being able to recognize where a child is developmentally will help the teacher know how to scaffold the child's learning across disciplines.

21. d. Teachers who model confidence in accepting challenges and solving problems can influence students' development of self-esteem. Self-esteem refers to how one values or feels about him- or herself, not others. We typically identify children as having high or low self-esteem. Interactions with others can influence one's self-concept, or how we think about ourselves.

22. a. When feeding an infant, positions do vary based on the age, physical size, movement patterns, and postural tone of the infant. Unless an infant is being bottle- or breast-fed, he or she should be positioned as upright as possible. Avoid causing the child's body to extend by applying hand pressure to the back of his or her head while feeding. Finally, use nipples with regular-sized holes to avoid causing the infant to choke by sucking too much liquid.

23. d. It is best to teach rudimentary communication behaviors by systematically manipulating and designing the environment to provide opportunities for the child to communicate his or her needs. For example, the teacher could display high-preference items the child typically desires. Ignoring, rewarding, and punishing the child are not positively effective methods for teaching communication behaviors.

24. b. One of the most important components of co-teaching is to schedule time to plan and evaluate the co-teaching experience. Co-teaching without planning what will be taught, who will do what, and what needs to be done to prepare for the experience can be highly ineffective. Evaluating the experience will encourage teachers to reflect on what is working and what should be adjusted. Through planning, the activities will be planned in detail. Most teachers do not find they need to practice or write out lesson plans for co-teaching. Finally, teaching with someone who has a different philosophy of teaching from your own can be enlightening. You might just learn something yourself!

25. a. John Dewey is credited with the learning-by-doing theory. It proposes that curriculum should be relevant to students' lives as they act in the world. In schools in the United States during Dewey's time, children typically sat quietly and were expected to learn. Dewey proposed that children should be involved in activities to learn and understand.

26. b. Self-esteem plays an important role in learning language. When students feel they, their family, and their culture are valued, self-esteem is enhanced. Self-esteem is particularly at risk for English language learners based on the power of language in our society. Choice **b** is correct because research tells us language learning benefits from high self-esteem. There is no evidence to support the other choices.

27. a. Attribution theory proposes that learners are motivated by the belief that they can succeed with effort. To motivate children to persist, we should encourage them to keep trying because they are capable and competent as long as they keep trying. Success involves effort; it is not ensured by luck or talent.

28. a. All of the activities across content areas revolve around the same theme: travel. Therefore, this is an example of a thematic unit. Individual lesson plans might be written for each activity, and mapping and collaboration might also be incorporated into the theme, but these are not the correct choices.

29. a. This choice extends the conversation so that students are asked to apply what they know about their own fire station to what they learned in the book about fire stations. By answering this question, students would show what they understand about fire stations and firefighters. The other questions do not probe the content understandings of the firefighters theme. They go in different directions, related to dogs' names, future dreams, and opinions about the story.

30. b. The three components are selection (choosing the appropriate tools for your purpose), administration (giving the test and collecting the data), and utilization (analyzing and using the data to inform instruction). The other choices are incorrect.

31. b. Choice **b** is the correct level because the child says one word to indicate her choice.

32. a. NAEYC stands for the National Association for the Education of Young Children, which is the world's largest organization that works with young children. It has nearly 80,000 members.

33. c. Choice **c** is correct. Students whose culture and cultural knowledge are not recognized tend to become oppositional. Schools often act in ways that put children who are not involved in the dominant culture to a disadvantage. School support and recognition of students' culture and language are prime factors in school success for these students. The other choices are not supported by evidence.

34. d. B.F. Skinner's operant conditioning refers to changing a behavior through the use of reinforcement that is given after the desired response. The hierarchy of need refers to Maslow's levels of personal growth. Self-esteem and punishment do not make sense here.

35. d. The child was identified as having a cognitive need, so the best person to collaborate with when planning this activity would be the special education teacher, who would best be able to help the teacher plan methods to manage the flow of the student from group to group so that he understands the process that is intended.

36. a. Giving students 3 to 5 seconds to process a question will increase the quality and quantity of their responses dramatically. We should not assume children who do not raise their hands do not know the answer. It is good practice to call on children with their hands raised as well as those who do not raise their hands. It's important to ask a variety of types of questions to encourage low- and high-level thinking. Inquiry questions are important, but it is also important to ask simple recall questions to check students' text comprehension.

37. d. With spiral questioning, the teacher leads students through a step-by-step process, working through basic questions to build a foundation for more interpretive questions. Inquiry questioning would be one of the higher levels of questioning that could be included in spiral questioning. Choices **b** and **c** are made up.

38. d. While restating, interpreting, and inquiring about something a student says all signify to the student that the teacher is actively listening, starting a new topic might indicate that the teacher was not even paying attention to what the child was talking about.

39. a. Assessment systems that identify students with developmental delays at an early age can inform a teacher's instruction and support children who are at risk with the aid of intervention services. Children with delays should be mainstreamed in the least-restrictive environment rather than removed from the regular classroom. The purpose is not to label students but to support them with needed interventions. Effective systems help teachers focus on the needs of all children.

40. b. NAEYC informs members and all early childhood educators about choice **b**, but not the other three choices, which are developmentally inappropriate for this age range.

41. a. The purpose of a mentor is to guide a colleague toward performance success. Typically, new teachers are assigned a mentor to model and counsel them through new experiences. The other choices are incorrect because they do not intentionally foster one's career.

42. b. The example of two girls reading together represents cooperative learning because they are learning by interacting with each other. They are not avoiding or competing. They are dependent on each other rather than independent of each other.

43. c. The power of choice is highly motivating for children. In this scenario, there is no evidence of a reward or punishment. We aren't told Rocky becomes tired, either.

44. a. Educators use learning standards to guide their instruction. Having learning standards helps educators know what children should be learning at various levels. Although they do help teachers identify where students should be at various ages and grades, and may indicate when a child is above, at, or below grade level, the standards are not an assessment in themselves. Therefore, choice **a** is the best answer.

45. b. This is an example of an all-class response system. This type of response helps the teacher quickly observe what students understand or know. It engages all students in the class. Choices **a** and **c** are made up. A Socratic seminar is a system of student-led, small-group discussion.

46. a. Proxemics refers to what we call one's "personal space." Choice **a** indicates that the teacher stands closer to the student than usual. She is invading his personal space to get his attention. Choices **b** and **c** do not relate to proxemics. Choice **d** mentions that the teacher touches the child's arm; this is an example of haptics—communicating through touch—rather than proxemics.

47. c. Directly observing the child in the library with a book and checking off evidence of print concepts is the most effective way. Parents may be able to give you some information, but they may not have the educational background to understand the components of concept of print. Paper-and-pencil quizzes are not developmentally appropriate for preschoolers, and anecdotal notes, while helpful, would not be feasible to do during a read-aloud.

48. b. While all of the topics are important, the best way to spend parent-teacher conference time would be to discuss the concerns that the parents have about the child's health, development, and behavior.

49. c. This description best meets the definition of a study group. Groups of teachers form a study group to support their practices and each other. The other choices are incorrect.

50. d. Tina Marie has the right to be able to easily maneuver around in her wheelchair and have the same advantages her peers have, like a table to eat or work at. Accommodations do not include being assigned to a male teacher for the purpose of helping with the wheelchair.

51. c. Choice **c** confirms for David that the grandmother values his developing conception of print. He already understands that there is a connection between marks people make on paper and what they say. The other choices do not reflect the grandmother's appreciation of his efforts.

52. a. Modeling and talking through the procedure, using the terms *sink* and *float*, would be the best way to ensure that the children understand the concepts. Young children of this age cannot yet read written instructions and may have difficulty following numerous directions without first seeing and learning the process through modeling. Allowing them to explore is a valid inquiry approach, but in this scenario, they would not necessarily learn the concepts and meet the teacher's objective.

53. c. Choices **a**, **b**, and **d** are all valid reasons for questioning children. We can use questioning as an informal assessment to determine what students know and do not know. Leading them through a series of questions can help them better understand a concept. When we use new vocabulary in our questions and model language usage, we can encourage children to use the new words in their responses, too, thereby encouraging their oral language development. Using questioning to interrogate children about their families, though, is an unethical use of the technique. While getting to know the family and its culture is helpful to teachers, the word *interrogate* connotes prying into the personal life of a family.

54. d. The only choice supported by research is that nonverbal communication does vary between cultures, but facial expressions are largely similar across cultures.

55. a. This practice is an example of getting students to assess themselves by reflecting on what they have learned each day. Divergent thinking refers to thinking in an unusual way. Problem solving relates to the process of working through details of a problem in order to reach a solution. Risk taking is the tendency to engage in unsafe behaviors.

56. d. An example of choice **d** would be to use results from a screening tool to determine the cause of a child's developmental delay. Choice **a** is incorrect because diagnostic tools can help identify the cause of a child's developmental delay, but they should not be conducted to determine the child's readiness for kindergarten. Choices **b** and **c** are incorrect because each assessment tool exists for a specific purpose.

57. b. A reflective journal is a record or diary of professional and personal reflections that a teacher keeps to inform and improve her teaching. The other choices are incorrect.

58. c. Choice **c** is correct because effective communication must be present to even begin discussion of choices **a** and **b**. Choice **d** may not be a goal or concern of a collaboration. Members may take turns leading the group.

59. b. If the students have never experienced the seashore, the teacher should build their prior knowledge by showing them pictures and having them talk about playing on any beach. Just reading the story will not prepare them for the vocabulary they will hear in the story. Quizzing them would not be age appropriate for early childhood. Playing in the sandbox would be beneficial if beach toys, shells, and other ocean artifacts are included, and students could learn the vocabulary to identify these items, but that is not mentioned in this choice.

60. a. Protection from bullying and harassment would be included under equal access to education. Equal access also covers disability, gender, and age issues. The other choices are incorrect because they do not refer to bullying.

61. d. In choice **d**, the student is asked to transfer what he knows about animals' heights in the real world to what he remembers about the storybook character Clifford. Therefore, he is being asked to transfer knowledge from one context to another. Choices **a** and **b** are low-level responses. Choice **c** is an inquiry question.

62. a. An incident analysis involves the description and analysis of an authentic and experienced incident for the purpose of reflecting on what happened, how it could be avoided, or what should be done to solve any remaining problem. None of the other choices fits this description.

63. d. Choice **d** is developmentally appropriate. Gathering information through ongoing observation data over time provides an authentic, contextualized picture of the child's progress. The other choices are developmentally inappropriate for early childhood settings.

64. d. There is no evidence in the second passage that the writer supports the use of developmentally inappropriate tools or standardized tests with young children. Yes, the author supports testing, but he could also believe that the testing must be authentic and appropriate. The author of the first passage might remark that the second author has never been in a classroom before, but we have no proof of that. The only choice that is supported by evidence from the second passage is choice **d**.

65. b. Generally, the first author is concerned about developmental appropriateness in instruction and assessment. That is why choice **b** is correct. There is no evidence in the passage to support any of the other three choices.

66. c. Choice **c** is correct because both authors are voicing strong opinions and advocating for their educational beliefs. While the other three choices are roles that teachers can take as educational leaders in the greater community, the expression of their opinions connects most closely to advocacy.

67. a. Confidentiality and privacy refer to the entrustment of anonymity. Schools take confidentiality and privacy issues very seriously.

68. b. The most effective choice is **b** because the mathematics workshop is not related to what she is currently teaching, the photography course does not relate directly to her teaching, and we don't know the nature of the blog. Working in a professional learning community with preschool teachers would be the most direct plan for Martha at this time.

69. d. Research shows that the availability and modeling of the use of books in the home does support a child's interest in them. Taking away Jon's toys or buying him books in place of a birthday present might make him resistant to reading and be counterproductive.

70. c. While some say biting is a normal part of childhood development, you want to take the parent's concern very seriously. Inviting the parent to talk with you and the school psychologist or a health official is the best first step. The parent is looking for your help with solutions. Choices **b** and **d** may be used as follow-up recommendations.

Praxis II Scoring

Evaluate how you did on this practice exam by scoring your constructed responses and your multiple-choice answers. Bring your constructed responses and the scoring guide to a trusted friend to score so you can better see how you did. Reflect on the types of questions you missed most frequently.

The key to doing well on the Praxis II is to practice, read widely, and stay organized and focused. You have self-assessed your strengths and weaknesses and learned how to manage the various types of questions on the test. Enter the exam with confidence, knowing you are ready and equipped to do your very best!

PRINCIPLES OF LEARNING AND TEACHING STUDY CHART PRACTICE EXAM 3	
STUDENTS AS LEARNERS	QUESTIONS
Student Development and Learning Process	4, 7, 9, 14, 20, 22, 25
Students as Diverse Learners	6, 15, 26, 33, 42, 50, 59
Student Motivation and Learning Environment	11, 16, 21, 27, 34, 43, 51
INSTRUCTIONAL PROCESS	
Planning Instruction	17, 28, 35, 44, 52
Instructional Strategies	3, 5, 8, 13, 19
Questioning Techniques	36, 37, 45, 53, 61
Communication Techniques	12, 23, 29, 38, 46, 54
ASSESSMENT	
Assessment and Evaluation Strategies	2, 18, 30, 39, 47, 55, 63
Assessment Tools	1, 31, 40, 48, 56, 64, 65
Professional Development, Leadership, and Community	10, 24, 32, 40, 41, 57, 58, 60, 62, 66, 67, 68, 69, 70
ANALYSIS OF INSTRUCTIONAL SCENARIOS	
Students as Learners	CR1
Instructional Process	CR2
Assessment	CR3
Professional Development, Leadership, and Community	CR4

ANSWERS AND EXPLANATIONS FOR PRACTICE EXAM 4

Scoring the Constructed-Response Case History Questions

Constructed responses are scored on a range from 0 to 2. First, this section presents the criteria for scoring constructed responses to the PLT case histories. Then, it provides sample level 2 responses for each question based on the scoring criteria that follow.

Criteria for Scoring
For a score of 2, the response must

- show that the writer has a thorough understanding of the parts of the case history that relate to the question.
- appropriately address all components of the question.
- provide a strong explanation (if requested) and support it with relevant evidence.
- provide evidence that the writer possesses strong knowledge of pedagogical concepts, facts, theories, methodologies, or procedures relevant to the question.

For a score of 1, the response must

- show that the writer has a basic understanding of the parts of the case history that relate to the question.
- appropriately address one component of the question.
- provide a weak explanation (if requested) but still be supported with relevant evidence.
- provide evidence that the writer possesses some knowledge of pedagogical concepts, facts, theories, methodologies, or procedures relevant to the question.

For a score of 0, the response must

- show that the writer misunderstood the parts of the case history that relate to the question.
- fail to address the question.
- not be supported by relevant evidence.
- provide little evidence that the writer possesses some knowledge of pedagogical concepts, facts, theories, methodologies, or procedures relevant to the question.

Answers and Explanations

PLT Case History 4.1: Misao Tanaka

1. Mr. Sato should be careful not to instruct and measure only the skills and abilities valued by the dominant culture but to be flexible and respectful of individual differences. Misao's background and experiences are quite different from those of his new environment. Careful instruction and assessment must take into consideration information about Misao's development to date, the sociocultural values and context of his family, and his family's cultural background. Active family involvement in the learning process should be encouraged to minimize cul-

tural biases. Also, rather than comparing Misao's development to what his English-speaking peers are doing, he should be viewed in relation to the developmental patterns of children from similar backgrounds. When possible, his comprehension and skills should be assessed in his first language rather than expecting him initially to demonstrate his understandings through oral or written English. Response expectations may be readjusted as Misao becomes increasingly confident and competent in English. In this way, Mr. Sato will get the most comprehensive view of Misao's learning strengths and needs.

There are various theories related to the best practices for instructing and assessing multilingual learners. Some believe that second-language learners learn best when immersed into the second language; others see a more guided transition as better suiting the needs of young learners. Mr. Sato's classroom has its advantages and disadvantages for Misao. Mr. Sato knows some Japanese language and is aware of many of the cultural traditions and practices that have formed Misao's background. This connection between teacher and learner should benefit Misao's ability to make sense of his new world and Mr. Sato's understanding of what Misao is going through. On the other hand, in a regular classroom instruction and communication among adults and peers will largely be in English. Misao's content and skills learning and his ability to assimilate into the classroom culture will be hindered by his inability to comprehend the language.

2. First, we know that the concepts of print knowledge that children bring with them from their native language can be transferred to second-language writing. For example, if Misao understands that a complete sentence has a subject and a verb, he can transfer that knowledge when he writes in English. Also, we know that strong

first-language literacy is a significant factor in second-language acquisition. One strategy that would encourage Misao to transfer this knowledge would be to have him write the names of his classmates on separate index cards. Then, he could begin a collection of action verbs cards. He could play games with the children where he chooses and reads one name and one verb. The classmate performs the action that Misao reads. Misao could practice forming sentences using this strategy of constructing sentences from sentence parts. Second, we know that children's writing appears to pass through phases of spelling development. This holds true for learning a second language, also. One strategy that would facilitate Misao's spelling development would be to encourage him to use drawings to express himself and meanings he wants to convey. Then he should be helped to use letters to label his drawings and to represent words. Eventually, he can learn common spelling patterns as he moves into conventional spelling.

PLT Case History 4.2: Ms. Isabella

3. Ms. Isabella can help students develop their reading comprehension skills by providing structured lessons on how to find the main idea in a social studies content passage; how to take notes by asking themselves who, what, when, where, how, and why; how to analyze key concepts and vocabulary in a passage; and how to summarize content. Through explicit instruction while learning about the content, students will be taught to break text down into small component parts and how to determine the features of each. Students will practice activating their prior knowledge before reading and making predictions about what they read. They will be given models of the skills and then will be guided as they practice the skills themselves. Generally, rather than teaching comprehension skills in isolation through decontextualized ac-

tivities, students will learn these skills along with and through content knowledge.

Ms. Isabella can help students improve their writing skills through content instruction by teaching students the components of specific writing genres, such as reports, poetic forms, folk tales, journals, and so on. For example, she could teach students how to write in a narrative voice. Students could keep a personal journal in the voice of an eighteenth-century child as the class reenacts crossing the country in a covered wagon. Students can demonstrate their content knowledge and employ the vocabulary of the content area as they internalize the construction of knowledge.

4. Two advantages of integrating computer technology into content learning are its motivating appeal to most students and the fact that it includes a wealth of information that is geared toward a range of developmental levels and skills. To capitalize on the motivational advantage, Ms. Isabella could promote learning by having students use iPads or smartphones to research information; students could also be assigned to take pictures related to something they are learning in math, science, or social studies, and bring them to share in class. These forms of technology have become part of the students' identity. Many students today have this kind of technology at their fingertips and are motivated when allowed to use it in class. To capitalize on the advantage that technology offers a wealth of perspectives and information, Ms. Isabella could assign students to research multiple perspectives on selected topics online and prepare an oral group presentation on the topic to the class representing, comparing, and contrasting multiple views. These types of opportunities help students practice their language skills and use newly acquired vocabulary in appropriate contexts. These types of activities will help students internalize concepts as they add to their content-area understandings.

Multiple-Choice Questions

1. c. Gardner originally presented eight multiple intelligences. Children who possess bodily-kinesthetic intelligence learn well through sensations received from their body, such as moving and touching. They tend to be physically gifted. The other intelligences are verbal/linguistic, logical/mathematical, visual/spatial, musical, interpersonal, intrapersonal, and naturalist.

2. d. Current philosophy emphasizes that children learn best when they actively collaborate with peers to construct meaning during hands-on manipulation and creation. While all of the choices would most likely cause learning, choice **d** would be most effective.

3. b. It is the teacher's responsibility to search his or her extensive repertoire of teaching strategies to find which work best with children with special needs. There won't be one solution to meet their needs; however, the teacher should rely on the strengths of the children to determine which strategies will work best. Typically, the special education teacher writes IEPs. Mainstreaming children with special needs among children with no special needs is the best method to foster social and academic growth among all children.

4. a. IDEA mandates that each child with a disability must receive appropriate public education that is free and reflects the least restrictive environment for the child based on his or her needs. The statute also mandates that children with disabilities be educated alongside children without disabilities unless the severity or nature of the disability interferes with the ability to successfully provide services and aid.

5. a. Classroom design can be used to meet instructional goals and should reflect students' needs (e.g., students with visual or hearing impairments may be best suited sitting near the front of the room). It is a good idea to change seating at least every couple of months so that children are shuffled from the periphery to the center of the classroom, from the back to the front, and from one group of peers to another. Sometimes it is a good idea to group students with unfamiliar peers so they can make new friends. Provide ample space for mobility between seats; however, hopefully you will want to encourage children to communicate and collaborate with peers throughout the day. There is no evidence to support a preference for alternating boy-girl seating.

6. a. Lesson plan objectives should align with national and state learning standards. They may need to be adjusted to the needs of some students, so it cannot be said that they meet all needs. Objectives describe what the student will know or be able to do at the completion of the lesson, and they should align with appropriate assessment criteria to determine if the objectives have been met.

7. b. The best example of a way to activate prior knowledge is by interactively reading and discussing a book about the seashore with the child. Teacher guidance and scaffolding will help to pull out key concepts and themes of the sea. The other choices will also activate prior knowledge, but the added guidance from the teacher makes choice **b** the best answer.

8. a. According to Moll, funds of knowledge are the bodies of knowledge that underlie a family's household activities. The knowledge may be productive in that it is related to getting something done; it may be lived in that it relates to daily living practices; it may also relate to learning something. Funds of knowledge are accumulated historically and developed culturally.

9. d. With holistic scoring, which is usually very appropriate for evaluating projects and written pieces, the scorer assigns a score based on his or her overall impression or quality of the piece. Elements (e.g., grammar, spelling, content, and clarity of a written essay) are not separated out or scored separately. In contrast, analytic scoring breaks the elements down and scores them separately.

10. c. *Brown v. Board of Education* was a 1954 Supreme Court decision that struck down the "separate but equal" policy that blacks and whites should be housed in separate schools. It was not the first attack on this policy. As early as 1849 a suit was filed against school racial segregation. The decision did have far-reaching implications. It is credited as having galvanized civil rights issues not only across the United States but around the world. It is said to have been a catalyst in having launched the Civil Rights movement in America.

11. a. John Dewey (1859–1952) promoted progressive education that spawned experiential education, such as outdoor learning and authentic applications for learning. Visiting a "living museum" would allow students to experience firsthand how people lived during the Colonial Period.

12. c. The *McGuffey Readers*, published by Truman and Smith's publishing company in the nineteenth century, were written by an educator named Rev. William Holmes McGuffey. The series of eclectic readers included readings from the Bible, contained pictures and lessons, and were highly moralistic in nature.

13. a. Blended literacy instruction combines the emergent literacy and scientifically based reading research approaches to early literacy instruction. Emergent literacy programs promote developmentally appropriate activities that promote literacy learning, while scientifically based reading research targets instruction that helps children learn necessary skills.

14. d. Computers can benefit all children, not just high achievers. However, when used inappropriately in a classroom, computers can not only be unsafe—even when schools use advanced filtering systems—but they can also distract students from reaching instructional objectives. Many teachers feel ill prepared to use technology effectively in the classroom.

15. c. Allowing students to demonstrate their understandings of a topic in a variety of ways (e.g., creating a model, writing a poem, taking a test) is an example of differentiated instruction. This approach allows students to show what knowledge they have constructed to the best of their ability. The other choices may lead to differentiated instruction if approached in such a way by the instructor, but the choices do not indicate they will be as they stand.

16. b. Measurement theory encourages educators to think about what their data (i.e., test scores, rubric grades, observations) mean. Educators must consider the measurement's validity, reliability, scoring procedures, and biases. It applies across the grade levels and does not assume all tests are either valid or invalid.

17. a. A primary resource is an original account or record of an event. It provides firsthand information from someone who was there when the event occurred. Eleanor Roosevelt's letter is the only choice that represents firsthand experience of the original event.

18. a. Visual literacy represents the ability to understand and communicate through visual means, such as maps, drawings, symbols, hypertext, and videos. K–6 instruction in visual literacy should include the analysis of advertisements because lives are infiltrated with them. Students should learn to critique advertised messages to be informed consumers. Visual literacy views students as constructors of knowledge who interpret what they view to make personal meanings rather than simply receive knowledge.

19. b. Simply put, formative assessments assess *for* learning, whereas summative assessments are assessments *of* learning. Choices **a**, **c**, and **d** all assess what was learned from a particular unit of study. Choice **b** would be used by a teacher to inform his or her instruction.

20. d. Graphic organizers may be used before, during, and after reading and instruction to clarify, organize, and generate ideas and thinking. Choices **a**, **b**, and **c** are all good examples of ways to use graphic organizers.

21. c. Scope and sequence refers to the organizational structure of curriculum that accounts for what and when content and skills should be taught over time, as exemplified in choice **c**. Choice **a** refers to scientific curriculum making. Think-Pair-Share is a teaching strategy to encourage participation and critical thinking, not a type of curriculum design. Choice **d** is an example of cooperative learning, but it does not imply any learning over time or any sequence to learning.

22. d. Phonological awareness refers to the ability to hear and manipulate the sounds in oral language. It includes the examples listed in choice **d**.

23. d. The postings are from a blog, which means that Casie does not know the authority with which the bloggers post. She does not know the bloggers' background, knowledge of the topic, biases, and so on. So, rather than take any stance on the issue now—either for or against foreign language classes—she should research and investigate the issue further, exploring multiple perspectives. She should consult peer-reviewed professional journals and other reliable resources.

24. a. The author of the second passage would most likely feel that Spanish-speaking children should learn English, based on the blogger's last two sentences. Choices **b**, **c**, and **d** sound like statements that the first author would more likely support.

25. a. The student draws on her rich knowledge base to apply the prior knowledge she has about word analysis and context clues.

26. d. Macy may be allowed a private location, a scribe, and additional time. These are accommodations that allow students identified with learning disabilities to complete the same assignments and tests as other students. They do not alter the content or give students any unfair advantages over other students. Macy would not be excluded from being expected to take the test altogether. Accommodations make it possible for students to show what they know or are capable of without being impeded by their learning disability.

27. c. Thorndike's theory of learning was based on his work with animals. He conducted experiments and observed that learning is incremental, reward is a stronger motivator than punishment, and cause and effect influence learning.

28. c. When educators base instruction on standards and connect lesson objectives to them, they guide instruction and curriculum. The purpose of standards is not to test students or to teach theory. They also do not motivate students.

29. a. Choice **a** reflects the evaluation level of Bloom's Taxonomy, which is the highest order of thinking. Choice **b** is the knowledge level, choice **c** is the comprehension level, and choice **d** is the application level. From lowest to highest levels of thinking order, Bloom's levels are knowledge, comprehension, application, analysis, synthesis, and evaluation.

30. b. Including all students in classroom discussions shows they are all valued contributors to the dialogue. However, calling on a student to make him feel uncomfortable in any way is a detrimental communication technique.

31. a. Formal assessments are standardized, as are norm- and criterion-referenced tests. Choices **c** and **d** are informal assessments.

32. d. A subtest may consist of just a few questions. The fewer the number of questions in a subtest, the less reliable the scores are. The other choices are not real components of standardized tests.

33. a. A mentor is usually assigned to a new teacher to "show her the ropes" and introduce her to school policies during her first years in a new school. Whereas this mentee would have her own classroom, an intern would work under the supervision of a supervising teacher. A critical friend is a collaborating colleague. Critical friends may work on research or self-study together as equal partners.

34. b. Choices **a** and **d** could be answered with either *yes* or *no*. Good research questions can lead to improved teaching. They should be higher-order questions that seek reasons and relationships. Of course, choice **c** would not be an action research question to explore in a classroom setting.

35. d. Choice **d** is correct. Choices **a** through **c** refer to reliability.

36. a. The description reflects curriculum-based measurement. It is used to give the teacher a fast and frequent method to measure progress in the basic academic subjects.

37. b. Personal space is all about the physical proximity of one person to another. It doesn't relate to head positions or eye contact. Just handing a student a pencil would most likely not threaten his personal space.

38. c. Never put a student on the spot or try to embarrass him, especially in front of his peers. Questioning purposes do involve all of the other choices, though.

39. d. Watson emphasized the nurture side of the nature versus nurture debate by believing that nothing was instinctual, including love. He believed that love was a conditioned response. He proposed that children should be treated like young adults and not coddled by their parents. Showing too much love would not prepare them for the real world.

40. b. Cindy is a cooperative learner because she learns by interacting with others. She is not avoiding or competing. She is dependent on others rather than independent of them.

41. d. To encourage students' motivation to perform uninteresting, inauthentic learning activities, teachers should explain why the tasks are valuable. Providing a rationale for why the activities are useful to them either now or in the future helps motivate students to engage their efforts.

42. b. Research shows that a longer wait-time causes decreased interruptions, increased student-to-student interactions, lengthened responses, and a greater number of higher cognitive responses.

43. a. It is true that in some cultures direct eye contact can be a sign of disrespect or intimacy. This could explain why a student avoids making eye contact with a teacher. The other choices are inaccurate.

44. c. Criterion-referenced testing measures specific and relevant behaviors that have been mastered, not the person's relative standing in the class or group. It measures what Molly is capable of spelling compared to her own past performance, not compared with the scores of other children in the class.

45. d. This is a description of a scaled score, which is a converted raw score. The purpose of scaled scores is to provide a consistent way to report scores on a test.

46. a. Choice **a** is the most complete response. To prepare for the observation, the peers should talk about the lesson planned and a focus for the observation. After the observation, the peers should meet to share, discuss, and reflect on the feedback that is offered. Choices **b** through **d** do not reflect the most beneficial process for peer observation. They do, however, offer suggestions to complement the process.

47. b. Choice **b** is correct because the media specialist has the knowledge needed to survey the availability of resources in the school and also in the community. If the media specialist knows ahead of time, he can arrange for interlibrary loans of the materials the library is lacking.

48. d. Peer assessment can be influenced by many factors, including social relationships among students. It may be too difficult for students to give their friends critical feedback if they perceive it as negative rather than helpful.

49. a. Teachers should go over scoring rubrics before using them to grade students' writing. Choices **b** through **d** reflect advantages of such a system.

50. c. When children learn song lyrics or mnemonic devices (i.e., "I before E except after C or when sounding like A as in neighbor and weigh"), they tend to remember the information longer. The other choices reflect other intelligences.

51. b. In choice **b**, the teacher provides feedback to redirect Carolina's thinking. She also recognizes that New York City is a viable response, which encourages Carolina to try again. Feedback encourages achievement when it redirects, probes, and acknowledges.

52. a. The prize awarded to the best poem in choice **a** is an example of extrinsic motivation. The other choices are all intrinsic motivators because they value the enjoyment of writing and sharing the poems with others.

53. d. Statistics show that poverty, or low socioeconomic status, greatly influences the academic achievement across cultures, races, and ethnicities.

54. b. This child is exhibiting Kohlberg's Level 1.1 obedience and punishment orientation, in which he focuses on the direct consequences of an action on himself. The other stages represent higher levels of moral development.

55. a. Teachers should avoid competing with parents in any way. If educators use strategies to build respect and trust, then teachers and families can work together to solve any problems as they arise and to promote a rich learning experience for all.

56. d. IRA stands for the International Reading Association. Choice **b** stands for the Association of Childhood Education International, which is a large professional association related to elementary teachers, but not specifically a language arts and reading group. The other acronyms are not related to professional reading associations.

57. c. Choice **c** is precise. The other choices do not identify stanine scores.

58. b. Choices **a**, **c**, and **d** would cause students to retell or relate rather than reflect on their learning.

59. a. Prediction strategies can help the listener prepare for the story. Choices **b** through **d** are effective listening strategies also, but they are not prelistening strategies done before listening.

60. a. Ms. Lassonde is most likely asking this question to see what the students already know about the subject.

61. d. The traditional classroom setting of rows of student desks facing the teacher's desk is the least inclusive setup for a classroom. Choices **a** through **c** are examples of ways to arrange the physical space in a classroom to accommodate the needs of diverse learners.

62. c. It was Section 504 that first guaranteed certain rights to children and people with disabilities. The other choices are incorrect.

63. b. During the industry versus inferiority stage of Erikson's stages of psychosocial development, students focus on the relationships they form in school and with neighbors. The essential question during this stage is: "Am I capable of surviving in the world?" The other choices represent earlier stages.

64. d. Whether educators support or do not support a bill, there are avenues for advocating for or against it throughout the process.

65. a. Since the theme will benefit her students and she did make a commitment to her colleagues, the best choice would be to openly communicate the situation with her colleagues. If they agree that the project can be postponed, Candice can pick up with the group when the conference is done. Always keep communication open, be up front with your colleagues, and stand by your commitments.

66. c. Choice **c** would be the best way because the other three choices would not allow the teacher to assess whether the objective was met. It would be difficult for a student to portray a passage's main idea through a performance or a portfolio. A teacher would not be able to observe the student's understanding of a passage's main idea.

67. c. We cannot assume children know how to listen respectfully until we teach them how to do this and provide ample opportunities for them to practice their body language in authentic listening situations. Providing a self-assessment checklist that identifies components of respectful listening (i.e., eye contact, relaxed facial expression, sitting calmly) is an effective way to encourage students to develop these skills.

68. a. Although grades should be de-emphasized, holding grades back and not providing feedback will not motivate students. Students need to know whether they are on the right learning path in order to continue exerting effort. Choices **b** through **d** are effective ways to help students develop self-motivation.

69. d. Intellectual freedom is the idea that in a democracy, every individual has the right to access material, even if it represents strong opinions. Teachers and librarians must protect their students' rights to intellectual freedom by not restricting them to one chosen perspective that might represent their own perspective or bias.

70. c. Due process is required under the Individuals with Disabilities Education Act. A free, appropriate education is determined by assessment and educational needs. The other choices are inaccurate.

Praxis II Scoring

Evaluate how you did on this practice exam by scoring your constructed responses and your multiple-choice answers. Bring your constructed responses and the scoring guide to a trusted friend to score so you can better see how you did. Reflect on the types of questions you missed most frequently.

The key to doing well on the Praxis II is to practice, read widely, and stay organized and focused. You have self-assessed your strengths and weaknesses and learned how to manage the various types of questions on the test. Enter the exam with confidence, knowing that you are ready and equipped to do your very best!

PRINCIPLES OF LEARNING AND TEACHING STUDY CHART PRACTICE EXAM 4	
STUDENTS AS LEARNERS	**QUESTIONS**
Student Development and Learning Process	1, 11, 12, 16, 25, 54, 63
Students as Diverse Learners	3, 4, 15, 26, 40, 53, 62
Student Motivation and Learning Environment	8, 27, 39, 41, 52, 61, 68
INSTRUCTIONAL PROCESS	
Planning Instruction	2, 6, 14, 21, 28
Instructional Strategies	5, 7, 13, 17, 18, 20, 22
Questioning Techniques	29, 38, 42, 51, 60
Communication Techniques	30, 37, 43, 50, 59, 67
ASSESSMENT	
Assessment and Evaluation Strategies	31, 36, 44, 49, 58, 66
Assessment Tools	9, 19, 32, 35, 45, 48, 57
Professional Development, Leadership, and Community	10, 23, 24, 33, 34, 46, 47, 55, 56, 64, 65, 69, 70
ANALYSIS OF INSTRUCTIONAL SCENARIOS	
Students as Learners	CR3, 4
Instructional Process	CR2
Assessment	CR1
Professional Development, Leadership, and Community	

19 ▶ ANSWERS AND EXPLANATIONS FOR PRACTICE EXAM 5

Scoring the Constructed-Response Case History Questions

Constructed responses are scored on a range from 0 to 2. First, this section presents the criteria for scoring constructed responses to the PLT case histories. Then, it provides sample level 2 responses for each question based on the scoring criteria that follow.

Criteria for Scoring

For a score of 2, the response must

- show that the writer has a thorough understanding of the parts of the case history that relate to the question.
- appropriately address all components of the question.
- provide a strong explanation (if requested) and support it with relevant evidence.
- provide evidence that the writer possesses strong knowledge of pedagogical concepts, facts, theories, methodologies, or procedures relevant to the question.

For a score of 1, the response must

- show that the writer has a basic understanding of the parts of the case history that relate to the question.
- appropriately address one component of the question.
- provide a weak explanation (if requested) that is still supported with relevant evidence.
- provide evidence that the writer possesses some knowledge of pedagogical concepts, facts, theories, methodologies, or procedures relevant to the question.

For a score of 0, the response must

- show that the writer misunderstood the parts of the case history that relate to the question.
- fail to address the question.
- not be supported by relevant evidence.
- provide little evidence that the writer possesses some knowledge of pedagogical concepts, facts, theories, methodologies, or procedures relevant to the question.

Answers and Explanations

PLT Case History 5.1 Mr. Tenace

1. Mr. Tenace's project plan depicts these two strengths of effective planning. His plan, which is based on a state science learning standard, is well sequenced and provides various grouping opportunities. Students will construct understandings of the living systems by reading widely about them from self-selected texts and sources. They will bring what they learn to a class discussion. They will work with the support of others in small groups to illustrate one system; then, they will illustrate the other system independently. This provides the opportunity for students to learn in the safety of a small group and then practice the process independently. The plan provides modeling and supportive grouping, as well as opportunities to work independently, reflect, and self-assess. These are all recommended aspects of effective planning.

2. Mr. Tenace could try to equalize the roles of males and females in his science classes by modeling equal treatment of both sexes and by assigning same-sex lab partners. Based on Mrs. Parker's observation, it appears that Mr. Tenace perhaps unintentionally models unequal treatment of the sexes. He refers to the females as "young ladies that we don't want to hurt" and doesn't address the boys' banter about there being no ladies present. In essence, he is modeling for the boys that the girls are different and should be treated differently in his class. When asked if the girls had to participate in the dissection, he sidesteps the issue by saying that partners can make these decisions. Mr. Tenace should set high expectations of participation for all of his students and discuss the value of being knowledgeable about science. He could also try assigning same-sex lab partners. He stumbled upon this possible anecdote during his interviews with the students. It appears that some girls relinquish some of their power to the boys during labs and take on a helpless role themselves. It might be helpful to observe the dynamics that occur between same-sex lab partners.

PLT Case History 5.2 Kim

3. Based on what Ms. Lee has observed so far, she should begin assessing Kim, especially her ability to hear, listen to, and understand oral conversations and directions. Ms. Lee should check Kim's permanent school record to see if there has been any history of hearing loss in the past. She should check to see that a hearing examination was completed recently. If not, she may ask the school nurse if he or she could check into the

matter. Ms. Lee should also continue to observe Kim's behaviors to determine if Kim responds appropriately to one-on-one conversations. It may be that Kim has difficulty focusing in large-group situations. Or perhaps she would benefit from having her seat moved to a quieter or more central place in the room. Ms. Lee should talk with Kim to inquire if there is anything she can do to help Kim. Ms. Lee should arrange for a parent-teacher conference, in which she would share her concerns in a sensitive way, not to alarm the parent but to gain insight. She may even consult Kim's past teachers.

4. After further assessment, Ms. Lee has determined that Kim would benefit from learning listening strategies to help her be a more active listener. Two listening strategies that might help Kim develop her active listening skills are:

 a. Avoid physical distractions. Kim should learn to cut out physical distractions so that she can focus on the content of the message. She may find that closing her eyes and visualizing a story as it is being read will help her focus. Or she should try to look directly at the speaker's eyes or mouth and think about what the speaker is saying. If she does lose track of what the speaker is saying, she should just pick up the conversation or story from where the speaker is right then. It is better to refocus on the rest of the story than just give up. She will probably still be able to pick up what is being said even after a lapse in active listening. Kim could practice applying this strategy by using audiotapes of books in order to practice closing her eyes and visualizing stories. This way, she could practice self-monitoring her comprehension. When she realizes she missed something, she could rewind the tape and listen again.

 b. Write down key words that the speaker is saying to keep track of the steps, sequence, or

procedure. It may be helpful to graphically organize thoughts in a personally meaningful way as she listens. Kim could practice applying this strategy by recording the speaker. The first time Kim listens—while the recording is being made—she could apply the strategy. Then she could rewind the recording and listen again, adding to her notes.

Multiple-Choice Questions

1. c. A norm-referenced test does all of the things listed in the description of what Mr. Fortuin is describing to the parent.

2. d. Piaget's concrete operational stage is characterized by logical and concrete reasoning, organized thinking, the loss of egocentric thinking, and an inability to handle abstract reasoning.

3. a. Gagne's *The Conditions of Learning* outline the relation of appropriate instructional designs to learning objectives. There is no evidence that any of the other choices are accurate.

4. d. The No Child Left Behind Act of 2001 supports standards-based education reform. Goals 2000, which identified eight national educational goals for U.S. students that were to be achieved by the year 2000, stated that all children in the United States would start school ready to learn.

5. c. In writing workshop approaches, students select topics and participate in the writing process by reading their drafts to peers, conferring with others, and learning what it is like to be a writer and an author.

6. a. Constructivism views learning as a process whereby learners actively construct new concepts.

7. b. Accommodations are adjustments to presentation, responses, setting, timing, and pacing that help children with special needs participate in regular classrooms. They do not, however, lower the level of difficulty or the standards of achievement. Not all children with special needs require accommodations.

8. c. Scientifically-based research is required by schools seeking to use federal funds to support educational programs according to the No Child Left Behind Act of 2001.

9. d. The practices described are all excellent examples of differentiated instruction that will help the teacher respond to variances among skill levels in his classroom.

10. a. Discovery learning, a constructivist approach to learning, is based on inquiry. Jerome Bruner and John Dewey's philosophies of learning support discovery learning.

11. a. Divergent thinking involves the ability to think creatively and brainstorm many answers or solutions. The best example is choice **a** because all of the other questions have "right" and "wrong" answers.

12. b. While the six kingdoms are accurate, the concept map does not show that the student understood that the map meant to show the connections between the concepts he filled in. Concept maps illustrate the relationships among ideas. "The Six Kingdoms of Biology" heading should be in the center, with each kingdom in a circle around the main heading. There is no evidence that the student copied the information.

13. c. Culturally responsive teaching is characterized by instruction that encourages children to understand and welcome their own and other's cultures. Multiculturalism should be integrated into all subjects and skills rather than focused on only during a special themed unit. Children should be viewed as individuals, not representatives of their race who are expected to respond to questions about the race in general.

14. a. Direct instruction emphasizes carefully planned lessons that are designed around very small increments of learning. Direct instruction often involves the use of a script. It is based on the philosophy that when taught properly, all children can learn.

15. d. Choice **d** encourages the student to reflect on how his actions affected his mother. His response to this question will most likely help him understand that he is the one in control of his mother's reaction. If he wants to make his mother proud next time, he needs to take different action.

16. a. The complexity of a concept might require more time to ensure that all students understand the lesson. Unfortunately, teachers and students are not limited to teaching and learning only those things they hold particular interest in. A grade 5–9 curriculum can mandate lessons that are required content.

17. d. Choice **d** encourages the male to think about the female's reaction to the term rather than demanding he apologize or punishing him with a writing assignment.

18. a. Children are motivated by choice; therefore, choice **a** provides the most options for student selection. Choice **a** allows students to take ownership and engage themselves in meaningful learning.

19. c. Self-actualization refers to one's desire to be self-fulfilled.

20. b. Readers gain a great deal of information about a text by previewing it and making predictions about its contents before reading.

21. a. Deductive thinking moves from specific observations to broader theories and conclusions.

22. d. When in doubt, a teacher should always consult the building administrator who may be aware of policies and circumstances in which information should or should not be shared. In general, it is best not to speak of school matters outside of school and to guard the confidentiality of one's students and their families.

23. c. The author of the first passage would most likely agree that national standards should be set and adhered to by all states so that consistency exists across the nation.

24. d. Choice **d** is the only response that is feasible. The second passage suggests that state control takes into consideration the economic needs of a state when it refers to funding.

25. a. The characteristics described reflect the brain development of typical adolescents. They are capable of retaining only about five to seven bits of information at a time, are moving from concrete to abstract thinking, and are beginning to develop the ability to think critically and control impulses.

26. b. The examples given are symptoms of a visual sequencing disorder. Visual memory reflects retention, visual discrimination refers to being able to distinguish items, and visual figure-ground discrimination means the ability to distinguish something from its background.

27. c. These questions and the theme of identity closely align with Erikson's identity versus role confusion stage in which children come to understand their own identities.

28. d. Choice **d** is correct because adolescents' short-term memory can generally only retain a few items at a time. Cramming in large amounts of information won't work because students will forget previous information to deal with the new. The other choices are all recommended practices to encourage brain development in adolescents.

29. c. All of the choices are sound ways to communicate objectives to adolescents except choice **c**. Teachers should not expect adolescents to follow the rules without being reminded of them consistently.

30. b. Standardized tests are formal assessments. The other three choices are informal assessments.

31. a. An achievement test assesses the skill or knowledge a learner has achieved. An intelligence test measures potential. Proficiency is measured by an achievement test, not a proficiency test. An aptitude test measures a general cognitive trait.

32. d. Professional educational associations exist to provide networking and professional development for educators across content areas. Most of them offer choices **a** through **c**, but not choice **d**.

33. a. Teachers must understand that Cici's cultural identity defines who she is. Asking her to leave it behind or ignoring its existence will not enhance her academic success. Teachers should use a multicultural teaching approach and embrace diversity in the classroom.

34. b. With learned helplessness, people feel helpless when they feel powerless to change a situation. So, choice **b** is correct. Learning as experience is a basic concept of constructivism. Reciprocal determinism is a concept of social learning theory. Choice **d** is made up.

35. c. Colinda is "intently" watching the demonstration, so attention doesn't seem to be a factor. She refers to the handout, so retention is not a problem. She "knows she can do this," so we know she is motivated. The problem lies in choice **c**, reproduction. Additional practice of the learned behavior should lead to success.

36. a. While the other choices are summative, recall, and interpretive, choice **a** would lead students to think about an aspect of the relationships among Atticus, Jem, and Scout that they may not have previously considered.

37. b. If the classroom is secure and noncritical, even shy students will be willing to participate. The other choices will not encourage the shy student to participate and may even make the matter worse.

38. c. Do not avoid talking with someone from another culture just because you don't know her culture. While choices **b** and **d** may be true, they don't relate to the phrase "context is key" that we are trying to understand. Choice **c** is correct because it's saying that in two different contexts, you would use two different forms of communication.

39. d. State tests are standardized, which means that all teachers across the state have to provide the same conditions for their students in order for the results to be valid. Skipping over the directions would make the test invalid. Therefore, choice **d** is correct.

40. a. These are criterion-referenced tests. Norm-referenced tests are referenced against a defined reference group of students. Achievement tests assess learning in a specific content area. Aptitude tests measure what a student can acquire through future training or learning.

41. b. While choices **a**, **c**, and **d** are valuable examples of data for action research, Wikipedia should not be used as a resource.

42. d. While behaviorists believe learning leads to permanent change in behavior, social learning (i.e., the work of Albert Bandura) proposes that people can learn without the new learning changing their behavior permanently. Choices **a** through **c** are the three core concepts of social learning theory.

43. a. This exemplifies negative reinforcement, which occurs when a desired behavior (reading a good book) is strengthened by the removal of a contingent stimulus (homework).

44. c. Psychomotor domain relates to skills. This objective reflects a skill. Cognitive domain refers to knowledge. Affective domain relates to attitudes. Choice **d** is not a domain of learning.

45. d. Ms. Peek is using reflective-listening statements, which offer the idea back to the speaker to confirm that the idea has been understood by the listener.

46. a. Losing even 10 minutes a day because of connectivity issues can dissuade teachers from using technology in the classroom. Choices **b** through **d** are advantages of using technology.

47. b. An analytic rubric would allow the teacher to evaluate separate components of the collaboration, the research, and the panel presentation. Choices **a**, **c**, and **d** would not match this type of presentation outcome.

48. d. The tests are valid because the scores correlated. Validity refers to whether a test measures what it is supposed to measure.

49. a. It can be difficult to look critically at ourselves and our practices. Inviting a colleague to reflect on both of your practices collaboratively will provide you with the ability to see yourself from someone else's perspective. While choices **b** through **d** might also work, the most effective method is using a critical friend.

50. c. Metacognition involves thinking about the processes one is engaged in. In other words, Stacey is thinking about what she is thinking about. Her memory is involved, but the skills she uses are metacognitive in nature. Choices **b** and **d** are made up.

51. b. Choices **a**, **c**, and **d** reflect appropriate rules for the classroom. Choice **b** is not appropriate because it is for outside of school.

52. a. While it would be motivating for students to have the power to choose the genre of their final product, the resources they will use, and who they will work with, it would not be appropriate or fair to allow students to determine their own grades or those of their peers. Students may choose to work toward a particular grade by fulfilling certain criteria, but the teacher should be the one to determine the final grade.

53. d. Choices **a** through **c** would all encourage high levels of thinking, but choice **d** would not.

54. b. When the listener does not understand what the speaker or the sentence means, he can ask a clarifying question. While choices **a**, **c**, and **d** are other effective strategies for active listening, they do not fit this situation.

55. a. Choice **a** is correct because formative assessment is used to evaluate progress and inform teaching. The other choices do not match this description.

56. d. Standard deviation represents the degree of distribution among the responses around the mean. Quantitative data is numerical data. Frequency distribution relates to the frequency of each response. Code patterns is a made-up term.

57. c. The para educator is the choice least likely to be a member of the IEP team.

58. b. Diagnostic tests do all of the following except label students.

59. a. While adolescents experience self-consciousness, sensitivity, and anxiety as a result of their rapid physical growth and change, hypersensitivity reaction is not a condition associated with adolescent growth.

60. a. Ms. Carter is a teacher advocate because she is supporting teaching and learning and the policies that improve them. She would be considered a stakeholder and is offering her perception as a teacher. She is also collaborating with the Board, but the best answer is choice **a** because she is promoting teaching.

61. d. The KWL chart will help students activate their prior knowledge about the topic and motivate them to think about what they want to learn about the topic. Choices **a** through **c** may be secondary goals for using a KWL, but the primary goal is stated in choice **d**.

62. c. The assault should have been foreseeable by Mr. Livingston; therefore, he may face a liability suit. Liability involves being responsible.

63. b. Setting SMART goals and evaluating their progress is an example of self-assessment. Metacognition is thinking about one's thinking. While some metacognition is involved in this process, it is not the correct choice. The other choices do not align with the SMART description.

64. d. Choices **a** and **b** are made up. Analytic scoring rates, choice **c**, projects on separate criteria.

65. a. Choice **a** is correct because that is how these test scores should be interpreted. Grade level reflects how a student at that grade level would perform on this test, but it doesn't indicate that the student could do the work of that grade level.

66. c. If child abuse is suspected, the teacher is mandated to report it to the authorities. Telling the parents or asking the child about it may make the situation worse if the parents are involved.

67. c. Adelphia demonstrates creativity and abilities characteristic of students who are gifted and talented. She should be referred to the gifted-and-talented teacher.

68. a. A conference is described here. The description does not meet the definition of an interview, a debriefing, or a diary.

69. d. Focusing on student achievement rather than just discussing problems creates a positive, open dialogue among teachers and parents. Choices **a** through **c** would not foster open communication.

70. c. Teacher licensing is governed by each state. Gwen would have to check the licensing regulations and reciprocity conditions that exist between Alabama and New York.

Praxis II Scoring

Evaluate how you did on this practice exam by scoring your constructed responses and your multiple-choice answers. Bring your constructed responses and your scoring guide to a trusted friend to score so you can better see how you did. Reflect on the types of questions you missed most frequently.

The key to doing well on the Praxis II is to practice, read widely, and stay organized and focused. You have self-assessed your strengths and weaknesses and learned how to manage the various types of questions on the test. Enter the exam with confidence, knowing that you are ready and equipped to do your very best!

PRINCIPLES OF LEARNING AND TEACHING STUDY CHART PRACTICE EXAM 5	
STUDENTS AS LEARNERS	**QUESTIONS**
Student Development and Learning Process	2, 3, 6, 25, 42, 50, 59
Students as Diverse Learners	7, 9, 13, 17, 20, 26, 33
Student Motivation and Learning Environment	18, 19, 27, 34, 43, 51, 52
INSTRUCTIONAL PROCESS	
Planning Instruction	8, 16, 28, 35, 44
Instructional Strategies	5, 10, 11, 12, 14, 21
Questioning Techniques	36, 37, 45, 53, 61
Communication Techniques	15, 22, 29, 38, 46, 54
ASSESSMENT	
Assessment and Evaluation Strategies	30, 39, 47, 55, 58, 63, 68
Assessment Tools	1, 31, 40, 48, 56, 64, 65
Professional Development, Leadership, and Community	4, 23, 24, 32, 41, 49, 57, 60, 62, 66, 67, 69, 70
ANALYSIS OF INSTRUCTIONAL SCENARIOS	
Students as Learners	CR2
Instructional Process	CR1, 4
Assessment	CR3
Professional Development, Leadership, and Community	

20▶ ANSWERS AND EXPLANATIONS FOR PRACTICE EXAM 6

Scoring the Constructed-Response Case History Questions

Constructed responses are scored on a range from 0 to 2. First, this section presents the criteria for scoring constructed responses to the PLT case histories. Then, it provides sample level-2 responses for each question based on the scoring criteria that follow.

Criteria for Scoring

For a score of 2, the response must

- show that the writer has a thorough understanding of the parts of the case history that relate to the question.
- appropriately address all components of the question.
- provide a strong explanation (if requested) and support it with relevant evidence.
- provide evidence that the writer possesses strong knowledge of pedagogical concepts, facts, theories, methodologies, or procedures relevant to the question.

For a score of 1, the response must

- show that the writer has a basic understanding of the parts of the case history that relate to the question.
- appropriately address one component of the question.
- provide a weak explanation (if requested) but still be supported with relevant evidence.
- provide evidence that the writer possesses some knowledge of pedagogical concepts, facts, theories, methodologies, or procedures relevant to the question.

For a score of 0, the response must

- show that the writer misunderstood the parts of the case history that relate to the question.
- fail to address the question.
- not be supported by relevant evidence.
- provide little evidence that the writer possesses some knowledge of pedagogical concepts, facts, theories, methodologies, or procedures relevant to the question.

Answers and Explanations

PLT Case History 6.1: Mr. Granato

1. There are advantages and disadvantages to parents being highly involved in their children's academic lives. One advantage is the belief that any attention is better than no attention. "Helicopter parents" watch over their children and advocate for them. They model good behaviors and ways to get things accomplished. In this case, the narrative indicates that Mrs. Maynard is modeling organization and follow-through, and how to talk with teachers and others in positions of authority. The disadvantages would include the issue that helicopter parents often seem to overstep their bounds by talking for the student when he or she should be advocating for him- or herself. There comes a point where Cody has to become responsible for himself. In life there probably won't be someone who is always supporting, pushing, and looking out for him. He has to learn to do this himself. In the narrative we see that Cody doesn't get a chance to speak up. His mother does all the talking.

   By the definition of a helicopter parent given in question 1, Mrs. Maynard can be identified as one. She has micromanaged Cody's academic life over the past 13 years by constantly contacting his teachers, checking his homework, and checking up on his progress. Although she is doing her job as a parent, she seems to be overbearing. One could presume she has caused Cody to be semi-interested in school. He can actually sit back and let his mother do things for him that he should be doing. For example, if he has a question about homework, he, not his mother, should be the one asking the teacher. To be motivated, students should feel they are in positions of power, authority, and ownership to be engaged in meaningful learning.

2. So far, the meeting is not going as well as one might hope. Mrs. Maynard seems to be in charge and ready to spring at Mr. Granato, putting him on defense. The purpose of the meeting is to share ideas and get to know each other, though. Hopefully, Mr. Granato can have a chance before Mrs. Maynard has to leave to (a) talk with both parties to come up with a plan to improve Cody's motivation and enthusiasm about the academic focus of twelfth grade, and (b) help Cody articulate what would motivate him to be more in command of his own learning. To accomplish these goals, he should treat Mrs. Maynard respectfully and give her credit for trying to support Cody. To accomplish the first goal of coming up with a plan to improve Cody's motivation, Mr. Granato could ask Cody what he likes about school now or what he has

liked about it in the past. If Cody can't readily come up with anything, he could ask the same question of Mrs. Maynard to see if she remembers anything that engages Cody. Mr. Granato could also have Cody complete an interest survey. Perhaps if he learns more about Cody's interests and incorporates them into the curriculum, Cody will respond. To accomplish the second goal of making Cody, rather than his mother, responsible for his learning, Mr. Granato could encourage Cody to write a list of short- and long-term academic goals that reflect what would make him feel good about himself.

PLT Case History 6.2: Ms. Strub

3. Ms. Strub should be concerned about (a) Annie's self-concept and her feelings of isolation, and (b) how they will influence her confidence and academics. Ms. Strub should continue to observe and write anecdotal notes in her journal to document specific behaviors, comments, and interactions that seem positive or troublesome. (Note that the positive should also be documented so Ms. Strub can analyze contexts that cause positive responses and can capitalize on them.) Adolescence can be a troublesome time. Perhaps Annie is just going through a rough stage. Ms. Strub should check with past teachers, and when she has enough evidence to support any concerns she has, she should talk with Annie's family to gain further insight. Ms. Strub's main concerns should be Annie's mental health and how Ms. Strub can best meet Annie's learning needs as a result.

We don't know enough about Annie and about how Ms. Strub runs her classes at this point to predict how Annie's social and emotional status might influence her learning in Ms. Strub's class. If Ms. Strub values collaboration, cooperation, and group work in her class, Annie could react in two ways: She could recoil and not participate due to her shyness, or she could become more comfortable working in small groups intimately with people. Annie seems to crave authentic friendship, which may develop as a result of getting to know people in safe contexts, such as small groups. Ms. Strub will have to keep a close eye on how Annie reacts to various methods so that she can design lessons that will help Annie develop socially, emotionally, and academically.

4. During adolescence, young women like Annie are susceptible to developing drug or alcohol dependence. Adolescence is depicted as a time young people demonstrate risky behaviors and recklessness. They are trying out their new-found independence from their families and trying to shape identities for themselves. They try new things, sometimes to be accepted as part of a group of peers. Acceptance into peer groups is extremely important to adolescents as shown in Annie's poem. Furthermore, although most young people are psychologically healthy, they can begin to exhibit signs of mental illness. Mood disorders (i.e., clinical depression, bipolar disorder, and anxiety disorders) may emerge during late adolescence. Suicide is a leading cause of death in adolescence, so it is an educator's responsibility to watch for signs of teens who are dealing with what they consider to be severe emotional trauma (i.e., struggling with peer relationships, being bullied, pressure from parents, and feelings of not belonging). Adolescence can be a time of turmoil and self-doubt. It appears Annie is struggling, as evidenced in her poem and behaviors.

Multiple-Choice Questions

1. **a.** With reciprocal teaching, students learn to use these four interrelated strategies when reading across the content areas: question, clarify, summarize, and predict.

2. b. GIST is a summarization strategy students use. In the GIST approach, students write a 15-word summary of an article, then work to delete trivial propositions to choose the main idea. They then select topic statements that fit the 15-word summary.

3. a. An anticipation/reaction guide assesses students' knowledge before they begin a unit of study or a lesson and again after they participate in the unit or lesson. The guide consists of a list of statements that the student marks as true or false. They indicate what the students know or anticipate being true or false and then what they learned about the topic after study.

4. d. An inquiry chart is used to look at critical questions by integrating what the student already knows about a topic and what information is gained from various resources.

5. d. A network tree is used to represent a problem, its possible or attempted solutions, and their results.

6. c. Content-area teachers, in order to be effective, must know how to improve the literacy levels of struggling readers and writers whom they work with in their classes.

7. b. A self-regulated reader or writer understands the tasks of an activity and uses effective strategies that help him or her complete the tasks. Self-regulation refers to understanding the task so that the reader or writer knows how to perform to achieve his or her goals.

8. b. Teacher questioning is the most common form of formative assessment. Questioning may occur orally or in writing. However, teachers should not rely solely on questioning techniques.

9. d. Morphology refers to the linguistic ability to identify and describe the components of a word, such as its root and affixes (prefixes and suffixes).

10. b. The psychologist G. Stanley Hall referred to the years of adolescence as those of storm and stress, reflecting the turbulence experienced due to the adolescent's transitioning from childhood to adulthood.

11. a. Between 2000 and 2008, the dropout rates of high school students differed by race and ethnicity. While the rates decreased overall, the rates were lower for Whites and Blacks than for Hispanics and Asians/Pacific Islanders.

12. a. Due process hearings may be requested by either the parent or school when there is a dispute regarding the eligibility, placement, supports, or services necessary to ensure a free and appropriate public education that meets the student's needs. Due process is one of the six principles of the Individuals with Disabilities Education Act (IDEA) of 2004.

13. a. Word identification or decoding is the ability to read a word or sound it out.

14. c. An IEP must include current performance, annual goals, special education and related services, participation with nondisabled children, participation in state and district-wide tests, dates and places for services, transition service needs, needed transition services, age of majority, and statement of how progress will be measured.

15. b. Erikson's stage for adolescents refers to identity versus role confusion, in which development depends on what they do versus what others do for or to them.

16. a. The main objective of PL 94-142 is to mainstream and integrate students with handicaps into general education classes as appropriate.

17. d. The curriculum guide is based on the state or local learning standards and typically describes the goals of a program as well as the topics that will be taught over a span of time, such as an academic year. Curriculum guides vary in the degree of specificity and content, but basically they articulate what will be taught.

18. b. Reviewing material from the previous class with the students allows the educator to determine what the children remember and understand from the previous class. If misunderstandings or gaps are revealed, the educator can reteach as needed. There is no evidence to support the other three choices.

19. c. Choice **c** is the only one that requires only the recall of factual information. Other choices require the use of analysis and critical thinking skills. Factual recall questions/prompts typically start with words such as *define, describe, explain, identify, locate, who, when, where,* and *what.*

20. c. Families are important connections to make. Schools should always attempt to accommodate families' schedules, transportation issues, and feelings of isolation.

21. a. Constructivist approaches require the "guide on the side" to be knowledgeable and skilled in facilitating students' learning to make sense of new information using what they already know. Constructivism does not require that direct instruction or memorization be eliminated from instruction.

22. c. Typically, nonfluent speakers can understand written English text before they can accurately pronounce all of the words out loud. The teacher should not make assumptions about the reading abilities of any student; rather, the teacher should review the permanent records of the student and follow up daily with formal and informal assessments of reading skills. Readers benefit from good models, and nonfluent speakers benefit from hearing others model accurate pronunciations.

23. d. The first passage does not imply that teachers should open their classrooms to any discussions. Choice **d** is the best choice because it refers to careful planning of the class discussion. The teacher would want to avoid scaring students with speculative hearsay, especially the day it occurred.

24. b. The most important thing to know is how the authors are defining the term *controversial issues.* Readers don't know what the authors consider controversial. They could be very conservative and think teaching biology is controversial. Or, they could be very progressive and think that sex-change operation methods are appropriate to discuss with adolescents in a classroom situation.

25. a. Learning grows from the knowledge we already have. The first step of the process of learning is to activate prior knowledge so we can determine how the new information connects with it. The learning process continues through the steps represented in choices **b**, **c**, and **d**.

26. b. Graphic organizers are helpful for visual learners because they provide a simplified visual display to represent key terms and how they relate to each other. The other choices represent an auditory learning style.

27. c. Students are motivated by book clubs because they provide opportunities for them to interact socially with their peers as they share their reading experiences. While the other choices may be reasons why book clubs are an effective method to use in the grades 7–12 classroom, they do not explain why book clubs motivate students.

28. d. Directly teaching students the complex steps as she models and thinks aloud through the process would all be effective strategies and methods to use. However, the jigsaw model relies on student groups teaching parts of something to their peers. Because the math process is described as a series of steps, it would be best to teach it as a procedural sequence from start to finish.

29. c. Various cultures have different norms for acceptable personal space and touching. Gender and the familiarity between the parties can influence personal space. Time of day is least likely to affect it.

30. b. A concept map would be an effective assessment tool to use at the end of a chapter study because it would show how students understood the key concepts and how the concepts relate to each other. It would not be effective for choices **a**, **c**, and **d** because the nature of a concept map is to show relationships among concepts.

31. b. The evaluation is norm-referenced because Mr. Montez is comparing individual students' results to the results of the rest of the class. It is also summative because the results sum up students' performance on the objectives.

32. d. It is most likely, presuming Mr. Kite and the researcher followed the same procedures and practices, that other factors and variables influenced the results. Choices **a** and **b** address student motivation, which may be one of the influential variables. It is also possible that the researcher's interpretation of the results influenced his conclusions, but an ethical researcher would not intentionally skew the results.

33. a. The idea of least-restrictive-environment was developed to normalize life for students with disabilities who were previously segregated from students without disabilities. Choices **b** through **d** do not reflect the rationale behind this mandate for students with disabilities.

34. b. Marco perceives finishing promptly and being given more work as a punishment. Rewarding him instead would encourage him to develop efficient work habits. Choice **a** would likely discourage all students because no one would be able to finish the problems. Choice **c** would most likely distract students who were still working on the worksheet. Choice **d** would not address the issue described.

35. d. Vicarious extinction is correct. It involves learning that the consequence of a behavior can influence anyone who is observing the behavior and its consequence. If the consequence is negative as in this example, the behavior is extinguished. Discovery learning is a type of inquiry-based instruction. Learning as experience is a basic concept of constructivism. Problem-based learning refers to learning through the experience of problem solving.

36. a. Interruptions actually decrease, interactions increase, responses are lengthened, and a greater number of higher cognitive responses occur.

37. b. This question will help Ms. Abermann assess whether students understood the article, since this was the main purpose of the article. It does not reflect divergent or critical thinking. It also does not require students to interpret the author's meaning.

38. c. If a student is not engaged in the conversation, the culture shows respect that way, or the teacher is confronting the student, it might even be expected the student would not make eye contact. However, if the student is intentionally showing disrespect for the teacher, this avoidance of eye contact would be the least acceptable choice.

39. d. All of these choices are advantages for essays, but choice **d** is the best reason because it explains how essays encourage deep thinking.

40. a. The author would least likely support choice **a** because he or she notes that sports encourage adolescents to erroneously "seek extrinsic rewards." The author supports self-determination, which is setting goals for oneself, and attribution, which promotes intrinsic motivation.

41. b. The main idea of this passage revolves around school culture. Adding *adolescent* to the search would narrow it to this age group. The other choices are too broad and would not render as effective a search.

42. d. Peer culture refers to the set of norms created and accepted within peer relationships. The author would promote changing the peer culture so that it primarily values and supports academic achievement. A clique, choice **a**, is a small, highly interdependent group within a school culture. Choices **b** and **c** are too general.

43. a. Choice **a** does not allow students the choice about what or how they will write, so it is least likely to inspire students to enjoy writing. Choice **b** allows choice, choice **c** allows the opportunity to enjoy writing without the pressure of grades, and choice **d** allows the opportunity to explore personal interests through writing.

44. c. Choice **c** is the correct definition for scope. Typically, publishers provide scope and sequence charts for programs that lay out what will be taught and when to teach it. This overall guide helps teachers fit the program into their academic curriculum. Choices **a** and **d** do not make any sense in relation to the definition of scope. Choice **b** defines sequence.

45. d. Choices **a** through **c** are all disadvantages of thematic units. Choice **d** is correct because transfer knowledge is one of the advantages of working with units.

46. a. Teachable moments occur in a classroom when conversations or situations lead to brief digressions to follow issues or concepts that have captured students' collective interest. The teacher may not have planned to discuss the moral issues, but the students' interests lead to extended conversations about it. Choices **b** through **d** are fictitious choices.

47. b. When writing essay questions, choices **a**, **c**, and **d** are all good suggestions because they promote learning and fairness. Choice **b**, however, is not a good suggestion because the teacher would be creating a routine where studying is not rewarded.

48. d. Although students may think they are brilliant because they get the same results, this is not the correct answer. Accuracy relates to how close the results are to what the real answer is. Validity refers to the results matching up with known values. The correct choice is **d** because reliability refers to how close the results are when the experiment is repeated.

49. a. Choice **a** might lead to discussion of students' math learning or it might not, so that is why it is the least valuable. The other choices all directly link to improving students' math performance.

50. c. Self-determination involves all of the suggestions in choices **a, b,** and **d.** Choice **c** is the correct response because it is the only choice that discourages students with disabilities from taking an active role in their futures.

51. b. Creativity allows adolescents to explore their personal aptitudes and interests, endeavors that fit with the adolescent's developmental tendencies to seek and form their identities. Although pursuing creative endeavors may lead adolescents to avoid schoolwork, reflect on their learning, and learn from adults, these choices do not link to what we know about personality development and theories.

52. a. Cognitive dissonance involves the reconstruction of knowledge that challenges the learner's basic beliefs and values. Extrinsic motivation refers to external rewards that motivate learners. Attribution is the idea that learners are motivated by feeling good about themselves. Self-determination is the concept that all individuals have the right to run their lives.

53. d. When students work at their zone of proximal development and receive scaffolding, they should be able to successfully complete the task and achieve the objective. Operant and classical conditioning refer to behaviorist concepts of reward and punishment. Choice **c** is made up.

54. b. Research evidence indicates that reasoning develops interactively rather than through isolation and independent thought. Research does support choices **a, c,** and **d.**

55. a. Guided thinking is a grid students use to identify their thinking of the concept, process, and facts. Each column is described in the choices. Choice **a** would be where the teacher can assess learning.

56. c. Mean refers to adding up all the numbers and dividing them by the total number of numbers. *Mode* is the value that occurs most often. *Median* is the middle value in the list of numbers. *Range* is the difference between the smallest and largest values.

57. c. All of the other choices are more confidential and formal. Facebook is an informal social network.

58. b. Plagiarism is fraud because the plagiarizer is stealing another's ideas or work and claiming it as her own. It is not just copying or borrowing someone else's work. Plagiarism is scandalous in that it is disgraceful, but the best response is choice **b** because it explains why it is illegal.

59. a. Choice **a** is correct because the question stem describes Section 504. EHA was renamed in 1990 as IDEA. NCLB supports standards-based education reform. IDEA covers children in special education with individualized educational plans. Terry's disability does not qualify him for an IEP but rather a 504 plan.

60. a. A 504 plan falls under a civil rights law. Its intent is to remove barriers that keep students with disabilities from participating freely. It levels the playing field. An IEP falls under IDEA. It provides educational services for significant remediation and assistance. An IEP does more than level the playing field.

61. d. Although the teacher's feedback is positive, it goes beyond just praising the student. If the student responds to the feedback positively and productively, his or her writing would take on a more critical perspective. Critical thinking and writing involve looking at and analyzing alternative perspectives on a topic. The feedback has nothing to do with establishing rules for behavior in the classroom. And, although the teacher isn't telling the student that he or she has to include her suggestions in the essay, she also is not really including the student in instructional decisions.

62. a. A holistic rubric does not list separate levels of performance for individual criterion like an analytic rubric does. Choice **b** describes an analytic rubric. Choice **c** reflects percentages. Choice **d** describes a checklist.

63. b. Choices **a**, **c**, and **d** are all good examples of authentic assessment because they gauge students' understanding of material and objectives. However, choice **b** is not aligned with the objectives.

64. d. Percentiles show how a student's scores compare to the scores of other students who were tested. Stanine scores range from 1 to 9, with the average at about 4.5. The raw score is the total number of points received based on the number of correctly answered questions.

65. a. Choice **a** is correct. If 1,000 students took the test, the student scored higher than 870 students. Percentile does not represent percent correct scores, though. With percentile scores, educators and parents can compare a student's scores with the scores of other students who took the same test.

66. c. The question describes an assessment portfolio. A showcase portfolio is also called a display portfolio. It displays the students' best work. A working portfolio contains work in progress and finished samples of work.

67. c. Choices **a**, **b**, and **d** are all good examples of active listening strategies that would work in this case. Choice **c** is not a good strategy, though, because a listener shouldn't make assumptions about the conversation.

68. a. A teacher's feedback should be sincere but specific. It should extend the student's thinking while confirming, correcting, challenging, encouraging, and acknowledging efforts already spent.

69. d. The characteristics described represent Piaget's formal operational stage of cognitive development, which involves students from age 11 through adulthood. Choice **a** represents how infants from birth to age 2 experience the world through their senses. Choice **b** involves children from 2 to 7 years of age; these children begin to represent the world through words and images. Choice **c** is for children 7 to 11 years of age who can classify objects.

70. c. Choice **c** is correct because Bandura's theory is stated accurately in this choice. Choice **a** really describes Vygotsky's theory. Choice **b** explains Erikson's identity conflict stage of psychosocial development. Choice **d** actually describes Bowlby's social child development theory.

Praxis II Scoring

Evaluate how you did on this practice exam by scoring your constructed responses and your multiple-choice answers. Bring your constructed responses and your scoring guide to a trusted friend to score so you can better see how you did. Reflect on the types of questions you missed most frequently.

The key to doing well on the Praxis II is to practice, read widely, and stay organized and focused. You have self-assessed your strengths and weaknesses and learned how to manage the various types of questions on the test. Enter the exam with confidence, knowing that you are ready and equipped to do your very best!

PRINCIPLES OF LEARNING AND TEACHING STUDY CHART PRACTICE EXAM 6	
STUDENTS AS LEARNERS	**QUESTIONS**
Student Development and Learning Process	7, 10, 15, 25, 53, 69, 70
Students as Diverse Learners	16, 22, 26, 33, 42, 50, 59
Student Motivation and Learning Environment	27, 34, 40, 43, 51, 52, 61
INSTRUCTIONAL PROCESS	
Planning Instruction	5, 21, 28, 35, 44
Instructional Strategies	1, 2, 3, 4, 9, 13
Questioning Techniques	18, 19, 36, 37, 45
Communication Techniques	29, 38, 46, 54, 67, 68
ASSESSMENT	
Assessment and Evaluation Strategies	8, 31, 39, 47, 55, 63, 66
Assessment Tools	30, 48, 56, 62, 64, 65
Professional Development, Leadership, and Community	6, 11, 12, 14, 17, 20, 23, 24, 32, 41, 49, 57, 58, 60
ANALYSIS OF INSTRUCTIONAL SCENARIOS	
Students as Learners	CR3,4
Instructional Process	CR2
Assessment	
Professional Development, Leadership, and Community	CR1

APPENDIX: PRAXIS II SUBJECT ASSESSMENTS AND TEACHING FOUNDATIONS TESTS

PAPER-DELIVERED TEST CODE	COMPUTER-DELIVERED TEST CODE	NAME OF TEST	HOURS ALLOTTED	FEE
0700	n/a	Agriculture	2	$115
0900	n/a	Agriculture (CA)	2	$115
0780	n/a	Agriculture (PA)	2	$115
0135	n/a	Art: Content and Analysis	2	$139
0134	5134	Art: Content Knowledge	2	$115
0341	n/a	Audiology	2	$115
0342	n/a	Audiology	2	$115
0030	n/a	Biology and General Science	2	$115
0233	n/a	Biology: Content Essays	1	$139
0235	5235	Biology: Content Knowledge	2	$115
0231	n/a	Biology: Content Knowledge, Part 1	1	$115
0631	n/a	Braille Proficiency	4	$139
0101	5101	Business Education	2	$115
0242	n/a	Chemistry: Content Essays	1	$139

PAPER-DELIVERED TEST CODE	COMPUTER-DELIVERED TEST CODE	NAME OF TEST	HOURS ALLOTTED	FEE
0245	5245	Chemistry: Content Knowledge	2	$115
0070	n/a	Chemistry, Physics, and General Science	2	$115
n/a	5665	Chinese (Mandarin): World Language	3	$150
0087	5087	Citizenship Education: Content Knowledge	2	$115
0800	n/a	Communication	2	$115
0811	n/a	Cooperative Education	2	$115
0867	n/a	Driver Education	2	$115
0022	5022	Early Childhood: Content Knowledge	2	$115
0020	n/a	Early Childhood Education	2	$115
0571	5571	Earth and Space Sciences: Content Knowledge	2	$115
0911	n/a	Economics	2	$115
0271	n/a	Education of Deaf and Hard of Hearing Students	2	$139
0021	5021	Education of Young Children	2	$139
0411	5411	Educational Leadership: Administration and Supervision (ELAS)	2	$115
0014	5014	Elementary Education: Content Knowledge	2	$115
0011	5011	Elementary Education: Curriculum, Instruction, and Assessment	2	$115
n/a	5015	Elementary Education: Instructional Practice and Applications	2	$139
0044	5044	English Language, Literature, and Composition: Content and Analysis	2	$139

PAPER-DELIVERED TEST CODE	COMPUTER-DELIVERED TEST CODE	NAME OF TEST	HOURS ALLOTTED	FEE
0041	5041	English Language, Literature, and Composition: Content Knowledge	2	$115
0043	n/a	English Language, Literature, and Composition: Pedagogy	1	$139
0361	n/a	English for Speakers of Other Languages (ESOL)	2	$115
0831	n/a	Environmental Education	2	$115
0121	5121	Family and Consumer Sciences	2	$115
n/a	5174	French: World Language	3	$150
0511	5511	Fundamental Subjects: Content Knowledge	2	$115
0433	n/a	General Science: Content Essays	1	$139
0435	5435	General Science: Content Knowledge	2	$115
0432	n/a	General Science: Content Knowledge, Part 2	1	$115
0921	n/a	Geography	2	$115
n/a	5183	German: World Language	3	$150
0357	n/a	Gifted Education	2	$115
0931	n/a	Government/Political Science	2	$115
0856	5856	Health and Physical Education: Content Knowledge	2	$115
0550	5550	Health Education	2	$115
0023	5023	Interdisciplinary Early Childhood Education	2	$115
0601	n/a	Latin	2	$115
0311	5311	Library Media Specialist	2	$115
0234	n/a	Life Science: Pedagogy	1	$139

PAPER-DELIVERED TEST CODE	COMPUTER-DELIVERED TEST CODE	NAME OF TEST	HOURS ALLOTTED	FEE
0561	n/a	Marketing Education	2	$115
0061	5061	Mathematics: Content Knowledge	2	$115
0065	n/a	Mathematics: Pedagogy	1	$139
0063	n/a	Mathematics: Proofs, Models, and Problems, Part 1	1	$139
0146	5146	Middle School: Content Knowledge	2	$115
0049	5049	Middle School English Language Arts	2	$139
0069	n/a	Middle School Mathematics	2	$139
0439	n/a	Middle School Science	2	$139
0089	5089	Middle School Social Studies	2	$139
0112	n/a	Music: Analysis	1	$139
0111	n/a	Music: Concepts and Processes	1	$139
0114	n/a	Music: Content and Instruction	2	$139
0113	5113	Music: Content Knowledge	2	$115
n/a	5152	PA Grades 4–8 Core Assessment	3.5	$140
n/a	5153	PA Grades 4–8 Core Assessment: Pedagogy	1.5	$50
n/a	5154	PA Grades 4–8 Core Assessment: English Language Arts and Social Studies	1.5	$50
n/a	5155	PA Grades 4–8 Core Assessment: Mathematics and Science	1.5	$50
n/a	5156	PA Grades 4–8 Subject Concentration: English Language Arts	1.5	$75
n/a	5157	PA Grades 4–8 Subject Concentration: Social Studies	1.5	$75
n/a	5158	PA Grades 4–8 Subject Concentration: Mathematics	1.5	$75

PAPER-DELIVERED TEST CODE	COMPUTER-DELIVERED TEST CODE	NAME OF TEST	HOURS ALLOTTED	FEE
n/a	5159	PA Grades 4–8 Subject Concentration: Science	1.5	$75
0095	5095	Physical Education: Content and Design	2	$139
0091	5091	Physical Education: Content Knowledge	2	$115
0092	n/a	Physical Education: Movement Forms—Analysis and Design	1	$139
0481	n/a	Physical Science: Content Knowledge	1	$115
0483	n/a	Physical Science: Pedagogy	1	$139
0262	n/a	Physics: Content Essays	1	$139
0265	5265	Physics: Content Knowledge	2	$115
0531	5531	Pre-Kindergarten Education	2	$115
0621	5621	Principles of Learning and Teaching: Early Childhood	2	$139
0622	5622	Principles of Learning and Teaching: Grades K–6	2	$139
0623	5623	Principles of Learning and Teaching: Grades 5–9	2	$139
0624	5624	Principles of Learning and Teaching: Grades 7–12	2	$139
0421	5421	Professional School Counselor	2	$115
0390	n/a	Psychology	2	$115
0201	5201	Reading Across the Curriculum: Elementary	2	$139
0306	n/a	Reading for Virginia Educators (RVE): Elementary and Special Education	2.5	$80
n/a	5306	Reading for Virginia Educators (RVE): Elementary and Special Education	2.5	$130
0304	n/a	Reading for Virginia Educators (RVE): Reading Specialist	3.5	$80

PAPER-DELIVERED TEST CODE	COMPUTER-DELIVERED TEST CODE	NAME OF TEST	HOURS ALLOTTED	FEE
n/a	5304	Reading for Virginia Educators (RVE): Reading Specialist	3.5	$130
n/a	5301	Reading Specialist	2	$139
0860	n/a	Safety/Driver Education	2	$115
0420	n/a	School Guidance and Counseling	2	$115
0401	n/a	School Psychologist	2	$115
0211	n/a	School Social Worker: Content Knowledge	2	$115
0951	n/a	Social Sciences: Content Knowledge	2	$115
0086	5086	Social Studies: Content and Interpretation	2	$139
0081	5081	Social Studies: Content Knowledge	2	$115
0950	n/a	Sociology	2	$115
n/a	5195	Spanish: World Language	3	$150
0354	5354	Special Education: Core Knowledge and Applications	2	$115
0543	5543	Special Education: Core Knowledge and Mild to Moderate Applications	2	$139
0545	5545	Special Education: Core Knowledge and Severe to Profound Applications	2	$139
0272	n/a	Special Education: Education of Deaf and Hard of Hearing Students	2	$115
0691	n/a	Special Education: Preschool/Early Childhood	2	$115
0881	n/a	Special Education: Teaching Speech to Students with Language Impairments	2	$115
0371	n/a	Special Education: Teaching Students with Behavioral Disorders/Emotional Disturbances	1	$115
0383	n/a	Special Education: Teaching Students with Learning Disabilities	2	$115
0321	n/a	Special Education: Teaching Students with Mental Retardation	1	$115

PAPER-DELIVERED TEST CODE	COMPUTER-DELIVERED TEST CODE	NAME OF TEST	HOURS ALLOTTED	FEE
0281	n/a	Special Education: Teaching Students with Visual Impairments	2	$115
0282	n/a	Special Education: Teaching Students with Visual Impairments	2	$115
0221	n/a	Speech Communication: Content Knowledge	2	$115
0330	5330	Speech-Language Pathology	2	$115
0048	n/a	Teaching Foundations: English	4	$139
0068	n/a	Teaching Foundations: Mathematics	4	$139
0528	n/a	Teaching Foundations: Multiple Subjects	4	$139
0438	n/a	Teaching Foundations: Science	4	$139
0204	5204	Teaching Reading	2	$139
0051	n/a	Technology Education	2	$115
0641	n/a	Theater	2	$115
0890	n/a	Vocational General Knowledge	2	$115
0941	5941	World and U.S. History: Content Knowledge	2	$115
0841	n/a	World Languages Pedagogy	2	$139

PRAXIS II: MULTIPLE SUBJECTS

	COMPUTER	NAME OF TEST	HOURS	FEE
n/a	5031[3]	Elementary Education: Multiple Subjects	3.5	$150
	5032	Elementary Education: Reading and Language Arts Subtest	1	$50
	5033	Elementary Education: Mathematics Subtest	50 min.	$50
	5034	Elementary Education: Social Studies Subtest	50 min.	$50
	5035	Elementary Education: Science Subtest	50 min.	$50
n/a	5141[3]	Middle School: Multiple Subjects	4	$150
	5142	Middle School: English Language Arts Subtest	1	$50
	5143	Middle School: Mathematics Subtest	1	$50
	5144	Middle School: Social Studies Subtest	1	$50
	5145	Middle School: Science Subtest	1	$50

ADDITIONAL ONLINE PRACTICE

Whether you need help building basic skills or preparing for an exam, visit the Learning-Express Practice Center! Using the code below, you'll be able to access additional Praxis online practice exams. This online practice will also provide you with:

Immediate Scoring
Detailed answer explanations
Personalized recommendations for further practice and study

Log in to the LearningExpress Practice Center by using the URL: **www.learnatest.com/practice**

This is your Access Code: **9308**

Follow the steps online to redeem your access code. After you've used your access code to register with the site, you will be prompted to create a username and password. For easy reference, record them here:

Username: _____ Password: _____

With your username and password, you can log in and access your additional practice materials. If you have any questions or problems, please contact LearningExpress customer service at 1-800-295-9556 ext. 2, or e-mail us at **customerservice@learningexpressllc.com**.